BUSINESS RESEARCH METHODS

CHRISTINA QUINLAN

BUSINESS RESEARCH METHODS

SOUTH-WESTERN
CENGAGE Learning™

Australia • Brazil • Japan • Korea • Mexico • Singapore • Spain • United Kingdom • United States

SOUTH-WESTERN
CENGAGE Learning

Business Research Methods
Christina Quinlan

Publishing Director: Linden Harris
Publisher: Thomas Rennie
Editorial Assistant: Charlotte Green
Content Project Editor: Lucy Arthy
Senior Production Controller: Paul Herbert
Marketing Manager: Amanda Cheung
Typesetter: Integra, India
Cover design: Adam Renvoize
Text design: Design Deluxe

For product information and technology assistance, contact
emea.info@cengage.com.
For permission to use material from this text or product,
and for permission queries,
email **emea.permissions@cengage.com.**

British Library Cataloguing-in-Publication Data
A catalogue record for this book is available from the British Library.

ISBN: 978-1-4080-0779-2

Cengage Learning EMEA
Cheriton House, North Way, Andover, Hampshire, SP10 5BE
United Kingdom

Cengage Learning products are represented in Canada by Nelson Education Ltd.

For your lifelong learning solutions, visit
www.cengage.co.uk

Purchase your next print book, e-book or e-chapter at
www.cengagebrain.com

Printed in China by RR Donnelley
2 3 4 5 6 7 8 9 10 – 15 14 13

BRIEF CONTENTS

1 INTRODUCING BUSINESS RESEARCH   2

2 DEVELOPING RESEARCH SKILLS   34

3 UNDERSTANDING RESEARCH ETHICS   66

4 UNDERSTANDING RESEARCH PHILOSOPHY   92

5 DEVELOPING A RESEARCH PROPOSAL   124

6 REVIEWING THE LITERATURE   150

7 UNDERSTANDING RESEARCH METHODOLOGY AND DESIGN   174

8 UNDERSTANDING RESEARCH METHODS, POPULATIONS AND SAMPLING   202

9 USING SECONDARY DATA AND ARCHIVAL SOURCES   238

10 USING OBSERVATION   260

11 USING INTERVIEWS AND FOCUS GROUPS   284

12 USING QUESTIONNAIRES AND SCALES   320

13 MANAGING DATA AND INTRODUCING DATA ANALYSIS   350

14 ANALYZING QUANTITATIVE DATA   378

15 ANALYZING QUALITATIVE DATA   416

16 DRAWING CONCLUSIONS AND WRITING RESEARCH   444

CONTENTS

Preface   x
Introduction   xi
Acknowledgments   xxii
About the Author   xxiii
Walk through Tour   xxvi
About the Website   xxviii

1 INTRODUCING BUSINESS RESEARCH   2

Learning Objectives   3
Research Skills   3
Introduction   4
The Four Frameworks Approach   5
The Four Frameworks And
   The Research Process   9
Keeping A Research Diary   10
The Development of Social Research   12
The Different Social Research Paradigms   12
An Introduction To Research Methodology   14
A Brief Introduction To Research Ethics   25
Case Study   28
Chapter Review   31
End Of Chapter Questions   32
References   32
Recommended Reading   32

2 DEVELOPING RESEARCH SKILLS   34

Learning Objectives   35
Research Skills   35
Introduction   36
Research Ideas   37
Turning Research Ideas Into Research Projects   39
The First Step: Developing A Research Statement   40
Aims And Objectives   44
Source Appropriate Literature   47
The Different Approaches To Research   49

Data: What Constitutes Evidence?   49
Plagiarism   50
Compiling A Bibliography   52
The Uses Of Appendices   54
Keeping The Research Diary   54
Case Study   59
Chapter Review   62
End Of Chapter Questions   63
References   63
Recommended Reading   64

3 UNDERSTANDING RESEARCH ETHICS   66

Learning Objectives   67
Research Skills   67
Introduction   69
Ethics In Business Research   70
Other Ethical Issues In Research   82
Case Study   88
Chapter Review   89
End Of Chapter Questions   90
References   90
Recommended Reading   91

4 UNDERSTANDING RESEARCH PHILOSOPHY   92

Learning Objectives   93
Research Skills   93
The Research Process   95
The Philosophical Underpinnings Of Research And
   Research Methodologies   98
The Research Project And The Philosophical
   Frameworks   99
The Methodological Pyramid   103

The Use Of Theory In The Generation Of
Knowledge   106
The Importance Of Theory In Research   108
How To Create A Theoretical Framework: The Second
Of The Four Frameworks   112
How To Generate Theory From Your Own
Research   116
The Links Between Research, Theory And
Knowledge   117
Case Study   118
Chapter Review   120
End Of Chapter Questions   121
References   121
Recommended Reading   121

**5 DEVELOPING A RESEARCH
PROGRAM   124**

Learning Objectives   125
Research Skills   125
Introduction   126
Generating Ideas For Research Projects   128
A Conceptual Framework: The First Step   137
Refining Research Ideas   138
Limiting The Scope Of A Research Project   139
Aims And Objectives   140
Create A Theoretical Framework For A Project, And
Provide A Sample Literature Review   141
Outline A Methodological Framework For A Research
Project   142
Developing A Research Proposal   143
Case Study   145
Chapter Review   148
End Of Chapter Questions   149
References   149
Recommended Reading   149

6 REVIEWING THE LITERATURE   150

Learning Objectives   151
Research Skills   151
Introduction   152
Literature In Research   156
The Conceptual Framework As A Guide To The
Review Of The Literature   156
Create A Theoretical Framework   157
Writing The Literature Review   158
Reading Literature: Some Key Points   165
Referencing The Work   168
Case Study   169

Chapter Review   171
End Of Chapter Questions   172
References   172
Recommended Reading   172

**7 UNDERSTANDING RESEARCH
METHODOLOGY AND DESIGN   174**

Learning Objectives   175
Research Skills   175
Introduction   177
Research Methodologies   178
Deciding On The Most Appropriate Methodology For
Your Own Research   189
Create A Methodological Framework, The
Third Of The Four Frameworks   191
Case Study   194
Chapter Review   199
End Of Chapter Questions   200
References   200
Recommended Reading   201

**8 UNDERSTANDING RESEARCH
METHODS, POPULATIONS AND
SAMPLING   202**

Learning Objectives   203
Research Skills   203
Introduction   205
Samples And Sampling In Research   208
Research Methods   217
Data Collection Methods   220
Case Study   232
Chapter Review   234
End Of Chapter Questions   235
References   235
Recommended Reading   236

**9 USING SECONDARY DATA AND
ARCHIVAL SOURCES   238**

Learning Objectives   239
Research Skills   239
Introduction   240
Secondary Data   242
Differentiating Between Primary And Secondary
Data   243
Sourcing Secondary Data Sets   246
Evaluate The Utility Of The Data Available   249
Use Secondary Data Appropriately   252

Case Study   253
Chapter Review   256
End Of Chapter Questions   257
References   257
Recommended Reading   258

10 USING OBSERVATION   260

Learning Objectives   261
Research Skills   261
Introduction   262
Understanding Observation   263
The Different Kinds Of Observation   266
Using Observation   269
The Need For Rigour In Observation   272
Critique The Use Of Observation In Research   273
Designing An Observation Study   274
Case Study   278
Chapter Review   281
End of Chapter Questions   282
References   282
Recommended Reading   282

11 USING INTERVIEWS AND FOCUS GROUPS   284

Learning Objectives   285
Research Skills   285
Introduction   286
Interviews And Focus Groups   289
Critique The Use Of Interviews And Focus Groups In
   Other Research Projects   311
Case Study   314
Chapter Review   316
End Of Chapter Questions   317
References   317
Recommended Reading   318

12 USING QUESTIONNAIRES AND SCALES   320

Learning Objectives   321
Research Skills   321
Introduction   322
Questionnaires And Scales   326
Projective Techniques   330
The Issues Of Validity And Reliability   335
Designing Questionnaires And Scales   336
The Politics And Practicalities Of Asking A Question   338

A Pilot study   341
Response Rates   342
Case Study   344
Chapter Review   347
End Of Chapter Questions   348
References   348
Recommended Reading   348

13 MANAGING DATA AND INTRODUCING DATA ANALYSIS   350

Learning Objectives   351
Research Skills   351
Introduction   352
Data And Data Management   356
An Introduction To Data Analysis   358
The Four Stages Of Data Analysis   365
Case Study   371
Chapter Review   374
End Of Chapter Questions   375
References   375
Recommended Reading   376

14 ANALYZING QUANTITATIVE DATA   378

Learning Objectives   379
Research Skills   379
Introduction   380
Working With Quantitative Data   382
Questionnaire Used In Street Intercept Interviews With
   High Street Fashion Shoppers   385
Coding Key For High Street Shoppers' Questionnaire
   (Lian's Research)   388
The Variable In Quantitative Data Analysis   397
Basic Statistical Analysis   399
Graphing Data   403
The Four Stages In The Data Analysis Process   408
Case Study   411
Chapter Review   413
End Of Chapter Questions   414
References   414
Recommended Reading   415

15 ANALYZING QUALITATIVE DATA   416

Learning Objectives   417
Research Skills   417
Introduction   418

Qualitative Data Analysis 420
The Four Stages Of Data Analysis 422
Data Analysis In Case Study Research: An
 Introduction 428
Case Study 438
Chapter Review 441
End Of Chapter Questions 442
References 442
Recommended Reading 443

16 DRAWING CONCLUSIONS AND WRITING RESEARCH 444

Learning Objectives 445
Research Skills 445

Introduction 446
The Final Chapter – Writing Conclusions And Drawing
 Recommendations 448
The Recommendations Of The Study 453
Writing The Research Project 457
Case Study 463
Chapter Review 465
End Of Chapter Questions 466
References 466
Recommended Reading 467

Bibliography 469
Glossary 479
Index 485

PREFACE

This new textbook aims to provide a balanced introduction to research methods for today's undergraduate business students. It does this by synthesizing rigorous coverage of methodologies with an accessible 'real-world' approach. The text follows course learning objectives for undergraduates in business and provides examples drawn from the full range of business subjects from marketing and strategy to human resource management.

The text has unique features: for example, it introduces the four frameworks approach to the research project. The four frameworks approach provides beginner researchers with direction in terms of the development of their research projects. It facilitates beginner researchers in the task of developing properly focused, fully integrated research projects. The textbook is very sympathetic to the challenges facing a student engaging with the subject for the first time, and provides an integrated and balanced approach to quantitative and qualitative research. The writing is simple and direct and the examples and case studies presented were selected particularly with an undergraduate readership in mind. In summary, the text provides a unique, simple and empathic yet comprehensive introduction to research methods for business students.

Business Research Methods is a valuable resource for all undergraduate business students, and particularly for second- and third-year students on business research methods courses. It provides an excellent introduction to the work of undertaking research in an academic environment. This text is essential reading for all business students required to undertake research projects. Postgraduate students, and indeed students from other non-business disciplines, will also find the text very helpful.

Christina Quinlan
May 2010

INTRODUCTION

FOR STUDENTS

Business Research Methods sets out to help students design and develop their research projects from inception to completion. The text has been written in an accessible style and will provide useful support for those undertaking investagative projects for the first time. Covering all aspects of the reseach process in some detail, this is an ideal introductory 'how-to-do' text. The book introduces a new model called the four frameworks approach designed to help researchers with the process of undertaking research. The icon on the right appears in the text every time the four frameworks approach is discussed. The narrative of the text is enhanced with a number of key features, among them skills activities, chapter reviews, end-of-chapter questions and case studies of real world research.

The Four Frameworks

Conceptual Framework

Theoretical Framework

Methodological Framework

Analytical Framework

This book is designed and written in such a way as to take you, the reader, through the subject of business research methods in a comprehensive but very clear, simple and straightforward manner. If you read the book to the end, you will have a complete understanding of business research methods and the confidence and the capacity to competently undertake a business research project. Whether you read the book from beginning to end, or choose to read particular chapters, you will find this book an invaluable companion as you undertake your study or thesis.

FOR LECTURERS

Business Research Methods is designed to fill a perceived gap in the European market in terms of teaching research methods to undergraduate business students. This is a vast market, with all undergraduate and postgraduate students undertaking research projects at some time in their academic career. This text closely follows the learning objectives of business research method programmes and will complement the academic support received during the research process, providing a useful point of reference for students. The text aims to match balanced coverage with accessibility

This text recognizes the institutional pressures on business research courses, including: (a) large class cohorts; (b) the issue of plagiarism; (c) increasingly diverse and international student profiles with different learning approaches; and (d) increasing demands for lecturers to employ virtual learning environments (VLEs) in their teaching. To accommodate these pressures, the book utilizes unique skills and real-world relevance emphasis matched with blended content, so that both students and lecturers will be more engaged with the material and many of the current anxieties over course delivery will be overcome.

KEY FEATURES

The following key features are included:

- Balance of coverage and accessibility: the text's structure has evolved from close examination of the standard learning objectives on undergraduate business research methods courses, ensuring all of the key topics are addressed in a balanced and thorough way. Matching this is a strong awareness of the realities of undergraduate courses, in terms of student interest and difficulties with some areas of the curriculum, meaning there is a focus on accessibility and engaging the student throughout.

- Wide-ranging examples: recognizing that students on research methods courses come from a wide range of business disciplines, the text uses wide-ranging examples including examples from SMEs, the public sector as well as not-for-profit business undertakings.

- Clear coverage of research theory: many research methods texts either avoid, gloss over or over-integrate questions of research theory. This text provides a clear and accessible chapter for undergraduates which lecturers can integrate into the teaching to the level required. 'Real World Research' boxes throughout the text also provide examples of theoretical issues which, again, can be used or avoided based on the direction of the course.

- Outward looking: recognizing that undergraduate students should be introduced to as wide a range of research methods and methodologies as possible. One of the key objectives of this textbook is to detail a wide variety of research methodologies and methods, including documentary analysis, content analysis, discourse analysis, archival research, life histories, narratives, semiotics, image-based research, projective techniques and field notes. The field of social research is very broad. The researcher within the field is concerned with producing methodologically sound research. Within that endeavour there is scope for great creativity and individuality. The methodologies and methods detailed here are some of the ways in which researchers creatively conduct sound systematic research.

- Emphasis on research skills: Chapter 1 sets out the practicalities of actually conducting research (formulating arguments, referencing skills, negotiating access, etc.). This chapter provides a clear pathway, at the start of the text, for students to begin moving on their research project. This chapter can be linked into earlier study skills modules provided during the students' course of study and it can be linked with wider institutional emphasis on student skills development.

- The emphasis on research skills development is enhanced by an accompanying online platform that contains a series of practical exercises, skills activities, that are 'called out' throughout the text. In addition to developing research practice, the platform also hosts all of the supplementary materials packaged with the text (including an eBook if adopted) and is fully compatible with major VLEs.

- Integration of online research methods: online research methods (ORMs) are integrated throughout the text in order to provide an up-to-date introduction to business research methods.

- Blended delivery: The text is available in different electronic formats, ranging from individual chapters through to the entire text. This provides students with an affordable and flexible option to access the text as and when required.

At the end of this learning exercise the student should be able to:

- Discuss many ways of engaging in research.
- Use a variety of methodologies and methods.
- Explain the creative scope of scientific research.
- Outline the constraints on creativity within scientific research.
- Design multi-method research projects.
- Critique the design of research projects.

THEORETICAL AND APPLIED ORIENTATIONS

As some students are required to use a more theoretical orientation than others, the text is designed to be read in different ways. The following models outline the ways in which the proposed text can be used by both more and less theoretically oriented students.

Model 1 details a useful approach to this book for more theoretically oriented students:

Model 1 How to use this book – an academic/theoretical approach to research

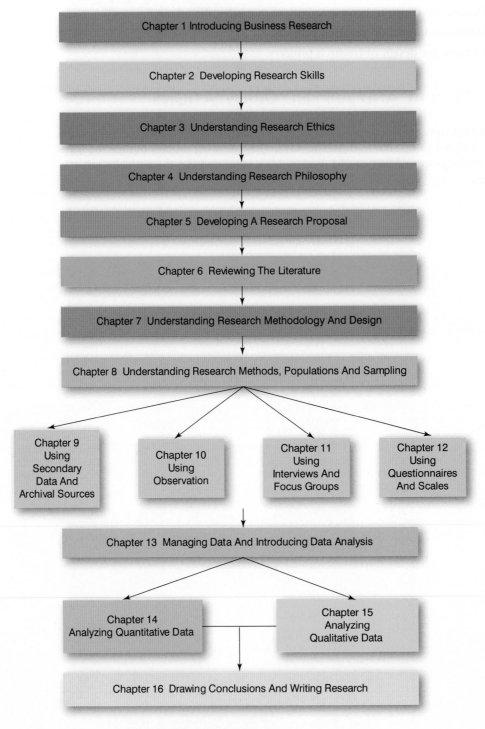

Model 1   How to use this book – an academic/theoretical approach to research

Model 2 details a useful approach to this book for students less theoretically oriented:

Model 2 How to use this book – an applied approach to research

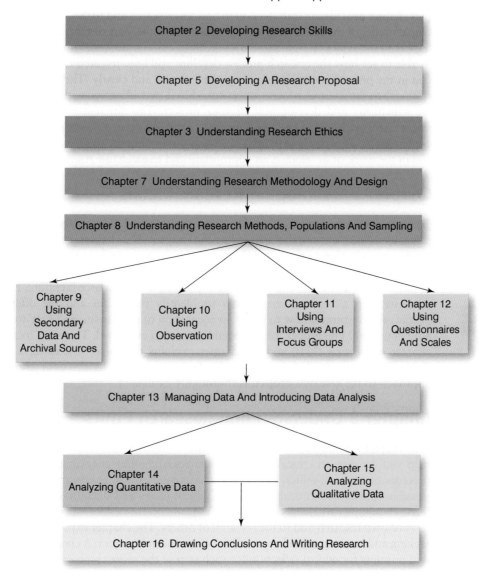

Model 2   How to use this book – an applied approach to research

DETAILED OVERVIEW

Chapter 1 Introducing Business Research

This chapter provides an introduction to business research and to the research process. A simple model of the research process is presented at the start of this chapter and at the start of all subsequent chapters in the book. Using this simple model you, the student, will be able to see how the research process develops and how research is carried out. Each step in the process is outlined and explained simply and clearly. The four frameworks approach to the research process is also introduced, providing you with a simple guide to the structuring and development of your project. The different paradigms in social research are briefly introduced and the ways in which these different paradigms can be used in social research are explored. The focus throughout the chapter is on encouraging you in the work of developing an appropriate and researchable research project.

Chapter 2 Developing Research Skills

To begin with, you are encouraged to assess the standard of your basic research skills, using an online short test, before reading the chapter. The chapter provides a clear and concise introduction to the key skills required to be a researcher. The chapter explains how to formulate an argument, how to develop a research statement or question, how to outline a research aim and a series of objectives, how to source literature, how (and why) to keep a research diary, how to identify plagiarism and the offence that plagiarism constitutes, how to avoid an accusation of plagiarism, and how to compile a bibliography. The proper use of appendices is also explained. There is a focus in this chapter on writing skills, and the chapter explains the value of keeping a research diary. The conceptual framework, the first framework in the four frameworks approach to the research project, is thoroughly explained.

Chapter 3 Understanding Research Ethics

This chapter introduces you to research ethics. A fundamental aim of the textbook is to help you develop an ethical perspective on research. The chapter explains the basic precepts of research ethics, exploring fundamental ethical issues and detailing some possible approaches to dealing with the ethical issues and dilemmas of research projects. The chapter will help you develop a critical reflective ethical approach to research, to your own research and to the research of others. The chapter explains the process of seeking and securing ethical approval for your research project. A checklist of questions and prompts for ethical reflection for each step of the research process is provided.

Chapter 4 Understanding Research Philosophy

This chapter provides a deeper exploration of the philosophical underpinnings of research introduced in the previous chapters, by discussing and developing earlier themes. The philosophical topics covered are positivism, constructionism, interpretivism, functionalism, critical inquiry, feminism and postmodernism. Reading this chapter will provide you with an understanding of the different world views represented in the different philosophical perspectives, and the ways in which these different perspectives shape the research process. The theoretical framework, the second of the four frameworks approach, is introduced here. The chapter highlights the importance of theory in research, and explains how knowledge and theory are generated through research. The links between research, theory and knowledge are discussed.

Chapter 5 Developing A Research Proposal

This chapter focuses on the development of research proposals. As well as teaching you how to develop formal proposals for research projects, this chapter focuses on generating ideas for research projects. The two key skills in generating ideas for viable projects are considered, the first is the ability to come up with ideas for research projects, and the second is the ability to critically evaluate those ideas. A guide to developing a research proposal is provided. This guide clearly outlines and explains the steps in the research proposal. The chapter explains and demonstrates how to: create a conceptual framework for the project; define and refine the question or statement; develop a research aim and objectives; write an appropriate sample literature review; select and justify a methodology; outline a methodological framework. The third framework in the four frameworks approach to the research process is the methodological framework. The chapter demonstrates how all of these different aspects of the research process are brought together in the formal research proposal.

Chapter 6 Reviewing The Literature

This chapter provides an in-depth introduction to the process of compiling a literature review. The chapter explains how to source research literature, evaluate that literature, review the literature and write the literature review. The chapter explains that the theoretical framework, the second framework in the four frameworks approach, is contained in the literature review. In the case study at the end of the chapter, two sample literature reviews are presented in order to provide you with a simple, clear and readily accessible guide to writing a literature review. The first is an example of a poorly written literature review and the second an example of a better literature review.

Chapter 7 Understanding Research Methodology And Design

This chapter provides you with a comprehensive introduction to research methodology and design. The chapter describes many of the different methodologies commonly used in social and business research, and explains how these different methodologies are deployed. The importance of using the most appropriate methodology and the necessity of justifying the choice of methodology used in the research project is explained. The third framework in the four frameworks approach to the research project, the methodological framework, is further explained.

Chapter 8 Understanding Research Methods, Populations and Sampling

This chapter focuses on data collection methods, research populations and samples and sampling methods. These are fundamental elements of the methodological framework, the third framework in the four frameworks approach to the research project. The means by which a research population is selected is explained, as is the means by which a sample is selected from a research population. Both probability and non-probability sampling methods are explained. A detailed introduction to the different research methods, i.e. the different ways of gathering data, is provided. The chapter explains how the choice and design of data collection method(s) used in the research project are fundamentally influenced by the aim of the research being undertaken, the population of the study, the kind of data required for the study and the location and form of that data. The importance of selecting and designing appropriate data collection methods is stressed.

Chapter 9 Using Secondary Data And Archival Sources

This chapter explains the value of secondary data and archival sources. The differences between primary and secondary data are explained and the relative advantages and disadvantages of both are explored. How and where to find secondary data sets and how to use secondary data sets appropriately is explained. The chapter highlights the necessity of critically evaluating secondary data sets, in order to clearly identify any limitations in them in relation to the requirements of the research project being undertaken. The chapter shows how to evaluate the utility and quality of the secondary data available, and explains the importance of such evaluations.

Chapter 10 Using Observation

This chapter explores observation as a data gathering method, demonstrates how to use observation in a small scale research project, and explains how to design and carry out a small observation study. Observation is one of the key data collection methods in social science research. Observation in data gathering is defined as the observation of the phenomenon under investigation, the recording of that observation, and the subsequent analysis of that recording of the observation. The different kinds of observation used in data gathering, participant observation, non-participant observation (or simply observation) and covert observation are explored. The chapter explores in detail how these different kinds of observation can be used in business research and explains how to critique observation methods.

Chapter 11 Using Interviews And Focus Groups

This chapter introduces and explains the data collection methods, interviews and focus groups. The ways in which to structure and carry out interviews and focus groups are demonstrated. Both face-to-face (F2F) focus groups and interviews, and focus groups and interviews conducted online, using computer mediated communication (CMC) are explored. The different types of interviews and their relative advantages and disadvantages are described: one-to-one, in-depth, telephone, group and online interviews. The chapter demonstrates how to design and develop appropriate interview and focus group schedules and explains how to critique the use of interviews and focus groups in research.

Chapter 12 Using Questionnaires And Scales

This chapter explains the use of questionnaires, scales and projective techniques in data gathering. Questionnaires and scales are structured means of data gathering and are used primarily for the production of quantitative data. Quantitative data are numerical data or data that can readily be converted into numerical form. The chapter explains that qualitative data, as well as quantitative data, can be gathered using questionnaires, through the use of open, rather than closed, questions. The chapter explains how to create questionnaires, scales and projective techniques, and when and how to use them. The issues of validity and reliability are explained, and the use and value of a pilot study is explored. The impact of response rates on the research project is considered.

Chapter 13 Managing Data And Introducing Data Analysis

This chapter explains the importance of managing data and introduces you to the processes and procedures of data analysis. The proper management of data is essential in every research project and there are many ways in which data can be lost or damaged or corrupted throughout the research process. A well thought-out plan for the proper management of data can help you avoid these threats to the validity and the quality of your research project. The analytical framework, the fourth and final framework in the four frameworks approach to the research project, is thoroughly discussed. The chapter shows you how to begin the process of data analysis and explains the four stages of data analysis. The four stages of data analysis is a simple model of the data analysis process developed to help you learn how to engage in data analysis and how to analyze your data.

Chapter 14 Analyzing Quantitative Data

This chapter focuses on quantitative data and quantitative data analysis. The chapter demonstrates quantitative data analysis and basic statistical analysis. Simple and more complex examples of quantitative data analysis are presented. The chapter explains what a coding key is and how coding keys are used in the process of analyzing data. The chapter presents an example of a student questionnaire and the coding key developed for that questionnaire. An extract from the data set from this student's research project is presented and explored. The value of SPSS in quantitative data analysis is outlined and the way in which SPSS is used to analyze quantitative data is explained. The value of visual displays of quantitative data analysis, figures, charts and graphs, is explored. The four stages in the data analysis process, which were introduced in Chapter 13, are discussed. The emphasis throughout is on ensuring that you understand all of the concepts and processes presented.

Chapter 15 Analyzing Qualitative Data

This chapter focuses on qualitative data and is designed to teach you how to engage in qualitative data analysis. The key concepts and issues in qualitative data analysis are explained. The chapter demonstrates the processes and procedures of qualitative data analysis. Both simple and more complex approaches to qualitative data analysis are presented. The use of CAQDAS (computer assisted qualitative data analysis software) is explored. Different approaches to analyzing qualitative data are explained. The four stages in the data analysis process are again explored and the chapter demonstrates ways in which you could present your analyzed data. There is a focus on mixed methods research, and on presenting the analysis of data from mixed methods research.

Chapter 16 Drawing Conclusions and Writing Research

The concept of conclusions in research and the manner in which conclusions should be drawn are explained in detail. The chapter shows how conclusions are conceptualized and how they are presented. Examples of how to conceptualize and present appropriate conclusions drawn from the analyzed data are provided in the chapter. The chapter explains what recommendations are, and how they are developed. The chapter explains how the final chapter of the thesis (or the final section of the research report) is designed to answer fully and completely the research question, or designed to respond fully and completely to the research statement, to the aim of the research project. It is in this way, as the chapter explains, that the research project is brought full-circle. A simple guide to the completion of the research project is provided.

PEDAGOGICAL FEATURES

Strong pedagogical features are essential for undergraduate students and the text includes the following range of features:

The Value of Good Research – These boxed features appear consistently throughout the text providing 'real-world' examples of research projects. This boxed feature appears at beginning of each chapter and focuses on reports of research in the media. There is also one of these box features in the middle of every chapter focusing on demonstrating the link between theory and research. In each of these box features an article from an academic journal is used to demonstrate this link.

Your Research – These boxed features explore common research issues and problems students encounter while undertaking research and propose solutions to them or provide a means to deal with them.

Real World Research – This boxed feature appears in every chapter and discusses real life examples of research in a variety of business examples. This feature discusses the real issues faced by researchers and the methods they use.

Research in Practice – This boxed feature focuses on exploring in detail a different research methodology, providing examples of research projects developed using the methodology. Further resources are provided on the methodology in question in each of the boxed features.

Chapter Review – Each chapter contains a brief review of the material covered in that chapter.

End of Chapter Questions – There are questions at the end of each chapter. These questions are designed to encourage the students to check their progress and to review the material covered in the chapter.

Case Studies – There is a case study at the end of each chapter. Each case study draws on a student examples or on a recently published business research project. These examples are drawn from across all business disciplines.

References – There is a complete and comprehensive bibliography at the end of the textbook, with references and a list of recommended readings at the end of each chapter.

Glossary – There is a comprehensive glossary of terms.

ACKNOWLEDGMENTS

For my family

I would like to acknowledge the support I have received from my family and friends throughout the work of writing this textbook. I am particularly indebted to Tom Rennie, formerly of Cengage Learning, for encouraging me to undertake this project and for having confidence in my capacity to produce a textbook which makes a useful contribution to knowledge in the field of social and business research. I am also indebted to Anna Carter for the patience she has shown me throughout the writing of this textbook and for all the encouragement and advice she has given me. I would like to thank Claire Martin for her diligent work in copy-editing the text, and Lucy Arthy and Charlotte Green at Cengage Learning for their courteous engagement with me in the process of finally getting this book to publication.

The publisher would like to thank the following reviewers for their contribution:

Don Keithley, University of Sunderland
George Knox, Faculty of Business and Economics Administration,
    Tilburg University
David Longbottom, University of Derby
Dorothy Macfarlane, Caledonian Business School, Glasgow Caledonian University
Yvonne Moogan, Liverpool Business School
Lenart Persson, Department of Business Administration and Social Sciences,
    Luleå University of Technology
Colin Rigby, School of Economic and Management Studies, University of Keele
Lorna Stevens, Faculty of Business and Management, University of Ulster
Argyrios Syntetos, Salford Business School, University of Salford
Godwin Tetteh, Faculty of Business, Computing and Information Management,
    London South Bank University
Martin Wetzels, Department of Marketing, University of Maastricht
Stephen Woods, Leeds Business School, Leeds Met University

ABOUT THE AUTHOR

CHRISTINA QUINLAN

Dr Christina Quinlan is a social scientist. She has taught research methods to both undergraduate and postgraduate students at Dublin City University for several years. She is interested in both quantitative and qualitative research and she has a particular interest in visual methods. Her PhD research was a study of women's experiences of imprisonment in Ireland. Using critical ethnography, discourse analysis and semiotics, Christina explored the manner in which the identities of imprisoned women are constructed and represented in different discourses, historical discourses, architectural discourses, organizational/managerial discourses and media discourses. Christina also engaged with the imprisoned women themselves and explored with them, using in-depth interviews and photography, the manner in which they constructed and represented their own identities. Christina's book on women's experiences of imprisonment in Ireland was published in 2011 by Irish Academic Press. Her current research interests include: Qualitative and Quantitative Research Methods, Image Based Research, Feminist Research, Media and Communications, Social Control, Prisons and Penality, Narratives of End of Life Experiences, Cross Cultural Communication, Development Issues, Poverty and Marginalized Populations.

SUPPLEMENTS AND BLENDED LEARNING

Research methods courses typically have large student numbers and consequently require the core textbook to supply a robust set of supplementary materials. Using a companion website, this textbook provides the following supplements:

- ExamView testbank – For lecturers containing questions created specifically for the text.
- PowerPoint slides – A full set of slides matched to each chapter and including all of the main figures from the text.
- Instructor's manual – A detailed manual provides suggested answers to the end-of-chapter questions and case study questions.
- Extra tutorial questions – Gives lecturers a set of extra discussion questions with answers for use in tutorials and assignments.

- Software guides – Detailed student guides to NVivo and SPSS are available for download.
- Multiple choice questions
- Online glossary
- Extensive weblinks
- Interactive "research diary" – Containing activities, study notes and a section for students to reflect on their own research. The research diary is fully downloadable and encourages students to record their own findings. A marginal logo throughout the book directs students to make entries into their research diaries or complete activities in relation to their own research.

Students taking business research methods courses often require flexibility in accessing textbook material, calling on chapters when required in an ad hoc and remote fashion (from home, while researching in the library, etc.). This new text recognizes this by offering an electronic version via the cengagebrain platform (see: **www.cengagebrain.com**) whereby students can purchase the entire e-textbook; individual chapters and/or simply subscribe to the etextbook for a set period of time. The emphasis throughout in the text is on accessibility, on rendering research methods and methodologies more accessible to all students.

WALK THROUGH TOUR

Learning Objectives: Listed at the beginning of each chapter, these emphasise the key topics that need to be understood before progressing to the next chapter.

The Value of Good Research: Provides 'real-world' examples of research projects throughout the text. Reporting on research in the media, they demonstrate the link between theory and research.

Your Research: Explore the common research issues and problems students may encounter while undertaking research, including the solutions they need to overcome these issues.

Real World Research: Discusses a variety of 'real life' research projects and demonstrates the range of research methods and methodologies used in business environments.

Research in Practice: Focuses on exploring in detail different research methodologies, providing examples of research projects developed using the methodology.

Chapter Review: Each chapter contains a brief summary of the material covered in that chapter and presents students with the opportunity to recap thier knowledge.

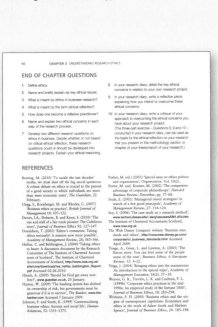

End of Chapter Questions: Designed to encourage the students to check their progress and to review the material covered in the chapter.

References: A complete and comprehensive bibliography at the end of the textbook, with references and a list of recommended readings at the end of each chapter.

Case Studies: At the end of each chapter draw on student examples and recently published business research, from across all business disciplines.

About the Website

All of our Higher Education textbooks are accompanied by a range of digital support resources. Each title's resources are carefully tailored to the specific needs of the particular book's readers. Examples of the kind of resources provided include:

- A password protected area for instructors with, for example, a testbank, PowerPoint slides and an instructor's manual.
- An area for students including, for example, multiple choice questions and weblinks.

To discover the dedicated digital support resources accompanying this textbook please go to:
www.cengage.co.uk/quinlan

For Students

- Downloadable software guides for NVivo, Excel and SPSS
- Multiple choice questions
- Online glossary
- Weblinks
- Interactive research diary

For Lecturers

- ExamView testbank
- PowerPoint slides
- Instructor's manual
- Extra tutorial questions

CHAPTER 1

INTRODUCING BUSINESS RESEARCH

LEARNING OBJECTIVES

At the end of this chapter the student should be able to:

- Detail the research process and explain the utility of the four frameworks approach to the research project.

- Outline and briefly explain each of the stages in the research process.

- Explain the different paradigms in social research.

- Apply different research paradigms in designing research projects.

- Know how to formulate a researchable problem.

RESEARCH SKILLS

At the end of this chapter the student should, using the exercises on www.cengage.co.uk/quinlan, be able to:

- Outline the steps in the research process.

- Differentiate between a research idea and a research statement or question.

- Trace the elements of the research process in a given sample project.

The aim of this chapter is to introduce you, the student, to the process of carrying out research. As you will see, this step in the process is generally the same in every research project. However, the approaches taken to each step in the process vary a great deal, and are in many cases, unique to each research project.

INTRODUCTION

Research process
The means by which research is carried out.

Figure 1.1 is a model of the **research process**. It appears at the start of each chapter to illustrate which element in the research process is the focus of the content of the chapter. As you can see, the process of undertaking research involves a number of steps. In the first place, you begin with an idea for a research project. You then start to refine that idea, by thinking about it, reflecting on it, and by engaging with the literature in the area to explore and examine how other researchers have engaged with this idea in their own research. You engage with the literature in the area in order to explore and examine how other researchers have engaged with this idea in their own research.

In the context of a research project, literature is research that has already been carried out and published may published in books, articles in scientific journals, theses, conference reports, government reports, the reports of NGOs (non-governmental organizations), and in the media.

Literature review
Always undertaken in order to embed the researcher and research project in the body of knowledge.

As you reflect on your research idea and engage with the literature, you will refine your idea. While you are engaging in this work, of refining your idea, it is a good discipline to try to express your idea in one sentence. This sentence can be a statement or a question. This one sentence becomes the conceptual framework for your research project. It contains all of the key concepts, all of the key words and phrases, in your research.

When you have gotten to the point of stating your research idea in one sentence, you will begin the process of developing an aim and a series of objectives for your research. Then you will start to write a review of the literature for your research project. This is a review of all of the published literature (theory) that you have read for your research. The **literature review** that you develop becomes the theoretical framework that your research project will be built upon.

Methodology
The way in which the research is carried out, as means of supporting the philosophical assumptions that underpin the research project.

You then select a research **methodology** for your research project. Examples of research methodologies include case study, survey, attitude research, action research, ethnographic research, grounded theory research, image-based research and feminist research. The different research methodologies used in social research and in business research are explored in detail in this textbook. You will then decide on the **data collection methods** to be used in your research. Examples of data collection methods include observation, questionnaires, interviews and focus groups. Other

Data collection methods
The means by which data is gathered for a research project, e.g. observation, interviews, focus groups, questionnaires.

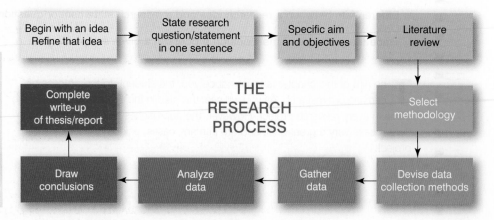

Figure 1.1   The research process

data collection methods you might choose from include scales, projective techniques, diaries, images, narratives, life histories, the use of documents, archives, printed material, film and symbols. These data collection methods are also considered in this textbook.

Then you will begin to gather **data**. Data in a research project are information or evidence that the researcher gathers in order to be able to explore the phenomenon under investigation or to prove or disprove the research hypothesis. The data gathered allow you to build a picture on the phenomenon under investigation; the more data and the better their quality, the more complex and richer the picture of the phenomenon you can present in the written report of the research. If you can gather data from several sources or perspectives, you can use comparisons to produce an even richer view of the phenomenon. When the data are gathered, you begin the work of analysing it. This involves first describing the data and then interpreting it. When the data are analyzed you conclude the research. **Conclusions** are drawn from the analyzed data. These conclusions are then theorized; this means that you knit them into the body of knowledge, and in this way the body of knowledge in this field grows and develops. Finally you complete the writing of the thesis or the report of the research.

The model of the research process above starts with 'begin with an idea, refine that idea', and then follows the arrows all the way around to the last element 'write thesis/report'. In practice, researchers do not wait until all of the steps have been taken to begin to write the report of the research, the thesis. Instead, they begin writing as they start the research process. As the research process develops and becomes more complex, so too does the written account of the research. Research projects are very creative endeavours; they might be said to be perhaps one part creative and one part **rigorous** and scientific.

THE FOUR FRAMEWORKS APPROACH

The **four frameworks approach** was developed specifically for students in order to provide them with a simple guide to help them develop their research projects. Using the four frameworks approach to the research project, the researcher uses their (very well-conceptualized) research question or statement (the first of the four frameworks, the conceptual framework) to direct the development of the research. The first framework, the conceptual framework, directs the development of the other three frameworks, the theoretical framework, the methodological framework and the analytical framework.

The four frameworks approach to the research process helps students avoid the confusion, uncertainty and even fear that can beset them when they are confronted with undertaking independent research. Students sometimes perceive independent research to be a mammoth task, an exercise in scholarship and knowledge creation that is seemingly without boundaries. I have found in my teaching that the four frameworks approach gives students a model with which they can map the boundaries of their own project. The four frameworks approach helps them maintain focus as they undertake their research. At the same time, the model does not prevent students from taking on board any new shift in direction that may naturally occur as their research develops. Students are able to incorporate any new insights or ideas they might develop through their review of the literature, their experiences while gathering data, or through their reflections on their research.

Data
Information or evidence gathered for a research project.

Conclusion
Essentially a judgement or a final decision.

Rigorous
For a research project to be rigorous, it must adhere to the scientific principles of research. The research must be systematic and valid.

Four frameworks approach
An approach to carrying out research whereby the conceptual framework, shapes, supports and directs the other three frameworks.

Figure 1.2   The four frameworks

The four frameworks approach to the research project is shown in Figure 1.2.

As can be seen, the first framework in the four frameworks approach is the conceptual framework. This, as previously stated, is contained in the one-sentence research question or statement which you, as the researcher, develop from your reflection on your research idea and from your reading of the literature published in the area of your research. Each key word and phrase in that one sentence is a **key concept** in your research.

The second framework is the theoretical framework. This is contained in the literature review undertaken and written for the research project. The key concepts in the conceptual framework help to guide the researcher towards an appropriate structure and the content for the literature review.

The third framework is the methodological framework. It is contained in the research methodology chapter or the thesis, in the research methodology section of the report of the research. This contains all of the information and detail relating to the research methodology and methods used in the research project. It is a complete and thorough account of how the research was carried out.

The final framework is the analytical framework. This framework is contained in the data analysis chapter of the thesis, or in the data analysis section of the report of the research. It contains all of the detail of the analysis carried out for the research that is to be presented in the written account of the research project. The researcher is guided in the work of carrying out and presenting the **data analysis** by the conceptual framework and the theoretical framework constructed for the research project, and also by the methodological framework, which provides the means through which data for analysis are to be gathered.

The four frameworks approach is explained in detail throughout this textbook. It provides a simple framework to guide researchers in the development and completion of thoroughly integrated and sound research projects. As Figure 1.3 shows, the conceptual framework for the research project informs and shapes the three subsequent frameworks; the theoretical framework, the methodological framework and the analytical framework.

While all of this represents quite a lot of information to take on board, each of these topics is dealt with in this textbook in a relatively simple and straightforward manner. In order to read the material presented in this textbook for understanding, it is best to skim the material quickly to begin with, then read the material through thoroughly and for meaning, then finally read it through fluently for understanding and learning. You will find that such an active engagement with the material will help you throughout this book, and indeed throughout your studies generally.

Key concept
A key idea, a word, or phrase.

Data analysis
The process of exploring and examining data with a view to uncovering meaning. Data is analyzed in order to uncover patterns and trends.

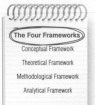

The Four Frameworks
Conceptual Framework
Theoretical Framework
Methodological Framework
Analytical Framework

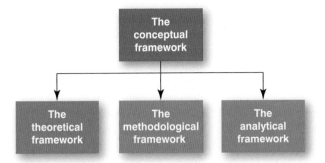

Figure 1.3   The four frameworks approach to the research project

The box below contains an extract from an article published in *The Observer* newspaper. In the article the authors highlight the view that simply relying on economic measures, such as measures of gross domestic product (GDP), is an inadequate way of measuring the well-being of people or the state of a nation. The article calls for the development of measures of happiness by researchers, heads of state and economists. It is useful for our purposes here in that it provides an example of some of the ways in which research can be used. It highlights one of the debates which are currently being held within the world of social scientific research. Perhaps you might develop an idea for a research project from your reading of the article.

The article suggests that GDP is an inadequate measure of a nation's well-being and highlights the fact that endless growth in consumption is having adverse climatic effects on the planet. It might be interesting to design a research project to examine the work of economists who have tried to come up with alternative measures of well-being. You could focus on one economist in particular, and examine the relative successes and failures of their theories. Through a research project, you could attempt to develop a measure of well-being. This would require a study of the different measures of well-being that have already been developed. You could conduct a survey among your classmates in order to establish what it is that they think contributes to their overall sense of well-being, and the contribution that economic well-being makes to it. Through research projects such as these, it might be possible to make a contribution to economic theory in this area.

THE VALUE OF GOOD RESEARCH

Research in the media

'Growth loses its place in the pursuit of happiness', Seager, A. and Stewart, H. *The Observer*, 10th January 2010

Britain has got the shopping habit back. We may only now be clambering out of the worst recession in living memory, but John Lewis has scored its best Christmas ever, Next clocked up a healthy festive season, and Boxing Day kicked off with jostling queues of bargain-hunters outside shopping centres, determined not to miss a moment of the sales.

For long-suffering retailers, and the gleeful shoppers themselves, that feels like good news, but should we welcome the return of the spendthrift habits that plunged us into crisis in the first place, or is it time to ask if traditional metrics of economic success – retail sales, house prices, even GDP growth – really point us in the right direction?

Indeed, with the issue of climate change becoming ever more urgent and a growing recognition that economic growth does not make people any happier, there are growing calls for growth and the endless consumption of ever more material goods to be downgraded as political goals.

The pursuit of growth and endless rises in consumption every year have become part of the national psyche, since Harold Macmillan told the electorate they had 'never had it so good'. The idea that more, bigger and cheaper is better is a powerful one, and it will be hard to dislodge. It affects the way we think, the things politicians aim for and how journalists report events.

Rises in economic output, a company's sales or house prices are invariably considered good, rises in petrol prices bad. But debate is growing. Just as he sparked a furore last year about whether the activities of the City were good for society, Financial Services Authority chief Adair Turner last week

Buses and illuminated decorations on Oxford Street, London © Justin Kase zsixz/Alamay

questioned whether economic growth was a 'false god'. He said that not only did growth harm the climate by increasing emissions of greenhouse gases, but 'all the evidence shows that beyond the sort of standard of living which Britain has now achieved, extra growth does not automatically translate into human welfare and happiness'.

This is an area some economists have tried to deal with for several decades, by attempting to subtract from GDP figures the social or environmental consequences of growth. Cleaning up an oil spill counts towards GDP, but the environmental damage it causes does not; pumping the oil out of the ground counts as economic activity, but the resource depletion it implies is not accounted for.

One of the oldest advocates of an alternative approach is Herman Daly, an American ecological economist who decades ago developed a measure called the 'index of sustainable economic welfare' and the idea of a 'steady state economy', which argues that the world has to develop a way to live within its means and the limitations of its resources. Another supporter is Chilean economist Manfred Max-Neef, who works on development and poverty issues, and argues that conventional models of development increase poverty and ecological disaster.

Professor David Blanchflower of Dartmouth College, New Hampshire – better known in Britain for being the only member of the Bank of England's monetary policy committee to see the recession coming – has spent decades working on measures of happiness and well-being which, he says, offer politicians much more useful ways to think about what policy they should aim for, rather than merely expanding GDP.

Blanchflower rejects the idea that happiness is difficult to measure. Not only are there huge amounts of survey data over decades asking people about how they feel, he says, but cross-checks with other disciplines such as psychology or medicine and their data on metrics such as blood pressure work very well. And the fundamental truth the data reveal is that, despite decades of economic growth in the western world, people have not got happier.

Sensing that GDP measures might have outlived their usefulness, last September French President

Nicolas Sarkozy commissioned a report by a panel of experts, headed by Nobel prize-winning economist Joseph Stiglitz, to look at how to ensure governments take full account of their citizens' happiness and well-being, not just the country's economic growth.

References

Seager, A. and Stewart, H. (2010) 'Growth loses its place in the pursuit of happiness', The Observer, 10 January © Guardian News & Media Ltd 2010. Reproduced with permission.

THE FOUR FRAMEWORKS AND THE RESEARCH PROCESS

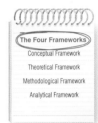

As explained above, using a four frameworks approach to any research project provides structure to the research project and guidance for the researcher in structuring the project. To recap, the four frameworks are the conceptual framework, the theoretical framework, the methodological framework and the analytical framework (see Table 1.1). The conceptual framework is contained in the research statement, question or hypothesis developed by the researcher for the research project. The theoretical framework is contained in the literature review. The methodological framework details how the research was conducted, and it is contained in the methodology section of the research report or thesis. The analytical framework is the structure of the detailed analysis of the data presented in the report or thesis. Each of these sections of the research project is dealt with in detail in the relevant chapter(s) of this book.

Once you have decided on your topic for your research project it is a good discipline to express this idea in one sentence. This then becomes the conceptual framework, clearly and simply defined, for the research project. An example of a research statement:

 This research project is a case study designed to facilitate the development of a new induction programme for new employees of Mannings Manufacturing Ltd.

Defining of the research project in one sentence helps exclude all of the concepts which are not relevant to the research, and facilitates the researcher in considering and exploring every concept which is relevant. All of the key concepts in the research

Table 1.1 Detail of the four frameworks	
The conceptual framework	Contained in the research statement, question or hypothesis
The theoretical framework	Contained in the literature review
The methodological framework	Contained in the methodology section
The analytical framework	Contained in the data analysis presented in the thesis

project should be included in this sentence. This notion of key concepts is something that we will be returning to again and again throughout the research process. You will notice that the statement of the research previously also contains a statement of the methodology to be used. It tells us that the research methodology used in (or proposed for use in) the research project was a case study methodology. Through this one sentence we now know exactly what this research project is about, and we also know what methodology was used in the research.

The research statement or question contains the conceptual framework for the research project. This one sentence contains all of the key concepts of the research project. Concepts are fundamental to research; they are the building blocks of theory, which is fundamental to all academic research. It is through building theory, that bodies of knowledge develop.

All academic researchers undertake a review of the literature in the field of their study. They do this in order to assess the state of knowledge in the field, and to identify any gaps in this knowledge. Another reason to conduct a literature review is for the researcher to develop their own expertise in the area or field of their research. In writing a review of the literature, the researcher constructs a theoretical framework for the research they are carrying out. The key concepts in the conceptual framework give the researcher guidance and direction in terms of the reading they need to undertake in order to develop a literature review, or a theoretical framework, for their research project. For example in the research statement on page 9, the key concepts are the key words and phrases; they are 'induction programme', 'the creation of an induction programme', 'new employees', and 'Mannings Manufacturing'. While 'Mannings Manufacturing' is not itself a key concept, Mannings Manufacturing is a small-to-medium-sized enterprise (an SME), and SME is a key concept in this research statement.

These key concepts are used by the researcher to direct the search for literature for the literature review. In other words, the researcher is searching through the literature for research that has been published on the areas of new employees, induction programmes, induction programmes for new employees, and induction programmes for new employees in SMEs. The literature found through these key-word searches represents the body of knowledge within which this research project is situated. Each research project is situated within a body of knowledge, and in turn, when completed, each research project makes a contribution to that body of knowledge.

KEEPING A RESEARCH DIARY

As you begin to engage with the process of creating, designing and developing your research project, it is important to begin to record your thoughts, ideas, inspirations, references, and resources in your research diary. This is a notebook which you have set aside solely for this purpose. It is best to use a hardback notebook as your research diary will be used a lot throughout the project and you don't want it to fall apart and you certainly don't want to lose any pages from it. This written, often scribbled, record of your thoughts and decisions will be invaluable to you when you are writing the formal written account of the research. You will be able to refer back to the research diary for inspiration and ideas and this will save you a lot of time in the writing process, as well as radically improving the formal written account of the research.

YOUR RESEARCH
The research diary

In the research diary, the researcher records his/her thoughts and ideas about their research project, his/her observations, understandings and reactions to the phenomena they witness, experience and study in the field. Researchers usually find that as their research project develops it changes, and as their acquaintance with the field develops, their perceptions and experiences of it change. These changes occur naturally as the research project deepens and develops. As this happens, records of initial perceptions and experiences are very useful. They provide a point of comparison with more mature experiences, and they provide a challenge to the 'naturalness' of more mature field experiences. In other words, experiences and phenomena that appear extraordinary to researchers fresh to a field can become naturalized as the researcher's field experience deepens and develops. In addition to this, thoughts, impressions and ideas recorded in the research diary often provide researchers with the means to begin the process of writing up different elements, aspects and chapters of the research report/thesis. Take this opportunity to update your interactive research diary, available at www.cengage.co.uk/quinlan.

When you begin thinking of a research project, you start by identifying an area within which you would like to conduct some research. This might concern marketing, human resources, or perhaps product development. The important thing is to decide on an area that interests you. In writing a report or a thesis on a topic in this area, you are in effect writing a book on that topic, which may ultimately contain anything from 10 000 to 90 000 words. By the time you have finished, you will become quite expert on your topic and it is therefore important that you work on a topic that is of particular interest to you. Perhaps this is an area in which you already have some particular expertise, or would like to develop some expertise. You may even be planning a career in this area.

YOUR RESEARCH
Common research problems

It is important to be able to distinguish between an area of interest, and a topic for a research project.

Once you have decided on your area, you need an idea for a topic within that area which you can develop into your research project. A common mistake that many beginning researchers make is to define their research project too broadly.

For example, you might be interested in human resources, but your topic for your research project might be, for instance, 'The Development of a New Induction Programme for New Employees of Mannings Manufacturing Ltd', where Mannings Manufacturing Ltd is the company or business within which you will work on your college placement, or it is the company you will work with in your summer job, or it is the company you have your part-time job with, or indeed your full-time job, if you are in full-time employment.

So you see, while your area of interest can be, and probably will be, quite broad, your research project will be very focused, and quite small in relation to the broad area.

It is essential that your research project be very focused and limited in scope.

- Is it possible to set these sentences as bullet points? It must be completed within the time allowed for the research.

- It must be completed within the word count allowed for the project. It must be 'do-able' or 'researchable' within the scope of the resources available to you.

- It must be to the standard required by your programme of study.

- It must 'fit' with the requirements of your degree programme.

THE DEVELOPMENT OF SOCIAL RESEARCH

Social research
Research conducted by social scientists on some aspects of the social world. Can be inductive or deductive.

Social research is about investigating some aspect of the social world. The process of social research, as we have seen, involves developing a question or a statement and then gathering data on the particular phenomenon being investigated in order to answer the question or respond to the statement. Anthony Giddens (2001: 639) says that good researchers try to make the (research) question or statement posed as precise as possible, and then they gather **empirical** evidence (data) on the topic before coming to conclusions. An empirical statement or theory, according to *The Penguin Dictionary of Sociology* (Abercrombie *et al.*, 2000: 117), 'is one which can be tested by some kind of evidence drawn from experience'. The word empirical is used to describe information, evidence or data gained from observation, experience or experiment.

Empirical
Information or evidence gained from observation, experience or experiment.

As individuals, we all draw our own conclusions in relation to the social world and our experiences of it. These conclusions are often influenced by our social class, gender, race, age, religious beliefs and formation, the socialization process we have undergone, the education we received, the family life we have experienced and are experiencing, our roles within that family, and so on. The personal perspectives that we have of the social world can seem to us so natural and normal that we may not really see that they are subjective. When we undertake a research project, it is important to explore our own motivations. As researchers we try to identify our patterns of perception in terms of the social world, and by identifying them and acknowledging them, attempt to transcend them. In this way, we try in our research to develop an 'objective' view of the world as it is. Or, we may attempt to develop an understanding of the world or a particular experience of the world as it is experienced, or lived, by a particular social group. The social world is extremely complex. It may be viewed differently from different perspectives, different theoretical perspectives and different research methodologies are used to study to social world. Every researcher must be aware of this complexity, and of their own particular perspectives on the world and how these perspectives can shape and influence the ways in which they approach and conduct social research.

THE DIFFERENT SOCIAL RESEARCH PARADIGMS

The social sciences were founded in the 1800s by Auguste Compte and developed into the 1900s by pioneering sociologists, among them: Emile Durkheim, Max Weber and Karl Marx. At its beginnings, the new science of sociology was positivistic. It initially attempted to model itself on the natural sciences and for over a hundred years

YOUR RESEARCH
Your research diary

Start and maintain a research diary. It is important to do this as you are beginning to think about your research project. Start your research diary by recording your own thoughts in relation to the areas and fields of business and business research that particularly interest you, and the issues and questions that come to mind when you focus on these areas. The purpose of this exercise is to help you move towards selecting an area within which to develop your research project.

The notes that you jot down during your reflections do not need to be very elaborate. They are simply notes you write to yourself in order to maintain a record of your thoughts and ideas with regard to your research. These notes will be very helpful when you begin the process of designing, carrying out and writing up your research project. Take this opportunity to update your interactive research diary, available at www.cengage.co.uk/quinlan.

endeavoured to establish its research credentials by adopting a 'scientific' or 'objective' approach. For example, Durkheim, in his work, used inferential statistics on suicide to measure social and moral integration. He did this perhaps because sociology was at that time endeavouring to define itself as a science in the way that botany is a science, or physics is a science. In scientific work at that time, only data after the positivist school were accepted as legitimate. The *Penguin Dictionary of Sociology* has a useful section on positivism (2000: 269).

Positivism in social research is associated with quantitative research, the production and study of numbers and statistics. However, much social research is not concerned with numbers at all, rather with social situations and with the manner in which groups and individuals experience and interpret them. So social research, as well as providing for the production of statistics in terms of the social world, also uses interviews, participant observation, oral histories and life histories, historical data, visual images, and so on, in order in order to study people's experiences and expressions, and the meanings people make, of social phenomena and social experiences. Such social research is referred to as qualitative research. It is research conducted within an interpretivist paradigm framework, a social constructionist paradigm framework, as opposed to a positivist paradigm framework.

Social constructionists and positivists are said to understand the world differently. Positivists see the world as having one reality of which we are all a part. Social constructionists see the world as being co-constituted, co-created, socially constructed, and made up of many different realities. For the interpretivist we each interpret the world in our own way, and through our individual and unique interpretation, we construct our own realities. In this way, reality is said to be multiple. Interpretivists and social constructionists can be critical of the positivists' view that there is one singular objective reality. The interpretivist and the social constructionist hold that reality is unique to each individual and to the manner in which each individual, given their own unique set of circumstances and life experiences, constructs, experiences and/or interprets their world.

The divide between the paradigms of positivism, social constructionism and interpretivism presents researchers with a substantial epistemological question. Epistemology is the theory of knowledge; it is the branch of philosophy concerned with

Multiple realities – an example

L ook at your own situation. Your experience of your family is uniquely your own. Your brother/sister/mother/father/daughter/son all have different perspectives on that family. They each have their own, individual and unique, reality in terms of their experience of the same family. Such is the complexity of the social world. Even at the level of one family, the complexity of human experience is extraordinary. Now multiply that complexity to a broader social situation, such as the study, for example, of induction programmes for new employees in a SME, and you will get a sense of just how complex social science research can be.

what knowledge is and how it is created. A researcher who conducts research with a view to presenting that research as some scientific record of an experience or a phenomenon, is presenting the world with new knowledge. The objective in all research conducted within an academic setting is to contribute to a body of knowledge. Because of this, it is important to establish the validity of any newly-created knowledge. The researcher must be in a position to substantiate claims made in their research and the manner in which new knowledge is created becomes critical. If the manner in which the knowledge was created can be examined, the new knowledge can be judged, critiqued and finally accepted or rejected.

The divide between positivism, social constructionism and interpretivism presents researchers with another substantial philosophical question, and that is the question of ontology. Ontology is the study of the nature of reality. As we have discussed, positivists and social constructionists and interpretivists hold different views on the nature of reality: positivists hold reality to be singular and objective; interpretivists hold reality to be multiple and subjective; social constructionists hold reality to be socially constructed, in other words phenomena develop within social contexts. Social constructionists study the ways in which individuals and groups participate in the creation of their own subjective realities, and individuals and groups are said to co-create their realities (see Berger and Luckman, 1966).

In order to cope with these and other issues in the creation of knowledge within the complex nature of reality, social research provides a number of **social research paradigms** within which social scientists may conduct research. These are called research methodologies and, as previously discussed, they include survey, case study, ethnography, oral history, action research, phenomenology, grounded theory, content analysis, and semiotics. Some of these methodologies call for entirely, or predominately, qualitative data while others demand quantitative data. Quantitative data is positivistic and qualitative data is interpretivist or constructionist.

Social research paradigms
Different perspectives taken by social scientists on the social world e.g. interpretivism and social constructionism.

AN INTRODUCTION TO RESEARCH METHODOLOGY

The methodological framework, the third framework in the four frameworks approach to the research project, is contained in the methodology section of the

RESEARCH IN PRACTICE

Multiple and subjective realities – an example

Imagine that you are reading this paragraph in a seminar or lecture on research methods. Let us say that there are 20 students participating in the seminar, or attending the lecture. If this is the case, then there are 20 students attending or participating. This is a fact. It is indisputable. This is the way in which reality can be said to be singular and objective. Then think about how the 20 students are experiencing the seminar or lecture. No two students will experience the seminar or lecture in the same way. Perhaps many of the students spend the time applying all that is being said to their own research project. Each project will be very individual and so each application of the science will be very unique. Perhaps there are students in the seminar or lecture who are really enjoying the experience. This may be, but the reasons why they are enjoying the experience, and ways in which they are enjoying the experience, and the complexity of that enjoyment, will be entirely individual and uniquely their own. Perhaps there are students who spend the time of the seminar or lecture simply wishing that the experience was over. This may be the case, but the reasons for this will be individual and unique for each student. This is an example of the way in which reality can be said to be multiple and subjective.

Now think of the researcher who has to try to document these experiences, to explore the patterns and trends in these experiences, to detail all that is unique in these experiences. The tools that you will learn from this textbook and from undertaking your own research will provide for you real skills in undertaking such research, and a real insight into how such research is accomplished.

thesis or report, and it contains all of the detail on how the research was conducted. As explained above, there are many different methodologies used in conducting research, examples include including case studies, surveys, experimental design, meta-analysis, attitude research, action research, ethnography, feminist research, grounded theory, semiotics, image-based research, phenomenology, and so on. Each of these methodologies has particular application, or use. The different research methodologies are dealt with more thoroughly in Chapter 7 of this textbook. Traditionally among business students, the common methodologies tended to be surveys and case studies. The other methodologies mentioned, and others besides, are now being used more frequently.

Some research projects can appear to have elements of more than one methodology. You might think that your own project is a survey with case study elements, for example. Or it may be that it is a case study but there is a semiotics element in it. This is frequently the case with social research. As research projects begin and develop, they can often seem to fit quite well with more than one methodology. However, it is essential for the purposes of clarity that the researcher decides which methodology is most appropriate for the project. The decision about the appropriateness of any methodology for any and every research project is a decision around 'fit': how well does the proposed methodology fit the proposed research project?

Along with methodology, the researcher is concerned with data collection methods, the means by which data are gathered. Data are presented as evidence in the research project in order to establish the argument, or the hypothesis of the research. Some data collection methods are very familiar; we have all filled in questionnaires, and some of us have participated in interviews and focus groups. Every data collection method is designed to focus on, observe and record observations of some phenomenon. Observation itself is another key data collection method, along with questionnaires, interviews and focus groups. Other data collection methods include scales and projective techniques, visual methods, photographs, pictures, maps, videos, films, the gathering of narratives, the use of field diaries, and documentary evidence. The data collection method(s) to be used in any research project is indicated to the researcher by the type of data required, by the population or sample population used, and by the methodology proposed for the project.

The Cyclical Process of Action

The research process, as stated above, is generally the same for every research project, but there are one or two exceptions. Among these exceptions is action research, where the research process is more cyclical than linear.

The model below (see Figure 1.4) is a simple model of the **cyclical process** of action research. As you can see, the process is quite different from the linear process detailed in the model of the research process (see Figure 1.1). Action research is a research methodology that has particular application in the work of improving practice. It is an appropriate methodology if a researcher wants, through their research project, to improve their own work performance, or the performance of a team, or performance in any other setting.

As can be seen from the model below, the process of action research is cyclical or spiralling. The research process moves from:

Cyclical process
A cycle of research, as opposed to a linear (or straight line) process.

- planning some change and the ways in which to measure it
- to acting, carrying out the planned change and measuring it
- to critically reflecting, thinking in a critical way about the change that was made, and the data from the measurement of the change
- to evaluating the change, deciding what impact the change has had, and weighing the value of the impact of the change.

When the researcher gets to the end of evaluating the change, they can go back to the planning stage and re-iterate each of the steps in the action research process. The

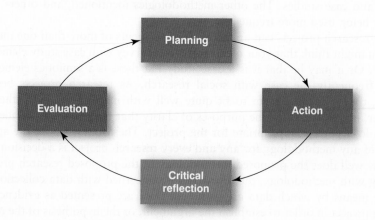

Figure 1.4   The process of action research

THE VALUE OF GOOD RESEARCH

Focus on action research

Action research is one of many research methodologies used in social science research. Research, has particular use when the focus of the research is on bringing about change and development.

In her article in the academic journal *Action Research* Grant (2007), details the action research project she developed for her PhD research. In the article, Grant makes important points about learning in the process of undertaking research, and she emphasizes the value of reflection in that process.

Grant explains in the article that the process of action research is not a linear process. She explores, in detail, the nature of action research.

She describes her plans for her research project, she describes how those plans sometimes failed, and how, when they failed, the decisions she made and actions she took in order to move her research project on.

The case study at the end of this chapter details a student's research proposal for a research project to be developed using an action research methodology.

References

Grant, S. (2007) 'Learning through "being" and "doing"', *Action Research* 5(3): 265–274.

cyclical process can be re-enacted as often as is necessary, or as often as is practicable. For a very simple overview of action research, find the YouTube clip *Action Research Made Simple*. This video was created for educators by Dr Margaret Farren, of Dublin City University. There are other YouTube videos on action research on the internet that you might like to view. Participatory Action Research (PAR) is another methodology that is used a lot in development work. For examples of this type of research in action see the case studies on the website of the organization *Research for Development* (**www.research4development.info/index.asp**), supported by the *UK Department for International Development* (DFID).

The fact that the research process is generally the same for many research projects means that once you have learned the basics of the research process, you can apply your knowledge to every research project that you undertake. Understanding the basic processes of the research process will also allow you to critique the research of others, perhaps research commissioned by your organization, or research carried out by some body or group commenting on your work or on an area of your expertise. Everyone working in a professional capacity should be able to read and understand basic research, and to have the ability to critically engage with research relevant to their interests and their work, and also possess some skills in carrying out research themselves.

Some problems business students typically encounter when approaching research methods for the first time

Many students new to research methods allow themselves to be put off by the new words, terms and concepts they encounter when they first begin to read into the subject. This is a great pity because with a little effort to become familiar with the terminology and the concepts, each student can relatively easily begin to develop a valuable new skill. Skilled researchers are highly prized in every organization, in multinational corporations, in small businesses, in the public sector and in not-for-profit organizations. As stated earlier, it is important for every professional to have the skills required to undertake research. It is important too to have the skills required to read and understand other people's research, and the research of other organizations. Such research might have important or critical implications for your own work and organization. Every organization needs people who can make this kind of contribution.

Research is essentially a creative undertaking. In general, the academy, university or college does not impose a research project on any student, beyond restricting them to researching their own academic field. So students are free to decide for themselves what to research. This means that while all the other subjects which must be undertaken for a qualification or credential at college or university are created and developed by someone else, this is the one subject which each student themselves designs, creates and develops. It is very important to be creative in research. The entire research endeavour at university is dedicated to the creation and development of knowledge. In undertaking your research project you are undertaking to create something new, to create some new knowledge, perhaps a new product, or a new training programme, or a new marketing strategy, or a new theory, or a new concept, or a new idea about an area of business.

Once started on a course of study in research methods, usually undertaken to prepare for the practical exercise of designing and carrying out a research project, many students make the mistake of trying to research something that is too big. It is important that as you yourself are designing the research project that you will have to conduct, you design a project that it will be possible to complete. You yourself are designing the mountain that you will have to climb; so do not make that mountain too big or too difficult to conquer. As stated earlier, a very common problem is that of students trying to research their idea, instead of first turning their idea into a research question or statement and then researching that question or statement.

Another mistake that students sometimes make is to create a research question or statement that has an '*and*' in the middle of it. Take the following research statement, for example:

> *This research project is a survey examining the attitudes of the employees of Swinton Records to the company's new business plan* and *the proposed relocation of the company to a new green field site.*

In effect, this is two research projects. The first project proposed is a survey examining the attitudes of the employees of Swinton Records to the company's new business plan. The second project proposed is a survey of the attitudes of the employees of Swinton Records to the proposed relocation of the company to a new green field site. It is neither necessary nor wise to attempt to undertake two research projects. It is sufficient to do one or the other of these. While each alone seems perhaps quite a simple study, each will grow and grow in complexity as each study develops. If you find yourself in such a position with your proposed research, with an '*and*' in the middle of the research question or statement, make a decision and move your project forward. You might decide to pick the project that most appeals to you, the one that makes most sense to you, the one that is perhaps the most useful for the company you are working with or researching, or the one that works for you in terms of taking you in a direction you wish to go in, with the company or with your career. It could happen that you might decide to keep the 'and' and do the bigger project because you feel that both aspects to the project are essential. It may be that this is the case. Then you will undertake the project as outlined in the research statement above. It is important, however, to have an understanding of the size of the project you are undertaking, and the resources you have available to you. Whichever decision you make, the important thing is to make a decision. Then once you have made a decision, move on.

Making decisions is, in itself, a problem for many students. To be a good researcher you must be able to decide what to include in your research and what to exclude. You must also be able to move quickly on from a decision and leave behind whatever you have decided to leave behind. As soon as a decision is made to exclude something from the research, your focus must move on from it. If it is excluded, it is no longer relevant. Focus only on what is relevant. It is in this way that your research project becomes more focused and more organized, through all of the decisions, big and small, that you make about it.

It is very useful, as the project develops, to have these decisions, and your reflections about them, recorded in the research diary. You can re-visit your research diary at any time and read through your thinking and reasoning in relation to any decision made. The record kept in the research diary will provide you with material for writing up your research project. At the very least, the material in your research diary will give you ideas for your writing.

How to formulate a researchable project

A researchable project is a project that the researcher could possibly undertake and complete. Many students develop ideas for projects that could not possibly be undertaken or completed. The simple test on below can establish very quickly whether or not a research project is researchable.

THE TEST OF RESEARCHABILITY

In this simple test you examine whether or not you have the resources to complete the research project you are thinking of undertaking. The resources you need are:

- The time needed to conduct the research: to design the project, carry out the field work, analyze the data, write up your findings, draw conclusions and make recommendations.

- The money needed to conduct the research. In general with small-scale research projects, funds may be required for the field work, for example, for posting questionnaires, for travelling to interviews and organising focus groups.

- Access to data. Many students underestimate the difficulties that researchers can encounter in accessing data, in attempting to access data, in securing access to data, and in maintaining access to data over the time period required to complete the field work.

From time to time you may ponder many issues and questions in relation to the business world. However, while all of these areas interest you, it may perhaps not be possible to conduct research on them. The reason for this may be one of practicality, because research is time-consuming and often very expensive. So, while you might think you would like to research the contemporary global experience of the rock music industry, it is unlikely that you will have the necessary resources at your disposal. A research project of this kind would involve a very long set-up period, a lot of privileged access to the world of the global rock music industry, and a great deal of expense in terms of travel, accommodation and subsistence. It might be possible to do some research around this idea on the internet, but this would probably be the only practical option for a researcher working on such a project.

It might be that you feel very strongly that an industry in your locality is causing serious and substantial environmental damage, and you might decide that you would like to explore this issue in your research project. This project may also be impossible to conduct. This time the issue is access to data. The industry, if it is causing environmental damage, is unlikely to give you the access you would require to gather the data that you would need in order to be able to carry out this study. Access to data is a critical issue in all research projects. Researchers are not the police; they do not have any rights of access, but are entirely dependent on the goodwill of the gatekeepers facilitating their research for access to the data they require. It is very important to remember that access to data can be withdrawn at any point throughout the lifespan of the research project.

Researchers sometimes think that as soon as they actually have the data they require, access can no longer be denied them. This is not the case. Even when the researcher has gathered the data, analyzed it and drawn conclusions from it, permission to use the data can be withdrawn. In an academic institution, if there is a dispute over rights to data used in a research project, the project will generally not be accepted by the institution until the differences have been resolved. Your own ethical principles, as a researcher, would probably prohibit you from proceeding with a research project where such a dispute over permission had arisen. The withdrawal of access to data can be a disaster for any researcher, as without that access the research project cannot be completed.

Gatekeepers are the people who have the capacity to provide and deny access to data. Gatekeepers can have formal roles in an organization or entity. They can be CEOs of companies, their PAs and/or secretaries, HR managers, marketing managers and so on. Gatekeepers can also have informal roles in social settings, such as opinion-leaders within groups who can facilitate or deny access to data for a researcher as easily and as quickly as can any formal gatekeeper. The important thing to remember is that a researcher who does not have access to data, or who cannot get access to data, or who cannot maintain access to data, does not have a research project. The project, because there is no guaranteed access to data, is not researchable.

So how does a researcher create and develop a researchable project? The researcher does this by ensuring from the start and for the duration of the project that they have the necessary time, money and access to data. Generally, for an undergraduate thesis, students spend 6 to 10 months completing the project, depending on the requirements of the programme. This represents quite a substantial amount of time. Usually, as indicated above, there are only relatively minor costs associated with such research, such as the cost of sending out questionnaires, or the costs of getting to and from interviews, the costs of printing and binding the final draft of the thesis. However, for the student living off a grant and/or the income from a small part-time job, such relatively minor expenses can represent quite substantial draws on their income. It is important when designing the research project to take account of such expenses.

I suggest that you source this journal article online and read it. When you do so, you should use the model of the research process outlined in Figure 1.1, to examine the different steps in the research process, and the ways in which those steps are accomplished in the research project presented in this journal article. If you have ideas around a research project of your own, you should now think about how, using the model of the research process outlined above, you would like to develop it, and think about the steps in the research process that you will have to take.

REAL WORLD RESEARCH

Often, however, the most problematic resource for undergraduate researchers is access to data. First of all the researcher must find out where the data are. It could be in the testimony of potential participants in the research, in records and archives, in documents or published material, or in some setting or activity. When the researcher has located the data and discovered what form it takes, he or she must then devise a method by which to gather or collect it. As with research methodologies, it is essential that the researcher select the appropriate data collection method or methods for the research project (see Chapter 8, 'Understanding Research Methods, Populations and Sampling').

The article detailed opposite explores the concept of corporate citizenship. It describes a good example of a research project which has a well structured and well-written literature review. The research was developed using an interesting research methodology and the data collection methods used in the research project are clearly detailed, as are the data analysis methods used in analysing that data. The conclusions drawn from the research are clearly and simply outlined and explained.

How theory influences research

In the article detailed below, the authors explore the concept of corporate responsibility. Corporate responsibility is a key concept in their study. It is interesting to note how this key concept is used by them to structure the entire research project.

We will see as we read the synopsis below, the different steps in the research process, detailed in Figure 1.1 at the start of this chapter. I suggest that you source the original article and while reading it, you should trace the steps in the research process as they were undertaken for this study.

Sector-based corporate citizenship

Timonen, L. and Luoma-aho, V.
Business Ethics: A European Review (2010)

In the introduction to the journal article, the authors explore, outline and define the concept of corporate responsibility. They say that corporations are now expected to conduct business in a responsible way. Corporate responsibility, they suggest, has links to profits, image, legitimacy, reputation and competitive edge. The authors highlight the importance of corporations communicating and reporting their actions in a transparent manner. They say that recent research shows that corporate citizenship is considered important but that it is often left without proper implementation. The authors suggest that this may be because corporations do not see the full potential of corporate citizenship (CC) as a tool for gaining competitive advantage. The authors state that the search in the literature for a good definition of CC is ongoing. They suggest that without a clear definition of CC or its relation to the more commonly used corporate social responsibility (CSR), it is difficult to utilize the full potential of the concept. The authors point to a lack of research in the areas of CC and CSR and they call for more studies to be undertaken to help uncover how these concepts work in reality in business life.

The authors engage in an extensive review of the literature, through which they explore in great detail the concepts of CC and CSR. There is a considerable body of knowledge in this field. Much of it is detailed by the authors in the literature review presented in the article. Although there is an extensive body of knowledge in this field, the authors call for further research, and they highlighted gaps in knowledge in the field.

The authors used a case study methodology in the research. They developed three cases based on internationally operating corporations headquartered in Finland: Metso, representing the engineering and technology industry; Marimekko, representing the textile and clothing design industry; and Nokia, representing the information technology industry.

Their approach to the case studies involves a narrative analysis of available responsibility reports and their contents. In other words, the authors used reports compiled by the individual companies as their data, and used a narrative analysis approach to analyze that data; they identified, examined and analyzed

the different narratives they found in the reports. A narrative, as the authors state, is a story. Very usefully, the authors of the article explain narrative analysis in great detail. They also provide extensive discussion of their three cases and the ways in which CC and CSR are dealt with in each of the three companies.

Finally, the authors draw conclusions from their analysis of their data. They call for the development of a more sophisticated definition of CC and for more studies of CC and CSR. You will note from your reading of the original article that the authors theorize their work well. In other words, they knit the findings of their work into the body of knowledge in the field, They demonstrate in their writing how their work fits with, or contradicts, other studies conducted in this field.

CC and CSR are very interesting areas of research. Are they areas you would consider investigating for your research project? You will find that you get many ideas for research projects of your own as you read published accounts of the research of others.

References

Timonen, L. and Luoma-aho, V. (2010) 'Sector-based corporate citizenship', *Business Ethics: A European Review* 19(1) January: 1–13.

Writing up the research: The thesis/report

Like the research process itself, the structure of the thesis or research report follows a conventional pattern an accepted pattern. The steps of the research project are sequential, as outlined at the start of this chapter; however, there are frequent overlaps in that the researcher moves back and forth through the steps as the project develops. Research projects are very organic, they are living and growing entities and they change all the time. Generally, the changes happen in tiny shifts in emphasis, rather than giant changes or u-turns. All these changes can affect the entire project, and the researcher is constantly engaged in a process of editing the thesis or report as it develops, in order to ensure that any changes made are properly incorporated, that they are made to 'fit' properly into the thesis. It is of course, very useful to record the changes made in the thesis, or report, and the reasons and reflections behind them, in the research diary. The thesis is the written account of the research project. It is a synopsis of the work that was carried out. As the word count is always quite constrained, it is not possible for this written record to be anything more than a synopsis of all of the work that went into the research project.

The thesis or report is written following particular social science conventions. The basic layout is shown in Tables 1.2–1.4. The word counts given are simply guides.

Table 1.2 Layout for a 20 000 word thesis	
Title pages	**Pages with name of project, research, supervisor, dedication, and appreciation**
Abstract	Three hundred-word summary of the entire project, generally presented in one paragraph.
Table of Contents	Including lists of tables, figures, photographs.
Chapter One – Introduction 2000 words	A brief introduction to the entire thesis or report.
Chapter Two – Literature review 5000 words	Contains the theoretical framework for the research project.
Chapter Three – Research methodology 5000 words	Contains the methodological framework for the research project.
Chapter Four – Data analysis 5000 words	Contains the analytical framework for the research project.
Chapter Five – Conclusions and recommendations 3000 words	Contains the fully-developed, well-conceptualized conclusions from the research and usually a bullet point list of the recommendations drawn from the conclusions.
Bibliography	A complete list, using a referencing system, of the books, articles, etc. referred to in the text.
Appendices	Each appendix contains a document/table/figure relevant to the research, and referenced and discussed in the research. Typically copies of letters seeking and granting permission for the research are contained in appendices; letters inviting participation in the research; copies of forms designed for the research such as informed consent form; copies of any data collection methods used in the research, for example a copy of the questionnaire, interview/focus group schedule. Long lists, and large tables and figures can be placed in appendices.

Note: The word count detailed above is an approximate sharing of the word count between the sections of the project based on a 20 000 word count.

You can play around with your overall word count, perhaps giving some extra words to the data analysis chapter, and taking those words from some other chapter in the work. It is generally the rule that you must complete the entire thesis/report of the research, within the word count; there is usually a 10 per cent margin on either side of the word count. The word counts of the bibliography and the appendices tend not to be included in the overall word count.

The Gantt chart (see Table 1.5) shows a timeline for a thesis carried out over an 8-month period. It is a good idea to create a model of this kind to plan the progress of your own research. As can be seen from the Gantt chart, and from the model of the research process outlined at the start of this chapter, the research project is developed in phases, and it takes a substantial amount of time. It is helpful therefore to develop a timeline for your research project and to use it to monitor your progress.

Table 1.3 Layout for a 15 000 word thesis	
Title pages	**Pages with name of project, research, supervisor, dedication and appreciation**
Abstract	Three hundred-word summary of the entire project, generally presented in one paragraph.
Table of Contents	Entire content Including lists of tables, figures, photographs.
Chapter One – Introduction 1500 words	A brief introduction to the entire thesis or report.
Chapter Two – Literature review 3500 words	Contains the theoretical framework for the research project.
Chapter Three – Research methodology 4000 words	Contains the methodological framework for the research project.
Chapter Four – Data analysis 4000 words	Contains the analytical framework for the research project.
Chapter Five – Conclusions and recommendations 2000 words	Contains the fully-developed, well-conceptualized conclusions from the research and usually a bullet point list of the recommendations drawn from the conclusions.
Bibliography	A complete list, using a referencing system, of the books, articles, etc. referred to in the text.
Appendices	Each appendix contains a document/table/figure relevant to the research, and referenced and discussed in the research. Typically copies of letters seeking and granting permission for the research are contained in appendices; letters inviting participation in the research; copies of forms designed for the research such as informed consent form; copies of any data collection methods used in the research, for example a copy of the questionnaire, interview/focus group schedule. Long lists, and large tables and figures can be placed in appendices.

Note: The word count detailed above is an approximate sharing of the word count between the sections of the project based on a 15 000 word count.

You will also find it helpful to look at a number of bound theses in the library. You can use these theses to study title pages, abstracts, tables of content, bibliographies and referencing methods. It is also helpful to examine the appendices of these theses in order to develop an understanding of the kind of material that goes into them. It is essential that you get some guidance, either from your lecturer in research methodologies or your thesis supervisor, on the word count required, on the format and layout requested, and on the referencing method that should be used. Your lecturer in research methodologies and/or your thesis supervisor will be able to provide you with guidance on all of the other issues and questions that will arise as you carry out your research. You should avail yourself of all the help and support that they can offer you.

Table 1.4 Layout for a 10 000 word thesis	
Title pages	**Pages with name of project, research, and supervisor, dedication and appreciation**
Abstract	Three hundred-word summary of the entire project, generally presented in one paragraph.
Table of Contents	Including lists of tables, figures, photographs.
Chapter One – Introduction 1200 words	A brief introduction to the entire thesis or report.
Chapter Two – Literature review 2500 words	Contains the theoretical framework for the research project.
Chapter Three – Research methodology 1800 words	Contains the methodological framework for the research project.
Chapter Four – Data analysis 3000 words	Contains the analytical framework for the research project.
Chapter Five – Conclusions and recommendations 1500 words	Contains the fully-developed, well-conceptualized conclusions from the research and usually a bullet point list of the recommendations drawn from the conclusions.
Bibliography	A complete list, using a referencing system, of the books, articles, etc. referred to in the text.
Appendices	Each appendix contains a document/table/figure relevant to the research, and referenced and discussed in the research. Typically copies of letters seeking and granting permission for the research are contained in appendices; letters inviting participation in the research; copies of forms designed for the research such as informed consent form; copies of any data collection methods used in the research, for example a copy of the questionnaire, interview/focus group schedule. Long lists, and large tables and figures can be placed in appendices.

Note: The word count detailed above is an approximate sharing of the word count between the sections of the project based on a 10 000 word count.

A BRIEF INTRODUCTION TO RESEARCH ETHICS

Social research is the means by which people find out new things about the social world. In order to do this, researchers engage with the theory in the field, by undertaking a review of the literature, and observe the phenomenon under investigation systematically, by gathering data, and by using their imagination creatively. Researchers must be informed, organized and systematic. They should must be sensitive to the people involved in the investigation and must engage with them, and with the entire research process, in an ethical manner.

Table 1.5 Gantt chart for a student research project	Oct	Nov	Dec	Jan	Feb	Mar	April	May
Focus on identifying research area. Develop idea in this area for research project. Turn this idea into a research question/statement.	██							
Commence reading of literature. Develop aim and objectives for research project. Decide on appropriate methodology for research, and develop the data gathering methods to be used.		██						
Write research proposal. Secure permissions needed to conduct the research. Secure ethical approval for the research.		██						
Write Chapter 1, introduction (this chapter is based on the research proposal). Begin writing literature review for the research (generally Chapter 2 in the thesis).			██					
Write research methodology chapter (usually Chapter 3 in the thesis).			██					
Complete writing of literature review. Finalize data gathering techniques (do this with reference to the literature). Gather data.				██				
Analyze data.					██			
Write data analysis chapter/findings chapter (generally Chapter 4 of the thesis).						██		
Write conclusions and recommendations chapter (generally Chapter 5 of the thesis).						██		
Complete first draft, and submit for feedback.							██	
Complete second draft.								██
Final review of thesis. Submit thesis.								██

YOUR RESEARCH
A research diary exercise

Jot down in your research diary some notes in response to these ethical issues and questions.

Consider for a moment any research project in which you have participated. Think about how you felt. Did you feel vulnerable at all? If so, why did you feel vulnerable? What was it about the research, the researcher, or the research process that made you feel like this? Think for a moment about yourself as the researcher. How do you want people to perceive your research project? What impression do you want to give people of you yourself as a researcher? How do you want them to feel about participating in your research? How do you want them to feel as they participate in your research?

Write a short reflective piece on how these reflections will help you when you are designing and carrying out your research. Also write a couple of sentences on how these reflections will help you in

writing the 'ethics' section of your thesis. The reflection that you engage in for this exercise may appear, in an edited form, in the ethics section of your research project. The ethics section is usually placed in the research methodology chapter of the thesis (this is usually Chapter 3 in the thesis or report of the research).

In your research diary, develop an ethics checklist for your research and for you yourself as a researcher working on that research project.

Try to find in your reading of journal articles particularly good ethical reflections on business research projects. Use these reflections, along with your own reflections, to help you develop your own knowledge and skills in terms of research ethics, ethical reflection and writing-up research ethics. Take this opportunity to update your interactive research diary, available at www.cengage.co.uk/quinlan.

The quality of every research project is dependent upon the **integrity** of the researcher. When you report your research, you will describe what you set out to do, how you did, what you found, and what that means. Obviously, the account of the research must be accurate and honest. It should give enough detail to allow the reader to evaluate the work. The literature review must be comprehensive, complete and up-to-date. The data should be properly gathered and properly managed, and analyzed appropriately. The conclusions drawn from the research should be drawn from the findings of the research, and these findings must emerge from the data gathered.

> **Integrity**
> The honesty and scholarship of the researcher in engaging with, conducting and concluding research.

Every researcher has responsibilities to a number of constituencies. These include the institution under whose auspices the research is being carried out and all individuals, groups, institutions and organizations participating in the research. The researcher has a duty of care towards all participants, and must, above all, do no harm. The researcher must accurately represent the research to participants, all of whom must participate on an informed, voluntary basis. Covert research can raise particular ethical issues. If you are thinking of engaging in covert research you should discuss this as soon as possible with your research methods lecturer and/or your thesis supervisor.

It is important in writing your research to reflect broadly any moral issues and imperatives of the project. This reflection should be detailed in the final report of the research, or in the thesis, and will enhance the quality of your work. It is important to remember that while there are general ethical principles and issues for all research and all researchers, every individual research project will have ethical issues which are unique to that project and which should be recognized, acknowledged and addressed.

CASE STUDY

Malik's action research project

Malik has a part-time job working as a weekend manager in a restaurant. She has decided that she is going to situate her research project in the restaurant. The owner of the restaurant has given her permission to do this. Malik feels that the team she manages in the restaurant could improve their performance and she feels that such an improvement in performance would lead to an enhanced customer experience. Malik's team in the restaurant consists of ten waiting staff. They have all agreed to participate in the research.

Before commencing the work of developing this research proposal, Malik discussed her idea for her research project with her thesis supervisor. Her supervisor agreed that this was an interesting and useful research project, and she accepted this research as appropriate in terms of the programme of study Malik is undertaking, which is for a BSc. in Business Management.

© webphotgrapheer/iStock

Having secured this approval, Malik developed the following research proposal. She submitted this research proposal to her thesis supervisor, who formally approved it.

A research proposal

Research statement: This research project is an action research project designed to improve the performance of a team of waiting staff at the *Bon Viveur Restaurant.*

Aim and objectives

The aim of the research is to improve the performance of a team of waiting staff at the *Bon Viveur Restaurant.*

The objectives of the research are as follows:

- to measure current performance of the team of waiting staff
- to establish which aspects of the performance warrant improvement
- to design a process by which performance might be improved
- to implement this process
- to measure the performance of the team following implementation
- to evaluate the efficacy of the improvement process
- to develop a model for the development of small teams in business enterprises.

The population of the study

The population of the study consists of the ten members of the team of waiting staff the researcher supervises in her work as weekend manager at the *Bon Viveur Restaurant.*

Sample literature review

This research project is focused on team performance. The focus of the review of the literature for this research project is on performance, on team training and development for improved performance. Following the work of Katzenbach and

Smith (2003), this research project will provide a model for the development of small teams in business. According to Katzenbach and Smith, team performance is one of the single largest untapped resources of most organizations. Katzenbach and Smith, state that 'commitment to goals' and 'shared purpose' is critical to team success. Leadership, according to them, is key. Yuki (2010), holds that leadership is in part about the organization of work activities and the motivation of people (the team) to meet objectives.

The use of teams has increased in organizations, as shown by Morgeson *et al*. (2010). They outline how research in management has begun to focus on the role of leadership in developing teams and in team success.

The literature review for this research project will explore:

- the nature of teams in business organizations
- the critical issues in team success
- the nature of team leadership in relation to successful teams.

Research methodology

The methodology to be used in the study is action research (McNiff and Whitehead, 2009; Brydon-Miller *et al*., 2003). Action research (see Chapter 1 of this text, 'Introducing Business Research') is a research methodology designed in particular to bring about change and development. As the focus of this research project is on performance a team, the methodology action research is an appropriate methodology.

Action research methodology follows a cyclical rather than a linear process, whereby the researcher first plans the research to be undertaken, and then acts, putting the plans into action. When the action has been completed, the researcher critically reflects on the action, and on what was accomplished by the action. Finally, the researcher evaluates the action. Having evaluated the action, the researcher may begin the cyclical process again, by planning the next stage of the research, then implementing the plan, then reflecting on the imple-

mentation and the impact of the implementation, and finally evaluating the effect of the process. The researcher can repeat the cyclical process as often as possible, or as often as is necessary, in order to bring about the desired change.

The data collection methods to be used in the study are as follows:

- focus group
- observation
- questionnaire.

To begin with, the researcher will convene a focus group with the ten members of the team. The purpose of the focus group is to explore the views of the team in relation to the improvements in performance needed and the improvements in performance possible. The focus group will be audio-recorded. The researcher will transcribe the audio-recording and, from the transcript, develop a plan for the implementation of the improvements decided on by the members of the focus group.

During the implementation phase of the research, the researcher and the team will observe the impact of the changes in performance. Two observation schedules will be developed for this purpose. The first observation schedule will be used to record the implementation of the proposed changes in performance. The second observation schedule will be used to measure the impact of the changes.

Finally, the researcher will develop a questionnaire designed to measure the impact of the changes in performance on the customer experience. This questionnaire will be administered to ten regular customers on two Saturday nights before the changes are implemented, and on two Saturday nights after the changes have been implemented. In all, 40 regular customers will participate in the study. The questionnaire will also be administered to all ten members of the restaurant's management team. The data will be analyzed using SPSS. SPSS is a computerized statistical analysis package, used for the analysis of social science data. The responses to the before and after questionnaires will be compared and conclusions will be drawn regarding the impact of the research on the customer experience.

Context for the research

The research is being undertaken for a BSc. in Business Management. The research will be conducted as a training and development exercise with the team of ten waiting staff the researcher supervises in her role as weekend manager at the *Bon Viveur Restaurant* in the village of Martens, in Upper Lakelands.

Rationale for the research

In undertaking the research, the researcher hopes to contribute to the development of her team and her workplace. Through the research, she hopes to develop some expertise in action research and the use of action research in training and development. Finally, she hopes through the research to make a contribution to knowledge in relation to small team management. The researcher plans to publish an account of the research in the trade magazine *Restaurants Today*. A copy of the thesis, the formal account of the research, will be placed in the university library.

References

Brydon-Miller, M., Greenwood, D. and Maguire, P. (2003) 'Why action research?', *Action Research* 1: 9–28.

Katzenbach, J.R. and Smith, D.K. (2003) *The Wisdom of Teams: Creating the High-Performance Organization,* New York: McKinsey & Company.

McNiff, J. and Whitehead, J. (2009) *Doing and Writing Action Research*, London: Sage.

Morgeson, F.P., Scott DeRue, D. and Karam, E.P. (2010) 'Leadership in teams: A functional approach to understanding leadership structures and processes', *Journal of Management* 36(1): 5–39.

Yuki, G. (2010) (7th edn), *Leadership in Organisations*, New Jersey, USA: Prentice Hall.

Question What do you think of Malik's research proposal? Do you think the project is researchable, using the test of researchability outlined in this chapter? Explain your answer. Does Malik's research proposal give you any ideas for your own research project?

CHAPTER REVIEW

In this chapter you were introduced to social and business research and to the research process. Research was defined in the chapter as a process which makes discoveries about social reality through the application of theoretical ideas and methods of research. The manner in which social research developed was briefly addressed and the different social science paradigms, positivism and interpretivism, as well as different types of social and business research methodologies, such as survey, case study, ethnography, action research, were introduced. The manner in which research projects are developed was briefly addressed. A model was presented of the research process. This process was seen to begin with an issue or an idea. This was developed into a researchable problem. This was then stated as a research statement or question or hypothesis. A specific aim and a series of objectives (usually no more than six) are developed for the project, a review of the literature is undertaken, the research methodology is decided upon, data collection methods are designed, the data are gathered, it is analyzed, conclusions are drawn and the report of the research or the thesis is written. The four frameworks approach to conducting research was introduced and explained. The four frameworks are the conceptual framework, the theoretical framework, the methodological framework and the analytical framework. The four frameworks approach to social research is a tool for researchers. The four frameworks approach helps researchers develop well integrated, sound, research projects. The chapter presents models of the layout of research projects with different word counts (20 000, 15 000 and 10 000 words). A Gantt chart is presented of a typical timeline for a student research project. Finally, some of the ethical imperatives in conducting business research were considered. This chapter was designed to introduce you to social and business research, to help you start your research diary and to set you on the path of designing, carrying out and completing your first business research project.

Now update your interactive research diary with your notes and findings at www.cengage.co.uk/quinlan. Complete the activities provided to reinforce your understanding of this chapter.

END OF CHAPTER QUESTIONS

1   Detail the steps in the research process.

2   Outline and explain the use of the four frameworks approach in the research project process.

3   When can a research project be deemed researchable?

4   What is a key concept in research?

5   What is a research diary?

6   List three different research methodologies.

7   List five different data collection methods.

8   Outline and briefly explain the key differences between the social-science paradigms positivism, interpretivism, and social constructionism.

9   Discuss the relevance and value of business research, using a range of examples of business research projects to support your answer.

10 Write a short reflective piece on research ethics.

REFERENCES

Abercrombie, N., Hill, S. and Turner, B.S. (2000) *Penguin Dictionary of* Sociology (5th edn), Penguin Books.

Action Research Made Simple URL http://www.youtube.com/watch?v=Qg83f72_6Gw Accessed 31.08.2010.

Berger, P. and Luckman, T. (1966) *The Social Construction of Reality*, New York: Anchor Books.

Brydon-Miller, M., Greenwood, D. and Maguire, P. (2003) 'Why action research?', Action Research 1: 9–28.

Giddens, A. (2001) *Sociology*, Cambridge: Polity.

Grant, S. (2007) 'Learning through "being" and "doing"', *Action Research* 5(3): 265–274.

Katzenbach, J.R. and Smith, D.K. (2003) *The Wisdom of Teams: Creating the High-Performance Organization*, New York: McKinsey & Company.

McNiff, J. and Whitehead, J. (2009) *Doing and Writing Action Research*, London: Sage.

Morgeson, F.P., Scott DeRue, D. and Karam, E.P. (2010) 'Leadership in teams: A functional approach to understanding leadership structures and processes', *Journal of Management* 36(1): 5–39.

Research for Development, a free-to-access online database containing information about research projects supported by the Department for International Development UK, Department for International Development (DFID), **www.research4development.info/index.asp** Accessed 02.06.2010.

Seager, A. and Stewart, H. (2010) 'Growth loses its place in the pursuit of happiness', *The Observer*, 10 January 2010.

Timonen, L. and Luoma-aho, V. (2010) 'Sector-based corporate citizenship', *Business Ethics: A European Review* 19(1) January: 1–13.

Yuki, G. (2010) (7th edn), *Leadership in Organisations*, New Jersey, USA: Prentice Hall.

RECOMMENDED READING

Bell, J. (2005) *Doing Your Research Project*, Maidenhead: Open University Press.

Collis, J. and Hussey, R. (2009) *Business Research: A Practical Guide for Undergraduate and Postgraduate Students*, Houndsmill: Palgrave Macmillan.

Creswell, J. W. (2003) *Research Design, Qualitative, Quantitative and Mixed Methods Approaches* (2nd edn), London: Sage.

Davies, D. (2005) *Business Research for Decision Making*, Mason, OH: Cengage South-Western.

Denscombe, M. (2002) *Ground Rules for Good Research*, London: Open University Press.

Easterby-Smith, M., Thorpe, R. and Jackson, P.R. (2005) *Management Research* (3rd edn), London: Sage.

Jankowicz, A.D. (2005) *Business Research Projects*, London: Cengage.

Kent, R. (2007) *Marketing Research, Approaches, Methods and Applications in Europe*, London: Cengage.

Locke, K. (2001) *Grounded Theory in Management Research*, London: Sage.

Lüscher, L. (2009) *Working Through Paradox: An Action Research on Sensemaking at the Lego Company*, Saarbrücken, Germany: VDM Verlag.

Methodspace: Connecting the Research Community, Sage, www.methodspace.com.

Murray, R. (2003) *How to Write a Thesis*, Maidenhead: Open University Press.

Neuman, W.L. (2000) *Social Research Methods: Quantitative and Qualitative Approaches*, Boston, MA: Allyn & Bacon.

RAPAR, Refugees and Asylum Seekers Participatory Action Research, www.rapar.org.uk/.

White, B. (2000) *Dissertation Skills for Business and Management Students*, London: Cengage.

Zikmund, W.G. (2003) *Business Research Methods*, Mason, OH: Cengage South-Western.

CHAPTER 2

DEVELOPING RESEARCH SKILLS

LEARNING OBJECTIVES

At the end of this chapter the student should be able to:

- Recognize their existing level of research skills and identify areas for improvement and the accompanying relevant chapter sections.

- Create a conceptual framework, the first of the four frameworks.

- Develop a research statement or question for a research project, and outline appropriate aims and objectives for the project.

- Identify and source appropriate literature.

- Compile a bibliography and properly use appendices.

RESEARCH SKILLS

At the end of this chapter the student should, using the exercises on the accompanying online platform, be able to:

- Generate ideas for research projects.

- Identify, source and use appropriate literature.

The aim of this chapter is to help the reader assess the standard of their basic research skills (using a short review test on the online platform) before setting out these skills in detail throughout the chapter. The chapter covers issues such as how to formulate an argument, how to develop a research statement or question, how to outline a research aim and a series of objectives, how to source literature, how to keep a research diary, how to identify plagiarism and the offence that plagiarism constitutes, how to compile a bibliography and the proper use of appendices. There is a focus in the chapter on writing skills and on note keeping. As in all of the chapters in this textbook, key words and terms are explained, and they are listed for convenience in a glossary of terms at the end of the chapter.

INTRODUCTION

The focus of this chapter is on the key skills needed by every researcher. The key skills relate to the different steps in the research process, as outlined in Figure 2.1.

It takes time to develop the skills of a good or competent researcher. The process involves reading text books on research methodologies and research methods, and gaining experience in working on research projects. The work of every researcher in academia is both theoretical and applied. Theory is to be found in literature, and literature as we know from Chapter 1, is found in books and journal articles, in theses, in government reports and papers, in the published work of NGOs, and in the reports of conference proceedings. The applied aspect of the research task is in the actual workings of real research projects, carried out in the field.

There are five basic skills required in conducting research. They are detailed in Table 2.1.

Table 2.1 The basic skills required by every researcher	
The five basic skills required	
1	The ability to generate ideas for research projects.
2	The ability to identify, source and use appropriate literature.
3	The ability to develop research projects with a good fit, i.e. where the different parts of the research project fit well together.
4	The ability to gather and analyze data.
5	The ability to write well, to be able to communicate clearly, thoroughly and simply through writing.

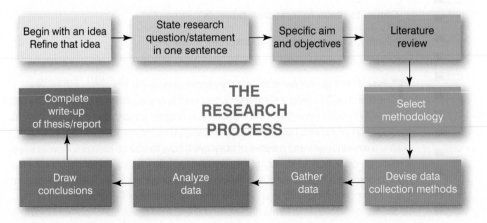

Figure 2.1   The research process

RESEARCH IDEAS

The article in the box feature below focuses on the favourite fast food in Britain, fish and chips. Some detail is given in the article on research carried out annually to identify the best fish and chip shop in the UK. Some quantitative data are presented in the box feature. Very simply, quantitative data in numerical form.

Can you identify some of the issues addressed in the article that could be used to develop ideas for good research projects? Among those ideas, is there an idea for a research project that you would consider developing.

One of the most important and fundamental skills every researcher requires is the ability to generate ideas for research projects. There are possibilities for research projects everywhere. For example, the news article below from *The Times Online* details a competition for the best fish and chip shop. This article could generate several ideas for research projects. Possibilities might include a research project focused on establishing which restaurant is 'the best', an investigation of the factors that make a restaurant 'the best', or perhaps a research project designed to create a campaign to turn a restaurant into 'the best' restaurant.

The key to developing an idea for a research project is to focus on an area of interest and/or of use to you. In general, when students begin to think in this way about ideas for research projects they find it relatively easy to decide on an idea. An idea for a research project is often simply a statement of the general area within which you wish to situate your research. You might, for example, decide that the area that interests you most is internet sales, or perhaps intercultural workplaces, or training and development, or any one of the very many areas you will have covered to a greater or lesser extent in your studies so far for your degree, in your reading for your degree, or in your work or place of employment.

Once you have decided on the area in which you wish to situate your research project, you need to begin to develop your idea for the research project from that area. Sometimes research projects come together readily and quickly, and sometimes they do not. It is important not to worry if your research project does not come to you immediately, because it is worth spending all the time needed in developing a research project. If the idea for the research project is fundamentally sound to begin with, there is a good chance that it will continue to be sound as it develops.

Your research project must be situated within your discipline. If you are taking a degree in business, then your research project must be undertaken on some aspect of business. Similarly, if your degree is in marketing or industrial relations, then your research project must be on some aspect of marketing or industrial relations. The third of the five basic skills required by every researcher, as outlined at the start of this chapter, is the ability to develop research projects with a good fit. One fundamental question is whether or not the research project you are thinking about fits with the requirements of your course of study. Other aspects of the notion of 'fit' relate to:

- whether or not the population you are using in your research is the appropriate population for that research project
- whether or not the research methodology you are using to develop the research project is the appropriate methodology
- whether or not the data collection methods you are using are appropriate to the requirements of the project

THE VALUE OF GOOD RESEARCH

Research in the media

It's a wrap

In an article in *The Times*, Wyke (2010) explains that the classic fish and chip shop has changed very little since they first opened for business. The first fish and chip shop is said by Seafish, an organisation dedicated to supporting the seafish industry, to have been opened in the 1860s on Cleveland Street in London by Joseph Malin. The research directorate of Seafish, which is based in Grimsby, provides in-depth data and research on a very broad range of topics to the seafish industry. Currently, according to the website of Seafish (**www.seafish.org**), almost 384 million meals are sold each year from around 11 000 fish and chip shops around the UK, and 49 per cent of these are fish and chips. Fish and chips, according to Seafish, remains the favourite take-away in the UK.

The annual competition organised by Seafish to identify the top chippies in the UK is highlighted in the article in *The Times*. The winner of the competition for the National Fish and Chip Shop of the Year for 2010 was named as The Atlantic Fast Food chippy in Coatbridge, Glasgow. The owner of the chippy, Giovanni Fionda, on being presented with the prestigious award at a gala ceremony in London, said that the award was recognition of dedication to customer service.

According to an article in *The Guardian* newspaper (Smithers, 2010), Atlantic Fast Food won after a rigorous judging process which involved customer votes, taste tests, shop inspections and a presentation to a panel of industry experts. In second place, according to this article, was Finnegan's Fish Bar in Porthcawl, South Wales, and in third place was The Great British Eatery, in Birmingham.

A classic fish and chip supper © Mike Bentley/iStock

References

Smithers, R. 'Scottish fish and chip shop named best in UK', *The Guardian*, 21.01.2010. Accessed 02.06.2010.

Seafish: The authority on seafood, **www. seafish.org** Accessed 02.06.2010.

Wyke, N.'The UK's Top 10 fish and chip shops 2010', *Times Online*, 19.01.2010, **http://www.timesonline.co.uk/tol/life_and_ style/food_and_-drink/ article6998138.ece** Accessed 02.06.2010.

⬤ whether or not the data analysis methods and procedures you are using are appropriate or congruent in terms of that research project.

The issue of 'fit' in relation to the research project is a very important one, and it is an issue that we will be returning to throughout this textbook.

It is important to be able to distinguish between a broad area for a idea for a research project and a research question or statement. Your idea is the broad area within which you want to conduct your research, for example internet sales, or the intercultural workplace, or perhaps training and development. You might be interested in examining the marketing of computer games, or recruitment and selection processes for human resource managers. Other ideas could include business plans for SMEs, or the experiences of women in senior management, or possible career paths for new business graduates. These are all ideas for research projects, and they are are good and useful and interesting ideas; but they are not research questions or statements. Each of these ideas is too broad to be a research project. Your carefully defined research project would be situated in one of these areas, or in such an area.

TURNING RESEARCH IDEAS INTO RESEARCH PROJECTS

Once you have decided on the broad area within which you want to situate your research, the next step is to turn your idea into a precisely defined research project. The key to this process is focus. The question to ask yourself as you engage in this process of refinement is this: what, precisely, am I interested in researching? What exactly do I wish to focus on in my research project?

In addition to focus, you must keep in mind at this stage the test of researchability. The test of **researchability** is explained in detail in Chapter 1 of this textbook. Using this simple test you ask yourself if your project is **researchable**, if you have the time needed, the money needed (if any money is needed), the **data** required and the level of access necessary to the **data** required to carry out the study.

This simple test can help you decide from the start whether or not it is worthwhile trying to develop your idea into a research project. If you think that you would have any difficulty with any one of the items in the test, then the chances are the research project you are proposing to undertake is not researchable. The project cannot be undertaken by you because it is too ambitious and cannot be completed in the time allowed, or it is too expensive for the budget you might be in a position to allocate to it, or the project could not be undertaken because you could not access the data required for the project, or you could not maintain access to the data for the length of time required to complete the field work. It is important to be very clear about these three issues from the outset, because a difficulty with any one could prevent you from completing your research.

Often students have very good and very interesting research projects in mind, but these research projects are, for one reason or another, beyond their capacity or resources. If you find yourself in this situation, the important thing is to accept that the project cannot, for whatever reason, be undertaken and to quickly move on to develop a research project that is possible.

Researchability
A project is deemed researchable if the researcher has the time needed, the money required, if any money is required, and the access to data necessary to carry out and complete the research project.

Researchable
A project is **researchable** if you have the time, money, data and the level of access to the data needed.

THE FIRST STEP: DEVELOPING A RESEARCH STATEMENT

Hypothesis
A predicted or expected answer to a research question.

When you have decided on the broad area within which you wish to situate your research project, the first step is the develop a simple research statement which clearly expresses your idea for your research project. This statement becomes the conceptual framework for your research project. The first framework in the four frameworks approach to the research project, outlined in Chapter 1, is the conceptual framework. The conceptual framework for the research project is contained in the research statement or question, or in the research **hypothesis**. As discussed above, it might be that you are interested in internet sales, or the intercultural workplace, or training and development. Let us say, for example, that you are interested in examining the marketing of computer games. This is your idea for your research project. The next step is to take this idea and turn it into a research project by creating a research question or statement. This research question or statement will contain **the conceptual framework** for the research project. The conceptual framework for any research project contains all of the key concepts within that research project.

The Four Frameworks
Conceptual Framework
Theoretical Framework
Methodological Framework
Analytical Framework

If we take, for example, the idea of researching the marketing of computer games, and we decide to develop this idea into a research statement or question, we have to do two things: we have to ensure that the research statement or question we develop is researchable, and we have to ensure that all of the key concepts that interest you as the researcher are contained in the conceptual framework, the research statement or question.

The idea is the marketing of computer games. The research statement might read something like this:

The conceptual framework
The entire research project rests on the conceptual framework, which is contained in the research statement or question.

> *This research project is a case study examining the marketing of computer games by three computer games companies: the companies are Zenith Computer Games Ltd, Orbit Computer Games Ltd and Galaxy Computer Games Ltd.*

This research statement is a simple statement of a research project. As a researcher, you should aim for a simple clear statement of the research. While it is clear and simple, the research statement contains all of the key concepts in the research project. The key concepts here 'marketing', 'computer games', 'computer games companies' and 'marketing computer games'. These four key concepts are the essential focus of this research project. We will see in the subsequent chapters how the entire research project rests upon this conceptual framework and how these four key concepts provide the entire focus of this study.

Case study methodology
Useful in the in-depth study of bounded entities, such as an organization, or a single incident or event.

The proposed research methodology, case study, as indicated in the research statement, would seem to be an appropriate methodology for the research proposed. **Case study methodology** (see Chapter 7, 'Understanding Research Methodology and Design'), is particularly useful in the in-depth study of bounded entities, such as a company, team, class, organization, a single incident or event, or any entity that is clearly bounded. The organization, incident or event provides the case that is to be studied. In the case study above, there are three cases: these are the three computer games companies, Zenith Computer Games Ltd, Orbit Computer Games Ltd and Galaxy Computer Games Ltd. The proposed case study methodology is a good fit for this research project.

In this case study, the researcher has clearly outlined the focus of the study, and the researcher has limited the **scope** of the study to three different computer games companies. The focus of the study is on the different marketing campaigns of each of these three companies. The researcher has decided to use three cases in this study, based on the three companies named in the research statement. This decision was not made arbitrarily; the decisions the researcher makes regarding the **scope** of the project are dictated by what it is possible to do, and what is necessary. It is up to the researcher to decide the scope of the project, with guidance from the research supervisor.

There are two dimensions to scope in every research project: breadth and depth. The researcher might decide to undertake a broad study, and include three or more companies. Alternatively, the researcher might decide to do a more in-depth study on a single company, or perhaps two companies, and examine their marketing campaigns in greater detail and depth than would be possible if there were more companies included in the study. In a small scale research project, resource constraints mean that there is always a trade-off between breadth and depth, the broader the study the less depth is possible. More depth in a study means less breadth.

In terms of this proposed study, which involves the examination of marketing campaigns, access to data may not be an issue. This is because the researcher could decide to use as data only material that is in the public domain, in this case the advertising undertaken by the companies. Such a decision might require a small change to the research statement. The research statement might now read something like this:

> *This research project is a case study of the advertising campaigns undertaken for the marketing of computer games by three computer games companies: the companies are Zenith Computer Games Ltd, Orbit Computer Games Ltd and Galaxy Computer Games Ltd.*

It is also possible to limit the temporal span (the timespan) of the research in the research statement. In the following version of the research statement, the proposed timescale for the study is 1 year. The researcher is proposing to study the 2010 marketing campaigns of the three companies. The reasons for limiting the timespan should be detailed in the brief discussion of the research statement or question that usually follows it, as in the example on page 40.

Scope
In relation to scope, there are two dimensions in every research project. The two dimensions are breadth and depth. In deciding the scope of the project, the researcher does not want to attempt to do too much; however, the researcher does need to do enough.

YOUR RESEARCH
The value of a research diary

There is generally a need for a rationale for every decision made in the research process, and that rationale should be logical, reasoned and reasonable. It should be possible to argue the case for every decision made throughout the research process This is an essential requirement of all research projects, because research projects are essentially exercises in reason and logic.

This requirement provides another good reason for keeping a research diary.

The researcher can record, briefly or at length, the decisions made in the process of developing the research project, and the reasoning behind those decisions.

These notes are very helpful in the writing of the research. They can provide starting points for the writing and they can become the basis for substantial sections of the thesis or report of the research. The researcher's notes, scribbled in the research diary, can be helpful in tackling writer's block, when the researcher does not know what to write about, or where to begin.

> " *This research project is a case study of the advertising campaigns undertaken in the year 2010, for the marketing of computer games by three computer games companies: the companies are Zenith Computer Games Ltd, Orbit Computer Games Ltd and Galaxy Computer Games Ltd.*

The research will focus on the 2010 marketing campaigns of the three companies in order to examine and compare and contrast the most current and up-to-date marketing of the three companies.

In another example, let us consider the student who wishes to examine recruitment and selection process for human resources managers. Once again the student must be able to access data on this topic. If the student works in a company with a HR department, the company may be prepared to allow the student access to their recruitment and selection processes. If so, then this can be the focus of the student's research. If this is not the case, perhaps the student might develop an ideal recruitment and selection process for a fictitious company, using information on recruitment and selection processes available in books and journal articles and online.

Use your imagination when you are considering the research project you will develop. You are, however, constrained by the requirements of the study programme within which you are engaged. You are also constrained by the standards of **validity** which are applied to all research projects.

Perhaps the key issue in all research projects is the degree of validity of the research. The concept of validity in research is the issue of how valid the research is; in other words, how logical, truthful, robust, sound, reasonable, meaningful and useful the research is. All of these issues are aspects of the validity of a research project. A related issue is the issue of **reliability**. In social science research, reliability relates to the degree to which the research can be repeated while obtaining consistent results. Validity and reliability are fundamental issues in social science research and we will return to them throughout this textbook.

Another fundamental issue in social science research is the issue of **triangulation**. The concept of triangulation and the processes of triangulating research call for more than one approach to answering the research question or responding to the research statement. There are different ways of triangulating research; theoretical triangulation, researcher triangulation, methodological triangulation and within method and between method (data collection method) triangulation (Denzin, 1970). Using between method triangulation, for example, the research question might be explored using a questionnaire and a series of interviews, or using a series of observations and a focus group. Using within method triangulation the research issue or phenomenon might be explored, for example, using two different, and perhaps sequential questionnaires, or using two different sets of interviews.

Essentially, triangulation means examining the research issue or phenomenon from more than one perspective. One of the critiques of triangulation is that it contributes to a naïve realist position by suggesting that social science research can provide an account of what is 'real', thereby implicitly suggesting that there can be a single definitive account of the issue or phenomenon under investigation. We know from Chapter 1 of this textbook that there are different understandings of the nature of reality. Those defending the concept of triangulation would argue that while there cannot be a single definitive account of the phenomenon under investigation, the process of triangulating research provides a broader view or perspective of the phenomenon under investigation, and consequently a (potentially) more valid view

Validity
Relates to how logical, truthful, robust, sound, reasonable, meaningful and useful the research in question is.

Reliability
The dependability of the research, to the degree to which the research can be repeated while obtaining consistent results.

Triangulation
Studying the phenomenon under investigation from more than one perspective, e.g. researcher, theoretical, methodological triangulation.

of that phenomenon. The concept of triangulation is explored in detail in later chapters.

A research statement for the project outlined above might read something like the following:

> *This research project is a case study designed to facilitate the development of a model recruitment and selection process for a fictitious company, 'People for Places Ltd'.*

Once again, the research statement contains the conceptual framework for the research project. The conceptual framework is made up of all of the key concepts in the research project. By outlining the research project in such a disciplined manner, the entire project is stated in one sentence – a question or a statement. In that one sentence the researcher focuses on precisely what the research project is concerned with, while excluding from the research project, by excluding from the conceptual framework, all that the research project is not concerned with. The key concepts in the above research statement are 'recruitment and selection process', 'model recruitment and selection process', and 'development of a model recruitment and selection process'.

Let us now consider two more research projects. The research statement for the project of the student who is interested in the business plans of SMEs might read as follows:

> *The research project is a survey of the business plans of 50 SMEs in the Greater Galloway area.*

As you can see, this research project is a **survey**, whereas the two previous projects were **case** studies. In other words, the research methodology to be used to develop this project is a survey. The key concepts within the conceptual framework outlined above are 'business plans', 'SMEs', and 'the business plans of SMEs'. These key concepts are the focus of this research; everything else is excluded from the research. The discipline of this focus is important at this stage in the research process because as the research project develops, it will naturally become more complex. Clarity, precision and simplicity at the start of the research process will pay dividends as the research project develops. The scope of the research is 50 SMEs in the particular geographic area indicated. The decisions made around how many SMEs to include and the geographic area or scope of the research should be outlined briefly in a short explanation of the research statement, which should appear underneath the research statement.

The research statement for the student interested in the experiences of women in senior management positions might read something like the following:

> *This research project is a survey of the experiences of 100 women in senior management positions in multinational corporations in the UK in relation to their rise to those senior positions.*

The focus of this study is on women in senior management positions and their rise to those positions. The key concepts in the project are 'the experiences of women managers', 'senior management positions', 'the struggle for women to reach senior management to senior management', 'women in senior management positions', and 'women in senior management in multinational corporations'. These key concepts

Survey
Used to denote survey research methodology in order to also used is particularly useful in facilitating the study of big populations and geographically scattered samples.

are essentially the focus of this research project. The research statement indicates the **scope** of the project, 100 women are included. The geographic scope of the project is all of the UK. The broad geographic scope can be readily facilitated through survey research.

Survey research methodology facilitates the study of big populations and samples, and populations and samples that are geographically scattered. Using a survey methodology it is easy, for example, to post a questionnaire to 100 women in different parts of the UK. Using a survey methodology, it would also be feasible also to conduct interviews, in particular telephone interviews, with 100 women located in different parts of the UK. Survey methodology is quite different from case study methodology. While survey methodology readily facilitates very broad studies, case study methodology readily facilitates the in-depth study of clearly defined bounded entities.

The scope of the research project above is limited to 100 women in senior management positions in multinational corporations. All of the decisions which have been made for the research project by the researcher, for example why there are 100 women, why it is a nationwide study, should be explained in the brief outline of the research project which should appear in the research report or thesis underneath the research statement or question.

It is easy to re-state a research statement as a question. Re-stated as a question, the above project might read as follows:

 What are the experiences of women in senior management positions in multinational corporations in the UK in relation to their rise to those senior positions? This research project is a survey of the experiences of 100 women in senior management positions in multinational corporations in the UK in relation to their rise to those senior positions.

Each research project should begin with a statement of the research. Your well-conceptualized research statement or question, the conceptual framework for your research project, should be the first sentence in the first chapter of your research report or thesis. In this way, the reader/examiner is brought immediately, without preamble, into your research project. On reading the first sentence the reader/examiner knows exactly what your research project is about. They know what methodology you have used, they know the scope of the project and they have a sense straightaway of the value of your research.

AIMS AND OBJECTIVES

Aims and objectives
A general statement of what you intend to accomplish.
Objectives specify how you intend to accomplish this aim.

Once the research statement or question has been delineated clearly, the next step is the development, from the research statement/question, of **aims and objectives**. The simplest way to do this is to develop one aim and a series of objectives, no less than two and no more than six objectives. While you can have more than one aim and more than six objectives, it is simpler to stay within these limits. Opposite are detailed examples of research aims and objectives. The case study at the end of this chapter details a student's experience in developing an idea for a research project into a research statement, an aim and a series of objectives.

The aim of the research is simply the research statement or question re-stated as an aim. For example, the research statement reads as follows:

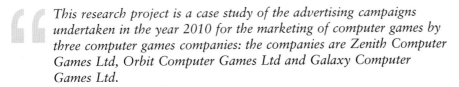

> *This research project is a case study of the advertising campaigns undertaken in the year 2010 for the marketing of computer games by three computer games companies: the companies are Zenith Computer Games Ltd, Orbit Computer Games Ltd and Galaxy Computer Games Ltd.*

The aim of the research is as follows:

> *The aim of this research is to examine the advertising campaigns undertaken in the year 2010 for the marketing of computer games by three computer games companies: the companies are Zenith Computer Games Ltd, Orbit Computer Games Ltd and Galaxy Computer Games Ltd.*

The objectives of the research emerge from the aim of the research. The objectives of the research are the steps the researcher intends to take in order to accomplish the aim of the research. Objectives are generally written in short phrases presented as bullet points. Each phrase uses at least one active verb, for example, consider, explore, examine, compare, contrast, develop. The objectives of the above study might read as follows:

- To examine the advertising campaigns of the three companies.
- To compare and contrast the advertising campaigns of the three companies.
- To explore the different advertising appeals used by the three companies.
- To examine the fitness for market of each of the marketing campaigns.

In another example:

> *This research project is a case study designed to facilitate the development of a model recruitment and selection process for a fictitious company, 'People for Places Ltd'.*

The aim of this research is to develop a model recruitment and selection process for a fictitious company 'People for Places Ltd'.

The objectives of the research are as follows:

- To examine the recruitment and selection processes of recruitment companies published on the internet.
- To explore models of recruitment and selection processes published in textbooks.
- To develop a model recruitment and selection process for a fictitious company 'People for Places Ltd'.

In another example:

> *The research project is a survey of the business plans of 50 SMEs in the Greater Galloway area.*

THE VALUE OF GOOD RESEARCH

Focus on survey methodology

Survey methodology is a very popular methodology with business students. Basically, surveys involve researchers asking questions of research participants. In survey research, information is gathered using standardized means. This is in order to ensure that every participant is asked the same questions in the same way. The requirement for standardization means that, usually, survey research involves the use of simple question formats. Questions are either closed or open. Using a closed format, the respondent is required only to give a 'yes' or 'no' or 'not applicable' response to questions, for example, 'Do you use this product?' Using an open format, the respondent is required to briefly explain something in response to questions, for example, 'Why do you use this product?'. Survey questionnaires can be very short or very long.

Surveys tend to involve relatively big populations and samples. For example, 30 respondents would be a small number of respondents in a survey.

As surveys tend to engage large populations of respondents, and as they tend to gather terse responses to questions (a lot of questions in survey research simply require the respondents to tick a box in order to answer the question). Surveys are useful ways of generating quantitative data.

Surveys can be carried out in different ways, online, by email, by post, by telephone, or in person.

A census of the population is a survey where every member of the population is included in the study.

In general, when carrying out survey research, a sample of the population (a small sub-section of the population), rather than the entire population, participates in the research. The sample is selected using an appropriate sampling method such as simple random sampling. If the sampling method is used correctly, then the sample can be said to be representative of the entire population and the findings of such a survey can be said to be valid for the entire population of the study. Sampling and sampling methods are dealt with

in detail in Chapter 8 of this textbook 'Understanding Research Methods, Populations and Sampling'.

In general, surveys tend to use questionnaires and/or interviews as data gathering methods. Questionnaires are effective in engaging with large populations. Sometimes the population is geographically scattered. A questionnaire can easily and relatively cheaply be emailed or posted to a geographically scattered or large population.

Survey research can be carried out using interviews. Telephone interviews can be used relatively easily and cheaply with geographically scattered populations. Surveys can also be developed using one-to-one in-depth interviews. One-to-one in-depth interviews may be possible with geographically scattered populations, if the population of the study is not too big, and if the researcher has the resources needed (time and money) to travel to interview all of the members of the population.

Many survey questionnaires are now created online, using tools such as *Survey Monkey* (**www.surveymonkey.com**) or *Instant Survey* (**www.instantsurvey.com**) or *Zoomerang* (**www.zoomerang.com**). All of these tools are quite easy to use and you can learn a lot about survey research from logging onto these websites and making attempts at developing questionnaires using the tools on the websites.

There are very many resources on the web for students of survey research. One of the most useful is the Princeton University Survey Research Centre (PSRC) (**www.princeton.edu/~psrc/**). This Centre provides a lot of information on how to conduct survey research. The PSRC refers students to the *American Statistical Association's* online guide 'What is a survey?' (**www.whatisasurvey.info/**). This is a free booklet which contains ten chapters, each of which deals with an aspect of survey research.

Another good resource on the web is The Research Methods Knowledge Base, 2nd edn (Trochim, 2006), (**www.socialresearchmethods.net/**).

Methodspace (**www.methodspace.com**) is also a good resource for research and researchers generally, as well as for those particularly interested in **survey** research.

References

Trochim, W.M. (2006) *The Research Methods Knowledge Base* (2nd edn), **www.socialresearchmethods.net/** Accessed 02.06.2010.

The aim of this research project is to survey the business plans of 50 SMEs in the Greater Galloway area.

The objectives of the study are as follows:

- To examine the business plans of the 50 SMEs.
- To compare and contrast the business plans of the 50 SMEs.
- To establish what the business plans have in common.
- To explore what is unique in each of the business plans.
- To develop and present, based on the findings of this survey, a model business plan for SMEs.

In another example:

> *What are the experiences of women in senior management positions in multinational corporations in the UK in relation to their rise to those senior positions? This research project is a survey of the experiences of 100 women in senior management positions in multinational corporations in the UK in relation to their rise to those senior positions.*

The aim of this research project is to examine the experiences of women in senior management positions in multinational corporations in the UK in relation to their rise to those senior positions.

The objectives of the research are as follows:

- To consider the experiences of women in senior management positions in multinational corporations (MNCs) in the UK.
- To explore the experiences of these senior managers of their rise to those positions.
- To detail the difficulties, if any, the women encountered throughout their rise.
- To examine the women's experiences in order to establish what experiences they had in common.
- To present an account of the critical experiences for women as they rise to senior management positions in MNCs in the UK.

As you can see, the objectives of the research detail the actions the researcher intends to take in order to accomplish the aim of the research. The objectives do not contain any statement about reviewing the literature, or any indication of the methodology or data gathering methods to be used in the research. The objectives, as stated, emerge from the aim. They are not new aims or other aims; they are the means by which the researcher intends to accomplish the aim of the research.

SOURCE APPROPRIATE LITERATURE

Your idea for your research project guides you in terms of the literature you need to begin to read. You have to have read some of the literature before you can fully and thoroughly outline a research question or statement for your research project. Literature, in the context of research projects, as was established in Chapter 1, is research that has already been carried out and published. Appropriate literature is literature that has been published in journal articles, in books, in government papers and reports, in theses, in reports of conference proceedings.

Your research project should emerge from the literature of the area within which your research project is situated, and in the end it should make a contribution to the literature, to the theory, in that area. It is by reading the literature that you develop an understanding of the kind of research being carried out in your area, and the focus of that research and any gaps it may contain, where little or no research has been carried out, or where there are unanswered questions. A gap in the research means that there is a need for research in this area and it would be a very good idea to develop your project as a response to a gap in the literature.

When you have finally decided, following an initial reading of the literature, on the research question or statement for your research project, you then begin to read the literature in order to develop your literature review. The key concepts in the research statement or question will indicate the areas within which you should focus your reading for your literature review. The written literature review in your thesis or in the report of your research contains **the theoretical framework** for the research project. The theoretical framework is the second framework of the four frameworks approach to the research project. The theoretical framework emerges from the conceptual framework. The example below illustrates this process.

The theoretical framework
The framework the researcher builds from the literature (theory) s/he reviews for the research project.

> *This research project is a case study of the marketing of computer games by three computer games companies: the companies are Zenith Computer Games Ltd, Orbit Computer Games Ltd and Galaxy Computer Games Ltd.*

The Four Frameworks
Conceptual Framework
Theoretical Framework
Methodological Framework
Analytical Framework

As stated earlier in this chapter, the key concepts in this research project are 'marketing', 'computer games', 'computer games companies' and 'marketing computer games'. These four key concepts are the essential focus of this research project and they are also the essential focus of the search for literature. You will use these key concepts to search for appropriate literature and to structure your literature review.

The ability to source appropriate literature is the second of the five basic skills needed in undertaking research. Each researcher must have the ability to source appropriate literature. While not all research is theorized, research conducted in an academic setting is always theorized. Theorized research is research that emerges from a body of knowledge and in turn makes a contribution to a body of knowledge. Academics are fundamentally engaged in developing theory and adding to the body of knowledge in their field. The researcher reads the literature in order to understand the area within which they are conducting their research, in order to develop some knowledge and expertise in this area, in order to develop an awareness of what is known in this area and in order to identify gaps in the knowledge in this area.

In general, published accounts of research projects make recommendations for further research. These recommendations are useful places to explore when attempting to develop an idea for a research project. For an example of a student project developed from the recommendations of another study, see the case study at the end of this chapter.

It is important when conducting a literature search to be able to identify good research. You need to be discerning. Check the date of the publication and try to be as up-to-date as possible in your reading, while including in your research any seminal writers in the field. Seminal writers are writers who have made an original and very substantial contribution to their field. Check the credentials of the authors. What qualifications and experience do they have? Establish whether or not they have a reputation in this field. Check the credentials of the place from where the work originated. Read the account of the research. Try to be critical in your reading, because you need to evaluate the value of the research. Examine the validity of the research. Is population of the study appropriate? What sampling **method** has been used, if a sample of a population has been used in the research? What data gathering methods were used? Were they appropriate? What data were gathered? What data analysis methods and procedures were used? Consider the findings of the research and the conclusions drawn from the research. Examine the standard of the writing, the substance of the contribution to the academic debate in the field that the work makes, and the overall quality of the work.

> **Method**
> Used to denote methodology and data collection such as data collection methods such as observation, interviews, focus groups, and questionnaires.

THE DIFFERENT APPROACHES TO RESEARCH

You will find in your reading that there are different approaches to research. It is useful from the start to begin to develop a sense of these different approaches. These different approaches reflect the different philosophical underpinnings of research projects.

In this chapter we have seen examples of proposed research projects to be developed using survey and case study methodologies. Survey and case study are examples of two different methodological approaches to research. We have seen that a survey approach to research facilitates the broad study of phenomena, the study of big populations and samples, and the study of populations and samples that are geographically scattered. We have seen that a case study research facilitates the in-depth study of phenomena, the study of clearly bounded entities, such as incidents or events or a particular business or company, or perhaps two or three businesses or companies. Clearly bounded entities can be studied in depth in a way that very scattered subjects cannot. Case study and survey research are examples of just two of the many different methodological approaches to research.

There are different philosophical frameworks within the world of social research and these frameworks facilitate different kinds of research. There are many different methodologies that can be used in carrying out research and there are also many different data collection methods. These different approaches to research and the ways in which they fit together are summarized in *The Methodological Triangle* detailed in Figure 2.2 (see Chapter 3 for a full explanation). The pyramid helps you see how the fundamental philosophies fit with the different methodologies, and how the different data collection methods fit with the different methodologies.

DATA: WHAT CONSTITUTES EVIDENCE?

Every researcher in undertaking a research project is exploring a phenomenon and/or attempting to establish a case. Conducting research is like going into a court of law and trying to prove a case. In the courtroom you would present as much evidence as possible. You would be very concerned to ensure that the evidence you presented was valid, trustworthy and correct. In your research project, you are concerned with the validity of the evidence you present. So what, in terms

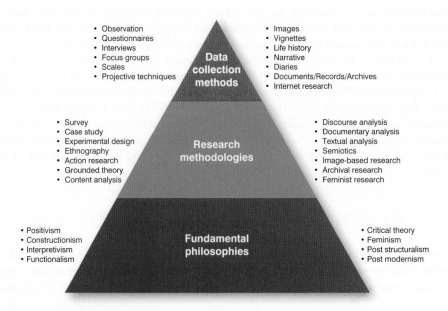

Figure 2.2   The methodological pyramid

of research projects, constitutes evidence? The answer is that it really depends on the phenomenon you are investigating.

In the context of research evidence is called data. Data can take many forms. It can be the testimony of human participants in a project, in, for example, the transcripts of interviews or focus groups. It can be in the responses to a questionnaire. It can also be found in documents, archives, records and reports. Data can be found in maps and charts, field diaries, narratives, photographs or film. It can be in the content of newspapers. In fact, data can take almost any form. The constraint is that the data must be valid. For data to be valid it must represent that which it is presented as representing. So if, for example, a researcher develops an interview schedule designed specifically by the researcher to measure, let us say, satisfaction levels among the participants in a training programme, then the interview schedule developed must do precisely that. The interview schedule must be a valid measure of those satisfaction levels. This issue of validity in the design and development of data collection methods is explored in detail in the chapters on methodology and method in this textbook.

PLAGIARISM

Plagiarism
The use and/or presentation of somebody else's work or ideas as your own. A serious offence and avoidable through proper referencing.

Plagiarism is the use and/or presentation of somebody else's work or ideas as your own. It is a most serious offence. Students who engage in **plagiarism**, even unwittingly, can be expelled from their colleges and institutions. This can have seriously detrimental effects on their careers. It can also be devastating for them personally, and for their families. You can avoid an accusation of plagiarism by properly referencing everything that you take from any and every source and then use in your own writing, or in any work that you present as your own.

REAL WORLD RESEARCH

How theory influences research

In the article detailed below, the researcher uses a survey methodology to explore the impact of different advertising appeals on consumer purchase decisions. The article is useful in that it presents some detail on the manner in which this particular survey was carried out. If you are interested in survey research you should source the original article and trace through the article the steps of the research process, as detailed in the model of the research process presented at the start of this chapter.

'Do all advertising appeals influence consumer purchase secision: An exploratory study',
Verma, S. (2009) Global Business Review, Vol. 10, 1:33–43

In this survey, the author sets out to examine the influence of different advertising appeals on consumer decision-making. According to the author, the review of the literature that he carried out showed that although advertisers use different ways of attracting and retaining customers, less work is done on evaluating the impact of the various appeals on customer decisions. This is a gap in the literature that the author found when he carried out his review of the literature.

In the article, the author presents a literature review on advertising and its impact on consumers. Following the literature review, he details and explains the research methodology used in the study. The methodology is survey methodology. In all, 1200 questionnaires were used in personal interviews with respondents. The respondents, we are told, belonged to different demographic groups in terms of gender, level of education, marital status and profession.

Some points worth noting with regard to this research:

- The methodology used in the study was survey, and the data collection method was interview questionnaire. The questionnaire was administered to participants through one-to-one interviews.

- An extensive review of the literature was undertaken before the questionnaire was designed. The review of the literature informed the development of the questionnaire and the creation and development of the questions in the questionnaire.

- A pilot study was carried out to help validate the questionnaire. A pilot study is a small preliminary study carried out before the main study to ensure that the data collection method designed for the research works as it is meant to work.

- The questionnaires were analyzed and a lot of quantitative data from that analysis are presented in the article. (In this textbook, we focus on quantitative data analysis in Chapter 14).

- The analyzed data are presented, discussed and explored.

- The findings of the research are presented. One of the findings of the research is that not all advertising is equally appealing.

- Conclusions are drawn. The author suggests that, given this finding (the finding detailed in the bullet point above), managers should generate different advertising strategies designed to appeal to specific market segments.

In your reading of the above article, consider the manner in which theory is used in the article. Consider in particular the way in which the literature review was constructed and presented.

References

Verma, S. (2009) 'Do all advertising appeals influence consumer purchase decision: An exploratory study', *Global Business Review* 10(1): 33–43.

It is vitally important that you learn to reference properly. When you get into the habit of referencing, you will no longer find it a chore, or at least it will certainly become less onerous. As you practise referencing properly, you will quickly learn to distinguish between somebody else's work and ideas, and your own. Where your ideas have developed from somebody else's, you simply reference the ideas that you have built your work upon. As stated earlier in this chapter, all research is built upon other research, and in turn all research becomes built upon. This is the way in which knowledge is created and the way in which a body of knowledge develops. You do want to add your own contribution and in doing this, you also want to acknowledge the contribution of others before you. You do this by referencing their work and their ideas.

If you want to read more about plagiarism there is a great deal of information about it and how to avoid it, on the internet. The University of Leeds provides a very useful resource on plagiarism awareness on its website at **www.ldu.leeds.ac.uk/ plagiarism/**. The University of Oxford provides a lot of information too on plagiarism on its website at **www.admin.ox.ac.uk/epsc/plagiarism/**. Your own institution will also have guidelines on plagiarism. If you need further information, do discuss this with your research supervisor or research methodologies lecturer. If you have a particular concern about plagiarism regarding something you've written, you can always submit it to your supervisor or mentor for comment and feedback.

Universities and colleges are now using software for example, *Turn it in* (**www. turnitin.com**) or *Check for Plagiarism* (**www.checkforplagiarism.net**) to examine for plagiarism in assignments and projects submitted by students. There is also free-to-download software now available to check for plagiarism in your own work. One example of this free-to-download software is *Viper The Anti-plagiarism Scanner* (**www.scanmyessay.com**).

Plagiarism really is a serious offence, and it does carry very serious penalties. The way to avoid plagiarism and accusations of plagiarism is to submit work that you have written yourself, work that is properly and thoroughly referenced.

COMPILING A BIBLIOGRAPHY

Bibliography
A list of all of the published work cited in the research project must all be listed in the bibliography.

The **bibliography** for any research project is one of the most critical elements of the research project. A good bibliography is a resource for any scholar interested in the topic of the research and helps demonstrate the scholarship of the project and its researcher. Readers and examiners tend to read through bibliographies before they read any other aspect of the research project. A quick read through the bibliography gives the reader a sense of the quality and standard of the work overall.

The bibliography is a list of all of the published work used in the research project: all of the books, chapters in books, journal articles, government reports and papers, theses, conference reports and proceedings, web references, newspaper and magazine articles, radio and television programmes and films, published photographs and other visual material referenced in the thesis or report of the research. Every reference detailed in the research project should be listed in the bibliography, and every reference in the bibliography should be detailed in the text.

The reading that you have done for the research is evidenced in your referencing throughout the work and in the bibliography. Try to ensure that your referencing and your bibliography adequately evidence the work that you did in reading for the research. The bibliography demonstrates the breadth and depth of your reading, shown by the variety of sources you have used in your research. Ensure that your references are up-to-date, including sources published in the year you present your thesis. Also ensure that you include any seminal writers on your topic. It may be that a key paper or a key book which influenced and shaped the direction of your area was presented 20 or more years ago, but it is important to reference this work. It is critically important that your research should reflect the current state of knowledge in the field. You should include all of the seminal works, but focus on the contemporary debate(s) in your area.

In compiling the bibliography:

- ensure that you are using the style required by your institution
- ensure that you have copied the details of the reference correctly
- be scrupulous about punctuation
- ensure that there are no spelling errors
- place the information for each reference in the bibliography in the correct order, according to the convention you are using
- do not use bullet points or any other styling or formatting in the bibliography.

Although the work of referencing is painstaking, and it must always be clear, consistent and correct, you will very quickly learn how to reference and get into the routine of referencing. You will learn a great deal about your area of study from the routine work of citing and referencing. You will learn the names of the theorists and become very familiar with their theories. If you apply yourself to this work of referencing properly, you will in no time be readily identifying theorists and their contribution to your field. If you are in doubt as to which referencing method is used in your institution, check with your research or thesis supervisor or your research methods lecturer. They will be able to advise you on the method used in your institution and on the correct way of using it.

There are many books and booklets which can help you in compiling your bibliography. It is useful, as always, to visit the library and to examine the bibliographies in the theses held there and the ways in which the bibliographies in those theses are presented. Dublin City University library has an online booklet, prepared by Dublin City University librarian Julie Allen, that provides a guide to referencing every kind of resource using the Harvard Referencing Method. The booklet has a sample bibliography on the last page. It is available at **www.library.dcu.ie/LibraryGuides/ citing&refquide08.pdf**. Another good resource is the very useful online library research skills tutorial provided by the University of London Research Library Services. This can be accessed at **www.ulrls.lin.ac.uk**.

Finally, there are software packages which can help you in compiling your bibliography. Among them are the software packages *EndNote*, *ProCite*, *Papyrus* and *Reference Manager*. Information on *EndNote* is available from the website **www.endnote.com**. This website gives free online tutorials as well as access to the software. It is possible that one of these software packages is available in your university or college. It is possible too that if the package is available within the university, the university is hosting workshops or tutorials to teach staff and students how to use the software. It is important to develop your computer skills as much as possible, and whenever possible. So if the college is offering any training on any software relevant to any area of your study, you should participate in that training.

THE USES OF APPENDICES

Appendices
Used to detail any
document or artefact
relevant to the
research but not
detailed in the body of
the research project.

Appendices are used to detail any document or artefact relevant to the research but not detailed in the body of the research project. Copies of letters written for the research project are placed in appendices. These letters might be letters written to, or received from, formal gatekeepers. These are the people you have sought and received permission from to conduct your research in, for example, their company, or with their employees. Copies of data collection methods and instruments are also detailed in appendices. For example, copies of questionnaires, interview schedules, observation schedules, focus group schedules, and Likert scales would be placed in appendices. Appendices are placed after the bibliography in the final written report of the research project. The pages of the bibliography are not numbered, and neither are the pages of the appendices. Each appendix is numbered at the top and given a title or heading.

It is neither useful nor helpful to place copies of completed data gathering instruments such as completed questionnaires or scales, or transcripts of interviews or focus groups, in appendices. In general, you will not be asked to present your raw data. If you are asked to do this, you will not be asked to do so by presenting it in appendices. It is unwise to pad the appendices with any material. Only place appendices material that is of relevance to the research project. Ensure that all of the material placed in appendices is discussed and explained in the body of the work and thoroughly embedded.

It is a good idea to display any long lists that you have used in appendices rather than in the body of the work. Very large tables or figures can also be displayed in appendices. These items tend to interrupt the narrative flow of your written account of your research project and so it is best to place them in appendices.

While you should not pad your appendices in any way, and you certainly should not load the appendices with raw data, you should use the facility of appendices as much as you can. The word count in appendices, as with the word count in the bibliography, is not included in the overall word count for the research project. This means that the appendices are a way for you to include elements in your research project without using up the word count. Students generally find it difficult to present research projects within the word count allocated for the project; 10 000 words, 15 000 words or 20 000 words can seem like a lot of words until you actually start to write the project up. It is when you are writing up the research project that you quickly see how few words you really have with which to express the entire experience of the research project.

It is a good idea to keep a note in your research diary of the documents and artefacts, the lists and models and figures you wish to place in the appendices of your research project. You should also visit the library and look at the appendices in the theses there. This exercise will give you some ideas for your own appendices.

KEEPING THE RESEARCH DIARY

The research diary is a valuable tool for any researcher. It is a simple notebook within which the researcher records all of their reflections and decisions throughout the duration of the research project. Ideally, the researcher starts the diary as soon as they begin to think about their research project, and they continue writing notes in the diary until the research project has been completed.

The completed research project represents all of the parts of the research process, as well as the creative, reflective engagement of the researcher with the research project. Throughout the process, the researcher is actively engaged with the work of developing the project. This engagement is sustained through the development of the conceptual, theoretical, methodological and analytical frameworks of the research project and the outlining of the conclusions and recommendations from the research.

The reflection that is recorded in the research diary is informal. As ideas arise, through active and reflective engagement with the issues and problems posed in conducting and completing the research project, the researcher records them quickly in the research diary. These ideas can be jotted down in one form, and then quickly jotted down again in another form as they develop in the researcher's mind. In this informal way, the researcher develops streams of ideas and inspirations about the research, which can be built upon as the project develops and is completed.

The formal written account of the research is the thesis or report of the research. As the ideas and inspirations recorded in the research diary are moved to the thesis or the research report, they become more polished and are formalized and integrated into the various chapters. In this way, the notes that the researcher makes in the research diary help with the process of writing up the research.

There is no right or wrong way to keep a research diary. You may decide for yourself how much detail you want to record. The notebook you choose as the research diary can be as big or as small as you wish. It is important to use a well-bound notebook, because you don't want pages to fall out of the notebook and get lost.

It is important to keep a record of the dates and places of all of the entries. These details may be needed in presenting the information in the thesis or report of the research, where they will lend support and credibility, and so validity, to the written account.

You might decide to just use a free-flow method in keeping the diary. Using this method each entry is entered on a new page. If you are recording something that happens during the course of the research, the page is dated and the place is recorded. You might record who was present and write a brief account of what happened. You should also record your impressions. What struck you most about the experience? What did you expect to happen? Why did you expect that to happen? What did happen? What meaning did you make of what happened? Perhaps what happened had different meaning(s) for different people. How? Why?

It is useful to record in the diary the names and roles of the people you encounter throughout the research. You should also record exactly where you encounter each person, and the context within which the encounter takes place. You will easily forget detail like this, and it can be very useful to have it to hand as the research develops. Some of the people you encounter will be gatekeepers in terms of your research and will be in a position, formally or informally, to permit your research to go ahead, or to disrupt, delay or even stop your research. Your encounters with these people will help shape your research. The record in the research diary will help you remember the influence each person had on your research. If necessary, you can use the record in the research diary to help in relation to them.

You use the research diary to record your engagements with the participants in your research. You will have data collection methods, such as questionnaires and/or interview schedules and/or focus group schedules and/or perhaps other methods to record the engagements with participants formally. There will also in some cases be audio recordings of your engagements with participants, perhaps photographs and maybe even video recordings. The research diary will help supplement these records. Your research diary is for your eyes only. It is your personal record of your own thoughts and ideas, your intuitions and experiences of the people and places you encounter throughout the research process. Use it as you see fit and record as much or as little detail as you wish.

You can use your research diary to help you generate ideas around your research. You can scribble down any ideas you have and then use your notes to develop these ideas. You can develop ideas for your research statement or question, reflecting on the key concepts you wish to include and how you might do this. You can develop the aim of your research and play around with ideas for objectives. You can think about the issues you want to explore with your participants when you engage in data gathering with your participants and experiment with questions you might ask in the field work for the research. You can also develop lists of questions and issues you would like to explore in the data gathering phase of your research and begin to develop lists of names of potential participants in your research. You can record any thoughts or ideas you have in relation to the ethical issues in your research. You can note your insights into your research project as they come to you. You can begin to create and develop structures for the different chapters of your project. You can jot down insights that you get regarding possible findings and conclusions from the research and recommendations you might make following your research. In short, you can use the research diary to record any aspect of your research project and any thought or idea you have in relation to it. The research diary becomes one of the most useful tools in the research process and it is a tool that researchers create by themselves for themselves (see Figure 2.3).

You may prefer to use a more formal method of recording your thoughts in your research diary. It may help you to devise a series of questions to ask yourself to facilitate a flow of ideas. It is important throughout the research process to stay focused on your research question or statement. Three of the questions outlined in the form below relate to checking the relevance of the experiences you are documenting in your diary to your research statement or question. A format such as the following might be useful.

Figure 2.3a   Example of spidergram included in research diary

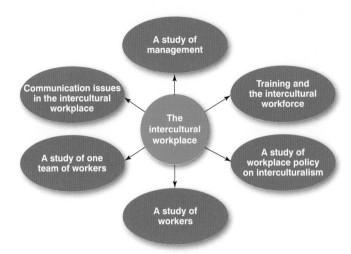

Figure 2.3b   Example of spidergram included in research diary

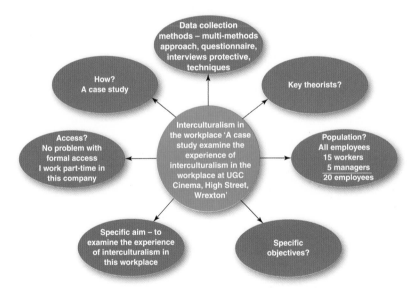

Figure 2.3c   Example of spidergram included in research diary

Here are some useful websites to help you develop skills in creating and generating spidegrams and thought map:

- www.mdx.ac.uk/WWW/STUDY/Spider.htm

- www.bbc.co.uk/schools/gcsebitesize/art/ao1/3personalexperiencesrev2.shtml

- www.mindtools.com/pages/article/newISS _01.htm

- www.avizsoft.com/Thoughtmapper_ example_Meeting_Minutes.htm

- (All websites accessed 02.06.2010)

RESEARCH DIARY

Place:

Participants:

Date:

Action: (Briefly record what happened.)

What was good in this meeting/interaction?

What was not so good?

What do I now know?

How can I now progress?

What should I do next?

How relevant is this to my research statement/question?

Will this help me answer my research statement/question?

How will this help me answer my research statement/question?

Notes:

CASE STUDY

Jack's survey research

A research proposal

Jack has an idea for a new product. The new product is a weekly online news bulletin which will be a guide to what's on in the university every week during semester. The news bulletin will alert students and staff to all the special events on campus for the week ahead, all of the academic, cultural, artistic and sporting events on campus for the week. The news bulletin will be called *What's On?* It will go online on Monday morning every week during semester. The bulletin will carry advertising and the advertising will generate revenue. Jack believes that every organization could develop a *What's On?* bulletin, based on his model.

Jack has decided that for his thesis for his degree, a BSc in Business Studies, he would like to undertake some research with students and staff in his university in order to try to establish whether or not there is a market for this new product.

Jack has explained his idea for his research project to his thesis supervisor and his thesis supervisor supports his idea. He has been asked by his thesis supervisor to develop a formal research proposal, based on this idea.

Jack developed the following research proposal.

A research proposal

Research statement: This research project is a survey of the perspectives of 100 people on campus, students and staff, on whether or not there is a market on university campuses for an online weekly news bulletin which would contain a listing of all of the events, academic, cultural, artistic and sporting, to be held on campus each week during semester.

Aim and objectives

The aim of this research project is to examine the views of 100 people on campus, university students and members of staff, in relation to whether or not there is a market on university campuses for an online weekly news bulletin which would contain a listing of all of the special events, academic, cultural, artistic and sporting to be held on campus during that week.

The objectives of the study are as follows:

- to survey participants with a view to establishing whether or not they think there is a market for a weekly online news bulletin on university campuses
- to determine the level of support that there might be for the proposed new product
- to gather feedback from participants on the proposed format, content, style and presentation of the new product
- to make recommendations in relation to new product development, based on the views of those surveyed.

The population of the study

The population of the study will be 100 people on campus, university students and staff, at the University of Illingham. In order to gather the sample of 100 people, a non-purposive sampling method will be used, quota sampling. With quota sampling the researcher will gather the 100 participants using different quotas, (see Chapter 8, 'Understanding Research Methods, Populations and Sampling').

In this research, there will be four quotas, the first quota will be made up of 25 female students, the second quota will be made up of 25 male students, the third quota will be made up of 25 female members of staff, and the fourth and final quota will be made up of 25 male members of staff. The researcher will secure the agreement of the participants to participate in the study.

The researcher has decided to limit the study to 100 participants in order to protect to some extent his idea for this new product.

Sample literature review

This research project is focused on new product development and on establishing whether or not there is a market for a particular new product, a university online weekly news bulletin detailing the special events scheduled to be held on campus at the university each week. The focus of the review of the literature for this research project is on new product development, and marketing new products.

According to Trott (2008: 403), the early stages of the new product development process are most usually defined as idea generation, idea screening, concept development and concept testing. The early stages of new product development are referred to by Trott (2008: 405), as the 'fuzzy front end'. This is because the early stages of the process of new product development are messy. In the early stages the developer is developing the concept and deciding whether or not to invest resources in further developing the idea.

According to Chou (2008), to be in a position to form strategic alliances with potential investors and suppliers, new product development (NPD) people and teams need to understand the factors that may influence investors and suppliers in decisions of whether or not to invest. The critical factors in such decisions, according to Chou, are trust, knowledge sharing, and collaboration in the NPD development process.

Another important issue, particularly for new businesses, and highlighted by Holt and Macpherson (2010), is the difficulty of creating and sustaining novel business ideas within, or even against, established market environments.

The literature review for this research project will explore:

- the key issues in NPD as they are currently detailed in the literature
- the critical issues in establishing strategic alliances with investors and suppliers
- the potential obstacles to establishing and sustaining a new business idea within an established market.

Research methodology

The research methodology to be used in the research project is survey research (Trochim, 2006). Survey research is an appropriate methodology for this research project because the population of the study is relatively large. There will be 100 participants. The focus of the study is on the exploration of the views of the population of the study on the viability of a proposed new product. The research will involve the exploration of three key issues with respondents. Both quantitative and qualitative data will be gathered on each of the issues. The researcher has a clear understanding of the data required for the project. The researcher will construct a questionnaire which will be specifically designed to gather the required data. A survey methodology is consequently justified. It is the appropriate methodology for this research project.

The data collection method to be used in the survey is an online questionnaire. The researcher will develop the online questionnaire using the software package Survey Monkey (**www.surveymonkey. com**). Each of the 100 participants in the study will be contacted by email and invited to participate in the research. Each will be told of the confidential nature of the research, and asked to observe confidentiality in terms of the proposed new product. As participants agree to participate in the research, and agree to observe confidentiality, they will be sent an email containing a link to the online survey. Each respondent will be asked to complete the survey online. The researcher will continue to contact potential participants until each of the four quotas has been filled.

Context for the research

The research is being undertaken for a BSc. in Business Studies. The research will be undertaken with students and staff on campus at the University of Illingham.

Rationale for the research

The researcher hopes through this research to establish that there is a market for the proposed new product. The researcher will use the opportunity of the research to test responses in the market to the proposed new product and the researcher will use any ideas generated by the research to further develop the new product. The researcher hopes to use the findings of the research to help secure investment for the new product.

References

Chou, A.Y. (2008) 'The role of knowledge sharing and trust in new product development outsourcing', *International Journal of Information Systems and Change Management*, 3(4) June: 301–313.

Holt, R. and Macpherson, A. (2010) 'Sensemaking, rhetoric and the socially competent entrepreneur', *International Small Business Journal* 28(1): 20–42.

Trochim, W.M. (2006) *The Research Methods Knowledge Base* (2nd edn), 'Survey research', **www.socialresearchmethods.net**

Trott, P. (2008) *Innovation Management and New Product Development*, Harlow: Pearson.

Questions What do you think of Jack's research proposal? What do you think of his research statement? Do you think it provides a good conceptual framework for the project? Explain your answer. What do you think of his aim and objectives? Can you see how the objectives clearly emerge from the aim? Explain your answer.

Students outside a university faculty building © Images-USA/Alamy

CHAPTER REVIEW

In this chapter the five basic skills of the research project were detailed and discussed. The five basic skills are the ability to generate ideas for research projects; the ability to identify, source and use appropriate literature; the ability to develop research projects with a good fit; the ability to gather and analyze data; and the ability to communicate research through very clear, very simple and very direct writing.

The chapter explored research ideas and the means by which they are turned into research projects. The well-conceptualized research statement or question was seen to be of the most fundamental importance. It was established that it should be possible to express the well-conceptualized research project in one sentence, a statement or a question. Such precision of expression calls for absolute clarity in relation to the proposed research project. A number of examples of well-conceptualized research projects were presented and explored in the chapter.

The well-conceptualized research statement or question was said to be the conceptual framework for the research project. On this framework, the other three frameworks in the four frameworks approach to the research project were said to rest. The conceptual framework contains the key concepts in the research project. The key concepts guide the creation and development of the theoretical framework for the research project. The conceptual framework for the research project emerges from the researcher's idea for the research project and the initial reading of the literature carried out by the researcher. The theoretical framework for the research project is contained in the literature review. The sourcing of literature for the research project was discussed, and the kind of literature needed for the literature review was outlined.

The need for evidence, or data, in the research project was discussed and the nature of evidence and the kinds of evidence possible in research projects were examined. The dangers of plagiarism were highlighted. The uses of bibliographies were outlined and the ways in which to compile a bibliography were considered. Some tools to help with the work of compiling bibliographies were presented and discussed. The meaning and uses of appendices were detailed. The research diary was discussed in some detail and its value explained. The uses of the research diary were explored and two different approaches to keeping the research diary were presented. The function of spidergrams and other conceptual maps in the generation and development of ideas was considered.

Now update your interactive research diary with your notes and findings at www.cengage.co.uk/quinlan. Complete the activities provided to reinforce your understanding of this chapter.

END OF CHAPTER QUESTIONS

1 Differentiate between a research idea and a research question.

2 Create a conceptual framework for a research project.

3 Detail a strategy, using the four frameworks approach to research, to source appropriate literature.

4 Detail, describe and explain some of the different approaches to research.

5 Initiate a research diary using a template on the online platform.

6 Evaluate the evidence presented in the research projects presented on the online platform. Critique the bibliography outlined.

7 Visit the library and find copies of theses which report research projects which students in your university have carried out using case study and survey methodologies. Be critical in your examination of these projects. Critique the theses in terms of their overall quality. Critically examine the standard of writing in the theses. Critically examine the bibliographies in the theses.

8 Read the research statements or questions or hypotheses. As conceptual frameworks for their research projects, how well do you think they work? Read the research methodology chapters.

9 Read the research methodology chapters. What initial thoughts do you have about them?

10 What research methodology was used?

11 What was the population of the research?

12 Was a sample used, and if so what sampling method was used?

13 How is the sampling method described? Is enough detail given to allow the reader to critically evaluate the method used?

14 What data collection methods were used?

15 How are these presented in the thesis?
It would be useful to keep a record in your research diary of your critical assessments of the theses. Record briefly in your research diary your reflections on these theses.

REFERENCES

Allen, J. Dublin City University, 'DCU library citing and referencing: A guide for students' (2nd edn), http://www.library.dcu.ie/LibraryGuides/citing&ref quide08.pdf Accessed 02.06.2010.

American Statistical Association's online guide 'What is a survey', www.whatisasurvey.info/ Accessed 02.06.2010.

Chou, A.Y. (2008) 'The role of knowledge sharing and trust in new product development outsourcing', *International Journal of Information Systems and Change Management*, 3(4) June: 301–313.

Denzin, N.K. (1970) 'The research act in sociology', Chicago, IL: Aldine.

Holt, R. and Macpherson, A. (2010) 'Sensemaking, rhetoric and the socially competent entrepreneur', *International Small Business Journal* 28(1): 20–42.

Methodspace: Connecting the Research Community, Sage, www.methodspace.com Accessed 02.06.2010.

Princeton University Survey Research Centre (PSRC), www.princeton.edu/~psrc/ Accessed 02.06.2010.

Smithers, R. 'Scottish fish and chip shop named best in UK', *The Guardian*, 21.01.2010. Accessed 02.06.2010.

Seafish: The authority on seafood, www.seafish.org Accessed 02.06.2010.

The University of Leeds 'Plagiarism awareness', www.ldu.leeds.ac.uk/plagiarism/ Accessed 02.06.2010.

The University of Oxford 'Plagiarism', www.admin.ox.ac.uk/epsc/plagiarism/ Accessed 02.06.2010.

Trochim, W.M. (2006) *The Research Methods Knowledge Base* (2nd edn), www.socialresearch-methods.net/ Accessed 02.06.2010.

Trott, P. (2008) *Innovation Management and New Product Development*, Harlow: Pearson.

Verma, S. (2009) 'Do all advertising appeals influence consumer purchase decision: An exploratory study', *Global Business Review* 10(1): 33–43.

Wyke, N.'The UK's Top 10 fish and chip shops 2010', *Times Online*, 19.01.2010, http://www.timesonline.co.uk/tol/life_and_style/food_and_drink/article6998138.ece Accessed 02.06.2010.

RECOMMENDED READING

Bell, J. (2005) *Doing Your Research Project*, Maidenhead: Open University Press.

Berman Brown, R. (2006) *Doing Your Dissertation in Business and Management*, London: Sage.

Denscombe, M. (2002) *Ground Rules for Good Research: A 10 Point Guide for Social Researchers*, Maidenhead: Open University Press.

Easterby-Smith, M., Thorpe, R. and Jackson, P.R. (2008) *Management Research* (3rd edn), Ch. 2, 'The Ingredients of Successful Research', London: Sage.

Hart, C. (1998) *Doing a Literature Review: Releasing the Social Science*, London: Sage.

May, T. (2005) *Social Research: Issues Methods and Processes*, Maidenhead: Open University Press.

Murray, R. (2003) *How To Write a Thesis*, Maidenhead: Open University Press.

Punch, K.F. (2005) *Developing Effective Research Proposals*, London: Sage.

Zikmund, W.G. (2003) '*Business Research Methods*', Ch. 4, 'The Research Process: An Overview', Mason, OH: Cengage South-Western.

CHAPTER 3

UNDERSTANDING RESEARCH ETHICS

LEARNING OBJECTIVES

At the end of this chapter the student should be able to:

- Appreciate the importance of research ethics.

- Critique research from an ethical perspective.

- Engage in critical reflection on the ethics of their research.

- Consider, explain and resolve the ethical issues and dilemmas in their research.

- Seek and secure formal ethical approval, where necessary, for their research project.

RESEARCH SKILLS

At the end of this chapter the student should, using the exercises on the accompanying online platform, be able to:

- Provide an ethical reflection on a given project.

- Critique a given ethical reflection.

The aim of this chapter is to explain ethics, to introduce the student to ethics in business research, and to help the student develop an ethical perspective on research in general and business research in particular. The chapter explains the basic precepts of research ethics, explores fundamental ethical issues and details some possible approaches to dealing with the ethical issues and dilemmas of research projects. The chapter will help you, the student, develop a critical reflective ethical approach to research.

THE VALUE OF GOOD RESEARCH

Research in the media

I n this newspaper article, Bunting discusses *Citizen Ethics*, a 60-page online pamphlet on ethics presented by the *Citizen Ethics Network* (**www.citizenethics.org.uk**) in association with *The Guardian* newspaper. She outlines what has recently been described as a crisis in ethics highlighted by, among other things, the global economic downturn. Reading the extract from the article presented here, will give you a good sense of what is meant by the word ethics.

'To tackle the last decades' myths, we must dust off the big moral questions: A robust debate on ethics is crucial to the pursuit of a

The World Economic Forum in Davos © RIA Novosti/Alamy

good society in which individuals are more than mere economic units.' Bunting, M. *The Guardian*, 22 February 2010 © Guardian News & Media Ltd 2010. Reproduced with permission.

Bunting writes 'The central premise of the *Citizen Ethics* supplement … is that we have lost a way of thinking and talking about some very important things. The preoccupation with market efficiency and economic growth has loomed so large that other activities, and other values, have been subordinated to its disciplines. "You can't buck the market", said Mrs. Thatcher, and no government has disagreed since. It was the adage that was to justify soaring pay for the highest earners and stagnant earnings for the low-paid. The market ruled, and questions of injustice, honour or integrity were all secondary or irrelevant.'

A poll for the World Economic Forum (2010) found in 10 G20 countries that two-thirds of respondents attributed the credit crunch and its ensuing economic recession to a crisis of ethics and values. Sir Thomas Legg declared in his final report on MPs' expenses that there had been a failure of ethics.

Citizen Ethics was a project to ask nearly four dozen prominent thinkers what this was all about. Did ethics really have a role to play, and had it failed? First, despite plenty of disagreements, on one thing there was a clear consensus: ethics are crucial. They are vital to the civic culture in which both politics and economics are ultimately rooted …. If we really want to understand how some of the incredible myths perpetrated over that last couple of decades have gone unchallenged, we have to get back to some basic arguments of philosophy. What is justice? Who deserves what? What constitutes human flourishing?

Too many of these questions have been shelved for too long. Questions of justice and reward were left to the market to resolve; questions of human flourishing were privatized.

One explanation for this abandonment of the debate is that we lost a language in which to think and argue about ethics.

Ethics is a word that derives from two Greek words, *ethos* for habit and *ethikos* for character, and it better fits what *Citizen Ethics* proposes rather than "morality", which comes from the Latin word *mores* for social institutions and customs. This is not about reasserting conventions, a preconceived code, but about reinvigorating a habit, a process of reasoning to the perennial question: what is the right thing to do?

References

Bunting, M. (2010) 'To tackle the last decades' myths, we must dust off the big moral questions: A robust debate on ethics is crucial to the pursuit of a good society in which individuals are more than mere economic units', *The Guardian*, 22 February 2010.

INTRODUCTION

Ethics can be defined very simply as a process of reasoning in terms of the right thing to do. There are ethical issues in every aspect of the research process. The model below provides a useful tool to aid reflection on the ethical issues that can arise in the different phases of the research process.

Consider each of these stages in the research process, as detailed in Figure 3.1. Ask yourself:

- What are the **potential harms** that might arise from your research, and from the manner in which you engage with the research and the standard you set for your research, throughout every stage of the research process?

- What are the potential risks that might arise from your research, and from the manner in which you engage with the research and the standard you set for your research, throughout every stage of the research process?

Potential harms
A potential harm is a harm that might occur.

The researcher reflects on the ethical issues in each phase of the research process. Then the researcher writes a reflection on these issues and the way in which each of them has been addressed. This ethical reflection becomes part of the methodological framework for the research project. Within the four frameworks approach to the

The Four Frameworks
Conceptual Framework
Theoretical Framework
Methodological Framework
Analytical Framework

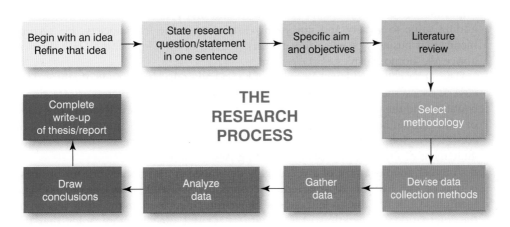

Figure 3.1   The research process

research process, the methodological framework is the third framework. The researcher deals explicitly with the ethics of the research project in the methodology section of the written account of the research.

There are many ethical issues in the recent global financial collapse. While some of the activities that led to the collapse were illegal, a great deal more of the activity was unethical.

Ethics can also be defined as the moral principles governing the conduct of an individual, a group or an organization. This definition provides a good point on which to begin a reflection on ethics. In research, as in business, there are fundamental ethical principles.

Ethics
Moral principles governing the conduct of an individual, a group, or an organization.

ETHICS IN BUSINESS RESEARCH

Ethics in business research is simply the application of ethical principles and standards to business research. Essential in ethics and ethical standards is a capacity to distinguish between right and wrong. YouTube has a number of videos of different people engaging in the Davos Debates on ethics. For 5 days in January every year top politicians and business people meet in Davos in Switzerland at the World Economic Forum (**www.weforum.org**). The people running global corporations attend the World Economic Forum, include Bill and Melinda Gates, Michael Dell and Evan Williams, co-founder of Twitter. Also in attendance are those running not-for-profit businesses, as well as the politicians and prominent concerned global citizens like Bono, Youssou N'Dour and Angelina Jolie. The World Economic Forum (WEF) is itself a not-for-profit foundation.

The YouTube videos show some of these people outlining briefly their understanding of ethics and business ethics. In particular, the YouTube video of Rakesh Khurana, Professor of Leadership Development at Harvard Business School, is of interest. In his video, Professor Khurana considers the question of whether business and management personnel should, like doctors, have an ethical oath. If you search for 'Harvard Business School's Rakesh Khurana on ethics' you will be able to view the video. It is just over 30 seconds long. Professor Khurana concludes that business and management personnel should have an ethical oath. He says that business is too important to be run by and for self interest and that business should be engaged in adding value to society and not simply extracting value from society. He recommends that business people adopt the first maxim of the Hippocratic Oath, first or above all, 'do no harm'.

The American Marketing Association has a highly developed code of ethics. This covers issues such as the responsibility of the marketer; marketers' professional conduct; and the principles of honesty, fairness and transparency. Reading this code of ethics would be a useful exercise. It would help you develop an understanding of ethical principles in practice. You will find this code online if you search for 'Statement of Ethics – American Marketing Association'.

Another good example of a very highly developed ethical framework for business is that of The Institute of Chartered Accountants Scotland (**www.icas.org.uk**). The Institute's Code of Ethics is laid out on the website. It is based on the 2005 version of the International Federation of Accountants (IFAC). The Institute holds that the code applies to all members, including students, in their professional and business activities whether those activities are paid or voluntary. The Code of Ethics is useful for our purposes in that it provides guidance on five fundamental ethical principles, among them integrity, professional competence and due care, confidentiality and professional behaviour. These, as you will see as you read on through this chapter, are also fundamental ethical principles in research.

The ethical framework of the Institute of Chartered Accountants of Scotland is presented in a report of the research committee of that institute (Helliar and Bebbington, 2004). This report contains a synopsis of a research project carried out by the research committee for the Institute. The research project was designed to examine the ethical standards of accountants. The title of the report is 'Taking Ethics to Heart: A Discussion Document by the Research Committee of The Institute of Chartered Accountants of Scotland'. In the document, the authors lay out the approach taken to the research and the findings of that research. One of the main findings was that there was no clear framework for accountants to use in ethical decision-making. The report proposed such a framework makes for interesting and very detailed reading on ethics and the profession of accountancy. The report provides a very good starting point for any student wishing to study ethics and business.

Ethical issues and dilemmas in business research

Ethics in business, and consequently in business research, has in recent years become a critical issue. It has become a critical issue globally, because basic ethical standards have not been adhered to in some businesses, even perhaps in some business sectors. Where ethical standards were not adhered to, a culture of greed flourished within which dishonest and fraudulent activities and behaviours were tolerated, and perhaps even encouraged. Writing in *The Banker* (05.01.2009), Will Hutton highlighted what he called the 'by now familiar roll call of villains', among them, fabulous bonus systems, poor regulation of financial markets and extraordinary international financial relationships. Globally, we are all now living with the consequences of these unethical practices. The processes being put in place to correct these 'mistakes' are costly and painful, and the effects are likely to be felt for a long time into the future. The financial readjustments that have taken place and are taking place have prompted a questioning of ethical standards and practices in business. This questioning has led to more vigorous engagements in ethics in business and in business research. As the processes of adjustment develops so too will standards and practices in business ethics and in ethics in business research.

Writing in *The Guardian* (20.01.2009) on this issue of offences against ethical standards and criminal offences, Afua Hirsch explored the criminal investigations in the USA of banks and businesses and some of the people working in them. She highlighted investigations into Washington Mutual, Freddie Mac and Fannie May and AIG as well as the criminal charges which were brought against four executives from Bear Stearns and Credit Suisse, all of whom were charged with fraud for misleading investors. In the article, Hirsch contrasted this US approach to these cases with the approach taken in the UK to Sir Fred Goodwin, former chairman of the Royal Bank of Scotland. Goodwin retired, according to the article, 'with a knighthood in the bag as well as an £8.4m pension'. He had been forced to step down from his post as chairman of the bank as a non-negotiable condition for the

£20bn bail out of Royal Bank of Scotland, and was facing a threat of possible sanctions. Hirsch describes this treatment of Goodwin as mild:

> *... in the context of a chairman who oversaw losses of £28bn in investments and purchases in a single year, at a cost to the taxpayer so gargantuan it becomes increasingly impossible to grasp.*

Unethical, and in some cases illegal, behaviour in economics has caused a global economic downturn. The fact that unfettered markets and unregulated financial systems are responsible for this early twenty-first century economic recession makes this chapter on ethics in business research particularly interesting.

The importance of ethics in research

When we undertake research, we are representing ourselves and our institution or organization in the wider community and must consequently adopt in our research endeavour the highest ethical standards. As we mature and become adults every action we take, and are seen to take, contributes to our reputation within our own community and beyond. As this is the case, we should always try to present ourselves as ethical practitioners and professionals.

So how do we undertake research ethically? To begin with, we must understand the basic concepts of research and the basic steps in the research process. It is unethical to present yourself as a researcher if you do not know how to conduct research. In order to be able to present yourself to your community as a researcher, you must have the necessary skills and competencies to carry out the research you are proposing to carry out.

Ethics and your research

It is important to begin to think as an ethical practitioner. It is likely that you have been guided all your life by ethical principles. To become an ethical practitioner requires a formal, open and acknowledged critical engagement with ethical standards and behaviours. In research, this critical engagement is formalized through the ethical reflection every researcher engages in and writes about their research project, and through the ethical standards reflected throughout the research project in the manner in which the research project is carried out and written up.

As stated in Chapter 1, the written formal account of the ethical reflection the researcher engages in, in relation to the research, is usually placed in Chapter 3 of the thesis, which is generally the methodology chapter. While the formal ethical reflection appears as a written section in the methodology chapter, the ethical standards of the research project are apparent to the reader of the research project in every element of the written record of a research project. They are evident in the way in which the project was conceptualized, designed and developed, and in the research-er's engagement with the population of the research and the way in which the fieldwork for the research is managed. The degree of scholarship which the researcher developed in undertaking the research is also reflected in the written account of the research and provides further evidence of the ethical standards of the researcher.

REAL WORLD RESEARCH

How theory influences research

The article below is from the *British Journal of Management*. In the article the authors explore business **ethics** as practice.

'Business Ethics as Practice', Clegg, S., Kornberger, M. and Rhodes, C. *British Journal of Management* (2007) © Wiley-Blackwell; 18:2: 107–122. Reproduced with permission via Rightslink.

The authors consider the individual within the business workplace using his/her own conscience as the appropriate standard in ethical and moral judgements. The authors consider the norms and practices of the organization as the arbiter of the appropriate standard in ethical and moral judgements.

They argue that what managers actually do is central to how the individual's sense of the appropriate standard in ethical and moral judgements is formed and challenged within organizations. They examine how the ethics of the individual are shaped by the culture of the organization, and how the ethics of individuals shape the ethical culture of organizations.

The article is very useful on a number of levels:

- It is useful in that it is an engaging study of management ethical practices. The focus is on the ethics, or the behavioural ethics of individuals situated within business organizations.

- The article is useful in that it presents a highly developed theoretical framework focused on how ethics 'play out in practice'.

- A careful reading of the article gives a good sense of how theory influences research, and vice versa, how research in turn makes a contribution to theory.

- The list of references at the end of the article is a very useful resource for both classical and contemporary references on ethics.

- Finally, this article might give you some ideas for your own research project.

The authors present the article as follows:

> In this article we develop a conceptionalization of business ethics as practice. Starting from the view that the ethics that organizations display in practice will have been forged through an ongoing process of debate and contestation over moral choices, we examine ethics in relation to the ambiguous, unpredictable, and subjective contexts of managerial action.

The article concludes by discussing how the 'ethics as practice' approach that we expound, provides theoretical resources for studying the different ways that ethics manifest themselves in organizations as well as providing a practical application of ethics in organizations that goes beyond moralistic and legalistic approaches.

In recent years, business scandals, ranging from Enron to the Parmalat disasters, have once again redirected the attention of both managers and organization theorists to a consideration of ethics and the moral dilemmas that corporations face in the context of contemporary capitalism (see Donaldson, 2003; Johnson and Smith, 1999; Parker, 2003; Porter and Kramer, 2002; Soule, 2002; Tonge, Greer and Lawton, 2003; Veiga, 2004; Weaver, Treviño and Cochran, 1999b; see also Werhane, 2000). Despite such a renewed focus, as Donaldson suggests, the theoretical tools employed to analyze and understand ethics require further development. In the same vein, as Wicks and Freeman argue, 'organization studies need to be fundamentally reshaped ... to provide room for ethics and to increase the relevance of research' (1998, p. 13). It is an aim that we subscribe to.

The goal of this article is to develop a theoretical framework with which to explore ethics in organization theory that moves beyond being either prescriptive or morally relative. To do so, we argue that ethics is best understood and theorized as a form of practice. Our approach is concerned with theorizing ethics in relation to what managers actually do in their everyday activities.

Finally, this research article concludes with 'a new research agenda' for the practice of ethics for business managers and in business organizations.

When you have read this synopsis you should source the original article and read it. Does this article give you any ideas for your research project? Does this article give you any ideas for your reflection on the ethical issues in your own research?

References

Clegg, S., Kornberger, M. and Rhodes, C. (2007) 'Business ethics as practice', *British Journal of Management* 18: 107–122.

Donaldson, T. (2003) 'Editor's comments: Taking ethics seriously? A mission now more possible', *Academy of Management Review*, 28; 363–366.

Johnson, P. and Smith, K. (1999) 'Contextualizing business ethics: Anomie and social life', *Human Relations*, 52: 1351–1375.

Parker, M. (ed.) (2003) 'Special issue on ethics politics and organization', *Organization*, Vol. 10(2).

Porter, M. and Kramer, M. (2002) 'The competitive advantage of corporate philanthropy', *Harvard Business Review*, December, pp. 37–68.

Soule, E. (2002) 'Managerial moral strategies? In search of a few good principals', *Academy of Management Review*, 27: 114–124.

Tonge, A., Greer, L. and Lawton, A. (2003) 'The Enron story: You can fool some of the people some of the time', *Business Ethics, A European Review*, 12: 4–22.

Veiga, J. (2004) 'Bringing ethics into the mainstream: An introduction to the special topic', *Academy of Management Executive*, 18(2): 37–39.

Weaver, G. R., Treviño, L. K. and Cochran, P. L. (1999b) 'Corporate ethics practices in the mid-1990s: An empirical study of the fortune 1000', *Journal of Business Ethics*, 18: 283–294.

Werhane, P. H. (2000) 'Business ethics and the origins of contemporary capitalism: Economics and ethics in the work of Adam Smith and Herbert Spence', *Journal of Business Ethics*, 24: 185–198.

Wicks, A. C. and Freeman, R. E. (1998) 'Organization studies and the new pragmatism: Positivism, anti-positivism and the search for ethics', *Organization Science*, 9: 123–141.

Do no harm In terms of your own research project, a good place to begin might be to adopt the first maxim of the Hippocratic Oath, above all, 'do no harm', as highlighted by Professor Rakesh Khurana in the YouTube video referred to above. In designing and carrying out your research, you must endeavour, above all, to do no harm. In order to accomplish this, you will find it useful to think about the potential harms that could arise while you are conducting your research project. Think about the field within which you are situating your research and the institutions, organizations and individuals who have agreed to participate in your study. Try to think of all the different kinds of harm that might possibly befall your participants by your research. Then try to think of how that harm might be circumvented or avoided. You will find your research diary very useful in recording these thoughts and ideas.

Integrity A second or allied basic tenet of research ethics is integrity. The value of every aspect of the research project is predicated upon the integrity of the researcher. The integrity of the researcher is evident in every aspect of the research and in practically every word written in the research project. The expertise the researcher displays in the way in which they carry out their research and write about it evidences their integrity.

In the final analysis, the reader of the research must be able to trust that the researcher actually carried out the research as they say they did. The reader will take a critical perspective and search through the research project for evidence of the integrity of the researcher, and also for evidence any of any absence of integrity. Examiners, in particular, are masters of the craft of critical examination of the thesis or the report of the research project.

Plagiarism As we read in Chapter 2 of this textbook, plagiarism is a most serious offence. It is the presentation of somebody else's work as your own. Suspicions of plagiarism can completely undermine perceptions of the integrity of the researcher. It is essential that you clearly understand plagiarism. It is essential that you learn to reference properly. The opportunity to undertake supervised research is a valuable opportunity to learn useful marketable skills. This opportunity should not be wasted.

Validity The most fundamental critique levelled at research projects, as detailed in the preceding chapters of this textbook, is the critique of the validity of the research project. Above all, the research project must be a valid research project. As defined in Chapter 2, the concept of validity in research is a question of how logical, truthful, robust, sound, reasonable, meaningful and is useful the research. In order to be valid, a research project must make a contribution to knowledge. The evidence gathered for a research project must be valid. The issue of validity in terms of the methodology, data gathering methods and data, are dealt with in detail in subsequent chapters.

Power The next fundamental ethical issue is power. This is an ethical issue in all research. Every researcher whether they are undergraduates, postgraduates or professional researchers, should critically examine their engagement with their research project in terms of their own power as researchers. The very title of 'researcher' confers a degree of power on the holder because it implies a high degree of expert skill and knowledge. All researchers conducting research within the context of a third level institution do under the auspices of that institution. This situating of the researcher, and the research, within a third level institution confers a degree of power on the researcher. The power that accrues to every researcher from these sources is very useful and it is particularly helpful in field research, where the researcher engages with real people and organisations in the process of carrying out their research. However, this power also presents a substantial ethical issue. Researchers must consider the potentially powerful effect in the field of the title of researcher and the affiliation with the university or college. It is likely that both the title and the affiliation will confer on the researcher a degree of power in the field in dealing with gatekeepers and potential research participants. How the researcher uses this power can be a substantial ethical issue.

Transparency One tried and tested way of avoiding potential harms in the design and development of a research project is through the use of openness and transparency. If you openly, honestly and clearly communicate your research with everyone involved in the project, including your research supervisor, the gatekeepers and the participants in your research, you are likely to uncover potential harms before they become harmful. Once you have uncovered them, you can take steps to ensure that they are neutralized or rendered harmless.

In open discussions around your research, potential issues and pitfalls will arise, and they can be dealt with immediately. Any reservations any stakeholder has about your research can be aired and then responded to and dealt with. If this is done, these potential problems can be dealt with properly. If they are not dealt with, they are likely to lead to difficulties which may not become manifest as substantial issues until the research project is very well advanced. As the research project develops it becomes increasingly difficult to deal with such issues and problems. If the research project is allowed to develop without dealing with the issues and potential problems, these issues and/or problems may even become substantial enough to undermine the research, and/or the researcher. They might even cause the research to be stopped.

YOUR RESEARCH
One student's ethical dilemma

I once had an MD (Managing Director) of a company telephone me to insist that an MSc student, who was conducting research under my supervision, did not have ethical approval for the research. The student had conducted the fieldwork for the research in this MD's company. Obviously and clearly the student had to have ethical approval from the organization on some level in order to be able to access the site and conduct the fieldwork in the site. The problem was that, for whatever reason, there was some loss of trust in the project within the organization, and this loss of trust manifested itself in the MD's official comment on and complaint about the research. By the time the MD did officially comment and complain about the project, the student had completed the research, finished writing up the project, and had just submitted the hardbound thesis.

The response of the university to this situation was to insist that the hardbound thesis be immediately returned to the student. The university would not allow the student to re-submit the thesis until this ethical dilemma was formally resolved. The student could not graduate until the thesis was submitted to the university and accepted by the university. The student had to go back to the MD and re-negotiate ethical approval for the research. Ethical approval was eventually given, but before it was, some changes had to be made to some aspects of the text. When these changes were effected, to the satisfaction of the MD, the thesis had to be re-bound and then re-submitted, and eventually, and finally, examined.

This is not a situation within which any student would want to find themselves.

THE VALUE OF GOOD RESEARCH

Focus on case study research

Case study is a research methodology. It is used a lot in business research. Case study methodology, as explained in Chapter 2, is particularly useful in the in-depth study of bounded entities, for example a company, or a team, or a class, or any organization, or a single incident or an event; any entity that is clearly bounded. The organization, incident or event provides the case that is to be studied. Case study research can focus on one case, or on a number of cases. Decisions about the number of cases to be studied are made in relation to the requirements of the research, the time

available for the research, and the level and degree of access available to potential cases.

Case study research is holistic. Generally, it involves the study of the case under investigation in great detail, or in its entirety.

Case studies tend to involve data from different sources. Case studies can draw on both quantitative and qualitative data. The key to data gathering in case studies is the data requirement in order to illustrate or explain the phenomenon under investigation. The researcher using a case study methodology, gathers as much data as necessary from as many sources as possible, in order to respond to the research question or statement.

For further information on case study research read Yin (2009), *Case Study Research: Design and Methods*. See also the guides to case studies provided by the Colorado State University (**www.writing. colstate.edu/guides/research/casestudy**), and Soy

(2006), *The Case Study as a Research Method* (**www.ischool.utexas.edu/~ssoy/useusers?l391.d1b.htm**).

The research article below details an interesting research project which was developed using a case study methodology.

'The Rise and Stall of a Fair Trade Pioneer: The Cafédirect Story', Davies, I. A., Doherty, B. and Knox, S. *Journal of Business Ethics* (2010) 92: 127–147.

In the article, the authors, using a case study methodology, investigate the growth of fair trade pioneer Cafédirect.

The authors state that Cafédirect secured a prominent position in the UK mainstream coffee industry based on its ethical positioning. In their research, the authors explored the marketing, networks and communication channels of Cafédirect which led the brand from a position of niche player to the mainstream. The authors report a slowdown in the brand's meteoric rise, and they ask in the article if the brand can resume its momentum with its current marketing strategy.

The article is interesting on a number of points:

- It presents a useful review of the literature on fair trade.

- It outlines the rise of the brand in question, Cafédirect.

- It presents a lot of detail on the methodology used in the research (in Appendix 1) and on the very wide variety of data that was were used in the study.

- The article provides a teaching appendix (Appendix 2) with interesting questions designed to promote further learning from the case study.

- Finally the article provides useful references for further reading.

Find the original article online and read it. It is, I think you will agree, an example of a very good case study.

Does the article give you any ideas for your own research project?

References

Davies, I.A., Doherty, B. and Knox, S. (2010) 'The rise and stall of a fair trade pioneer: The Cafédirect story', *Journal of Business Ethics* 92: 127–147.

Soy, S. (2006) 'The case study as a research method', **www.ischool.utexas.edu/~ssoy/useusers/l391.d1b.htm**

Yin, R.K. (2009) *Case Study Research: Design and Methods* 4, London: Sage.

RESEARCH IN PRACTICE

Shen's research project – a case study

Shen is studying for a degree in Strategic Management.

He has decided on the topic for his research project. He read an article in a newspaper about the key issues in taking a venture to market. He was very interested in the article, and as he read the article, he began to think about designing a research project on the topic of bringing new ventures to market.

He decided to read a little more around this topic and to consider how he might develop this idea into a viable research project. He spoke about this to his lecturer in Research Methodologies, and his lecturer was very encouraging. He/she advised Shen to develop the idea further and to try to develop the idea into a proposal for a research project.

Shen, after some reading and reflection, came up with the following:

This research project is a case study of the key issues that contribute to success when taking a venture to market.

The research will focus on ten successful start-up companies, each of which will have started-up in or after 2005. The ten companies will be identified with the help of key informants from the university, and information from media reports.

To be included in the study, each of the new businesses will have to be a 'successful' business. In the first place 'successful' new businesses will be identified. Then the 'successful' businesses will be contacted. The research will be explained to them, and they will be invited to participate in the study. This process will continue until ten successful new companies have agreed to participate in the study.

Data for the research will come from financial reports and marketing plans for each of the ten companies. In addition, in-depth interviews will be conducted with three key informants in each of the ten companies, the CEO, the financial controller, and the director of marketing.

The research when complete will make an important contribution to knowledge in relation to the issues that contribute to success when taking a venture to market in an economy experiencing a downturn.

Before he goes any further with this work, Shen intends to discuss his research project with his newly-appointed thesis supervisor. He is hoping for some positive and encouraging feedback.

What do you think of Shen's research project?

Do you see any potential problems in the proposed research? I think that Shen needs to define more clearly what is meant by the term 'successful' in relation to this research. Otherwise, I think his research has potential.

Do you think Shen's supervisor will support his idea for his research project?

The ethically reflective practitioner

It is important for standards in ethics in research that each researcher becomes an ethically reflective practitioner. This means that they need to take the time to think critically about the standard of their research, their code of conduct and behaviour as researchers, and in particular their conduct in relation to their engagement with participants in the field. Researchers should critically reflect on the manner in which they gather, manage and store their data. They should critically reflect on the means and processes through which they analyze these data and they should critically reflect on the way they decide to write up their research. As you can see, research ethics are a part of every aspect of the research process.

Over and over again throughout this textbook, you will find yourself encouraged to critically engage with every aspect of your research. If there are faults in your research in the language, in the words used, in the syntax, the spellings, the punctuation, you would obviously correct them. In the same way, if there are issues with the proposed research, including issues with the research population, the sample of the population, the sampling method, methodology, data gathering methods, the data itself, the means and processes of analysis, or the findings of the research and the conclusions drawn or the recommendations made, you must address them.

As a researcher, you should critically engage with each and every one of these aspects of your research project, and you should do the same with every other research project with which you are presented. Remember, one of the most important reasons why anyone would want to develop research skills is in order to be able to critique (to critically engage with) other peoples' research, particularly if their research has implications for you, for the way that you live or work, for your profession and/or for your career.

Researchers often start out with very simple research projects. Then, through the scholarship they bring to these projects, through their engagement with the literature, their work on research methodology and data analysis, and through the expert way in which they develop insights into their data, and draw conclusions from their data, these simple research projects become extraordinarily complex. The key to developing a good research project is to keep it simple to begin with. This simple research project will, through your scholarly engagement with each and every step of the research process, become quite complex. It is therefore best to begin with a very simple research statement or question. This is particularly important for undergraduate researchers.

Undergraduate researchers are inexperienced researchers. The opportunity to undertake supervised research is offered to students in order to facilitate them in the development of research skills. It is therefore particularly important for undergraduate researchers that they begin with a very simple, very clear, ethically unambiguous, and very useful research statement or question (or hypothesis). It is important too that they, as students and beginner researchers, make the most of every opportunity available to them for supervision and feedback. The process of **reflexivity** in research will encourage you as a researcher to reflect on your research and to openly discuss your research with all of the participants and stakeholders in the research project. Through this essential reflexive process, the issues, problems and ethical dilemmas, real and potential, in your research project will be acknowledged, discussed and ultimately resolved. If you actively and critically engage in this process you will become a reflective ethical research practitioner.

> **Reflexivity**
> Researcher's active thoughtful engagement with every aspect and development of their research, e.g. self-reflection, self-consciousness, self-awareness.

The ethical issues of anonymity and confidentiality

Two important and basic precepts in research ethics are those of **confidentiality** and **anonymity**. Two aspects of these precepts are those of **informed consent** and data protection. Confidentiality in research generally refers to the guarantee that researchers make to participants, whether they are individuals or organizations, that their contribution to the research project will be confidential. The guarantee is that only the researcher, and perhaps the supervisor of the research project, will have access to the data that participants provide for the research project. Anonymity is a guarantee that researchers make to participants, individuals and/or organizations, that they will not be identified at any time during the research, and that they will not be identifiable in any way in any written account of the research, the thesis and any other publications based on the research. Often participants consent to participate in research only when these guarantees have been given. It is easy to issue these guarantees, but ensuring that participants remain anonymous and their contributions to research remain confidential is often much more difficult than researchers anticipate.

> **Confidentiality**
> The non-disclosure of certain information.

> **Anonymity**
> means free from identification.

Informed consent

The principle of informed consent is another ethical concern. When a researcher invites a potential participant to participate in their research, they are ethically obliged to inform that potential participant of the nature of the research, the nature and extent of their participation in the research, and any possible consequences for them that might arise from their participation. The potential participant will then consent, or not, to participate in the research. The participant should indicate in an informed consent form, (see page 79) that they have been advised about the nature and intent of the research and the nature and extent of their engagement with it, and

> **Informed consent**
> Agreement given by a person to participate in some action, after being informed of the possible consequences.

YOUR RESEARCH

Common research problems

Examples of potential difficulties in guaranteeing confidentiality and anonymity

Let us say, for example, that you decide to conduct your research within your university or college, and as part of your research you decide to interview the president of the university or college. You may then, in the written account of the research, wish to highlight a quote or a particular viewpoint given to you by the president. It can be difficult then, if not impossible, not to identify the president as the holder of this particular viewpoint. In fact it might be essential to the research and the meaning of the research that the quote or the viewpoint be attributed to the president. The quote or the viewpoint may have meaning only in the context of it being a quote from the president.

This presents an ethical dilemma. For the quote to be meaningful, it must be attributed. If it is attributed, there will a breach of the guarantees of confidentiality and anonymity.

How can this be resolved? The easiest way to resolve these issues is to critically reflect on your research as you design it. Discuss your research with your supervisor. Try, if at all possible, to anticipate such dilemmas and deal with them.

You might perhaps interview other members of senior management within the college or university, or perhaps you might interview the presidents of other universities and colleges, as well as your own. Both of these approaches would help you maintain your guarantees of anonymity and confidentiality, as you can hide the identity of individual presidents or senior managers in a group of presidents or senior managers. It is worth noting, however, that in such a small group it can be difficult to maintain anonymity and confidentiality.

If you discuss your concerns regarding anonymity and confidentiality with the participants or potential participants in the study, you may find that they are happy to go on the record and so will not require that their identities remain anonymous and their contributions confidential. This is another means by which these ethical issues can be overcome.

This brief example illustrates clearly the necessity for openness and dialogue around research and it demonstrates some of the advantages of developing a reflexive critical (questioning) engagement with any proposed research, research strategy or research design.

---

they should then sign the form. The informed consent form is a record of the fact that the participant understands what the research is about, and understands what is required of them as a participant. The form also records the fact that the participant is a willing, informed participant, who understands that he/she may withdraw from the research at any time without question or consequence.

Research ethics committee are convened by organizations to monitor and police the ethical standards of research projects in which the parent organization has some gatekeeping role.

The template of the informed consent form opposite is useful in that it functions as an information sheet and an informed consent form. Sometimes researchers develop separate information sheets and informed consent forms. This happens usually when the research is very complex, and requires a lot of explaining. It also happens when it is a requirement of a **research ethics committee** (REC). RECs and their requirements are explained at the end of this chapter. The template informed consent form below informs the potential participant about the nature of the research and about the participation in the research required of participants. The form also provides a structure for the participant to indicate that they have been properly informed and that they have given their informed consent to participate in the study.

As well as informing potential participants about the research and providing a record of their consent to participate in the research, the informed consent form can serve the researcher as a prompt for ethical reflection. It also provides an insight into the ethical standards of the research project.

YOUR RESEARCH

An example of an informed consent form

(SAMPLE) INFORMED CONSENT FORM

Research study title: ————————————————————————————

Researcher name: ——————————————————————————————

Researcher's status: ——————————————————————————————
(E.g. Final year student BSc. Management, University of Bellejour)

Researcher's contact telephone number: ————————————————————

Researcher's email address: ——————————————————————————

Dear Sir/Madam,

You are invited to participate in a research study designed to explore the overall satisfaction of customers of *The Beat Box Music Store* with the store's overall product. If you would like to participate in this research I would very much appreciate it if you would read this form and sign the bottom of the form. Participation in this study will involve an interview, which will last approximately 15 minutes. At the end of the interview you will be asked to complete a short questionnaire. The questionnaire will comprise ten questions, nine of which require yes or no answers. The final question is an open question, using a sentence completion format.

All information will remain confidential and your identity will remain anonymous. The interview will be audio-recorded; the information gathered will be transcribed by the researcher. Only the researcher will have access to the transcripts, and all of the transcripts will be coded. Your name will not appear on any transcript or questionnaire. All of the data gathered for the research will be adequately and properly disposed of on completion of the study.

Please read the following statements and if you understand the statements, and if you wish to participate in this study, please indicate your agreement to take part by ticking the boxes:

☐ I have read and I understand the description of the study.

☐ I willingly consent to participate in the study.

☐ I understand that I may withdraw from the research at any time without consequence.

☐ I understand that the interviews will be audio-recorded and the researcher will take notes.

☐ I understand that my identity will remain anonymous and my contribution will be confidential.

Participant's signature: _____

Name in block capitals: _____

Researcher's signature: _____

OTHER ETHICAL ISSUES IN RESEARCH

Privileged access
Access to an individual or site which provides an advantage to those in securing access.

Intrusion
Unwarranted, unnecessary or unwelcome engagement on a person or place.

Vulnerable populations
Populations which have some vulnerability, in terms of their social position or their age or their state of well-being.

Other ethical issues in research include the issue of **privileged access**; the issue of **intrusion**; and the issue of **vulnerable populations**. Sometimes there can be ethical dilemmas in carrying out research in areas in which you have privileged access. For example, you might in your work be in charge of a group of people. You might be a team leader or a manager, and this position places you in a privileged position in relation to that team, if you decided to conduct your research on or with the team. It might be that the team would welcome any research initiative that you might propose, but if you are in a leadership position, it might be that they do not feel that they can freely refuse to participate in your research. They may also feel that to refuse to participate in the research might have consequences for them, either in their work with the team or in their relationship with you. This is an ethical dilemma. While it does not mean that you cannot or should not conduct research in such circumstances, it does mean that you should actively and critically engage with the ethical issues in such research.

Care is needed in asking intrusive questions. These might include questions about how much money a participant earns, about sexual orientation or behaviour, about experiences of imprisonment or experiences in other closed institutions, about criminal activities or potentially criminal activities or about deviant behaviour. All of these areas, and many more, are potentially sensitive and can be ethically problematic. Great care is needed when undertaking research on topics such as these. The advice, guidance and support of a research supervisor is essential.

The issue of intrusion relates also to the degree of intrusion on the time, goodwill, and privacy of participants the research requires. Potential participants have a right to privacy. One question you should ask yourself is whether or not your research is sufficiently important to justify the level of intrusion you are proposing on potential participants. The issue of intrusion has ethical consequences in terms of researchers asking too much of participants. Researchers can trespass too much on the time and goodwill of research participants. You should keep your engagement with participants to the minimum required in order to gather the necessary data. Be careful of the amount of time and effort you require of participants. Gathering unnecessary data is another ethical issue. Often researchers gather unnecessary data, or even the wrong data, when they are unclear about the data they require for their research project. This is one of the reasons why it is important to be properly prepared for the fieldwork, the data gathering phase of the research.

The issue of vulnerable populations is a substantial ethical issue. Some populations are researched a lot, and some are not. Powerful people tend not to be the subjects of research projects. This is often because they feel powerful enough to refuse to participate in research projects, or they are powerful enough to have **a gatekeeper** protecting them and deflecting invitations to participate. Children are considered a vulnerable population in terms of research. People in institutions, hospitals or other care settings are also considered vulnerable populations in terms of research. The issue of vulnerable populations can sometimes be a more substantial issue in not-for-profit business research, where researchers may have very laudable intentions, but their research agendas may involve sensitive, ethically problematic research with vulnerable populations. This is of course not to say that such research should not take place, but such research warrants substantial critical engagement and ethical reflection on the part of the researcher. Critical reflection on the research project can bring the researcher to the point where they decide, on reflection, to change or even to substantially change the project in some way or to some degree.

> **Gatekeeper**
> Any person or structure that governs or controls access to people, places, structures and/or to organizations.

One critical question that should be asked of every research project is whether the project warrants all the work, expenditure of resources, and trespass on the time and experiences of potential participants. In order to be worth all of this, the research project must make a substantial contribution to knowledge. Once again, the best way to ensure a good ethical standard for your research project is to be open and honest about the research design as it develops and to engage in dialogue, with your peers and your supervisor and any other advisors you can access, about your research. Remember to keep notes of all of these discussions in your research diary; these notes will be invaluable when you are writing up.

This degree of reflexivity in terms of your research project will help you to identify and deal with ethical issues and potential pitfalls before they become problems. This reflexivity will also make you a better and more skilled researcher. Remember, the point of the exercise of undertaking a research project for a programme of study is to develop research skills.

Table 3.1 provides a shortlist of the ethical issues and principles we have discussed in this section. It is a useful reminder of the key aspects of a critical ethical reflection on any research project.

Research ethics committees

Many organizations now have (RECs). These committees are made up of people appointed by the organization to oversee the ethical standards of research conducted within the organization. The people on RECs generally have some degree of expertise in relation to research. Most universities, if not all, have RECs. Many other institutions do too, including hospitals. In general, researchers who wish to conduct research within an institution which has a REC, or under the auspices of such an institution or organization, will be obliged to submit a formal application for ethical approval to this committee.

The requirements of RECs can be substantial and you would be wise to establish from the very beginning whether or not you will be obliged to seek permission to

Table 3.1 Shortlist of important ethical issues and principles		
Do not harm	Power issues	Engaging in a critical reflexive manner with every aspect of the research process
Integrity of the researcher and the research	Maintaining confidentiality	Engaging with vulnerable populations
Scholarship of the researcher	Right to privacy of potential participants	Intrusion – being careful not to intrude too much on the goodwill of participants
Issue of validity	Guaranteeing anonymity to participants	Ethical issues in privileged access
Developing the research in an open and transparent manner	Providing for informed consent	Gaining and maintaining ethical approval for the study

conduct your research from one or more RECs. If it happens that you must secure ethical approval from an REC before you may commence gathering data for your research, then you should, as soon as possible, familiarize yourself with the require-ments and the forms (in the plural, as there is usually more than one form to be completed) of those committees. The informed consent form shown above is a good, and typical, example of one of the forms that such committees generally require applicants to complete. Other forms frequently required by RECs include letters informing potential participants about the nature of the research and inviting them to participate and copies of any recruitment material or advertisements used to engage participants in the research. RECs usually want copies of any data gathering instrument to be used in the research, such as a copy of the questionnaire to be used, a copy of the interview schedule to be used.

There are two dates that have great significance in relation to any engagement with an REC. The first date is the date of the deadline for submission of an application for ethical approval to an REC. The second date is the date of the meeting of the REC, which is the date on which a decision will be made as to whether or not ethical approval will be granted to your study. Usually, the deadline for submission to the REC is 2 to 3 weeks before the actual meeting. RECs tend to meet relatively infrequently, perhaps six or eight times a year. As this is the case, it is important to be aware of the dates that concern you and your application for ethical approval. If you miss the deadline for submission, you have to wait for the next deadline, and the delay could have significant implications for your research.

Research ethics checklist of questions/prompts for ethical reflection

The questions below are designed to prompt you in terms of your ethical reflection on your research project. The sets of questions relate to different

YOUR RESEARCH
Common research problems

Gaining ethical approval for your study

You must of course, to begin with, establish the ethical standards of your own institution. Ensure that in your research you meet the requirements of the ethical standards of your own institution. Ensure too that you have formal acknowledgement, in writing and from the appropriate source, that you have met the requirements of the ethical standards of your own institution.

In presenting research projects to RECs for ethical approval, some research projects require a full ethical review and some research projects require expedited ethical reviews.

In general, undergraduate research projects are automatically subject only to a simple expedited review. Postgraduate research projects tend to be subjected to more rigorous ethical review.

It would be a very good idea to establish as early as possible the level of formal ethical review to which your project is likely to be subjected.

As an exercise, visit the websites of some of the university RECs and try to read and understand their requirements. You will find this a very useful exercise

in terms of prompting you in ethical reflections on your own research project.

Some examples of university research ethics web pages:

Cardiff Business School at Cardiff University has a very comprehensive and detailed section on ethics on their website (**www.cardiff.ac.uk/carbs/research/ ethics**).

So too does the Faculty of Law, Business & Social Sciences at the University of Glasgow (**www. gla.ac.uk/bss/research/ethics**).

And so too does the School of Business and Economics at Swansea University (**www.swan.ac. uk/sbe/research/ethics.asp**).

The University of Derby on its website presents a very useful *Directory of Research Ethics Web Links* with very many links, among them links to the research ethics publications of global organizations such as *The World Health Organization*, and national government organizations such as *The Scottish Office* (**www.derby.ac.uk/research/ethics/ links**).

phases of the research process, as outlined in the model of the research process detailed in Figure 3.1 at the start of this chapter. You can use these sets of questions to examine your ethical engagement with your own research and also to help you develop the formal ethical reflection you will need to properly engage with your research.

Questions for the planning phases of the research process

- Is the research useful?
- Will the research make a contribution to knowledge?
- Do I know enough about the topic to conduct this research?
- Do I know enough about research methodology, have I learned enough about research methodology, to conduct this research to a high standard?

Questions for the literature review

- Have I engaged properly and thoroughly with the literature on this topic?
- Have I scrupulously avoided presenting a skewed perspective on the literature?

Questions for the population and sample

- Is the population chosen for the research the appropriate population?
- Is the sample selected, if using a sample, an appropriate sample?
- Is the sampling method used the appropriate sampling method?

Questions for Research Methodology

- Is the proposed research methodology appropriate?
- Does it fit with the aim of the research and with the population of the study?

Questions for data gathering

- Are the data gathering techniques chosen for and/or designed for the research appropriate?
- Will the data gathering methods chosen yield the data required for the research?
- Are the data gathering methods too intrusive?

Questions for negotiating access

- Do I have all the permissions needed for access for the fieldwork?
- Do I have good working relationships with all of the gatekeepers and all of the participants in the research?
- Am I being as open and honest as possible about the research? Are there any ethical issues in the openness and transparency with which the research was conducted?

Questions for an ethical engagement with participants

- Have I ensured as much as possible to explain and neutralise any potential harms and risks for participants?
- Do I have a clear understanding of the potential risks to participants through their participation in the research?
- Have I thoroughly communicated these potential risks to potential participants?
- Have all of the participants read and signed an informed consent form?

- Have I guaranteed the participants confidentiality and anonymity?
- Can I guarantee confidentiality and anonymity?
- How can I guarantee confidentiality and anonymity?
- Have I provided participants with my contact details should they have any concerns at any stage about the research?
- Do my participants know that they can withdraw from my research at any time without any consequence to them or for them?

Questions for data management

- Do I have a plan for the management of data?
- Where will the data be held?
- Is this a secure place?
- Who will have access to the data?
- Will the data be coded for anonymity and confidentiality?
- Do I have a plan for the appropriate disposal of data?

Questions for data analysis

- Have I the necessary skills to properly analyze the data?
- Do I have enough time for data gathering and data analysis?
- Are my conclusions rooted in my data and have they clearly emerged from my data?

Questions for completing the research

- Are my conclusions insightful?
- Do my conclusions add substantially to knowledge in this field?
- Are my recommendations reasonable and achievable?
- Have I properly and thoroughly referenced my work?
- Is my research of a high standard?
- Is my research ethical?

Questions for disseminating the research

- How is my research to be disseminated?
- How will I provide feedback on the findings of my research, if required, to individual and institutional participants?

CASE STUDY

The Walt Disney Company

Ethics in business is the application of ethical standards in business throughout every aspect and element of the business. The Walt Disney Company provides a good case study of ethics in business. On their website they detail their ethical framework for their business. They call this framework *Business Standards and Ethics* (**http://corporate.disney.go.com/corporate/cr_business_standards.html**).

The framework covers:

● hiring practices with a particular focus on equal opportunities without bias

● human resources with a focus on Disney's culture and values

● policies to prevent harassment and discrimination.

The company states on this webpage that it 'incorporates best-in-class business standards as a key pillar of its business practices'.

It is worth taking a little time to read through these pages. They give a good overview of a highly structured, carefully developed ethical framework for business.

In your research diary briefly record the key elements of Disney's business ethics framework. If you think any aspect of this framework is of use to you in relation to your own research, write a short paragraph about this.

Question What are the key ethical issues that the Disney Company focuses on in relation to its hiring practices?

Disneyland Magic Kingdom Castle © Travelshots.com/Alamy

CHAPTER REVIEW

This chapter deals with research ethics. The particular focus of the chapter is on research ethics in business. The critical nature of ethics in business and in business research was highlighted in this chapter. The concept and practice of ethics was explored and defined. The ethical standards of different organizations were considered. A journal article on business ethics in practice was considered in some detail. The article was deemed useful in that the focus of the article is on the behavioural ethics of individuals situated within business organizations and this focus is presented in the journal article within a highly developed theoretical framework. The article gives a good sense of how theory influences research and vice versa. The main ethical issues in designing and carrying out research were examined. Two fundamental ethical issues in research, as explained in the chapter, are the integrity of the researcher and the quality of the research. The work of RECs, in universities and colleges and other institutions was considered. The processes of gaining ethical approval from RECs were explained. Students were asked to reflect on the potential risks and harms attendant upon their research projects with regard to every stage of the research process. Finally, a useful checklist of research ethics questions was provided.

Now update your interactive research diary with your notes and findings at www.cengage.co.uk/quinlan. Complete the activities provided to reinforce your understanding of this chapter.

END OF CHAPTER QUESTIONS

1   Define ethics.

2   Name and briefly explain six key ethical issues.

3   What is meant by ethics in business research?

4   What is meant by the term ethical reflection?

5   How does one become a reflexive practitioner?

6   Name and explain two ethical concerns in each step of the research process.

7   Develop two different research questions on ethics in business. Decide whether or not based on critical ethical reflection, these research questions could or should be developed into research projects. Explain your ethical reasoning.

8   In your research diary, detail the key ethical concerns in relation to your own research project.

9   In your research diary, write a reflective piece explaining how you intend to overcome these ethical concerns.

10 In your research diary, write a critique of your approach to overcoming the ethical concerns you have about your research project.
    (The three-part exercise – Questions 8, 9 and 10 – conducted in your research diary, can be used as the basis for the ethical reflection on your research that you present in the methodology section or chapter of your thesis/report of your research.)

REFERENCES

Bunting, M. (2010) 'To tackle the last decades' myths, we must dust off the big moral questions: A robust debate on ethics is crucial to the pursuit of a good society in which individuals are more than mere economic units', *The Guardian*, 22 February.

Clegg, S., Kornberger, M. and Rhodes, C. (2007) 'Business ethics as practice', *British Journal of Management* 18: 107–122.

Davies, I.A., Doherty, B. and Knox, S. (2010) 'The rise and stall of a fair trade pioneer: The Cafédirect story', *Journal of Business Ethics* 92: 127–147.

Donaldson, T. (2003) 'Editor's comments: Taking ethics seriously? A mission now more possible', *Academy of Management Review*, 28; 363–366.

Helliar, C. and Bebbington, J. (2004) 'Taking ethics to heart: A discussion document by the Research Committee of The Institute of Chartered Accountants of Scotland', The Institute of Chartered Accountants of Scotland, http://www.icas.org.uk/site/cms/download/res_helliar_bebbington_Report.pdf Accessed 02.06.2010.

Hirsch, A. (2009) 'Should Sir Fred get away scot-free?', www.guardian.co.uk, 20 January.

Hutton, W. (2009) 'The banking system has shirked its ownership of risk, but governments must be generous if it is to survive', *The Banker*, www.the-banker.com Accessed 5 January 2009.

Johnson, P. and Smith, K. (1999) 'Contextualizing business ethics: Anomie and social life', *Human Relations*, 52: 1351–1375.

Parker, M. (ed.) (2003) 'Special issue on ethics politics and organization', *Organization*, Vol. 10(2).

Porter, M. and Kramer, M. (2002) 'The competitive advantage of corporate philanthropy', *Harvard Business Review*, December, pp. 37–68.

Soule, E. (2002) 'Managerial moral strategies? In search of a few good principals', *Academy of Management Review*, 27: 114–124.

Soy, S. (2006) 'The case study as a research method', www.ischool.utexas.edu/~ssoy/useusers/l391.d1b.htm

The Institute of Chartered Accountants Scotland, www.icas.org.uk

The Walt Disney Company website 'Business standards and ethics', http://corporate.disney.go.com/corporate/cr_business_standards.html Accessed April 2009.

Tonge, A., Greer, L. and Lawton, A. (2003) 'The Enron story: You can fool some of the people some of the time', *Business Ethics, A European Review*, 12: 4–22.

Veiga, J. (2004) 'Bringing ethics into the mainstream: An introduction to the special topic', *Academy of Management Executive*, 18(2): 37–39.

Weaver, G. R., Treviño, L. K. and Cochran, P. L. (1999b) 'Corporate ethics practices in the mid-1990s: An empirical study of the fortune 1000', *Journal of Business Ethics*, 18: 283–294.

Werhane, P. H. (2000) 'Business ethics and the origins of contemporary capitalism: Economics and ethics in the work of Adam Smith and Herbert Spence', *Journal of Business Ethics*, 24: 185–198.

Wicks, A. C. and Freeman, R. E. (1998) 'Organization studies and the new pragmatism: Positivism, anti-positivism and the search for ethics', *Organization Science*, 9: 123–141.

World Economic Forum, http://www.weforum.org/en/index.htm

'Writing case studies', provided by the Colorado State University, www.writing.colstate.edu/guides/research/casestudy

Yin, R.K. (2009)*Case Study Research: Design and Methods* 4, London: Sage.

RECOMMENDED READING

Bell, J. (2005) *Doing Your Research Project*, Ch. 3, 'Ethics and Integrity in Research', Maidenhead: Open University Press.

Collis, J. and Hussey, R. (2009) *Business Research, A Practical Guide for Undergraduate and Postgraduate Students* (3rd edn), 'Ethical Issues', pp. 45–47. Houndsmill: Palgrave Macmillan.

Davis, D. (2005) *Business Research for Decision Making*, Ch. 16, 'Ethical Considerations in Business Research', Mason, OH: Cengage South-Western.

Denscombe, M. (2003) *The Good Research Guide: For Small-Scale Social Research Projects* (2nd edn), Ch. 9, 'Ethics', Maidenhead: Open University Press.

Donovan, R.J., Jalleh, G., Fielder, L. and Ouschan, R. (2009) 'Ethical issues in pro-social advertising: The Australian 2006 White Ribbon Day Campaign', *Journal of Public Affairs*, 9: 5–19.

Journal of Business Ethics, Springer.

Neuman, W.L. (2000) *Social Research Methods: Quantitative and Qualitative Approaches*, Ch. 5, 'The Ethics and Politics of Social Research', Boston, MA: Allyn & Bacon.

Qualitative Market Research (2005) Special Issue 'Ethics in Marketing', Vol. 8(4).

Stake, R.E. (1995) 'The Art of Case Study Research', Sage, Thousand Oaks, CA.

'Studying The Ethical Consumer: A Review of Research' (2007) Editorial, *Journal of Consumer Behaviour*, 6: 253–270.

Vijayan, S., Wilkinson, M. and Worth, P. (2009) 'Conducting research within the NHS: A guide for medical students and a closer look into the ethical approval process', *Reinvention: A Journal of Undergraduate Research*, 2(2) (online), www2.warwick.ac.uk/fac/sociology/rsw/undergrad/cetl/ejournal/issues/volume2/vijayan/

Webley, S. and Werner, A. (2008) 'Corporate codes of ethics: Necessary but not sufficient', *Business Ethics: A European Review*, 17(4) October: 405–415

Zigmund, W.G. (2003) *Business Research Methods*, Ch. 5, 'Ethical Issues in Business Research', Mason, OH: Cengage South-Western.

SCHOLA MORALIS PHILOSOPHIAE

CHAPTER 4

UNDERSTANDING RESEARCH PHILOSOPHY

LEARNING OBJECTIVES

At the end of this chapter the student should:

- Understand the philosophical underpinnings of research and research methodologies.

- Understand the different world views represented in the different philosophical approaches.

- Understand the use of theory in the generation of knowledge.

- Understand the importance of theory in research.

- Understand how to apply theory in their own research.

- Be able to create a theoretical framework, the second of the four frameworks.

- Understand the links between research, theory and knowledge.

RESEARCH SKILLS

At the end of this chapter the student should, using the exercises on the accompanying online platform, be able to:

- Explain the philosophical underpinnings of sample research projects.

- Outline an appropriate theoretical framework for a given project.

- Critique a proposed theoretical framework.

The aim of this chapter is to explore the philosophical underpinnings of research and research methodologies. This chapter reminds students of the discussions of these issues in earlier chapters and develops some of these themes. Among the topics covered in this chapter are positivism, constructionism, interpretivism, functionalism, critical inquiry, feminism and postmodernism. Each of these represents a different perspective on the social world and a fundamental framework within social science research. They have all been written about extensively elsewhere and this chapter contains a brief introduction to them. The chapter highlights the importance of theory in research, and explains how through research, knowledge and theory are generated.

THE RESEARCH PROCESS

Figure 4.1 details the research process. It is outlined at the start of each chapter. As this is the fourth chapter in the textbook, this is the fourth time we have encountered the figure. You should by now be quite familiar with it.

In this chapter, the focus is on understanding philosophical frameworks. Every research project is underpinned by a **philosophical framework** which evidences the worldview within which the research is situated and which can be seen in every step of the research process. This is where the issue of **'fit'** becomes critical. Each step in the research process, as designed by the researcher, should be appropriate to, or should fit with, the purpose and focus of the research. Every aspect of the research project, as it is developed by the researcher, should 'fit' with the philosophical framework within which the research project is situated.

When beginning the process of developing a research proposal, the questions you must ask yourself are:

- what am I going to do? (the research statement/question – the aim of the research)
- how am I going to do it? (the methodology and methods to be used)
- where am I going to do it? (the site of the research)
- why am I going to do it? (the rationale for the research).

The first question is clearly the most important, 'what am I going to do?'. The second question, 'how am I going to do it?', relates to (research) methodology and (data collection) methods. In deciding what methodology and methods you will use, it is important to bear in mind that you must **justify** these decisions. In answering these questions, you must consider the research question or statement, that is, the purpose of the research, and the methodology and the methods you choose must be capable of supporting the research question or statement.

Our choice and use of particular methodologies and methods, as Crotty explains (2005: 2), relates to the assumptions about reality that we bring to our work and consequently to our theoretical perspective. Questions about the nature of reality are questions of **ontology**. Questions about the methodology and methods used in

Philosophical framework
The worldview within which the research is situated.

'Fit'
Every step in the research project, should 'fit' with the purpose and focus of the project, including the philosophical framework.

Justify
The researcher is obliged to justify, or explain the choices they make in relation to the research they decide to undertake and their methodological choices.

Ontology
relates to the study of being, the nature of being and our ways of being in the world.

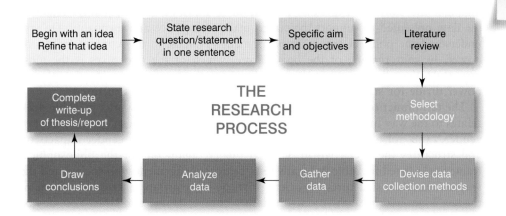

Figure 4.1   The research process

the research project relate to our understanding of knowledge and how it is created, and to the value we ascribe to knowledge. In particular, such questions relate to the validity of new knowledge generated by research projects. These are questions of **epistemology**. Table 4.1 outlines three epistemological positions that concern us.

Epistemology
Relates to knowledge, to what constitutes knowledge, and to the processes through which knowledge is created.

As we know from our reading of Chapter 1, and the discussion above, ontology relates to the nature of reality, to the study and nature of being, and to our ways of being in the world. There are different understandings of the nature of reality. As explained in Chapter 1, positivists see the world as having one reality of which we are all a part. Social constructionists see the world as being co-constituted and socially constructed, and made up of many different realities. For the interpretivist, we each interpret the world in our own way, and through our individual and unique interpretations, all of us construct our own realities. As there are different understandings about the nature of reality, the nature of being in the world, ontology and ontological issues are important issues in social science research.

Table 4.1   Three epistemological positions
Positivism Positivism holds that there is one objective reality; reality is singular and separate from consciousness.
Social constructionism Social constructionism and social constructivism hold that social phenomena develop in social contexts and that individuals and groups create, in part, their own realities.
Interpretivism Interpretivism is related to constructivism. It holds that social reality is a subjective construction based on interpretation and interaction.

The box feature below contains a discussion of the concept of feminism. The discussion is interesting in that it highlights the concerns that some feminists have in relation to the roles and representations of women in the film industry. Feminists operate within particular assumptions about the nature of reality and the social world. Feminism, as detailed in Table 4.2 (see page 97), is a philosophical framework. It is also an intellectual and political movement that seeks justice and equality for women. As you read through the discussion in the box feature, highlight the concerns expressed in relation to injustice and inequality. Examine the data presented to support the claims made of injustice and inequality. Do you understand the political argument being made? Politics, in this context, relates to power. In your reading of the box feature, which of the two sexes is the most powerful? Very briefly, what do you think are the implications (if any) of that power divide for society, and for the way in which society is structured?

The term functionalism (see the list of philosophical frameworks in Table 4.2), relates to the way in which society is structured. Using, for example, the concept of gender, think for a moment about some of the ways in which gender impacts on and structures the social world. Critical theory, again one of the philosophical frameworks listed in Table 4.2, calls for a critical engagement with society and the way in which the structures in society privilege some groups over others. Some of the key issues in critical theory are the issues of race, gender and class. You may be able to think of ideas for a business studies research project that you might like to carry out using feminism as your philosophical framework. One example might be

THE VALUE OF GOOD RESEARCH

Research in the media

Sex and the City – US HBO TV series © Pictorial Press Ltd/Alamy

Is it time to kill the chick flick?

'Hollywood thinks that all women care about is weddings and shopping. Can anything stop the inane decline of the chick flick?' *Maher, K., The Times,* **3rd February 2009**

This headline is from an article by Kevin Maher published in *The Times* in February, 2009. In the opening sentence, Maher quotes Simone de Beauvoir's famous announcement from her book *The Second Sex*, 'One is not born a woman, but becomes one'. He goes on to say that de Beauvoir might have added: 'But it takes Hollywood to turn one into an hysterical fashion-mongering man-craving anorexic caricature'. He says that, increasingly, the Hollywood chick flick has become essentially a kind of 'regressive pre-feminist stereotype and misogynistic cliché'. To make this point Maher highlights films such as *Bride Wars* and *Confessions of a Shopaholic* which he states are made for women, but which feature key female characters who are 'variously neurotic, idiotic, label-obsessed, weight-obsessed, man-obsessed or wedding-obsessed, and often all at the same time'.

The contemporary representation of women in chick flicks, which is said to have deteriorated in recent years, has been widely critiqued by feminists in the industry and in academia. Chick flicks have been accused (Ferriss and Young, 2008) of re-introducing and often validating traditional and even subjugated roles for women in contemporary society. Maher quotes Diane Purkiss, feminist historian and Fellow of Oxford University, who said that 'The heroines are getting dumber and dumber'. He also quotes Melissa Silverstein, movie marketing consultant and founder of the company Women & Hollywood who said that what we are seeing in chick flicks is a white male version of women, which, she said, is just unacceptable.

According to the statistics quoted on the Women & Hollywood blog (**www.womenandhollywood.com**), and taken from The Motion Picture Association of America, in 2009 there were 217 million filmgoers in the USA which generated a total of 1.4 billion dollars in ticket revenue; women accounted for 113 million filmgoers and they bought 55 per cent of the tickets while men accounted for 104 million filmgoers and they bought 45 per cent of the tickets. The Women & Hollywood blog quotes statistics from The Center for the Study of Women in TV and Film, San Diego State University, that highlight the fact that in 2009 women directed 7 per cent of the top 250 grossing films, and women wrote 8 per cent of them; women comprised 17 per cent of all executive producers and women made up 23 per cent of all producers, only 2 per cent of all cinematographers were women. Writing in *The Observer* (16.05.2010), Rachel Millward, director of the Birds Eye View Film Festival, noted that not one of the 19 competition films at the Cannes Film Festival 2010 was directed by a woman. Many observers hold that, in order to be able to fundamentally influence film-making and to change contemporary mainstream representations of women in films, women must undertake creative roles in film-making.

References

'Women & Hollywood: from a feminist perspective', www.womenandhollywood.com

Maher, K. (2009) 'Is it time to kill the chick flick? Hollywood thinks that all women care about is weddings and shopping. Can anything stop the inane decline of the chick flick?', *The Times*, 3 February.

Ferriss, S. and Young, M. (2008) *Chick Flicks: Contemporary Women at the Movies*, London and New York: Routledge.

Millward, R. and Shoard, C. (2010) 'Does it matter that there are no women up for the Palme D'Or?', *The Observer*, 16 May.

a project designed to study the experiences of business women working in a predominately male environment. Can you think of ideas for a research project that you would like to carry out using critical theory as your philosophical framework? One example might be a study of power, what it is and how it is exercised, from the perspectives of male and female business managers from different ethnic and cultural backgrounds.

THE PHILOSOPHICAL UNDERPINNINGS OF RESEARCH AND RESEARCH METHODOLOGIES

The epistemological positions we are concerned with are positivism, constructionism and interpretivism. Some of the philosophical frameworks commonly used in social science research are functionalism, symbolic interactionism, feminism, critical inquiry and postmodernism. Each of these represents a particular framework for viewing the social world and each represents particular ontological and epistemological standpoints. The philosophical framework within which each research project is situated evidences the world view within which the research is situated and tells us something of the ontological position of the researcher, their understanding of the nature of reality, in relation to the research being undertaken.

It is of course possible for a researcher to situate one research project within one epistemological position, and another project within another. For example, one research project might be situated within a framework of positivism, and the next within a framework of constructionism. Decisions around the epistemological position used in the research are dictated by the research being undertaken, its aim, and the kind of data required in order to properly conduct and complete the research.

Table 4.2 contains brief definitions of a number of philosophical frameworks or perspectives. It is not possible to simply define complex concepts. Every discipline and theory is made up of concepts, e.g. key ideas and key words. such as those below, but it is useful to list some of them to give students a sense of the immensity and complexity of this area of science and thought. As you can see, the three epistemological positions of positivism, constructivism (or constructionism) and interpretivism are here as philosophical frameworks. Positivism is the framework within which science originally developed, and a great deal of scientific endeavour is carried out today within a framework of positivism. The epistemological positions of constructivism and interpretivism emerged from critiques of positivism and its limitations in relation to social science research. The other philosophical frameworks listed below are embedded in one or other of the three epistemological positions.

Table 4.2 Some philosophical frameworks	
Positivism	Positivism holds that there is one objective reality; reality is singular and separate from consciousness.
Constructivism	Social constructionism or social constructivism holds that social phenomena develop in social contexts and that individuals and groups create in part their own realities.
Interpretivism	Interpretivism holds that all knowledge is a matter of interpretation.
Hermeneutics	Hermeneutics is the theory of interpretation and the study of the processes of interpretation.
Symbolic interactionism	Symbolic interactionists hold that people derive meaning from interaction, that reality comes into being through the shared meaning that develops from human interaction.
Functionalism	Functionalism within sociology is the study of the structures of society and the manner in which those structures serve societal needs.
Structuralism	Structuralism holds that human culture can be understood as a system of signs, that meaning is produced and reproduced in society through systems of signs, such as different structures, for example economic structures, different practices, and ways of doing things.
Critical theory	Critical theory is the examination and critique of society, with a view to exposing systems of domination through a focus on values and norms.
Feminism	Feminist theory holds that there should be political, social, sexual and economic equality between women and men.
Post-structuralism	Post-structuralism derives from a critique of structuralism.
Post-modernism	Post-modernism means after modernity, after the period of modernity. In the period of modernity, which developed from the time of the Enlightenment, scientists attempted to explore, analyze and explain the world in empirical objective rational terms. Post-modernists challenge and reject the simplicity of such approaches.

It is important to think a little about these frameworks and to develop some sense of their meaning and their contribution to the ways in which we understand the social world. The list provides a starting point for an exploration of the various theoretical and philosophical perspectives on the social world. For further detail and discussion see Crotty (2005); see also the chapter, Competing paradigms in qualitative research, by Egon Guba and Yvonna Lincoln, in the *Handbook of Qualitative Research,* available to download as a pdf document in Google Scholar.

THE RESEARCH PROJECT AND THE PHILOSOPHICAL FRAMEWORKS

In considering the methodology and the data collection methods to be used in the research project, you must consider the kind of knowledge needed in order to respond to the research question or statement. Research is undertaken in order to make a contribution to knowledge; it is fundamentally concerned with the nature of knowledge and the means of knowledge creation. These are questions of epistemology.

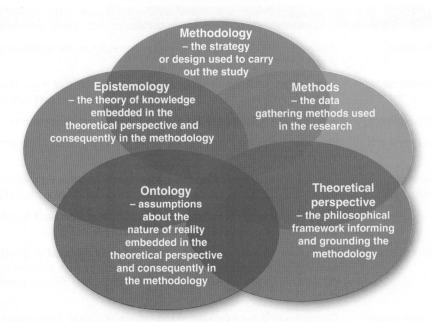

Figure 4.2   The five basic elements of the research process

Knowledge is created within the research project through the researcher's exploration of the phenomenon under investigation, by the means of the methodology and the methods, which must be adequate for the research project. They must 'fit', and be capable of generating the knowledge required for the research. In order to answer epistemological questions, the researcher must explain and justify the methodology and methods used in the research project. Such explanations and justifications help to establish the validity of the research. In Figure 4.2 (developed from Crotty, 2005), we can see the five basic elements of the research process. The epistemological and ontological assumptions embedded in the research project are embedded in the theoretical perspective deployed in the research and this is embedded in the research methodology used in the study.

In developing the research project, first we state what it is that we are going to do, the research statement or question, the aim of the research. We then explain how we are going to do it and state the methodology to be used. We say, for example, that this research project is a survey, or a case study, or an action research project, or a grounded theory study, or a phenomenological study, and so on. These are statements of methodology. Embedded in each statement of methodology are assumptions about the nature of reality (ontological assumptions) and implicit statements about the kind of knowledge that will be generated by the research (epistemological assumptions). If, for instance, we say we are going to conduct survey research, using that methodology we will produce a particular kind of knowledge (see Research in Practice box – Carol's research project). If we say that we are going to conduct phenomenological research, using that methodology we will produce a different kind of knowledge to the kind of knowledge produced by, for example, a survey methodology (see Research in Practice box – Fiona's research project). In explaining and justifying the methodological decisions made in the design of the research project, we explain and outline the theoretical perspective informing the research, the philosophical underpinnings of the research, and consequently the ontological and epistemological embedded in the research.

In Carol's research project below, the methodology proposed is survey and the method is a questionnaire. There is a sample of participants, all of them female managers working in management roles in SMEs. The study is designed to explore and examine their work experiences as managers. The elements of the project 'fit' well together. The philosophical framework for the study is positivism. This is implicit in the statement of the methodology and methods. Survey research fits within a framework of positivism. Implicit within the statement of the methodology survey are ontological assumptions, or assumptions about the nature of reality. As stated at the beginning of this chapter, positivists see the world as having one reality of which we are all a part. Also implicit are epistemological assumptions, about the nature of knowledge and about the kind of knowledge that will be generated by this research project. This

RESEARCH IN PRACTICE

Carol's research project – a survey

Carol attended a guest lecture recently on the topic of women in management. She was really interested in the area and found the lecture very stimulating. She decided to situate her research project in the area of women in management. She mentioned this to her lecturer in research methods who encouraged her to come up with a specific research project in this area. Carol produced the following:

This research project is a survey of the work experiences of 100 women in management in SMEs in Liverpool.

The aim of the research is to examine the work experiences of 100 women in management in SMEs in Liverpool.

The objectives of the study are as follows:

- to explore the work experiences of the women
- to document the work experiences of the women
- to highlight any particularly good or bad work experiences the women have had

- to record what the women learned from those experiences
- to understand why the women had those good or bad experiences
- to provide an account of the lessons learned by the women in their work experiences.

The methodology is survey (Fowler, 2002). The data collection method is a questionnaire. The questionnaire will comprise both open and closed questions, and there will be two sentence completion exercises. The sentence completion exercises will be used to allow the women to document a particularly good work experience and a particularly bad work experience. The use of survey methodology is justified in this research project because the sample size is relatively big, 100 women will participate in the study, and the population of the study is geographically scattered, the participants are located in 100 different companies. A survey methodology will allow for the participation in the study of such a large and scattered population. A mixture of quantitative and qualitative data are required for the study. The open and closed questions and the sentence completion exercises in the questionnaire will provide the required data.

Reference

Fowler, F.J. (2002) *Survey Research Methods*, Thousand Oaks, CA: Sage.

research project will generate knowledge about the single reality that each of the participants share, the reality of their work experience as female managers within SMEs.

In Fiona's research project detailed below, the same topic is explored using a different methodology.

RESEARCH IN PRACTICE

Fiona's research project – a phenomenological study

Fiona also attended the guest lecture on the topic of women in management. She was also really interested in the area and found the lecture very stimulating. She too decided to situate her research project in the area of women in management. She mentioned this to her lecturer in research methods who encouraged her to come up with a specific research project in this area. Fiona produced the following:

This research project is a phenomenological study of the work experiences of 20 women in management in an SME in Liverpool. A sample of 20 is a relatively small sample. Phenomenological studies, according to Smith *et al.* (2009: 3) are conducted with relatively small samples. This is in order to be able to examine the experiences of the small sample of participants in great detail.

The aim of the research is to examine the work experiences of 20 women in management as explained and detailed by the women themselves. All 20 participants work in Hibernia Incorporated, an SME in Liverpool. (The name of the SME has been changed in order to preserve confidentiality.)

The objectives of the study are as follows:

- to explore with the participants their work experiences

- to facilitate the women in reflections on the lessons learned by them in their work experiences.

The methodology is phenomenological. Phenomenology is a research methodology that facilitates the study of lived experience from the perspective of those living the experience. Phenomenology in social science research developed from the work of Edmund Husserl (Moustakas, 1994), who held that although there was 'a real' world which each of us can perceive, there is also an intersubjective world which each of us experiences individually, or in our own unique way.

Two data collection methods will be used in the study. They are as follows:

1 The first data collection method to be used is in-depth interviews. The in-depth interviews will allow the researcher to explore in-depth with the women their experiences of work as managers in the SME.

2 The second data collection method will provide a photographic element to the research (Rose, 2007). Each of the participants in the study will be asked to provide a photograph to the study that illustrates for them their work experience within the company. Each photograph will be accompanied by a short narrative written by the participant explaining the meaning for them of the photograph.

Taken together, these two data collection methods will facilitate the participants in explaining and detailing their work experiences as women in management.

References

Moustakas, C.E. (1994) *Phenomenological Research Methods*, Thousand Oaks, CA: Sage.

Smith, J.A., Flowers, P. and Larkin, M. (2009) *Interpretative Phenomenological Analysis*, London: Sage.

Rose, G. (2007) *Visual Methodologies: An Introduction to the Interpretation of Visual Materials*, London and Thousand Oaks: Sage.

In Fiona's research project below, the methodology proposed is phenomenology and there are two data collection methods: in-depth interviews and a photographic method. There is a sample of 20 participants, all of them female managers and all of them working in management roles in one SME. The study is designed to explore and examine 'the lived experience' of their work experiences as managers. Phenomenological research focuses on lived experience from the perspectives of those living the experience. The elements of the project 'fit' well together. The objectives detailed for the phenomenological study are clear but less explicit than the objectives detailed for the survey (Carol's study). This is because the phenomenological researcher allows the participants in the research to explain and describe their own experiences. The phenomenological researcher does not impose any preconceived ideas that they might have on the experiences of the women. This is the case even when the researcher shares the experience with the participants, as Fiona does by being, as are all the participants, a female manager in the company within which the study will be undertaken.

Although both studies detailed above have focused on exploring the same topic, they are designed differently. Each project will produce different data and make its own unique contribution to knowledge. Carol's study is being developed from an epistemological position and theoretical framework of positivism. This is implicit in the statement of methodology in Carol's research project. The methodology Carol is using is survey research. As we know, implicit in the statement of the methodology and methods, is a statement of the theoretical framework within which the study is embedded. Survey research engages with participants in order to explore the single 'objective' reality that they all experience. Within a framework of positivism there is one objective reality and survey research is an appropriate methodology to use in examining and exploring such experiences.

Phenomenological research engages with participants in a different way, exploring the multiple realities of their unique lived experiences. Instead of a large sample such as you would have in survey research, phenomenology works at a deeper more complex level with smaller samples. The philosophical framework for Fiona's study is symbolic interactionism, from the work of American sociologist George Herbert Mead and the Chicago School. Symbolic interactionism comes from an epistemological position of constructivism and interpretivism (see Table 4.2). The epistemological position is implicit in the statement of the methodology. The methodology for Fiona's research project is phenomenology. Phenomenological research fits within a framework of constructivism. Within such a study, no one reality is more valid than any other, and no one person's understanding of 'reality' is more valid than any other person's understanding. Also implicit in the statement of the methodology are epistemological assumptions, assumptions about the nature of knowledge and about the kind of knowledge that will be generated by this research project. This research project will generate knowledge about multiple realities, the different reality that each participant experiences in her work as a female manager within an SME.

Concepts
Every discipline and theory is made up of concepts, e.g. key ideas and key words.

THE METHODOLOGICAL PYRAMID

In order to help with understanding these key philosophical **concepts** and how they fit with each other and emerge one from the other, we now consider the **methodological pyramid** (see Figure 4.3), detailed initially in Chapter 2 of this textbook.

Methodological pyramid
Shows how the fundamental philosophies and different data collection methods fit with the different methodologies.

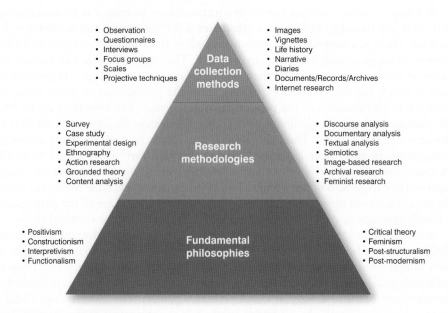

- Observation
- Questionnaires
- Interviews
- Focus groups
- Scales
- Projective techniques

Data collection methods

- Images
- Vignettes
- Life history
- Narrative
- Diaries
- Documents/Records/Archives
- Internet research

- Survey
- Case study
- Experimental design
- Ethnography
- Action research
- Grounded theory
- Content analysis

Research methodologies

- Discourse analysis
- Documentary analysis
- Textual analysis
- Semiotics
- Image-based research
- Archival research
- Feminist research

- Positivism
- Constructionism
- Interpretivism
- Functionalism

Fundamental philosophies

- Critical theory
- Feminism
- Post-structuralism
- Post-modernism

Figure 4.3   The methodological pyramid

In the pyramid the fundamental philosophies support the (research) methodologies which in turn support the data collection methods. Another way of saying this is that (research) methodologies emerge from the fundamental philosophies, and data collection methods emerge from (research) methodologies. See Crotty (2005) for another account of this complexity. This is the way in which the concept of fit works within social science research. The pyramid helps you see how the fundamental philosophies fit with the different methodologies, and how the different data collection methods fit with the different methodologies.

The philosophical framework within which the research project is situated emerges during the process of developing the conceptual framework for the research project. The conceptual framework, as we know, is contained in the research statement or question.

When your idea for your research project becomes focused, you can begin to make decisions about the methodology you want to work with for the project. Decisions about which methodology is most appropriate (which is the best fit) for the project are made in light of the aim of the project, what it is that the project is to accomplish, what knowledge the project is designed to provide.

If the aim of the project is to establish the fact(s) of some phenomenon, there is scope for the project to be situated within a framework of positivism. Within a framework of positivism reality is singular, objective, and apart from participants. This is quite a simple understanding of the social world. For example, let us say that you want to carry out a study of cigarette smoking among your classmates at college and you ask them whether or not they smoke cigarettes. They respond, they either do or they do not smoke cigarettes. There is one objective reality, there is no ambiguity, they either do or they do not smoke cigarettes. This study could be described as positivistic. Within such a research project it is often possible to answer the research question or respond to the research statement with **quantitative data**. Quantitative data are numeric data.

Quantitative data
Data in the form of numbers, numerical data.

The interpretivist and the constructivist hold that reality is unique to each individual, and to the manner in which each individual, given their own unique set of circumstances and life experiences, construct, experience and interprets their world. If it is intended that the research project will explore thoughts and feelings and beliefs about the phenomenon under investigation, then the project may be developed within a framework of interpretivism or constructionism. In this case, each participant will respond to the research or engage with the research in a unique and individual way. Using the cigarette smoking study again, let us suppose that now that you know how many of your classmates smoke cigarettes, you decide that you would like to establish why they smoke cigarettes. In responding to the question of why they smoke cigarettes they will give subjective answers. They will each have their own individual and unique reasons and/or justifications for smoking cigarettes. These unique and individual responses may be quite complex and it may be that such complexity cannot readily or adequately be represented quantitatively and so the data gathered will be **qualitative data**.

Each of the classmates who smoke will have a different reason for smoking, and a different understanding of their smoking. It is possible that one or two of the respondents will feel guilty about smoking, however the nature of, and reasons for, that guilt will be unique to each of them. One or two of the respondents might be defensive about their smoking; and, again their defensiveness and the reasons for it will be unique to each individual and their own experience of smoking cigarettes. It may be that others simply enjoy the pleasure of smoking cigarettes, but the explanations for and descriptions of enjoying cigarette smoking are likely to be different for each respondent. In any case, the responses you get to the question of why they smoke will present you with data of a completely different order to the data received in response to the question of how many smoke. This data is qualitative in nature. It is rich and descriptive. It is not numerical and, while it might be possible to code the data numerically, this may not serve richness, depth and complexity of the data. A simple number cannot convey the complexity of why, for example, a person smokes cigarettes.

There are two types of data that can be collected for any research project, quantitative data and qualitative data (see Table 4.3).

Quantitative data are data that is numerical. For example, you might ask a participant in a research project to tell you their age, and they respond to the question and answer that they are 25 years old. This is numerical data, it is quantitative data.

If you ask the same participant to indicate to you their gender, for the most part there are two possible answers. They will answer that they are male or they are female. Now you have data that is not numerical in form, but it is data that can readily be coded numerically. As there are, generally, only two possible answers to that question on gender, the researcher can assign a code to each

> **Qualitative data**
> Non-numerical data.

Table 4.3 Quantitative and qualitative data	
Quantitative data	Data in the form of numbers; or data that can readily be coded numerically
Qualitative data	Data that represent feelings, thoughts, ideas, understandings non-numeric data

of the possible answers. In this case female might be coded 1, and male might be coded 2. In this way, the non-numerical data has easily been converted to numerical data, female = 1 and male = 2. We now have numerical values for the data on gender. Positivism holds that there is one objective reality; reality is singular and separate from consciousness. For example, you either are 25 years old, or you are not. There is no ambiguity. You either are female, or you are not. There is, again, no ambiguity. This is the simplicity of the singular reality.

Qualitative data are not numerical, although, as we have seen, relatively simple and concise qualitative data can easily be coded numerically. If you have a small number of qualitative responses, it is easy to assign a numerical code to each one as we did above with the data on gender. If you have little variation in the qualitative responses that you receive and they are short and concise, it is a simple procedure to assign a numeric code to each response.

However, often qualitative data are too complex to be coded numerically, and sometimes coding qualitative data numerically serves neither the data nor the research project. This is because qualitative data can lose richness, depth and complexity through numerical coding. It may be that the research project actually requires densely descriptive data. If this is the case, reducing the complexity of qualitative data to the level of a numeric code may substantially damage the research project, and at the same time raise ethical issues regarding the management of data.

It is important to note that distinctions between qualitative and quantitative occur within data collection methods, at the uppermost point of the methodological pyramid.

In considering your research statement or question, you should ask whether this research project fits within a framework of positivism or a framework of constructionism or interpretivism. You should consider the kind(s) of data that you will need to elicit for the research project in order to be able to answer the research question or in order to be able to respond to the research statement. Ask yourself whether it is likely that you will need quantitative data or qualitative data. It may be that you will need a mixture of both. If this is the case, ask yourself whether you are likely to need predominantly qualitative or predominantly quantitative data. Ask yourself where the data is to be found, and how the data might best be gathered. In answering these questions, you will be able to move towards making a judgement with regard to which research methodology and data gathering methods to use in order to gather the data required to adequately and properly accomplish the aim of the research.

Theory
Research that has already been carried out, completed and published, sometimes in the context of the research project.

THE USE OF THEORY IN THE GENERATION OF KNOWLEDGE

All research is about the generation of knowledge. All research, certainly all research conducted within an academic setting, is embedded in **theory**. Every academic research project emerges from a particular body of knowledge, a particular body of theory, and it in turn makes a contribution to that body of knowledge. As every research project concludes and makes its own contribution to theory, to the body of knowledge, the body of knowledge grows.

Wherever within theory you decide to situate your research project, you will be entering a theoretical debate that has likely been ongoing for some time. The theoretical debate is conducted by all of the theorists (researchers) working in the field. These researchers conduct research and they publish their findings in theses, in academic journals, in conference papers and proceedings, in government reports and papers, in newspaper reports, in books and online. Through the publication of their research, researchers facilitate other theorists/researchers in an engagement with their research. Other theorists critically examine the research to establish its validity. They explore the philosophical framework within which the research is situated and examine the methodology used in the research. They critique the data gathering methods and the data gathered. Finally, they examine the findings of the research, the conclusions the researcher drew from the research and the insights into the phenomenon under investigation presented by the researcher as a result of the research. They do all of this to establish the validity of the research. When the validity of the research is established, the research is accepted as making a contribution to knowledge. It is in this way that, through each and every research project, theory is developed and and the knowledge base is expanded. This is how research is used to expand knowledge. Every research project becomes part of the knowledge base, part of the 'what is known' about the particular phenomenon investigated by the research project.

REAL WORLD RESEARCH

How theory influences research

In the summary of the journal article presented below, it can be seen that the authors of the article clearly situate their research within a body of knowledge, a particular area of marketing theory, and they clearly outline the contribution that their research makes to the body of knowledge. Source the original article online and read the 'conclusions and implications' section of the paper to examine the way in which the authors knit their research into the research in the body of knowledge in this area. This is the process of theorizing research, and it is the way in which research makes a contribution to knowledge.

'Brand extension feedback: The role of advertising', Martinez, E., Montaner, T. and Pina, J. M. (2009) © *Journal of Business Research*, Vol. 62: 405-414. Reprinted with permission from Elsevier.

Abstract

'Firms often use brand extensions as a way of introducing their new products, although they also risk diluting their brand image. In order to understand how consumers assess extensions and extended brands, the present work proposes and estimates a theoretical model, using the structural equation methodology. The results of the estimation indicate that the attitude towards the extension influences brand image and that this attitude is a consequence of the initial brand beliefs and the coherence of the new product. A multi-sample analysis also reveals that favouring the introduction of extensions through adequate advertising constitutes an efficient way of protecting brand image.'

The authors detail in the introduction to the article some of the theory on launching new products, on branding and on brand extension strategies.

They outline why they think it is important to analyze the reciprocal transfer of associations between product brands and brand extensions.

They state that their research proposes a theoretical model which explains the consumer assessment of brand extensions and the subsequent effects on brand image.

They write that previous research has analyzed the effects of brand equity leveraging and feedback as independent phenomena. They explain that their study 'proposes a comprehensive model that considers the process as a whole'.

Reference

Martinez, E., Montaner, T. and Pina, J.M. (2009) 'Brand extension feedback: The role of advertising', *Journal of Business Research* 62(4): 405–414.

THE IMPORTANCE OF THEORY IN RESEARCH

Theory is of the most fundamental importance in research. However, not all research is embedded in theory. You yourself may have conducted research for your workplace that did not have a theoretical base. Perhaps you examined sales graphs to establish patterns of sales, peaks and lulls in sales over periods of time, or perhaps you examined employee absenteeism records in order to establish patterns of absenteeism among particular employees or particular groups of employees, or patterns of absenteeism over particular times, days of the week, or days of the month, and so on.

This is of course research. It is not, however, research that has a theoretical base; it does not have a theoretical framework and so is of limited use. It is limited because it has not emerged from a theoretical framework, a particular body of knowledge. The findings of such research are generally confined to the specific context within which the research was conducted and can make a contribution only in this very limited context. While this contribution may be very useful within that particular context, the contribution is absolutely limited to that context. Such research cannot make a contribution to theory. It cannot go towards developing the knowledge base.

As such research generally makes no attempt to connect with what is known on the topic of the research, it makes no contribution to the broad debate. The findings from such research projects are by-and-large not known in any broad context and do not become part of the 'what is known' within the body of knowledge about the phenomenon investigated in the research project. As stated above, all research conducted in an academic setting is embedded in theory. It emerges from a theoretical framework and it, in turn, makes a contribution to the body of theory in that field.

Concepts, the building blocks of theory

Concepts are the building blocks of theory. What are concepts? As we have seen in our exploration and use of the conceptual framework, the first of the four frameworks in the four frameworks approach to research, concepts are key ideas, key words, often the big words in a sentence, a paragraph, in an idea. Every discipline and every theory is made up of concepts. Marketing is a concept. We only have to hear the word marketing, and immediately all the complexity of the concept that is 'marketing' inhabits our minds. We 'know' what marketing is, what is meant by the word (or concept) 'marketing'.

The concept 'marketing' is part of everyday language within Business Studies. But there wasn't always a concept in business called 'marketing'. The concept of 'marketing' was created and developed by theorists working in the field of sales. So the concept 'marketing', emerged from the body of knowledge that is 'business sales'. It is part of the theory of business sales. As a concept it makes and has made a very substantial contribution to theory in that field. It has facilitated the development of countless more concepts and countless research projects, all of which have made their own contribution to the marketing body of knowledge. It is in this way that concepts emerge from theory through research, and it is in this way that in turn, again through research, they make a contribution to theory.

The same can be said for the concepts 'human resources', 'branding' or 'globalization'. The same can be said for any and every concept in every discipline that there is or ever was in existence. Somebody somewhere had to see the pattern or activity, identify the pattern or the activity, and then label it with a name. Somebody somewhere had to come up with the name for the concept. The name, through debate, came to be accepted as representing the concept. It is in this way that concepts come into being.

Concepts, as stated, are key words or key ideas. They each contain a great deal of meaning. Each theory is made up of a number of concepts. It is created from different concepts and from the way in which different concepts are grouped together or aligned. This process of developing theory from concepts is not a simple linear process, but a very complex process of creation, development and reflection. It is, as is all creative endeavour, one part inspiration and nine parts perspiration. Each theorist is immersed in the concepts that make up the body of knowledge within which they are working. Through their active engagement with the theories and concepts it contains, they try to develop the body of knowledge, to create new concepts, to develop old concepts and to move the discipline along. Concepts, created and developed, and aligned with other concepts, are the means through which theory is created. Concepts are the building blocks of theory.

The uses of theory in research

The conceptual framework for every research project is contained in the research question or statement created and developed for that research project. The conceptual framework contains all of the key concepts in the research project.

There will be many other key concepts which are relevant to the research project, and many too of keen interest to the researcher, but the fact that they are excluded from the conceptual framework means that they are not part of the research project, and so they are of no concern to the researcher in their engagement with this particular project. As it develops, the research project will become complex enough and it is not possible, nor even desirable, to engage with concepts and bodies of knowledge that are not part of the conceptual framework created and developed for the project.

The theoretical framework is the framework created by the researcher from theory relevant to the research project. It is designed by the researcher to support the research and it emerges from the conceptual framework. The theoretical framework

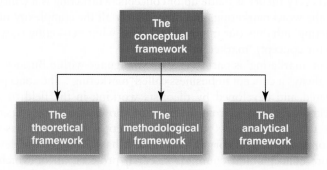

Figure 4.4   The four frameworks approach to the research project

for every research project is contained in the literature review. The key concepts in the conceptual framework indicate for the researcher the literature that needs to be sourced for the literature review for the research project. In this way, the theoretical framework emerges from the conceptual framework, using the four frameworks approach above (see Figure 4.4), to the research project.

REAL WORLD RESEARCH

How theory influences research

'Training failure as a consequence of organizational culture', Bunch, K.J. (2007)
Human Resources Development Review, Vol. 6:2: 142–164.

This article is a literature review. Researchers sometimes carry out only a review of the literature. Researchers do this in order to develop their knowledge or expertise on a topic or on a field of knowledge and to establish what is known, and to establish any gaps in what is known.

This article is worth reading because it is an example of a very good literature review. It is an extensive review of the literature in this field.

What do you think the author means when she writes that the literature review is intended to be 'representative'? She means that she has selected literature that she has judged to be representative of the entire body of literature for inclusion in this article.

The article is worth reading too for an exploration of the way in which theory influences research, in this context, in relation to the issue of training failure as a consequence of organizational culture.

The review has a very substantial bibliography.

As an exercise, critique the bibliography. Read the bibliography and examine it. How extensive are the references in the bibliography? Are the references up-to-date? What period of time do the references cover? Where do the references come from? Are they from books, from journal articles? Are there any web references? What would you say about the quality overall of the references? What would you say about the quality overall of the literature review?

Focus on the writing in the article. Is it clear and to the point? Take note of the structure of the article, the introduction, the body of the work and the final conclusions. Take note of the paragraph structure in the article.

This bibliography is an example of a good and useful, properly compiled bibliography.

The author has used the Harvard referencing method in the article. If you are required to use this referencing method in your research, you might use this article as a guide.

You might also use the bibliography as a guide to help you develop an understanding of how you should present your bibliography in your own research project.

Reference

Bunch, K.J. (2007) 'Training failure as a consequence of organizational culture', *Human Resource Development Review* 6(2): 142–164.

If we look at the research projects we examined in this chapter we can see clearly the conceptual frameworks, and within them the key concepts that the authors of the articles chose to focus on for their research. The key concepts that Bunch (2007) in her work focused on were training, training failure, and training failure as a consequence of organizational culture. The key concepts that Martinez *et al.* (2009) focused on in their work were branding, brand extension and the role of advertising in brand extension. In your own research, you should focus on an area that has interest and meaning for you. You should develop your research project around a question or a statement based on your interest and your reading of the literature in this area. The key concepts of this well-conceptualized research statement or question provide you with the focus of your research.

THE VALUE OF GOOD RESEARCH

Focus on image-based research

Image-based research refers to the use of images in research. The images can be photographs or pictures, drawings, cartoons, maps, charts, graphs; they can be images in advertising or other marketing or business material. In fact, any kind of an image can be used in image-based research.

In image-based research, the image or images used in the research form the data, or a part of the data for the research project. Sometimes images are used as data in the research project in conjunction with data from one or more other sources, for example, from observations, interviews, or from questionnaires.

The key issue with data from images, as with data from other sources, is the issue of validity. This is the degree to which the data are representative of the phenomenon under investigation.

In the article below, the authors situated their research within a feminist framework, and they conducted the study using image-based research. They used a content analysis approach to data analysis.

'Female role stereotypes in print advertising: identifying associations with magazine and product categories', Plakoyiannaki, E. and Zotos, Y. (2009) *European Journal of Marketing*, Vol. 43:11/12: 1411–1434

According to the abstract, the study was undertaken for three reasons:

- to provide up-to-date evidence in the UK on the frequency of appearance of female role portrayals in print advertisements

- to compare female role stereotypes across magazine types
- to explore the interface between female role stereotypes and product categories.

The researchers analyzed the content of 3830 advertisements, published in ten high circulation UK magazines.

They said that their findings indicate that women in UK magazine advertisements are mainly portrayed in decorative roles, and that female role stereotypes vary significantly across magazine types. They also said that their findings suggest that there is an association between product categories and female role stereotypes.

Based on the findings of the study, they conclude that there is a need for the advertising industry in the UK to adjust its communication practices to the changing role of women in society.

The student project (see Research in Practice box – Ian's research project, pages 113–114), proposes a research project using image-based research. Based on your reading of the previous project, and Ian's project, can you think of any ideas for research projects using image-based research?

The Sage web-resource Methodspace (**www. methodspace.com**), provides useful resources for researchers. In relation to image-based research, there are videos on the website from such experts in image-based research as Sarah Pink, Marcus Banks and Jon Prosser.

Reference

Plakoyiannaki, E. and Zotos, Y. (2009) 'Female role stereotypes in print advertising: Identifying associations with magazine and product categories',

HOW TO CREATE A THEORETICAL FRAMEWORK: THE SECOND OF THE FOUR FRAMEWORKS

In practice, the work of creating a theoretical framework begins the moment the researcher begins to think about creating and developing a research project. Every research project, as has been stated, emerges from a body of knowledge and must make a contribution to knowledge. It is not possible to know what contribution your research project might or could make unless you know what is already known in that body of knowledge.

You must enter the debate within that body of knowledge where that debate is currently. If you do not do this, you may end up conducting research on a topic that has already been well researched, or you may end up conducting research on a topic that is out-of-date, perhaps a topic which the debate in the field has already dealt with and from which it has already moved on. It is for all of these reasons that you begin reading around a topic as soon as you have an idea for your research project.

You begin reading to develop a sense of what it is that the researchers working in this field know, and what it is that the researchers working in this field would like to know. This will indicate where you can make a useful contribution to research in this field.

Through all of this work you create a conceptual framework for your research project, which contains all of the key concepts in the research project. Each of the key concepts then guides you in terms of your reading for your theoretical framework. For example if the research question or statement which you have created and developed for your research project contains the key concept 'marketing' then your reading will be in the area of marketing.

RESEARCH IN PRACTICE

Kate's research project

This is an example of a research statement (a conceptual framework). This conceptual framework was developed for Kate for her research project. Kate works in the human resources department of the company, Greene's Biscuits Ltd, which is an SME in the town of Lillington. Kate is interested in her research in examining in detail the training and development provision made in the company for all employees.

" This research project is a case study of the training and development provision for the employees of Greene's Biscuits Ltd., Lillington.

Conceptual frameworks for research projects contain, of course, several key concepts. The researcher decides on the way in which the key concepts are put together then aligns the key concepts in such a way as to provide the most apt, the most appropriate, conceptual framework for the research project.

Read the detail given above on Kate's research project. Examine the research statement. The research statement contains the conceptual framework for the research project. There are several key concepts in this conceptual framework. One of the key concepts is not of relevance to the theoretical framework; this is the key concept 'case study'. The words 'case study' tell the reader what methodology was used in the research. This is relevant to the methodological framework, the third of the frameworks within the four frameworks. We will discuss that framework in later chapters of this book.

The key concepts that are of relevance to the theoretical framework are the concept of training, the concept of development, the concept of training and development, and the concept of training and development for employees. Another key concept of relevance is the concept of a SME. The business within which the research took place is Greene's Biscuits Ltd, Lillington, which is an SME. As this is the case, the theoretical framework that needs to be developed is one around training and development for the employees of SMEs.

The areas of search for literature for the theoretical framework for the project outlined above are: training and development; training and development for employees; training and development for employees for SMEs. As you can see, each strand of the theoretical framework comes from the conceptual framework. In this way the conceptual framework provides a guide in the search for literature for the theoretical framework. The literature review is usually Chapter 2 of the thesis or report of the research. Tables 4.4, 4.5 and 4.6 contain a sample structure for the literature review (with different word counts) for the project detailed in the conceptual framework outlined above.

The theoretical framework, or literature review, contains a discussion, or review, of the literature in the area of the research project. Each theoretical framework is unique because each is created and designed to support an individual research project. The theoretical framework provides theoretical scaffolding for the research project. The reading that the researcher undertakes for the literature review is focused on the areas indicated by the key concepts in the conceptual framework.

Table 4.4   Example of structure for the literature review (based on 5000 word count)

First section 300 words – in 2 paragraphs	Introduction (a brief introduction to the chapter and the contents of the chapter)
Second section (first subheading) 1400 words – in 3 paragraphs	Training and development
Third section (second subheading) 1400 words – in 3 paragraphs	Training and development for employees
Fourth section (third subheading) 1400 words – in 3 paragraphs	Training and development for employees of SMEs
Fifth section 500 words – in 2 paragraphs Word count total = 5000 words	Summary (a brief summary of the main points and the main argument developed throughout the chapter)

Table 4.5   Example of structure for the literature review (based on 3000 word count)

First section 200 words – in 1 paragraph	Introduction (a brief introduction to the chapter and the contents of the chapter)
Second section (first subheading) 800 words – in 3 paragraphs	Training and development
Third section (second subheading) 800 words – in 3 paragraphs	Training and development for employees
Fourth section! (third subheading) 800 words – in 3 paragraphs	Training and development for employees of SMEs
Fifth section 400 words – in 2 paragraphs Word count total = 3000 words	Summary (a brief summary of the main points and the main argument developed throughout the chapter)

Table 4.6   Example of structure for the literature review (based on 1000 word count)

First section 100 words – in 1 paragraph	Introduction (a brief introduction to the chapter and the contents of the chapter)
Second section (first subheading) 250 words – in 2 paragraphs	Training and development
Third section (second subheading) 250 words – in 2 paragraphs	Training and development for employees
Fourth section (third subheading) 250 words – in 2 paragraphs	Training and development for employees of SMEs
Fifth section 150 words – in 1 paragraph Word count total = 1000 words	Summary (a brief summary of the main points and the main argument developed throughout the chapter)

In undertaking the literature review:

1 the researcher first sources the literature
2 then he/she downloads and saves the literature
3 then he/she reads the literature
4 finally, he/she begins to construct from the literature he/she has read the theoretical framework for the research project.

As we have stated, the researcher creates the theoretical framework:

- to provide the theoretical framework for the research project
- to establish their expertise in this area
- to detail the current state of knowledge in the area
- to highlight what is known and to highlights any gaps in what is known
- to detail the theory from which the research has emerged
- to outline the theory to which the research will ultimately contribute.

It is important to remember that your conceptual framework is not written in stone. Indeed, practised researchers often change and rearrange their conceptual frameworks a great deal before finally deciding on the format. It can happen that you, through your reading or through your reflection, come up with a new key concept that must be included in the theoretical framework. If this is the case then you simply change your conceptual framework so that it encompasses this new concept. Remember that each new or additional concept adds to the complexity of your research project. Unnecessary complexity at the start is inadvisable and undesirable and it is best to keep the conceptual framework simple. The project will become complex enough as it develops. You will see as you read on through this textbook that even the most practised researchers often begin with very simple ideas for their research projects and that these initially very simple research projects become extremely complex through the scholarship of the researchers and their engagement with the research.

The theoretical framework is considered in more detail later in Chapter 6, where more examples are provided.

RESEARCH IN PRACTICE

Ian's research project – an image-based research project

Ian is undertaking an undergraduate degree in Business Studies. He is spending the summer working in New York, returning to the summer job he held last year working as a business intern in Bloomberg Tower in mid-town Manhattan. He is going to undertake his research for his degree there. He was so impressed by the new building housing Bloomberg enterprises in New York city that he decided to focus his research on the building and on how the building itself facilitates Bloomberg's business agenda. He has been given permission to conduct his research in Bloomberg by his manager there and is now in dialogue with his thesis supervisor in relation to the research project he is proposing.

Ian is particularly keen to focus his research on demonstrating how, through innovative design, the new Bloomberg building (Bloomberg Tower), fosters innovation, team building and knowledge spillovers.

He has decided to use image-based research as his methodology. He intends to photograph the structure and organization of the interior of the building and has also been given access to and permission to copy the architects' designs for the organization and structure of the interior of the building. He intends to use these resources as the data for his project. He is particularly keen to focus on actually demonstrating how, in practice, the interior organization and structure of the building operates as a facilitator of the work of the business.

His research statement is as follows: This research project is a study of the new Bloomberg building in New York city, and of the manner in which the design of the interior of the building facilitates and fosters innovation, team building and the exchange of knowledge between individuals within the company.

The literature review for the project will draw on literature in the areas of organizational structure and the impact of organizational structure on innovation, team building and communication.

The methodology will be image-based research.

The data will comprise of photographs of the interior of the building taken by the researcher, and designs for the building drawn by the team architects who designed the building.

The rationale for the study is the unique perspective the study will provide on the manner in which organizational design can impact on and foster innovation, team building and knowledge spillovers in a major company.

Ian's thesis supervisor has approved the study provisionally, and has asked Ian to develop a full research proposal for the study.

HOW TO GENERATE THEORY FROM YOUR OWN RESEARCH

The literature that you review gives you material from which you develop in part the questions that you ask in the data gathering phase of the research. This is one of the reasons why you must have an understanding of the literature, before you develop your research question or research statement.

The questions you ask in the data gathering phase of the research emerge from your research question or statement. At all stages through the research, you should be clear as to the relevance of what you are doing to the aim of your research.

Theorizing data
Explaining and demonstrating how research findings and conclusions support or contradict the current research.

When you get to the stage of data analysis, you begin the process of theorizing your data. The process of **theorizing data** is the process of establishing how your data fits with theory in the field. You do this by establishing where and how your data supports, and contradicts, the theory in the literature review. This is the process of establishing how your data fits with the theory in the field. To theorize your research you knit your findings into the findings of published research, which is laid out in the literature review created for the research project. We saw this work of theorizing findings in practice earlier in this chapter, when we studied the work of Martinez *et al.* (2009) as reported in their journal article 'Brand extension feedback: The role of advertising'.

Sometimes students worry if their findings contradict the findings of other theorists. However, as long as your research was thorough and valid, your findings are your findings, and they stand with the findings of other researchers. There can be many reasons why your research would contradict the research of others. It might be that you are working in a different temporal framework, or a different geographic area, or in a different cultural setting. It might be that the organization or entity that you are studying is unique in some way, and this then might account for the differences you are finding in your study. It might simply be that things have changed since the other studies were conducted, and those changes account for the differences that you are uncovering in your research. In any case, the important thing is to conduct the research properly and to report your findings thoroughly. It is important too to be alert to those aspects and elements of your research project, such as the context for the research and the population or sample of the study, which make your research different from the research that has already been carried out. It would be useful to record these insights as they come to you in your research diary.

THE LINKS BETWEEN RESEARCH, THEORY AND KNOWLEDGE

Every research project is designed to make a contribution to knowledge. The researcher creates the conceptual framework for the research project, and from that develops the theoretical framework for the research project.

The conceptual and theoretical frameworks guide the researcher in the data gathering phase of the research in terms of the areas to be explored and/or the questions to be asked. This data are analyzed and the findings and conclusions drawn are theorized. The data are theorized by knitting the findings and conclusions into the research detailed in the literature review. The researcher makes a contribution to knowledge by knitting their research into the body of knowledge in the area within which they have situated the research project. What results from this process of theorization is a new theory, or a new extension of existing theory, which is laid out in the final chapter of the thesis or report of the research.

The new theory or new extension to existing theory is brought into being through the creative engagement of the researcher with the key concepts of the research, with the theory in the field, with the insights they have into the data gathered for the research project. This creative engagement through the reflective process leads the researcher to develop new concepts, and concepts, as we know, are the building blocks of theory.

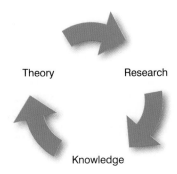

Figure 4.5   The cycle of theory, research and knowledge

CASE STUDY

The research diary

Student keeping a research diary © Catherine Lane/iStock

Nadin and Cassell (2006) in their journal article write about the use of a research diary as a tool for reflexive practice, drawing on reflections from management research.

This is a useful article in that it demonstrates some of the utility of the research diary in practice.

The focus of the article is on the use of the research diary as an aid to reflexivity in management research.

In the article, the authors state that while there have been calls for reflexivity in management research, there has been very little written on how to 'do' reflexivity in practice.

They define reflexivity as involving 'reflecting on the way in which research is carried out, and understanding how the process of doing research shapes its outcomes'.

The authors go on to state 'whilst more commonly associated with the disciplines of sociology and ethnography, reflexivity is emerging as a key issue for qualitative researchers within management'.

Drawing on empirical work in the field of small businesses, the authors 'outline a practical example of a research diary in use, and (they) analyze the extent to which it enables reflexivity in practice in the research process'.

The research diary 'was simply an A5 lined notebook'. The entries were made by hand. Each time a firm was visited and data gathered, a new entry was made. This was done as soon as possible after each visit. Reflections on the research, the process and the experience of gathering data were recorded in the diary.

Some of the items recorded were as follows:

- methodological issues
- supplementary thoughts and insights to the interview data gathered
- ideas and thoughts on general themes as they emerged in the data analysis process
- non-verbal aspects of the social encounter (the interview/the site visit)
- thoughts and insights into the management style. Anything that the researcher found strange – anomalies or contradictions
- the researcher's reactions to the encounter (how she felt/responded)
- the researcher's engagement with the encounter (researcher's own assumptions, values and beliefs and how they impact on the research)
- the diary was used to record concerns which might, as the authors state, otherwise have been lost, or simply not considered.

In addition to all of this, the research diary acted for the researchers as a useful organizational aid to help keep track of the research process as a whole.

In their conclusions the author's state: 'the use of a research diary was grounded in the epistemological position of social constructionism and the need for reflexivity in research'.

Question Can you briefly explain the meaning of the concluding statement outlined above?

References

Nadin, S. and Cassell, C. (2006) 'The use of a research diary as a tool for reflexive practice: Some reflections from management research', *Qualitative Research in Accounting and Management* 4(4): 208–217.

CHAPTER REVIEW

his chapter introduces the reader to the philosophical underpinnings of research. Some key philosophical frameworks are highlighted and discussed. A model of the methodological pyramid is presented and discussed. The model details the philosophies, the methodologies and the methods of social research and the manner in which these fit together in the research project. The two types of data, quantitative and qualitative data are introduced and explained and the differences between them explained. The use of theory in the generation of knowledge is discussed, as is the importance of theory in research. The role of concepts in theory is explored and the function of concepts as the building blocks of theory is discussed. The theoretical framework is presented as the second framework in the model of the four frameworks approach to the research project. The uses of the theoretical framework are detailed and the process of constructing a theoretical framework is explored. The means by which a researcher generates theory from their research are outlined and the importance of generating theory from research is detailed and highlighted, as are the links between research, theory and knowledge.

Now update your interactive research diary with your notes and findings at www.cengage.co.uk/quinlan. Complete the activities provided to reinforce your understanding of this chapter.

END OF CHAPTER QUESTIONS

1 What is meant by the term philosophical framework in relation to social research?

2 Name and briefly explain three philosophical frameworks used in social research.

3 What is quantitative data?

4 What is qualitative data?

5 Give an example of how simple and concise qualitative data can be coded numerically.

6 Explain why the numerical coding of qualitative data can be inappropriate.

7 Explain the limits of research developed without a theoretical base.

8 Explain what is meant by the statement 'concepts are the building blocks of theory'.

9 Briefly explain the process of developing theory, as detailed in this chapter.

10 Explain why it is necessary to engage with the literature before making final decisions regarding the focus of the research project.

REFERENCES

Bunch, K.J. (2007) 'Training failure as a consequence of organizational culture', *Human Resource Development Review* 6(2): 142–164.

Crotty, M. (2005) *The Foundations of Social Research*, London: Sage.

Ferriss, S. and Young, M. (2008) *Chick Flicks: Contemporary Women at the Movies*, London and New York: Routledge.

Fowler, F.J. (2002) *Survey Research Methods*, Thousand Oaks, CA: Sage.

Guba, E.G. and Lincoln, Y.S. (1994) 'Competing Paradigms in Qualitative Research', in N. Denzin and Y. Lincoln (eds), *Handbook of Qualitative Research*, Thousand Oaks, CA: Sage.

Maher, K. (2009) 'Is it time to kill the chick flick? Hollywood thinks that all women care about is weddings and shopping. Can anything stop the inane decline of the chick flick?', *The Times*, 3 February.

Martinez, E., Montaner, T. and Pina, J.M. (2009) 'Brand extension feedback: The role of advertising', *Journal of Business Research* 62(4): 405–414.

Methodspace: Connecting the Research Community, Sage, (**www.methodspace.com**)

Millward, R. and Shoard, C. (2010) 'Does it matter that there are no women up for the Palme D'Or?', *The Observer*, 16 May.

Moustakas, C.E. (1994) *Phenomenological Research Methods*, Thousand Oaks, CA: Sage.

Nadin, S. and Cassell, C. (2006) 'The use of a research diary as a tool for reflexive practice: Some reflections from management research', *Qualitative Research in Accounting and Management* 4 (4): 208–217.

Plakoyiannaki, E. and Zotos, Y. (2009) 'Female role stereotypes in print advertising: Identifying associations with magazine and product categories', *European Journal of Marketing* 43(11/12): 1411–1434.

Rose, G. (2007) *Visual Methodologies: An Introduction to the Interpretation of Visual Materials*, London and Thousand Oaks: Sage.

Smith, J.A., Flowers, P. and Larkin, M. (2009) *Interpretative Phenomenological Analysis*, London: Sage.

'Women & Hollywood: from a feminist perspective', **www.womenandhollywood.com**

RECOMMENDED READING

Banks, M. (2007) *Using Visual Data in Qualitative Research*, London: Sage.

Denscombe, M. (2004) *Ground Rules for Good Research*, Part One, 'Foundations for Social Research', Maidenhead: Open University Press.

Grant, P. and Perren, L. (2002) 'Small business and entrepreneurial research: Meta-theories, paradigms and prejudices', *International Small Business Journal* 20(2): 185–211.

Jameson, D.A. (2009) 'Economic crises and financial disasters: The role of business communication', *Journal of Business Communication* 46(4): 499–509.

Jankowicz, A.D. (2005) *Business Research Projects* (4th edn), Ch 5, 'Basic Assumptions about Research', London: Cengage.

Kent, R. (2007) *Marketing Research: Approaches, Methods and Applications in Europe*, Ch. 2, 'Academic Research in Marketing', London: Cengage.

Lee, N. and Lings, I. (2008) *Doing Business Research: A Guide to Theory and Practice*, Ch. 2, 'The Scientific Approach to Research' and Ch. 4, 'The Interpretive Approach to Research', London: Sage.

May, T. (2005) *Social Research, Issues Methods and Process*, Ch. 1, 'Perspectives on Social Scientific Research' and Ch. 2, 'Social Theory and Social Research', Maidenhead: Open University Press.

Neuman, W.L. (2000) *Social Research Methods: Qualitative and Quantitative Approaches*, Ch. 2, 'Theory and Research', Boston, MA: Allyn & Bacon.

Pink, S. (2006) *Doing Visual Ethnography*, London: Sage.

Prosser, J. (ed.) (2003) Image-based Research: A Sourcebook for Qualitative Researchers, London: Routledge Falmer.

Rose, G. (2007) *Visual Methodologies: An Introduction to the Interpretation of Visual Materials*, London and Thousand Oaks: Sage.

CHAPTER 5

DEVELOPING A RESEARCH PROPOSAL

LEARNING OBJECTIVES

At the end of this chapter the student should be able to:

- Generate ideas for research projects.

- Develop research questions/statements, define and refine them.

- Provide a sample literature review for a research proposal.

- Outline a methodological framework for a research project.

- Develop a research proposal.

RESEARCH SKILLS

At the end of this chapter the student should, using the exercises on the accompanying online platform, be able to:

- Generate research ideas.

- Outline researchable problems.

- Develop research proposals.

In this chapter the focus is on the development of research proposals. This is a very important chapter. As well as teaching you how to develop formal proposals for research projects, this chapter looks again at how to generate ideas for research, and how to critically evaluate those ideas to make sure they are researchable.

INTRODUCTION

As a social science researcher, the first thing you need to be able to do is to generate ideas for research projects. As you have probably gathered from your reading of this textbook, ideas are all around you. You just need to be able to identify them as potential research projects.

Figure 5.1, the model of the research process shows that the first step is to come up with an idea for the research project and the work of refining that idea. The process of refining the idea should result in you being able to state your research project in one sentence. This one sentence can be phrased as a statement or a question. This sentence, as we know, contains the conceptual framework for the research project, which is the first framework in the four frameworks approach to the research project.

The research statement or question, the conceptual framework for the research, drives every element of the research process. All of the decisions made for every element of the research process are determined by the research statement/question.

The newspaper article detailed below explores the issue of free products and in particular free products on the internet. As you will read in the article, media mogul Rupert Murdoch has referred to this as a flawed business model. Why, in Murdoch's view, is the model flawed?

The article concludes with a discussion of different ways of making money from the internet. It seems that, with business leaders like Murdoch engaged in the topic, the development of profitable business models for web-based businesses is of major interest to businesses and business leaders globally. Is this an area that might be of interest to you? Can you think of an **idea for a research project** based on this article? On what side of this particular divide do you think you stand? Are you an advocate of free access to content on the web or do you favour a pay-for-content model? Do you know of any other web-based businesses that are free or fee-based? Do you know what business model(s) it/they use? Consider whether there is a possibility of developing a useful research project around an in-depth study of one or more of these web-based business models. Is this an area that would interest you? You might think about developing a research project about how your friends and colleagues

The Four Frameworks
Conceptual Framework
Theoretical Framework
Methodological Framework
Analytical Framework

Idea for a research project
Your idea for your research project is properly expressed in your very well-conceptualized research statement or question.

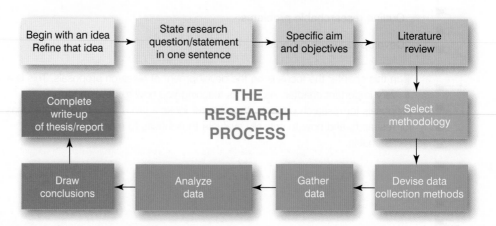

Figure 5.1 The research process

THE VALUE OF GOOD RESEARCH

Research in the media

Rupert Murdoch – Chairman and CEO of News Corporation © jeremy sutton-hibbert/Alamy

'The end of the age of FREE!', Thorpe, V. *The Observer*, 10th May 2009

'**F**or a decade now, consumers have become accustomed to having free access to music, films and information, thanks to the internet. But with many of the media's biggest players starting to talk of charging for content, is the tide about to turn?'

The article goes on: 'In art as in commerce, a price tag traditionally has magical powers. With the flick of a wand, a pound sign confers desirability on an item that might be thrown away if it was handed out for nothing.'

Consumers who have grown up during the past 15 years are completely at home in a world where much of what they want to hear, see or read will cost them nothing. True, in the case of some films and TV shows, the practices involved may skirt around the law a bit. Generally speaking, though, culture has become a happy free-for-all. Now may be the time to pay the bill.

Chris Anderson, a leading American commentator on the web and editor-in-chief of *Wired* magazine, puts the matter concisely: "Somehow an economy had emerged around "free" before the economic model that could describe it." Anderson's next book, *Free: The Future of a Radical Price*, will both celebrate and analyze the effect of all this giving-away. The author of the influential 2006 book *The Long Tail*, Anderson is to suggest that few of the conventional rules of commerce, such as "supply and demand" and "economies of scale", apply any longer. While some suppliers, such as Sky Sports, might still get away with charging their audience, they would have to be pretty sure they offered a unique product.

One of the biggest players in the game last week questioned the rationale behind the current give-away culture. Rupert Murdoch, head of News Corp, even went so far as to refer to it as a "flawed" business model when he spoke to reporters in New York. The media mogul – who owns the *Times*, *Sunday Times*, *Sun* and *News of the World* in Britain, as well as *Fox News* and the *Wall Street Journal* in America – announced that he was considering charging for more of his internet sites.

"We are now in the midst of an epochal debate over the value of content and it is clear to many newspapers that the current model is malfunctioning," Murdoch said. His volte-face followed background news that profits from News Corp newspapers were down year-on-year from $216m to $7m and that British newspaper advertising revenues were down 21 per cent.

'The upshot was, Murdoch concluded, that within a year the web would have utterly changed its financial model and his titles would be leading the pack. Earlier in the week, reports that the Guardian Media Group, the owner of this newspaper, was thinking along similar lines had ricocheted around the globe. While GMG management has no plans to charge for content on its sites, the group's chief executive, Carolyn McCall, did suggest that a subscription system was conceivable for some specialist areas.'

The article goes on ...

'The dominant force in the market, Google, has now provided so much free that it no longer has to worry whether it will make money. Free information is its very brand and that is why the advertising on its search engines is so lucrative. In some ways, it resembles the old business model of offering a "loss leader" or distributing complementary freebies: consumer interest grows and everyone wins.'

Anderson gives 'the pioneering example of the Prince album that was handed out with copies of the *Mail on Sunday* in 2007. Although the singer lost money on the deal, his follow-up London concerts sold out. The newspaper lost money, too, yet its management could put no value on the huge business advantage of being seen as pioneers on the music scene.'

References

Thorpe, V. (2009) 'The end of the age of FREE?', *The Observer*, 10 May © Guardian News & Media Ltd 2009. Reproduced with permission.

engage with the internet? What content do they pay for and why? What content might they pay for and why? Is there scope for the development of a research project around the kinds of applications your friends and/or colleagues use, or even the kinds of applications they would like to use? Are there applications your friends and/or colleagues would like to be able to use, but can't, because they're not (yet) available? Is there scope for the development of a research project focused on new product development? Is there scope for the development of a research project around new business models for internet-based products and companies?

An interesting case study might be the Arctic Monkeys, and the way in which they developed their market. Do you think there might be some scope there for the development of an idea for a research project for business studies?

I am sure you use different web-based social networking products. I use Twitter, because I enjoy using it, and it is free. Is there, do you think, scope for developing a research project around the study of the business model of Twitter? What is the business rationale underpinning Twitter? Does it have a business rationale? Does Twitter make money? If so, how does Twitter make money? It might be interesting to develop a research project on the means through which revenue might be generated from or by Twitter?

Questions that you have about people, or businesses, or aspects of business, provide good starting points in the search for an idea for a research project.

GENERATING IDEAS FOR RESEARCH PROJECTS

The example of the internet and the debate around business models for the internet are useful in that they demonstrate clearly that potential research projects are all around us. It is important to begin to develop some skills in identifying potential research projects, because you will have to do so to satisfy the requirements of your course of study, and because 'ideas' are simply new ways of thinking about things. Developing your capacity to think in new ways will help you become innovative, which is a key skill, particularly in a knowledge-based economy.

You can generate ideas for research projects from:

- everything you have studied so far in your work toward your qualification
- everything you have seen, watched and experienced in your work
- everything that interests or intrigues you about the business world
- every person that you have encountered in the business world.

The problem should not be one of having no ideas; the problem should be in deciding on which idea to focus for your research project.

Think about what you have studied so far in your work for your qualification(s). Are there any thoughts that come to you straightaway about ideas for research projects? If there are, jot them down in your research diary; try to capture them right away, before you forget them. Think about the subjects and topics you studied that really interested you, and jot them down. Now think about the subjects that you did well in. Write the names of these down in your research diary. Now think about any issues, or unanswered questions, or outright problems, that you came across in your reading for your subjects. Was there anything that particularly interested you? Was there anything that you think would be worth thinking about in more detail? If there is, write it down in your research diary.

The next step is to begin to think critically about your ideas for research projects. Think about them in terms of the kinds of problems you would encounter trying to develop these into research projects. Some of the questions you need to ask yourself at this point are detailed in the following list.

Questions in relation to the proposed research idea/research project

- Are there any particular problems, sensitivities, issues, about this **research idea** that stand out from the start?
- Do you think that these problems, issues and sensitivities would be substantial enough to stop such a research project, or to substantially delay such a research project? If the answer is yes to this, you may need to move on quickly from this idea.

> **Research idea**
> This broad area within which you want to situate your research.

Questions in relation to the literature in the area or field of the proposed research

- Is there anything written about this issue or topic (is there any literature, any published research, on this research or topic)? There may be a great deal, there may not. If there is little literature on the topic, you should seek advice as to whether or not you should continue with the topic. It is likely that you will be advised against continuing if there is little literature.
- Who has been writing on this topic? When did they write on this topic? Recently?
- Where is the topic being written about? In journals? In newspapers? Online?
- What is being written about the topic?

- If the topic has been or is being written about in journal articles, this is really useful. This means that the topic has been addressed and developed theoretically. This would be particularly helpful for a beginner researcher working within an academic institution.
- Try to locate the journal articles online.
- Make a file on your computer and in that file save copies of the journal articles you have found on this topic.
- When you have saved the journal articles to your computer, scan them quickly and then read them closely. Record the thoughts and ideas that come to you as you read in your research diary.
- What are the authors of those journal articles saying about the topic? What is known about the topic? What issues and aspects have been thoroughly explored? What issues, aspects, questions do the authors of the journal articles recommend for further research? What issues are yet to be explored?
- Is there any issue among those issues that you would/could/should explore?

Questions in relation to research methodology and methods for the proposed research

- What methodologies did the researchers in the literature you've read use in their study of this issue/phenomenon?
- Did they study human populations? If so, what populations did they work with? Were they big populations or small? Did the researchers encounter any particular problems in working with these populations?
- What kind of data collection methods did they use?
- If you were to conduct research on this topic, where would you conduct the research? Do you have access to a site, an organization, a population, where or with whom you could conduct your research on this topic?
- What kind of data would you look for in order to produce some new knowledge in this field?
- Where are these data? Are they, for example, in records and reports? Are they, for example, in the testimony of people which you might gather through interviews or focus groups?
- How would you go about gathering the data?
- Why would you gather the data in that manner? Why is that the best way to gather the data?

Try to answer these questions. Scribble your notes in response to these bullet points, statements and questions into your research diary. Then, in your research diary, quickly organize your notes. Think about the ideas and insights you have had during this exercise. Using more scribbles, arrange them and rearrange them. Are more ideas coming to you through this process? Now try to put your thoughts, ideas and insights into some kind of order.

Now quickly analyze your notes. What are they telling you about this possible research project? Is there potential in your notes for more than one idea for a research project or does one idea stand out? How does this idea strike you? Does it seem reasonable and do-able? As you think about it, is this research project becoming more and more interesting? Perhaps your notes are warning you in some way about this research project. What do you now feel about this research project? Do you think that this is something on which you would like to spend some more time, or should you move onto another idea? If your instincts are telling you that this is not the way to go with your research project, then perhaps you should listen to your instincts. Do not be afraid to ask for advice. Talk to your research supervisor or your lecturer in research methods and air your ideas. You may have an opportunity to run your idea very quickly by your lecturer at the end of a lecture. If there is a major issue or problem with your idea, they may be able to spot it right away. If they do, this can save you a lot of time and bother.

It is important not to become too attached to an idea for a research project until you have been given some indication that, in general, the idea you are developing is viable, and that your proposed research idea is acceptable. There is no point in getting attached to an idea for a research project which, for one reason or another, is not acceptable to your supervisor/potential examiner. It may be that there is some ethical issue, or the scope of the research idea may not be broad enough or deep enough for the standard required by the programme of study. Perhaps the area has been studied too much, or has not been studied enough and there really is nothing written on the topic; while this can be an intriguing and engaging challenge for experienced researchers, it is not the best starting point for beginner researchers.

In addition to the areas detailed above, there may be some other experience or area in your life that you can explore with the view to generating an idea or ideas for research projects. The media, TV, the internet, newspapers and magazines, as we have seen, are all very useful areas of exploration in terms of ideas for research projects. Hobbies and pastimes as well as sporting and social endeavours, clubs and organizations are all potentially fruitful, too.

THE VALUE OF GOOD RESEARCH

Focus on documentary research/ documentary analysis

Documentary research or documentary analysis, as it is often called, is research focused on analysing documents. Examples of the kinds of documents used in documentary analysis include company reports, government reports, archives, files, records of meetings, other records, memos and diaries. Documentary research can be used in internet research, in researching websites and web pages and other documents on the internet. Any document can be used as the focus of documentary research. Both quantitative and qualitative approaches can be used to gathering and analysing data in documentary research.

Documentary research can be used as the methodology in the research project and/or it can be used as a data collection method in the research project.

The journal article detailed on the next page provides an interesting example of case study in which documents were gathered and used as data.

'European constructions of an American model: Developments of four MBA programmes', Mazza, C., Sahlin-Andersson, K. and Strandgaard Pedersen, J. (2005)

In the article the researchers created four case studies of MBA programmes. The four cases were the MBA programmes offered by:

- Copenhagen Business School, Copenhagen, Denmark
- IESE Business School Barcelona, Spain
- SDA-Bocconi, Milan, Italy
- Uppsala University, Uppsala, Sweden.

In the first stage of data collection for the study, the researchers gathered and analyzed documentary material on the four MBA programmes. In their analysis they examined the presentation and content of the documents. The documents they analyzed included the homepage presentations on the internet of the MBA programmes, brochures on the programmes, detail in alumni magazines on the programmes, detailed descriptions of the programmes of study, guidelines on the programmes and the curricula of the programmes.

The researchers expanded the study by supporting the data from the documentary sources with data from interviews with key informants. They also gathered data on the context within which the MBAs were offered, data on the educational institutions hosting the MBA programmes. You should source this article and read it through. Focus in particular on the methodology section. What do you think of the methodology used in the research project? Does it give you any ideas for a research project that you might undertake?

Some useful resources on documentary research include:

World History Sources, *Scholars Analysing Documents,* George Mason University, (**http://chnm. gmu.edu/worldhistorysources/whmdocuments.html**).
Denscombe, M. (2007) *The Good Research Guide for Small-scale Social Research Projects*, 3rd edn, Chapter 12, 'Documents', Maidenhead: Open University Press.
Scott, J. (1990) *A Matter of Record: Documentary Sources in Social Research*, Oxford: Blackwell.

The first of the three resources above is a history resource. It would be interesting to think about a research project focused on some aspect of business history. There are a number of academic journals dealing with business history, among them are *Business History, Business History Review, Business and Economic History, Accounting, Business and Financial History*. The US Library of Congress provides a very good guide to business history resources (**www.loc.gov/rr/business/guide/guide1/sharp13.html**).

The Cancer Council of New South Wales, Australia, presents on its website a documentary analysis study of the tobacco industry. The study is called 'The Tobacco Industry – A History of Denial' (**http://www.cancercouncil.com.au/editorial.asp?pageid=377**). The study details the documents used in the analysis, and it explains how access to the documents was possible.

The case study presented at the end of this chapter contains a research proposal for a research project to be carried out using a documentary analysis methodology.

References

Mazza, C., Sahlin-Andersson, K. and Strandgaard Pedersen, J. (2005) 'European constructions of an American model: Developments of four MBA programmes', *Management Learning*, 36(4): 471–491.

Figure 5.2 details some ideas for research projects developed around a (fictitious) cricket club. If you belong to any kind of club, is there any research that you could conduct in the club and/or for the club that would be useful? Four ideas have been jotted down in the spidergram below for research projects for this particular cricket club. Perhaps you will find in the spidergram some inspiration in terms of ideas of your own. Perhaps you can think of other potential research projects for this club, or for another club or for a different enterprise or organization. Figure 5.3 is another spidergram

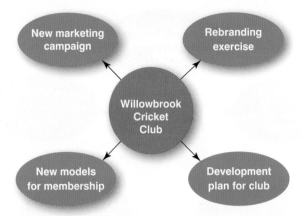

Figure 5.2   Research diary research project ideas: Willowbrook Cricket Club

which presents five ideas for potential research projects all focused on the World Wildlife Fund (WWF).

The five (scribbled) ideas for the WWF are as follows:

- a study of the brand recognition
- a study of the web presence of the WWF, by this I mean a **critical analysis** of the website of the WWF
- a new marketing campaign for the WWF
- a marketing campaign for the WWF aimed specifically at third level students
- a study of new fundraising models for the WWF, or perhaps the development of a fundraising model designed specifically for the WWF.

> **Critical analysis**
> Critical analysis is a questioning analytical approach to any phenomenon.

It may be that one or more of these ideas appeals to you and perhaps gives you an idea for your own research project. If so, that's good. It may be that reading this and reflecting on the ideas presented here helps you to decide that you would like to go in a different

Figure 5.3   Research diary research project ideas: World Wildlife Fund (WWF)

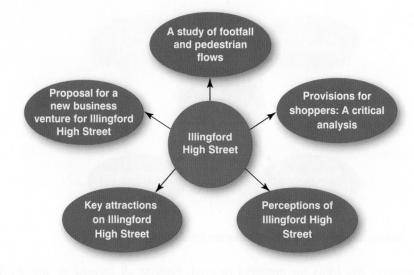

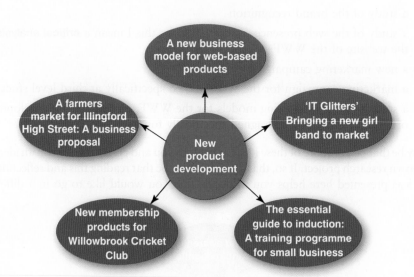

Figure 5.4   Two spidergrams from a research diary

direction entirely in developing your own research idea(s). This is good too. The important thing is that you take some action and actively engage with the development of your research project. Figure 5.4 shows two spidergrams copied from a research diary.

The first spidergram, at the top of the page, is a study of a (fictitious) high street. The student who prepared this spidergram is thinking about conducting his research project on the local high street. In this spidergram there are ideas for five potential research projects:

- A new business venture for the high street.
- A study of the key attraction on the high street.

- A study of perceptions of the high street. (It doesn't say whose perceptions. It might be the perceptions of shoppers, or shopkeepers, perhaps the perceptions of both, or perhaps the perceptions of another group entirely.)
- A critical analysis of the provision for shoppers on the high street.
- A study of footfall, or pedestrian flows on the high street.

In the second spidergram we can see that the student who created it is thinking about designing a research project around developing a new product. This student is interested in new product development. The five ideas depicted in the spidergram are as follows:

- An idea for a research project based on the development of a new business model for web-based products.
- An idea for a farmer's market for Illingford high street.
- An idea for the development of a marketing campaign for a new (fictitious) girl band, 'It Glitters'.
- An idea for a research project focused on the development of new membership products for the (fictitious) Willowbrook Cricket Club (above).
- An idea for a research project focused on the development of a generic induction programme for small businesses, 'The essential guide to induction: A training programme for small businesses'.

Having read through all of these ideas for research projects, are there any ideas that appeal to you? If not, the ideas presented here may suggest ideas for research projects to you that you do find interesting.

REAL WORLD RESEARCH

How theory influences research

The journal article outlined below is from the journal *Marketing Theory*. In the article, the authors explore the old record collections of their participants as a means to examining the ways in which their participants structure or construct their own identities. The study draws on, and makes a contribution to, consumer research theory. The study is particularly useful in that it illustrates that data for research are everywhere; and as researchers, what we need is the skill and imagination to be able to identify valid data and then the skill to use it to full effect in research projects.

'Identity, consumption and narratives of socialization', Shankar, A., Elliot, R. and Fitchett, J. A. (2009)

According to the article: 'numerous studies have demonstrated that possessions symbolize issues of identity (e.g. Belk, 1988; Csikezentmihalyi and Rochberg-Halton, 1981; and Ditmar, 1992), but as people progress through the stages of their lives, as their identities develop and change, many, if not most, of their possessions come and go as a result. Through use and over time, possessions get worn out or outgrown, or are simply "not me" anymore'.

The article continues, 'unlike other possessions that come and go, we identified records and CDs as a suitable site to explore the processes of identity formation and development. The highly symbolic nature of music means that its consumption represents an ideal site though which to examine the development of identity. Simon Frith (1996a: 110), the world-renowned sociologist of rock, argues that "music seems to be a key to identity, because it offers so intensely a sense of both self and others, of the subjective in the collective". From the perspective of the individual, listening to music performs a number of functions, including the management of self-identity, interpersonal relationships, and mood (Hargreaves and North, 1999). For example, the consumption of music, and especially love songs, "offer people the romantic terms to articulate, and so experience their emotions" (Frith, 1988: 123); they provide people with ready-made narratives to enable them to give meaning to their emotions of love, "to place ourselves within imaginative cultural narratives" (Frith, 1996b: 275). Music in this sense, is a Foucaldian technology of self, enabling "emotional work" and the care of self to be carried out (De Nora, 1999: 37). At the social level, the music that people like, the bands that they see perform live, and the records that they buy, symbolize the social groups that they belong to, and, in so doing, those groups that they reject or do not want to belong to (Bourdieu, 1984).'

'Consequently, we suggest, that a person's past of popular music, embodied or represented in his or her records, is a site through which to examine the historical and social dynamics of identity. Our participants were selected because they had kept many, but inevitably not all, of their records since their childhood. Now in their forties, these records represent a document of their lives (Plummer, 2001).'

'We pursued a narrative approach to data collection that assumes that telling and/or writing stories has an ontological status. This means that the process of telling stories is an act of creation and construction and not simply an act of remembering or retelling. In this view, the goal of the researcher is to help the participant in this process, and consequently we encouraged our participants to reflect on their old records, play and listen to them again, and then discuss these reflections with the researcher (Shankar et al., 2009).'

'A convenience sample of 12 people was approached and asked to take part in this research – the main criterion for selection simply being that they still had their old records.'

The researchers detail that the process of data collection was two-fold. In the first place the participants were asked to put their records into what were for them meaningful piles. Then they were to listen to the records while speaking and recording their thoughts about the records. The tapes were transcribed by the researchers and the themes related to issues of identity which emerged from the transcripts were used to inform the in-depth one-to-one interviews which the researchers subsequently conducted with the participants.

The researchers outline some very interesting theories of consumption throughout the article, and they conclude the article with some insights into new business models for digitized and web-based music.

The research question or issue in this research is interesting. So too is the population of the research and the criterion for inclusion in the research. The theoretical framework for the study is clearly developed and clearly outlined in the article. The methodology and data collection methods used in this research are also interesting and they are clearly explained in the article. What is evident is the manner in which the research emerged from a sound theoretical base, and the way in which in turn the research makes a contribution to that body of knowledge.

The researchers conceptualized a very simple research project which became complex through the scholarly way in which the researchers engaged with the different steps of the research process; with the review of the literature, with the development of the research methodology, with their engagement with data gathering and data analysis, and with the insight that they brought to the process of analysing the data and concluding the research.

References

Shankar, A., Elliot, R. and Fitchett, J.A. (2009) Identity, consumption, and narratives of identity', Marketing Theory, 9(1): 75 © 2009 by Sage Publications. Reprinted with permission.

The article explored above demonstrates each stage of the research process, and also clearly shows all of the elements of the research proposal. The rest of this chapter is focused on the different stages and elements of the research proposal and culminates with an example of a student research proposal.

A CONCEPTUAL FRAMEWORK: THE FIRST STEP

The conceptual framework is the first of the four frameworks in the four frameworks approach to research, as outlined in Chapter 2. The conceptual framework is contained in the research statement or research question. In a properly conceptualized research statement or question, the entire conceptual framework for the research project should be stated in one sentence. This one sentence should contain all of the key concepts of the research project.

Drawing on the spidergrams detailed above, it is useful here to explore the conceptual frameworks of the ideas for research projects presented in them.

In the cricket club example (Figure 5.2), a useful conceptual framework might be as follows:

> *This research project is a case study designed to examine the branding of Willowbrook Cricket Club.*

Another example might be:

> *This research project is a case study designed to produce a new marketing campaign for Willowbrook Cricket Club.*

Another example might be:

> *This research project is a survey designed to explore perceptions of the members of Willowbrook Cricket Club of the image and branding of the club.*

As can be seen from these examples, each research project is expressed in one sentence which captures all of the key concepts and issues in the project and also contains an expression of the methodology to be used. One of the studies uses a survey methodology while the other two use case study methodology.

Each research project is a relatively simple study. As has been said many times, it is a good idea to begin with a very clear simple research statement or question. Each or any of the research projects outlined above would be a useful starting point for any student. Through their engagement with the relevant literature, and their development of a methodological framework for the project, their engagement with the analysis of the data gathered, the simple project outlined above would develop into a complex and scholarly work.

Let us take the next spidergram and attempt to develop those research ideas into conceptual frameworks for research projects. The next spidergram (Figure 5.3) is concerned with the WWF. The issues that emerged were:

- issues of awareness of the fund
- issues of perceptions of the fund
- the issue of the branding of the fund
- the market presence of the fund.

Appropriate conceptual frameworks for these issues and ideas are as follows.

> *This research project is an image-based research project designed to measure brand awareness among undergraduates at Hazelbrook University of the brand of the WWF.*

Another example might be:

> *This research project is a survey of perceptions of the WWF among 50 shoppers in Hazelbrook Shopping Centre, Illingford.*

Another example might be:

> *This research project is a case study designed to critically examine the web presence of the WWF.*

Another example might be:

> *This research project is a survey examining awareness of and perceptions of the WWF among students at Hazelbrook University.*

Once again, each of the research statements detailed above contains all of the key concepts in the research project and provides an appropriate conceptual framework for the research project. Each of the research statements contains a statement of the methodology to be used in the research. Each of the research statements is simple and concise.

Let us consider the final spidergram (Figure 5.4) which focused on developing ideas for a research project around a study of a high street. An example of a research statement for such a project might be as follows:

> *This research project is a case study of Illingford High Street with a view to producing a new development plan for that high street.*

Each of the sample research statements outlined above represents an appropriate research statement for a research project for business studies. You could adapt any of these research statements to your own research idea, and in this way produce a good, simple and clear statement for your own research project.

REFINING RESEARCH IDEAS

Every research idea needs to be properly defined and refined. It often happens that students have really great ideas for their research projects, but those ideas are too big, too broad or too ambitious. Telling yourself, and your thesis supervisor, that you want to examine your cricket club, or you want to study the WWF, or you want to study your home town for your research project is great. It means that you know at least what it is you want to study, and this is often a big step forward. However, this is just your research idea. You now need to get from your research idea to a properly defined and refined research project. For example, where studying your hometown is your research idea, 'a case study of Illingford High Street with a view to producing a new development plan for that high street' is your specific research project.

It is important to understand clearly the difference between research ideas and research projects. Your research idea is the broad area within which you want to work. Your research project is your carefully defined and refined research statement or question. It is the conceptual framework for your research project and it contains all of the key ideas, all of the key concepts of your research project. Use the research statement/question to help you maintain your focus. This is not to say that your research will not grow or develop. It will and it should. But every shift and change in the research must be reflected in a shift and change in the research statement/question.

It is worth spending as much time as is necessary at the conceptualizing stage of a research project, because this will save you time in the long run. It is better to spend time thinking about it and reflecting on it at the start and ensuring that when you do begin to work on the research that you are working on the right research project.

This level of engagement with your research project will facilitate the development of a research project of the depth and complexity appropriate to your course of study. This reflective engagement with your research project will help to ensure that, from the start, you design and develop the right research project for you. Remember it is essential that you have the support of your thesis supervisor for your research idea, your research statement/question, your research project.

LIMITING THE SCOPE OF A RESEARCH PROJECT

One of the most critical steps in any research project is the process of limiting its scope. The critical question is whether or not the research is do-able, given the resources available. If you remember, in Chapter 1 we defined a researchable problem as one where the researcher has the time, money, and the access to the data required to complete the project. If the research project is one assignment of many to be completed in the course of the academic year, then there are implications in terms of the amount of time available for the research project. This will obviously have implications for the scope and size of the project.

The word count allowed for the research project is a useful indicator of the expected scope of the project. Clearly a research project of 10 000 words will be of a different magnitude to a research project of 20 000 words or 50 000 words. It is useful, in developing a sense of the scope of a project, to have some sense of what is expected from the research. You should be able to answer the following questions:

- What is the word count allocated to the work?
- Is the research for an undergraduate degree or a postgraduate degree?
- Are you tasked with simply designing a research project, or do you have to also conduct the research, to gather and analyze data and produce findings?
- Are you restricted in any way in terms of the kind of research you can undertake? Are you, for example, expected to engage in survey research?

It is important to be very clear on the standard expected, the magnitude or scope expected, and any expectations or requirements in terms of populations, methodologies and data gathering techniques.

It is also important to know what it is that you, as the researcher, want to accomplish with the research. Once you know what is expected, and what it is that you want to do, it often becomes somewhat easier to decide on which particular research project to develop.

AIMS AND OBJECTIVES

When you have the fully and properly conceptualized research statement or question, the next step is to develop aims and objectives. For the sake of simplicity and clarity, you can re-state your research statement/question as an aim. Your project then has one aim.

For example, your research statement reads as follows:

> *This research project is a case study of Illingford High Street with a view to producing a development plan for that high street.*

Then the aim of your research reads as follows:

> *The aim of this research is to develop a case study of Illingford High Street with a view to producing a development plan for that high street.*

Another example of re-stating the research statement or question as the aim of the project is as follows. First detail the research statement:

> *This research project is a survey examining awareness of and perceptions of the WWF among students at Hazelbrook University.*

Aim of your research
To keep things simple, the aim of your research is your research statement/ question re-stated as an aim.

Then state the **aim of your research** as follows:

> *The aim of this research is to examine awareness of and perceptions of the WWF among students at Hazelbrook University.*

This simple approach of re-stating the well-conceptualized research statement or question as the aim of the research project helps to maintain the focus of the research.

The **objectives of the research** flow from the aim of the research. They are not additional aims, but the steps you, as the researcher, are going to take in order to accomplish the aim of the research. An example of an aim and objectives is as follows:

Objectives of the research
The steps the researcher takes in order to accomplish the aim of the research.

> *The aim of this research is to develop a case study of Illingford High Street with a view to producing a new development plan for that high street.*

The objectives of the research are as follows:

- In the first place Illingford High Street will be mapped, and all of the businesses on the high street will be detailed on the map.
- An analysis will then be undertaken of the nature of all of the businesses on the high street, any gaps in retail and service provision will be identified.
- The perspectives of the owners and managers of the businesses on the high street will be gathered in terms of the development needs of the high street.

- The perspectives of the local government representatives will be gathered in terms of the development needs of the high street and in terms of any development plans already in existence for the high street.

- The perspectives of the general population of the High Street will be gathered in terms of thoughts and/or ideas they might have for the development of the high street.

- Finally, following a detailed analysis of the data above, a new development plan for the high street will be created and presented.

As you can see, six objectives were conceptualized and outlined and they flow from the aim.

Let us now consider the idea for research on the WWF. An example of the aim and objectives of one of the studies is as follows:

The aim of the research is to examine awareness of and perceptions of the WWF among students at Hazelbrook University.

The objectives of the research are as follows:

- To examine levels of awareness of the WWF among students at Hazelbrook University.

- To examine perceptions of the WWF among students at Hazelbrook University.

As you can see, this research project has only two objectives. Two objectives are enough for this research project. They will allow the researcher to accomplish the aim of the research.

In general, it is a good idea to have no less than two objectives and no more than six objectives.

Sometimes conceptualizing the objectives of the research project can take as long as conceptualizing the research statement. It is important to take time and to engage actively and reflectively with the process of developing appropriate objectives for the research. Remember, the objectives of the research are essentially the steps you are going to undertake in order to accomplish the aim of the research. You should not include reviewing literature as an objective of the research, or outlining an appropriate methodology, or creating and developing a bibliography. These are all aspects of the research process that every researcher must complete. The objectives of any research project are specific to that project.

In an academic environment, the researcher is relatively free to decide on the topic of the research. It is important not to be overly ambitious. Remember that the researcher must accomplish whatever they set out to achieve. It is important that the researcher creates for themselves an acceptable research project that is meaningful to them, and which they can comfortably accomplish within the time constraints of the project.

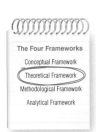

The Four Frameworks
Conceptual Framework
Theoretical Framework
Methodological Framework
Analytical Framework

CREATE A THEORETICAL FRAMEWORK FOR A PROJECT, AND PROVIDE A SAMPLE LITERATURE REVIEW

The second framework of the four frameworks approach to the research project is the theoretical framework. The theoretical framework for the research project is contained, as detailed in Chapter 4 of this textbook, in the literature review.

The conceptual framework for the research project, contained in the well-conceptualized research statement or question, gives the researcher direction in terms of their reading for the literature review. The researcher starts by developing a search strategy which is based on the key concepts in the conceptual framework. If, for example as in the research project explored above, your research statement reads as follows: this research project is a case study of Illingford High Street with a view to producing a development plan for that high street. Then your key concepts are: high street; small town (Illingford); development plan; development plan for a high street; development plan for a high street in a small town.

These key concepts are the focus of your research, and consequently of your literature search.

A sample literature review, which is what you are required to write for a research proposal, is a sample, or a small example, of the actual or proposed literature review. In general, the sample literature review would consist of 300–800 words, depending on the overall word count given for the research proposal. If you wish to know what a literature review looks like, you can read any of the journal articles presented and discussed throughout this textbook. They all have good literature reviews. Remember that a literature review is not a listing of relevant literature; it is a review of relevant literature. Reviewing literature in the context of a research project involves reading the literature relevant to the research project, and critically evaluating it.

It is not really possible to finally outline a research statement for a research project until you have undertaken some reading of the literature. Until you have undertaken the reading around a topic, you cannot know what is known, and what is not known on a topic and where the focus of your research should be. When you are familiar with the literature, then you can create and develop a useful research project, one that makes a meaningful contribution to knowledge.

The Four Frameworks

Conceptual Framework

Theoretical Framework

Methodological Framework

Analytical Framework

Methodological framework
An outline and a justification of the methodology selected for the research project; e.g. justification of population, sample.

OUTLINE A METHODOLOGICAL FRAMEWORK FOR A RESEARCH PROJECT

The **methodological framework** for the research project is the third framework within the four frameworks approach. It is fully detailed in the chapter on research methodology in the thesis or in the report of the research. In general, this is Chapter 3 of the thesis, or the written account of the research. A synopsis of the methodological framework is presented in the research proposal.

The first element of the methodological framework is the research methodology selected by the researcher for the research project. As you know, the researcher does not arbitrarily select the research methodology for the project. The appropriate methodology is indicated to the researcher by the nature of the research, the kind of data required for the study, the population of the study, and the geographic spread of the population. As is explained in detail in Chapter 4 of this textbook, implicit in the statement of the methodology and methods is a statement of the philosophical framework within which the study is embedded. The philosophical framework makes ontological assumptions about the nature of reality, and epistemological assumptions about knowledge and the kind of knowledge to be created by the study.

YOUR RESEARCH

Common research problems

Beginner researchers are often confused as to what is required of them in producing a research project. A template or a guide for your research can help resolve a lot of this confusion.

It is always a good idea to try to find a published research project, or two or three such projects, in books or in journal articles, which have researched the phenomenon you intend to research. You can then use these published research projects as guides or templates for your own research. From these research projects you will get a good example of a literature review, some good insights into research design, and some useful ideas for the methodology for your own research, some helpful insights into the proper approach to data analysis and some guidance in terms of outlining findings, drawing conclusions and making recommendations.

The templates will also help you by providing a guide to the writing, structuring and referencing of a research project.

If the study has a human **population** this will have a substantial influence on the design of the study. If the population of the study is big, a **sample** may be drawn from the population. A sample is a small subset of a population, said to be representative in some way of the population. The process of selecting a population for a research project and the different sampling methods are dealt with in detail in Chapter 8, 'Understanding Research Methods, Populations and Sampling'. In the research proposal, what is needed is a statement of the research methodology, a description of the population of the study, the number of people in the population, and the size of the sample drawn from the population, as well as an outline of the sampling method used (see Chapter 8).

Some detail of the data collection methods to be used in the research is given in the research proposal. The data collection methods are named and explained. The questions asked are detailed, explained and justified.

Four important issues/concepts to keep in mind when writing a research proposal are the issues of validity and reliability, the concept of triangulation, and the ethical issues and potential ethical issues in the proposed research. The concept of validity in research, as defined in Chapter 2 of this textbook, is a question of how valid the research is, how logical, how truthful, how robust, how sound, how reasonable, how meaningful and how useful. The term reliability in research, as defined in Chapter 2 of this textbook, relates to the degree to which the research can be repeated while obtaining consistent results. Triangulation in research, as defined in Chapter 2 of this textbook, involves the use of more than one approach to the research. Chapter 3 of this textbook deals in detail with research ethics.

> **Population**
> Every person who, or every entity which, could be included in the research.

> **Sample**
> A sample is a subset of a population. If probability sampling is used, the sample said to be representative of the population.

DEVELOPING A RESEARCH PROPOSAL

The following is a template for the research proposal. The case study at the end of this chapter provides an actual example of a research proposal.

TEMPLATE FOR A RESEARCH PROPOSAL

This research project is a case study of Illingford High Street with a view to producing a new development plan for that high street.

Aim and objectives

The aim of this research is to conduct a case study of Illingford High Street with a view to producing a development plan for that high street. The objectives of the research are as follows:

- In the first place Illingford High Street will be mapped, and all of the businesses on the high street detailed on the map.

- An analysis will be undertaken of the nature of all of the businesses on the high street, with a view to exploring possible areas for development.

- The perspectives of the owners and managers of the businesses on the high street will be gathered in terms of the development needs of the high street.

- The perspectives of the local government representatives will be gathered in terms of the development needs of the high street, and in terms of establishing if any development plans already exist for the high street.

- The perspectives of the general population of the high street will be explored in terms of any thought or ideas they might have for the development of the high street.

- Finally, following an analysis of the data above, a new development plan for the high street will be developed and presented.

Sample literature review

Read Chapter 6 of this textbook 'Reviewing the Literature'. See also the sample literature review in the case study presented at the end of this chapter.

Research methodology

The research methodology is a case study. (You must detail, explain and justify the research methodology proposed for the research. In this proposal you would explain what a case study is, and why it is the appropriate methodology for this research project. In doing this, you have to read about this methodology in the research methodology textbooks and in your writing you have to try to demonstrate your scholarship in relation to this methodology. You apply the theoretical knowledge you have developed about case study methodology to the research project you are undertaking. For an example, read the research methodology section of the case study at the end of this chapter.

Detail the population of the study, if the study has a human population.

Population of the study (this is the subheading)
Detail, explain and justify the proposed population, sample and sampling method.

Data collection methods (this is the subheading)
Describe and justify the data collection methods to be used.

Context for the research (this is the subheading).
Describe the context for the research.

The context for the research would read for example as follows:

This research project is being undertaken for the award of BSc. in Management at the University of Newforge. The focus of the research is on Illingford High Street. Illingford is a town in Castleward County. The town has a population of 20 000 people. The high street in the town has grown a little in the past five years. Five years ago, there were 20 businesses on Illingford High Street. Currently there are 25 businesses on the high street. While there are signs of growth and development in the town and on the high street, there is scope for further growth and development. This research project is designed to produce a new development plan for Illingford High Street.

(See also context for the research in the case study detailed at the end of this chapter.)

Finally the rationale for the research.

Rationale for the research (this is the subheading)

(see rationale for the research detailed in the case study outlined at the end of this chapter.)

Tom's research project (using a documentary analysis methodology)

Mobile phone shop © Yuri Arcurs/Shutterstock

Tom is undertaking a part-time degree in Business Studies. He works full-time for a recruitment agency. Tom has decided to focus his research project on the agency's business plans. He has been given access to the most recent business plans of the company, the business plans covering the past 3 years. Tom intends to use the three business plans as data in his research. He has decided to use documentary analysis as his research methodology. Tom has prepared the following research proposal.

This research project will critically examine the business plans of the past 3 years of Company A

(the name has been changed in order to maintain confidentiality), an SME selling mobile phones. The methodology to be used in the study is documentary analysis.

Aim and objectives

The aim of the study is to critically examine the business plans of the past 3 years of Company A.

The objectives of the study are as follows:

- to examine any changes and/or developments in the plans over the 3 years
- to highlight any shortcomings in the business plans
- to highlight any particular strengths in the business plans
- to determine the effectiveness of the business plans
- to provide recommendations for the drawing up of business plans in the future.

Sample literature review

There are very many different kinds of business plans, and business plans are written for many purposes and for many audiences. The business plans this research is concerned with are business plans written as guides for the management of the business. Business plans are important. They provide a complete guide to the strategic management of the business. They signal important messages about care, diligence and effective management within the company.

This literature review will focus in particular on business plans for SMEs. The review will consider the determinants of good business plans as they are presented in the literature. The review will focus on strategies for effectiveness in business plans, and will highlight in particular those strategies deemed in the literature to be most effective.

The ultimate purpose of developing a business plan, according to Abrams and Barrow (2008), is to have a successful business. DeThomas and Derammerlaere (2008), suggest that the components of a complete business plan should include an industry analysis, a market and sales analysis, a marketing plan, an operating plan, an organization plan and a financial plan. These key components of the business plan have been reduced by Prinson (2008), to three elements: the organizational plan, the marketing plan and the financial plan.

The well-written business plan, according to Prinson (2008), provides a pathway to profit for any new business. She states that the business plan, to be of value, must be up-to-date, and it must provide detailed information on the company's operations, as well as its projections (see also Johnson, 1993 and Blackwell, 1996). According to DeThomas and Derammelaere (2008), the business plan's assumptions, forecasts and projections should be clearly stated and they should be supported with evidence, explanations and detail as to their basis.

In a study of owner-managers of small firms in Sheffield in the UK, Richbell *et al.* (2006), found a correlation between high levels of education and possession of a business plan. In addition, they found that possession of a business plan had a positive association with a growth orientation. In other words, those business managers with business plans also had an orientation towards growth for their businesses.

There are clearly advantages in having business plans. However, in order to be effective, business plans must be well-written and comprehensive and thorough, and the assumptions, forecasts and predictions outlined in the plans must be supported with detailed, accurate and up-to-date data.

The research proposed here is a critical analysis of the business plans for the past 3 years of Company A.

Research methodology

The proposed methodology for this research project is documentary analysis (see *The Methodological Pyramid*, Quinlan (2010), Chapter 4). Documentary analysis is a relatively unobtrusive form of research, it does not require engagement with human participants, and it is one that provides opportunities for valuable and often unique insight into organizational policy and practice. Jameson (2009), citing research on Enron and Lehman Brothers, highlighted the utility of documentary analysis in providing important insights into the role that communication plays in major business events. Any document, such as journals, letters, records, can provide the data for a documentary analysis methodology. In this study, the documents to be analyzed are the business plans for the past 3 years of Company A. The data from the documents will be analyzed using a content analysis approach.

According to Neuman (2000), content analysis is a technique for analysing the content of texts. The texts in this case are the documents detailed above. The content within a content analysis approach to data analysis is any content, texts, images, figures, tables, charts, graphs, in the documents.

The proposed methodology is an appropriate methodology for this research project. The project is designed to critically examine the business plans for the past 3 years of Company A. Therefore the study is a study of different documents. As this is the case, a documentary analysis methodology is an appropriate methodology.

Context for the research

The research is being undertaken for a BSc. in Business Studies. The research will be undertaken in Company A. Company A is the workplace of the researcher. Permission to carry out the research has been formally given by the CEO of the company.

Rationale for the research

The research is being undertaken in order to provide a critical assessment of the business plans over the past 3 years of Company A. The research will provide insight into the effectiveness of the business plans of Company A. The research will also produce recommendations for the development of business plans in the future in Company A. A copy of the completed thesis will be placed in the university library and will be available to other researchers. The hope for the research is that it will make a valid contribution to knowledge in relation to the writing of business plans for SMEs.

References

Abrams, R. and Barrow, P. (2008) *The Successful Business Plan, Secrets and Strategies*, Capstone Publishing Ltd., Chichester: John Wiley & Sons.

Blackwell, E. (1996) *How to Prepare a Business Plan* (2nd edn), London: Kogan Page.

DeThomas, A. and Derammelaere, S. (2008) *Writing A Convincing Business Plan* (Barron's Business Library), New York: Barron's Educational Series.

Jameson, D.A. (2009) 'Economic crises and financial disasters: The role of business communication', *Journal of Business Communication* 46: 499–509

Johnson, R. (1993) *The Perfect Business Plan: All You Need To Get It Right First Time*, The Perfect Series, London: Century Business.

Neuman, W.L. (2000) *Social Research Methods: Quantitative and Qualitative Approaches* (4th edn), Boston, MA: Allyn & Bacon.

Prinson, L. (2008) *Anatomy of a Business Plan: The Step-by-Step Guide to Building a Business and Securing Your Company's Future*, California: Out of Your Mind … and into the Marketplace Publishing Company.

Richbell, S.M., Watts, H.D. and Wardle, P. (2006) 'Owner-managers and business planning in the small firm', *International Small Business Journal* 24(5): 496–514.

Question Based on your reading of the methodology and methods outlined in the research proposal above, what can you say about the epistemological and ontological assumptions underpinning this research? (You would need to have read Chapter 4 of this textbook to be able to answer this question.)

CHAPTER REVIEW

T his chapter explores the development of research proposals. The chapter begins with some suggestions for ways of developing ideas for research projects and emphasizes the fact that ideas for research projects are everywhere, and that researchers simply need enough imagination to be able to see the possibilities that exist within their own work and life experience for research projects. The issues and potential problems in designing research projects and in carrying out research projects are considered. The process of generating conceptual frameworks for research projects are explored in some detail. The processes through which research ideas are defined and refined are examined and the means through which the scope of a research project can be limited are explored. The theoretical framework for the research project is explained briefly, as is the methodological framework. These are dealt with in detail in later chapters of this textbook. The different elements of the methodological framework are briefly considered for the purposes of developing a research proposal; those elements are research methodology, population of the research, and data collection methods. The issues of validity and reliability are considered in relation to the research proposal; so too is the issue of triangulation and the area of research ethics. The chapter ends with a template for a research proposal.

Now update your interactive research diary with your notes and findings at www.cengage.co.uk/quinlan. Complete the activities provided to reinforce your understanding of this chapter.

END OF CHAPTER QUESTIONS

1 What are the key elements of a research proposal?

2 What constitutes a viable research project?

3 Outline three research statements/questions for three viable research projects.

4 Explain why these research projects are 'viable'.

5 Develop an aim and a series of objectives for each of the research projects.

6 Propose a research methodology for each of the three research projects.

7 Explain why the proposed methodologies are appropriate.

8 Explain what is meant by literature in the context of a research project.

9 What is a theoretical framework in the context of a research project?

10 Which framework of the four frameworks approach to the research project provides direction for the theoretical framework?

11 Develop and detail a search strategy for literature for the literature review for your research project.

REFERENCES

Abrams, R. and Barrow, P. (2008) *The Successful Business Plan, Secrets and Strategies*, Capstone Publishing Ltd., Chichester: John Wiley & Sons.

Blackwell, E. (1996) *How to Prepare a Business Plan* (2nd edn), London: Kogan Page.

DeThomas, A. and Derammelaere, S. (2008) *Writing A Convincing Business Plan* (Barron's Business Library), New York: Barron's Educational Series.

Jameson, D.A. (2009) 'Economic crises and financial disasters: The role of business communication', *Journal of Business Communication* 46: 499–509

Johnson, R. (1993) *The Perfect Business Plan: All You Need To Get It Right First Time*, The Perfect Series, London: Century Business.

Mazza, C., Sahlin-Andersson, K. and Strandgaard Pedersen, J. (2005) 'European constructions of an American model: Developments of four MBA programmes', *Management Learning*, 36(4): 471–491.

Neuman, W.L. (2000) *Social Research Methods: Quantitative and Qualitative Approaches* (4th edn), Boston, MA: Allyn & Bacon.

Prinson, L. (2008) *Anatomy of a Business Plan: The Step-by-Step Guide to Building a Business and Securing Your Company's Future*, California: Out of Your Mind … and into the Marketplace Publishing Company.

Richbell, S.M., Watts, H.D. and Wardle, P. (2006) 'Owner-managers and business planning in the small firm', *International Small Business Journal* 24(5): 496–514.

Shankar, A., Elliot, R. and Fitchett, J.A. (2009) Identity, consumption, and narratives of identity', *Marketing Theory*, 9(1): 75.

Thorpe, V. (2009) 'The end of the age of FREE?', *The Observer*, 10 May.

RECOMMENDED READING

Bell, J. (2005) *Doing your Research Project*, Open University Press.

Collis, J. and Hussey, R. (2009) *Business Research: A Practical Guide for Undergraduate and Postgraduate Students*, Ch. 7, 'Writing Your Research Proposal', Houndsmill: Palgrave Macmillan.

Punch, K.F. (2005) *Developing Effective Research Proposals*, London: Sage.

Robson, C. (2000) *Real World Research*, Ch. 3, 'Developing Your Idea', Oxford: Blackwell.

White, B. (2000) *Dissertation Skills*, Ch. 6, 'Writing a Proposal', London: Cengage.

CHAPTER 6

REVIEWING THE LITERATURE

LEARNING OBJECTIVES

At the end of this chapter the student should be able to:

- Source appropriate literature.

- Evaluate the quality and utility of literature sourced.

- Review literature.

- Create a theoretical framework.

- Write a literature review.

RESEARCH SKILLS

At the end of this chapter the student should, using the exercises on the accompanying online platform, be able to:

- Create a theoretical framework for a given research project.

- Critique a given literature review.

The aim of this chapter is to consider and explain the literature review. The chapter begins with a definition of 'literature' in the context of research. This is followed by a discussion on where to source literature and a discussion on the importance of exercising discernment in relation to literature he/she reviewed. There are explanations of how to select appropriate literature and how to use literature. The way in which to construct the theoretical framework, the second of the frameworks within the four frameworks approach to the research project, is also discussed. There is a demonstration of how to write a literature review. In the case study at the end of the chapter two sample literature reviews are presented, the first is an example of a poorly written literature review, the second an example of a better literature review.

INTRODUCTION

Literature
Research that has already been carried out and published of research.

Literature in the context of research is research that has already been carried out and published. Such research is published in journal articles, books, theses, government reports, the reports of NGOs, conference reports, online and in the media. The literature in a field or area of research constitutes the body of knowledge in that field or area of research; it contains the theory in that field. The researcher undertakes a review of the literature in order to:

- develop their own expertise and scholarship on the topic or phenomenon
- to establish what is known and what is not known in the field
- highlight gaps in the knowledge base in the area or on the topic; the researcher may decide to use their research project to try to fill in one or more of those gaps
- create a theoretical framework for the research project, contained in the literature review.

Figure 6.1, the model of the research process, suggests that the literature review is the fourth stage in the research process. In fact, the process of reviewing the literature begins as soon as the researcher has decided to undertake a research project. As soon as s/he decides on an area of research, or on a particular topic within an area of research, the researcher begins to read literature around that topic or that broad area. Reading for the research project begins as soon as the researcher decides to undertake a research project, and the reading continues all the way through the research project.

The news article detailed on page 151 was taken from *The Guardian Online* (**www.guardian.co.uk**). *The Guardian Online* has a number of blogs under various headings; one of the headings is Science and Technology. Under this heading there are five subheadings, one of which is *Datablog*. *Datablog* is a very interesting blog for any researcher, particularly a beginner researcher. The blog presents all kinds of data, and it presents it in different ways. In the article detailed below, *Datablog* presents data designed to measure well-being for each of the G20 nations. In the first instance the data are presented in table format, and then the same data are presented in a visual format (see Table 6.1). The economic philosophy outlined in the article is both engaging and timely, and the two different representations of the same data provide a useful learning exercise. In later chapters of this textbook we will focus in more depth on the different ways of representing data.

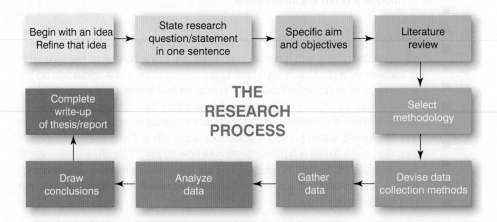

Figure 6.1   The research process

Do you know why data are sometimes presented in tables and sometimes presented in graphs and figures? If you study the table and the figure above, you may be able to answer this question. There are a lot of data on many different topics in *Datablog*. If you spend some time browsing this website, you will learn a great deal about data and about the different ways of presenting it. You might also get some new ideas for your own research project.

THE VALUE OF GOOD RESEARCH

Research in the media

Amartya Sen, Nobel Prize winning economist © Jeff Morgan 10/Alamy. Now update your interactive research diary with your notes and findings at www.cengage.co.uk/quinlan. Complete the activities provided to reinforce your understanding of this chapter.

'There's more to life than GDP: Nations can be ranked in many different ways – money is just one of them', *The Guardian,* 2009. Posted by Rogers, S. © Guardian News & Media Ltd 2009.

'It's time to give up our blind faith in economic growth', Chakrabortty, A. *The Guardian,* Sunday 22nd March, 2009 http://www.guardian.co.uk/business/2009/mar/22/gdp-economic-growth-happiness-wellbeing. © Guardian News & Media Ltd 2009.

In the article Charkrabortty argues that 'It's time to give up our blind faith in economic growth. The harsh realities of global warming and financial meltdown have given us an ideal opportunity to look beyond GDP when it comes to assessing how well we are doing.'

He writes, 'For all its prominence, GDP is only one yardstick of economic performance and it is no guide to social progress. It simply indicates the market value of all goods and services produced in an economy. It takes no account of how income is shared out, or of how it is generated. Few would celebrate a boom in costly divorce cases – but it would be great for GDP. And there is mounting evidence that, beyond a certain point, greater prosperity does not make us feel any better. Over the past 50 years, western standards of living have soared, yet survey after survey shows the Britons and Americans are no happier now than they were half a century ago.'

'This focus on growth fails to take account of what the social and psychological evidence tells us,' says the economist Richard Layard. Our well-being depends on three things, he says: family relationships, satisfaction at work and strong communities: 'Many policies to drive up income harm precisely those things from which we derive our quality of life.' Layard wants to make the pursuit of happiness part of government policy – and he's not alone. An all-party parliamentary group on Well-being Economics (including Layard) holds its first meeting today, while next month a commission launched by the French President, Nicolas Sarkozy, and led by Nobel laureates Amartya Sen and Joseph Stiglitz will report on how to incorporate quality of life into objective measures of economic activity.

'Increasing GDP is obviously important in a recession – and it remains essential for the developing world. But over the long run it is unclear why rich countries with static or falling populations – like much of continental Europe – should obsess about earning ever greater levels of income. Why shouldn't they work less, spread their wealth more evenly and enjoy themselves? We may be nearing the condition predicted 160 years ago by John Stuart Mill in his *Principles of Political Economy*, in which he suggested that there is "as much room for improving the Art of Living and much more likelihood of it being improved, when minds ceased to be engrossed by the art of getting on".'

The article goes on and it is worth reading to the end.

References

Guardian (2009) 'There's more to life than GDP', **http://www.guardian.co.uk/news/datablog/2009/mar/24/g20-economics**

Table 6.1   In *Datablog* the first link is called Data: In it the table below is presented. The table contains data on the different countries.

Country	GDP per capita. $. 2009	Life expectancy	Happy planet index (New Economics foundation)	UN human development index	Inequality - Gini coefficient (high score = less equal)
Argentina	9,843.33	75	52.2	0.860	51.3
Australia	50,053.16	82	34.1	0.965	35.2
Brazil	8,168.57	72	48.6	0.807	57
Canada	46,799.36	81	39.8	0.967	32.6
China	3,576.69	73	56	0.762	46.9
France	48,293.08	81	36.4	0.955	32.7
Germany	45,999.09	80	43.8	0.940	28.3
India	1,122.19	63	48.7	0.609	36.8
Indonesia	2,393.20	68	57.9	0.726	34.3
Italy	40,297.96	81	48.3	0.945	36
Japan	37,644.48	83	41.7	0.956	24.9
S.Korea	20,954.72	79	41.1	0.928	31.6
Mexico	11,102.91	74	54.4	0.842	46.1
Russia	14,688.46	66	22.8	0.806	39.9
Saudi Arabia	22,291.33	70	42.7	0.835	41.3
South Africa	6,647.80	55	27.8	0.670	57.8
Turkey	11,193.98	73	41.4	0.798	43.6
United Kingdom	44,719.53	79	40.3	0.942	36
United States	47,335.21	78	28.8	0.950	40.8
SOURCE	IMF	WHO	NEF	UNDP	UNDP

http://spreadsheets.google.com/ccc?key=phNtm3LmDZEMsp17d1VuoJQ. © Guardian News & Media Ltd 2009.

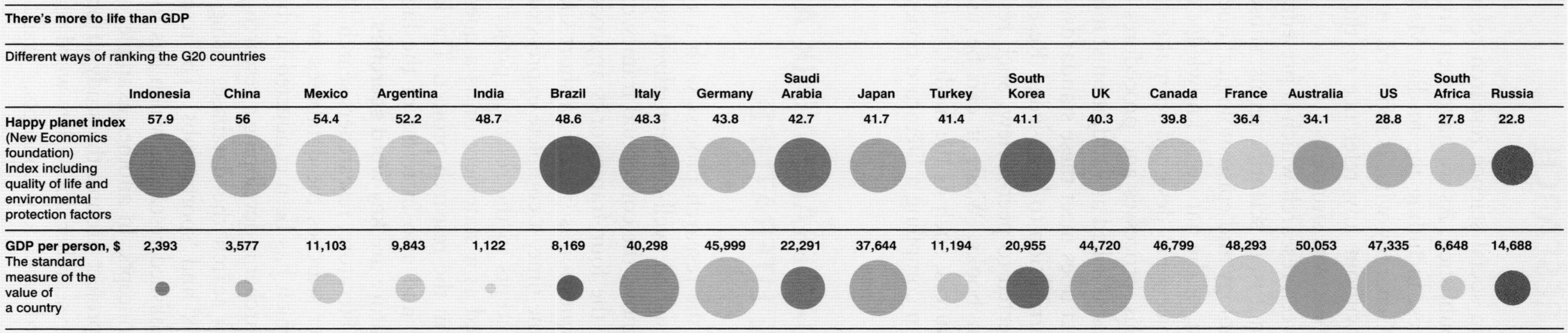

There's more to life than GDP

Different ways of ranking the G20 countries

	Indonesia	China	Mexico	Argentina	India	Brazil	Italy	Germany	Saudi Arabia	Japan	Turkey	South Korea	UK	Canada	France	Australia	US	South Africa	Russia
Happy planet index (New Economics foundation) Index including quality of life and environmental protection factors	57.9	56	54.4	52.2	48.7	48.6	48.3	43.8	42.7	41.7	41.4	41.1	40.3	39.8	36.4	34.1	28.8	27.8	22.8
GDP per person, $ The standard measure of the value of a country	2,393	3,577	11,103	9,843	1,122	8,169	40,298	45,999	22,291	37,644	11,194	20,955	44,720	46,799	48,293	50,053	47,335	6,648	14,688

Figure 6.2   The second link is called Graphic: In the figure below the data from the table above is presented in a visual format. http://image.guardian.co.uk/sys-files/Guardian/documents/2009/03/24/HAPPY_index_DPS_2303.pdf. © Guardian News & Media Ltd 2009.

LITERATURE IN RESEARCH

The word 'literature' in social science research refers to research that has already been carried out and published. As we have seen above, such literature is published in many different places, including the media. Media reports of research projects tend to be very short. Generally what is reported in the media is a brief synopsis of the research, usually without any reference to the theoretical framework within which the research project was situated.

The distinction between research which is presented within its theoretical context and research which is not is, in scientific terms, substantial. In previous chapters we have discussed epistemology and epistemological questions, i.e., questions of knowledge, of what is known, of the nature of knowledge and of the means of knowledge creation. Research projects are designed to make a contribution to some body of knowledge and the rules, processes and procedures of research are rigorous. For a research project to be established as valid, it must meet rigorous scientific standards. When a research project does meet these standards, the findings of the research are accepted as a valid contribution to knowledge. Research which has been established as valid has been subjected to peer-review. Such research is published primarily in journal articles and in books. While it can be useful and interesting to source material from other sources, such as the media, it is primarily these **peer-reviewed sources** that are used in compiling a literature review for a research project.

Peer-reviewed sources
Are published accounts of research which have been subjected to critical review by the peers of the authors of the research.

THE CONCEPTUAL FRAMEWORK AS A GUIDE TO THE REVIEW OF THE LITERATURE

The researcher begins the research process with a research idea and s/he develops this into a properly designed, well-conceptualized research project. The outcome of this process is, as we know, the conceptual framework for the research project. It is the first framework in the four frameworks approach to the research project. The research statement or question is (ideally) a short succinct sentence. It is simple and clear, and is, at the same time, a complete expression of the research project.

Each of the key concepts in the research project is articulated in this sentence, which may be expressed as a statement or as a question. The key concepts are the key words or phrases in the research project. The key words are important in the conceptual framework and also in terms of the literature review. This is because most searches for literature are **key word searches**.

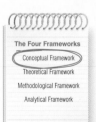

The Four Frameworks
Conceptual Framework
Theoretical Framework
Methodological Framework
Analytical Framework

When searching for literature, researchers search library databases using key word searches. The researcher searches the databases for published research i.e published accounts of research which has been conducted in the same field, on the same topic. For example, if the researcher is developing a research project around a marketing plan for a sports club, they search the databases using those key words, 'marketing', 'marketing plan', 'sports' and 'sports clubs'. The researcher tries to source all of the literature, all of the published research, which has focused on one or more or all of these key words and concepts. In another example, if the researcher is, for instance, developing a research project around the study of brand recognition of a big brand such as the WWF, the researcher does a key word search in the library databases for the following key words and key concepts, 'brands', 'brand recognition', 'World

Key word searches
The researcher uses key words and/or concepts when searching for relevant literature.

Wildlife Fund', 'brand recognition World Wildlife Fund'. You will know from your previous experience in doing **key word** searches in library databases that single word searches such as 'marketing' or 'brands' or 'sports' yield too many results to be useful.

In order to generate useful and thorough key word searches, the researcher develops a **search strategy**. The search strategy can be developed and outlined in the research diary. In the diary the researcher devises and decides on the key word searches. The researcher then carries out the searches and records a summary in the research diary of the results of those searches. The researcher then has a record in the research diary of the searches carried out and a summary of the results of those searches. This can help the researcher to avoid duplicate searches. This exercise also provides a record of searches which the researcher can reflect on when developing ideas for further searches, which may be more complex or more in-depth.

A key objective of the search is that the researcher sources and develops an awareness of all of the literature relevant to their study. In the first place, the researcher identifies all of the relevant literature. Then the researcher sources that literature and saves it in a folder on their own computer. Then the researcher begins the process of reading the literature, developing an understanding of it, and about the body of knowledge represented in the literature. The researcher reads the literature with a view to developing from it a theoretical framework for their own research.

> **search strategy**
> The plan the researcher makes for their search of the body of knowledge for relevant literature for their literature review.

CREATE A THEORETICAL FRAMEWORK

The theoretical framework is the second framework within the four frameworks approach to the research project. Below is the figure of the four frameworks approach that is detailed in Chapter 1 of this textbook (see Figure 1.2, page 6).

Within the figure, each of the frameworks rests on the first framework. So the second framework, the theoretical framework rests on, and emerges from, the conceptual framework. This process is demonstrated in the figure below.

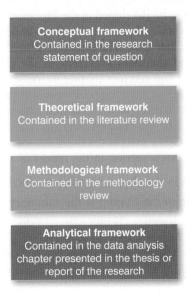

Figure 6.3   The four frameworks

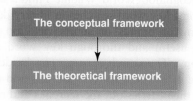

Figure 6.4   The theoretical framework emerges from the conceptual framework

As can be seen from the figure above, the theoretical framework emerges from the conceptual framework. In practice, what this means is that the researcher uses the conceptual framework to provide direction and focus for their literature search, and for the layout and the construction of the theoretical framework.

WRITING THE LITERATURE REVIEW

Structure
The structure of a chapter, or any written work, is the way in which it is organized.

The first thing to be done when starting to write the literature review is to develop a plan for its **structure**. Plan the literature review first, and then write the literature review to that plan. Sketch the structure for the literature review in the research diary. For the literature review the structure will be as follows. To begin with there is the introduction; this is followed by a number of sub-sections and the chapter ends in a summary.

- The introduction is an introduction to the chapter, nothing else, nothing more.
- The summary is a summary of the chapter, nothing else, nothing more.

It is important that the introduction and the summary be effective. The introduction should thoroughly and succinctly introduce the reader to the content of the chapter and to the main argument to be developed in the literature review. The argument will be an argument for the research that you are about to undertake and you will develop it from your critique of the literature. The summary should thoroughly and succinctly summarize the chapter and the main argument of the chapter for the reader. Use journal articles to find brief and succinct chapter introductions and summaries, which you may use as models for your own introductions and summaries.

Each literature review chapter is divided into sub-sections, each of which is headed by a subheading. The subheading indicates the content of the sub-section. The following example details a sample structure for the literature review chapter in a thesis, or the literature review section in the report of the research project.

- The first sub-section in the chapter is the introduction.
- The final sub-section in the chapter is the summary.
- There are then three sub-sections between the introduction and the summary. There might in fact be four or five sub-sections, or even two sub-sections; however, a model of three sub-sections between the first sub-section (which is the introduction) and the final sub-section (which is the summary) generally works well.

The sub-sections in between the introduction and the summary represent the body of the literature review. Here, the researcher presents the theoretical framework for the research project. The main sections of the literature review are each developed around individual subheadings, which are derived from the conceptual framework and the reading of the literature undertaken for the review. The subheadings are presented in the literature review in the order which makes most sense.

Each subheading is carefully conceptualized and developed to reflect the content of that sub-section. Each sub-section contains a carefully developed, cogently expressed and well-laid out argument. Each section contains two, three, four or five paragraphs, each of which contains substantial amounts of information. Finally, each subsequent sub-section further develops the main argument presented in the literature review.

Given this structure, it should be possible to plan the layout of the chapter in great detail before actually beginning to write the chapter. With a very detailed plan, and a comprehensive and critical reading of the literature, the writing of the literature review should be a relatively simple and straightforward task. Everything written in the chapter must be clearly relevant to the research project that you are undertaking and explicitly related to the argument that you are developing in the chapter. The argument that the researcher is expressing in the chapter, ultimately, is an argument for the research that they are carrying out.

RESEARCH IN PRACTICE

Sara's research project

Sara is undertaking a degree in business management. She wants to conduct her research within the area of human resource management. She is particularly interested in recruitment practices. Sara has no way of gaining access to a human resource department within which to conduct her research. As this is the case, Sara has decided to study the recruitment practices of a major company as they are published on the company's website on the Internet. Sara has developed the following research statement for her research project:

 This research project is a content analysis study of the recruitment practices of the BBC (the British Broadcasting Company) as they are outlined on the BBC website.

Given this example of Sara's research statement, the three sub-sections that form the body of Sara's literature review chapter will be drawn from this conceptual framework. The focus of the above study is on recruitment, on recruitment practices, and on recruitment practices in a major media organization, the BBC.

- All of these key concepts, taken from the conceptual framework, are used to guide the search for literature.
- They are used to construct a theoretical framework for the research project.
- They are used to structure the literature review, the chapter that is the literature review.

So in the case of the research project detailed in the conceptual framework outlined above, the chapter that is the literature review could be structured, for example, as shown in Tables 6.2, 6.3 and 6.4.

Table 6.2	Example of structure for the literature review for Sara's research project (based on 5000 word count)
First section 300 words – in 1 paragraph	Introduction (a brief introduction to the chapter and the contents of the chapter)
Second section (first subheading) 1400 words – in 4 paragraphs	The Internet and contemporary recruitment and selection practices
Third section (second subheading) 1400 words – in 4 paragraphs	The use of the Internet and the company website in recruiting employees
Fourth section (third subheading) 1400 words – in 4 paragraphs	Issues in contemporary Internet-based recruitment practices
Fifth section 500 words – in 2 paragraphs Word count total = 5000 words	Summary (a brief summary of the main points and the key argument developed throughout the chapter)

Table 6.3	Example of structure for the literature review for Sara's research project (based on 3000 word count)
First section 200 words – in 1 paragraph	Introduction (a brief introduction to the chapter and the contents of the chapter)
Second section (first subheading) 800 words – in 3 paragraphs	The Internet and contemporary recruitment and selection practices
Third section (second subheading) 800 words – in 3 paragraphs	The use of the Internet and the company website in recruiting employees
Fourth section (third subheading) 800 words – in 3 paragraphs	Issues in contemporary Internet-based recruitment practices
Fifth section 400 words – in 2 paragraphs Word count total = 3000 words	Summary (a brief summary of the main points and the key argument developed throughout the chapter)

Table 6.4	Example of structure for the literature review for Sara's research project (based on 1000 word count)
First section 100 words – in 1 paragraph	Introduction (a brief introduction to the chapter and the contents of the chapter)
Second section (first subheading) 250 words – in 2 paragraphs	The Internet and contemporary recruitment and selection practices
Third section (second subheading) 250 words – in 2 paragraphs	The use of the Internet and the company website in recruiting employees
Fourth section (third subheading) 250 words – in 2 paragraphs	Issues in contemporary Internet-based recruitment practices
Fifth section 150 words – in 1 paragraph Word count total = 1000 words	Summary (a brief summary of the main points and the key argument developed throughout the chapter)

Table 6.5 Approximate word count for the literature review	
In a 20 000 word thesis	Literature review is 5000–7000 words
In a 15 000 word thesis	Literature review is 3500–4000 words
In a 12 000 word thesis	Literature review is 3000 words
In a 10 000 word thesis	Literature review is 2500 words

The Four Frameworks
Conceptual Framework
Theoretical Framework
Methodological Framework
Analytical Framework

The word count given to the literature review is dependent on the word count given to the research project. Table 6.5 details approximate word counts for literature reviews based on the word count of the research project.

This model of the structure of the literature review chapter for the research project, based on the conceptual framework above that Sara developed for her research, demonstrates the simplicity and the utility of the four frameworks approach to the construction and developmentof the research project. This was also demonstrated in Chapter 4 of this textbook when we considered Kate's research project which was situated within the HR department of the SME Green's Biscuits Ltd. This approach to the construction and development of the research project may be applied to any research project. Because the entire research project rests on the conceptual framework, it is critical that this conceptual framework is very well-constructed. It is of the utmost importance that the researcher properly, actively and thoroughly engages with the process of conceptualizing the research project. This active and thorough engagement with the process of conceptualization will produce a well-conceptualized project.

YOUR RESEARCH
Common research problems

The standard of writing

There is an expectation in every academic institution that the students registered in that institution can read and write fluently and properly in the language of the institution. If the language of the institution is English, there is a presumption that the students registered in the institution can write correct English. There is no tolerance of misspellings, poorly constructed sentences or grammatical errors. This rule applies regardless of whether or not English is the first language of the student. Any student who is not confident that their written English is up to the standard required should have their thesis proofread before they submit it for examination. A great many marks are needlessly lost by students to poorly written and badly presented work.

When the researcher uses the conceptual framework as a guide in the literature search, the focus of the research is maintained. While meandering off on tangents through research literature is often a very pleasant and engaging pastime, it can lead to time being wasted, and in the worst-case scenario, can lead to a loss of focus in the research. To avoid losing focus, it is useful to have a copy of the research statement/ question to hand, perhaps written on the first page of your research diary, which you should always have with you when you are working on your research project. Refer to the research statement/question regularly when you are searching for and reading literature. Check that the material you are sourcing and reading is relevant to your research project. If it is not, move on from that literature to literature which is clearly relevant.

When sourcing literature, check the theoretical content of the literature. Ask the following questions:

1 Does the material you are reading clearly have a theoretical framework?

2 Does the material you are reading reference other research?

The literature that you source in or through the university or college library will be the most useful because it will be academic material and will almost certainly have been developed for the purpose of contributing to scientific knowledge.

A quick search of the library, using electronic means, will establish whether a great deal has been written on this topic, or not. It will also establish when the material was written. It is important to establish the seminal authors in any field. These are the authors who made a founding contribution to any area of knowledge. It is also important to establish which contemporary authors are writing on the topic. You need to situate your work in relation to the most up-to-date work. Between the seminal authors and the most up-to-date authors, there may be other authors who have made a noteworthy or significant contribution to the development of the concept that you are researching.

THE VALUE OF GOOD RESEARCH

Focus on content analysis

Content analysis is a research methodology that is used when the research calls for the analysis of the content of any text or set of texts. Using content analysis, researchers search the text for the presence of particular words, phrases and concepts. Any text that is language-based can be used as data in a research project using content analysis as the research methodology. Examples of texts include advertising, records, books, chapters, newspaper content, speeches, transcripts of conversations, advertising.

Content analysis can also be used within a different research methodology as an approach to data analysis. We saw an example of that in the case study at the end of Chapter 5, where Tom in his research proposal used documentary analysis as his research methodology, and content analysis as his approach to analysing his data. The information from Neuman (2000), detailed below, if you remember was quoted in Tom's research proposal.

According to Neuman (2000), content analysis is a technique for analysing the content of texts. Neuman states (2000, 283), that using content analysis the researcher can compare content across different texts and analyze the content using quantitative techniques.

When used quantitatively, content analysis can establish the objective meaning in texts from the manifest content in texts. The researcher interprets what is written in the texts.

Content analysis can also be used qualitatively. When used qualitatively, content analysis can establish the subjective meaning in the latent content in texts. Using content analysis qualitatively, the researcher attempts to read between the lines, and tries to uncover the meaning underlying the written lines of text.

The article detailed below details a study undertaken using content analysis.

'Biting the hand that feeds: Social identity and resistance in restaurant teams', Richards, J. and Marks, A. (2007)

The focus of this study is on teamwork as a means of work organization, and on employee resistance to team-work. The teams the researchers studied were hotel restaurant teams. The lead researcher in the study secured paid employment in a hotel restaurant and he/she carried out the research from this paid position.

The main data collection method used in the study was observation. The researcher observed the phenomenon under investigation, (teamwork and employee resistance to teamwork), and noted those observations in daily entries in a field diary. Data collection for the study went on for 12 weeks. In the end there were over 30 000 words in the field diary. The researchers supplemented their observation data with a study of company documentation.

The daily field diary entries and the company documentation were analyzed using a qualitative content analysis approach. The content of both the diary and the company documentation were analyzed for keywords and phrases and themes. The authors state that the qualitative content analysis approach used in the study provided 'an effective portrayal of the broader culture and work structures in the organization'.

The study is interesting on a number of levels. It is an interesting study carried out using an interest-ing methodology. The field work for the study was covert, the hotel teams studied did not know that they were participating in a research project and were being observed, in a data gathering exercise, for that research. The covert (hidden) nature of the study is considered by the authors and they highlight in their discussion in the journal article the ethical issues in such covert research.

It would be a useful exercise to source the original article and to examine it in relation to the different elements of the research process as they are dealt with in the article, and in particular it would be useful to examine section 4 of the article, the section on methods.

Some useful resources on content analysis include:

The Colorado State University, 'Introduction to content analysis' (**www.writing.colostate.edu/guides/research/content/index.cfm**)

Deacon, D.H., Golding, P., Pickering, M. and Murdock, G. (2007) *Researching Communications: A Practical Guide to Methods in Media and Cultural Analysis*, London: Hodder Arnold.

BBC World Service Trust, 'Using content analysis to measure the influence of media development interventions: Elections training for journalists in Yemen' (**http://downloads.bbc.co.uk/worldservice/trust/pdf/bbcwst_research_series_yemen.pdf**).

Research Methods Knowledge Base, 'Unobtrusive measures (indirect measures, content analysis, and secondary analysis of data') (**www.socialresearchmethods.net/kb.unobtrus.php**>) Accessed 02.06.2010.

References

Richards, J. and Marks, A. (2007) 'Biting the hand that feeds: Social identity and resistance in restaurant teams', *International Journal of Business Science and Applied Management* 2(2): 41–57.

Neuman, W.L. (2000) *Social Research Methods: Qualitative and Quantitative Approaches*, Ch. 3, 'Theory and Research', and Ch. 16, 'Reviewing the Literature and Writing a Report', Boston, MA: Allyn & Bacon.

One question that is often asked by students is 'how much literature'? The short answer to this question is 'a warehouse-full'. However, the researcher must be realistic in terms of what it is possible to accomplish, given the time available for the research.

The expectation on the part of the supervisor(s) and the examiner(s) is that the work will be excellent. The student strives to reach this standard, balancing the requirements of the standard of excellence with the time available for the study

REAL WORLD RESEARCH

How theory influences research

'Employer Preferences for Résumés and Cover Letters', Schullery, N. M., Ickes, L. and Schullery, S. E. (2009)

The abstract of the article reads as follows.

Abstract

'This article reports the results of a survey of employers' preferences for résumé style, résumé delivery method, and cover letters. Employers still widely prefer the standard chronological résumé, with only 3% desiring a scannable résumé. The vast majority of employers prefer electronic delivery, either by email (46%) or at the company's website (38%), with only 7% preferring a paper copy. Cover letters are preferred by a majority (56%). Preferences regarding résumé style and cover letters were independent of national (USA) vs multinational geographic range, company size, type of industry, or respondent's job function. Smaller companies prefer résumé delivery by email, and human resources workers prefer delivery using the company's website.'

The article begins:
'Preparation for employment searches is a standard component of most business communication courses and textbooks. Over recent years, however, numerous anecdotal experiences relayed by student job applicants have caused us to question the wisdom of spending classroom time teaching multiple résumé formats and cover letters. Company representatives at our career fairs have increasingly declined even to accept a printed résumé while speaking with the student. Instead, students are directed to company websites for employment application and résumé submission. There, the applicants are prompted to enter their

education, skills and experience directly into a proprietary series of labelled boxes, which gather information into the employers' databases for sorting convenience. A similar option for prompted entry of résumé information into searchable databases is provided at job websites, such as Monster.com. Students return to the classroom confused about whether they really need a prepared résumé of any kind. The scannable résumé seems to be particularly problematic.'

Then the review of the literature begins:
'In the late 1990s, the scannable format was the most up-to-date style for a résumé (Baker, DeTienne & Smart, 1998; Quible, 1995; Roever & McGaughey, 1997) and is still included in business communication textbooks (e.g., Locker & Kienzler, 2008; Thill & Bovée, 2007). The scannable résumé offered employers the ability to sort large numbers of applicants quickly and without bias by any criteria desired, but not without a price. The scanning equipment was expensive and required an extra step of manual paper handling to scan a printed copy into the scanner's memory, where optical character recognition software could then convert the printed text into digital code. Companies that could afford neither to develop their own proprietary systems nor to purchase a commercial package had to contract to have the work done. Although usage was widespread – even described as a revolution (Kennedy & Morrow, 1995) – it was not universal. A 1998 survey of Fortune 500 companies found that one-third of the respondents had no plans to adopt an electronic résumé management system (Baker et al., 1998). The majority (61%) of those that did use such a system did not 'scan' the data in at all, but input it manually by keyboard. Further, a 1996 study of 236 companies in a rural Missouri community found that most were unaware of the résumé management technology, none used it, and only three had plans to use it in the future (Roever & McGaughey, 1997). Even for companies possessing the technology, anything short of 100% compliance left it necessary to maintain redundant systems for handling applications.'

At the end of the literature review, the research question is presented as follows:

'**Research Question**: What are employers' preferences regarding résumé style, résumé delivery method, and having a cover letter accompanying the résumé?'

As you can see from the journal article, the research question clearly emerged from the review of the literature. You will also notice that the research question is very simple. It is stated in one sentence, and in this case the sentence is phrased as a question.

The research question detailed in the journal article is a good example of a very well-conceptualized research question, and of a well-conceptualized conceptual framework. All of the key concepts in the research project are detailed in this conceptual framework.

This conceptual framework will provide good support and direction for this research project. It will keep the research focused, and it will act as a guide for the researcher throughout the research process.

References

Schullery, N.M., Ickes, L. and Schullery, S.E. (2009) 'Employer preferences for résumés and cover letters', Business Communication Quarterly 72(2): 163–176. © 2009 by Sage Publications.

The journal article detailed above is a good example of a simple and effective, conceptual framework providing guidance and direction for the development of the theoretical framework for the research project. The first three or four pages of the article address the literature in the field. It is important that you source this article and read the content of the article. Begin by reading the literature as it is laid out in these first pages. The review of the literature continues for some pages. The study was conducted in the USA, and there are some cultural differences evident. At the end of the review of the literature, the authors of the study detail the study's research question. The research question, as we know, contains the conceptual framework for the research project.

> **Critical perspective** Is a reflective, thoughtful, evaluative perspective or view.

READING LITERATURE: SOME KEY POINTS

In reading literature the researcher engages in an evaluation of the literature. The researcher is trying to establish the value of the literature in terms of their own research. The literature review is undertaken in order to provide for the development of a theoretical framework for the research project. The literature has relevance only to the degree that it is relevant to the research being undertaken. This is the first and the most fundamental measure of value in terms of the literature being sourced, read and reviewed. How relevant is the literature to the research?

> **Critical engagement** The process by which the researcher takes a critical perspective on the research being reviewed.

The next question is how dated is the literature sourced? If the literature is quite dated, is it from seminal sources? Is there any very up-to-date literature? The next questions then relate to the author(s) of the literature. Who authored the literature? What qualifications do they have? Do they have other publications? These questions will help the researcher to discern quality in publications.

When reading published research, it is important to take a **critical perspective**. When developing such a critical perspective it is helpful to draw on the model of the research process. Using the model of the research process, read and critically examine every element of the research as it is presented in the published research. The following bullet points are useful in helping with the development of the **critical engagement** needed when appraising literature.

Questions for the introduction to the research

- Critically examine the research question/statement, the research hypothesis.
- Does it seem useful and appropriate?
- Are the aim and objectives of the research clearly outlined?
- Do they seem reasonable and appropriate?
- Do the aim and objectives 'fit' with the research statement/question/hypothesis?

Questions for the literature review

- Critically examine the literature review, the theoretical framework.
- Is it comprehensive?
- Does it include seminal authors?
- Is it up-to-date?
- Does it adequately support the research project as it is detailed in the research statement/question, in the hypothesis?

Questions for the research methodology

- Examine the methodology. Is it appropriate?
- Has enough detail been given on the methodology to allow for a critique of the research?
- Is the population of the research detailed, if there is a human population?
- Was a sample used? If so, is the sampling method detailed?
- Are the data collection methods outlined?
- How well did the data collection methods serve the research?
- Do the data collection methods 'fit' with the aim of the research?
- Is there a copy of the data collection method(s) in the appendices?

Questions for data analysis

- How was the data analyzed?
- Was the means of analysis adequate and appropriate?

Questions for the findings of the research

- Are the findings from the data clearly drawn from the data? Is it clear that the findings did emerge from the data?
- Are the findings reasonable, useful, interesting and insightful?
- Are the findings theorized? Did the author(s) knit the findings from the research back into the body of knowledge? Did the author(s) connect the findings with the theory laid out in the literature review, in the theoretical framework for the research project constructed and presented in the literature review?

Questions for the conclusions drawn from the research

- Are there conclusions? Are they reasonable?
- Do the conclusions emerge clearly from the findings?
- Are the conclusions meaningful?
- Do they evidence a deep level of reflection on the part of the researcher?
- Are they useful, interesting and insightful?

Questions for the recommendations made at the end of the study

- Are there recommendations?
- Are the recommendations clear and simple?
- Do the recommendations make sense?
- Are the recommendations achievable, are they do-able?
- Are there recommendations for further research?

Questions for an overall critical appraisal of the study

- Overall, is the report of the research well-written?
- Is the research well-presented?
- Has the research been carried out to a high standard?
- Does the research make a contribution to knowledge?
- Is it a valid contribution to knowledge?
- Is it a valuable contribution to knowledge?

These are generic questions that may be asked of any research project. Use these questions to develop a critical perspective on the research (literature) that you are reviewing.

You can expect your supervisor(s) and your examiner(s) to take a critical perspective on your research. As this is the case, you might use the bullet points above to critically appraise your own research before you submit it for examination.

YOUR RESEARCH
Common research problems

There are some common mistakes that students make when writing the literature review:

- Students do not review enough literature.
- Students review irrelevant literature.
- Students present unnecessary detail in their review (the case study at the end of this chapter presents an example of a poorly written literature review and an example of a better literature review).

● Students fail, in writing their literature review, to present and then develop a main argument in the review.

Try to ensure that you are reading and reviewing enough literature, and that the literature you are reviewing is relevant to your research. In ensuring that the literature is relevant, be guided by the conceptual framework for the research project. The research statement or question contains the conceptual framework for the research project. The structure for the literature review should emerge from the conceptual framework.

When you are planning the writing of the literature review, decide precisely what your main point is (what your main argument is) in the review. Then outline and develop that argument throughout the chapter. The key points to remember are that:

1 You are presenting a review of the literature.

2 This review of the literature is your take on the literature, your appraisal of the literature.

3 It is your appraisal of how the literature pertains to your research project as it is detailed in the research question or statement.

In accomplishing all of this, your review of the literature must be open, balanced and critical, because you cannot be seen to have any bias in relation to the literature. You must be open to contradictions and contradictory arguments. Your appraisal of the literature must be logical. Your critique must be reasonable and your argument must be clear and coherent. It will be much easier to write a reasoned and logical argument if you reflect on it critically before you start to write. You can clarify your argument in notes in the research diary.

REFERENCING THE WORK

Referencing is critically important and much of the work of the **literature review** is in referencing all of the relevant research that you have used in developing the theoretical framework for your study. It is essential that the literature review be properly referenced. Establish with your lecturer and/or your supervisor which referencing system is to be used in the work and learn how to use that system. The system of referencing will be standard across the institution so the theses in the library will all have been written using that system. These theses are a good source of information regarding referencing, although it is important to take a critical perspective on them. It is often the case in academic institutions that all of the theses are placed in the library, the poorly written theses as well as the outstanding ones. Try to be discerning when you read, so that the standards you are absorbing as you read are high. Try to avoid picking up bad habits from poorly written works. Your lecturer and/or supervisor may provide you with an official guide to referencing. If not, the library may provide this. There are some useful resources in terms of referencing in Chapter 2 of this textbook, under the heading of Plagiarism. Chapter 2 of this textbook also explains in detail the way in which to compile a bibliography.

> **References**
> Give details of the source of ideas or theories or models within literature.

It is important to try to reference as much as possible throughout the literature review. Include all of the **references** you can in writing the review. These references evidence the amount of reading undertaken for the research. While referencing as many theorists as possible, it is important to lead the review with your own voice. Remember, it is your take on the literature, as it pertains to your research project, that you are presenting in this chapter. This is important. Try not to begin a paragraph with a reference. Opening sentences in paragraphs should lead the reader into the paragraph. Do not deploy references in the introduction or the summary. The introduction gives the reader a broad introduction to the chapter. The summary summarizes the chapter. There should not be any new information in the summary. The summary is simply a summary of the main points, and the main argument, presented in the chapter.

CASE STUDY

Two literature reviews

Siemens offices on Hong Kong island. © T. Lehne/Lotuseaters/Alamy

I n this case study, two examples of sample literature reviews are presented. The first is an example of a poorly written literature review. The second is an example of a better literature review.

In reading the two examples try to see why one is a poor example and the other a better example. In your research diary, write down, in short phrases, why one is a poorly written review, and the other a better review.

Remember to use the lessons learned in undertaking this exercise when writing the literature review for your research project. This exercise is designed to help you write a better literature review.

Idea taken from Neuman, W. (2000) *Social Research Methods: Quantitative and Qualitative Approaches*.

Example of a bad literature review

Induction programmes for new employees at work come in many forms. Williams and O'Brien (2008) in their study of induction programmes in SMEs found that, in general, the programmes used by the firms tended to be short 2-hour induction programmes designed simply to introduce new employees to their new workplace and their new work colleagues. They found too that employees who participated in the short induction programmes felt that the induction programmes were too short, and that sometimes, because they were too short, the programmes failed to introduce new employees to key people and key processes within the organization. Their research project was a case study, and in the case study they examined the induction programmes of 20 SMEs in the greater Middleton area. Bradley and Finch (2009), in their study of the induction programmes of 5 MNCs found that the induction programmes of the MNCs tended to be longer than those of the SMEs studied by Williams and O'Brien, and they tended to be generic, with each MNC developing their own generic induction programme. The MNCs of the Williams and O'Brien study each had highly structured and highly detailed induction programmes, each of which was designed to thoroughly introduce new employees to their new work environment. Cooper *et al.* (2009), detail in their work three main models of induction programme: the Large model, the Medium model, and the Small model. In their work, Cooper *et al.* presented a review of the literature on induction models presented in business journals, conducted over the last 20 years. They found that, over the years, different models of induction were in vogue at different times. They state in their work that while contemporarily an integrated model of induction, encompassing elements of the Large, Medium and Small models is in vogue internationally among businesses of every size, in fact, each of the models is suited, they believe, to different kinds of businesses and different sizes of businesses. Frank and Lyden (2009), in a survey of 300 British firms, found that the majority of the firms (63%) had week-long induction programmes. Of the rest of the firms, 20% had 3-day induction programmes and 20% had induction programmes that lasted 3 weeks. The remaining 7% had either no induction programme (2%) or induction programmes that lasted longer than 3 weeks. Frank and Lyden used a random sampling technique in their research and only businesses with 15 or more employees were included in the sample.

Example of a better literature review

There are many different kinds of induction programmes and many different models of induction programmes currently in use in different businesses and different firms; some last for a number of hours and some last for a number of weeks (Williams and O'Brien, 2008; Bradley and Finch, 2009; and Frank and Lyden, 2009). The model of induction programme generally used by SMEs tends to be a short 2-hour model of induction (Williams and O'Brien). This model was established by Williams and O'Brien as being flawed. They suggest that the model is too short and, as a consequence, it does not properly address the task of induction. The model of induction used by MNCs is a long generic model, designed for use internationally (Bradley and Finch). A potential flaw in this model might be the lack of cultural nuance that the model allows for.

The model is a generic model, as detailed by Bradley and Finch, it is designed for operation across different national and cultural borders and boundaries.

The different models of induction have evolved over recent decades, Cooper *et al.* (2009). There are currently, as established by Cooper *et al.*, three main models, Large, Medium and Small. The model which is currently in vogue among firms internationally is a hybrid model, encompassing elements of each of the three main models. Following their extensive review of existing models, Cooper *et al.* suggest that each of the three main models has particular application in particular kinds of businesses and in different sized businesses. It is important to note that, in Britain, almost all firms have developed some kind of induction programme for new employees (Williams and O'Brien; Frank and Lyden), only 2% of the 300 firms studied by Frank and Lyden had not.

Question

Having read both of the sample literature reviews above, can you explain why one of the reviews is better than the other?

References

The idea of creating sample literature reviews is based on a similar exercise in: Neuman W., Social Science Research: Quantitative and Qualitative Approaches, "How Big Should a Sample Be?" © 2000 Allyn & Bacon.

CHAPTER REVIEW

This chapter provides an exploration and explanation of the literature review. In the chapter, literature in the context of social science research, is shown to be research that has already been carried out and published. This research is published in conference papers and reports, in theses, in journal articles and in books. The chapter explains that it is research which has been established as valid research, through a peer review process, that is published in books, in journal articles, in conference reports, in government publications and in theses. These publications are said in the chapter to be the main sources for literature for the literature review of the research project. The chapter explains how the conceptual framework is used to provide direction and focus to the literature review. The literature review is developed around the key concepts in the conceptual framework. The chapter shows how the researcher develops a search strategy, using the key words and key concepts from the conceptual framework to search for and locate appropriate literature. The steps the researcher takes in compiling the literature review are as follows: the researcher searches for relevant literature; the researcher saves the literature; the researcher reads the literature; the researcher plans the literature review and creates a structure for the chapter of the literature review; the researcher writes the literature review. In writing the literature review, the researcher presents a critical analysis of the literature, as it pertains to the research that they are conducting. The researcher in writing the review leads with their own voice, and they construct an argument from the literature review. In writing the literature review the researcher makes a point, this is the key point of the literature review, or the key argument of the literature review. This key point or key argument becomes clear to the researcher through their reflection on the literature and their planning of the literature review. The researcher ensures that as many references as possible are included in the literature review. The references demonstrate the breadth and depth of the reading carried out for the research. The quality of the literature review is a demonstration of the knowledge and expertise of the researcher in the theoretical field of the research.

Now update your interactive research diary with your notes and findings at www.cengage.co.uk/quinlan. Complete the activities provided to reinforce your understanding of this chapter.

END OF CHAPTER QUESTIONS

1   What is the relationship between the conceptual framework and the theoretical framework?

2   What is a theoretical framework?

3   Outline a literature search strategy.

4   What is meant by a critical engagement with the literature?

5   Explain the role of references in the literature review.

6   What is a bibliography?

7   Name and explain the referencing style used in your institution.

8   Explain why the researcher plans the literature review.

9   How does the researcher develop the key argument of the literature review?

10 Demonstrate, by means of an example, an appropriate structure for a literature review.

REFERENCES

BBC World Service Trust, 'Using content analysis to measure the influence of media development interventions: Elections training for journalists in Yemen', http://downloads.bbc.co.uk/worldservice/trust/pdf/bbcwst_research_series_yemen.pdf Accessed 02.06.2010.

Colorado State University, 'Introduction to content analysis', www.writing.colostate.edu/guides/research/content/index.cfm

Deacon, D.H., Golding, P., Pickering, M. and Murdock, G. (2007) Researching Communications: A Practical Guide to Methods in Media and Cultural Analysis, London: Hodder Arnold.

Guardian (2009) 'There's more to life than GDP', http://www.guardian.co.uk/news/datablog/2009/mar/24/g20-economics

Trochim, William M. The Research Methods Knowledge Base, 2nd Edition. Internet WWW page, at URL: http://www.socialresearchmethods.net/kb/ (indirect measures, content analysis, and secondary analysis of data) (www.socialresearchmethods.net/kb.unobtrus.php)

Richards, J. and Marks, A. (2007) 'Biting the hand that feeds: Social identity and resistance in restaurant teams', International Journal of Business Science and Applied Management 2 (2): 41–57.

Schullery, N.M., Ickes, L. and Schullery, S.E. (2009) 'Employer preferences for résumés and cover letters', Business Communication Quarterly 72 (2): 163–176.

RECOMMENDED READING

Bell, J. (2005) 'Doing Your Research Project', Maidenhead: Open University Press.

Collis, J. and Hussey, R. (2009) Business Research: A Practical Guide for Undergraduate and Postgraduate Students, Ch. 6, 'Searching and Reviewing the Literature', Houndsmill: Palgrave Macmillan.

Creswell, J. (2003) Research Design: Qualitative, Quantitative and Mixed Methods Approaches, Ch. 2, 'Review of the Literature', Thousand Oaks, CA: Sage.

Easterby-Smith, M., Thorpe, R. and Jackson, P.R. (2008) Management Research, Ch. 3, 'Doing a Literature Review', London: Sage.

Gill, J. and Johnson, P. (2006), Research Methods for Managers, Ch. 3, 'The Role of Theory in Research Methods', London: Sage.

Hart, C. (2005) Doing a Literature Review, London: Sage.

Jankowicz, A.D. (2007) Business Research Projects, Ch. 7, 'Reviewing and Using the Literature', London: Cengage.

Kent, R. (2007) *Marketing Research, Approaches, Methods and Applications in Europe*, Ch. 2, 'Academic Research in Marketing', London: Thomson.

Lee, N. and Lings, I. (2008) *Doing Business Research: A Guide to Theory and Practice*, Ch. 4, 'Reviewing Existing Literature', London: Sage.

Methodspace: Connecting the Research Community, Sage, **www.methodspace.com**

Neuman, W.L. (2000) *Social Research Methods: Qualitative and Quantitative Approaches*, Ch. 3, 'Theory and Research', and Ch. 16, 'Reviewing the Literature and Writing a Report', Boston, MA: Allyn & Bacon.

White, B. (2000) *Dissertation Skills for Business and Management Students*, Ch. 7, 'Using the Literature', London: Cengage.

CHAPTER 7

UNDERSTANDING RESEARCH METHODOLOGY AND DESIGN

LEARNING OBJECTIVES

At the end of this chapter the student should be able to:

- Understand, discuss and write about research methodology.

- Understand how research methodologies are deployed in research.

- Decide on the methodology most appropriate for their own research and create a methodological framework for that research.

- Critique the use of methodologies in other research projects.

RESEARCH SKILLS

At the end of this chapter the student should, using the exercises on the accompanying online platform, be able to:

- Evaluate the utility, value and limitations of the methodologies deployed in given research projects.

- Design a research project with an appropriate methodology.

The aim of this chapter is to introduce the student to research methodology, to give the student an understanding of how to use research methodologies and to outline some of the methodologies used in research. The chapter details and explains the third framework in the four frameworks approach to research, the methodological framework, and shows how to develop an appropriate methodological framework for a research project. The different elements of the methodological framework are highlighted and explained.

THE VALUE OF GOOD RESEARCH

Research in the media

In April 2009 Channel 4 in the UK presented a *Dispatches* documentary 'Crash: How Long Will it Last?'. The description of the documentary below was taken from the Channel 4 website (**http://www. channel4.com/programmes/dispatches/episode-guide/ series-13/episode-2**).

You will notice from the way that Will Hutton talks about the two films made for the documentary that, although he is an economist, the opportunity to research the crash presented to him by the making of the films, gave him an opportunity to study the crash and to critically reflect on it to a much greater extent than he had previously.

Researching the crash for the films made Will Hutton even more of an expert. When you think about your research project, think about it as providing you with an opportunity to become quite expert on an area or on a subject or topic that interests you.

Reporter, Will Hutton, on making the films (20.04.2009):

'I've been writing and broadcasting about the credit crunch ever since it first broke in September 2007 – the fateful weekend we watched the first bank run since the nineteenth century. I thought I had a pretty good grip about what had happened and why. But making these two *Dispatches* films was the first time I'd had the opportunity to stand back and look back at the last 20 months as a whole – and talk both on and off the record to many of the people involved. It was highly revealing.'

'What is striking is how long it took most of the banking, regulatory, official and ministerial world to come to grips with the profundity of what was happening. I remember saying to a senior economic minister in the autumn of 2007 that he needed to set up an economic war room to monitor lending and the condition of the interbank markets, but there was no appetite for anything so dramatic. The hope was still that Northern Rock was just a little local difficulty. Like the 1914–1918 war, it would be over by Christmas.'

'The American government was no different. One of the advantages of looking back is that you see the extent to which there was a transatlantic ping pong throughout the credit crunch – although Britain was

Bank of England. © Pete Tripp/iStock

very much the little 'ping' and the US a giant 'pong' (stretching the analogy to breaking point). Bear Stearns hedge funds going bust in the summer of 2007 is the pong that generates the ping of Northern Rock; then Bear Sterns itself goes bust, creating shock waves in Britain in the spring of 2008. But the biggest American pong of them all was the near calamitous bank run in the first fortnight of September 2008 that nearly brought down the American banking system. It so spooked London that we had our very own bank run in the money markets too – that led to Gordon Brown's best moment of the year; when he saved the British banks and persuaded others round the world to follow suit.'

'This is one of the biggest – perhaps biggest economic event since the war. It has crippled the banking system, and although there are signs that the economy is beginning to decline at a much less rapid rate, the consequences were grave and will stay with us for years.'

References

Channel 4 (2009) 'Crash: How long will it last?', *Dispatches* documentary, **http://www.channel4.com/programmes/ dispatches/episode-guide/series-13/episode-2** Reproduced with kind permission of Will Hutton and Channel 4.

INTRODUCTION

In this chapter the focus is on **research methodology**. As you can see, in the model of the research process below (see Figure 7.1), research methodology is situated after 'literature review' and before 'data collection' methods. As we will see in this chapter, 'data collection methods' are a major part of the methodological framework for the research project. As we have discussed in earlier chapters, thoughts and ideas in relation to the research methodology and data collection methods to be used in the project should develop as the idea for the research project develops. This is because all of the elements of the research project have to fit together. The research methodology used must be capable of supporting the research, capable of enabling and facilitating its completion. The research methodology must be the appropriate research methodology for the research project; it must fit with the research project.

You may remember we discussed research methodology in Chapter 3 of this textbook where we explored the philosophical frameworks of social research and the philosophical underpinnings of different research methodologies. As we saw in

Research methodology
Signals to the reader how the research was conducted, and what philosophical assumptions underpin the research.

The Four Frameworks
Conceptual Framework
Theoretical Framework
Methodological Framework
Analytical Framework

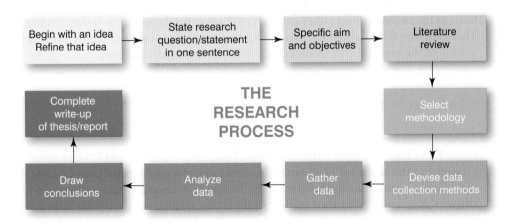

Figure 7.1   The research process

YOUR RESEARCH
Common research problems

Sometimes students have absolutely no idea what to focus on for their research project.

The challenge of making a decision regarding the focus of the research project often seems to students, and to beginner researchers in general, to be substantial. Sometimes students are a little in awe of the research process and feel overwhelmed by the assignment they have been set.

The best way to overcome some of these fears and issues is to practice developing ideas for research projects in your research diary.

As we know, the first thing to do when designing a research project is to decide on an area or an issue on which to focus your research. The next thing to do is to create a research statement or question around this area. This research statement or question becomes the conceptual framework for your research. The next task is to quickly detail the context for the research, where the research will take place. Then it would be helpful to write a note about the likely population of the research, if there is a human population in the research, who they are

and where they are. If it does not involve human participants, it would be helpful to write a note on the data to be gathered for the project, what form or format the data are in, and where it is to be located. Then quickly estimate the kind of data gathering method(s) required. For example, will you need to conduct interviews? Would a questionnaire be helpful? Will there be documentary evidence? When you have this done, read quickly through the summaries of the different research methodologies listed in Table 7.2, and try to pinpoint the most appropriate methodology for your research. If you cannot do this, try at any rate to identify the most likely research methodologies for your research. It is important to remember that although you may use more than one data gathering method, you will use only one research methodology in your research project.

The important thing is to get started and begin to engage with the process. When you get started, you might be surprised at how quickly the design of your research project begins to come together for you.

that chapter, there are many different approaches to research, and a number of different philosophical frameworks within which you might situate your work.

Every research project is designed to make a contribution to knowledge. The process or processes through which knowledge is created are of fundamental importance in research. A researcher poses a question, and then conducts research in order to be able to answer that question. When the researcher develops some clarity in relation to the focus of the research project, they can start to develop the design of the research project. The researcher thinks about the nature and purpose of the study and begins to develop a sense of the best research methodology to use in the research project.

RESEARCH METHODOLOGIES

There are very many different methodologies in social research. You have seen examples of many of these in the accounts of published research and student projects presented in this textbook. You have also seen examples and explanations of some of the different research methodologies in the *Research in Practice* feature in each of the chapters. You know from your reading of the earlier chapters in the textbook, that the decision on the methodology to be used in a research project is informed by the focus of the research, the research question or statement or the research hypothesis, and by the type of data required for the research, and by the location of that data.

You will remember that in Chapter 4 we examined the methodological pyramid (see Figure 7.2). You will remember from our in-depth study of the model in that chapter that the fundamental philosophies support the research methodologies, and that the research methodologies in turn support the data collection methods. This means that the research methodology must fit with the fundamental philosophies of the research project, and the data collection methods must fit with the project's research methodology. Through your study of different research proposals, you have seen the way in which the different elements of the research project are designed by the researcher to fit together in such a way as to properly and adequately support the research project.

Figure 7.2 is a list of the main research methodologies used in social science research. It is by no means a complete list. There are very many different research methodologies, all of which are interesting and all of which have been used by researchers in important, creative and engaging research projects. It is important to read a little about these methodologies in order to develop some understanding of the ways in which they are used in research projects. This reading will help you in the work of deciding which research methodology best fits the research project you are designing. The research methodology used in the research project is the most fundamental aspect of the research project's methodological framework. You will remember that, in the four frameworks approach to the research project, the methodological framework emerges from the conceptual framework.

Figure 7.3 illustrates the way in which the methodological framework emerges from the conceptual framework. The decision on which methodology to use in the research

The Four Frameworks

Conceptual Framework

Theoretical Framework

Methodological Framework

Analytical Framework

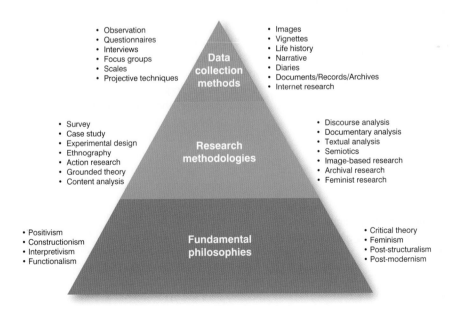

Figure 7.2   The methodological pyramid

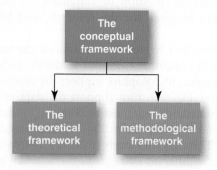

Figure 7.3   The methodological framework emerges from the conceptual framework

Longitudinal Research
Research that takes place over a long period of time.

Interviews
The social science researcher develops a series of questions or a series of points of interest to discuss with the interviewees.

project is made based on the focus of the research. The focus of the research is outlined, clearly and simply, in the conceptual framework for the research project. The conceptual framework for the research project is contained in the research question or statement.

The research project below details a study of decision-making among three entrepreneurs. The study was a **longitudinal** study; it took place over 1 year and 6 months. The aim of the study was to examine 'sensemaking' among entrepreneurs. The population of the study was three entrepreneurs. The study involved the researchers engaging each of the three entrepreneurs in three **interviews**. The interviews with each of the entrepreneurs were undertaken at 6-monthly intervals over the time period of the study. The methodology used in the study was **narrative research**, or narrative analysis. This methodology calls for the analysis of different narratives (or stories) in the data gathered for the research project. The research methodology narrative research or narrative analysis is

REAL WORLD RESEARCH

How theory influences research

The article below is taken from the *International Small Business Journal*.

'Sensemaking, rhetoric and the socially competent entrepreneur', Holt, R. and Macpherson, A. (2010)

In this article, the authors describe the research they carried out using a narrative research methodology. The research focused on the accounts that three participating entrepreneurs gave of the ways in which they negotiated uncertainty in their work.

The methodological approach to the research is laid out clearly in the journal article. The research methodology used was narrative research. The data gathering method used was longitudinal interviews. The data gathered was triangulated by using within-method triangulation; using this method three different interviews were conducted with each of the three participants in the study.

The authors state that 9 interviews in all were conducted for the study, 3 open-ended, in-depth interviews with each of the 3 manufacturing entrepreneurs. Each of the 3 interviews, conducted with each of the 3 entrepreneurs, took place at 6-monthly intervals and each lasted between 1.5 to 2 hours.

The article details that the main questions asked in the interviews were framed in terms of what Sole and Edmundson (2002) called 'significant learning episodes'; they say that significant learning episodes are an extension of the critical incident technique developed by Flanagan (1954). The authors state that, although initially a way of collecting data for quantitative analysis, critical incident technique is now commonly used to orient interviews around particular events that have meaning for the participants (Kokalis, 2007; Chell and Allman, 2003).

In the interviews, each entrepreneur was asked to recount moments at which their experience of creating and sustaining their firm changed significantly, moments within their experience which culminated in a particular insight, a change of direction, or the review and revision of existing understanding.

The interviews were recorded and fully transcribed and then sorted into accounts of learning episodes.

The interviews, according to the authors, allowed the entrepreneurs to construct stories (narratives) about their experiences and to make sense of those experiences by reflecting on them.

The brief synopsis of the journal article presented here clearly demonstrates how theory influences research. This is evident in the way in which the work of other researchers and theorists influenced and informed the way in which the authors of this study designed their research project.

References

Holt, R. and Macpherson, A. (2010) 'Sensemaking, rhetoric and the socially competent entrepreneur', *International Small Business Journal*, 28(1): 20–42.

---

the research methodology in focus in the text box, The Value of Good Research, on pages 188–189 of this chapter.

One of the most important decisions to be made in any research project is the decision about methodology. The research methodology used in the research must be capable of supporting the research, of facilitating the accomplishment of the aim of the research, the completion of the research. Practiced, experienced researchers can make decisions around appropriate methodologies for research projects relatively quickly. For the beginner researcher, the decision-making process is slower and needs to be supported by some study of the different research methodologies.

Some of the many different research methodologies used in social science research are listed in Table 7.1. The list, although by no means exhaustive, is useful. It gives some indication of the depth and complexity of this area of social science research, while providing for a succinct introduction to the more frequently used social science research methodologies. Reading a little about all of the methodologies listed below will help you decide which research methodology to use in your own research. It will also facilitate you in the work of critiquing the methodological choices made in the research of others.

Each of the research methodologies listed is dealt with in detail in this textbook, in the examples of research projects from journal articles and from student research projects. Each of the research methodologies listed features in one of the research methodology in focus box features, which appear in each chapter of this textbook. Table 7.2 contains brief summaries of each of the research methodologies listed in Table 7.1. Enough detail is given in the table on each of the methodologies to enable you to decide which of the methodologies might be a good fit for the research project you are designing. In addition, at least one reference is given for further reading on each of the methodologies.

> **Narrative research**
> Narrative inquiry or narrative analysis is a research methodology that is used in the gathering and analysis of narratives (stories).

Table 7.1 List of research methodologies	
Survey	*Life history*
Case study	*Phenomenology*
Experimental design	*Narrative analysis*
Ethnography	*Semiotics*
Action research	*Attitude research*
Grounded theory	*Image-based research*
Content analysis	*Archival analysis*
Discourse analysis	*Textual analysis*
Documentary analysis	*Meta-analysis*
Historical analysis	*Feminist research*

Table 7.2 Detailed research methodologies	
Survey	Surveys tend to be quantitative research projects or largely quantitative, research projects that is quantitative with some qualitative element. In general, the data collection methods that tend to be used in surveys are questionnaires or scales. It is often the case that the population or population sample used in surveys is big, and a questionnaire and/or a scale is an effective method to use in engaging with large research populations. Sometimes the population is geographically scattered. A questionnaire can generally easily be posted or emailed or made available on the Internet for a geographically scattered population. The use of the Internet in survey research is very common, and online surveys are commonly used. Fowler (2009), has written on survey research methods. Survey methodology is the methodology in focus in Chapter 2 of this textbook, 'Developing Research Skills'. Questionnaires and scales are explored in detail in Chapter 12 of this textbook, 'Using Questionnaires and Scales'.
Case study	If the research is located in a bounded entity, in a specific space or place, in a particular incident, it may be possible to conduct the research using a case study methodology. Within a case study methodology, the case to be studied could be a class in a school, it could be a school, and it could be an office, or a shop, or a factory, an enterprise of some kind. It could be a study of a particular practice, for example recruitment and selection processes or a marketing campaign. Case study research can involve the study of one case, or the study of a number of cases. Using this research methodology, the researcher engages in an in-depth examination of the phenomenon under investigation. A case study generally does not have the substantial population in terms of numeric size or geographic spread of survey research. Instead of breadth, i.e. numeric size and geographic spread, case study research calls for depth; it calls for the deeper investigation of some bounded entity. A simple definition of case study methodology is that it is the in-depth study of a bounded entity. A case study methodology can draw on quantitative or qualitative data, or it can draw on a mixture of both. Yin (2009), has written on case study methodology. Case study methodology is the research methodology in focus in Chapter 3 of this textbook 'Understanding Research Ethics'.
Experimental design	Experimental design is the methodology used when conducting experiments. True experiments are rarely conducted in business research or in social science research generally. This is because of the difficulties in controlling all the different variables in

Table 7.2   Detailed research methodologies (continued)

	social science situations and phenomena. Properly designed experiments can be very effective in laboratories or in laboratory conditions. Laboratory conditions are difficult to replicate in the social world or in the study of social phenomena. The experiments which are conducted in real-life settings are called field experiments.
	In an experiment, two groups are established, with individuals or units being randomly assigned to both groups. The two groups are pre-tested, and the dependent variable is measured. Then a program or application, the independent variable, is applied to one group, the experimental group, and not to the other group, the control group. Both groups are tested again; again the dependent variable is measured. If there is a difference in the experimental group but not in the control group, the program or application applied to them, the independent variable, is said to account for the difference. There can be more than one dependent variable in an experiment but there should only be one independent variable.
	There is further discussion of experiments in Chapter 8, see Table 8.4 Detailed data collection methods. In addition, experimental design is the methodology in focus in Chapter 14 of this textbook, 'Analysing Quantitative Data'. You may also find Trochim's (2006) website 'Research Methods: Knowledge Base', useful in this context. It provides a clear introduction to experimental design (**www.socialresearchmethods.net/kb/desexper.php**).
Ethnography	Ethnographic research is used when a researcher wants to carry out an in-depth examination of a culture. Ethnographic research calls for the observation in the field of the phenomenon under investigation. Using ethnography the researcher goes inside the culture being investigated in order to develop a very deep understanding of it. The researcher must be inside the culture enough to be able to document the culture, but also (and at the same time) outside of the culture enough to be able to document the culture. This means that when an individual is part of a culture, when they are immersed in that culture, they are in a position to properly and thoroughly document that culture and all its complexities. Yet because they are immersed in the culture they often cannot see the strangeness of the culture; the culture can appear to them to be 'natural'. In order to be able to conduct ethnographic research, the researcher must have the capacity to see the 'strangeness' of the culture they are attempting to document and analyze. This methodology can draw on quantitative or qualitative data, or a mixture of both. Fetterman (2010), has written on ethnographic research. Ethnography is the research methodology in focus in Chapter 10 of this textbook, 'Observation'.
Action research	Action research (AR) is used to bring about change, improvement and development in the quality of any organization and/or in the practice or performance of any team or group or organization. AR follows a cyclical or spiral process of planning, action, critical reflection and evaluation. AR can be a particularly effective approach to problem-solving in organizations. One form of AR, participatory action research (PAR) is widely used in development research. PAR was developed from the teaching theories of Paulo Freire, the revolutionary twentieth-century Brazilian educator. AR was developed by MIT Professor Kurt Lewin in the 1940s. This methodology can draw on quantitative or qualitative data, or on a mixture of both. AR is the methodology in focus in Chapter 1 of this textbook, 'Introducing Business Research'.
Grounded theory	Grounded theory (GT) methodology is used when the specific focus of the research is on building theory from data. This methodology is very useful when researching phenomenon about which little is known. In the thesis of a GT research project, there is sometimes a very short literature review, as little has been written on the

(Continued)

	Table 7.2 **Detailed research methodologies (continued)**
	phenomenon under investigation. In some grounded theory research projects there is no literature review at all, this is because some methodologists hold that within a grounded theory methodology, studying the literature gives the researcher preconceived ideas about what is to be found in the data. Within the GT research project, theory is generated from data, and so, within a grounded theory research project, the concluding chapter in the report of the research/the thesis is theoretically very rich. This chapter contains the theory developed from the data gathered for the research project. A GT approach to data analysis involves three stages: the first stage is open coding, the second stage is selective coding and the third stage is theoretical coding. This approach to data analysis is used in research projects which have been designed using other research methodologies. GT was developed by Barney Glaser and Anselm Strauss (1967). Glaser and Strauss later split in their understanding of the methodology. Within Glaser's GT methodology, the methodology can draw on quantitative or qualitative data, or on a mixture of both. Strauss and Corbin (1997), have more recently written on this methodology; they have presented the methodology as a qualitative methodology. GT is the research methodology in focus in Chapter 15 of this textbook, 'Analysing Qualitative Data'.
Phenomenology	A phenomenological research methodology is used in the social sciences to examine lived experience. Phenomenology is the study of lived experience from the first-person point of view. It is the study of experience or consciousness. Phenomenology is one of the most qualitative of the social science methodologies. Using a phenomenological research methodology the researcher spends a great deal of time developing accounts of lived experience from the perspective of those living the experience. The lived experience can be any lived experience: that of the worker in a factory, that of the CEO of a company, that of the undergraduate business student, and so on. Very powerful phenomenological accounts of personal experience can be used to bring about change; phenomenological accounts of, for example, experiences of bullying in the workplace or experiences of working in a racist or a sexist workplace, can highlight and challenge such behaviours and practices in a way that can quickly lead to change. Moustakas (1994), has written about phenomenological research methods. Phenomenology is the research methodology in focus in Chapter 11 of this textbook, 'Using Interviews and Focus Groups'.
Narrative research/ Narrative analysis	This methodology is used in the gathering and analysis of narratives. The narratives gathered as data and analyzed are often narratives (or stories) of personal experience told to the researcher by the person who has had the experience. Narrative research is frequently used in marketing and consumer behaviour research in order to understand consumption and consumer behaviour. Narrative analysis can be used to analyze textual data, in written or visual texts. This methodology can be used to examine and analyze the narratives or stories created or developed around products for marketing purposes. Such narratives are often developed around a character(s) real or fictional, with attributes or characteristics which the product developers want consumers to associate with their product(s). An example would be the fictional character Lara Croft and the use of her image in promoting such diverse products as video games, magazines, credit cards and soft drinks. Narrative research and narrative analysis has been written about by Gubrium and Holstein (2009) (see also Andrews *et al.*, 2008). Narrative analysis is the research methodology in focus in this chapter of the textbook, Chapter 7, 'Understanding Research Methodology and Design'.
Historical research/ Historical analysis	This methodology involves exploring and analysing the history of some phenomenon. The subject of the research might, for example, be a particular industry, such as coalmining in Wigan, or brewing in Wiveliscombe. There might, for example, be useful lessons to be learned from the study of the history of Apple Computer Inc. or the history of the Microsoft Corporation. The different historical

	Table 7.2 Detailed research methodologies (continued)
	periods of trade, such as an aspect of colonial trading history, or a history of some aspect of globalization, might prove illuminating in terms of some issue in contemporary business studies. Some contribution to the study of the history of economic thought might be valuable, perhaps a study of the lessons of Marxist economics for contemporary society. An interesting idea for a research project might be the study of Guinness advertising over the last fifty years, or perhaps a study of the most popular Guinness advertising campaign ever. It is worth remembering that recent history is as valid as ancient history in terms of historical research. There might be some aspect of recent business history that you could study that would count as a valuable contribution to knowledge. There are very many possibilities for the useful application of this methodology in business research. This methodology can draw on quantitative or qualitative data, or on a mixture of both. Danto (2008), has written about historical research. Connor (2004), has written about women, accounting and book-keeping in eighteenth-century England. Historical research is the research methodology in focus in Chapter 9 of this textbook, 'Using Secondary Data and Archival Sources'.
Life history	This methodology is used to compile life histories of different people or different companies. This methodology could be used, for example, to understand the changes that have occurred in the lives of a group of people, or the changes that have occurred in the life of a company. This methodology can draw on quantitative or qualitative data, or on a mixture of both. One particular kind of life history research is oral history. Oral history has been written about by Thompson (2000). An oral history is a vocalized account of some historical experience given by a witness or participant in that experience. An interesting and useful oral history research project might be one of the vocalized accounts of the experiences of people involved in the contemporary crisis in banking. The most fundamental data collection method within a life history and an oral history research methodology is the life history interview. The life history interview has been written about by Atkinson (1998). Life history research is the research methodology in focus in Chapter 16 of this textbook, 'Drawing Conclusions and Writing Research'.
Content analysis	Content analysis is a research methodology used to analyze the content of any text. Content analysis can be used to examine the tenor of a text, and both the explicit and the latent content of texts. It can be used to calculate the frequency with which particular words, or phrases, or concepts or ideas appear in the text being analyzed. It can be used to examine the placing within the text of particular aspects and elements of the communication. It can be used to examine the strength of the communication, through the force given to aspects of the communication, evident in the size of the font, in the organization of the communication, and in any highlighting, for example through the use of colour, in the text. Texts can be documents, interview transcripts or the transcripts of speeches, newspapers, conversations, advertising, websites and web pages, and so on. Any text that is language-based can be analyzed using a content analysis approach. Content analysis is used a great deal in media analysis. An interesting research project using content analysis might be the study of the website of a company. You could study a company's website in order, for example, to examine their positioning in the marketplace, or to examine their brand, or perhaps to examine their business ethics. Although traditionally a quantitative methodology, this methodology can draw on quantitative or qualitative data, or on a mixture of both. Content analysis has been written about by Krippendorf and Bock (2009). Content analysis is the research methodology in focus in Chapter 6 of this textbook, 'Reviewing the Literature'.

(Continued)

Table 7.2 Detailed research methodologies (continued)	
Discourse analysis	Discourse analysis is a research methodology that facilitates the identification of discourses in the social world and the analysis of those discourses. According to Fairclough (1995), discourses can be written texts, spoken words and/or cultural artefacts. Discourses are, he suggests, embedded in social events and social practices. Foucault (1970, 1972), believed that public discourses can be shaped by powerful individuals and groups and he also believed that such discourses have the power to shape individuals and their experience of the social world. Foucault believed that powerful discourses could bring about particular realities. You might, by way of an example, think about the discourses that prevailed in international economics before the recent global economic turmoil. Then think about the discourses that prevail in international economics since the recent global economic turmoil. Think about the powerful forces creating, propounding and perpetuating those discourses, and think about the impact of those discourses on you, your family and your friends, and on every individual on the planet. Discourse analysis calls for the identification and analysis of discourses. Discourse analysis is the methodology in focus in Chapter 8 of this textbook, 'Understanding Research Methods, Populations and Sampling'. In Chapter 8 see also the detail on discourse analysis in Table 8.4 Detailed data collection methods.
Documentary analysis/ Documentary research	Documentary analysis is the methodology designed to facilitate research on documents. Documentary analysis involves the systematic analysis of data in the form of documents or data drawn from documents. The documents used can be written documents, books, papers, magazines, notices, letters, records, and so on. Documentary research is the research methodology in focus in Chapter 5 of this textbook, 'Developing a Research Proposal'. Scott (1990), has written in detail about documentary research.
Semiotics	Semiotics is the study of signs, their form, content and expression. Semiotics is and has long been widely used in media analysis. In recent years the study of social semiotics has become prominent. Signs in society are signs because they signify something. Anything that has signifying power can be studied semiotically. If you consider, for example, the following sign: £, you will immediately recognize the sign and you will know immediately what it signifies. The social world, and the world of social interaction, is full of signifying signs. Semiotics is the study of such signs. Semiotics can be used, for example, to uncover the meaning of the image of a company, or a brand, or a product. Semiotic data can be analyzed both quantitatively and qualitatively. Erving Goffman published a (now classic) study, *Gender Advertisements* (1979), in which he engaged in a semiotic analysis of advertising. Chandler (2007), has written about semiotics. Semiotics is the research methodology in focus in Chapter 13 of this textbook, 'Managing Data and Introducing Data Analysis'. See also the detail on semiotics in Table 8.4 Detailed data collection methods in Chapter 8 of this textbook, 'Understanding Research Methods, Populations and Sampling'.
Attitude research	Attitude research is the methodology used in the measurement of attitudes. Attitude research can be used to measure the attitudes of people to anything: to a product, to an advertising campaign, to a company, to spending, to saving, anything. Attitude research has traditionally been a quantitative methodology, or a methodology that uses quantitative data, however qualitative data can also be used in attitude research, as can a mixture of both quantitative and qualitative data. There are many scales that have been specifically designed for attitude measurement, research. Some examples of the different scales used in attitude measurement include Likert scales, semantic differential scales and social distance scales. These scales are illustrated and explained in Chapter 12 of this

Table 7.2 Detailed research methodologies (continued)	
	textbook, 'Using Questionnaires and Scales'; attitude research is the research methodology in focus in this chapter. All of these scales and many more, are explained in detail by Oppenheim (1998) in his book on measuring attitudes.
Image-based research	Image-based research is the use of images in social research. Using this research methodology, a researcher can draw on data from photographs, film, videos, advertising, cartoons, drawings, maps, charts, and any other kind of image. Visual data can be analyzed using a quantitative or a qualitative approach, or a mixture of both. Banks (2007), Pink (2006), Prosser (1998) and Rose (2001), are among those who have written on this methodology. As detailed in Chapter 4, the web-resource Methodspace (www.methodspace.com) has a number of video interviews with research methodologists, among them Jon Prosser, Sarah Pink and Marcus Banks, experts in image-based research. An interesting example of image-based research in business studies is the work of Pullman and Robson (2007), who in one of their research projects used image-based research to examine hotel guests' responses to the design of a hotel. Pullman and Robson said that because design is a visual medium, image-based research was the most appropriate research methodology for their research project. You might in your own research think about taking some photographs of the phenomenon you are investigating. Using image-based research, the images might be the only data in the research project, or they might be used to supplement data from other sources. If there is no opportunity to take photographs to use as data in your research project, you might think about using photographs, or other images, already in existence that you could draw on as data for your research project. Image-based research is the research methodology in focus in Chapter 4 of this textbook, 'Research Philosophy'.
Archival research	Archival research is research carried out on the content of archives. Archives are documents or stores of documents. Archives can be very small and they can be very extensive. Libraries, for example, can store archives. The stored records and/or documents of a company or a business would constitute an archive. According to the website of The National Archive of the UK (www.nationalarchives.gov.uk), 'archives are documents in any medium that have been created by an individual, family, business or organization during its existence and have been chosen to be kept permanently because they are considered to be of continuing value'. Researchers when they conduct archival research, gain access to the archive and then conduct their research on the contents of that archive. It is often the case that different data collection methods are used in archival research, for example content analysis, documentary analysis, image-based research. The methods used, as always, depend on the data available in the archive, on the requirements of the study, and they depend in this case on the imaginative way in which the researcher engages with the archival material. Archival research is considered in detail in Chapter 9 of this textbook, 'Using Secondary Data and Archival Sources'.
Textual analysis	Textual analysis is the analysis of any text. Texts can be books, magazines, other documents or images or film, TV programmes, DVDs, videos, websites and web pages, advertisements, clothes, graffiti, the décor, layout and organization of rooms, and so on. The researcher analyzes the texts in order to develop some interpretation of the meaning of the text in relation to the aim of the research. The researcher analyzes and interprets the text in order to try to make some meaning of the text. There is a short introduction to textual analysis on the website of The University Writing Centre at Wright State University, Ohio, USA.

(Continued)

Table 7.2 Detailed research methodologies (continued)	
	You will find it at **www.wright.edu/academics/writingctr/resources/textualanalysis.html**. The Media and Communications Studies site on the website of Aberystwyth University provides some reading on the different kinds of textual analysis. You will find this resource at **www.aber.ac.uk/media/Sections/textan.html**.
Meta-analysis	Meta-analysis is a research methodology which involves the quantitative analysis of amalgamated previously existing research data sets. This methodology involves the bringing together of quantitative data sets from previously conducted research projects, combining them, and then analysing them. The possibility of error is quite large in using this methodology. This is because the meta-analysis is dependent upon the validity of the existing data sets. The researcher conducting the meta-analysis generally will not have been involved in the design or conduct of any of the research projects which produced the data sets. As this is the case, the researcher cannot guarantee the validity of the data. Another issue in terms of validity in meta-analysis is that the process of amalgamating the data sets could alter or damage in some way the data in the data sets. Despite these issues, meta analysis are conducted. In an article published in the *International Business Review*, Kirca and Yaprak (2010), investigate how often meta-analysis techniques have been used in the international business literature over the past 30 years, they provide an overview of the process of meta-analysis research, they examine the role of meta-analysis in the synthesis of research in international business, and they suggest guidelines for future applications of the technique. Lipsey and Wilson (2000) have written in detail about meta-analysis, as have Borenstein *et al.* (2009).
Feminist research	Feminist research can be undertaken to highlight the experiences of women, as well as to highlight gender inequality. Feminism, as detailed in Chapter 4 of this textbook, is a philosophical framework and it is an intellectual and political movement. Feminists hold a particular standpoint in relation to the nature of the social world. Feminists hold that the world is structured around gender inequality, with men holding more power than women. Feminist research is research conducted from that standpoint. Pierre Bourdieu (2001), is one of many theorists to have written on this topic. The web-resource Methodspace (**www.methodspace.com**), has two video interviews (Parts 1 and 2), with Sharlene Nagy Hesse-Biber on feminist research. Feminist research can be undertaken using any kind of data collection methods; the requirement being, as always, that the data collection methods used fit the population and the data requirements of the study. Hesse-Biber (2007) has edited a handbook of feminist research. With Leavy, Hesse-Biber (2007), has co-edited a very useful primer on feminist research practice.

Table 7.2 may help you clarify your thinking in relation to the decision you have to make regarding the research methodology to use in your research project. In order to confirm your decision, you will need to do further reading and engage in further

YOUR RESEARCH

Common research problems – learning more about research methodologies

You will need to read a little more about the methodologies outlined above. A good way to begin would be to do an internet search using the name of the research methodologies that seem particularly relevant to your research. For example, search the Internet using the word 'ethnography', or 'feminist research', or 'grounded theory'.

The next step would be to locate some textbooks in the library on the methodology. In a couple of hours in the library you could have a good look at a number of different textbooks covering a number of different methodologies. You will find the reading lists at the end of the chapters in this book very helpful in such searches.

The next step is to locate journal articles which feature the research methodology, or methodologies, that seem particularly relevant to your research. The research articles in academic journals are relatively short synopses of research projects which have been carried out and completed. The first thing to do is to identify the journals relevant to your research. You will find that there are a number of journals dedicated to every aspect of social science and business research, for example, the *International Small Business Journal*, *Gender and Society*, *Journal of the Academy of Marketing Science*, *Journal of Business Communication*.

You can use the search mechanism within each journal to search for articles on research projects which have used the methodology or methodologies that are relevant.

You can download copies of the articles from your library's online e-resources. If you do not know how to do this, the librarians will help you, or they will direct you to someone who can help you. Do not be afraid to ask for help and direction.

You could ask for a mentor. You might be able to connect with a more senior student who could support and direct you.

You could develop a research project around a mentoring system for undergraduate students. Remember, ideas for research projects are all around you.

reflection. You will need to do further reading in any case, in order to develop the level of expertise required by your programme of study in terms of the research methodology you decide to use in your research project.

DECIDING ON THE MOST APPROPRIATE METHODOLOGY FOR YOUR OWN RESEARCH

It is very important that you decide as quickly as possible which methodology you intend to use in your own research. Take the time that you need to get this right, but try to get it right as quickly as you can. Again, do not hesitate to ask for guidance in selecting a research methodology and for feedback in relation to any decision you make regarding research methodology from your lecturers and your thesis supervisor.

It often happens that a research project has elements that seem to fit with more than one research methodology. It is important, however, that you make a decision and choose one methodology. If you can see aspects of more than one methodology in your work, decide which one will work best in relation to what it is that you want to accomplish with your research and work with that methodology. The decision around which research methodology to use in the research project must be a reasoned logical decision which can stand up to scrutiny from readers and examiners.

YOUR RESEARCH

Common research problems – deciding on a research methodology

The best way to learn how to decide on an appropriate research methodology for a research project is to practise. The following exercise is a research diary exercise.

Imagine that you are a professional researcher and you have been asked to conduct a research project on the following: 'Key principles of Britain's top strategic managers'.

Using your research diary, propose three different methodologies for the research and detail the data collection methods to be used in each.

As you will see, there are usually a number of options in terms of the design of any research project. The key is to select the best option for the project in relation to what it is that you want to accomplish with the research.

I once asked a class of 15 students to design a research project around the concept of Santa Claus. Each one of the 15 students designed a unique research project. From the exercise 15 very different research projects were outlined, each of them viable, valid and interesting.

The best way to learn how to design and develop research projects is to practise designing and developing research projects. The research diary exercise in the Your Research box is designed to encourage you to begin to do this. It also demonstrates to you that many research projects can be carried out using one of a number of different research methodologies. The choice of research methodology shapes the research project; different research methodologies will produce different research projects.

THE VALUE OF GOOD RESEARCH

Focus on narrative research/ narrative inquiry/narrative analysis

Narrative research, narrative inquiry or narrative analysis is a research methodology that is used in the gathering and analysis of narratives (stories). Human beings communicate by telling stories. They narrate their lives and their experiences; they narrate their work, their experiences, knowledge and understanding of their workplaces. According to Kohler Riessman (2008), the storytelling impulse is natural and universal across the globe. Narratives are socially situated. As Kohler Riessman, states, they are composed for particular audiences at particular points in time. They draw on the taken-for-granted discourses and values circulating in the culture from which they are drawn. Consequently, they don't speak any essential truth; they don't evidence any essential reality. Based on this statement, can you say something about the philosophical framework within which a researcher is working when using narrative analysis? These issues of truth and reality are, as we know from our reading of Chapter 4 of this textbook, epistemological and ontological issues.

The researcher gathers the narratives (the stories), as data or the researcher extracts narratives from data. Data in narrative research can be in the form of texts such as diaries, interviews, letters, documents, webpages, and so on. It can also be in the form of orally told stories. The researcher explores and analyzes the narratives in the data. Kohler Riessman, presents four different approaches to analysing narratives: thematic analysis, structural analysis, dialogic/performance analysis and visual analysis. It would be useful to read about these different approaches to narrative analysis, outlined in Kohler Riessman's book, if you think you might use narrative research as your research methodology in your research project.

Rajan's research project

Rajan is thinking of using a narrative research methodology in his research project. He has been following, in the media, accounts of an episode of industrial unrest in the national postal service. He is thinking about using narrative research to explore, with the different parties in the dispute, the different ways in which each party is constructing and representing the dispute within their own narratives. Rajan wants to situate his research project within the regional offices of the national postal service. The offices are located in the city in which he lives. The different

parties to the dispute, as he has identified them, are postal workers, trade unionists, and postal service managers. Rajan also wants to study the dispute as it is narrated in the media. He believes that the narratives of the dispute presented in the media have had, and are having, a substantial impact on the dispute.

What do you think of Rajan's idea for his research project? Do you think his thesis supervisor will support the research?

The following are some useful resources for narrative research.

Boje, D.M. (2001) *Narrative Methods for Organizational & Communication Research,* Sage Series in Management Research.

Colorado State University Guide to Narrative Inquiry **(http://writing.colstate.edu/guides/research/observe/com3a2.cfm)**

Fletcher, D. (2007) '"Toy Story": The narrative world of entrepreneurship and the creation of interpretive communities', *Journal of Business Venturing,* 22(5): 649–672.

Kohler Riessman, C. (2008) *Narrative Methods for the Human Sciences,* Sage.

CREATE A METHODOLOGICAL FRAMEWORK, THE THIRD OF THE FOUR FRAMEWORKS

The methodological framework for the research project contains all of the detail in relation to how the research was carried out. It is contained in the research methodology chapter of the thesis, or in the research methodology section of the research report. In this chapter/section the researcher begins by introducing the research methodology used in the research project and then, drawing on (and referencing) research methodology textbooks, justifies that research methodology, explains why it was chosen and how it was used.

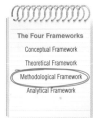

The Four Frameworks

Conceptual Framework

Theoretical Framework

Methodological Framework

Analytical Framework

In the research methodology chapter in the thesis, or section in the report of the research, following an explanation and justification of the research methodology used in the research project, the researcher details and explains the population of the study and the sample drawn from that population, that is if the research project had a human population. If a population sample was used, the researcher details and explains the sample, and the size of the sample in relation to the size of the population. The sampling method used is clearly outlined and justified. The next chapter in this textbook, Chapter 8, deals in detail with populations, samples and data collection methods.

The next issue to be dealt with is data collection. The researcher thoroughly details, explains and justifies, the data collection methods used in the research project. Usually a copy of each of the data collection methods, such as the questionnaire, or the **interview schedule** or the **observation schedule**, is placed in appendices. Each of

Interview schedule The list of questions the researcher develops to ask participants, or the list of points, or the key issues, the researcher develops to discuss/explore with participants.

Observation schedule
An observation schedule, like an interview schedule, is a form or series of forms on which the results of an observation are recorded.

Observation
A data collection method where the researcher engages in observing and recording the phenomenon under investigation, or some part of the phenomenon under investigation.

Questionnaires
Questionnaires are structured means of gathering data.

the data collection methods used is discussed and explained and justified in detail. The level of detail given is important as this allows readers and examiners to fully understand the research project, and to critically engage with it and evaluate it.

The issues of validity and reliability are then addressed. As stated in Chapter 2, perhaps the key issue in any research project is that of validity. Validity in social research is the degree to which a research project measures that which it purports to measure. This means that if, for instance, the researcher develops a research project designed to measure levels of industrial unrest in a particular workplace, then the research project must do that if it is to be valid. The data collection methods used in the research project must be valid measures of industrial unrest in the workplace, and the researcher must be able to establish the validity of the data collection methods used.

The term reliability in social science research, as explained in Chapter 2, relates to the degree to which the research can be repeated while obtaining consistent results. A measurement instrument in social science research is deemed reliable if it produces consistent results again and again.

The issue of reliability has more application to quantitative than to qualitative research. Within quantitative research the data gathering instrument is designed before the researcher goes into the field to accomplish a specific purpose. Therefore, the instrument is to a degree independent of the context for the research. Such an instrument, if used again, should yield consistent results. On the other hand, qualitative research is context specific, and the data collection methods developed for qualitative research are developed specifically for the context within which the research is situated. As this is the case, it would not be meaningful to test whether or not data collection methods developed for qualitative research would yield consistent results over time, with different populations. Rather than attempting to establish the validity of their data gathering methods, qualitative researchers focus on establishing the rigour of their research; they focus on establishing the soundness, the dependability of their research (see Guba and Lincoln, 1994; Riege, 2003; see also Table 11.4. Issues of validity and reliability in qualitative research, in Chapter 11, 'Using Interviews and Focus Groups').

The next issue to be addressed in the research methodology chapter/section is the issue of triangulation. Triangulation in social science research, as explained in Chapter 2 of this textbook, is the use of more than one approach to answering the research question or responding to the research issue. It means looking at the phenomenon under investigation from more than one perspective. As we have said before, completing a research project is a bit like going into a court of law. If you were in court to win a case, you would amass as much evidence as you could in order to do so. It is the same in research. You want to amass as much evidence as possible in order to prove or establish your case. You set out in your research project with a research question or statement, a research hypothesis that you hope to prove or disprove. In triangulating the research, you can use as many data gathering methods as feasible and necessary to gather data in order to have different perspectives on the phenomenon you are investigating. In analysis, the data from each method is compared in order to produce within the research a more comprehensive description and understanding of the phenomenon under investigation. Limits on the number of data collection methods used in any research project arise from the resources at the researcher's disposal: the amount of time the researcher has in which to conduct the research; the amount of money the researcher can spend on the research; and, above all, the level and degree of access the researcher has to relevant data.

YOUR RESEARCH

Common research problems – the need for triangulation

Let us use as an example a HR manager working with a multi-ethnic multiracial workforce. Let us say that the manager believes that there are intercultural issues and barriers among the workforce. He/she decides to introduce training in intercultural communication in order to challenge these issues and break down the barriers.

The manager carries out the training and then asks the employees who participated in the training to complete a questionnaire. The questionnaire was designed to establish how useful or beneficial the training was to the employees in terms of helping them overcome the intercultural barriers in their workplace relationships. The employees respond very positively to the questionnaire indicating in their responses that the training was beneficial or very beneficial.

The manager then engages in a series of observations, noting the level and nature of intercultural communication taking place among the workers. The observations establish that there has been little or no change in the situation, that the intercultural issues and barriers that the training was designed to challenge and overcome still exist.

The data are apparently inconsistent, in that the responses to the questionnaire contradict the findings of the observations. There can be a number of reasons for this.

The positive responses to the questionnaire might indicate a degree of political correctness among the respondents, where the employees who responded to the questionnaire gave what they believed to be the 'correct' response. The positive responses might evidence issues in terms of power in the organization. The employees might have been afraid to give real responses, afraid for their jobs, afraid of repercussions, afraid of presenting themselves to management in a poor light, afraid that they might have been identifiable from their responses and that there might be negative repercussions for them, and so on.

It could be that the employees really did find the training helpful, but there are other issues in employee relations that need to be addressed; issues that have been highlighted by the observations carried out.

In research terms, using only one of the methods, either one, would not have given a valid insight to the situation. The use of two methods yielded a more complex representation of the phenomenon under investigation, a more comprehensive, a more correct, a more valid representation of the phenomenon under investigation.

As explained in Chapter 2, using between-method triangulation for example, the research question might be explored using a questionnaire and a series of interviews, or using a series of **observations** and a focus group. Using within-method triangulation the research issue or phenomenon might be explored, for example, using two different, and perhaps sequential **questionnaires**, or using two different sets of interviews. The data collection method in the Holt and Macpherson (2010) study, outlined in the *Reflecting on Research – How theory influences research* box feature in this chapter uses within-method triangulation, whereby three different interviews were conducted sequentially with each of the three entrepreneurs who participated in the study.

Finally, it is important within the methodology chapter to have a very good reflective section on ethics which deals with the ethical issues in the design and conduct of the research project. Research ethics are dealt with in some detail in Chapter 3 of this textbook.

Table 7.3 summarizes the structure for the methodological framework. As stated at the start of this chapter, the methodological framework is contained in, or is the content of, the research methodology chapter of the thesis or the research

The Four Frameworks

Conceptual Framework

Theoretical Framework

Methodological Framework

Analytical Framework

methodology section of the report of the research. The table below gives a breakdown of the word count for this chapter in the thesis or section in the report of the research. The word counts are given simply as guides. If you need any clarification around the word count required for your work, speak to your lecturer and/or your research supervisor.

Table 7.3 Structure for methodological framework (the content of the research methodology chapter or section)			
	20 000 word thesis/report	15 000 word thesis/report	10 000 word thesis/report
Introduction (to the chapter/section)	100 words	100 words	50 words
Research methodology	600 words	200 words	150 words
Population of the study	200 words	100 words	50 words
Sample and sampling method	300 words	200 words	150 words
Data collection methods	900 words	700 words	400 words
Issues of validity and reliability	300 words	300 words	200 words
Triangulation	200 words	100 words	50 words
Ethics	400 words	300 words	150 words
Total word count	3000 words	2000 words	1200 words

CASE STUDY

Genji's case study research project: The methodological framework

In this case study, we examine Genji's research project and the methodological framework she developed for the project.

Genji is being sponsored in her studies for her degree by an international NGO. The NGO sponsoring Genji's studies has asked her to examine in her research project, strategies for the promotion of the uptake of low-carbon technologies in developing countries. This is an issue which the NGO in its work is currently addressing.

Genji developed the following research statement (conceptual framework) for her research project.

'This research project is a case study designed to identify key strategies that can be used to pro-

mote the uptake of low-carbon technologies in developing countries.'

When Genji's research supervisor approved this research statement, Genji then developed the following aim and objectives for the study.

'The aim of the research project is to identify key strategies that can be used to promote the uptake of low-carbon technologies in developing countries.

'The objectives of the study are as follows:

- To identify the different strategies used to promote the uptake of new technologies.

- To establish which of these strategies would be useful in promoting the uptake of low-carbon technologies in developing countries.

- To produce a template of key strategies that can be used to promote the uptake of low-carbon technologies in developing countries.'

Genji carried out a literature review. She constructed the theoretical framework (contained in the literature review/the content of the literature review) using the structure detailed opposite:

Wind turbines © N Vasuki Rao/iStock

- Introduction.
- *First subsection heading* 'Promoting new technologies in developing countries'.
- *Second subsection heading* 'Strategies for the promotion of new technologies in developing countries'.
- *Third subsection heading* 'Strategies for the promotion of new low-carbon technologies in developing countries'.
- Summary.

Genji developed the following methodological framework for the Genji's project. (The word count of Genji's methodological framework, from here to the end excluding references, is 1571 words.)

Research methodology

This research project will be developed using a case study methodology (Yin, 1989, 2008; Bell, 2005). Case study research calls for the in-depth study of the phenomenon under investigation (Yin, 2008). The phenomenon under investigation can be an issue, or a number of issues, an organization, or a number of organizations, an individual, or a number of individuals, an event or incident, or a number of events or incidences. As Yin states (1989), the case can be an event, an entity, an individual or even a unit of analysis; 'it is an empirical enquiry that investigates a contemporary phenomenon within its real life context using multiple sources of evidence'.

The phenomenon under investigation in this proposed case study is the key strategies that can be used for the promotion of low-carbon technologies in developing countries. A case study approach to this research is appropriate as the research calls for the in-depth study of strategies for the promotion of particular technologies, and for the development of a template of key strategies for the promotion of these technologies. A case study methodology will allow for the in-depth study of the strategies used to promote particular technologies, and it will allow for the identification of key strategies. When the key strategies have been identified through this case study, a template of the key strategies will be developed and presented. This template of key strategies that can be used to promote the uptake of low carbon technologies in developing countries will be presented in the final chapter of the thesis.

Population of the study

This case study will draw on multiple sources of data (Yin, 2008) and the study will use two different populations.

The first population will be a population of senior managers involved in the development of strategies for the promotion of low-carbon technologies. These managers will be drawn from commercial companies producing low-carbon technologies.

The second population in this study will be a population of development workers engaged in the promotion of low-carbon technologies in developing countries.

Sample and sampling method

Five participants for the research will be selected from each of the two populations. A judgemental sampling method will be used in selecting participants in the research. Using a judgmental (or purposive) sampling technique (see Chapter 8, 'Understanding Research Methods, Population and Sampling'), the researcher decides, or makes a judgement, about who to include in the research. The criterion for inclusion in the research lies in the capacity of the participant to inform the research. The participants chosen by the researcher to be included in the study must have a contribution to make to the research in terms of the focus of the research. In this study, the focus of the study is on key strategies used to promote low-carbon technologies in developing countries.

The people chosen to participate in the study will be key informants on this topic.

Data collection methods

This research project, as stated above, will involve a multi-method approach (Creswell, 2003, Den-

scombe, 2003). It will involve multiple sources of data.

First, an Internet search will be undertaken in order to develop a comprehensive portfolio of documents (see Duffy, in Bell, 2005), detailing:

- strategies used in the promotion of new technologies
- strategies used in the promotion of low-carbon technologies
- strategies used in the promotion of low-carbon technologies in developing countries.

Second, the strategies found in the Internet search will be compared with the strategies detailed in the review of the literature. The data from this exercise will help inform the engagement with the ten participants in the research, the five senior managers from companies producing low-carbon technologies, and the five development workers engaged in promoting low-carbon technologies in developing countries.

In the next phase of data gathering for the case study, each of the ten participants in the research will be sent a short questionnaire which they will be required to fill in prior to interview. The questionnaire will contain five questions on key strategies to promote low-carbon technologies in developing countries.

In order to complete the questionnaire, participants will have to compile a list of key strategies. They will give the researcher a copy of this list prior to the in-depth interview in which each will participate, and they will refer to the list during the interview.

Finally, in the in-depth interviews with each of the ten participants, the interview schedule will focus on the key strategies in promoting low-carbon technologies in developing countries.

A copy of the questionnaire and a copy of the interview schedule will be placed in the appendices of this thesis.

Triangulation

As stated, the study involves multiple sources of data (Yin, 1989, 2008). Data gathering for the research project involves a study of documentation of the strategies used in the promotion of low-carbon technologies available on the Internet. In addition, there will be a short survey of the strategies used by the key informants in the study. The key informants in the study will supply documentation on the key strategies they use and recommend to the researcher. Finally, the researcher will engage the ten participants in the study in in-depth interviews.

Altogether, the research will draw on two different kinds of documentary evidence, survey data and interview data. Taken together, these data will provide the research project with the in-depth and triangulated perspective necessary in case study research.

Data analysis

The data gathered for the research project will be analyzed. A thematic approach to data analysis will be used (Bryman and Burgess, 1994; see Table 15.2: A simple approach to qualitative data analysis in Chapter 15, 'Analysing Qualitative Data'). The core aspects of the strategies to emerge in data gathering will be identified. Key strategies will be identified. The relative strengths and weaknesses of the different strategies will be analyzed. Finally, the key strategies to be used in the promotion of low-carbon technologies in developing countries will be highlighted. New strategies will be developed from the analysis of the existing strategies, their core aspects, their relative strengths weaknesses and their utility in a developing world context.

Issues of validity and reliability

The issue of validity is perhaps the key issue in research Chapter 2, 'Developing Research Skills'. A measurement of the validity of the research is the degree to which the research project measures what it set out to measure, the degree to which the research project accomplishes what it set out to accomplish. The validity of this research project is evident in the manner in which a strict focus has been maintained throughout the research project. This strict maintenance of the focus of the research

project has been facilitated by the deployment throughout the design of the research project of the four frameworks approach to the design of the research project (see Quinlan, 2011). The validity of the research is evident in the multi-method approach taken to the research, and outlined above. This case study will be triangulated using a between-method approach to triangulation (Denzin, 1970). The data collection methods used in the study include documentary research, survey data and interview data. The data collection methods are the correct data collection methods for the case study. They will yield the data required. The population of the case study is an expert population in relation to the phenomenon under investigation.

The issue of reliability in the research project (see Quinlan, 2011), relates to the degree to which the research can be repeated while obtaining consistent results. The validity of this case study has been established above. The case study has been well constructed. The populations used in the case study and the data gathering methods deployed in the case study are appropriate to the case study and appropriate to the phenomenon under investigation in the case study. This case study could be repeated and the same results would be achieved. It would seem, therefore, that the case study is reliable.

Ethics

The ethical issues in this research project are substantial. The research has been requested by an NGO working in a developing country. The research, when it is complete, will go to shape the work of that NGO and it will go to shape the experiences of development of the people of that developing country. As this is the case, the case study must be properly and thoroughly conducted. It must be well designed. The findings of the research, the conclusions drawn from the research and the final product of the research, the template of key strategies designed to promote the use of low-carbon technologies in developing countries, must be meaningful and useful.

There are ethical responsibilities in the conduct of this research to the two populations of the research, the population of senior managers involved in the development of strategies for the promotion of low-carbon technologies, and the population of development workers engaged in the promotion of low-carbon technologies in developing countries. The participants in the research must be dealt with in a professional manner. Their contribution to the research will be acknowledged. They will be made aware of the fact that by participating in the research they will be making a substantial contribution to the international development work of the NGO. The participants will be made fully aware of the extent of the participation in the research required of them before they agree to participate.

The individual identities of the participants in the research will remain anonymous. The organizations they represent will not be identified.

The data gathered for the research will be held safely and securely. The names of the participants and their organisations will be coded and only the reseacher and her supervisor will have access to the codes.

Correct data analysis procedures will be used in the analysis of the data.

The research, when it is completed, will be presented to the NGO. An article from the research will be published on the website of the NGO. A copy of the thesis will be placed in the university library.

References

Bell, J. (2005) *Doing your Research Project*, Maidenhead: Open University Press.

Bryman, A. and Burgess, R.G. (1994) *Analysing Qualitative Data*, London: Routledge.

Creswell, J. (2003) *Research Design: Qualitative, Quantitative and Mixed Methods Approaches*, London: Sage.

Denscombe, M. (2003) *The Good Research Guide: For Small-scale Social Research Projects* (2nd edn), Maidenhead: Open University Press.

Denzin, N. (1970) *The Research Act in Sociology*, Chicago: Aldine.

Duffy, B. (2005) 'The Analysis of Documentary Evidence', in J. Bell *Doing Your Research Project*, Ch. 7, Maidenhead: Open University Press.

Yin, R.K. (1989) *Case Study Research*, London: Sage.

Yin, R.K. (2008) *Case Study Research: Design and Methods*, London: Sage.

Questions What do you think of Genji's research project? What do you think of the methodological framework that she developed for her research project? Using this chapter as a guide, do you think you could design a methodological framework for your own research project?

CHAPTER REVIEW

The focus in this chapter was on research methodologies. A number of different research methodologies were listed and described. The different ways of applying the various research methodologies were considered. The means by which an appropriate methodology is selected for a research project were explored. It was established in the chapter that the decision with regard to which research methodology to use in the research project rested on the focus of the research and the intention of the researcher in terms of what they hoped to accomplish in undertaking the research. Decisions on which research methodology to use in the research project are influenced by the population, if any, of the study, and the size and geographic spread of the population. The data requirements of the study and the data available for the study were also shown to influence the choice of research methodology for the research project. The fact that the decision around the appropriate methodology to be used in any given research project is often complex and sometimes ambiguous was acknowledged. Although many research projects can be undertaken using one of a number of research methodologies, it was recommended that the researcher decide on one research methodology for the research project. It was advised that the researcher should discuss their ideas and thoughts with their lecturer and/or their research supervisor before finally making a decision about the choice of methodology. The fact that the researcher must become quite expert in relation to the research methodology used in their research project was detailed and explained in the chapter.

Now update your interactive research diary with your notes and findings at www.cengage.co.uk/quinlan. Complete the activities provided to reinforce your understanding of this chapter.

END OF CHAPTER QUESTIONS

1 The methodological framework emerges from the conceptual framework. Explain this statement.

2 Name and briefly explain five different research methodologies.

3 Name the research methodology you intend to use in your research project and explain why it is the most appropriate research methodology for your research.

4 Name two other research methodologies that you could use to develop your research project and explain why you have decided not to use them.

5 Outline and briefly explain the key elements of the methodological framework.

6 Can you detail and defend the methodological framework you intend to use in your research project?

7 Explain the meaning of the word triangulation and the use of triangulation in social science research.

8 Explain the key differences between survey research methodology and case study research methodology.

9 Explain the term narrative inquiry in relation to social science research.

10 What are the key ethical concerns you now have in relation to your research project?

REFERENCES

Andrews, M., Squire, C., and Tamboukou, M., (eds), (2008) *Doing Narrative Research*, Sage, London and Thousand Oaks, CA.

Atkinson, R. (1998) *The Life Story Interview* (Qualitative Research Methods Series 44), London: Sage.

Banks, M. (2007) *Using Visual Data in Qualitative Research*, London: Sage.

Bell, J. (2005) *Doing Your Research Project*, Maidenhead: Open University Press.

Boje, D.M. (2001) *Narrative Methods for Organizational & Communication Research* (Series in Management Research), London: Sage.

Borenstein, M., Hedges, L.V., Higgins, J.P.T. and Rothstein, H.R. (2009) *Introduction to Meta Analysis*, Chichester: John Wiley & Sons Ltd.

Bourdieu, P. (2001) *Masculine Domination*, California: Stanford University Press.

Boje, D.M. (2001) *Narrative Methods for Organizational & Communication Research*, Series in Management Research, London: Sage.

Bryman, A. and Burgess, R.G. (1994) *Analysing Qualitative Data*, London: Routledge.

Chandler, D. (2007) *Semiotics: The Basics*, London: Routledge.

Channel 4 (2009) 'Crash: How long will it last?', *Dispatches* documentary, **http://www.channel4.com/programmes/dispatches/episode-guide/series-13/episode-2**

Colorado State University, 'Guide to narrative inquiry', **http://writing.colstate.edu/guides/research/observe/com3a2.cfm**

Connor, R.E. (2004) *Women, Accounting and Narrative: Keeping Books in Eighteenth-Century England*, London: Routledge.

Creswell, J. (2003) *Research Design: Qualitative, Quantitative and Mixed Methods Approaches*, Ch. 2, 'Review of the Literature', Thousand Oaks, CA: Sage.

Danto, E.A. (2008) *Historical Research*, Oxford, UK: Oxford University Press.

Denscombe, M. (2003) *The Good Research Guide: For Small-scale Social Research Projects* (2nd edn), Part 1, 'Strategies for Social Research', Milton Keynes, Buckingham: Open University Press.

Denzin, N. (1970) *The Research Act in Sociology*, Chicago: Aldine.

Duffy, B. (2005) 'The Analysis of Documentary Evidence', in J. Bell *Doing Your Research Project*, Ch. 7, Maidenhead: Open University Press.

Fairclough, N. (1995) *Critical Discourse Analysis*, London, UK: Longman.

Fetterman, D.M. (2010) *Ethnography: Step-by-Step* (3rd edn), Thousand Oaks, CA: Sage.

Fletcher, D. (2007) '"Toy Story": The narrative world of entrepreneurship and the creation of interpretive communities', *Journal of Business Venturing* 22 (5): 649–672.

Foucault, M. (1970) *The Order of Things*, New York: Pantheon.

Foucault, M. (1972) *Archaeology of Knowledge*, New York: Pantheon.

Fowler, F.J. Jr (2009) *Survey Research Methods* (4th edn), Thousand Oaks, CA: Sage.

Glaser, B. and Strauss, A.L. (1967) *The Discovery of Grounded Theory*, Chicago: Aldine.

Goffman, E. (1979) *Gender Advertisements*, New York: Harper and Row.

Guba, G.G. and Lincoln, Y.S. (1994) 'Competing paradigms in qualitative research', http://ctl.iupui.edu/common/uploads/library/CTL/IDD443360.pdf Accessed 02.06.2010.

Gubrium, J.F. and Holstein, J.A. (2009) *Analyzing Narrative Reality*, Thousand Oaks, CA: Sage.

Hesse-Biber, S.N. (ed.) (2007) *Handbook of Feminist Research: Theory and Practice*, Thousand Oaks, CA: Sage.

Hesse-Biber, S.N. and Leavy, P.L. (2007) *Feminist Research Practice: A Primer*, Thousand Oaks, CA: Sage.

Holt, R. and Macpherson, A. (2010) 'Sensemaking, rhetoric and the socially competent entrepreneur', *International Small Business Journal*, 28(1): 20–42

Kirca, A.H. and Yaprak, A. (2010) 'The use of meta-analysis in international business research: Its current status and suggestions for better practice', *International Business Review* 19(2): 160–177.

Kohler Riessman, C. (2008) *Narrative Methods for the Human Sciences*, Thousand Oaks, CA: Sage.

Krippendorf, K. and Bock, M.A. (2009) *The Content Analysis Reader*, London: Sage.

Lipsey, M.W. and Wilson, D. (2000) *Practical Meta Analysis*, Thousand Oaks, CA: Sage.

Media and Communications Studies, Aberystwyth University, 'Textual analysis', www.aber.ac.uk/media/Sections/textan.html Accessed 02.06.2010.

Methodspace: Connecting the Research Community, Sage, www.methodspace.com

Moustakas, C.E. (1994) *Phenomenological Research Methods,* Thousand Oaks, CA: Sage.

Oppenheim, A.N. (1998) *Questionnaire Design, Interviewing and Attitude Measurement,* London: Pinter.

Pink, S. (2006) *Doing Visual Ethnography* (2nd edn), London: Sage.

Prosser, J. (1998) *Image-based Research*, London: Routledge.

Pullman, M.E. and Robson, S.K.A. (2007) 'Visual methods: Using photography to capture customers' experience with design', *Cornell Hotel and Restaurant Administration Quarterly*, 48(2): 121–144.

Riege, A.M. (2003) 'Validity and reliability tests in case study research: A literature review with "hands-on" applications for each research phase', *Qualitative Market Research*, 6(2): 75–86.

Rose, G. (2001) *Visual Methodologies*, London: Sage.

Scott, J. (1990) *A Matter of Record: Documentary Sources in Social Research*, Oxford: Blackwell.

Strauss, A. and Corbin, J. (eds) (1997) *Grounded Theory in Practice*, London: Sage.

The National Archive of the UK, www.nationalarchives.gov.uk

The University Writing Centre, Wright State University, Ohio, USA, 'Textual analysis', http://www.wright.edu/academics/writingctr/resources/textualanalysis.html Accessed 02.06.2010.

Thompson, P. (2000) *The Voice of the Past: Oral History* (3rd edn), Oxford: Oxford University Press.

Trochim, W.M. *The Research Methods Knowledge Base*, 'Experimental design', www.socialresearchmethods.net/kb/desexper.php

Yin, R.K. (2009) *Case Study Research: Design and Methods* (4th edn), Thousand Oaks, CA: Sage.

Yin, R.K. (1989) *Case Study Research*, London: Sage.

Yin, R.K. (2008) *Case Study Research: Design and Methods*, London: Sage.

RECOMMENDED READING

Bell, J. (2005) *Doing Your Research Project, Ch. 1*, 'Approaches to Research' Maidenhead: Open University Press.

Bignell, J. (2002) *Media Semiotics: An Introduction*, Manchester: Manchester University Press.

Collis, J. and Hussey, R. (1997) (repr. 2003, 2009) *Business Research: A Practical Guide for Undergraduate and Postgraduate Students*, Ch. 5, 'Choosing a Methodology', Houndsmill: Palgrave Macmillan.

Creswell, J. (1998) (repr. 2007) *Qualitative Inquiry and Research Design: Choosing Among Five Traditions*, London: Sage.

Hammersley, M. and Atkinson, P. (1995) *Ethnography*, London: Routledge.

Neuman, W.L. (2000) *Social Research Methods: Quantitative and Qualitative Approaches*, Ch. 4, 'The Meanings of Methodology', Ch. 6, 'Qualitative and Quantitative Research Designs', Boston: Allyn & Bacon.

Roberts, H. (1997) *Doing Feminist Research*, London: Routledge.

Robson., C. (2002) *Real World Research*, Part 11, *'Designing The Enquiry'*, Oxford: Blackwell.

van Leeuven, T. (2005) *Introducing Social Semiotics*, London: Routledge.

White, B. (2000) *Dissertation Skills*, London: Cengage.

UNDERSTANDING RESEARCH METHODS, POPULATIONS AND SAMPLING

LEARNING OBJECTIVES

At the end of this chapter the student should be able to:

- Define a research population.

- Select a sample from a population.

- Explain how the choice and design of data collection method(s) used in the research project are fundamentally influenced by the aim of the research being undertaken, the population of the study, the kind of data required for the study and the location of that data.

RESEARCH SKILLS

At the end of this chapter the student should, using the exercises on the accompanying online platform, be able to:

- Outline an appropriate population for a given research project and select a sample from that population using an appropriate sampling method.

- Select and design appropriate data collection methods for a given research project.

Data collection methods, research populations and samples, and sampling methods are fundamental elements of the methodological framework, the third framework in the four frameworks approach to the research project. The aim of this chapter is to explain how to select a population, and when and how to select a sample from a population for a research project. The chapter details different research methods, i.e. different ways of gathering data.

THE VALUE OF GOOD RESEARCH

Research in the media

'Moving from "what happened?" to "now what?" is vital for business', Rich, D., global managing director of the Accenture Analytics Group, *Financial Times*, 04.02.2010. Reproduced by permission of Accenture.

In this article, the author explains the value of good and timely data. The author highlights the findings of a survey carried out by his company with 600 senior managers in UK and US organizations. As you will see, the majority of those managers viewed the gathering of good and timely data as an urgent priority. The author of the article believes that good and timely data will account for the differ-ence between organizations that will survive the global economic downturn and flourish, and those that will not.

Extract

'As they emerge from a period of profound reces-sion and extreme volatility, organizations face a new competitive landscape – one in which rapid com-munications, proliferating data and fast-evolving customer segments are combining to create oppor-tunities, but also complex risks.'

'To succeed as agile and adaptable players in this environment, companies must be able to get the right information to the right people across the business – equipping them to understand their organization's current health and future potential.'

'This is underlined by recent Accenture research. In a 2009 survey of 600 senior managers at more than 500 UK and US blue-chip organizations, two-thirds of all respondents cited "getting their data in order" as an immediate priority.'

© Rudyanto Wijaya/iStock

'The next immediate need is for organizations to be confident that they have the right data – and are asking the right questions. All too often, in our experience, organizations that do make analytics-based decisions are making fundamental choices based on flawed data.'

'Our survey showed companies across most sectors accepting the importance of getting their data in order before undertaking any more ambitious analytics-based initiatives. Once their data is in order, they should move fast to develop a deeper understanding of customers, markets and competitors.'

'Cultural change is important too. To deliver value throughout the business, predictive analytics must be driven top-down. But with so much senior decision-making grounded in gut instinct, any broad-based commitment to analytics is still lacking.'

'For as long as companies only use analytics in limited ways, they will be limiting their capacity to succeed. The companies that thrived in the wake of earlier recessions were demonstrably those that used data-derived insights made by informed decision-makers to generate lasting competitive advantage.'

References

Rich, D. (2010) 'Moving from "what happened?" to "now what?" is vital for business', *Financial Times*, 4 February.

INTRODUCTION

This chapter explores the ways by which data can be gathered for a research project, and deals with research populations and sampling methods. The methodological framework of the research project comprises an account of all of the ways and means by which the research was actually carried out. The population used in the research, the sample selected from that population, and the means used to gather data for the research project are all fundamental aspects of this framework. As can be seen from Figure 8.1, at this stage in the research process we have decided on the research methodology to be used in the research project, and we have now come to the stage of defining the population of the research, deciding whether to work with the entire population or with a sample of that population, and deciding the data collection methods to be used in the research.

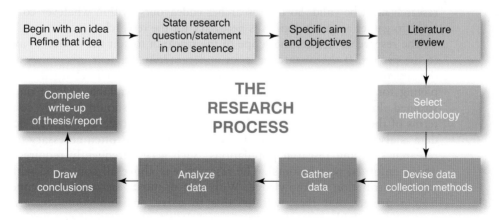

Figure 8.1   The research process

The population of a study is all of the individuals, items or units relevant to the study. The population comprises individuals, groups, organizations, documents, campaigns, incidents, and so on. The population of the research is also called 'the universe'. As this term implies, the population of a study comprises all of the units or individuals belonging to that population. The researcher designing the research project decides on and defines the parameters of the population of the study. If, for example, the researcher is interested in disposable income levels among undergraduate students at university, then the population of that research will be university undergraduates. As the global population of university graduates is enormous, the researcher uses some means to limit and more narrowly define that the population. The key point is that the researcher defines the population of the study.

The population could be defined, for example, as all of the students in one undergraduate class at university, or all of the undergraduate students at one particular university, or all of the undergraduate students at university in one town. The researcher might choose two different universities to work with, or all of the undergraduate students in the country. The researcher might decide to study only undergraduate students from EU countries, or from non-EU countries. The researcher might decide to compare levels of disposable income among:

- EU and non-EU undergraduate students at the University of Liverpool
- or among undergraduate students at university in Liverpool
- or among undergraduate students at university in England
- or among undergraduate students at university in the UK.

The researcher may decide to focus on the population of undergraduates in UK universities, or the population of undergraduates in the University of Westminster, or in the University of Edinburgh, or in Cardiff University. The researcher may decide to focus on the population of undergraduates in all three universities. All of these populations are valid.

The researcher defines the population of the study precisely, in order to ensure that the research project is researchable, as detailed in Chapter 1 of this textbook. The researcher must limit the scope of the research to what it is possible to do. The research must be valid. So the researcher endeavours, within whatever constraints exist, to gather as much data as is necessary for the research.

The researcher defines the scope of the research to suit the resources available to the project. If the researcher is an undergraduate student in a university, and the research project is one of many projects the student is charged with completing for their degree, then clearly the resources available will be quite constrained. In such a situation, the student researcher should be very concise in terms of the scope of the research project. As well as time and money, access to data is also a key resource. In order to access data, it is often necessary to access research sites and research populations. Such access frequently requires formal and/or informal permission(s). The researcher is above all concerned with making a contribution to knowledge. With that in mind, the researcher conceptualizes a project that they will be able to carry out and complete, given the resources available, a project that is useful and one that makes a very specific contribution to knowledge.

YOUR RESEARCH

Common research problems – Deciding on the scope of the research project

Remember that the student designs the project, and in so doing he/she designs the mountain they must climb. It is important that they do not design too challenging a mountain.

You must keep the scope of the research project relatively narrow. Ensure that the research project is properly focused. Keep the project design simple. The project will grow in complexity naturally. This will happen through your scholarly engagement with the literature, through your scholarship in research meth-odology, through your work on analysing the data gathered for the project, and through the insights and conclusions you draw from your analyzed data.

The research project you design should be simple. The research project you develop from that simple design will be complex. It will become com-plex through each step of the research process, and through the scholarship you bring to each step of that process as you develop and complete your research project.

There are many examples of research projects in this textbook, some of them use human **population**s and some do not. You can read back through the examples you have already examined to study the different populations of those projects. Table 8.1 provides examples of human populations of research projects.

The important issue to note from the list below is the necessity to define a population very clearly. Populations are defined in terms of a temporal span and/ or a geographic location. Some research projects do not have human populations. Instead their populations comprise collections of entities. Table 8.2 provides exam-ples of research projects focused on entities rather than people.

It often happens in the course of conducting the research project that the research shifts a little. Such a shift might involve a change in the scope of the research, perhaps the population becomes defined in a slightly different way, or the aim of the project changes slightly, perhaps the research question becomes a little clearer or changes slightly. Such changes are appropriate. They simply reflect the natural organic shifts

Table 8.1   Examples of human research populations
For the purpose of a national census, the entire population of a country is included in the research as the population of the research.
All graduates of the BA Business Studies at the University of Exeter (2005–2010).
All mothers of toddlers attending the 'Mothers and Toddlers Group' at the Village Community Club, Fernfield, Greater Heaton, Manchester, Thursday, 10 July, 2007.
All members of the 2009–2010 final year undergraduate class BA Business Studies, the University of Exeter, who have played the video game *Grand Theft Auto*.
All diners in Angie's Happy Haven café, Friday, 10 August, 2006.
All operational staff in Thompson's Conveyors and Elevators Ltd.
All HR managers in Hinton's Ltd.

Table 8.2   Examples of research projects without human populations
All businesses employing less than ten employees in the town centre, Oaklands, Sheffield.
All advertisements shown during the commercial breaks in *Coronation Street* for the month of October, 2009.
The advertisements used in TV advertising for Guinness in the year 2009.
The legislation governing the import and export of goods in the UK.
Levels of output in Milton's Joinery for the 6 months from January to June 2009 inclusive.
The HR policies of the multinational corporation *BrightCom*.

a research project goes through as it develops. The researcher must be flexible enough to allow these changes to occur and s/he should be competent enough to incorporate such shifts and changes into the design of the research project.

It often happens that the population of the research forces a shift or a change in the research. This can happen as a result of access issues. It can happen that the gatekeepers, the people in charge of access to the site of the research, officially, explicitly or perhaps tacitly, withhold access from the researcher. The role of gate-keepers in research is considered in detail in Chapter 3 of this textbook. Part of the responsibility of the researcher is to obtain access to the data required and the data sources, and then, most importantly, to maintain that access.

SAMPLES AND SAMPLING IN RESEARCH

When the researcher has precisely conceptualized the project and clearly defined the population of the project, the next decision that must be made is whether to work with the entire population of the research, or a sample drawn from that population. Research conducted on an entire population is known as a census. According to the UK Office for National Statistics (**www.ons.gov.uk/census/index.html**), a national census is a count of all people and households in the country. The 2011 census of England and Wales covers around 25 million households.

In social science research, it is often the case that the entire population of the research is too big, and as a result beyond the scope of the researcher. In such situations, the researcher clearly defines the population of the research, and then selects from that population a sample to study. The proposed research is then carried out on or with the sample, instead of the entire population. Some research is carried out using entire populations and some is carried out using sample populations or samples of populations.

Figure 8.2 illustrates the population, the sample and the unit/the individual/or the case. As can be seen from the figure, the population is all of the units in the figure. The sample is a small sub-set of the population. The population is made up of many individual units, cases or individuals.

Decisions with regard to whether to work with an entire population or a sample of the population are made based on the size of the population, the time available for the research, and the requirements of the research. Whichever decision is made, what is important is the clear definition of the population, and if a sample is used, a clear description of the sample selected and the sampling method used in making that selection.

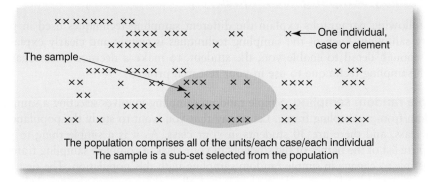

Figure 8.2   The population, sample and the unit/case/individual

When using a sample of a population in a research project, the researcher must clearly describe the sample. Then he/she must explain why that sample was selected and clearly describe the sampling method, the means by which that sample was selected. In describing the sampling method, the researcher aims to establish how *representative* the sample is of the research population. The key issue in sampling is this notion of **representation**. The concept of representation relates to the degree to which a sample drawn from a population can be said to be representative of the population. Another issue to be addressed is that of the **inclusion and exclusion criteria**. The inclusion criteria are the criteria potential participants must meet in order to be included in the study. Exclusion criteria are the criteria on which potential participants will be excluded from participation in the study. Outlining clear inclusion and exclusion criteria is a good way of achieving clarity in terms of what potential participants could and would contribute to the research. There are two kinds of sampling, **probability sampling** and **non-probability sampling**.

Probability sampling

Using probability sampling, the sample selected from the population is claimed by the researcher to be representative of the population. It is of fundamental importance that the sample selected be representative of the population of the study. This is because the researcher using a probability sampling technique wants to claim that the findings of research conducted with the sample are generalizable to the entire population of the study. Probability sampling is based on the theories of mathematics of probability. Probability sampling techniques include **simple random sampling**, **stratified sampling, systematic sampling** and **cluster sampling**. If used properly, probability sampling techniques yield precise results while working with samples a fraction the size of the original populations of research.

The basic rule of probability sampling holds that each member of the population has an equal probability of being selected for inclusion in the sample. As this is the case, the researcher, in order to engage in probability sampling, must have a complete list (or map, or chart), of every member of the population. The sample is drawn from this list. This list is known as a sampling frame. Each member or item in the sample is randomly selected from the population for inclusion in the study, using the sampling frame.

Representation
The degree to which a sample selected from a population can be said to be representative of that population.

Inclusion and exclusion criteria
The criteria potential participants must meet in order to be included in the study. Exclusion criteria is the criteria on which potential participants will be excluded from participation in the study.

Probability sampling
Each case, individual or element has an equal probability of being selected.

Probability sampling techniques

The following paragraphs explain the different sampling techniques used in probability sampling. Each of the sampling techniques is simply and clearly explained, with enough detail to enable you, the student, to make a decision with regard to which sampling technique to use in your research project.

Simple random sampling Simple random sampling involves selecting a sample at random from a sampling frame. Let us say that you want to study the population of your class, and there are 30 students in your class. As it is a simple thing to get a complete list of the names of the students in your class (a complete sampling frame), it is possible to engage in simple random sampling with this population. The first thing to do is to make a list on a sheet of paper of all of the names of the people in your class. Then tear off each name one by one, and place each one into a hat or a box. Then select one name at a time from the hat or box. You are now engaging in simple random sampling. Every time you select a name, note the name and then replace it in the hat or box. Then each time you select a name, you are selecting from a complete population. This is known as *sampling with replacement*. You continue this process until you have the complete sample required, the number of names required to complete the sample. The National Lottery uses a system of simple random sampling to compile the numbers in each game. In the game all of the numbers are placed into the machine and they are selected one at a time until the complete set of numbers is drawn. This is *sampling without replacement*, i.e. the ballls after they have been selected and the numbers on them noted are not placed back into the machine in order that the next number drawn is drawn from a complete set of numbers. In social science research, in order to generate random samples, researchers often use tables of random numbers. Books of mathematical tables contain tables of random numbers. Tables of random numbers can also be computer-generated. The case study at the end of this chapter focuses on random numbers, on the process by which random numbers can be produced in Microsoft Excel, and on the way in which a researcher would use such random numbers to generate a sample for a research project.

Systematic sampling Systematic sampling involves selecting items at systematic or regular intervals from the **sampling frame**. For example you might be working in a housing estate trying to establish which brand of washing powder is used in each house. Your sampling frame is made up of all of the houses in the housing estate. Suppose there are 500 houses in the estate and you begin at a random starting point and then sample every third house, or every fifth house, or whatever interval of house you decide on, until you complete your sample. Your complete sample is the number of houses or households you have decided to include in the study. You are engaging in systematic sampling. Alternatively you might spin a pen and then begin at the house toward which the pen is pointing when it stops spinning, and then call at every third house, or every fifth house, or whatever, in order to complete your sample. The random starting point is important. This is a systematic sampling technique.

Stratified sample A stratified sample is a sample selected based on some known characteristic of the population, a characteristic which will have an impact on the research. Using stratified sampling the researcher divides, or stratifies, the sample selected for use in the research using the characteristic which he/she knows will have an impact on the research. In the Real World Research box opposite, in the study of religious practice, the researcher uses first a simple random sampling technique and,

---

Non-probability sampling
In situations where it is not possible to compile a complete sampling frame, researchers use non-probability sampling techniques.

Simple random sampling
Involves selecting a sample at random from a sampling frame.

Systematic sampling
Involves selecting items at systematic or regular intervals from the sampling frame.

Sampling frame
A complete list or chart of every individual, unit or case within the population.

Stratified sample
A sample selected based on some known characteristic of the population, a characteristic which will have an impact on the research.

then a systematic sampling technique before finally deciding that a stratified sampling technique is really required for this particular study with this particular population. This example provides a good and simple explanation of stratified sampling.

Cluster sampling Cluster sampling is used when the units or the people who make up the population of the study are to be found in groups or clusters. Sampling is carried out by randomly selecting a sample of the clusters to study, rather than randomly selecting from the population. Cluster sampling is particularly efficient with populations that are geographically spread in clusters. Rather than randomly

> **Cluster sampling**
> Used when the population of the study can be divided into discreet groups based on any particular characteristic, e.g. geographic location.

REAL WORLD RESEARCH

The need for and the use of stratified sampling

A study of religious practice among your classmates

Suppose you as a researcher decided to examine religious practice among your classmates. Let us say that there are 30 students in your class.

You decide to select a sample of ten students from this population of 30 using a simple random sampling technique.

You obtain or create a list of the names of all of the students in your class. This is your sampling frame. You write all of the names on individual pieces of paper, put all of the pieces of paper into a box or a bag, and select pieces of paper at random, until you have selected ten names. This technique is a simple random sample technique. Now you have the ten names you need. All seems well.

Carrying out the same study you decide to use a systematic sampling technique. For this technique use your original list of 30 names, select a random start, and you then select every third name on the list until you have your sample of ten names. Again, all seems well.

In each of the two examples you have used different sampling techniques, and you have used them properly. However, your research could still go sadly awry.

What would happen if, for example, using the simple random sampling technique the ten students you selected, unknown to you, just happened to be devout Jehovah's Witnesses, or practising Bud-

dhists, or Sikhs, or Muslims, or Catholics, or Jews? What if the other 20 students in the class, none of whom were selected to be part of the sample for the study, just happened to be non-religious, atheists or agnostics? Well, certainly the sample that you have chosen to work with will not be in any way representative of religious practice among your classmates.

What you have here is a rogue sample, a sample that is not and cannot be representative of your population in terms of the phenomenon which you are investigating.

It is important for researchers to know enough about the population of their study before they begin to sample that population to know if there is something significant about the population in terms of the research being conducted.

In the case of the study of religious practice described here, the researcher might overcome the issues in sampling by conducting a census, in which case all 30 students are included in the study. In this way the religious practice of all of the members of the class will be explored in the research.

Alternatively, the researcher might overcome the issues by using a stratified sample. Using a stratified sampling technique, the researcher produces two lists of names, one list contains the names of the practicing students, the other list contains the names of the non-practicing students. The researcher puts all the names from one list into a hat, and selects five names. Then the student puts the names from the other list into a hat, and selects five names. Now the student has ten names. These ten names comprise the sample to be used in the research. This sample is a stratified sample. It is stratified along religious lines. The sample has been stratified in order to ensure that the sample selected is representative of religious practice in the population being studied, i.e. the population of 30 students in your class.

REAL WORLD RESEARCH

How big should a sample be?

A question students often ask is how big should a sample be?

For small-scale research projects, such as those undertaken by undergraduate students at university, a study undertaken using quantitative methods should have no less than 50 people or units in the sample. For studies undertaken using qualitative methods, a sample of 20 is considered substantial. Qualitative methods are designed to generate rich complex data. Such data are frequently, in terms of volume, quite substantial. Consequently, researchers using qualitative methods tend to keep the numbers of participants relatively low, in order to be able to cope with the large volume of data generated.

In relation to the question of how large should a sample be in quantitative research, Neuman (2000: 216) says that the answer is 'it depends'.

Neuman writes

> A large sample alone does not guarantee a representative sample. A large sample without random sampling or with a poor sampling frame is less representative than a smaller one with random sampling and an excellent sampling frame.

The question of sample size can be addressed in two ways. One is to make assumptions about the population and use statistical equations about random sampling processes. The calculation of sample size by this method requires a statistical discussion that goes beyond the level of this text. The researcher must make assumptions about the degree of confidence (or number of errors) that is acceptable and the degree of variation in the population.

A second and more frequently used method is rule of thumb – a conventional and commonly accepted amount. Researchers use it because they rarely have the information required by the statistical method. Rules of thumb are not arbitrary but are based on past experience with samples that have met the requirements of the statistical method.

One principle of sample sizes is, the smaller the population, the bigger the sample ratio has to be for an accurate sample (i.e. one with a high probability of yielding the same results as the entire population). Larger populations permit smaller sampling ratios for equally good samples. This is because as the population size grows, the returns in accuracy for sample size shrink.

For small populations (under 1000), a researcher needs a large sampling ratio (about 30 per cent). For example, a sample size of about 300 is required for a high degree of accuracy. For moderately large populations (10 000), a smaller sampling ratio (about 10 per cent) is needed to be equally accurate, or a sample size of around 1000. For large populations (over 150 000), smaller sampling ratios (1 per cent), are possible, and samples of about 1500 can be very accurate. To sample from very large populations (over 10 million), one can achieve accuracy using tiny sampling ratios (0.025 per cent), or samples of about 2500. The size of the population ceases to be relevant once the sampling ratio is very small, and samples of about 2500 are as accurate for populations of 200 million as for 10 million.

A related principle is that for small samples, small increases in sample size produce big gains in accuracy. Equal increases in sample size produce more of an increase in accuracy for small than for large samples. For example, an increase in sample size from 50 to 100 reduces errors from 7.1 per cent to 2.1 per cent but an increase from 1000 to 2000 only decreases errors from 1.6 per cent to 1.1 per cent (Sudman, 1976: 99).

References

selecting from all of the members of the population, the researcher identifies all of the clusters of units or individuals within the population, and then randomly selects clusters from all of the clusters to include in the study.

When the researcher is designing the research project, he/she should take note of any characteristics of the population that are or that might be significant in terms of the proposed research. In particular the researcher should be alert to patterning in those characteristics. It may be that the age range of the population has some significance for the research, or the work and employment of the population is organised in some significant way, or it might be that the gender or racial make-up of the population is significant. There may be some patterning in some characteristic in the population that will necessitate the use of a systematic sampling method. The task of gathering this kind of information would form part of the preliminary work conducted for a research project. The information gathered in this preliminary phase can be recorded in the research diary. The notes the researcher makes for themselves in the research diary can lead to insights which can fundamentally shape the design and quality of the research project.

Another key figure is the **response rate** to the research. A high response rate, as high a response rate as possible, is important to ensure that the research is **representative**. While the sample drawn may be relatively easily established as being representative, the research will falter if the response rate from the sample is not sufficiently high. It is very important in reporting research to include the response rate. This gives the reader of the research an understanding of the scale, the scope and the validity of the research. The most carefully designed research can be scuppered by a low or a poor response rate.

Non-probability sampling

In non-probability sampling, the sample is selected to *represent* the population, but it cannot be said to be *representative* of the population, in any statistical sense. The emphasis in non-probability sampling is on the capacity of a relatively small number of cases to clearly and comprehensively illustrate the phenomenon under investigation. It often happens with social science research projects, as stated, that it is not possible to produce a complete list of the population; when this is the case, it is not possible to develop a sampling frame. For example, a researcher might be asked to examine brand loyalty among consumers of *Cosmopolitan* magazine. It wouldn't be possible to compile a complete list of consumers of *Cosmopolitan* magazine. Without a complete sampling frame, it is not possible to engage in probability sampling, as without a sampling frame it is not possible to guarantee that every member of the population has an equally likely chance of being included in the study. The sampling approach used in such circumstances is non-probability sampling. Non-probability sampling techniques include judgemental sampling, **quota sampling, snowball sampling** and **convenience sampling.**

> **Response rate**
> The number of responses the researcher gets to their inquiry.

Non-probability sampling techniques

The following paragraphs explain the different sampling techniques used in non-probability sampling. As with the probability sampling techniques explained above, each of these sampling techniques is simply and clearly explained. Enough detail is given to enable you, the student, to make a decision with regard to which sampling technique to use in your research project.

> **Representative**
> A sample selected from a population, under certain circumstances, is representative of that population.

Judgemental or purposive sampling   Using a **judgemental** or **purposive sampling** technique the researcher decides, or makes a judgement, about who to include in the research. The criterion for inclusion in the research is the capacity of the participant to inform the research. Each person, or unit, chosen to be included

Quota sampling
The researcher fills a sample of participants in the research using different quota criteria.

Snowball sampling
The researcher finds a suitable participant, asks them to recommend another participant and so on.

Convenience sampling
Using a this technique the researcher engages conveniently located participants.

Judgemental sampling
The researcher decides who to include in the research.

Saturation point
Saturation point is reached when the researcher gathering data for the project no longer hears any new thoughts, feelings, attitudes, emotions, intentions, etc. At this point continuing to engage participants would not be useful, necessary or ethically sound, as further participants will not add to the knowledge being generated.

must have a contribution to make to the research. People chosen to be included in such a sample would be key informants on the topic under investigation. For example, Genji in her research, detailed in the case study at the end of Chapter 7 in this textbook, used a judgemental sampling technique in order to compile the **sample** for her study. Genji was researching key strategies used in the promotion of low-carbon technologies in developing countries. Her judgemental sample comprised five senior managers from companies producing low-carbon technologies, and five development workers engaged in promoting low-carbon technologies in developing countries.

Quota sampling Using a quota sampling technique the researcher develops a sample of participants for the research using different quota criteria. Jack in his research project, detailed in the case study at the end of Chapter 2 in this textbook, used a quota sampling method in order to compile the sample for his survey research. Jack needed 100 participants in his survey. The population of the study was a population of students and staff from his university. He decided that there would be four quotas. The first quota was to be made up of 25 female students, the second quota was to be made up of 25 male students, the third quota was to be made up of 25 female members of staff, and the fourth and final quota was to be made up of 25 male members of staff. In this way, Jack used a quota sampling method to develop, using four different quotas, the sample for his research.

Convenience sampling Using a convenience sampling technique the researcher engages those participants in the research whom it is easiest to include, for example people in the newsagents, people in the supermarket, and so on. The researcher knows how many people to include in the sample, then continues to engage people in the research until the sample has been filled.

Snowball sampling Using a snowball sampling technique the researcher finds one participant in the research, conducts the research with that participant, and then asks that participant to recommend the next participant. Participants must fit the inclusion criteria for the research project. The researcher goes through the procedure with the second participant and when finished, asks that participant to recommend another participant to be included in the research. The researcher continues in this manner until the sample is complete.

In some qualitative research projects the research is allowed to unfold, and so the population or the samples used are sometimes not defined from the outset. A frequently-asked question in such circumstances is, when does the researcher stop engaging participants in the research? The answer is when the researcher reaches **saturation point**. Saturation point is reached when the researcher, though continuing to explore the phenomenon with participants in the research, no longer hears any new thoughts, feelings, attitudes, emotions, intentions, etc. This is saturation point, the researcher is 'saturated' with knowledge on the topic and continuing to engage participants would not be useful, necessary, or ethically sound, as it will not add in any way to the knowledge generated.

There are substantial ethical issues involved in engaging some populations in research, in particular vulnerable populations such as children, people with impairments, and socially, culturally and materially disadvantaged people. Particular care should be taken in the design of research projects involving such participants. It is a

REAL WORLD RESEARCH

Detailing the population and sample

Both the population and the sample used in the research project raise issues of validity. In order for the research to be valid, the population used in the research must be a valid population in terms of the phenomenon under investigation. The research population must be the appropriate population, in terms of the focus of the research. It is a good idea to use your research diary to record your reflections on these issues and the decisions that you make in relation to them.

In your research diary describe the population of your research. Do this in the first instance in broad terms. Then do this in as insightful a manner as possible in order to highlight any potential issues or characteristics in the population likely to influence your research and the design of your research project. The diary should be filled with background details and with first and fresh impressions of the population. Background knowledge of the population is very useful to the researcher when making decisions on population and sampling issues. First impressions can provide insights which can contribute substantially to the richness of a research project.

Decide whether you are going to work with the entire population or a sample of that population. Record these decisions in your research diary and write clear and detailed explanations for those decisions.

In writing up the research, the researcher must clearly outline the population of the study, the sample selected, if sampling is used, and the sampling technique used. The researcher records and explains the decisions made with regard to the population and sample, and the rationale for those decisions. The size of the population and the size of the sample must be clearly and unambiguously stated in the report of the research.

well-established fact that social research tends to be conducted with less powerful populations. This is because more powerful individuals and populations are in a position to deflect research or refuse to participate. Less powerful individuals and populations are less likely to refuse to engage in research or to opt out of research. This is often because they do not possess the social capital (see Bourdieu; 1986) that such action would require.

As well as creating knowledge, every researcher is charged with disseminating the knowledge that they have created. In other words, researchers are obliged to publish their research. As a matter of course, students generally publish their work in theses in libraries. In addition to this, you might think about other ways of publishing your research. It might be possible to publish a synopsis of your research in a student newsletter or newspaper, in a trade newsletter or journal. You should consider submitting an article from your research to an academic journal. The *Reinvention Centre for Undergraduate Research* at Warwick University publishes an online peer-reviewed journal of undergraduate research, *Reinvention: A Journal of Undergraduate Research* (**www.warwick.ac.uk**). It would be a useful exercise to locate the journal online and read some of the articles published in it. In due course, you might think of submitting an article to the journal for publication, based on your own research.

THE VALUE OF GOOD RESEARCH

Focus on discourse analysis

Discourse analysis (DA) is a research methodology and a means of analysing data. Discourse analysis means simply the analysis of discourses. Traditionally, discourses have been understood to be language based, to be found in conversation, in written texts, in spoken words. More recently, discourses have been accepted as being more broadly based, and in fact, contemporarily, any kind of communication can be said to be discursive, to have different discourses embedded in it. For example, included among the different discourses that I have studied in the course of my work are historic discourses, managerial discourses, architectural discourses and media discourses. In the detail on discourse analysis presented in Table 8.4 below, discourse analysis is said to be a way of analysing the social world as it is produced and represented in language. As detailed in that table, according to Fairclough (1995), discourses can be written texts, spoken words and/or cultural artefacts, discourses are embedded in social events and social practices.

In their study of websites as tools of communication of a 'green' company, Biloslavo and Trnavŏeviĉ (2009), used content analysis and discourse analysis to examine the websites of 20 companies in Slovenia in relation to sustainable development.

'Websites as tools of communication of a "green" company', Biloslavo, R. and Trnavŏeviĉ, A. (2009)

The main purpose of the study was to analyze the 'green reputation' of a sample of Slovene companies based on their websites. The researchers found that the 20 companies in their sample did use their websites to present their values about environmental protection and social responsibility. They also found, however, that the companies did not max-

imize the potential of their green credentials as a tool for gaining competitive advantage.

This is an interesting study. The researchers present a useful literature review focused on corporate reputation, corporate identity and corporate image. They outline clearly and simply the sampling method used in the study, a purposive sampling method. They clearly explain the sample of companies used in the study and they outline the rationale they used in selecting those companies for inclusion in the sample. The researchers explain the way in which they used content analysis and discourse analysis in their examination of the company websites.

It would be useful to source the original article and to read it through for an example of how to conduct research using a content analysis and a discourse analysis methodology.

Another interesting research project is that of Wang (2006). Wang explored the use of questions as a means of exercising power in both casual conversation and institutional dialogue.

'Questions and the exercise of power', Wang, J. (2006)

Wang writes of power being overt in institutional dialogue, for example in business, and covert in casual conversation, and he writes that questions are used to exercise power differently in both forms of verbal interaction. He writes that questions are powerful in conversation and in dialogue because unequal distribution of questions leads to unequal turn-taking in conversation and dialogue. He writes that dominant questions control the conversation or dialogue, and questions that demand a 'yes' or 'no' answer and the 'wh' questions (who, what, where, why) exercise power in different degrees.

In his review of the literature, Wang explores the nature of power, the definition of a question, and the phenomenon of power in questions. If you examine the structure of Wang's literature review, his theoretical framework, you will clearly see how the structure for the literature review emerged from the conceptual framework of the research project.

For his data on conversational analysis, Wang used ten real casual conversations between college roommates and talks between close friends from two film scripts, *Sleepless in Seattle* and *Notting Hill*. For his analysis of institutional dialogue, Wang carried out analyzes on five different kinds of encounter, medical encounters, courtroom cross-examinations, classroom encounters, news interviews and service encounters.

It would be useful to source this article and to study how Wang uses discourse analysis in his exploration of power in questions. As much research involves researchers posing questions, this is an interesting article for all researchers in terms of the power they have in shaping and asking questions and the ways in which they use that power.

The website of CADAAD (Critical Approaches to Discourse Analysis Across Disciplines) is a useful resource (**www.cadaad.org/**). Hopefully you will remember reading about critical theory in Chapter 4 of this textbook, 'Understanding Research Philosophy'. In that chapter we read that critical theory is a philosophical framework that calls for a critical engagement with society, and in particular with the way in which power operates in society. The CADAAD website provides a glossary of terms and a bibliography as well as links to

resources. On the links and resources page, at the end of that page, there are ten papers, all of them classic studies in critical discourse analysis (CDA). The page provides links to many of the papers. One of the papers is particularly useful, for anyone interested in critical theory, it is van Dijk's (1993), paper, 'Principles of critical discourse analysis'.

There are a number of journals that specialize in research focused on discourses and discourse analysis. Among these journals are *Discourse Studies*, *Discourse and Society* and *Discourse and Communication*.

References

Biloslavo, R. and Trnavčevič, A. (2009) 'Websites as tools of communication of a "green" company', *Management Decision* 47(7): 1158–1173.

Fairclough, N. (1995) *Critical Discourse Analysis*, London: Longman.

van Dijk, T.A. (1993) 'Principles of critical discourse analysis', *Discourse and Society* 4(2): 243–289.

Wang, J. (2006) 'Questions and the exercise of power', *Discourse and Society*, 7(4): 529–548.

RESEARCH METHODS

The term **research methods** means data collection methods or data gathering techniques; data collection methods are the means by which researchers gather the data required for the research project. There are very many research methods that can be used in gathering data for the research project. Commonly-used research methods include questionnaires, interviews, focus groups, scales, projective techniques, diaries, documents, records, and visual methods such as photographs and/or videos. Each research method, or data gathering technique, each questionnaire, each series of interviews, and so on, must be either designed by the researcher specifically for each research project, or borrowed (and referenced) from another research project. The choice of data gathering method(s), is dependent on the aim of the research, the population of the study and the data required for the study and on the location of that data.

The researcher must know what kind of data are needed and where the data are to be found before decisions can be made about how to gather these data. The data could be in documents or written reports, or in the attitudes and beliefs of human participants, or in the behaviours of human participants in the research, and each of these examples would require the design of a different data gathering technique. It might be that there is some vulnerability in the human participants in the research or that participation in the research could potentially render the population vulnerable. If this is the case, the data gathering methods must be demonstrably sensitive to that vulnerability. If, for example, the human population in the study is made up of children, the age of the respondents and their potential vulnerability in participating

> **Research methods**
> Data collection methods.

in the research will require special consideration in the design of data gathering technique(s). The researcher might be working with a population with cultural issues, language issues or with literacy issues. Any or all of these will have an impact on the design of data gathering technique. The researcher must identify the data required, and then decide where the data are, and finally decide how best, within a framework of research ethics, to gather the data.

Researchers are very pragmatic when it comes to research methods. They use whatever method of data collection is most appropriate, or whatever data collection method will work best. In deciding on the most appropriate data collection method(s) to use, some of the typical considerations of researchers are:

- whether the data can be gathered by interviewing people
- if a questionnaire would produce the required data
- whether or not it would be useful to conduct a focus group, or a series of focus groups
- if the data required could be gathered from diaries in which participants in the research would record their experiences of the phenomenon under investigation
- if the data required is to be found in documents, in records or in archives
- if the data would best be gathered using a series of observations
- if the data could be gathered through taking a series of photographs, or using an existing series of photographs.

When the researcher knows what data are required for the research project, and how that data can best be gathered, the researcher designs the approach to data gathering to be used. The data gathering methods are designed in such a way as to ensure that they will yield the data required. The data gathered are the means by which the researcher establishes the thesis developed in the research, the means by which they accept or reject the hypotheses presented in the research project. They are the means by which they prove their case, the means by which they illustrate the phenomenon under investigation. As this is the case, the data gathered must be adequate and they must be valid.

REAL WORLD RESEARCH

How theory influences research

The research project detailed below explored youth electoral engagement. It is a multi-method research project. As well as the *questionnaires* used and *focus groups* conducted with young people, the researchers *interviewed* personnel from advertising agencies and they engaged in a *content analysis* of election posters. Read the synopsis below and then find the original article online. Use this article to develop your knowledge of data collection methods. In particular read the 'research design' section of the journal article. This section provides a good example of the level of detail required in writing up the research methodology chapter in the thesis, or the research methodology section in the report of the research.

'Exploring the value of party political advertising for youth electoral engagement: An analysis of the 2001 British General Election advertising campaigns', Dermody, J. and Scullion, R. (2004)

The authors of the article wrote that one of the key issues in the latter days of the 2001 British General Election was the issue of encouraging the electorate to vote. They wrote that turnout at British elections was in decline, particularly among young people. They said that British democracy appeared to be facing a crisis and stated that election advertising campaigns had been accused of failing to engage a disinterested young electorate.

The aim of their research paper was to explore youth attitudes to electoral advertising and to explore the value of electoral advertising for public servants tasked with increasing voter engagement and voter turnout among people.

Research design

A multi-method approach was taken to the research. This included a *survey* and *focus group* interviews with potential first-time voters aged 18–22. The population for the survey comprised British citizens who were eligible to vote for the first time. They were aged between 18 and 22 at the time of the 2001 British General Election. The *focus group* respondents also conformed to this pattern. The sample contained a mix of students. Some were employed and some were unemployed. There was an equal gender mix. There was a bias towards 21–22-year-olds. A greater proportion of the respondents said that they voted. The majority of the participants classified themselves as 'White British'. They were educated to GCSE standard, with a large cluster also holding A/AS qualifications. The students in the sample were typically studying for their first degree. The authors compared the sample against the national profile (of 18–22-year-olds), there is a slight bias towards students, young people who claimed they voted and alleged Labour supporters. The authors felt that, overall, the respondent 'fit' was 'reasonably tight', and they felt that this close fit helped to confirm 'the robustness of findings from the data'.

We are told that both the *survey* and *focus group* data were collected during the 3 week period immediately following the election on 1 June, 2001. The authors state that five *focus groups* were conducted

in a variety of regions over that time period. They detail that each of the *focus groups* typically consisted of 6–10 respondents and on average lasted 2.5 hours each. They state that all *interviews* were taped and the analysis conducted on the *interview* data was based on verbatim transcripts. The *interviews,* they write, explored respondents' attitudes to advertising generally before moving on to explore their attitudes to the election advertising and the election itself. The authors tell us that two *pilot focus groups* and a review of pertinent literature informed both the content and structure of the *focus group* interviews.

The authors state that a quasi-random sampling approach was adopted for the *survey.* They say that a filtering system was used to ensure all respondents fitted the sampling criteria – the interview was terminated if they did not. The data collection method was a *survey* involving *street intercept interviews*, using an *interviewer-administered questionnaire. Street intercept interviews* are *interviews* conducted in the street with people passing by in the street. The researcher intercepts the passers-by and engages them in an interview. The *street intercept interviews* took place in large towns throughout the UK. A total of 867 usable *questionnaires* were completed. The two *pilot focus groups* and literature review also informed the content and structure of the *questionnaire.* The *questionnaire* focused on the attitudes of the respondents to the election generally, before moving on to ask each of the respondents specifically about three advertisements used to encourage voting before the election. The respondents' attitudes to the three advertisements were measured using *semantic differential scales.* Statistical Package for the Social Sciences (SPSS) was used to analyze the data. SPSS is a computerized data analysis package used for the analysis of quantitative data. The analysis of quantitative data and the use of SPSS in analysing quantitative data are dealt with in detail in this textbook in Chapter 14 'Analysing Quantitative Data'.

All of the data collection methods used in the study are detailed in the text above. Using your research diary, list all of the data collection methods used in this study. Use the information on data collection methods outlined below in Table 8.4 to develop your understanding of each of the methods used in this research.

What sampling method was used in the above study? Could you write a short critique of that sampling method?

What population was used in the study? How well do you think the sample selected represents the population?

Do you agree with the authors' claim that there was a close fit between the population of the study and the sample of that population included in the study?

What do the authors mean when they state that this close fit helped to confirm the robustness of findings from the data?

References

Dermody, J. and Scullion, R. (2004) 'Exploring the value of party political advertising for youth electoral engagement: An analysis of the 2001 British General Election advertising campaigns', *International Journal of Nonprofit and Voluntary Sector Marketing* 9(4): 361–379.

DATA COLLECTION METHODS

The researcher is, as stated, a pragmatist when it comes to gathering data. The techniques that provide the most useful data, the most appropriate data, are the methods used. There are very many data collection methods at the disposal of the researcher, including those described in this chapter. In fact, the researcher is limited only by their own imaginations, and by the issue of validity, in terms of the data collection method(s) they use in their research project. Table 8.4 contains short descriptions of different data gathering methods. You will notice that some of the data gathering methods listed below are also listed in Tables 7.1 and 7.2 in Chapter 7 of this textbook. This is because these approaches to research can be used as research methodologies and/or as data collection methods. Some of them, such as discourse analysis, content analysis and narrative analysis can also be used as approaches to data analysis. We will encounter these terms again when we explore data analysis in later chapters of this textbook.

Table 8.3 List of data collection methods	
Observation	Scales
Participant observation	Projective techniques
Covert observation	Content analysis
One-to-one interviews	Field diaries
Telephone interviews	Visual methods
Group interviews	Narrative analysis
Postal questionnaires	Documentary evidence
Drop and collect questionnaires	Discourse analysis
Group administered questionnaires	Semiotics
Online questionnaires	Oral history
Focus groups	Archival research
Internet research	Experiments
Secondary sources	Unobtrusive methods
Case studies	Critical incident method

Table 8.4 Detailed data collection methods	
Observation	Observation is a data collection method used in order to record the observations of a phenomenon. The researcher engages in observation in order to gather data on the phenomenon under investigation. In conducting an observation, the researcher observes what is happening and records her or his observations. Observations can be carried out in an unstructured, semi-structured, or structured manner. In an *unstructured observation* the researcher has no pre-set criteria in terms of what it is that he/she is observing. This kind of observation is usually engaged in at the beginning of a study, when the researcher is not sure precisely what will happen, or what exactly he/she needs to be observing. Often, through unstructured observation, these things become apparent. In *semi-structured observation*, the researcher has a pre-prepared list of actions that he/she wishes to focus on through the observation. Generally this list will contain about eight points, each of which relates to the action to be observed. The researcher notes each time the action happens, and records, generally in field notes, his or her observations on and around the action. In *structured observation*, the researcher has a structured list of actions or points related to the action that he/she wishes to observe. A schedule designed for the recording of a structured observation can look like a highly structured questionnaire. The researcher ticks boxes on the schedule to record the actions he/she is observing, recording his or her thoughts in separate field notes. Chapter 10 in this textbook focuses on observation.
Participant observation	Participant observation is the same as observation, with one major difference, the researcher is a participant in the action he/she is observing. While the researcher participates in the action, he/she observes the action and records their observations on the action.
Covert observation	Covert observation is observation carried out covertly or secretly. The researcher observes the action and records their observations of the action covertly. There are substantial ethical issues in covert research. Chapter 3 of this textbook deals in detail with research ethics.
One-to-one interviews	One-to-one interviews are interviews carried out generally face-to-face and on a one-to-one basis between the interviewer and the interviewee. One-to-one interviews or face-to-face interviews are a very common data collection method. They have very many advantages. In a one-to-one interview, the interviewer has an opportunity to establish a rapport with the interviewee. The researcher has the opportunity to explain the research in detail to the interviewee. He/she can discuss the questions and issues with the interviewee. He/she can observe the interviewee's responses to the interview questions and issues. The interviewer can probe the interviewee in terms of any responses to questions. Interviews are usually audio-recorded and transcribed later. Every interview is a social engagement and the interviewer, the researcher, must have the capacity to engage the interviewee in the interview in an empathetic way. The interviewer must have the capacity to sustain that engagement for the length of the interview. In interviews there is a danger of interviewer bias. This is where the interviewer attempts to influence or lead the responses of the interviewee, intentionally or otherwise. Interviewing in research is a particular skill. The researcher must be empathetic, but he/she must not influence the responses in any way. Interviews can be time-consuming, and they can be exhausting for the interviewer. Interviewees can be very cooperative and sometimes they can be quite uncooperative. The interviewer must be prepared to deal with any contingency. What should he/she do if the interviewee suddenly terminates the interview? What should he/she do if a fire alarm goes off? Interviewers need to be very well-prepared for the social encounter that is the interview.

(Continued)

	Table 8.4 Detailed data collection methods (continued)
	Any equipment needed, electronic or otherwise must be in proper working order, prepared and ready, for the interview. The interviewer must ensure that sufficient time is given to each interview, to preparation, to set-up, to de-briefing and/or recovery after the interview. After the interview, there must be sufficient time for the transcribing of interview recordings. Transcribing interviews is the process through which recorded interviews are typed up into typed transcripts. Typed transcripts of interviews are complete and accurate typed records of the interviews, taken from (or transcribed from) the recordings of the interviews. The transcript becomes the data to be analyzed. Chapter 11 of this textbook focuses in detail on interviews.
Telephone interviews	Telephone interviews are interviews conducted, generally on a one-to-one basis, over the telephone. Telephone interviews can be very convenient and very time and resource efficient. They are relatively inexpensive when compared to the cost of actually visiting all of the respondents as is necessary in one-to-one interviewing. Telephone interviews can yield a substantial amount of data relatively quickly and easily. On the negative side, the interviewer in telephone interviewing is not face-to-face with the interviewee and so cannot observe the responses of the interviewee to the interview questions and issues. Neither generally can the interviewer establish the same level of rapport with the interviewee as is possible with one-to-one interviews. It can be more difficult in telephone interviewing to discern when more information needs to be given to the interviewee; it can be more difficult to discern whether or not it would be possible or appropriate to probe an issue with a telephone interviewee. It is, generally speaking, easier for an interviewee to terminate a telephone interview or to withdraw from a telephone interview than from a one-to-one face-to-face interview.
Group interviews	Group interviews are interviews conducted face-to-face between the interviewer and a group of interviewees. This type of face-to-face interview has all of the advantages of the one-to-one interview outlined above, as well as all of the issues. A key skill required in group interviewees is that of facilitating groups. Facilitating groups is a substantial and a complex task. It requires particular skill and diplomacy. A group interview is used by a researcher when the data required for the research project can best be gathered through a group interview. This means that there is something in the group processes, which generally occur naturally within group interviews, which will lead to the generation within the group interview of the data required for the research. The researcher chooses group interview as the data gathering method when there is something in the group process which will aid the generation of the data required.
Online interviews	Online interviews can be synchronous, in real time, using a chat room or using conferencing software, or asynchronous, outside of real time, using email or message boards or discussion boards, and so on. In synchronous interviewing the interviewer asks questions and the interviewee responds immediately. Synchronous interviews can be conducted very quickly, and this can have advantages. In asynchronous interviewing, the interviewer sends questions to the interviewee and the interviewee responds at a later time. Interviewers send one question at a time, or a very short number of questions at a time. A long list of questions is a questionnaire, not an interview schedule. Asynchronous interviewing can take time. This has advantages and disadvantages. One advantage is that respondents can take time to consider their responses and this can improve the quality of responses. A disadvantage can be the difficulty in keeping respondents engaged with the interview process. Online interviews are useful with geographically dispersed populations and with otherwise difficult to reach populations. Online interviews are very resource efficient, if all participants have

	Table 8.4 Detailed data collection methods (continued)
	ready access to the technology used in the interviews. The relative anonymity of the interviewee can facilitate openness and frankness in their responses to interview questions and probes. There is a possibility of respondents mistrusting online interviewing, some people feel that chat rooms for example are too open, sometimes people perform different identities online. Video links in online interviewing can intimidate respondents and consequently inhibit the quality of their engagement in the interview. On the other hand, where there is no video link, there is reduced chance of interviewer bias. Interviewer bias occurs when the interviewer influences the responses of the interviewee in some way. Bias is dealt with in detail in Chapter 11, 'Using Interviews and Focus Groups'.
Postal questionnaires	Questionnaires are among the most widely used data collection methods. I am sure that you have filled in a questionnaire at some point in your life. You have to fill in a questionnaire if you open a bank account, if you join a library. Questionnaires are generally highly structured data collection instruments. With highly structured data collection instruments, respondents are often simply required to tick boxes in order to respond to the research. This facilitates participants, and participants in large numbers, in participating in the research. The researcher in designing the data collection instrument has decided very precisely what data are required and they have structured the data collection instrument very precisely to provide that data. Questionnaires can be made up of both closed and open questions. Closed questions are questions that require a set response, for example, yes/no/don't know/not applicable. The respondent is given a set of possible responses and simply ticks a box to indicate the response that they have selected in response to the question posed. Open questions do not have a set of pre-defined responses. Open questions allow the respondent to express themselves. The following is an example of an open question: Please explain why you decided to introduce the new product.
	In response, respondents are invited to respond as they wish and they are given space in the questionnaire to respond openly to the question or issue. There are generally very few such open questions in questionnaires. This is because of the complexity posed by coding such responses. It is much easier to code the responses to closed questions. The more open questions there are in a questionnaire, the more complex, protracted and time-consuming will be the coding process. Questionnaires with closed questions can be readily and quickly coded and analyzed. Questionnaires are often used with big research populations. Questionnaires can readily and easily be administered to large populations. Postal questionnaires are questionnaires that are posted to respondents. A covering letter is sent with the questionnaire and a stamped addressed envelope (SAE) to facilitate the respondents in responding. The respondent is required to fill in the questionnaire and post it back to the researcher using the SAE. Often the researcher has to post a reminder to the respondents to encourage them to respond to the questionnaire. As the researcher does not meet with the respondents or engage with the respondents in any other way, there can be an issue with low levels of response rates using this method of data collection. The cost of this data collection method is the cost of the stationary and the cost of the postage. The *Value of Good Research* box feature in Chapter 2 of this textbook deals with survey research. Chapter 12 of this textbook focuses on questionnaires and scales.
Drop and collect questionnaires	A drop and collect questionnaire is where a researcher drops a questionnaire with respondents and then returns to collect the questionnaire when the respondent

Table 8.4 Detailed data collection methods (continued)	
	has completed filling in the questionnaire. The method of administering the questionnaire, drop and collect, can help boost response rates.
Group administered questionnaires	Group administered questionnaires are questionnaires which the researcher administers to a group. When the group is gathered together, the researcher administers the questionnaire to them. It might happen that the group assembles for a meeting, or for a class, or for a conference or for some other purpose. The researcher takes the opportunity of the gathering to administer the questionnaire. This is a very efficient means of gathering data. The data are gathered in one go. The collective nature of the data gathering, together with the presence of the researcher, helps boost response rates. Response rates of 100 per cent would not be unusual in group administered questionnaires.
Online questionnaires	Online questionnaires are questionnaires which are administered online. Such questionnaires can be sent to respondents via email, or respondents can be sent a link to the questionnaire, which can be uploaded to a website, and invited to respond to the questionnaire. Response rates can be a substantial issue using online questionnaires. Questionnaires can be created online using tools like Survey Monkey, Instant Survey or Zoomerang. The *Exploring Online Research Methods* web page of the University of Leicester is a useful resource for information on online questionnaires, (**www.geog.le.ac.uk/ORM/site/home.htm**). The *Value of Good Research* box feature in Chapter 2 of this textbook deals with survey research and with online questionnaires. There is some focus on online questionnaires in Chapter 12 of this textbook which focuses on questionnaires and scales.
Focus groups	In focus group research, the researcher brings groups of people together, to focus on a particular issue. The optimum number of participants in a focus group is eight, the lowest is six, and the highest is 12. The group generally meets around a table. This setting facilitates even contribution from all participants. The focus group is generally audio-recorded. The audio recording is transcribed. Transcribing focus groups is the process through which the recorded focus group is typed up into a transcript. Typed transcripts of focus groups are complete and accurate typed records of the focus groups, taken from or transcribed from the recordings of the focus groups. The transcript becomes the data to be analyzed. The researcher, and/ or any assistant researcher(s) may also record their observations of the focus group and their impressions of the focus group by hand. These observations and impressions can be used to supplement the data from the transcripts. Focus groups, like questionnaires, can be unstructured, semi-structured or structured. Usually, they are semi-structured. In a semi-structured focus group, the researcher has a list of questions or issues to be explored during the focus group. The researcher moderates the focus group, or may invite another expert to moderate. The moderator facilitates the focus group. The moderation of focus groups requires particular skills. The group dynamic in focus group research often produces unique insights and perspectives, and this is the real value of this particular method. The onus is on the moderator to get the discussion going, to maintain it, and to conclude it on time. Focus groups are dealt with in detail in Chapter 11 of this textbook.
Internet research	Internet research is research conducted on the internet. Obviously there is a great deal of information on the World Wide Web (WWW). The internet can be used to source literature and it can be used to source data, primary and secondary data. We have seen above where the internet can be used to develop and administer questionnaires. Interviews can be conducted on the internet, using email, chat rooms, discussion boards or through the use of video-conferencing (see Chapter 11, 'Using Interviews and Focus Groups'. The case study at the end of

Table 8.4 Detailed data collection methods (continued)	
	Chapter 9 in this textbook, 'Using Secondary Data and Archival Sources', is an example of how secondary sources available on the web can be used as data in a research project. In the case study, four different reports, all available on the internet, were used in order to study child poverty. The internet can be searched for information. Search engines on the WWW can help you find the information you need. Google is a very popular web search engine. Other web search engines include Yahoo, MSNSearch, ASK.com, Alltheweb, AtlasVista, Lycos. Key word searches can also help you find the information you need. Domain searches are also important. A domain on the internet is the home or area of authority or autonomy of an individual, an organization, an entity. You could search, for example, the domain of the OECD (Organization for Economic Cooperation and Development) for information and data, or the domain of the IMF (International Monetary Fund). The *Exploring Online Research Methods* web page of the University of Leicester is a useful resource for information on online research methods (**www.geog.le.ac.uk/ORM/site/home.htm**).
Secondary sources	A secondary source is, in a sense, a second-hand source. A secondary source is something that has been written about a primary source. When a researcher creates data themselves, what they have created is a primary source. When the data they are using have been created by someone else, the data are secondary data, data from a secondary source. A secondary source builds on a primary source, a secondary source interprets and analyzes a primary source. A secondary source is an account of something. The original material is the primary source. Secondary sources of data can be used very effectively by researchers in carrying out research. As we saw above, Chapter 9 in this textbook focuses on secondary sources. The case study at the end of Chapter 9 is a study of child poverty carried out using secondary sources. The data used in the case study are all drawn from reports published on the Internet.
Case studies	Case studies, as explained in Chapter 7, (Table 7.2 Detailed research methodologies), is research carried out on a bounded entity, on a specific space or place, on a particular incident, or on specific entities. Using a case study method the researcher studies one case or a number of cases. The researcher, drawing on all of the data sources possible, engages in an in-depth examination of the case(s). Yin (2009), has written on case study methodology. Case study methodology is the research methodology in focus in Chapter 3 of this textbook, 'Understanding Research Ethics'. Susan Soy (2006) has produced a good simple guide to case study research. You will find this at **www.ischool.utexas.edu/~ssoy/useusers/l391`d1b.htm**.
Scales	Scales and scaling techniques are used widely in attitude measurement research. Commonly used scales include Likert scales, Bogardus social distance scales, semantic differential scales. In the box feature 'Real World Research – How theory influences research' in this chapter, Dermody and Scullion (2004), used a semantic differential scale as one of the data collection methods in their multi-method research project. Scales are used to generate quantitative data. Scales are very interesting research techniques. They appear to be quite simple, but appearances can be deceptive. The production of a valid scale involves a great deal of work and preparation. Scales are dealt with in detail in Chapter 12 of this textbook, 'Using Questionnaires and Scales'.
Projective techniques	Projective techniques are used to explore people's instinctive responses to stimuli, stimuli such as, for example, advertising campaigns. Projective techniques are indirect ways of exploring attitudes. It is suggested sometimes that as the purpose of projective techniques is often less obvious than the purpose of attitude scales,

(Continued)

Table 8.4   Detailed data collection methods (continued)

	projective techniques can yield truer results. One example of a projective technique is sentence completion. This is an exercise whereby the researcher gives the respondent the first part of a sentence, and asks the respondent to complete the sentence. Scales and projective techniques can be used alone or as part of other research methods. They can, for example, be built into questionnaires. They can be used in interviews, or to help start or prompt discussions in focus groups. There is an introduction to projective techniques in Chapter 12 of this textbook, 'Using Questionnaires and Scales'. Oppenheim's (1992), book has a very good chapter on projective techniques.
Content analysis	Content analysis is a research method that involves the analysis of content, the analysis of any kind of content. Content analysis is widely used in communications research. Traditionally content analysis was used for the systematic quantitative description of the explicit content of any communication. Content analysis can also be used qualitatively. Content analysis generally means the analysis of some aspect of a particular type of communication. The communication might be a newspaper, a newsletter, a radio or TV programme. The research is focused on a particular phenomenon, and the researcher identifies that phenomenon in the communication. The researcher then examines the phenomenon within that communication. The researcher might explore for example how often a word or phrase is used. The researcher might analyze the content in order to come to some conclusion about the tone of the communication, about the message in the communication, about the ideologies expressed in the communication, and so on. Content Analysis is the research methodology in focus in Chapter 6 of this textbook, 'Reviewing the Literature'.
Field diaries	Field notes or field diaries are the traditional way in social research and in particular in anthropological and ethnographical research, through which observations in the field are recorded. Field diaries are diaries in which the researcher records all of their observations in the field. The field in social research is the site of the research. It is the site where the research takes place, or the site where the research is carried out. Field diaries are particularly useful for researchers in the writing-up phase of the research. They can be used by the researcher as a prompt to memory, an aide memoir, as a record more reliable than memory. They can be used for the descriptive passages they often contain regarding the research site, and these can greatly enhance a research project, adding richness and colour to the descriptions of the site, the phenomenon, and/or the participants (see Hammersley and Atkinson, 1995: Chapter 7). Research participants can be requested to keep diaries within which they record their observations and reflections on the phenomenon under investigation. These diaries can then be used as data in the research project.
Visual methods and image-based research	Visual methods is the use of any kind of visual image as data in the research project. Visual methods involves the analysis of visual images. Any kind of visual images can be used, maps, charts, photographs, drawings, paintings, cartoons, videos and films, and so on. The researcher can gather visual images or he/she can create visual images, or they can ask participants in the research to give visual images to the research project or to create visual images for the research project. As with every data collection method, data generated by the method must be valid. The data must be valid in terms of the purpose of the research project. As explained in the table on research methodologies in Chapter 7 of this textbook, Table 7.2 Detailed research methodologies visual data can be analyzed using a quantitative or a qualitative approach, or a mixture of both. Banks (2007), Pink (2006), Prosser (1998), and Rose (2001), are among those who have written on visual methods and image-based research. As detailed in Chapter 4, the

Table 8.4 Detailed data collection methods (continued)	
	web-resource Methodspace (**www.methodspace.com**) has a number of video interviews with research methodologists, among them Jon Prosser, Sarah Pink and Marcus Banks, Image-based research is the research methodology in focus in Chapter 4 of this textbook, 'Understanding Research Philosophy'.
Narrative analysis	Narrative analysis calls for the analysis of narratives. Narratives are collected as data, or narratives are identified in data and then analyzed. Narratives are stories. These stories can be oral histories or biographies; they can be folk tales or myths. They can be the stories participants tell about the phenomenon under investigation. Human beings tell stories. In fact much of human communication is accomplished through story-telling. The stories told about a culture or a phenomenon can be very revealing. People within a culture or people experiencing a phenomenon tell stories about that culture and/or that phenomenon. It is one of the ways through which they can make meaning of the culture and/or the phenomenon. The narratives that a culture tells about itself are also revealing. Such narratives can be discerned from the material published by organizations about their organization. The researcher gathers data for the research project. S/he identifies the narratives in the data and then he/she analyzes those narratives in order to explain or illustrate the phenomenon under investigation. As explained in Chapter 7 of this textbook, Table 7.2 Detailed research methodologies, narrative research and narrative analysis has been written about by Gubrium and Holstein (2009). Narrative analysis is the research methodology in focus in Chapter 7 of this textbook, 'Understanding Research Methodology and Design'.
Documentary evidence	Documentary evidence is data in the form of documents, or data drawn from documents. Documentary analysis involves the systematic analysis of data in the form of documents or data drawn from documents. The documents used can be written documents, books, newspapers, notices, letters, records, and so on. Documentary research is the research methodology in focus in Chapter 5 of this textbook, 'Developing a Research Proposal'.
Discourse analysis	Discourse analysis is a way of analysing the social world as it is produced and represented in language. According to Fairclough (1995), discourses can be written texts, spoken words and/or cultural artefacts. Discourses are, he suggests, embedded in social events and social practices. Foucault (1970, 1972), was concerned with the way in which individuals could be represented within powerful discourses. You might, for example, think about the powerful discourse that a multinational corporation might develop and circulate about itself. Another way to think about discourses is to think about the individual and how the individual might be represented within the discourses of the organization. For example, how are individuals represented within marketing discourses, within HR discourses? You can see how all of these discourses would differ. Discourses are embedded in the language we use, and in the way in which we use that language. Discourse analysis calls for the identification of such discourses within the ways through which we communicate, and the analysis of them. Discourse analysis is the methodology in focus in this chapter, Chapter 8, 'Understanding Research Methods, Populations and Sampling'. See also Wodak and Krzyzanowski (2008).
Semiotics	Semiotics is the study of signs in society. Signs are the words, pictures, symbols, etc. used by people in society to communicate, to make meaning. van Leeuwen (2005), explores social semiotics such as dress, everyday objects, artefacts and images. He defines semiotic resources (2005: 3), as the actions and artefacts we

(Continued)

Table 8.4 Detailed data collection methods (continued)	
	use to communicate. According to van Leeuwen (2005: 5), 'studying the semiotic potential of a given semiotic resource is studying how that resource has been, is, and can be, used for the purposes of communication'. In using semiotics in research, the focus is on the way in which people use semiotic resources, language, dress, artefacts, food, images, etc. to communicate. Social semiotics are loaded with meaning and cultural significance. Semiotics is widely used in market research. There are many articles detailing research projects carried out using semiotics in journals such as the *European Journal of Marketing*, *The Journal of Consumer Marketing*, the *Journal of Consumer Research* and the *International Journal of Market Research*. Semiotics is the methodology in focus in Chapter 13 of this textbook, 'Managing Data and Introducing Data Analysis'. See also the detail on semiotics in Table 7.2 Detailed research methodologies in Chapter 7 of this textbook, 'Understanding Research Methodology and Design'.
Oral history	Oral history is a data collection method by which oral testimony is gathered from the research participants on their experience of the phenomenon on which the research project is focused. Oral history is a systematic method of gathering such data. Oral historians are focused on establishing an historic record. They don't gather anecdotes or folk tales. Oral history is a history of the present or the recent past. This is because oral historians deal with the testimonies of living individuals. The Oxford journal *The Oral History Review* is a good place to look for examples of oral history research projects. The UCLA (University of California, Los Angeles) Anderson School of Management has an oral history research programme called *Entrepreneurs of the West* (**www.anderson.ucla.edu/x1194.xml**). Oral history and life history is the methodology in focus in Chapter 16 of this textbook, 'Drawing Conclusions and Writing Research'.
Archival research	Archival research, as explained in Chapter 7, (Table 7.2 Detailed research methodologies), is research carried out on the content of archives. Archives are documents or stores of documents. Archives can be very small and they can be very extensive. Libraries, for example, can store archives. The stored records and/ or documents of a company or a business would constitute an archive. According to the website of The National Archive of the UK (**www.nationalarchives.gov.uk**), 'archives are documents in any medium that have been created by an individual, family, business or organization during its existence and have been chosen to be kept permanently because they are considered to be of continuing value'. Archival research is considered in detail in Chapter 9 of this textbook, 'Using Secondary Data and Archival Sources'.
Experiments	As detailed in Chapter 7, (Table 7.2 Detailed research methodologies), in an experiment two groups are established, with individuals or units being randomly assigned to both groups. The two groups are pre-tested, and the **dependent variable** is measured. Then some programme or application, the **independent variable**, is applied to one group, the experimental group, and not to the other group, the control group. Both groups are tested again; again the dependent variable is measured. If there is a difference in the experimental group but not in the control group, the programme or application applied to them, the independent variable, is said to account for the difference. There can be more than one dependent variable in an experiment but there should only be one independent variable. In the social world, there are so many variables it can be difficult sometimes to isolate an independent variable. It can be difficult to establish precisely which

Table 8.4 Detailed data collection methods (continued)	
	variable(s) account for changes that occur in social science research. It can be difficult in social research, to absolutely establish cause and effect, to establish precisely what/which cause brought about what/which effect.
	The Hawthorne Experiments (1924–1933) are classical examples. Elton Mayo a professor of Industrial Management at the Harvard Business School studied worker behaviour at the Western Electrical Company's Hawthorne Works in Illinois, USA. The experiments Mayo carried out were designed to measure worker productivity. Mayo found that as he studied the workers, their productivity improved. What he realized was that the subjects of his experiments changed their performance in response to being observed. In other words, it was the experience of being observed that caused worker productivity to improve. This variable of being observed was an unforeseen variable in the experiments, yet it was the variable that brought about the change in worker behaviour. This discovery became known as 'the Hawthorne effect'. You can read about the Hawthorne experiments on the Harvard Business School website at **www.library.hbs.edu/hc/hawthorne/anewversion.html**. Trochim (2006), on his website *Research Methods: Knowledge Base*, provides a clear introduction to experimental design (**www.socialresearchmethods.net/kb/desexper. php**). Experimental design is the methodology in focus in Chapter 12 of this textbook, 'Using Questionnaires and Scales'.
Unobtrusive methods	Unobtrusive methods are data collection methods that can be employed by the researcher without the researcher intruding in any way on the site of the research or on the population of the research. Unobtrusive methods clearly have an important place in social research, given the impact of other methods on the behaviour of research participants, as highlighted in the Hawthorne Experiments detailed above. Unobtrusive methods avoid the reactivity generated by other data gathering methods. Many of the methods detailed above can be used unobtrusively, secondary sources are clearly unobtrusive. Potentially unobtrusive methods include content analysis and documentary analysis. Other methods can be used unobtrusively, such as observation and photography. In his book on unobtrusive methods in social research, Lee (2000), talks about 'found data', for example data in the form of material objects found which inform the research, data in the form of environmental damage or erosion, and accretion measures whereby the data are in the form of some physical evidence, such as graffiti or garbage. Garbage-based research, garbology, the study of what people throw away, is used in consumer research. Garbage analysis was used by Cote *et al.* (1985), in their study of the disparity between stated intention and actual behaviour in relation to 15 commonly consumed food and beverage products. There are clearly ethical implications in the use of many unobtrusive methods. There may also be legal issues. It is always a good idea to get feedback on your ideas for your research before you become fixed on them or committed to them. It is essential that you seek and secure approval from your research supervisor for those ideas before you put any of them into practice.
Critical incident technique	This method involves gathering data about a critical incident or a series of critical incidents and the consequences of that/those incident(s). The researcher generally uses observation and/or interview to explore the critical incident and its consequences. The researcher also uses reports, official reports, media reports, and any other reports and documentation available on the critical incident. The researcher gathers data on the critical incident in order to understand the incident. The researcher then applies their understanding of the critical incident to the

(Continued)

Table 8.4   Detailed data collection methods (continued)
phenomenon under investigation in order to develop further insight(s) into the phenomenon under investigation. One disadvantage of the critical incident method is that the focus on critical incidents may cause routine incidents to be overlooked. There is a chapter on Critical Incident (Gilbert and Lockwood, 1999), in *The Handbook of Contemporary Hospitality Management Research* (Brotherton, 1999). Kaulio and Uppvall (2009), used critical incidents to study leadership in R&D alliances.

You will already be familiar with many of the data collection methods detailed here, although some will be new to you. It is possible that the knowledge that you have of some of the data collection methods listed is 'common sense knowledge'. This kind of knowledge can be harmful rather than helpful in scientific undertakings. The rigorous use or application of data collection methods in social science research requires sophisticated scientific knowledge. For this reason it is important that you read the brief descriptions of the data gathering methods given in Table 8.3 List of data collection methods. It is important too that you follow this up with further reading, guided by the references and recommended readings given in this textbook. This is particularly important in relation to the data collection methods that you intend to use in your own research project.

> **Dependent variable**
> What is measured in an experiment. The variable that responds to the independent variable.

As stated previously in this textbook, you are only limited in terms of your own imagination in relation to the ways in which you use these data collection methods, and any other data collection methods you find or devise for your project. The only stipulations or constraints are that the data collection methods must be valid and they must fit the research. This means that they must fit the aim of the research, the population of the research and the data requirements of the research, and they must accomplish what it is that they purport to accomplish.

> **Independent variable**
> The **variable** that the variable introduced in order to produce some effect on the dependent variable.

In writing up your research it is important that you clearly detail as fully as possible all of the elements of the methodological framework. The methodological framework, as you know, is contained in, or it is the content of, the research methodology chapter of the thesis, or the research methodology section of the research report. The model in Figure 8.3 demonstrates again how the methodological framework emerges from the conceptual framework in the four frameworks approach to the research project.

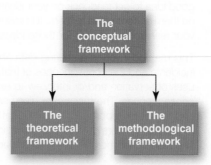

Figure 8.3   The methodological framework emerges from the conceptual framework

YOUR RESEARCH

Common research problems – Understanding the difference between quantitative and qualitative research and data

It is sometimes the case that students have difficulty in grasping the difference between quantitative and qualitative research and data. The following research diary exercise is designed to help you develop an understanding of both quantitative and qualitative research and data. Record this exercise in your research diary.

For this exercise we will revisit the table on research methodologies in Chapter 7 (Table 7.2 Detailed research methodologies). From your reading of the descriptions of the methodologies in the table, can you name the methodologies in which only quantitative data can be used? Can you name the methodologies in which only qualitative data be used? Can you name the methodologies which can draw on a mixture of quantitative and qualitative data?

Now think about your own research project. Think about the research methodology you are using in your research. Think about the data collec-

tion methods you are using in your research and the table on data gathering methods in Chapter 8 (Table 8.4 Detailed data collection methods). In your research diary, write a short paragraph on the contribution of both quantitative and qualitative data to your research. In your writing respond to the following questions:

What do you think of the contribution of both the quantitative and qualitative data?
In your research project, do you think one is more useful than the other?
Why do you think that?

Capture your answers and thoughts in your research diary. You will find these useful to look back on when you are designing your research project, when you are writing the research methodology chapter or section of your thesis and explaining the choices that you made in relation to the design of your research project.

In the research methodology chapter in the thesis or in the research methodology section of the report of the research, you must detail and explain the methodology used in the research and the rationale for choosing that methodology. You have to clearly outline the population of the study and sample used, if a sample is used. The sampling technique used and the manner in which the technique was operationalized or used in the research project must be explained. You must name and explain the data collection methods used; you must explain why those particular data collection methods were used, how they were designed, and how they were used. It is also important to clearly present the response rates to the different data collection methods used in the research.

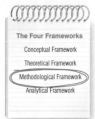

The Four Frameworks

Conceptual Framework

Theoretical Framework

Methodological Framework

Analytical Framework

CASE STUDY

How to use a table of random numbers to randomly select a sample

How to use a random number table.

1 Let us say that we have a population of 90 students, and in our study we want a sample of 30 students from that population of 90.

2 We get or we compile a complete list of the names of the 90 students. This is our sampling frame.

3 We assign each student a number, between 1 and 90.

Table 8.5 Part of a table of random numbers				
13245	12908	10987	63689	65789
90876	45387	66754	88975	22234
34512	76894	24674	34577	34688
20137	23144	23557	13567	98799
42378	34556	76889	32412	57886
76890	44321	35669	54678	35467
34667	78665	21332	23123	87923

Research at work © Andrew Rich/iStock

4 As we have a population of 90, and 90 is a two digit number, we need to use the first two digits of the numbers in the table of random numbers above.

5 To begin, we randomly point to a number on the table. This number becomes our starting point.

6 Let us say we pointed to the number 44321. We use the first two digits of this number, and the number becomes 44. The student who has been allocated the number 44 in our sampling frame becomes the first student to be included in our sample.

7 We then continue down that column to the end, selecting the first two digits of each number, and then including in our sample of 30 students, the student to whom that number has been assigned.

8 Then we move onto the next column, selecting each number, and using the first two digits of that number, and including in our sample the student to whom this number has been assigned.

9 We continue this process until our sample is complete, until we have selected the 30 students from the population of 90 students to be included in the sample for our study.

You will find tables of random numbers in maths books and in the appendices of books on statistics.

The web tutor Stat Trek (**http://stattrek.com**) has a very simple, easy to use, *random number generator* that you can use to generate any amount of random numbers., and including in our sample the student to whom this number has been assigned.

You can use Excel to generate random numbers using a mathematical formula, the RAND function. The RAND function in Excel generates a random number which is greater than or equal to 0 and less than 1. The syntax for the RAND function is: =RAND (). Every time you use the command, Excel will generate a new random number. You continue generating random numbers until you have enough.

Question The sampling method used in the exercise in this case study is systematic sampling. Can you define this sampling method and explain how it works?

CHAPTER REVIEW

This chapter focused on research populations, sampling and sampling methods and on research methods or data collection methods. The ways in which research populations are defined were considered in the chapter. The different ways of selecting a sample from a research population were outlined. The key issue in sampling, as explained in the chapter, is the issue of representation, the issue of how representative the sample selected is of the population of the study. There are two kinds of sampling, probability sampling and non-probability sampling. Probability sampling, as explained in the chapter, is based on the theories of mathematics of probability. Probability sampling techniques include simple random sampling, stratified sampling, systematic sampling and cluster sampling. If used properly, probability sampling techniques yield precise results while working with samples a fraction the size of the original populations of research. Probability sampling can only be carried out with the use of a sampling frame. A sampling frame helps guarantee that every member of the population of the study has an equally likely chance of being included in the study. In the absence of a complete sampling frame, the sampling approach used is non-probability sampling. In non-probability sampling, as explained in the chapter, the sample is selected to *represent* the population, but it cannot be said to be *representative* of the population, in any statistical sense. The emphasis in non-probability sampling is on the capacity of a relatively small number of cases to clearly and comprehensively illustrate the phenomenon under investigation. Non-probability sampling techniques include judgemental sampling, quota sampling, snowball sampling and convenience sampling. Different research methods or data gathering methods used in social and business research were listed and explained in the chapter. The chapter demonstrates how the researcher constructs the methodological framework for the research project. The methodological framework explains in detail how the research was carried out. The methodological framework is contained in the research methodology chapter in the thesis, or in the research methodology section of the report of the research.

Now update your interactive research diary with your notes and findings at www.cengage.co.uk/quinlan. Complete the activities provided to reinforce your understanding of this chapter.

END OF CHAPTER QUESTIONS

1 Explain what is meant by the term population of the research project.

2 Detail and explain the reasons why a researcher would engage in sampling with a research population.

3 Explain the difference between probability and non-probability sampling.

4 What is simple random sampling and how is it used?

5 Outline an example of a research project that should be developed using a stratified sampling technique. Explain why a stratified sampling method should be used in this research project.

6 What is meant by the term judgemental sampling method and how and when is such a method used in research?

7 Detail five different research methods available to the business researcher.

8 It is important that you use appropriate data gathering methods. Why is this the case?

9 In your research diary re-visit the data collection methods you had proposed for your project. Having read this chapter, are they still the same? Explain your answer.

10 What are random numbers? How are random numbers used in sampling in research projects?

REFERENCES

Banks, M. (2007) *Using Visual Data in Qualitative Research*, London: Sage.

Biloslavo, R. and Trnavčevič, A. (2009) 'Websites as tools of communication of a "green" company', *Management Decision* 47(7): 1158–1173.

Bourdieu, P. (1986) 'The Forms of Capital' in John-Richardson (ed.) *Handbook of Theory and Research for the Sociology of Education*, New York: Greenwood Press, pp. 241–258.

Brotherton, B.(1999) (ed.), 'The Handbook of Contemporary Hospitality Management Research', New York: John Wiley & Sons.

CADAAD (Critical Approaches to Discourse Analysis Across Disciplines), **www.cadaad.org/** Accessed 02.06.2010.

Cote, J.A., McCullough, J. and Reilly, M. (1985) 'Effects of unexpected situations on behavior-intention differences: A garbology analysis', *The Journal of Consumer Research* 12(2): 188–194.

Dermody, J. and Scullion, R. (2004) 'Exploring the value of party political advertising for youth electoral engagement: An analysis of the 2001 British General Election advertising campaigns', *International Journal of Nonprofit and Voluntary Sector Marketing* 9(4): 361–379.

Exploring Online Research Methods, University of Leicester, **www.geog.le.ac.uk/ORM/site/home.htm** Accessed 02.06.2010.

Fairclough, N. (1995) *Critical Discourse Analysis*, London: Longman.

Foucault, M. (1970) *The Order of Things*, New York: Pantheon.

Foucault, M. (1972) *Archaeology of Knowledge*, New York: Pantheon.

Gubrium, J.F. and Holstein, J.A. (2009) *Analyzing Narrative Reality*, Thousand Oaks, CA: Sage.

Lee, R.M. (2000) *Unobtrusive Methods in Social Research*, Milton Keynes: Open University Press.

Hammersley, M. and Atkinson, P. (1995) *Ethnography*, London: Routledge.

Kaulio, M.A. and Uppvall, L. (2009) 'Critical incidents in R&D alliances: Uncovering leadership roles', *European Management Review* 6(3): 195–205.

Methodspace: Connecting the Research Community, Sage, **www.methodspace.com**

Neuman, W.L. (2000) *Social Research Methods: Quantitative and Qualitative Approaches*, Boston: Allyn & Bacon.

Oppenheim, A.N. (1992) *Questionnaire Design, Interviewing and Attitude Measurement*, London: Pinter.

Pink, S. (2006) Doing *Visual Ethnography* (2nd edn), London: Sage.

Prosser, J. (1998) *Image-based Research*, London: Routledge.

Rich, D. (2010) Moving from "what happened?" to "now what?" is vital for business', *Financial Times*, 4 February.

Reinvention: A Journal of Undergraduate Research, **www.warwick.ac.uk**

Rose, G. (2001) *Visual Methodologies*, London: Sage.

Soy, S. (2006) *The Case Study as a Research Method*, http://www.ischool.utexas.edu/~ssoy/usesusers/l391d1b.htm Accessed 02.06.2010.

Stat Trek, Teach Yourself Statistics, http://stattrek.com

The National Archive of the UK, www.nationalarchives.gov.uk

Sudman, S. (1976) 'Applied sampling', New York: Academic Press.

Trochim, W.M. (2006) *The Research Methods Knowledge Base* (2nd edn), www.socialresearchmethods.net/.

UCLA Anderson School of Management, Oral History Research, 'Entrepreneurs of the West',

http://www.anderson.ucla.edu/x1194.xml Accessed 02.06.2010.

UK Office for National Statistics, http://www.ons.gov.uk/census/index.html Accessed 02.06.2010.

van Dijk, T.A. (1993) 'Principles of critical discourse analysis', *Discourse and Society* 4(2): 243–289.

van Leeuven, T. (2005) *Introducing Social Semiotics*, London: Routledge.

Wang, J. (2006) 'Questions and the exercise of power', *Discourse and Society*, 7(4): 529–548.

Yin, R.K. (2009) *Case Study Research: Design and Methods* (4th edn), Thousand Oaks, CA: Sage.

Wodak, R., and Krzyzanowski, M., (eds), (2008) *'Qualitative Discourse Analysis in the Social Sciences'* Hampshire: Palgrave Macmillan.

RECOMMENDED READING

Bell, J. (2005) *Doing Your Research Project*, Part 11, 'Selecting Methods of Data Collection', Maidenhead: Open University Press.

Bignell, J. (2002) *Media Semiotics: An Introduction*, Manchester: Manchester University Press.

Brotherton, B. (1999) *The Handbook of Contemporary Hospitality Management Research*, Chichester: John Wiley & Sons.

Deacon, D., Pickering, M., Golding, P. and Murdock, G. (1999) *Researching Communications: A Practical Guide to Methods in Media and Cultural Analysis*, Ch. 3, 'Selecting and Sampling', Oxford: Oxford University Press.

Denscombe, M. (2003) *The Good Research Guide: For Small-scale Social Research Projects* (2nd edn), Part 11, 'Methods of Social Research', Maidenhead: Open University Press.

Gilbert, D. and Lockwood, A. (1999) 'Critical Incident Technique', in B. Brotherton, *The Handbook of Contemporary Hospitality Management Research*, Chichester: John Wiley & Sons.

Neuman, W.L. (2000) *Social Research Methods: Quantitative and Qualitative Approaches*, Ch. 8, 'Qualitative and Quantitative Sampling', and Ch. 10, 'Survey Research', Boston: Allyn & Bacon.

Marshall, J. and Adamic, M. (2010) 'The story is the message: Shaping corporate culture', *Journal of Business Strategy* 31(2): 18–23.

Robson, C. (2000) *Real World Research*, Part III, 'Tactics: The Methods of Data Collection', Oxford: Blackwell.

Simpson, M. and Tuson, J. (2003) *Using Observation in Small-scale Research*, Glasgow: University of Glasgow.

CHAPTER 9

USING SECONDARY DATA AND ARCHIVAL SOURCES

LEARNING OBJECTIVES

At the end of this chapter the student should be able to:

● Differentiate between primary and secondary data.

● Source secondary data.

● Explain the importance of archives and archival sources.

● Evaluate and critique secondary data.

● Use secondary data and archival sources appropriately in their research projects.

RESEARCH SKILLS

At the end of this chapter the student should, using the exercises on the accompanying online platform, be able to:

● Source a set of secondary data.

● Explore and use that data set.

● Evaluate the utility and quality of the data in that data set.

The aim of this chapter is to introduce the student to the differences between primary and secondary data and to show the advantages and disadvantages of both data types. The chapter explores secondary data sets and explains how to obtain them. The chapter explains how secondary data sets are to be used. The chapter highlights and explains the potential limitations of secondary data sets. There are two research methodologies in focus in this chapter, they are historical research and archival research.

INTRODUCTION

Secondary data
Data that already exists; it not created by the researcher.

All the use of **secondary data** is particularly important for researchers who, for one reason or another, are not able to access primary data.

Primary data is data which the researcher makes or creates themselves. You should know when you decide to undertake a particular research project that the required data are available and accessible. As we have discussed, one of the fundamental requirements of every research project is that the project be 'researchable'. You cannot research a project if the data required are not available or not accessible. When beginning to consider data and different kinds of data, it is useful to consider again the model of the research process. Figure 9.1 clearly indicates the stage in the research process when the researcher makes final decisions about data. Throughout the research process the researcher is thinking about the kind(s) of data needed for the research project, and the likely sources of that data.

As can be seen from Figure 9.1, the data collection methods for the research project are devised when the researcher has decided on the research methodology to be used in the research project. Final decisions around methodology and (data collection) method(s) tend to be made when the literature review is completed, or nearly completed. This is because the researcher needs to learn from the literature what is already known in this area, and be able to more clearly see what is *not* known. The researcher will then develop their research project around some element of what is not known about the phenomenon under investigation, in order to ensure that the research makes a contribution to knowledge. Another reason why the researcher does not make final decisions around the methodology and methods to use in their research until they have nearly completed their review of the literature, is because they may get some new ideas or insights about the

REAL WORLD RESEARCH

Ensuring your research makes a contribution to knowledge

Many students worry unduly about having to make a contribution to knowledge with their research. In fact, it is very easy to make a contribution to knowledge.

Let us say for example that you might like to undertake a study of the life and work of Bill Gates of Microsoft for your research. You might hesitate to suggest this, because you believe that the life and work of Bill Gates has already been very well researched, and therefore you might think that you would not be able to make a useful and unique contribution to knowledge in your

proposed study. However, you would in your thesis focus on one small aspect of Bill Gates' life or work. You might, for example, study his early career or the early years of the development of his business. You might study his public statements and speeches about the contemporary business world. Perhaps he has spoken and written widely on business ethics, or business philosophy, or on starting a new business, or on strategic leadership or on a myriad of other topics relevant to your degree.

Can you get copies of these speeches and writings? If you can then you have a data set. If the data set is good enough, if it meets the standard required by your university or college for your thesis, then you have a viable research project.

Through a detailed presentation and analysis of that one small aspect of the work of Bill Gates, you would be able to draw some unique and insightful conclusions. Your insights and conclusions could make a very substantial contribution to knowledge.

The possibilities in terms of ideas for viable research projects are all around. You simply need to be imaginative enough to be able to see them.

In another example, you might decide that for your research project you want to examine the career trajectories (the career paths) of graduates who graduated from the programme of study that you yourself are undertaking. This is a good idea for a research project. You might find, however, that another student has the same idea, or you might find that a student examined exactly this topic 2 years ago. You can still undertake this research, and make your research project unique. You might be able to argue that in the 2 years that have passed since the last study, there has been substantial change in terms of the opportunities available to business graduates. You might decide to engage in your study only with

the female graduates, or only with the male graduates, or only with the graduates who have worked in business or in a specific area of business since they graduated, and so on. As I hope you can see, it is quite easy to ensure that your research is unique. You simply differentiate your research in some fundamental way from the research of others. When you have done this, it is important to ensure, through the scholarly manner in which you design, develop and conclude your research, that your research does make a contribution to knowledge.

It is important to clearly explain your rationale (your reason(s)) for the decisions you make in relation to your research project. These decisions have to be logical and reasoned. You can use your research diary to develop and record your decisions and the thoughts, ideas and insights behind these decisions. Such records will be very helpful when you are writing up your research.

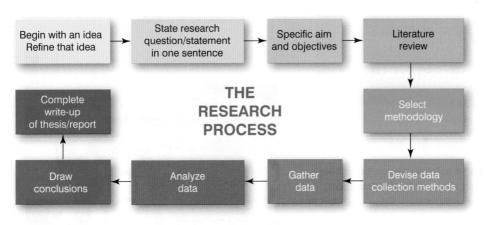

Figure 9.1   The research process

methodology and methods that they might use in their research project from their reading of the literature.

Decisions around the use of **secondary sources** and archival sources are part of the methodological framework for the research project. As we know, the methodological framework is one framework in the four frameworks approach to the research project. The methodological framework emerges from and forms part of the conceptual framework. In this way, methodological decisions for the research project are shaped by the focus of the project, by the aim of the research, by what it is that the research is trying to accomplish. Figure 9.2 demonstrates

Secondary sources
Places and organisations, libraries, websites, books, reports and so on, that contain data and/or commentary and discussion on data.

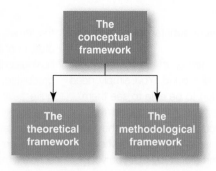

Figure 9.2   The methodological framework emerges from the conceptual framework

how the theoretical framework and the methodological framework emerge from the conceptual framework.

Primary data
Data directly observed or gathered by the researcher engaged in a research project.

SECONDARY DATA

Secondary data are data from secondary sources. They are data that already exist. Sometimes researchers use these data rather than creating data themselves. **Primary data** are data that researchers themselves create. Secondary data are data that have been created from a primary source. As detailed in the table on data collection

THE VALUE OF GOOD RESEARCH

Research in the media

'Cycling England scheme encourages bike users in towns', Richard Scott, Transport Correspondent, *BBC News*, February 23rd 2010

Extract

The British government wants the British nation to get on its bike, according to an article in *The Guardian's* Bike blog (28.10.2009); only 3% of people in Britain cycle to work, while in Copenhagen, according to figures from then Transport Secretary, Andrew Adonis, 40% of all journeys are made by bike. An article published by BBC News (2010) highlighted the Cycling England initiative which is designed to boost cycling in England's towns. Cycling England (**www.dft.gov.uk/cyclingengland**), is an independent expert body established in 2005 by the Department for Transport and designed to promote cycling in England.

© David Palmar/iStock

The BBC News article highlighted a study carried out by Cycling England to monitor people's cycling habits (see also the Cycling England website). The research was conducted using automatic counters and manual counters of cyclists; in addition, secondary data was examined, the sources of which included school and workplace travel surveys and case studies. The study found that in the first three years of operation of the Cycling England scheme the number of trips taken by cyclists in the (initial) five participating towns rose by an average of 27%.

References

BBC News (23 February, 2010) 'Cycling England scheme encourages bike users in towns' by Richard Scott.

Cycling England, **www.dft.gov.uk/cyclingengland/** The Guardian (28 October, 2009), 'Is the UK government's cycle-to-work scheme an empty gesture?', Alok Jha.

methods in Chapter 8 of this textbook (Table 8.2 Detailed data collection methods), a secondary source is, in a sense, second-hand. It is something written about a primary source.

The article below is from *BBC News*. It details the work of Cycling England, an initiative of the UK Department (**www.dft.gov.uk/cyclingengland/**) which was set up to encourage cycling in towns in England. The article details some of the sources of primary data gathered in order to evaluate the initiative. These data were gathered using both automatic and manual counters of numbers of cyclists. The extract also details secondary data sources used to evaluate the initiative. The secondary data sources used were school and workplace travel surveys and case studies. These surveys and case studies were carried out by other groups and organizations. Researchers at Cycling England accessed and used these surveys and case studies as secondary data sources in their own research, the evaluation of the Cycling England initiative.

DIFFERENTIATING BETWEEN PRIMARY AND SECONDARY DATA

The distinction between primary and secondary sources is not always obvious. A source can be primary in one context and secondary in another context. For example, a recent newspaper article is a secondary source and a newspaper article from 1929 used to examine the Wall Street Crash is a primary source. Will Hutton (2009), writing in *The Observer* newspaper, discussed the work of Japanese economist Richard Koo. This is a secondary source. (Will Hutton's article could be a primary source if the researcher used the article in conducting, for example, a content analysis study of major UK newspaper representations of leading economists throughout 2009.) The Japanese economist Richard Koo (2008), based his economic theory on his study of Japanese economics and the 1929 Wall Street Crash. He used both primary and secondary sources of data in his research. A primary source is a first-hand account of an experience or a phenomenon by a person who has had the experience or experienced the phenomenon. A secondary source is a second-hand account of an experience or phenomenon. **Primary sources** are said to be unmediated, or direct sources. A secondary source is something written about a primary source and often the secondary source builds upon the primary source. A secondary source is one created or compiled by a person who did not experience or witness the phenomenon, but who compiled an account of the phenomenon based on the witness or testimony of another or others.

Primary sources Primary sources are direct sources of evidence that the researcher creates and/or gathers themselves. A primary source is also called an original source. Primary sources provide original information or evidence and are the first evidence of a phenomenon being observed and recorded. A primary resource is a first-hand account of some phenomenon. Examples of primary sources include documents, letters, diaries, photographs, maps, charts, sound recordings, completed questionnaires, completed scales, interview transcripts, focus group transcripts, statistics, all kinds of research data, reports, original manuscripts, official documents and records, film and video, some newspapers and magazines, art works, stories, narratives, published first-hand accounts, folk tales, web content. As can be seen, almost any artefact can be a primary source. The essential criterion is that they must be original accounts of the phenomenon.

Secondary sources Secondary sources do not provide original information or evidence. They refer to original information or evidence published in primary sources. They comment on, analyze, interpret or discuss primary sources. Examples of secondary sources include publications, textbooks, newspaper and magazine articles, histories, criticisms, and commentaries on experiences, events, phenomena. The essential point is that these accounts are not first-hand accounts.

It is helpful perhaps, to think of secondary sources as second-hand material. Research journals, such as those that have been used extensively in this book, contain research articles, all of which are primary sources. They are first-hand accounts of research projects written by the researchers who have undertaken the research. The book reviews in the journals, on the other hand, are secondary sources. The book reviews are accounts of primary sources. The book review is an account (a secondary source) of the book reviewed (a primary source).

It is important when reading literature and writing literature reviews to be able to distinguish between primary and secondary sources, and to make the distinction when writing the review. Academic standards require the use of primary sources. Many students fail to meet this standard by drawing on and quoting secondary sources when they should be using primary sources. In other words, they read and use material from books, and other published sources, which write about primary sources, instead of reading, using and quoting from the primary source itself. Primary sources are original sources; secondary sources provide analysis, discussion or interpretation of primary sources. In a literature review it is not appropriate to present a theoretical framework based on secondary sources. It is important in researching and writing the literature review to find and use the primary sources.

For example, Michael Porter presented his **Five Forces Model for Industry Analysis** in his books *Competitive Strategy* (1983), and *Competitive Advantage* (1985). Michael Porter's writing on this model is a primary source. Porter's Five Forces Model has been written about extensively in business and management literature.

Primary sources
Sources that provide new insight into any phenomenon. Sometimes called original sources.

Five Forces Model for industry analysis
A framework for industry analysis and business strategy developed by Professor Michael Porter.

The writings of other writers and academics on Porter's Five Forces Model are secondary sources. However, any researcher writing about their own original research in which they used Porter's Five Forces Model, produces in their writing on their research new primary sources.

The journal article detailed below presents a research project which was based on secondary sources. The article is from the journal *Business & Society*.

REAL WORLD RESEARCH

How theory influences research

'The Invisible Work of Managing Visibility for Social Change: Insights From the Leadership of Reverend Dr Martin Luther King Jr', Roberts, D.D. *et al.* (2008)

In this article, the authors introduce the concept of tempered visibility as a lens through which to view Martin Luther King Jr's civil rights leadership. They review the academic literature on visibility and its implications for leadership. They outline key moral and socio-political factors that enabled King to become visible. They provide examples of how King intentionally increased and decreased his exposure while leading key events in the Civil Rights Movement. The authors use King's example to demonstrate the process by which leaders gain visibility, and the positive and negative outcomes of visibility for leaders and their change efforts. The authors hold that their analysis extends the understanding of the strategic management of visibility.

> I am conscious of two Martin Luther Kings. I am a wonder to myself. . . . I am mystified at my own career. The Martin Luther King that the people talk about seems to me somebody foreign to me. . . . There is a kind of dualism in my life. Martin Luther King, the famous man, is a kind of stranger to [me].

'He often stated that Martin Luther King, the famous man, was a kind of stranger to him.' (J. Pious Barbour, Martin Luther King Jr's Crozer Theological Seminary mentor, reflecting on conversations he had with Martin Luther King Jr in 1963; Garrow: 1986, p. 289).

The authors state that Reverend Dr Martin Luther King Jr, is best known through his work as a leader in the Civil Rights Movement in the US in the 1950s through the late 1960s. He employed strategies of non-violent direct action to challenge the discriminatory laws and social norms circumscribing the lives of African–Americans. The authors state that King's life is often hoisted up as an example of leadership that has inspired people around the world.

The authors state that, as the introductory quote indicates, King saw himself as to a degree disconnected from his highly visible persona. In order to manage his internal tension and to ensure leadership effectiveness, the authors says that King engaged in sophisticated thought and action regarding his public persona. Specifically, they say, King carefully managed his own visibility as a leader for the sake of his human, spiritual, and social needs and for the success of the Civil Rights Movement.

In the article, the authors review the literature on visibility and its implications for leadership. They explain the processes by which people gain visibility and they explore the positive and negative outcomes of such visibility. They review the leadership experiences of Martin Luther King Jr by way of illustrating the strategic management of visibility. They highlight the active role that King played in casting a public spotlight on his own experiences and values as well as on the experiences of those for whom he advocated. They review key moments in King's leadership of the Movement to illuminate the dynamic process through which King managed his visibility – heightening and reducing his exposure to preserve his humanity and to promote social change. They discuss the consequences of King's heightened visibility for leadership and social change. Finally, after reviewing a subset of King's strategies, they glean insight from his leadership example in order to extend our understanding of how and why leaders manage their visibility.

The methodology used was a case study. It was, as the authors state, a case study of Reverend Dr Martin Luther King Jr. The data used in the case study were from secondary sources. The authors stated that they reviewed several secondary sources (e.g., Batten, 1992; Branch, 1988; Dyson, 2004; Franklin, 1989; Garrow, 1986; Jackson, 2006; Raines, 1989; West, 1999) that recount key moments in King's life and the Civil Rights Movement to generate examples of how King strategically managed his visibility.

They authors state in the article that while this research is important, it also paves the way for future research – both theoretical and empirical. They suggest that their framework could be used to better understand how leaders' visibility directly influences the visibility of the people and causes that they lead. They also state that they believe that this research on tempering visibility can be generalized to leadership in corporate settings.

They suggest that future research could compare how African–American leaders (or leaders from any under-represented group) strategically manage visibility with majority leaders' approaches to strategically

managing visibility. They ask if generalizations hold when race, gender, or class differences are accounted for. They say that comparative research would illuminate differences in how leaders manage their visibility and aid in understanding whether Black leaders must manage their visibility differently from majority leaders. They suggest that differences may exist because Black leaders are more marginal from mainstream society and confronted with a history of discriminatory treatment whereas their White counterparts are most likely viewed as speaking to issues reflective of a mainstream society. Finally, the authors state that the risks of visibility when leading social change may be greater for minorities just as, they state, Kanter (1977), argued that the risks of visibility are greater for those in the numerical minority in corporations.

References

Roberts, D.D., Roberts, L.M., O'Neill, R.M. and Blake-Beard, S.D. (2008) 'The invisible work of managing visibility for social change: Insights from the leadership of Reverend Dr Martin Luther King Jr', *Bussiness & society* 47(4): December, 425–453.

SOURCING SECONDARY DATA SETS

Data set
A complete collection of interrelated data, e.g. all of the data in a research project.

There are many ways of sourcing secondary data sets and there are many places where secondary data sets can be sourced. A **data set** (sometimes written as dataset) is a collection of data. Data, as we know, can be in the form of numbers (quantitative data/numeric data) or in the form of thoughts, or ideas, or perceptions or beliefs (**a qualitative data set**).

The data set used in the case study on Martin Luther King, outlined above, was made up of several secondary sources. As the authors explained, they:

Qualitative data set
A complete set of qualitative data used or to be used in a research project.

> *Reviewed several secondary sources (e.g., Batten, 1992; Branch, 1988; Dyson, 2004; Franklin, 1989; Garrow, 1986; Jackson, 2006; Raines, 1989; West, 1999) that recount key moments in King's life and the Civil Rights Movement to generate examples of how King strategically managed his visibility.*

The bibliography presented in the journal article provides full references for the secondary sources that make up the data set for the research project. These secondary sources are detailed in Table 9.1. Table 9.1 contains the entire data set for a major research project that made a very substantial contribution to knowledge. Read through the data set as it is presented in the table. As you read, try to think of ideas for research

Table 9.1 The data set used in the Martin Luther King study (above), as detailed by the authors and as presented in the bibliography of the journal article.
Batten, C. E. (1992). Martin King. In C. Carson (series ed.), R. E. Luker, & P. A. Russell (vol. eds.), *The papers of Martin Luther King, Jr. Vol. 1. Called to serve.* (pp. 390–391), Berkeley: University of California Press.
Branch, T. (1988). Parting the waters: America in the King years 1954–1963, New York: Simon & Schuster.
Dyson, M. E. (2004). Mixed blessings: Martin Luther King, Jr., and the lessons of an ambiguous heroism. *The Michael Eric Dyson reader*, New York: Basic Civitas Books.
Franklin, R. (1990). Liberating visions: Human fulfilment and social justice in African American thought, Minneapolis, MN: Fortress Press.
Franklin, R. M. (1989). An ethic of hope: The moral thought of Martin Luther King, Jr. In D. Garrow (ed.) *Martin Luther King, Jr.: Civil rights leader, theologian, orator. Vol. 2. Martin Luther King, Jr. and the civil rights movement* (pp. 349–350), Brooklyn, NY: Carlson.
Garrow, D. (1986). *Bearing the cross: Martin Luther King, Jr., and the Southern Christian Leadership Conference*, New York: William Morrow.
Garrow, D. (1989). Martin Luther King, Jr. and the cross of leadership. In D. Garrow (ed.) *Martin Luther King, Jr.: Civil rights leader, theologian, orator. Vol. 2. Martin Luther King, Jr. and the civil rights movement* (pp.453–464), Brooklyn, NY: Carlson.
Jackson, T. (2006). Martin Luther King, Jr. (1929–1968). In J. Witte, Jr. & F. S. Alexander (ed.). *The teachings of modern Christianity on law, politics, and human nature. Vol. 1. The teachings of modern Christianity* (pp. 439–464), New York: Columbia University Press.
Raines, J.C. (1989). Righteous resistance and Martin Luther King, Jr. In D. J. Garrow (ed.). *Martin Luther King, Jr.: Civil rights leader, theologian, orator. Vol. 3. Martin Luther King, Jr. and the civil rights movement* (pp. 733–41), Brooklyn, NY: Carlson.
West, C. (1999). *Prophetic Christian as organic intellectual: Martin Luther King, Jr.* In C. West (ed.), *The Cornel West reader* (pp. 432–434), New York: Basic Civitas Books.

projects of your own using such a data set. As you read, think about your own research project and the contribution that secondary sources might make to it.

The data set is a list of books and chapters in books. It is not a long list, yet it does represent a very comprehensive data set, that contains a lot of data. This data set is made up of the writings about Martin Luther King, All of the sources were written by people who studied his life and work. Martin Luther King died on 4 April, 1968. All of the sources detailed above were published after 1986, years after his death. In writing the books and chapters in the data set, the authors drew on original sources, diaries and documents, and other sources, which detailed the life and work of Martin Luther King.

YOUR RESEARCH
Generating ideas for research projects

It is good practice to get into the habit of looking for ideas for research projects and recording those ideas for possible future use.

One of the activities we, as researchers, engage in all the time is the work of generating thoughts and ideas about research projects. These thoughts and ideas should be recorded for safe keeping and for future use in your research diary.

In relation to your own research project, perhaps there is a leader, in business or in civil society, that you would like to study. Perhaps there is a possibility of developing a research project around strategic, operational or even inspirational leadership that would be acceptable as your research project, to your programme of study and to your research supervisor and/or your lecturer in research methods.

Aja is a student of business management. There is a synopsis of his research proposal below.

Aja is a very keen football player and supporter. For his research project he wants to study football managers and their approach to strategic management. What do you think of Aja's research idea? Aja developed the following research proposal based on his idea for his research project:

Aja's research proposal

Research statement: This research project is a case study of four football managers and their approach to strategic management as evidenced in four different publications.

Aim and objectives: The aim of this study is to examine the strategic management styles of four different football managers as evidenced in four different publications. The study is being undertaken in order to explore the lessons, if any, for strategic business management knowledge and theory in the approaches to strategic management of the four managers to be studied.

The objectives of the study are as follows:

- to explore the strategic management styles of the four football managers
- to document the key principles of strategic management evident in the management styles of the four football managers

- to examine the strategic management styles and approaches of the four football managers in order to make a contribution to business strategic management knowledge and theory.

Research methodology

The research methodology is a case study. The data used in the case study will be secondary data.

Four football managers have been selected for study. They are Alex Ferguson, Arsène Wenger, Brian Clough and Bill Shankly.

The data for the case study are data from four published accounts, four books each of them biographies which detail the management styles of these four managers. The books are as follows:

- *The Boss: The Many Sides of Alex Ferguson* by Michael Crick (2002), London: Simon and Schuster UK Ltd.
- *Arsène Wenger: Pure Genius*, by Tom Oldfield (2008), London: John Blake Publishing Ltd.
- *His Way: The Brian Clough Story*, by Patrick Murphy (2009), London: Pan Books Ltd.
- *Shanks: The Authorized Biography of Bill Shankly*, by Dave Bowler (1996), London: Orion.

The four books will be critically examined with a view to providing detail and insight into the aim and objectives of the study as detailed above.

It is likely that Aja's research supervisor will approve the research. However, it is also likely that his research supervisor will ask him to broaden his data set. In order to do this, he should perhaps include more secondary sources; he could also decide to gather primary data, perhaps through interviewing key informants on the management styles of the four football managers.

In the previous chapters we considered very many ideas for research projects. One such idea was for the research project detailed below which appears in Chapter 5: 'Developing a Research Proposal'. The research statement for this research project was as follows:

This research project is a survey of perceptions of the WWF among 50 shoppers in Hazelbrook Shopping Centre, Illingford.

This research project will involve the gathering of primary data. The primary data gathered for this research project will be the responses to the questionnaire which the researcher will develop in order to carry out the survey of the 50 shoppers in Hazelbrook Shopping Centre in relation to their perceptions of the WWF. The responses to the questionnaire will become the data set used in the research. As explained in Chapter 8, questionnaires are generally made up almost entirely of questions designed to create quantitative data. The data set which will result from the survey for the above project will be primarily if not entirely a numeric/ a **quantitative data set**. The questionnaire will be developed and administered by the researcher. The responses to the questionnaire will become the data set. The researcher creates the data. The data are, therefore, primary data.

> **Quantitative data set**
> A complete set of quantitative data used or to be used in a research project.

There are very many online sources of data. Often these data are used by researchers as secondary sources. Examples of these online sources of data include The Office of National Statistics in the UK (**www.ons.gov.uk**), Marketing Online (**www.marketing-online.co.uk**), the International Monetary Fund (IMF), (**www.imf.org/external/index.htm**), the Organization for Economic Cooperation and Development (OECD) (**www.oecd.org**), the Human Development Index (**http://hdr.undp.org/en/**), even the Central Intelligence Agency (CIA) (**www.cia.gov/**). These are just some of the major organizations, both national and international, which provide very large amounts of data freely and online. Any student can access the data and browse it. You examine some of the data and data sets available online. This will help you become familiar with some of the different ways of accessing and using data and more practised and confident with large data sets.

EVALUATE THE UTILITY OF THE DATA AVAILABLE

While there are a lot of data available online, not all are good or useful. It is important that you develop the capacity to evaluate the utility or the value of data that you find online, particularly data that you are thinking of using in your research project. The first thing to do is to establish where the data come from and decide whether or not this is a reputable source. Then establish how the data were gathered, and how they were analyzed. Be critical in your appraisal. Consider the ways in which the data are presented. When were the data gathered? When were they analyzed and when, how and where were they published? Unless you want historic data, useful data are up-to-date data. Decide whether or not the data you have accessed are current enough. Old or out-of-date data may not be useful at all, because the world may have changed substantially since that data were published.

> **Data stream**
> Various data from different streams.

It is important when reading through the large data sets to think about the contribution, if any, large or small, the data might make to your own research project. It might be that you could develop a project based entirely on the data available. The case study at the end of this chapter presents an example of such a project. It might be that the data could provide one **data stream** for your research project. A data stream is data from one source. In the research project above on the WWF there was one data stream, from the questionnaire developed for the survey. In the research project above on Martin Luther King there was also one data stream, from the biographical writings on Martin Luther King's life and work. Aja, in his research proposal, is proposing to use data from secondary sources, again data from one stream. There is a recommendation at the end of Aja's proposal that he broaden his data sources and a suggestion that he could perhaps also gather primary data for the research project, in the form of interviews with key informants. Interview data would provide a second stream of data for Aja's project. Two streams of data is a form of triangulation. Triangulation in research, you will remember from Chapter 2 of this textbook, is the use of more than one approach to answering the research question or responding to the research issue. Triangulation means looking at the phenomenon under investigation from more than one perspective and is a means of ensuring robustness in a study.

It is important to have enough data, and data that are valid and useful. The validity of secondary data can be established through the reputation of the organization hosting the database and/or archive within which you find the data. It can also be established through an examination and explanation of the methodologies and data gathering methods used by the host organization in gathering the data. The kinds of questions that you should ask of such data are as follows:

- Where were the data published?
- When and where were the data gathered?
- Why were the data gathered?
- How were the data gathered and analyzed?
- What findings were drawn from the data?
- What conclusions were drawn from those findings?
- Do the data make sense?
- Do the data seem useful to you?
- How could or would you use the data?

The researcher should also look out for any other issues in the data. There may be research metholodgy, ethical or political issues. There can be, for example, ethnocentrism in data. Ethnocentrism is the belief that one's own ethnic or cultural group is superior and all other ethnic or cultural groups are seen as being 'other' than that group. As a result they are seen as being somehow less than that group. There can be geo-political issues, race issues, class issues, gender issues and other issues in published data.

THE VALUE OF GOOD RESEARCH

Focus on historical and archival research

The research methodologies in focus in this chapter are historical research and archival research. As explained in Chapter 7 (Table 7.2: Detailed research methodologies), historical research involves studying the history of some phenomenon while archival research is research on the content of an archive(s). According to the UK Business Archives Council (**www.businessarchivescouncil.org.uk**), every business is unique and the records or archive of every business can make a contribution to the bottom line. The Council suggests that good record keeping in business is an integral part of transparent corporate governance. They say that the past can be used to support present performance, that a good archive can add detail and depth to the public image of a company, that archives can facilitate companies in exploiting their heritage, and that archives can be used for education and training purposes within a company. At the end of the *Putting Records to Work* page on the Council's website, there is a case study entitled *The Memory Store*. It is a case study which draws on data from the archive of *The John Lewis Partnership,* a business that has grown from a single shop in London's West End into the UK's biggest department store.

In their study of the cultivation and marketing of flowers in Colorado, USA, Liu and Meyer (2008), used archival research. They used the *Records of the Colorado Flower Growers' Association* (CFGA). This, they tell us, is an archival collection documenting the Association from 1928 to 1980. The archive contains minutes from meetings, correspondence, newsletters, financial reports, scrapbooks, news clippings and photographic material. The archive is clearly a very important archive and this journal article, as well as detailing the business of growing and selling carnations in the flower industry of Colorado, outlines a collaborative project between the archive and the Colorado State University (CSU) libraries to make a selection of the scrapbooks, clippings, newsletters and photographic materials from the archive available online to researchers.

A newspaper article, taken from the *Irish Times* (O'Connell, 2009), presents an interesting research project which is being developed with the use of some very interesting data. As the newspaper article details, the research project is being developed:

> using 'eclectic' sources of data, including tide records, skippers' logs, ocean sediments and archaeological specimens. The newspaper article goes on to state that, probably the most unusual sources would be the restaurant menus.

The research project was designed to establish a baseline to evaluate the health of global ocean ecosystems, according to Poul Holm, Professor of Environmental History at Trinity College Dublin, and global chair of the History of Marine Animal Populations (HMAP), which he co-founded in 2000. The initiative feeds into the Census of Marine Life which involves around 100 researchers working in 15 oceanic regions. Professor Holm said that the most unusual data sources for the project would be the restaurant menus. He said that they are a very good source of information on how we have been eating

our way down the food web. He said that if you look at menus 100 years ago you would see a lot of species that today are endangered, like abalone, which would have been very abundant in American restaurants. Although we have fished down a lot of species so they are commercially extinct, Professor Holm says that they are not biologically extinct and he says that if the ecosystem is given some breathing space, the species will actually rebuild. He said that depleted herring stocks in the North Sea recovered in the 1970s when they were given a chance. Whales, he said, will need more time because mammals reproduce slowly. The professor suggests that we are looking at a century-long programme to rebuild whale stocks.

As you can see, there are very many interesting research projects in the area of business research, and there are very many ways of conducting business research. Historical business research and archival research are just two of those ways.

The National Archives of the USA has a very useful website with a specific resource for researchers. You can access these archives online at **www.archives. gov**. The National Archives of the UK can be located at **www.nationalarchives.gov.uk**. The National Archives of Australia can be located at **www.naa.gov.au**.

In considering the contribution that historical research can make to knowledge in business and management, let us consider what Walton (2010), had to say on the topic of business history in his article 'New directions in business history: Themes, approaches and opportunities'. In the article, Walton argues that the dominant focus in business history is unnecessarily narrow. The mainstream interests of capitalist economic practices, international business and traffic flows, big business, business groups and cartels, corporate governance and corporate management structures are, he states, marginalizing the study of other kinds of business endeavour. He suggests that this 'increasingly exclusive, monocultural version of economic activity' undermines any attention to or study of other ways and means of engaging in business activity. Walton mentions by way of example cooperatives, mutuals, collectives, not-for-profit societies, nationalized industries, business entities run by local and regional government, businesses selling intangibles, independent enterprises, small enterprises, local networks, organic businesses, local and regional markets, communal arrangements for the management of shared assets. He calls for researchers to make visible other forms of enterprise through the use of different research methods, methods such as oral history, archival research and image-based research. Walton talks of entrenched orthodoxies in business disciplines. He highlights the failures of existing business models, and he states that these failures need critical and systemic interrogation.

Whether or not you agree with Walton, I hope that you realise that there are many interesting and useful research projects in business and in business history that need to be carried out.

References

Reproduced with permission from 'Ocean census looks back to go forward', *Irish Times*, 28 May 2009.

USE SECONDARY DATA APPROPRIATELY

One of the problems of using secondary data is the sheer amount of data available. Often the published data sets are very large. It is very important that the data set gathered, created or selected for use in the research project be manageable. Keep the data set simple. Unless very confident, skilled and able in terms of research and research methods, researchers are wise to work with small sets of data or relatively small sets of data. This sometimes means that the researcher works with subsets of data sets. Subsets of data sets are small parts of the overall data set that the researcher selects from the data set. Again, the case study at the end of this chapter provides an example of the researcher working with subsets of data sets. The data presented in the case study have all been selected out of reports of much larger data sets.

One of the main problems with secondary data is that the data available may not be exactly the data required. When working with secondary sources every researcher is restricted to the data available. The main danger in selecting out subset of data from a large data set is that in selecting out data, you render the data invalid in some way. Try to ensure that when you do select out data, the logic of the data holds. In other words, try to ensure that you understand exactly what the data you have selected really means. It is a good idea to organize the data set you intend to use in your research project as quickly as possible. You should immediately begin the process of establishing the strengths and limitations of the data set, in terms of the research project you intend to undertake using the data.

When you write up your research you write an explanation and defence of your data set. The most important issue to be addressed in that defence of your data is the issue of validity. Try to establish the validity of the data selected out; validity in this context means that the data are valid, credible, reasonable, reasoned, justifiable and defensible. The validity of the data is the extent to which the data measures or represents that which it purports to measure or represent. Try to be clear about what it is that the data that you have selected measure and/or represent. Try to ensure that the data are credible and that they are useful and meaningful in relation to your research. In other words, try to ensure that the data really do explain or illustrate the phenomenon which you are investigating, as it is outlined in your research statement or question.

In using secondary data, the researcher must observe proper ethical standards. The source of the data should be properly and fully referenced. The data must not be misused or mis-represented in any way. If you have a data set that you intend to work with for your research, discuss it with your research supervisor and/or your research methods lecturer and ask them for some comment and/or feedback. Then listen to their advice.

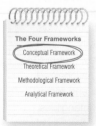

The Four Frameworks
Conceptual Framework
Theoretical Framework
Methodological Framework
Analytical Framework

CASE STUDY

Child poverty

The following case study uses secondary data from a number of sources to examine child welfare.

The research project – governmental approaches to tackling child poverty

In a European context, there are a great many reports and publications on child poverty and governmental approaches to tackling child poverty. Among these reports are the reports of Eurochild (2006) (2nd edn 2007). According to the 2006 report, 19 EU Member States have made 'tackling child

poverty and social exclusion' one of their key priorities. The report states however, that the clarity, comprehensiveness and specificity of the objectives of the 19 countries vary widely. The report puts forward the following countries' objectives, as examples of appropriate and clear child poverty objectives:

- *Austria* to offer all children and young people equal development opportunities, regardless of the income situation of their parents, their nationality or their health status.

- *Bulgaria* to limit the intergenerational transmission of poverty and social exclusion (with a focus on child poverty and social exclusion).

- *Estonia* to prevent and alleviate the poverty and social exclusion of children and families.

- *Hungary* to fight against child poverty by improving the income position of families with children through providing cash and in-kind allowances to them, and by facilitating the employment of parents; by strengthening the daytime care of small children and other child welfare and child protection services; by guaranteeing equal opportunities in the educational/training system; by protecting the health of children and young people.

- *Malta* to improve the social inclusion prospect of children and young persons.

- *Poland* to counteract the poverty and social exclusion of children and youth.

- *Portugal* to fight child poverty through measures that ensure their basic citizenship rights.

- *Slovakia* to reduce child poverty and solve the inter-generational reproduction of poverty by preventive measures and support to families with children.

While the UK does not feature in the Eurochild list of exemplary countries, the UK did perform very well in the OCED report on family support.

Figure 9.3 details OECD data on family support for 37 countries. As can be seen from the table, public

Breaktime at South London school © Janine Wiedel Photo-library/Alamy

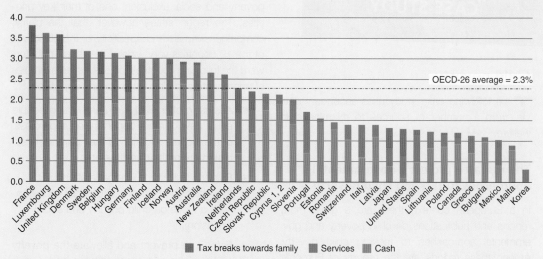

Figure 9.3   PF1: Public spending on family benefits, OECD Family Database: **http://www.oecd.org/els/social/family/database.** Reproduced with permission.

spending on family benefits falls into three broad categories, tax breaks, services and cash. The OECD-26 average is given in the table as 2.3%, as a percentage of GDP 2005. The UK is well above the OECD average at 3.6%, while France leads the table at (about) 3.8%. Of the EU countries, Greece is at the bottom of the table having spent just slightly more than 1% of GDP in 2005 on family benefits.

While it is a fact that, in the OECD scale, the UK is ranked in third place overall, the scale is a simple aggregated measure of family benefits.

In the study 'An Index of Child Well-being in Europe', the UK did very poorly, and was ranked 24th out of 29 countries in terms of child well-being (Bradshaw and Richardson, 2009). This research found that there are positive associations between child well-being and spending on family benefits and services and GDP per capita. In their conclusions they are critical of neo-liberal policies in the UK which, they state,

> resulted in decades of under-investment in children's services and benefits, and big increases in child poverty and inequality. . . .

That the UK is making such slow progress out of the bottom of this league table ('The Index of Child Well-being in Europe', see Table 9.2), is an indica-

tion of the long-term damage that can be done by neglecting children, especially in a recession.

References

Bradshaw, J. and Richardson, D. (2009) 'An index of child well-being in Europe', *Child Indicators Research* 2(3): 319–351.

Eurochild (2006) 'Ending child poverty within the EU: A review of the 2008–2010, National Strategy Reports on Social Protection and Social Inclusion', **http://www.eurochild.org/fileadmin/user_upload/files/NAP_2008-2010/Ending child poverty.pdf**

Eurochild (2007) 'Ending child poverty within the EU: A review of the 2008–2010 National Strategy Reports on Social Protection and Social Inclusion' (2nd edn), **http://www.icyrnet.net/User-Files/File/NAPs%20report%202006%20final.pdf**

OECD Family Database, Social Policy Division, Directorate of Employment, Labour and Social Affairs (2005) 'PF1: Public spending on family benefits', **http://www.oecd.org/dataoecd/45/46/37864391.pdf**

Child Poverty Action Group (CPAG) London, (2009) 'The child well-being index: Where the UK

Table 9.2 The child well-being index								
Rank	Country	Health	Subjective Well-being	Children's relationships	Material resources	Behaviour and Risk	Education	Housing and environment
1	Netherlands	2	1	1	7	4	4	9
2	Sweden	1	7	3	10	1	9	3
3	Norway	6	8	6	2	2	10	1
4	Iceland	4	9	4	1	3	14	8
5	Finland	12	6	9	4	7	7	4
6	Denmark	3	5	10	9	15	12	5
7	Slovenia	15	16	2	5	13	11	19
8	Germany	17	12	8	12	5	6	16
9	Ireland	14	10	14	20	12	5	2
10	Luxembourg	5	17	19	3	11	16	7
11	Austria	26	2	7	8	19	19	6
12	Cyprus	10			13			11
13	Spain	13	4	17	18	6	20	13
14	Belgium	18	13	18	15	21	1	12
15	France	20	14	28	11	10	13	10
16	Czech Republic	9	22	27	6	20	3	22
17	Slovakia	7	11	22	16	23	17	15
18	Estonia	11	20	12	14	25	2	25
19	Italy	19	18	20	17	8	23	20
20	Poland	8	26	16	26	17	8	23
21	Portugal	21	23	13	21	9	25	18
22	Hungary	23	25	11	23	16	15	21
23	Greece	29	3	23	19	22	21	14
24	United Kingdom	24	21	15	24	18	22	17
25	Romania	27	19	5		24	27	
26	Bulgaria	25	15	24		26	26	
27	Latvia	16	24	26	22	27	18	26
28	Lithuania	22	27	25	25	28	24	24
29	Malta	28	28	21		14		

Source: 'The Child Well-being Index', London (2009), http://www.cpag.org.uk/info/ChildWellbeingandChildPovertyl.pdf Reproduced with permission from Child Poverty Action Group (CPAG).

stands in the European table', http://www.cpag. org.uk/info/ ChildWellbeingandChildPoverty.pdf

Question Do you think that the data used in this case study are useful and appropriate data, in relation to the phenomenon under investigation? What do you think are the relative advantages and disadvantages of using these data in a study of child poverty?

Critique the research project presented above. Write a short report outlining, in bullet-point format, what you think is good about the research project and what you think is not good about the research project. Explain your thinking. Draw on your knowledge of research methodology when composing your critique.

CHAPTER REVIEW

The chapter establishes that there are essentially two kinds of sources of data, primary sources and secondary sources. As detailed in the chapter, a primary source is a first-hand account of an experience or a phenomenon by a person who has had the experience or experienced the phenomenon. A secondary source is something written about a primary source. A secondary source often builds on a primary source. Examples of primary sources include documents, letters, diaries, photographs, maps, charts, sound recordings, completed questionnaires, completed scales, interview transcripts, focus group transcripts, statistics, all kinds of research data, reports, original manuscripts, official documents and records, film and video, some newspapers and magazines (as above), art works, stories, narratives, published first-hand accounts, folk tales, web content. Almost any artefact can be a primary source. The essential criterion is that they must be original, original accounts or recordings of the phenomenon. Secondary sources do not provide original information or evidence. Secondary sources refer to original information or evidence published in primary sources. Secondary sources build on primary sources. There are so much data available in secondary sources that, as detailed in the chapter, it can be difficult to find secondary data to fit precisely the requirements of the research project. In using secondary sources, researchers often select and use small subset of data from large data. The case study at the end of this chapter provides an example. Selecting out subsets of data from large data sets poses some problems for researchers. The biggest problem is the need to ensure that when selecting a subset of data from a large data set the logic or meaning of the data is not lost. It can be difficult sometimes to maintain the logic, and the validity of the data in such circumstances. It is important to understand exactly what the data selected really means. The data selected must be valid and meaningful and they must be valid and meaningful in terms of the use to which they are put in the research project. There are ethical issues in using secondary sources. A major ethical concern is that secondary source data should not be misused or misrepresented in any way.

Now update your interactive research diary with your notes and findings at www.cengage.co.uk/quinlan. Complete the activities provided to reinforce your understanding of this chapter.

END OF CHAPTER QUESTIONS

1   What is meant by the term primary sources?

2   What is meant by the term secondary sources?

3   Give three examples of types of primary sources.

4   Give three examples of types of secondary sources.

5   Secondary sources data are particularly useful to researchers who cannot access primary sources. Explain this statement.

6   Detail and explain three potential problems in using secondary data sources.

7   Briefly outline an idea for a research project to be developed using only secondary data sources.

8   Explain the utility of secondary sources in research. Use the case study at the end of this chapter to help with this exercise.

9   What is archival research?

10 Use the Internet to find a journal article detailing a business research project conducted using archival research. Critically appraise that research project.

REFERENCES

Bowler, D. (1996) *Shanks: The Authorized Biography of Bill Shankly*, London: Orion.

Bradshaw, J. and Richardson, D. (2009) 'An index of child well-being in Europe', *Child Indicators Research* 2(3): 319–351.

Business Archives Council, **www.businessarchivescouncil.org.uk**

Central Intelligence Agency (CIA), **www.cia.gov/**

Child Poverty Action Group (CPAG) London(2009) 'The child well-being index', **http://www.cpag.org.uk/info/ChildWellbeingandChildPoverty.pdf** Accessed 03.06.2010.

Crick, M. (2002) *The Boss: The Many Sides of Alex Ferguson*, London: Simon and Schuster UK Ltd.

Eurochild (2006) 'Ending child poverty within the EU: A review of the 2008–2010 national strategy reports on social protection and social inclusion', **http://www.eurochild.org/fileadmin/user_upload/files/NAP_2008_-_2010/Ending_child_poverty.pdf** Accessed 03.06.2010.

Eurochild (2007) 'Ending child poverty within the EU: A review of the 2008–2010 national strategy reports on social protection and social inclusion' (2nd edn), **http://www.icyrnet.net/UserFiles/File/NAPs%20report%202006%20final.pdf** Accessed 03.06.2010.

Hutton, W. (2009) 'Hail the man who argues Britain should stop worrying about its debt', *The Observer*, 5 July.

Human Development Index, **http://hdr.undp.org/en/site/** Accessed 03.06.2010.

Koo, R.C. (2008) *The Holy Grail of Macro Economics: Lessons from Japan's Great Recession*, Singapore: John Wiley & Sons.

Liu, S. and Meyer, L.M. (2008) 'Carnations and the floriculture industry: Documenting the cultivation and marketing of flowers in Colorado', *Journal of Archival Organization* 6(1): 6–23.

Marketing Online, **www.marketing-online.co.uk** Accessed 03.06.2010.

Murphy, P. (2009) *His Way: The Brian Clough Story*, London: Pan Books Ltd.

National Archives of Australia, **www.naa.gov.au** Accessed 03.06.2010.

National Archives of the UK, **www.nationalarchives.gov.uk**

National Archives of the USA, **www.archives.gov/**

O'Connell, C. (2009) 'Ocean census looks back to go forward', *Irish Times*, 28.05.2009.

OECD Family Database, Social Policy Division, Directorate of Employment, Labour and Social Affairs, (2005), 'PF1: Public spending on family benefits', **http://www.oecd.org/dataoecd/45/46/37864391.pdf** Accessed 03.06.2010.

Oldfield, T. (2008) *Arsène Wenger: Pure Genius*, London: John Blake Publishing Ltd.

Organization for Economic Cooperation and Development (OECD), **www.oecd.org**

Porter, M. (1983) *Competitive Strategy*, London: Collier Macmillan, Free Press.

Porter, M. (1985) *Competitive Advantage*, London: Collier Macmillan, Free Press.

Roberts, D.D., Roberts, L.M., O'Neill, R.M. and Blake-Beard, S.D. (2008) 'The invisible work of managing visibility for social change: Insights from the leadership of Reverend Dr Martin

Luther King Jr', *Business & Society* 47(4): December, 425–456.

Scott, R. (2010) 'Cycling England scheme encourages bike users in towns', Transport Correspondent, *BBC News*, 23 February.

UK Office of National Statistics, (**www.ons.gov.uk**).

Walton, J.K. (2010) 'New directions in business history: Themes, approaches and opportunities', *Business History* 52(1): 1–16.

RECOMMENDED READING

Best, J. (2001) *Damned Lies and Statistics*, California: University of California Press.

Davis, D. (2005) *Business Research for Decision Making* (6th edn), Ch. 4, 'Secondary Data Collection in Business Inquiry', Mason, OH: Cengage South-Western.

Denscombe, M. (2002) *Ground Rules for Good Research*, Maidenhead: Open University Press.

Kent, R. (2007) *Marketing Research Approaches, Methods and Applications in Europe*, Ch. 3, 'Accessing Secondary Data', London: Thomson.

Lee, R.M. (2000) *Unobtrusive Methods in Social Research*, Milton Keynes: Open University Press.

Levitas, R. and Guy, W. (eds) (1996) *Interpreting Official Statistics*, London: Routledge.

Metcalf, D. (2009) 'Nothing new under the sun: The prescience of W.S. Sanders' 1906 Fabian Tract', *British Journal of Industrial Relations* 47(2): 289–305.

Neuman, W.L. (2000) *Social Research Methods: Quantitative and Qualitative Approaches*, Boston, MA: Allyn & Bacon.

Oppenheim, A.N. (1998) *Questionnaire Design, Interviewing and Attitude Measurement*, London: Cassell.

Robson, C. (2000) *Real World Research*, Oxford: Blackwell.

Zikmund, W.G. (2003) *Business Research Methods*, Ch. 8, 'Secondary Data', Mason, OH: Cengage South-Western.

CHAPTER 10

USING OBSERVATION

LEARNING OBJECTIVES

By the end of this chapter the student should be able to:

● Understand the concept of observation in research and be aware of the different kinds of observation engaged in by researchers.

● Know how to use observation in data gathering and be able to design a method of data collection using observation.

● Understand the need to rigour in observation.

● Critique the use of observation in research studies generally.

RESEARCH SKILLS

At the end of this chapter the student should, using the exercises on the accompanying online platform, be able to:

● Design a small observation study.

● Create an observation schedule for that small study.

● Complete an ethical reflection on that observation study.

The aim of this chapter is to introduce the student to the concept of observation. Observation is a key data collection method in social science research. It involves the observation of the phenomenon under investigation, the recording of that observation and the subsequent analysis of that recording. The different kinds of observation used in data gathering are participant observation, non-participant observation (or simply observation) and covert observation. This chapter explores the ways in which observation can be used in business research.

INTRODUCTION

Data gathering techniques are part of the methodological framework, the third framework in the four frameworks approach to the design of the research project. The four frameworks approach to the research project is useful because the process of logically developing the research project from the research statement or question helps the researcher develop a logical and coherent, fully integrated research project. The first three frameworks of the four frameworks approach to research are laid out again in the model below, Figure 10.1.

The epistemological and ontological perspectives of the research project are, we know from our reading of Chapter 4, 'Understanding Research Philosophy', embedded in the philosophical framework of the research project, and consequently in the project's research methodology. As stated in Chapter 4, embedded in each statement of methodology are implicit statements or assumptions about the nature of reality (ontological assumptions) and about the kind of knowledge that will be generated by the research (epistemological assumptions).

Observation studies can be designed to produce both quantitative and qualitative data. Qualitative research is undertaken within a social constructivist or an interpretivist framework. The ontological perspectives within such philosophical frameworks hold reality to be multiple, individually interpreted or socially constructed. Qualitative data are generated by observation when semi-structured or unstructured observation schedules are used. Quantitative data are generated when highly structured observation schedules are used, and/or when a large number of observations are carried out. Quantitative research is situated within a positivist philosophical framework. The ontological perspective within this framework holds reality to be singular, objective, and apart from the individual. We will see, as we read through this chapter, how the researcher designs observations to fit within one or other of these different philosophical perspectives.

Observation as a data collection method must be used, as must all data gathering methods, in a rigorous and **systematic** manner. This means that the observation must be properly designed and there must be a system in place designed to facilitate the methodical collection of data.

In any data collection exercise, the first and arguably the most critical decision to be made is the decision on exactly what data to collect. The data gathered must answer or illuminate in some way the research question or statement.

Systematic
Systematic means there must be a system in place and the action is carried out in a systematic manner, using the system.

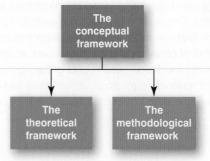

Figure 10.1   Three frameworks of the four frameworks approach to research

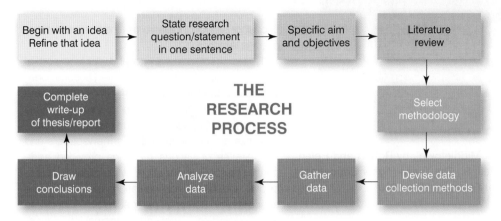

Figure 10.2 The research process

Above is the model of the research process (see Figure 10.2). The stage we are currently exploring is that of devising data gathering methods. We are at the stage of finally deciding on the data collection methods to use in the research project and we are about to start gathering data.

Observation as a data collection method is a traditional method in ethnographic research. Ethnography is the research methodology in focus in this chapter. Ethnography involves the researcher going into a culture to observe the phenomenon under investigation from the perspective of those experiencing the phenomenon. **Participant observation** is a data collection method in which the researcher participates in the action being observed. **Covert observation** is hidden observation.

The box feature below contains an extract from an article by Susan Currell which was published in *The Times Higher Educational Supplement*. In the article, Currell writes about a book called *Middletown* which was written by two social scientists, Robert and Helen Lynd, and published in 1929, the year of the Wall Street Crash.

The article is useful in that it details the different sources of data used by the Lynds in their study, and the article explains that this publication prepared the way for a new methodology for social science research, mass observation research.

Mass observation research was popular, particularly in the UK, in the mid-twentieth century. There was a mass observation social research organization in the UK from 1937 to the early 1950s. The archive of that organization is held by the University of Sussex. You can explore the archive at **www.massobs.org.uk**.

As you will note from your reading of the extract below, the researchers carried out the research for the study outlined in the book *Middletown* by participating in community life, and by recording the observations they gathered about life within that community through their participation in it.

Participant observation
Carried out by the researcher when the researcher does participate in the action or in the phenomenon being observed.

Covert observation
Carried out without the knowledge of those being observed.

UNDERSTANDING OBSERVATION

Observation in the context of research means watching or observing some action, activity or phenomenon, and recording it in some manner. Observation in research is

THE VALUE OF GOOD RESEARCH

Research in the media

'The Canon: Middletown', by Robert and Helen Lynd. Currell, S., *The Times Higher Educational Supplement* February 23rd 2010

Extract

'Unlike other social scientists of the early twentieth century who studied particular 'problem' or 'alien' groups and cultures, the Lynds consciously set out to make a case study of life in the most unproblematic and middle-of-the-road place, finally choosing Muncie, Indiana as their representative average America.

Researchers entered into and became part of the community, living locally in rented accommodation and attending dinners, meetings, rallies and parties, and then writing up records of these experiences. Census data, surveys, city records, business reports, local histories, newspapers and the minutes of various meetings provided additional statistical information, while diaries, scrapbooks and casual conversations provided more anecdotal or personal perspectives. Divided into six 'life activities' – working, homemaking, education, leisure, religion and community – *Middletown* (1929) was the first popular social analysis of the ordinary aspects of US life.

Setting the trend for mass observation research, the book was unique in the way that it examined various class, age and gender differentials in income, social and religious belief, diet, education, leisure, group memberships and other common aspects of human culture.

Offering detailed descriptions of the minutiae of everyday life, such as what people read, what their houses looked like, the art on their walls, whether they had carpet or linoleum, or servants or machines, as well as their pastimes, *Middletown* gently exposed the network of consensual and habitual activity that keeps capitalism functioning effectively, even when its rewards are unevenly distributed.

Published in the year of the Wall Street Crash, the Lynds' study of prosperous middle-American life reminds us that consumer credit had already become the ritualized glue that cohered national culture, but also pushed it to the edge of catastrophe: published at the onset of the worst economic crisis of the twentieth century, it is a most surprising and enduring bestseller.'

Small town of Winthrop, Washington © Gene Krebs/iStock

References

Currell, S. (2010) 'The Canon: Middletown, by Robert and Helen Lynd', *Times Higher Educational Supplement,* 11 February.

very simply watching or observing. The researcher observes the action or activity or phenomenon, and records his/her observation(s). Observation is a field research method, i.e. the researcher undertakes this data gathering method themselves, in the field. Thus observation yields primary data, Primary data, as we know from Chapter 9, are data which are observed or gathered first-hand, or directly, by the researcher. Observation yields empirical data, which are data gathered by observation or experience. Observation data are data gathered directly by the researcher in the field, which is the site or context of the research. The context for the research might be a business, or a classroom or an organization.

The decision to use observation as a data collection method in any research project is taken in response to the data requirements of the research project and the location of that data. The data may be in the action or activity of some person, or some people, or some organization or entity. The researcher identifies the action or activity or phenomenon to be observed and then designs the means by which to carry out the observation. In order to do this, the researcher must gain **access** to the people who are carrying out the action or activity. Usually, the researcher must ask for permission to enter the field and to carry out the observation. This almost always involves writing formal letters to the people in charge of the field, asking their permission to enter and to carry out the observation. When the researcher has secured access, the researcher can begin the observation of the activity.

Access
Access to data and access to the field of the research project.

The researcher's recorded observations of the phenomenon are the data, the evidence the researcher has created or developed on the phenomenon under investigation. The steps in this process are laid out in Table 10.1.

Now that we know what observation is, we now need to know how to carry out an observation in the field. As explained above, the researcher decides what to observe and where to observe it. When possible, the researcher will visit the field several times before commencing the observation in order to become familiar with the field and the action before finally deciding on precisely which action(s) or what parts of the action(s) to observe. The researcher can then design the means by which to carry out the observation.

The preliminary visits to the field are 'informal observations'. They are used by researchers to help them design the formal observation and to alert them to anything in the field that might interfere with, obstruct or delay it. If the researcher can identify potential obstructions or delays, s/he may be able to design the formal observation in

Table 10.1   Conducting an observation study
1   Identify the data required for the research
2   Gain access to the data
3   Decide on observation as an appropriate data collection method to be used to gather data
4   Design the means by which the observation will be carried out and recorded
5   Carry out the observation, by observing the action or the phenomenon and recording that observation
6   The record of the observation is the data gathered
7   Analyze the data

such a way as to circumvent or avoid these problems. Having said that, it is neither possible nor desirable that the researcher attempts to control the environment of the observation; the researcher simply needs to be familiar enough with the environment, and secure enough in it, to be able to carry out the observation.

THE DIFFERENT KINDS OF OBSERVATION

Non-participant observation
Carried out when the researcher does not participate in the action or in the phenomenon being observed.

In general, researchers engage in three kinds of observation, the first kind is called 'observation' or **'non-participant observation'**; the second kind is called 'participant observation'. The third kind of observation is called 'covert observation'. Covert observation is ethically problematic and as such, is used with caution by researchers.

Table 10.2 details the three kinds of observation, all of which can be used formally or informally. An informal study is less rigorously designed than a formal study. Informal studies can be used to inform, supplement and/or support formal studies.

There are three critical decisions that must be made in any observation study. The researcher must decide what exactly is to be observed, and how to conduct and record the observation. These critical decisions are listed in Table 10.3.

The Real World Research box below is an extract from a research project that was carried out using covert participant observation. The project is interesting for many reasons. In this article, the literature review consists of a review of the literature on the ethics of covert participant observation. The journal article details two case studies, both of which were developed using covert participant observation

Table 10.2 The different kinds of observation		
(Non-participant) observation **Formal/informal**	**Participant observation** **Formal/informal**	**Covert observation** **Formal/informal**
The first kind of observation that researchers engage in is called observation, or non-participant observation. Using this kind of observation the researcher observes some activity or action or phenomenon in the field, and records that observation. The recorded observation is the data gathered.	Using participant observation the researcher is part of the action or the activity or the phenomenon in the field. While participating in, or being part of, the action, activity or phenomenon, the researcher observes the action, activity or phenomenon, and records that observation. The recorded observation is the data gathered.	Using covert observation the researcher observes the action, activity or phenomenon in a covert manner. In other words, the fact that the action, activity or phenomenon is being observed is kept from the people who are part of, or who are generating, the action, activity or phenomenon. The observation is kept secret. It is covert. Such observations are ethically problematic. The researcher records the observation. The recorded observation is the data gathered.

Table 10.3 Critical decisions to be made in any observation study
1   Deciding what exactly is to be observed
2   Deciding how to conduct the observation
3   Deciding how to record the observation

YOUR RESEARCH
Using observation in your research

Think about your own research project. Is there any way that you could use observation as a data gathering technique (or method) in your research project? If you think that you could use observation in your research project, which of the three observation methods would you use? In your research diary, write a note detailing how, where, when and why you would use this means of observation.

In your research diary, write a short paragraph about covert observation. Use the Internet to search for examples of covert research projects. One of the most famous, or infamous, covert social science research projects is the Milgram Study. You can read about the Milgram Study at **www.experiment-resources.com/milgram-experiment-ethics.html**.

Another interesting example of covert research is Derren Brown's TV programme *The Heist*, first broadcast on Channel 4 in the UK, on 4 January, 2006. In the programme, the presenter Derren Brown invites a group of business women and men to participate in a documentary about motivational speaking. This was pretence. He was, in fact, using his engagement with the group of business people to examine whether or not he could persuade these people to participate in a real bank robbery.

Use the Internet to search for information on the TV programme *The Heist*. From your reading of this information, in your research diary describe the covert observation being undertaken by Derren Brown. Write a short summary on the ethics of that observation; critically examine the observation and in your short summary detail the ethical issues, if any, apparent to you in that observation.

as the data collection method. In the journal article, which you should source and read, both of the case studies are outlined in detail. The aim, the design of the research and the context within which it was undertaken, the data collection method, the data gathered for each study, the findings and the conclusions are all discussed and explained.

This study is particularly useful in that it was a covert research project, carried out using participant observation, and the authors of the article engage in an in-depth consideration of the ethical issues in covert research.

It is unlikely that as a student researcher you will get permission to use a covert method in your research project. If you are thinking about using such a method you should get advice and guidance from your thesis supervisor and/or your lecturer in research methods. However, it is important to have some knowledge and understanding of covert observational studies. In particular, you should have an understanding of the ethical issues and problems inherent in covert research.

REAL WORLD RESEARCH

How theory influences research

Covert participant observation in management research

'Re-evaluating the consequentialist perspective of using covert participant observation in management research', Oliver, J. and Eales, K. (2008)

The authors of the study write that the primary purpose of using participant observation in management research is to gain insight into and knowledge of organizational phenomena. They state that the critical issue in the research process is the need to collect data in an appropriate manner. They express their concern about the possibility of the method of data collection being unethical or creating difficult personal or emotional issues for the researcher. In the paper they ask whether engaging in extended periods of covert participant observation is an ethical way to learn about organizational problems.

They write that most of the literature regarding this research method concentrates on the epistemological methodological relationship (the relationship the method has with knowledge creation and the kind of knowledge created by the method) and the associated problems of researcher subjectivity, impressionism, bias and research outputs that are often idiosyncratic descriptions of the phenomena being investigated. However, they state when this research method is considered in ethical terms, the debate shifts from being one of distance and objectivity in the method to one of invasion of privacy, informed consent and deception. As a result, the higher principled debate concerning covert participant research is one based on research morals, not methodological validity.

The researchers state that while the ethics of management research and the research ethics involved in investigating organizational phenomena have been dealt with in the literature, little attention has been paid to the ethical considerations and consequences for the researcher pertaining to the collection and use of data. They state that their paper makes a contribution to the growing debate concerning the ethical nature of covert participant observation in management research. They suggest that researchers need to consider the consequences for themselves when choosing to conduct management research in a covert way.

An extensive review of the literature on the use of observation, participant observation and covert observation in business, management and organizational research is presented.

The researchers state that the ethical debate about the use of covert participant observation demonstrates real tensions between obtaining often exploratory and in-depth data in a covert way, and, obtaining these data in a way that is not deceptive, that does not infringe upon the rights of participants, and that doesn't result in unforeseen consequences and harm to participants.

In the journal article, the researchers go on to outline two case studies. The first case study details a covert participant observation in a small family business. The second case study details a covert participant observation with a national leisure service provider. The aim of both case studies is detailed. The findings from both research projects are outlined.

Read the journal article, and in your research diary, make a note of the way in which the participant observation was carried out. Then write a short paragraph on the ethical issues, as you see them, in the study.

References

Oliver, J. and Eales, K. (2008) 'Re-evaluating the consequentialist perspective of using covert participant observation in management research', *Qualitative Market Research: An International Journal* 11(3): 344–357.

USING OBSERVATION

There are a number of different ways in which observation can be used in data collection. Observation can be participant or non-participant, and covert or open. A researcher can also engage in human or mechanical observation. Mechanical observation is observation undertaken through the use of some kind of technology, such as mobile phone technology. A researcher can engage in natural observation, which is observation in a natural setting, or contrived observation, which is observation in a setting that has been contrived by the researcher. An example of a contrived observation would be if participants read a text or watched a film or video while the researcher observed and recorded their reactions and responses. In this case, the situation is not natural but has been contrived by the researcher. A researcher can engage in direct observation, where participants know that the researcher is watching them. In such observations participants tend to react to being watched. As a result, this kind of observation is sometimes known as reactive observation. A researcher can also engage in **Unobtrusive observation**, when participants may or may not have been told that the research is being undertaken. The researcher carries out the observation in an unobtrusive manner. Table 10.4 details these different ways in which researchers use observation.

As with every data collection method, the researcher makes a decision around which observation method to use based on the aim of the research, the population of the research, the data requirements of the research, the best way in which to gather the data required for the research, and the ethical issues in conducting the proposed observation.

As we discussed earlier in this chapter, observations can be unstructured, semi-structured, or structured (see Table 10.5). **Unstructured observations** are sometimes undertaken when the researcher is unsure about precisely which aspects of the phenomenon under investigation need to be explored or examined. Unstructured observations are sometimes used by researchers in the early stages of a research project. Often an unstructured observation leads to a more **structured observation**. The researcher uses the unstructured observation to get to know the field and/or the phenomenon under investigation. Then the researcher designs a semi-structured or structured observation in order to focus the observation on the precise phenomenon being investigated.

> **Unobtrusive observation** Carried out unobtrusively, with or without the knowledge of the research participants.

> **Unstructured observations** Carried out when the researcher does not know what aspects or elements of the action or the phenomenon should or could be observed.

> **Structured observation** Carried out when the researcher knows precisely what aspects or elements of the research project should or could be observed.

Table 10.4 The ways in which researchers use observation	
Participant observation	Non-participant observation
Direct observation	Indirect observation
Human observation	Mechanical observation
Covert observation	Open observation
Natural observation	Contrived observation
Direct (reactive) observation	Unobtrusive observation

Table 10.5 Unstructured, semi-structured and structured observation

Unstructured observation: in an unstructured observation the researcher goes into the field and simply observes the action or the phenomenon under investigation in the research project. The researcher records their observations of the phenomenon. The recorded observations are the data to be analyzed.

An unstructured observation can be recorded in a field diary.

Semi-structured observation: in a semi-structured observation the researcher knows which aspects or elements of the action or the phenomenon he/she wishes to observe and so he/she designs a semi-structured observation schedule in order to facilitate that observation. The researcher observes the elements or aspects of the action or the phenomenon and then records those observations in the semi-structured observation schedule he/she has designed for the research.

Structured Observation: in a structured observation the researcher knows very precisely which aspects or elements of the action or phenomenon s/he wishes to observe and so s/he designs a structured observation schedule in order to facilitate that observation. A structured observation schedule can look like a questionnaire. A questionnaire is a structured data gathering instrument. The researcher designs the structured observation schedule, or they use an observation schedule they have found in their reading of the literature. An example of a structured observation schedule is given in Figure 10.4.

An example of a semi-structured observation schedule is given below.

Health and Safety Research/Textile Style Ltd

(Record every incidence of the following:)
Date_____

Infringement of Health and Safety Regulations	Notes Record detail of infringement	Number of times infringement occurs

Figure 10.3 Semi-structured observation schedule

Semi-structured observation
Carried out when the researcher knows broadly speaking what aspects or elements of the research should or could be observed.

Figure 10.3 is an example of a schedule for a **semi-structured observation**.

Figure 10.4 is an example of a schedule for a structured observation.

A structured observation schedule can be a great deal more structured even than the example given below. Think of the degree of structure and design in questionnaires you have seen or completed. A structured observation schedule is designed in a similar way. The key is to design the data gathering instrument to meet the needs of the data requirements of the research project. The data gathering instrument is designed specifically for the job it is required to do.

Customer relations research/Willow Music Store
(Every occurrence observed of the activities listed below will be recorded.)

Date_____

Place a tick in box to record occurrence.

Engaging customers in conversation									
Active selling									
Smiling at customers									
Product promotion									
Good customer service									
Poor customer service									
Missed sales opportunities									

Figure 10.4   Structured observation schedule

THE VALUE OF GOOD RESEARCH

Focus on ethnography

The research methodology ethnography, as explained in Chapter 7, is used when the researcher wants to carry out an in-depth study of a culture. The researcher goes inside the culture in order to develop an in-depth view of the culture. Although inside the culture, the researcher has to maintain simultaneously an outsider perspective on the culture. This is in order to ensure that the researcher does not become acculturated, or so much a part of the culture that they can no longer critically engage with the culture. In ethnographic research, researchers use any data gathering method that will provide useful data on the phenomenon under investigation. The phenomenon under investigation will be a culture or some aspect or element of a culture.

Ken Anderson is an anthropologist who works at Intel Research. In 2009 he wrote about ethnographic research as a key to strategy in the *Harvard Business Review*. Anderson wrote that corporate ethnography is not just for innovation any more, it is central to gaining a full understanding of customers and the business itself. The ethnographic work at his company Intel and other firms, he wrote, now informs functions such as strategy and long-term planning. In the article Anderson states that ethnography is the branch of anthropology that involves trying to understand how people live their lives. He wrote of researchers visiting consumers in their homes and offices to observe and listen in non-directed ways. The goal, he stated, is to see people's behaviour on their terms, not on ours. While this observational method might seem inefficient, he wrote, in fact it informs the company about the context within which customers would use a new product and about the meaning the new product might hold for them in their lives.

Some of the research questions ethnographers are currently engaged with include: how long particular markets will play out, whether television and personal computer technologies will converge, whether or not consumers shift comfortably to new media, and whether or not smartphones will take over most of the functions of personal computers.

Anderson wrote that Intel can analyze data on the latest buying patterns and data from customer surveys but customers often can't articulate what they want in products and services. This is why a company like Intel employes ethnographers. So that they can study how people live in order to discover trends that will be used to inform the company's future strategies. You can read Anderson's article at **http://hbr.org/2009/03/ethnographic-research-a-key-to-strategy/ar/1**.

The Sage journal *Ethnography* has many articles detailing business research projects carried out using ethnography as the research methodology. A recent article in the journal is Lee's (2009), article on the professionalizing of the rap career. Lee's research involved 4 years of ongoing ethnographic field work with inner-city men who rap at an 'open mic' venue in South Central Los Angeles in California, USA. In the article Lee explains that the rappers in the study view the venue as a place to develop their skills and earn the respect of their peers, but they hope to move beyond the venue and make money in the music industry. The data for the article are from observations and interviews. In the article Lee provides an interesting account of the ethnographer's journey into that culture (2009; 480–484), a journey he had to make in order to be able to engage in ethnographic research.

Another Sage journal, the *Journal of Contemporary Ethnography* also has many articles detailing business research projects carried out using ethnography as the research methodology.

An interesting article on ethnographic research in the workplace is the article by Tope *et al.* (2005), 'The benefits of being there: Evidence from the literature on work'.

The University of Pennsylvania provides a simple guide on how to do ethnographic research (**www.sas.upenn.edu/anthro/anthro/cpiamethods**).

Another interesting and potentially useful website is that of Ethnographic Research, Inc. (**www.ethnographic-research.com**).

Colorado State University provides a writing guide on ethnography, observational research and narrative inquiry at **http://writing.colstate.edu/guides/research/observe/**.

THE NEED FOR RIGOUR IN OBSERVATION

Rigour
For a research project to be rigorous, it must adhere to the scientific principles of research, e.g. systematic and valid research.

One of the most basic principles in research is the principle of **rigour**. For a research project to be rigorous, as stated in Chapter 1 of this textbook, it must adhere to the scientific principles of research. The research must be systematic and it must be valid. The aim and objectives of the research must be clearly stated, and they must be valid. The researcher has to design a methodology for the research that will facilitate the accomplishment of the aim and objectives. The methodology must be the appropriate methodology for the proposed research. The population of the research must be clearly defined, and appropriate for the proposed research. The population of the study must also be appropriate to the study. If a sample is drawn from the population, the sampling method must be detailed, if a sampling frame is used, it must be detailed and it must be valid. The sample size must be clearly stated. The limitations of the research must be explored and outlined. If possible and appropriate, attempts to overcome the limitations of the research must be made, and then detailed and explained. The data collection methods designed and used must be appropriate and valid. The **field work** undertaken for the research must be systematic, rigorous and valid. The data gathered must be properly managed and stored, and in due course properly analyzed. The researcher must have the scholarship, the skills and the competencies necessary for the conduct of the research. This should be evident in the manner in which the researcher engages with the research project, and in the manner in which the researcher writes up the research.

As can be seen from the above, the researcher is required throughout the research process to make decisions regarding the design and development of the research project. A beginner researcher needs a good deal of guidance in making these decisions. Therefore it is important to have a research supervisor or a lecturer in research methods whose expertise in this area you can call on, as you develop your research project.

The discussion above of rigour in the research process highlights the fact that there are no clear-cut rules about rigour. It is not a case that one kind of observation, for example, is more rigorous than another. It is the way in which the observation is designed and carried out by the researcher that establishes the rigour of the observation. Similarly, one data gathering method is not more rigorous than another, but it is the way in which the researcher uses the data gathering method that establishes the rigour of the method. Research methodologies and data gathering methods are flexible and can be used in different ways to accomplish many different things is social research. We have seen this in detail in Chapters 7 and 8 of this textbook. Rigorous research uses appropriate methods systematically and consistently in order to thoroughly accomplish the aim and objectives of the research project.

An aid to improving the rigour and the validity of the research project is the **pilot study**. The researcher undertakes a pilot study to test the design of the research project. A pilot study can also be undertaken to test the data gathering method(s) designed for the research project. In a pilot study, the researcher tests the instrument to see how it works. For example, to test an observation schedule, the researcher engages in a practice observation to see how well the observation schedule records the data required for the study. This is a pilot study. Following the pilot study, the researcher can amend the data gathering instrument in order to improve the quality of the data the instrument will provide.

Field work
The means by which data gathering is undertaken in order to provide primary data for a research project.

Pilot study
An aid to improving the rigour and the validity of the research. This is a test of the data gathering instrument(s) designed for the research.

CRITIQUE THE USE OF OBSERVATION IN RESEARCH

As a researcher, when you critique the use of observation in someone else's research you should consider the validity of the observation proposed or carried out as a means of gathering data for that particular study. You should also consider the rigour with which the observation was designed, constructed and carried out. You should be concerned with the manner in which observation as a means of data gathering serves the data requirements of the study. You are also concerned with the means by which the data were analyzed.

You should also be concerned with the aim and objectives of the study, and whether, or to what degree, the observation carried out served to accomplish them. You should consider whether or not the observation data collection method used was the most appropriate data collection method in terms of the needs of the study. You might suggest that other data collection methods may have served the research better. You should consider the population of the study and whether or not observation was the best means of data collection with that population. If the study does not have a human population, you should consider the context for the study, and whether or not observation was the most appropriate means of data collection in that context given the data requirements of the study.

In reading such a research project you should think about the way in which the observation was designed. The observation should be as thorough, systematic and consistent as possible. Even when a data collection method is designed to be unstructured, it should be systematic. The observation should be clearly and thoroughly organized, and that organization should be thoroughly detailed, outlined and explained, in the written report of the research. The thorough reporting of the manner in which the observation was carried out facilitates the researcher in establishing the validity and the rigour of the observation This, thorough reporting, also allows readers to examine these issues.

When you critique an observation, you should examine the observation schedule, a copy of which should be included in the appendices of the study, in terms of the appropriateness and thoroughness of the observation. You should check what was included in the observation and note what, if anything, was omitted. Decide whether or not there was an error in what was included or omitted. Examine when, where and with whom the observation was conducted. Explore the manner in which the observation was conducted. Decide whether or not the conduct of the observation was appropriate to the needs of the study, and appropriate in terms of proper and appropriate ethical standards. Examine the manner in which the observation was recorded, and whether the recording of the observation was rigorous. Examine and critique the evidence presented in terms of the validity and rigour of the observation.

This is how you critique an observation study in a research project, and this is how any observation that you may design and carry out in the course of your own research will be critiqued. It is important to be aware of all of these points, and the critiques prompted by them, when designing and carrying out an observation as part of a research project. It is useful to remember too that many if not all of these issues are relevant to most data collection methods, as well as to observation and observation studies.

DESIGNING AN OBSERVATION STUDY

When designing an observation study, it is important to be sure to begin with, that observation is an appropriate data gathering method for the study. The researcher does not arbitrarily select the data collection method(s) for the research project. The data collection method(s) used in the research project are dictated by the data requirements of the study, by the location of that data, by the kind(s) of data available and the level of access possible to that data, by the aim and objectives of the research, by the population of the research, by the location of the population and by the context for the research. The researcher builds the research project, step-by-step, and each step taken in the design of the research project must be congruent with all of the previous steps taken. In other words, each step taken in the design of the research project must fit with all of the other steps already taken in the process of designing the research project. The example below provides an outline of Iona's research project in which observation was used as a data gathering method. What do you think of Iona's research and the methodology and data gathering methods she has proposed for it?

Proposed research methodology for Iona's research project

This research project is a case study examining employee relations in the SME, Techtron Inc. Techtron Inc is an SME in the east midlands with 50 employees. Almost half of the employees, 24 of them, are technicians, the rest are management and administrative staff. The focus of this study is on employee relations within and between these three groups of employees.

Aim and objectives

The aim of this research project is to examine employee relations in the company Techtron Inc.

The objectives of the research are as follows:

- To examine employee relations in Techtron Inc. in relation to the three groups of employees in the company: management, administrative staff and technicians.

- To examine within and between group employee relations in Techtron Inc.

- To document both within and between group employee relations in Techtron Inc.

This research project is a case study. The methodology used for the research is case study methodology.

Two different data collection methods will be used in this research, observation and interviews. The data collection methods will be used sequentially. First, a series of observations will be undertaken in order to facilitate the recording and documentation of employee relations in the firm. Second, issues in employee relations evidenced in the observations will be further explored in a series of in-depth interviews. It is anticipated that the interviews will allow the researcher to probe and further examine, or examine

in more detail, the findings of the observations. The in-depth interviews will also allow participants in the study to explain employee relations in the firm, as they are evidenced in the observations.

With the use of two different data collection methods in the research, triangulation can be accomplished. Triangulation in research is the examination of the phenomenon under investigation in the research from more than one perspective. In this research project, the findings of the observation will be triangulated with the findings from the in-depth interviews. The data from the two different data collection methods will together provide a richer, deeper, more nuanced and more complex insight into employee relations in the firm.

Observations: As the observations are to be conducted with all 50 employees in the firm, there is no sampling in this element of the field work. To begin with there will be a series of unstructured observations in the workplace. These observations will take place over a 2-week period, from June 10 to June 24. Each of these observations will take place in 2-hour slots. Over the 2-week period there will be two of these observations each day. These unstructured observations will be recorded in the field diary of the research in the following manner.

Date

Time

Venue

Population

Record observation

Unstructured observation schedule

Following these unstructured observations, there will be 4 weeks of semi-structured observations.

- The first week of these semi-structured observations will be spent observing within-group employee relations among the technicians in the firm.

- The second week will be spent observing within-group employee relations among administrative staff in the firm.

- The third week will be spent observing within-group employee relations among managers in the firm.

- The fourth and final week will be spent studying between-group employee relations generally within the firm.

The findings from the unstructured observation and the issues in employee relations in the firm evidenced by those observations will be used to structure the semi-structured observations.

The semi-structured observation schedule to be used to record these observations is detailed below.

Semi-structured observation

Date

Time

Venue

Observing

Evidence of good employee relations	
Apparent causes	
Evident consequences	

Evidence of bad employee relations	
Apparent causes	
Evident consequences	

Finally, a series of in-depth interviews will be undertaken with a sample of employees from each of the three groups of employees in the firm. A purposive sampling technique will be used, whereby the researcher will select the employees to be included in the sample for interview.

- Technicians – there are 24 technicians in the company. Twelve of these technicians will be interviewed for the research.

- Administrators – there are 12 administrators in the company. Six of these administrators will be interviewed for the study.

- Managers – there are 14 managers in the company. Seven managers will be interviewed for the research.

In all, 25 in-depth interviews will be conducted. The interview schedule will be semi-structured, as was the second observation schedule. The findings of both series of observations will be used to inform the construction of the interview schedule. It is anticipated that the interviews will shed light on the history of employee relations in the firm, as well as explaining and clarifying the firm's employee relations, as they were evidenced in the observations. The completeness of the proposed methodology for this research establishes in part the validity of the research. The rigour with which the research was carried out will be evident in the completeness of the data gathered for the research.

Iona has developed a very interesting research project. The methodology and the data collection methods designed for the project are congruent with the aim and the objectives of the research. The data gathering methods fit well with the population of the study and they are appropriate in terms of the data requirements of the research project. The project is simple but comprehensive. The research, when completed, will provide a rich insight into employee relations within the firm. Iona's project is situated within a social constructivist philosophical framework. Her data gathering methods will provide predominantly qualitative data. Through the data gathering methods she is using in the project, Iona will be able to develop an account of how employee relations within the company are socially constructed.

CASE STUDY

Dabir's research idea

Dabir is doing a degree in business management. He has decided to travel around Ireland over the summer holidays. He plans to conduct his research for his thesis while on that trip. Following his reading of Russell's (2008), journal article on nostalgic tourism, Dabir decided to model his research project for his thesis on Russell's research.

'Nostalgic Tourism', Russell, D.W. (2008)

In his article Russell wrote that the global tourism industry is experiencing unprecedented growth, as more people seek its services and as more compe-

Dublin Bus Tour, Ireland © Claude Thibault/Alamy

tition enters the marketplace. The article was written before the recent global economic downturn. Russell states that both the UK and the Republic of Ireland have experienced steady growth in tourism. He writes that due to increased competition, tourism companies have had to reassess their business models in order to look for new niche opportunities. These niche opportunities can, he states, positively benefit the tourism industry as a whole. One such niche opportunity, according to Russell, is to cater to nostalgic tourists. Such tourists are in search of authentic cultural experiences through which they can experience their ancestral roots. In order to conduct his research, Russell participated in a 23-day bus tour. He used a multi-method approach to the research. The data gathering methods used were observation, interview and survey.

(For the purposes of this chapter, with its focus on observation, in this case study we will focus on the observation data gathering method of the research project.)

Using participant observation, Russell made an effort to observe all the activities participated in by the tourists on the tour. He observed what they ate, what they bought and what they did. He also made a record of what they said when speaking aloud. He didn't engage in eavesdropping. Observation was conducted at all times in public places, on the bus, during visits to sites, during and after meals.

Russell also conducted brief interviews with the tourists before the tour commenced and he administered a questionnaire, of ten questions, to the group when the tour had ended and before everyone left. While he engaged in participant observation on the tour, he did not speak of the research on the tour. In this way, he managed to conduct the research relatively unobtrusively.

In the article, Russell wrote that nothing is more fundamental to a sound marketing strategy than understanding and catering to the needs and desires of consumers. He suggested that such understanding is important in order for travel companies to better target tourist sub-sets and to more appropriately position their travel package offerings, especially at a time when the global tourism market faces more intense competition. The ancestral tourism experience, he wrote, involves sustained immersion and active interpretation that continues even after conclusion of the tour. His research, he wrote, demonstrated that the perception of authenticity and the fulfilment of cultural experiences are important determinants in fostering repeat business and soliciting favourable recommendations from customers. He suggested that, in order to improve customer satisfaction, tour companies should consider integrating what are now supplemental tour options into the regular package offering, in an effort to improve authentic experience perceptions.

Dabir has decided to build on Russell's work. He is going to take a bus tour around Ireland. While on the tour he will explore the tourists' engagement with heritage tourism and he will consider the response of the heritage tourism industry to the heritage tourists.

Dabir plans to engage in participant observation on the tour. He will observe his fellow tourists in the manner in which they engage with and respond to the different elements of the tourist product offered to them.

He will also observe the manner in which the providers of the tourist product engage with and respond to the tourists.

Dabir also plans to use secondary sources in his research. He will examine the heritage tourist product as it is presented in tour company literature and on their websites.

From all of these data, Dabir hopes to provide an analysis of the needs of heritage tourists and the degree to which those needs are met by heritage tourism providers.

What do you think of Dabir's research idea? It seems a good idea. It is simple and interesting. An area of concern would be the validity of the research. Dabir must take great care in designing and carrying out his observations. He must ensure that the observations are conducted and recorded in a systematic and consistent manner. He must clearly make a contribution to knowledge with his research. He should clearly and explicitly establish that contribution when writing up his research.

The exercise below is based on Russell's journal article 'Nostalgic tourism'. You will find the exercise useful in terms of developing your understanding of the research process.

Read the journal article and examine the use of observation in the study. Detail in your research diary the manner in which observation was used in the study. Write a short note in your research diary about the contribution that the observation element of the research made to the study. In your reflection on the study in your research diary, engage with and respond to the following:

- How was the observation conducted?
- What data was gathered through the observation data gathering method?
- What contribution, if any, did the observation data make to the findings?
- Could another method of data gathering have been substituted for the observation method? If yes, state the method(s). If no, explain why not.
- Give five reasons why the observation data collection method, as it was deployed in this study, was useful.
- Take particular note of the manner in which theory is deployed in the writing of this journal article.
- In the journal article try to identify three of the four frameworks from the four frameworks approach to the research process:

  The conceptual framework
  The theoretical framework
  The methodological framework.

1 Read how the researcher clearly defines what it is that they are trying to do.

2 Can you see how the researcher creates, from the literature, a theoretical framework for the research that they are proposing to carry out?

3 Examine the way in which the researcher clearly outlines the methodology for the research, detailing the population of the study, and the data gathering methods to be used in the study.

4   Can you see how the data gathered evidences the phenomenon under investigation?

5   Examine the way in which the researcher uses the data gathered.

6   Read how the researcher theorizes the data gathered.

7   Can you see how, through theorizing the data gathered, the researcher knits their research into the body of knowledge? As you know, it is through theorizing the data gathered, through knitting their research into the body of knowledge, that the researcher makes their contribution to knowledge.

CHAPTER REVIEW

This chapter focuses on observation as a means of gathering data. The chapter establishes that observation is a fundamental and important method of gathering data in research. Observation in the context of research means watching or observing some action or activity or phenomenon, and recording in some manner that action or activity or observation. As outlined in the chapter, the researcher while observing the phenomenon under investigation, records their observation of that phenomenon. The recorded observations of the phenomenon represent the data of this data gathering method. The chapter explains that all data collection including observation must be carried out in a rigorous, systematic and consistent manner. In the written report of the research, this process must be thoroughly detailed and explained. The main types of observation in social research were detailed and explained in the chapter. They are participant observation, non-participant observation and covert observation. There are different ways of structuring observations; observations can be structured, semi-structured or unstructured. Examples are given of these different ways of structuring observations. The chapter concludes with an example of a student research project developed around two data collection methods, observation and interviews.

Now update your interactive research diary with your notes and findings at www.cengage.co.uk/quinlan. Complete the activities provided to reinforce your understanding of this chapter.

END OF CHAPTER QUESTIONS

1 Explain what is meant by observation in field research?

2 What is meant by the term rigour in social research?

3 Name the three main types of observation engaged in by researchers.

4 What are the three critical decisions to be made in any observation study?

5 Why would a researcher use unstructured observation as an observation method?

6 Why would a researcher use semi-structured observation as an observation method?

7 Why would a researcher use structured observation as an observation method?

8 What is unobtrusive observation in research?

9 What is covert observation in research and what are the main ethical issues in such research?

10 Detail and explain how would critique an observation study.

REFERENCES

Anderson, K. (2009) 'Ethnographic research: A key to strategy', http://hbr.org/2009/03/ethnographic-research-a-key-to-strategy/ar/1 Accessed 03.06.2010.

Colorado State University, 'Writing guide: Ethnography, observational research, and narrative inquiry', http://writing.colstate.edu/guides/research/observe/

Currell, S. (2010) 'The Canon: Middletown, by Robert and Helen Lynd', *Times Higher Educational Supplement*, 11 February.

Ethnographic Research, Inc., www.ethnographic-research.com

Lee, J. (2009) 'Open mic: Professionalizing the rap career', *Ethnography* 10(4): 475–495.

Mass Observation Archive, The Library, University of Sussex, www.massobs.org.uk

Oliver, J. and Eales, K. (2008) 'Re-evaluating the consequentialist perspective of using covert participant observation in management research', *Qualitative Market Research: An International Journal* 11(3): 344–357.

Russell, D.W. (2008) 'Nostalgic tourism', *Journal of Travel and Tourism Marketing* 25(2): October, 103–116.

Tope, D., Chamberlain, L.J., Crowley, M. and Hodson, R. (2005) 'The benefits of being there: Evidence from the literature on work', *Journal of Contemporary Ethnography* 34(4): 470–493.

University of Pennsylvania, 'How to do ethnographic research: A simplified guide', www.sas.upenn.edu/anthro/anthro/cpiamethods

RECOMMENDED READING

Berger, J. (1972) *Ways of Seeing*, Harmondsworth: London: Penguin.

Collis, J. and Hussey, R. (2009) *Business Research: A Practical Guide for Undergraduate and Postgraduate Students*, Houndsmill: Palgrave Macmillan.

Denscombe, M. (2003) *The Good Research Guide: For Small-scale Social Research Projects* (2nd edn), Maidenhead: Open University Press.

Easterby-Smith, M., Thorpe, R. and Jackson, P.R. (2008) *Management Research* (3rd edn), London: Sage.

Gill, J. and Johnson, P. (2006) *Research Methods for Managers*, Ch. 7, 'Ethnography: It's Origins and Practice', and Ch. 8, 'Issues in Ethnographic Research', London: Sage.

Hammersley, M. and Atkinson, P. (2001) *Ethnography*, London: Routledge.

Jankowicz, A.D. (2005) *Business Research Projects*, London: Cengage.

Kent, R. (2007) *Marketing Research, Approaches, Methods and Applications in Europe*, London: Cengage.

Lee, R. (2000) *Unobstrusive Methods in Social Research*, Milton Keynes: Open University Press.

Miles, M.B. and Huberman, A.M. (1994) *Qualitative Data Analysis: An Expanded Sourcebook*, London and Thousand Oaks: Sage.

Neuman, W.L. (2000) *Social Research Methods: Quantitative and Qualitative Approaches*, Ch. 13, 'Field Research', Boston, MA: Allyn & Bacon.

Paterson, M. (2006) *Consumption and Everyday Life*, Ch. 7, 'Mallrats and Car Boots: The Spaces of Consumption', London: Routledge.

Prosser, J. (1998) *Image-based Research*, London: Routledge.

Robson, C. (2002) *Real World Research*, Ch. 11, 'Observational Methods', Ch. 12, 'Additional Methods of Data Collection', Oxford: Blackwell.

Rose, G. (2001) *Visual Methodologies*, London: Sage.

Simpson, M. and Tuson, J. (2003) *Using Observations in Small-scale Research: A Beginner's Guide*, The SCRE Centre, Glasgow: University of Glasgow.

Van Leeuwen, T. (2005) *Introducing Social Semiotics*, London: Routledge.

Zikmund, W.G. (2003) *Business Research Methods*, Mason, OH: Cengage South-Western.

CHAPTER 11

USING INTERVIEWS AND FOCUS GROUPS

LEARNING OBJECTIVES

At the end of this chapter the student should be able to:

- Decide on the most appropriate use and design of interviews and/or focus groups for particular research projects.

- Use interviews and/or focus groups in their own research and design and develop appropriate interview and focus group schedules for their own research.

- Critique the use of interviews and focus groups in research.

RESEARCH SKILLS

At the end of this chapter the student should, using the exercises on the accompanying online platform, be able to:

- Decide when to use interviews and when to use focus groups to gather data.

- Design an interview schedule and a focus group schedule for a sample project.

- Critique the design of a proposed interview and focus group.

The aim of this chapter is to introduce and explain two data collection methods, interviews and focus groups. In the chapter, the ways in which to structure and carry out interviews and focus groups are explained. Both this face-to-face COMP (F2F) focus groups and interviews, and focus groups and interviews conducted using computer mediated communication (CMC) are explored. The different types of interviews, one-to-one interviews, in-depth interviews, telephone interviews, group interviews and online interviews and their relative advantages and disadvantages are described.

INTRODUCTION

The Four Frameworks
Conceptual Framework
Theoretical Framework
Methodological Framework
Analytical Framework

Data gathering techniques are part of the methodological framework, the third framework in the four frameworks approach to the design of the research project. The four frameworks approach to the research project facilitates the researcher in developing a logical and coherent, fully integrated research project. The first three frameworks of the four frameworks approach to research are laid out again in Figure 11.1.

The epistemological and ontological perspectives of the research project are, we know from our reading of Chapter 4, 'Understanding Research Philosophy', embedded in the philosophical perspective informing the research project, and consequently in the project's research methodology. As stated in Chapter 4 and Chapter 10, embedded in each statement of methodology are implicit statements or assumptions about the nature of reality (ontological assumptions) and about the kind of knowledge that will be generated by the research (epistemological assumptions).

Focus groups and interviews are often used in research undertaken within a social constructivist or interpretive philosophical framework. The ontological perspectives within such philosophical frameworks hold reality to be multiple, individually interpreted or socially constructed. Focus groups and interviews are most frequently used to generate **qualitative research.** Quantitative data can be generated when a highly structured interview schedule is used, and/or when a large number of interviews and/or **focus groups** are carried out. **Quantitative research** is situated within a positivist philosophical framework. The ontological perspective within this framework holds reality to be singular, objective, and apart from the individual. We will see, as we read through this chapter, how the researcher designs their interviews and focus groups to help accomplish the aim of the research, by engaging the population of their study in a data gathering exercise that will provide the data required for the study. The philosophical perspective within which the project is situated is indicated in the aim of the research and confirmed in the methodology used to carry out the research.

It is likely that you have at some time participated in an interview, and perhaps you have participated in a focus group. This chapter explores these two data gathering

Qualitative research
Qualitative research to focus on words rather than numbers in the collection of data. Qualitative research as a research strategy is inductive and subjective, constructivist and/or interpretivist.

Focus groups
Data collection where a researcher uses a group of participants in a focused discussion on the issue under investigation, designed to produce new knowledge and new insights

Quantitative research
Quantitative research usually focuses on the gathering of numeric data or data in numerical form, i.e. data in the form of numbers. Quantitative research is deductive. It is said to be objective and situated within a framework of positivism.

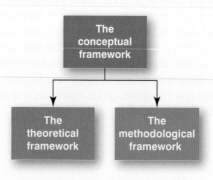

Figure 11.1　Three frameworks of the four frameworks approach to research

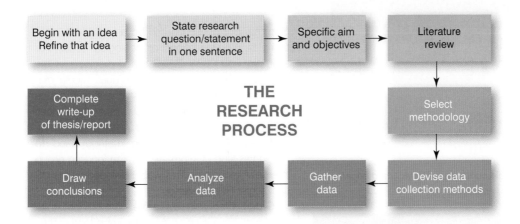

Figure 11.2 The research process

methods and explains how these data gathering methods are used in business research projects. As explained in the previous chapter, in any data gathering exercise the most critical decisions to be made are the decisions on exactly what data to gather and how to gather it.

Figure 11.2 details the place where, in the research process, the researcher uses data gathering methods. As can be seen from the figure, when the researcher has selected a methodology he/she begins to devise data collection methods. In this chapter, the data gathering methods to be examined are interviews and focus groups.

The article detailed below, taken from the Channel 4 website, explains how Channel 4 uses a multi-method approach, including **telephone interviews** and focus group research, in order to establish what their audiences think about their programmes. The programme featured in the article below is the Channel 4 programme *Big Brother*. The article gives a brief account of differences between quantitative and qualitative research; you will remember in Chapter 4 we explored the methodological pyramid and the differences between quantitative and qualitative data. The article on page 286 explains briefly why quantitative research is limited in some respects and why some research questions can best be answered through qualitative research.

In the article, Linda Hancock, research manager of market research organization *Quaestor*, explains that her organization used qualitative research methods in order to 'really get under the skin of viewers and viewing behaviour'. Three different qualitative data gathering methods are mentioned in the article, diaries, interviews and focus groups. As you read through the article note the different data needs of Channel 4 in relation to audience perceptions of their programming, and the different data gathering methods they used in order to provide data to meet those needs.

THE VALUE OF GOOD RESEARCH

'Focus groups' – from the Channel 4 website

www.channel4.com/culture/W/wtc4/audience/
focusgroups.html

Big Brother set © Dave Hogan/Getty Images

The television ratings produced by organizations such as the Broadcasters' Audience Research Board (BARB) (www.barb.co.uk) is quantitative data, and is to do mainly with numbers. Sometimes, however, broadcasters want qualitative data, information about media audiences.

The kind of issues that can benefit from qualitative analysis can be quite simple, such as what audiences like or don't like about a particular pro-

gramme. But questions can be asked about more complex, representational or ideological issues. For example, until 2001, BARB asked a sample of the television audience to keep individual 'media diaries'. They were used by researchers to produce an 'appreciation index' of how much audiences enjoyed particular programmes.

Today, the most common method used to obtain this kind of information is 'the focused group interview' technique. This was developed by the US sociologist Robert Merton.

Group interviews are more cost-efficient than individual interviews, but more importantly, they allow the researcher to observe the ways audiences make sense of the media through social interaction.

Big Brother – a case study

Channel 4 commissions market research organizations to produce qualitative data about its programmes.

Below is an example, an account by Linda Hancock, research manager of market research organization, *Quaestor*, of the research done on Big Brother Series 4.

❝ In order to go beyond merely asking, 'how many/who is watching Big Brother', we are using qualitative techniques to really get under the skin of viewers and viewing behaviour. Not only do we want to find out what they really think, but we also aim to understand what is driving their response to the show and how their response develops over the course of the series.

The research takes place every Monday and Tuesday evening, and on most weeks is in the form of four mini-group discussions.

Four sets of six people, fitting a specific set of criteria, are recruited by local qualitative recruiters to take part across two different UK locations. The criteria on which they are recruited relates to:

- their age, gender and socioeconomic profile
- whether they are in a terrestrial or multi-channel TV household
- their Big Brother viewing frequency

- their level of interaction with the show (voting, use of internet, SMS, interactive TV, etc.).

Typically, the four groups might be as follows:

- Group 1: 17–18 year old females, C4 and E4 viewers
- Group 2: 19–24, mixed gender, C4 only viewers
- Group 3: 25–34, mixed gender, C4 and E4 viewers
- Group 4: 35–44, mixed gender, C4 only viewers.

Every week, a different set of respondents is recruited in different locations.

An experienced moderator leads a 1 hour discussion within each group. At times the groups may be held in a viewing studio with a two-way mirror, to allow Channel 4 personnel involved in Big Brother to observe.

The discussion is semi-structured in that a discussion plan is used to guide the conversation. This plan covers key topics: the housemates, the weekly task, the Saturday live task, the eviction show, the schedule, viewing behaviour, etc. The discussion plan is adapted every week in conjunction with Channel 4, to ensure that relevant question areas are explored. To facilitate the discussion we use picture boards of the characters as well as cards with a range of adjectives written on them describing the series.

The respondents watch the programme just before going to the group interview. We recruit people with a mix of behaviour and attitudes ranging from, 'I wouldn't miss a show' to, 'I try to catch it if I'm in'.

Of the 11 weeks of research, three will comprise in-depth telephone interviews with individual respondents who have already participated in a group discussion. This allows us to find out how individual responses change through the series. In these weeks 12 interviews are conducted, each lasting half-an-hour.

A report detailing the key findings of the week is submitted to Channel 4 by Thursday lunchtime. After thorough and detailed analysis, the research will culminate in a 1–2 hour presentation of the cumulative findings from the 11 weeks of research. The presentation will include a series of recommendations to ensure that subsequent series can benefit from what we learned from this one.

INTERVIEWS AND FOCUS GROUPS

Interviews and focus groups, as stated above, are data gathering methods. They are two ways through which data can be gathered for a research project.

Interviews are generally used when the researcher can identify key respondents in relation to the phenomenon under investigation and can engage these respondents in an interview process.

Focus groups are generally used when the researcher wants the participants to focus on a particular phenomenon and, through that focus, generate some ideas about, and/or insights into, that phenomenon. Focus groups are efficient ways of gathering data simultaneously from a range of participants. Focus groups are also used when a **group dynamic** would be useful to the researsch agenda.

Group dynamic
Energy that develops naturally within a group. It can be positive or negative and is often affected by strong personalities.

Interviews

There are essentially five different types of interviews in research: the one-to-one interview, the group interview, the telephone interview, the online interview (see Chapter 8, 'Understanding Research Methods, Populations and Sampling'), and the photo-elicitation interview.

- The one-to-one interview: this is usually an in-depth interview, where the researcher (one researcher interviewing one interviewee) explores the phenomenon under investigation in-depth with the interviewee (the person being interviewed).

- The group interview: this is where the researcher interviews a group of people at the same time. This is not, as will be seen, the same as a focus group.

- The telephone interview: this is where the researcher (the interviewer) interviews the interviewee (the participant or respondent) over the telephone.

- The online interview: this is where the researcher conducts the interview using the internet or an intranet.

- In a photo-elicitation interview, the interviewer engages the interviewee in a discussion and analysis of a photograph or a series of photographs.

Photo-elicitation interview
The researcher takes the interviewee through an exploration and analysis of a series of photographs.

In a **photo-elicitation interview**, the researcher engages participants in their research in an exploration and analysis of a photograph or a series of photographs. As Harper states (1998, 35), in the photo-elicitation interview, interview/discussion is stimulated and guided by images. These images can be photographs taken by the researcher and/or the participants in the research or they can be other photographs or images. Becker (1974), said that photo-elicitation is a method whereby the researcher uses photographs to engage the informants in verbal commentary. Collier and Collier (1986) and Harper (1996, 1998), refer to this method as the photo-interview.

Photo-elicitation research has been used to explore many aspects of the world of work, for example to document the experiences of migrant workers, dairy farmers, industrial workers and child labourers. Venkatraman and Nelson (2008), used photo-elicitation in their research when they asked young urban Chinese consumers to photograph their experiences in Starbucks in Beijing. The researchers used the photographs in in-depth interviews to explore those experiences with the young people. You might think of the possibility of using photo-elicitation interviews in your own research. (Image-based research is the research methodology in focus in Chapter 4 of this textbook.)

One-to-one interview
The researcher interviews each participant, one at a time and in great depth and detail.

One-to-one interviews In the **one-to-one interview**, or face-to-face (F2F) interview, the researcher has the opportunity to develop a rapport, or comfortable communicative relationship, with the interviewee. This rapport helps the researcher engage the interviewee in the interview process, which calls for confidential, formal, open and honest communication between the interviewer and interviewees.

During a one-to-one interview, the researcher has the opportunity to observe the interviewee, including the manner in which they engage with, and respond to, the research questions. The researcher also has the opportunity to probe the responses. This probing is not usually done in any challenging way. The researcher uses gentleness, skill, discretion and respect to question the responses of the interviewee, asking for clarification where necessary or perhaps requesting a more detailed or more elaborate response to a question.

In the one-to-one interview the interviewee becomes the sole focus of the interviewer. This means that during the interview, the interviewee has the space and the time to express their individual perspective on, or experience of, the phenomenon under investigation. The one-to-one interview gives the researcher the opportunity to gather in detail the testimony of the one research respondent who is participating in the interview. This may be useful, or even essential, in terms of the data requirements of the research project. Or it may not. The researcher must decide how best to gather the data required for the research. The main disadvantage of one-to-one interviews is that they are time-consuming. There is also potential in a one-to-one interview situation for the interviewer to influence or lead the responses of the interviewee in some way. Such action is a source of **bias** in interview data (the issue of bias in research is explored in detail later in this chapter).

Bias
Anything that contaminates or compromises the research or data.

Group interviews In a group interview the researcher conducts the interview with a group of respondents/participants. Here, the same opportunities do not exist for the building of rapport with each respondent, or for each respondent to express at length and in-depth their own perspective on, or experience of, the phenomenon under investigation. The group interview has its own unique advantages. The group dynamic may produce data that would not be produced through a one-to-one interview process. The group setting may also serve to protect the interviewer and the interviewees. There is safety in numbers. The group setting may provide a sense of security for participants, and the group dynamic may encourage the participants to engage more fully and more freely in the process of creating data. However, the researcher must exercise caution. The group dynamic can also have completely the opposite effect. Participants can feel constrained or even intimidated by the group setting, and may as a consequence be less inclined to engage with the process. Once again, the researcher must make a decision about the optimum method to use to gather the data required within the constraints of the resources available.

Telephone interviews In a telephone interview, the researcher conducts the interview over the telephone. Usually this is done on a one-to-one basis, with one interviewee/participant/respondent. The telephone interview does not afford the researcher any opportunity to observe the interviewee. However, the telephone does offer convenience, for both the interviewer and the interviewee. The researcher does not have to travel to where the interviewee is in order to conduct the interview and the interviewee can take part in the interview in any location that has a telephone or access to a signal for a mobile phone. The use of the telephone also allows for some degree of privacy and anonymity, because the researcher cannot see the interviewee. Sometimes there is a requirement in the research for privacy and/or anonymity and sometimes there is simply a distinct benefit for the research in the researcher conducting the interviews by telephone; for example if the population of the research is scattered over a large geographic area, or if there is some sensitivity in the research question. It is important to remember that many people do not have telephones, and also that many people who do have telephones have unlisted telephone numbers. This can, in some research projects, have substantial implications for population sampling.

Online interviews
Interviews conducted online. Can be synchronous or asynchronous.

Online interviews **Online interviews** can be synchronous or asynchronous. Synchronous interviews are interviews undertaken in real-time; for example interviews carried out in chat rooms, when the interviewer asks a question and the interviewee responds immediately. Asynchronous interviews are interviews that are conducted out of real-time, for example using email or online discussion forums, bulletin boards, message boards, and so on. An email interview involves the interviewer in sending the interviewee a question or a short series of questions to which the interviewee responds; a long list of questions sent via email is a questionnaire (questionnaires and scales are dealt with in detail in Chapter 12). Asynchronous interviews can be carried out over extended periods of time. Using web-conferencing software, both synchronous and asynchronous one-to-one and **group interviews** can be carried out. The *Exploring Online Research Methods* web page of the University of Leicester is a useful resource (**www.geog.le.ac.uk/ORM/site/ home.htm**).

Group interviews
A researcher interviews the participants in a group.

How to conduct interviews

The researcher must decide on what interview technique to use and then plan the interviews. It is a useful exercise to do this step-by-step and the research diary should be used for this work, so that a secure record is kept of the process. This planning process will help you prepare properly for the interviews and it will help ensure that you spot any potential issues or problems in the interview process. The notes from your research diary will be of help when you write up this process in the research methodology chapter of your thesis, or in the research methodology section of the report of your research.

Interviews are conducted differently in quantitative and qualitative research. There are substantial epistemological and ontological reasons for this. As you know from your reading of Chapter 4, 'Understanding Research Philosophy', epistemology relates to the nature of knowledge, to what is known, and to how we know what we know, while ontology relates to the nature of being and reality. As explained in Chapter 4, the philosophical framework of positivism holds that there is one objective reality; constructivism holds that reality is subjective, individuals construct their own (multiple) realities, and interpretivism (which is related to constructivism) holds that social reality is a subjective construction based on interpretation and interaction.

In quantitative research, the researcher decides what needs to be known, and designs a very precise data gathering instrument to gather data in order to create knowledge. In designing such a precise instrument, the researcher controls and even shapes the information that is gathered, and consequently the knowledge generated by the research project. Quantitative research is said to be objective, and situated within a framework of positivism.

In qualitative research, the researcher loosely designs the research instrument. This is in order to allow the research participants to control and shape the information that is gathered, and consequently the knowledge generated by the research project. Qualitative research is said to be subjective and situated within a framework of constructivism and/or interpretivism.

In quantitative research, interviews are conducted in a structured systematic manner. The researcher designs a structured interview schedule, which is like a questionnaire, and follows it rigidly, asking each interviewee the same questions in the same order. The interview schedule is the list of questions to be asked or issues to be explored in the interview(s). If the interview schedule is long, questions are grouped into sections so that the issues raised can be dealt with thoroughly, efficiently and systematically. The interview schedule begins with background questions, then more general questions, before finally moving to specific questions on the phenomenon under investigation. Standardized probes are written into the interview schedule. This is to ensure that if probing is used, the same probing is used with each interviewee. When probing an interviewee, interviewers say things like 'could you tell me a little more about that', or 'could you say a little more about that', or the interviewer might simply make an encouraging noise, such as 'hmmmm'. The interviewer does not want to bias the interview by leading the interviewee in their responses. Such bias is known as interviewer bias or researcher bias (see separate section on bias below).

In quantitative research the interview schedule guides the interview, so that every interviewee is asked the same questions. This is necessary in ensuring that the data are gathered in a rigorous systematic manner. Structured interview schedules are comprised mostly **closed questions**. These are questions which provide respondents with a restricted set of options in terms of possible answers, for example yes/no, or sometimes/often/regularly. Closed questions elicit short responses and are often used to gather factual data. The possible responses to closed questions can be pre-coded to ensure that the data gathered can be easily and quickly analyzed.

Open questions are questions which do not anticipate particular responses; they are questions to which the respondents may respond in any, unique and individual, way. Open questions are used to explore respondents' understandings, feelings and beliefs. They often require thought and reflection on the part of respondents and they usually generate long responses.

In qualitative research, the interviews are more loosely structured. The interview schedule is either unstructured or semi-structured and the interview is conducted in a flexible manner. The focus of the interview in qualitative research is on exploring the interviewees' perspectives and the emphasis is on allowing or facilitating the interviewee to open up and express their ideas and thoughts on the phenomenon being explored. These interviews are more like conversations, where the interviewee is allowed to take the discussion in any direction they wish in order to explain or illustrate their perspective. The interviewer can probe responses, ask interviewees to elaborate or to illustrate an answer with an example. This loose structure and flexible approach to interviews in qualitative research allows for the production of rich and complex data.

Table 11.1 takes you step-by-step through the process of planning and conducting interviews for your research project.

Closed questions
Questions that elicit short responses, e.g. a yes/no. Often used to establish factual information.

Open questions
Used to explore understandings, feelings and beliefs. Usually require thought and reflection generate longer responses.

Table 11.1	How to conduct interviews
Decide on interview method	The first thing the researcher must do is decide on the interview method: one-to-one, group, telephone or online interview.
Devise interview schedule	The researcher must devise the interview schedule. The interview schedule, as explained above, is highly structured in interviews in quantitative research. It is unstructured or semi-structured in interviews in qualitative research.
Select interviewees using appropriate sampling method (see Chapter 8)	The researcher must decide on whom to interview. The researcher selects a sampling method for the interviewees based on the population of the study and the needs of the research. For example, if the population of the study is a large population and the researcher wants a sample representative of the population, the researcher may engage in simple random sampling in order to select the sample of interviewees. Sometimes the researcher knows precisely who in the population he/she needs to interview. In such a case, the researcher uses a judgemental or purposive sampling technique to select key informants on a topic to interview. It is

(Continued)

Table 11.1 How to conduct interviews (continued)	
	important to select the appropriate sampling technique for your research. Sampling methods are explored in detail in Chapter 8, 'Understanding Research Methods, Populations and Sampling'.
Contact interviewees and invite them to participate	When you have compiled a list of potential interviewees, and their contact details, you should contact them in order to invite them to participate in the interview. Remember that they are free to refuse to participate.
Provide interviewees with formal information on the research	Provide potential participants with information on your research. The decision they make with regard to whether or not to participate in your research is likely to be made based on this information. As this is the case, it is important to develop an information sheet on your research. The information sheet should clearly identify you and your organization and/or college or university. If you are undertaking the research in order to qualify for a diploma or degree, this should be stated on the information sheet. If the research is funded, this should be stated and the source(s) of the funding should be acknowledged. The information sheet should succinctly explain your research, the background to it, the context for it, and it should briefly explain why you are conducting the research and what you hope to learn/gain from it. It is a good idea to explain in the information sheet the benefits of participation in the interviews to the participants. The benefits may be related to them making a contribution to knowledge through their participation. You can also offer to provide feedback to them on the findings of the research. This may be beneficial for them in terms of their business and/or their career. With a little reflection, you may come up with other benefits to your participants that may accrue to them from participation in your research. It should be noted on the information sheet that their participation in the research is voluntary. Participants should be guaranteed anonymity as far as is legally and practically possible. They should be guaranteed confidentiality, and they should be guaranteed that they will not in any way be harmed or disadvantaged through participation. The issue of informed consent is considered in detail in Chapter 3, 'Understanding Research Ethics'. The chapter contains a template for an informed consent form.
Set up interviews	The work of setting up the interviews may, depending on the interview method, involve deciding on a mutually convenient location and time. If so, the location is critical. It must be suitable. It must be comfortable, quiet, reasonably private and if possible free from interruption. A noisy background will have a negative impact on any audio-recording of the interview. It may even render parts of, or even the entire, interview inaudible. If you are audio-recording the interviews you should ensure that the system you are using is dependable. You should test it and you should ensure that you have two power supplies, usually mains electricity and batteries, in case one runs out or suddenly becomes unavailable. It is a good idea to provide a copy of the interview schedule to participants before the interviews. This gives participants the opportunity to prepare in advance for the interviews. It also reassures participants that they are not going to be surprised by the interview questions/issues or find themselves unprepared for the interview questions/issues. Providing participants with the interview schedule before the interview signals frankness, openness and honesty and this can help the researcher in the work of establishing rapport with interviewees.
Conduct one-to-one interviews / face-to-face (F2F) interviews	Remember that you are being judged as a researcher as soon as you enter the location for the interview. It is important that you behave accordingly. Dress appropriately and present yourself in a professional manner. Be prepared for things to go wrong, allow that things may not go according to plan. When you are

	Table 11.1 How to conduct interviews (continued)
	prepared for this, you will react appropriately. Allow the interviewee the time they need to make whatever changes they need to make. The important thing for you is that you complete the interview and get the data required. Be patient. As soon as the interview does begin it is a good idea to switch the recorder on, if the interview is being audio-recorded. Test the recorder to make sure that it is recording. Then start the interview process. The interviewee usually quickly forgets that the interview is being recorded. Both the interviewer and the interviewee should have copies of the interview schedule. You should allow the interviewee the time he/she needs to answer the question. Remember that the responses the interviewees make to the questions and/or issues raised become the data gathered for the research project. Ensure that you use the opportunity of the interviews to gather as much data as you can. The data you gather should be good and useful data, pertinent to the research project.
Conduct telephone interviews	When conducting telephone interviews ensure that the interviewee has the time to engage properly with the interview. Ensure as much as you can that the interviewee has the privacy necessary to engage properly with the interview. As the interviewee must manage these issues themselves, allow them the time they need to manage these things. Be prepared for things not to go according to plan. Be prepared to be patient. Be prepared to ring back at another time or on another day if necessary. When the interview does commence, work systematically down through the interview schedule with the interviewee. Allow them the time they need to express themselves. If the interview is interrupted, wait patiently for the interview to resume.
Conduct group interviews	Ensure that the venue is suitable. Remember that the group dynamic is the thing that makes the group interview unique. Use the group dynamic to help you generate the data you need. You do this by encouraging the development of group interaction. You can ask a direct question. You can give the members of the group a minute or two of silence to think about their answers, you can then encourage them to confer in groups of two or three before encouraging them to speak out. It is often the case that the issue in facilitating groups is that of discouraging one or two individuals from speaking too much and dominating the group, rather than any difficulty with generating an energy or a dynamic within a group. Sometimes a group will police itself in this regard, and the dominant voices will be checked by members of the group. Sometimes the facilitator has to check the dominant voices. This must be done skilfully and diplomatically. You don't want to offend or alienate any member of the group. Even when you are checking a dominant member, you must make it clear that their contribution is very much valued. As a last resort you can use a system of allocating imaginary cards to each member of the group. Each member is given a number of imaginary cards, for example five cards. Every time they speak they use up a card. When all the cards are used up, they have to stop participating in the discussion. This method is not ideal, but as a last resort it is effective.
Conduct online interviews	When conducting interviews online, you must first establish that your population and sample are online or can get online, and that they have the information and communications technology (ICT) skills necessary to engage in an online interview. You must also establish that your population and/or sample is willing to engage in an interview online with you. In asynchronous interviews, you post a question one at a time, or a short series of questions, to your interviewees, and you allow them to respond in their own time. You can repeat this exercise until the interview is

(Continued)

Table 11.1 How to conduct interviews (continued)	
	completed. Using synchronous interviewing, the interview is in real-time, you ask the questions and the interviewee(s) respond immediately. Online communication is different to F2F communication. It tends to be faster and more informal. Written online communication tends to have a lot of abbreviations, like texting, and lots of spelling and grammatical errors. An advantage in written online communication is the immediate provision of a transcript of the interview, a transcript that can easily be converted into a word document. Keeping interviewees engaged in online interviews can be difficult. Participants can be distracted and the interviewer is not there with them and so cannot anticipate distraction or witness distraction and so cannot take action to keep the participant engaged. The interviewer should be prepared for this and have a plan to deal with it. The researcher has to motivate the interviewee to stay engaged. They may be able to do this by persuading the interviewee of the importance of the research, it may be possible to coax the interviewee to stay engaged, or the interviewee might be provided with some incentive to stay engaged. It is important to remember that exercising, or attempting to exercise, too much control over participants or potential participants raises ethical issues.
What to do if things go wrong	If the interview breaks down for any reason, try to establish why this has happened. It may be because there has been some loss of trust on the part of the interviewee. This can happen. It can happen accidentally and it can happen without the interviewer knowing or understanding why it happened. Do not insist on completing the interview. If the interviewee wants the interview to stop, allow that to happen. Try, if you can, to establish why this has happened. Offer to make adjustments. Offer to provide further information on the research. Offer apologies for any offence or upset that you may have unknowingly caused. Be ready if necessary to accept that the interview has broken down irretrievably. If you feel it is necessary, explain to the interviewee that you will write to them apologizing for any upset or offence you might have unwittingly caused, and outlining an account of what happened. Such a letter serves as a formal record of your perspective on what happened. Explain what happened to your thesis supervisor and ask them for their advice. Do not worry unduly. Researchers are very pragmatic people. If one approach to a research issue doesn't work, another approach will. If you do happen to lose one interviewee, replace this interviewee with another, assuming that you yourself, through your manner or behaviour, are not the cause of the breakdown in the interview. If you do lose a participant in your research, learn what you can from the experience. One of the most important lessons to learn is following such a set-back, how to move your research forward.
Conclude interview	When concluding interviewees it is important to ask the interviewee if they have anything more that they would like to say, or if there is anything that they would like to add. Often in these final moments of an interview, interviewees will sum-up their thinking on the phenomenon being investigated in a clear, succinct and useful manner. Sometimes interviewees will at this point remember and articulate something critical. It is important to note in your research diary any promise you make to the interviewee, for example in terms of feedback on the findings of the research. It is important to thank the interviewee for their participation. Be polite. Express your gratitude for the help and support you have been given with your research. Be open and communicative but careful. Do not identify or discuss other participants in the research. Do not engage in speculation with respondents about the possible findings, conclusions or implications of the research. Ensure that you have packed up all your equipment safely before you leave the venue. In particular, ensure that the data are secured.

Table 11.1　How to conduct interviews (continued)	
Manage data	The proper management of data is an ethical issue in every research project. The security of data is a fundamental aspect of the proper management of data. Data can be lost, left behind, misplaced or even stolen. Ensure that you have a mindful, careful plan in place for the secure transport and storage of data. The safety and security of your data is one of your main priorities.

YOUR RESEARCH
A common research problem

Sometimes beginner researchers go to extraordinary lengths in planning and organizing their field work, their interviews or focus groups or observations. Then when they are at home or back at their desks examining the data gathered in the field work, they find that the data are not adequate. The data do not address the phenomenon under investigation, or they do not address it in the detail required for the research, or it does not address every aspect of the phenomenon as the researcher had hoped.

This is very common, and it is a serious problem. The way to counter this problem is to ensure that you design the most appropriate data collection method(s) for your research project. You must also ensure that when you are in the field and actually carrying out your data collection, the data you are collecting really do address the phenomenon you are investigating, the phenomenon detailed in your research statement/question and in the aim and objectives of your research. The data gathered must address the phenomenon under investigation, and they must do this thoroughly. When you are planning and designing your field work you must keep the research statement/question close to hand and you should check constantly that your plan and design will allow you to accomplish and complete this research.

It is worth remembering that beginner researchers often panic unnecessarily over the data that they have gathered in the field work. If the field work has been properly prepared and carried out, it is likely that the process will produce a great deal of good, relevant data. It is always a good idea to ask for support and guidance from your supervisor and/or lecturer in research methods when undertaking an exercise as critical as the design and conduct of the field work for your research project.

Bias in research

As explained above, bias in research is anything that contaminates or compromises the research. Bias can be introduced to a research project at any stage, at the design stage, during sampling, data gathering, or data analysis, or at the stage of developing findings and coming to conclusions about the research. Bias can refer to a particular perspective that the research takes which highlights some aspects or findings of the research while ignoring or even hiding others. Bias can also refer to some systematic error that has somehow been introduced into the research.

Researcher bias Researchers can themselves be the cause of bias. For example, researchers can be biased in favour of a particular result or finding in their research. They can have a particular view and want that view confirmed by the study, rather than keeping an open mind as to what the study might confirm. They can influence the findings of the research through the design of the study. Through the use of what are known as leading questions, the researcher can influence participants in the study, through the wording of the questions, the emphasis they place on the different words and concepts in the questions, and through encouraging and/or affirming particular responses. Sometimes in qualitative research, the researcher is said to be the research instrument. The data gathered for the research project is filtered through their perceptions of the phenomenon under investigation, through their engagement with, and experience of the phenomenon under investigation. In such research, there are not more possibilities for bias than there are in other kinds of research, but there are different opportunities for bias. All researchers are in control of their own research. It is their responsibility as competent and ethical researchers to guard their research against bias.

Sampling bias Sampling bias occurs when the sampling procedure used in the research is flawed or compromised in some way. Researchers can introduce sampling bias into their study if the population or sample used in their study is biased in favour of a particular population or sample population. Population samples that under-represent some members of the population will bias research. Bias can be introduced through non-responses, when the non-respondents in the study differed in some significant way to respondents. When respondents are self-selecting, voluntary response bias can occur if the respondents have a particular agenda in the research. The population and/or the sample selected for the study should be appropriate for that study, and appropriate sampling methods should be used when selecting samples from study populations. Sampling methods are dealt with in detail in Chapter 8, 'Understanding Research Methods, Populations and Samples'. The online *Teach yourself statistics* website *Stat Trek* provides a simple tutorial on bias in survey sampling (**http://stattrek.com/AP-Statistics-2?Survey-Sampling_Bias.aspx?Tutorial=AP**).

Respondent bias Respondents can bias research in a number of ways. They can respond in a patterned way to each question, perhaps answering 'yes' to every question, or 'no' to every question. This is known as a response set. Acquiescence bias happens when a respondent agrees with everything the researcher says. Social desirability bias occurs when a respondent gives the socially desirable or the politically correct response, rather than an honest response. Prestige bias occurs when the respondent is influenced in responding through their perception of the prestige of a group or individual, for example the use of words like 'doctor' or 'president' or 'excellent' might introduce prestige bias.

Researchers try to eliminate bias from their research. If they find that despite their best efforts they have not managed to eliminate bias from their research, they acknowledge that their study is biased, or that it may be to some degree biased. Researchers try to identify possible sources of bias in their research, although it is not always possible to do this. When researchers do identify a possible source of bias in their research, they acknowledge it.

Focus groups

A focus group is used in research as a data collection method when there is some advantage, in terms of data gathering or data collection, in bringing a group of people together and facilitating this group in a focused discussion of the phenomenon under investigation in the research project. Clearly, the people invited to participate in the focus group must be expert in some way on the phenomenon under investigation.

A focus group is similar in some respects to a group interview, but it is very different in other respects. The key difference is that in a focus group, the researcher facilitates the group in focusing on the phenomenon under investigation in the hope of developing from that focus new information and new insights into that phenomenon. In a group interview, the interviewer interviews the group about the phenomenon under investigation.

In order to conduct focus group research, the researcher must have the capacity to properly facilitate the discussion, to ensure that the discussion stays focused, and to ensure that the discussion is fruitful in terms of the data required for the research. In any group discussion, focus can easily be lost. The researcher must have the confidence, ability and diplomatic skills necessary to facilitate the discussion, and to ensure that the group maintains the necessary focus in order to gather useful and pertinent data.

THE VALUE OF GOOD RESEARCH

Domino's Pizza and focus group research

In the Domino's Pizza 'Pizza Turnaround' advertising campaign, the company acknowledged that they had problems with their product. The company engaged in research, including focus group research, with its customers. The research, established that the company's customers wanted changes in the company's product. The company demonstrated their commitment to their customers by changing and improving their product. When the company had changed and improved the product they introduced a new advertising campaign to launch the improved product. The company called the new advertising campaign 'Pizza Turnaround'. The new TV commercials in the 'Pizza Turnaround' advertising campaign featured some footage from the focus groups. The footage from the focus groups was featured also in a documentary the company made about the process of changing the product. The documentary was called *The Pizza Turnaround Documentary*. You can view *The Pizza Turnaround Documentary* on the Domino's Pizza website at **www.pizzaturnaround.com**.

Focus groups can be F2F or they can be online. Online focus groups (OFG) can be synchronous, in real-time, or asynchronous, out of real-time. In synchronous OFG the focus group happens in real-time using chat rooms or focus group software. Using conferencing software, the participants in the focus group can see each other; using other software the typed contributions of participants are visible to all participants.

In asynchronous OFG the focus group happens out of real-time, using listservs, mailing lists or discussion groups. The focus group issues and/or questions are posted for participants, and participants engage with the issues and questions and respond to the focus group facilitator/moderator in their own time.

Table 11.2 sets out the key advantages and disadvantages of online interviews and focus groups.

Table 11.2   Advantages and disadvantages of online interviews and focus groups

Advantages	Disadvantages
No access issues if the population is online or can go online	Potential participants must have access to the technologies and capability to use them
Participants located anywhere in the world, with access to the technologies, can participate	Recruitment can be difficult
Very large numbers can participate	Authentic participant identification can be an issue
No time limits	Different levels of skill and ease with the technologies can disadvantage some participants
Can be very inexpensive	It can be difficult to establish and/or maintain rapport with participants
Without video link participants cannot be seen and consequently may engage more openly	Without video link participants cannot be observed so data on non-verbal cues/facial cues/ body language cannot be gathered
Can provide a lot of data very quickly	Quality of data may not be adequate to research requirements
Very convenient for participants	Participants may be easily distracted
Can be structured to guarantee participants anonymity and privacy	Level and quality of participant engagement can be problematic
Participants less likely to be intimidated/controlled/ controlling	Participants can easily/suddenly disengage from the research
Participants in asynchronous interviews and focus groups have more time to respond	Lack of depth in data compared to data gathered from in-depth F2F interviews and F2F focus groups
No recording necessary, so no recording issues or errors	Asynchronous interviews and focus groups can take a long time to complete
Accurate transcript provided, transcripts can readily be used in computerized data analysis	The facilitator/moderator may have to work very hard at facilitating and maintaining interaction
Safe and secure environment for researcher and participants	The technology can break down/the connection can be lost

Online focus groups have particular advantages and are useful in some research projects. For other research projects the traditional F2F focus group is the most suitable method. This was the finding of Reid and Reid (2005), who, using experimental design as their methodology, carried out a comparison of focus groups conducted using CMC and conventional F2F focus groups. According to Reid and Reid, the results of their experiment suggest that CMC is a viable alternative to F2F focus groups for certain purposes. Experimental design is the methodology in focus in Chapter 14 of this textbook.

Traditional F2F focus groups take place around a table, ideally a boardroom table or a table like a boardroom table. Figure 11.3 outlines the processes involved in undertaking a F2F focus group.

Figure 11.3   Conducting a F2F focus group

Decide on participants
The population of the study should be clearly outlined. If necessary, a sample of participants should be drawn from this population. An appropriate sampling method should be used. Ideally each **focus group** should comprise eight to 12 participants. Participants must be capable of making a useful contribution to discussion of the phenomenon under investigation. Participants should be contacted, invited to participate in the **focus group**. They should be provided with an information sheet and an informed consent form (see Chapter 3). The information sheet should succinctly explain your research, the background to it, the context for it, and it should briefly explain why you are conducting the research and what you hope to learn/gain from it. It is a good idea to explain in the information sheet the benefits of participation in the **interviews** to the participants. In order to participate in the research, participants must read and sign the informed consent form, indicating that they freely participate in the research, that they understand the research and that they consent to the data generated by their participation in the research being used by the researcher(s) for the purposes of the research.

Decide on venue
The venue should be convenient for participants. The **focus group** should take place in a comfortable room with a boardroom style table. This style of table facilitates equal participation. The room should be properly heated and ventilated. The room should be neither too big nor too small. In a very big room, electronic recording can become compromised

Prepare focus group schedule
The **focus group** schedule should be semi-structured. This structure will allow the researcher to guide the focussed discussion of the group while allowing for group discussion. There is an example of a **focus group** schedule below in the box feature labelled 'Research Project'.

Prepare recording mechanism
Focus groups should be recorded electronically, usually audio-recorded. If the **group dynamic** is of interest or if the physical, facial and/or bodily responses of participants are relevant the **focus group** might be video-recorded. There is too much discussion in a **focus group** for the discussion to be recorded adequately by hand. The transcript of the recorded **focus group** is the data gathered from the **focus group**. These data can be supplemented by any notes the researcher and/or research assistants make during the **focus group**.

Convene the focus group
The participants in the **focus group** should sit together around the table, in a boardroom table format. Drinking water and fresh drinking glasses or paper cups should be provided for participants. There should be no hierarchy. The participants should participate in the **focus group** as equals. The recording device should be switched on and checked to ensure that it is recording properly. When everyone is seated comfortably, the researcher introduces themselves and the research, and any research assistants. The researcher explains the process, what will happen and what he/she hopes to accomplish in terms of data collection through the process. The researcher might ask the members of the group to introduce themselves and to say a little about themselves. The researcher passes around copies of the **focus group** schedule. There should be one for every participant. Then the researcher takes the participants through the **focus group** schedule, familiarizing the participants with the schedule and answering any questions and queries they might have. The facilitator or moderator of the **focus group** (usually the researcher) starts the **focus group** discussion.

Figure 11.3 (Continued)

Starting the focus group

Ideally, when the **focus group** begins, everyone in the room should be sitting at the table. There should be room at the table for the researcher and any researcher assistant(s). When the researcher(s) sit with the group as part of the group, this has the effect of neutralizing their presence in the room. They become participants in the **focus group** rather than observers of the **focus group**. If participants in research feel that they are being observed, they may feel uncomfortable, and, more problematically, they may begin to perform and in doing so, they may introduce bias into the research. When research participants 'perform' for research, they try to give the researcher what it is that they think the researcher really wants, rather than clearly and simply, and openly and honestly engaging with the research questions and issues. This kind of **bias**, as explained above, is known as social desirability **bias**.

The focus group discussion

The **focus group** discussion should be very tightly focused on the phenomenon under investigation. The **focus group** facilitator or moderator controls and directs the discussion, using the **focus group** schedule and working methodically down through each of the different points and/or issues in the schedule. The facilitator should ensure proper time management of the group. If the **focus group** runs over time, members of the group may leave before the **focus group** is completed. The purpose of the **focus group** discussion can vary, according to the aim of the **focus group** and the overall aim of the research project. The outcome of the discussion should be an in-depth perspective on the phenomenon under investigation with some new understanding, new knowledge and/or new insight into that phenomenon.

Managing the group dynamic

The use of the **focus group** allows the researcher, as with a group **interview**, to benefit from **group dynamics**. When a group of people get together, any group of people, a natural dynamic develops between them and this dynamic will help drive the discussion within the group. It might happen that participants in the research are a little shy, of each other or of the research process. In this case, the **group dynamic** may be a little slow to develop and the researcher must encourage the development of the **group dynamic**. The researcher may pose a simple question or present a simple or slightly provocative statement to encourage the discussion to begin and to facilitate the development of the **group dynamic**. **Group dynamics** can be very tricky. Groups can naturally develop good dynamics, and they can as easily develop poor dynamics. The researcher should be sensitive to the nature of the dynamic within the group and should manage the group accordingly.

Concluding the focus group

At the end of the **focus group** discussion, the facilitator gives participants an opportunity to voice any further comments they wish to make. Then the facilitator thanks the participants for the contribution they have made to the research and the help and support they have given to the researcher. The researcher briefly explains when the research is due to be completed. The researcher should not be drawn into speculating about the findings or conclusions of the research or the possible implications of the research. The interviewer does not comment on or identify in any way any participant in the research, whether or not they are present. The researcher ensures that the data are secure. He/she packs up all the equipment and leaves the room in the condition agreed. The safe and secure transport of the data from the venue to the researcher's desk, office or home is a key priority now for the researcher.

Interview and focus group schedules

Data gathering instruments, whether they are observation schedules, as explored in the previous chapter, interview or focus group schedules, as discussed in this chapter, or questionnaires and scales as discussed in the following chapter, are designed to provide the necessary data for the research project. As this is the case, the overall aim of the research and the objectives of the research inform the content of the data gathering instrument. In addition, the review of the literature conducted by the researcher will inform the development of the research instrument.

Using the research diary, the researcher gathers together all of the issues they would like to explore, or all of the issues they believe should be explored, in the research. A long list of these issues can be developed in the research diary. Next, the researcher groups together the issues that appear to belong together. Then the researcher begins to reduce this long list by continuing to group together issues that belong together, and by collapsing together issues that are really about the same thing, perhaps conceptualizing a new concept (a new word or new phrase) to cover these issues. This is a process of conceptualization and reduction.

Sometimes researchers convene a panel to help in this process. This panel could comprise fellow researchers, or of researchers with expertise in the area, or of senior researchers, or a mixture of such individuals. A three-person panel is sufficient. Engaging such a panel in this exercise can help in establishing the validity of the research. Through repetitions and reiterations of the process of conceptualization and reduction, described above, the key issues to be examined in the data collection phase of the research begin to emerge. The researcher, working alone or with the help of a panel, decides on the key issues to explore in the schedule, and on the different aspects of those key issues to explore; decisions are also made on the order in which the issues should be explored in the schedule. The interview, focus group, or observation schedule is designed in accordance with these decisions.

An interview schedule is the list of questions to be asked or the series of points or issues to be discussed during an interview or a series of interviews. As explained in the previous chapter, data gathering schedules, whether they are used in observation interviews or focus groups, can be unstructured, semi-structured or structured.

Semi-structured interview and focus group schedules allow participants the opportunity to express themselves with regard to the phenomenon under investigation. The semi-structured design of the schedules provides an open approach to the research encounter. Using such an approach, the researcher does not, through the design of the research instrument, impose their own perspective on, or understanding of, the phenomenon on the participants in the research. The meaning of the phenomenon for participants, and their personal experience and understanding of it, are allowed to emerge in the interviews or focus groups through the semi-structured or unstructured design of the data gathering exercise.

The following box contains an example of a semi-structured focus group schedule, used in the study of brand loyalty among third-level students. The focus group schedule is simple, but the simplicity of the structure belies the amount of work and preparation that goes into the construction of such a schedule.

A structured interview schedule is like a questionnaire. It is comprised mostly of closed questions. As explained above, closed questions are often used to establish facts, for example a respondent's age, or gender, or to establish whether or not a respondent uses a particular product. Often closed questions can be answered with yes or no answers.

RESEARCH PROJECT

Brand loyalty among third-level students

Focus group schedule

Date_____ Venue_____ No. of participants _____

1   Introductions

2   The aim of the focus group

3   The focus group schedule – the conduct of the focus group, one speaker at a time, balanced discussion, the views of all participants, recording mechanisms

Issues for discussion

4   Brand loyalty

5   Loyalty to particular brands

6   Brands that tend to prompt loyalty among third-level students

7   Key elements and aspects of those brands

8   Ways of prompting and/or promoting brand loyalty among third-level students

9   Summing up

10 Thanks and feedback

There are often one or two, or a few, open questions in a questionnaire or in a structured interview schedule. Open questions are designed to allow the respondent to answer in any way they choose and tend to generate long answers. Respondents usually have to think and reflect on the issue raised in an open question in order to answer the question. Asking a respondent why they do something, for example, 'Why do you use that product?' will generate a long, and probably unique, response from every respondent. The question, 'Why do you use that product?' is an open question. The respondent may respond in any way to that question, and their response cannot be anticipated by the researcher. We will explore closed and open questions in more detail in the following chapter, Chapter 12 'Using Questionnaires and Scales'.

Structured interview schedules are useful where the interviewer has a limited amount of time for the interview, for example in street intercept interviews, where the interviewer intercepts passers-by on the street and engages them in interviews. Structured interview schedules are also useful where the interviewer is not audio-recording the interview, but recording the responses by hand. This often happens with telephone interviews; the researcher uses a structured interview schedule and records the responses of the interviewee by hand.

Audio-recorded F2F interviews are transcribed, typed up, and these typed transcripts become the data to be analyzed. Where the responses to the interview questions are recorded by hand, these hand written responses become the data to be analyzed. Obviously the quality of interview transcripts is of fundamental importance. It is common for researchers to give interviewees a copy of the transcript of their audio-recorded interview. When this happens, the interviewees are asked to read the transcript and verify that the transcript is an accurate account of the interview. This is known as **Interviewer verification.**

Interviewee verification is an aid to establishing the validity of the data, and consequently, the validity of the research. Having read their interview transcript, interviewees can also provide the researcher with feedback on the data gathered during the interview and can clarify points and correct errors.

Interview schedules and focus group schedules can be subjected to pilot studies. As explained in the previous chapter, a pilot study is a test of the design of the research project, or a test of the data gathering instrument(s) designed for the research. An interview schedule is piloted by engaging a small number of interviewees, perhaps three, four or five interviewees, depending on the size of the study, in interviews in order to pilot, or test, the interview schedule. The people interviewed in the pilot study are not the people who will be interviewed in the study, but they are people who are similar to the people who will be interviewed in the study itself. The pilot study demonstrates to the researcher how the interview schedule will work in a real interview. Based on the experience of the pilot, the researcher may amend the interview schedule as appropriate.

Similarly, a focus group schedule can be piloted by engaging in a pilot, or test, focus group. Three or four participants are enough in a focus group pilot. Alternatively, the researcher might engage a panel, as described above, to critique the design of the focus group schedule.

It is important to try out or test data gathering methods before using them to generate data for the research project. Many unanticipated issues and problems can emerge in piloting and when they do they can then be dealt with before data gathering commences for the research project. As explained in the previous chapter, a pilot study is an aid to establishing the rigour and the validity of the research project.

> **Interviewer verification**
> An interviewer gives each of the interviewees a transcript of their interview. Each interviewee then verifies that the transcript is an accurate record of their interview.

YOUR RESEARCH
Common research problems

It often happens that students and/or beginner researchers use the 'wrong' data collection method or an inappropriate data collection method in their research project. When this happens, it is usually because the student has some preconceived notion or idea about the data gathering method they wish to use in their research project. Often the student feels comfortable for some reason with their preferred data gathering method. It may be that the student has used the data gathering method before, or that the student has participated in a research project that required him/her to use that data gathering method. For whatever reason, the student has some degree of familiarity with that data gathering method. This familiarity leads the student to favour this data gathering method and, potentially problematically, to favour the use of this data gathering method in their research project.

There are many ways of gathering data, as we saw in Chapter 8. The data gathering method used should be the most appropriate data gathering method for the research project. The aim of the research gives an indication of the data required for the research project. The location of that data is the key to the kind of data gathering method to use. If the data can best be gathered by engaging in one-to-one interviews, then this is the method to use. If the data can best be gathered by facilitating a group of experts on the phenomenon under investigation in a focused group discussion, then a focus group or a series of focus groups is the method to use.

In order to be able to make good decisions about the data gathering method(s) to use in your research, you must have some knowledge of a variety of data gathering methods and the data that can be gathered using these methods.

Validity and Reliability in Qualitative and Quantitative Research

The issues of validity and reliability are engaged with differently in qualitative and in quantitative research (see Table 12.4 in Chapter 12). Many researchers object to the application of quantitative measures of quality to qualitative research. Indeed, Corbin (Corbin and Strauss, 2008: 301–302), suggests that even the words 'validity' and 'reliability' do not fit well with qualitative research; she believes that they carry with them too many quantitative implications. Even the word 'truth' is too dogmatic for Corbin in relation to evaluations of the quality of qualitative research; she prefers to use the word 'credibility' (Glaser and Strauss, 1967; Lincoln and Guba, 1985). Lincoln and Guba's terms for naturalistic inquiry (qualitative research) are laid out in Table 11.3 in relation to the comparable term in conventional inquiry (quantitative research). These terms are, as they are used in qualitative research, are explained and explored in more detail in Table 11.4 opposite.

Qualitative researchers are generally not concerned with measurement and often they do not support a scientific perspective that holds that the social world can be studied in a similar fashion to the ways in which the natural world is studied. They reject positivist approaches to social science and their approach to the study of the social world is either constructivist or interpretivist. They hold the philosophical

Table 11.3 Lincoln and Guba's (1985) terms for naturalistic inquiry	
Conventional inquiry	*Naturalistic inquiry*
Internal validity	Credibility
External validity	Transferability
Reliability	Dependability
Objectivity	Confirmability

Table 11.4 The issues of validity and reliability in qualitative research	
Validity	**Reliability**
The term validity in research, as defined in Chapter 2, is a question of how valid the research is, how logical, how truthful, how robust, how sound, how reasonable, how meaningful and how useful. Qualitative researchers are concerned with the **credibility**, the honesty and the truthfulness of their research. Above all they want their research to be trustworthy and authentic (see Lincoln and Guba, 1985 and Guba and Lincoln, 1994). Qualitative researchers regard qualitative data as being co-constructed, constructed by the researcher and the research participants together in the data gathering processes used in the research project.	The term reliability in research, as defined in Chapter 2, relates to **the dependability** of the research, to the degree to which the research can be repeated while obtaining consistent results. Rather than reliability in the quantitative research sense of achieving consistent results over time and with different populations (see Table 12.4, Chapter 12), qualitative researchers, as stated in Chapter 7, focus on establishing the rigour of their research. They focus on establishing the soundness, the **dependability of** their research (see Guba and Lincoln, 1994; Riege, 2003).
Qualitative researchers gather empirical data in the field and they use that data to present authentic, vivid and detailed accounts of the experiences of the people participating in their research. Qualitative researchers use a wide variety of data gathering methods. The focus is on developing a 'thick description' (Geertz, 1973), of the experiences of the social world that are the focus of the research. Guba and Lincoln (1994) argue that this thick description allows for judgements to be made in relation to whether or not the findings of the research are **transferable** to other contexts, rather than generalizable to other contexts in a quantitative research sense.	While rejecting standardized structured approaches to data gathering, qualitative researchers do try to gather data in a consistent manner. In order to help establish the **dependability** of the research, Guba and Lincoln recommend that an audit approach be adopted by the researcher (see Bowen 2009). Using such an approach, every decision made in the research project should be documented, explained and justified. Using Guba and Lincoln's approach to auditing, evaluators of the research (advisors, examiners and readers) then become auditors of the research, auditing the decisions made.
Respondent verification, (interviewee verification as outlined earlier in the chapter is an example) is a method used to help establish the validity of the research project; the researcher encourages research participants to verify the findings of the research. In qualitative research, the fundamental aim of research is to illustrate the experiences of the participants in the research of some aspect of the social world. The ontological position of qualitative researchers is that there is no objective reality in terms of experiences of the social world; rather, there are individually constructed or individually interpreted experiences of reality. The work of the qualitative researcher is to create in their research **credible**, i.e. truthful and authentic, accounts of the experiences of research participants.	An alternative approach to auditing can be developed using the research diary. The qualitative researcher can record an audit trail in their **research diary**. The audit trail is a documented trail of their experiences, insights, knowledge development, and decision-making, throughout the research project. The researcher can use this audit trail to help establish the **dependability** of the research project. A dense account of this audit trail can be included in the research methodology chapter of the thesis, or in the research methodology section of the report of the research. This account can be used to clearly document, outline, explain and justify the decisions the researcher made in relation to the research. Such an account can form part of the 'thick description' necessary in the writing up and reporting of qualitative research. It can provide for **confirmability** of the research.

perspective of experiences of the social world as being constructed or interpreted uniquely by every individual.

Qualitative researchers see data gathering as an interactive process, often as a co-constructed process, a process that the researcher co-constructs with the participants in their research. Their engagement with their field work tends to be prolonged and in-depth. They often use more multi-method approaches, and more varied approaches to field work. While they tend not to use fixed or standardized measures of any phenomenon, they do produce deeply complex and rich accounts of the phenomena they investigate.

In both quantitative and qualitative research, validity can be established through the depth and complexity of the research project; through the researchers prolonged engagement with the field and with the participants in the research; through the scholarship evident in the written account of the research; through the detailed description of the methodology and methods used in the research project; through the expert analysis of the data carried out by the researcher; through the knowledge

REAL WORLD RESEARCH

Differences in quantitative and qualitative research

Quantitative and qualitative researchers engage differently in research. Sometimes beginner researchers fail to adequately respect the differences, both in the way in which they conduct their research and in the way in which they write up their research.

Quantitative and qualitative researchers make different assumptions about the social world and they expect different results from their researches. Where a quantitative researcher is generally in search of facts, qualitative researchers explore experiences and perceptions and understandings. Very often, research projects will have elements of both kinds of research, both quantitative and qualitative research.

A problem that can arise is in the different languages used by the two different perspectives. Quantitative research generally employs a technicist, instrumental language, using words like instrument and subject. Qualitative research generally employs a softer language, using words like participant rather than subject, and data collection methods rather than data collection instruments.

A quantitative researcher will never refer to 'I' or 'me' or 'the researcher' in writing up their research. A qualitative researcher will.

A skilled researcher is able to use the appropriate language and approach to both quantitative and qualitative research. Really skilled researchers have studied and understand the different philosophical traditions underpinning both approaches.

Beginner researchers develop a capacity to nuance the language they use in writing up their research as appropriate, depending on whether the research being written about is quantitative or qualitative, or a mixture of both.

A good way to begin to develop this skill is to read reports of research published in academic journals. Find and read a report of a quantitative study and a report of a qualitative study and compare the different language used in both. Then find a report of a study which used a mixed methods approach, drawing on both quantitative and qualitative data, and consider the way in which language was used in that report. In your research diary note the differences in the style and language used in the reporting of quantitative and qualitative research.

the researcher has of the phenomenon; and through the contribution to knowledge the researcher makes through the publication of the research.

The journal article in the box feature below shows how the theory is put into practice. The project detailed is a study of customer relationship marketing in relation to a UK film festival. As you read the synopsis of the methodology used in the research project, you will see how the researchers used an in-depth interview and three focus groups in their research. Detail is given on the sampling frame used in

REAL WORLD RESEARCH

How theory influences research

'Getting the picture: Programme awareness amongst film festival customers', Unwin, E. (2007)

In this study, the researchers explore how film festival customers become aware of a festival programme compared to general release films. The purpose of the research was to understand customer decision-making processes and the role that customer relationship marketing (CRM) plays.

A case study methodology was used in the research. The case study was built on a single case, an established UK film festival 'IFF'. In carrying out the research, an in-depth interview was conducted with the marketing manager of the film festival and three focus groups were conducted with three different groups of film festival customers, infrequent customers, mid-range customers and frequent customers.

The researchers used a semi-structured interview schedule for the interview. The schedule focused on a number of questions regarding, for example, overall communications strategy, methods of customer relationship management, plans for future development and areas for improvement.

In the three focus groups held, following 'ice-breaker questions', the participants were asked about how they developed awareness for films on general release; their motivations in selecting particular films; their initial awareness of IFF; what they thought of the IFF logo; how they became aware of

films showing at IFF; if they chose films in IFF in a similar manner to those on general release and their perceptions of the 'personality' of IFF.

The article details that the sampling frame used was the IFF database, which was operational for 2 years prior to the research. The three focus groups were conducted with participants recruited to each group on the basis of their attendance at the previous year's film festival: 'infrequent' attendees (who saw 1–3 films); 'mid-range' attendees (4–6 films) and 'frequent attendees' (8+ films). The authors state that participants' frequency of attendance provided a degree of homogeneity within each group and that this 'allows for free-flowing conversations among participants' and 'also facilitates analyses that examine differences in perspectives among groups' (Morgan, 1997: 35)

We are told that convenience sampling was employed, and that this is a common strategy within focus group research. The focus group participants, we are told, were, due to resource constraints, selected primarily from local residents.

The journal article documents that the focus groups were recorded on to audiotape, and that the participants gave informed consent for this procedure understanding that their confidentiality would be respected (Stewart and Samdasani, 1990). We are told that the focus groups were semi-structured, following a focus group guideline, but allowances were made for expansion on interesting points raised by participants.

The article explains that for the purposes of data analysis, the audiotapes were transcribed and assembled with the moderator's notes.

References

Unwin, E. (2007) 'Getting the picture: Programme awareness amongst film festival customers', *International Journal of Nonprofit and Voluntary Sector Marketing* 12 (3): 231–245.

selecting participants for the focus groups and on the sampling method used. It is important to read the synopsis and to source the original article and read it through. The article provides an interesting literature review as well as a comprehensive overview of the methodology used in the research. When you read the article, look in particular for the justification the researchers provide for the methodology. As you read, critique their methodology and their justification of it.

The study is a relatively simple yet useful study in marketing. The study might help you develop ideas for your own research project. As you can see, it is possible to conduct important research, and research that will be published and widely read, using local resources. The authors of the study above conceptualized a simple research project. Through the scholarly way in which they engaged with the literature in the field of CRM and research methodology theory, they developed a research project that has made a substantial contribution to knowledge.

There are potential weaknesses in the study above. Can you identify them? What do you think of the decision the researchers made to conduct just one interview? Do you think the focus group approach to data gathering was appropriate? The researchers do not provide copies of the interview or focus group schedule used in the study. Providing copies in the appendices to the study would allow readers a closer and a more precise perspective on the study. What do you think of the sample and sampling method used? Was sampling carried out properly in the study? Within which theoretical perspective would you say the study was situated?

The box feature below focuses on the research methodology, phenomenology.

THE VALUE OF GOOD RESEARCH

Focus on phenomenology

Phenomenology, in social science research, is the study of lived experience from the first person point of view, i.e. from the view of the person living the experience. The aim of the phenomenological study is to examine and highlight the essences of the everyday lived experiences studied. Phenomenological research is situated within an interpretivist philosophical perspective. The philosophical perspective of the research project, as we know, is embedded in the methodological framework of the research project. Embedded in each statement of methodology are implicit statements or assumptions about the nature of reality (ontological assumptions) and implicit statements or assumptions about the kind of knowledge that will be generated by the research (epistemological assumptions).

Phenomenological research is in-depth research. Phenomenological researchers often work at great depth with a relatively small number of research participants. The kind of knowledge generated in phenomenological studies is knowledge about individual and unique lived experiences. The focus on individual lived experience within phenomenology renders the one-to-one in-depth interview a preferred method of gathering data within phenomenological research.

Any everyday lived experience is an appropriate topic for a phenomenological study. In business research, among other topics studied using phenomenology are project management and the emotions involved in project management, (Whitty, 2010); the work of managing groups and teams (Neale *et al.*, 2002); entrepreneurship and the nature of entrepreneurial learning (Cope, 2005); human resource development (Gibson and Hanes, 2003); and, within human resource development, career choices and career paths (Conklin, 2007). Phenomenology is widely used in research in healthcare management (Chan *et al.*, 2010), and phenomenology has been used in sports management research (Edwards and Skinner, 2009).

The philosophical and methodological issues in researching entrepreneurship through phenomeno-logical inquiry were the subject of the study carried out by Cope (2005). Cope explored 'the nature of entrepreneurial learning from a phenomenological point of view, i.e. from the level of lived experience'. Cope states in the journal article that he wanted to understand how the six participants in his study believed they had engaged with and responded to the challenges of small business ownership and the impact they believed these experiences had had on them, as business people and as individuals. Cope wanted to establish what the participants in his study had learned from their experiences as small business owners, how that learning and those experiences had impacted on them, and what they would do differently if they were confronted with similar situations in the future. He used a 'purpose-ful' sampling method (similar to a purposive sam-pling method), and a snowball sampling method. The majority of the sample, he writes, was chosen from personal networks within the Management School at Lancaster University. Each of the indivi-duals chosen to be included in the sample of six entrepreneurs was chosen 'for the unique and highly interesting story that they would bring to the research process'. Cope conducted six interviews, one with each of the entrepreneurs. The interviews were unstructured. The only structure provided was that each of the interviewees was told at the start of their interview of the focus of the research.

Cope provides a very interesting description of this study in this journal article. You should source the original article and read what the article has to say about this study in particular, and phenomen-ological research and phenomenological research in business management in general.

The resources below are also helpful.

Professor T.D.Wilson's online paper 'Alfred Schutz, phenomenology and research methodology for information behaviour', **http://informationr.net/ tdw/publ/papers/schutz02.html**

'Debating Phenomenological research methods', Linda Finlay, (2009) Open University, **www. phandpr.org/index.php/pandp/article/viewFile/40/80**

'A Phenomenological research design illustrated', T. Groenewald, (2004) *International Journal of Qualitative Methods*, **www.ualberta.ca/~backissues/ 3_1/pdf/groenewald.pdf**

References

Cope, J. (2005) 'Researching entrepreneurship through phenomenological inquiry: Philosophical and methodo-logical issues, *International Journal of Small Business Management* 23(2): 163–189.

Gibson, S.K. and Hanes, L.A. (2003) 'The contribution of phenomenology to HRD research', *Human Resource Development Review* 2(2): 181–205.

Neale, M.A., Mannix, E. and Sondak, H. (2002) *Toward Phenomenology of Groups and Group Membership*, Vol. 4, Research on Managing Groups and Teams, Connecticut: Jai Press Inc.

Whitty, S.J. (2010) 'Project management artefacts and the emotions they evoke', *International Journal of Mana-ging Projects in Business* 3(1): 22–45.

CRITIQUE THE USE OF INTERVIEWS AND FOCUS GROUPS IN OTHER RESEARCH PROJECTS

The first issue to examine when critiquing research is whether the data gathering method used, interviews or focus groups, is the most appropriate data gathering method in terms of the data requirements of the project. When this question has been answered, the critique moves on to an examination of the data collection method as it was used in the research project. At issue is the design of the data collection method(s) and the manner in which the method(s) were used.

Table 11.5   Critique an interview or focus group
How many interviews/focus groups were conducted?
How were the interviews/focus groups conducted? Was this appropriate?
Where did the interviews/focus groups take place?
Was the population appropriate? If sampling was used, how was the sample selected? Was the sampling method used appropriate?
How many interviews were completed? How many people participated in each focus group?
How long did the interviews/focus groups last?
Were they audio-recorded? If so, how were they audio-recorded?
Were they video-recorded? If so, was a reasonable rationale given for this?
Were the recordings transcribed? If so, how were they transcribed?
Was there an interview/focus group schedule?
Has the interview/focus group schedule been included in appendices in the published account of the research?
Were the issues/themes detailed for consideration and the questions asked in the interview/focus group schedule appropriate to the research? Were they likely to provide the data required?
Is there evidence of scholarship in the construct of the interview/focus group schedule?
Was the interview/focus group schedule appropriately structured?
Was anything omitted from the interview/focus group schedule? Could there have been useful additions to the schedule?
Was the presentation of the interview/focus group schedule of an appropriate professional standard?
Were the interviews/focus groups conducted in a professional manner?

YOUR RESEARCH
Common research problems

Every researcher engaged in a research project is vulnerable to charges and accusations of inappropriate and/or unethical behaviour. Beginner researchers or student researchers should ensure that their research supervisor and/or research methods lecturer reads and signs off on every aspect and element of the research process as they undertake it.

If a researcher has any grounds for concern about this, for example if you are conducting your research with particularly vulnerable people or engaging research participants on a particularly sensitive issue, it is a good idea to use a research assistant. This research assistant can be a classmate or colleague. Your research assistant simply accompanies you, the researcher, through the potentially vulner-

able encounter. They provide a chaperone service to the research, ensuring that the researcher and the research participants are not alone together while the research is being conducted. They provide witness to the correct and ethical conduct of the research.

Remember too that the audio or visual recording of the research encounter evidences the professionalism and appropriateness of any encounter in the field. As well as providing evidence in terms of data, the record can provide evidence of the professional and ethical conduct of the field work for the research.

Such caution and foresight is another aspect of the level of preparedness every researcher needs when engaging in field work with human participants.

Questions asked and issues considered in this critique would include the following (see Table 11.5).

The list of questions in Table 11.5 is useful in terms of developing a critique of any research that used interviews and focus groups. They also provide you with guidance in terms of the critique likely to be levelled at any interviews and/or focus groups you might carry out for your own research.

When you decide to use a series of interviews, a focus group or a series of focus groups in your research, it is a good idea to source sample interviews and focus groups in theses and in journal articles and examine how the interviews and focus groups were designed. Look at the interview and/or focus group schedules. Copies of these should be presented in the appendices of the research. In examining them, pay particular attention to:

- The appropriateness of the population of the study and/or the sample of that population and the sampling method used in the interviews and/or focus group(s).
- The length of the interview or focus group schedule and the level of complexity in the structure of the interview and/or focus group schedule. In general such schedules should be neither long nor complex.
- The areas and issues explored with participants in the interviews/focus group(s).
- The relevance of the areas explored in the interview/focus group schedule to the research question/statement and to the aim and objectives of the research.
- The capacity of the participants in the research to engage with and respond to the questions asked and/or the issues discussed.

Remember, the most important issue is the capacity of the data collection instrument to facilitate the production of the data required for the research. The participants in the research must be capable of participating fully and usefully in the research.

The ethical aspects of every element of every research project are of fundamental importance. When you are reading through the examples of interviews and focus groups you have located in the literature, pay particular attention to the manner in which the researchers dealt with the ethical issues they were grappling with in designing and carrying out their research. In your critique of the ethical standards they brought to their work, try to see if there is anything in those standards that you might bring to your own work. In addition, consider whether there are any ethical concerns that you can see that those researchers have not properly or thoroughly addressed.

CASE STUDY

The museum shop as a marketing tool for the Imperial War Museum

Imperial War Museum, London © Godrick/iStock

The research outlined here was an exploratory study undertaken by Kent (2010), to assess the role of the museum shop in extending the learning experience in the museum.

In his journal article, Kent explains that the research is situated in the theoretical framework of museum experiences and learning. He presents in the article a review of the literature on the role of museums, their commercial, educational and recreational orientations and the provision of visitor experiences. He explores the issues in marketing the museum, the tensions between the commercial aspect of the museum and the museum's educational remit, and the desire on the part of consumers for authentic museum experiences.

A mixed methods approach was used in the research to examine visitors' knowledge and experience of museums and their shops. Data collection for the study was undertaken at the Imperial War Museum (IWM) in London.

In the first phase of the research in-depth interviews were undertaken to examine the experience of museum shops and their contribution to learning. We are told that for the in-depth interviews, six respondents were selected for interview using a purposive sampling approach. Each of the six respondents was a regular museum visitor. A semi-structured interview schedule was used to guide respondents through the interview. In the interviews, respondents were asked questions about their visits to the museum and in particular their visits to and experiences of the museum shop.

In the second phase of the research a convenience sample of museum visitors was asked to complete a semi-structured questionnaire. A semi-structured questionnaire was devised, using different types of questions (open and closed) and a semantic scale assessment on store atmospherics. A semantic scale, or a semantic differential scale, uses opposite adjectives, such as hot/cold, good/bad, interesting/dull, and asks respondents to indicate which of the adjectives best describes the phenomenon under investigation. Questionnaires and scales are the focus of Chapter 12 of this textbook, and an example of a semantic differential scale is given in that chapter.

We are told that 150 responses were obtained during weekdays by intercepting visitors leaving the shop. The researcher noted that respondents appeared to have a positive relationship with the museum and were therefore willing to take part because they wanted to help.

Finally, the researcher states that observations were taken by the researcher about the ambience of the ground floor, in which the main hall and shop are located.

As you can see, a substantial amount of data were gathered for the research project using observations, in-depth one-to-one interviews and a questionnaire which incorporated a semantic scale.

You will notice that the researcher made notes to himself during the data gathering phase of the research. You will note also that those notes were used to supplement the data gathered. Researchers engaged in data gathering make notes to themselves in a field diary or in the research diary of the research project.

We are told in the journal article what sampling methods were used in the study. For the in-depth interviews, a purposive sampling method was used. For the questionnaires, a convenience sampling method was used.

Following your reading of Chapter 8 of this textbook, can you explain these two sampling methods? Can you outline the differences between them? Do you think that these sampling methods were the appropriate sampling methods to use? Why do you think that?

The researcher presents a useful analysis of the data gathered. Reading this analysis will help you prepare for the chapters on data analysis which are coming up.

In his discussion of the data analysis undertaken, Kent provides an interesting and a complex insight into the role of the museum shop.

He concludes that the museum shop is a significant destination for museum visitors. The museum shop is, he holds, a commercial space, a recreational space, and a space which supports informal learning.

Kent's research, as it is outlined in the journal article, provides a good model for a research project. When you read the article, read it in conjunction with the model of the research project outlined at the start of each chapter in this textbook. You will see in Kent's research how the different elements of that model come together in a real life research project.

References

Kent, T. (2010) 'The role of the museum shop in extending the visitor experience', *International Journal of Nonprofit and Voluntary Sector Marketing* 15(1): 67–77.

CHAPTER REVIEW

T he focus of this chapter is on the data collection methods interviews and focus groups. The chapter outlines the processes involved in undertaking the different kinds of interviews. The procedures for conducting F2F focus groups are detailed. The key advantages and disadvantages of online interviews and focus groups are presented. The chapter contains an explanation of the ways in which interview and focus group schedules are designed and constructed. Interviews are generally used when the researcher can identify key respondents and can engage these respondents in an interview process, and when interview data will serve the research agenda. Focus groups are generally used when a group dynamic would be useful to the research agenda, and/or to the participants in the research. There are essentially five kinds of interview, one-to-one in-depth interviews, telephone interviews, group interviews, online interviews and photo-elicitation interviews. One of the most fundamental tasks in every research endeavour is the decision around which data gathering method to use in the research. This decision is made based on the data requirements of the research project, with reference to any potential ethical issues. Focus groups were said in the chapter to be very similar to group interviews. The main differences, according to the chapter, are in the role of the researcher and in the structure of the two different methods. In a focus group the researcher is a facilitator. The focus group is structured by the researcher to focus on a particular phenomenon. In a group interview, the researcher takes the role of interviewer, and the group interview is structured as an interview. The chapter explains in detail how to structure and organize interviews and focus groups. Examples are given of unstructured, semi-structured and structured interview and focus group schedules. The design of focus group and interview research is explored and the means through which focus group and interview research can be critiqued is detailed.

Now update your interactive research diary with your notes and findings at www. cengage.co.uk/quinlan. Complete the activities provided to reinforce your understanding of this chapter.

END OF CHAPTER QUESTIONS

1 Name and briefly explain the five types of interview detailed in this chapter.

2 Outline the advantages and disadvantages of one-to-one in-depth interviews.

3 Design a simple flow chart for the design and conduct of a series of telephone interviews.

4 Detail and explain the reasons why a researcher would decide to conduct group interviews.

5 What are the key issues in conducting structured interviews?

6 What is a focus group and how is it different from a group interview?

7 Outline the key advantages and disadvantages of online interviews and focus groups.

8 Design a simple research project using a focus group using computer mediated communication (CMC).

9 Design a simple research project using a face-to-face (FTF) focus group.

10 What is bias in research? Name and explain three different kinds of bias.

REFERENCES

Becker, H.S. (1974) 'Photography and sociology', *Studies in the Anthropology of Visual Communication* 1(1): 3–26.

Bowen, G.A. (2009) 'Supporting a grounded theory with an audit trail: An illustration', *International Journal of Social Research Methodology* 12(4): 305–316.

Chan, G., Benner, P., Brykcynski, K.A. and Malone, R.E. (2010) *Interpretive Phenomenology in Health Care Research: Studying Social Practice, Lifeworlds, and Embodiment*, Sigma Theta Tau Intl., http://www.nursinglibrary.org/Portal/CMSLite/ GetFile.aspx?ContentID=103477&VersionID=115170 Accessed 03.06.2010.

Collier, J. Jr. and Collier, M. (1986) *Visual Anthropology: Photography as a Research Method*, New Mexico: University of New Mexico Press.

Conklin, T.A. (2007) 'Method or madness: Phenomenology as knowledge creator', *Journal of Management Inquiry* 16(3): 275–287.

Cope, J. (2005) 'Researching entrepreneurship through phenomenological inquiry: Philosophical and methodological issues, *International Journal of Small Business Management* 23(2): 163–189.

Corbin, J. and Strauss, A. (2008) *Basics of Qualitative Research*, Thousand Oaks, CA: Sage.

Edwards, A. and Skinner, J. (2009) *Qualitative Research in Sports Management*, Oxford: Butterworth-Heinemann.

Exploring Online Research Methods, University of Leicester, www.geog.le.ac.uk/ORM/site/home.htm Accessed 03.06.2010.

Finlay, L. (2009) 'Debating phenomenological research methods', *Phenomenology & Practice* 3(1): 6–25, www.phandpr.org/index.php/pandp/ article/viewFile/40/80 Accessed 03.06.2010.

'Focus Groups', Channel 4 website, http://www. channel4.com/culture/microsites/W/wtc4/audience/ focusgroups.html Accessed 03.06.2010.

Geertz, C. (1973) *The Interpretation of Cultures*, New York: Basic Books.

Gibson, S.K. and Hanes, L.A. (2003) 'The contribution of phenomenology to HRD research', *Human Resource Development Review* 2(2): 181–205.

Glaser, B. and Strauss, A. (1967) *The Discovery Of Grounded Theory*, Chicago: Aldine.

Groenewald, T. (2004) 'A phenomenological research design illustrated', *International Journal of Qualitative Methods* 3(1) 1–26. www.ualberta.ca/ ~backissues/3_1/pdf/groenewald.pdf Accessed 03.06.2010.

Guba, E.G. and Lincoln, Y.S. (1994) *Competing Paradigms in Qualitative Research*, http://create.alt.ed. nyu.edu/courses/3311/reading/10-guba_lincoln_94.pdf Accessed 03.06.2010.

Harper, D. (1996) 'Seeing sociology', *The American Sociologist* 37(3): 69–78.

Harper, D. (1998) 'An Argument for Visual Sociology', in J. Prosser (ed.), *Image-based Research*, pp. 24–41, London: Routledge and Falmer.

Kent, T. (2010) 'The role of the museum shop in extending the visitor experience', *International*

Journal of Nonprofit and Voluntary Sector Marketing 15(1): 67–77.

Lincoln, Y.S. and Guba, E.G. (1985) *Naturalistic Inquiry*, Newbury Park, CA: Sage.

Neale, M.A., Mannix, E. and Sondak, H. (2002) *Toward Phenomenology of Groups and Group Membership*, Vol. 4, Research on Managing Groups and Teams, Connecticut: Jai Press Inc.

Professor T.D.Wilson's online paper 'Alfred Schutz, phenomenology and research methodology for information behaviour', **http://informationr.net/tdw/publ/papers/schutz02.html**

Reid, D.J. and Reid, F.J.M. (2005) 'Online focus groups: An in-depth comparison of computer mediated and conventional focus group discussions', *International Journal of Market Research* 47(2): 131–262.

Riege, A.M. (2003) 'Validity and reliability tests in case study research: A literature review with

"hands-on" applications for each research phase', *Qualitative Market Research* 6(2): 75–86.

Stat Trek, Teach yourself statistics, 'Tutorial on bias in survey sampling', (**http://stattrek.com/AP-Statistics-2/Survey-Sampling-Bias.aspx?Tutorial=AP**) Accessed 03.06.2010.

Unwin, E. (2007) 'Getting the picture: Programme awareness amongst film festival customers', *International Journal of Nonprofit and Voluntary Sector Marketing* 12(3): 231–245.

Venkatraman, M. and Nelson, T. (2008) 'From servicescape to consumptionscape: A photo-elicitation study of Starbucks in the New China', *Journal of International Business Studies* 39(6): 1010–1026.

Whitty, S.J. (2010) 'Project management artefacts and the emotions they evoke', *International Journal of Managing Projects in Business* 3(1): 22–45.

RECOMMENDED READING

Bell, J. (2000) *Doing Your Research Project*, Ch. 9, 'Planning and Conducting Interviews', Maidenhead: Open University Press.

Collis, J. and Hussey, R. (2009) *Business Research: A Practical Guide for Undergraduate and Postgraduate Students*, Houndsmill: Palgrave Macmillan.

Denscombe, M. (2003) *The Good Research Guide: For Small-scale Social Research Projects* (2nd edn), Ch. 10, 'Interviews', Maidenhead: Open University Press.

Easterby-Smith, M., Thorpe, R. and Jackson, P.R. (2008) *Management Research* (3rd edn), Ch. 7, 'Creating Qualitative Data', London: Sage.

Hammersley, M. and Atkinson, P. (2001) *Ethnography*, Ch. 5, 'Insider Accounts: Listening and Asking Questions' London: Routledge.

Jankowicz, A.D. (2005) *Business Research Projects*, London: Cengage.

Jones, S. (1999) *Doing internet Research: Critical Issues and Methods for Examining the Net*, London: Sage.

Kvale, S. and Brinkmann, S. (2008) *InterViews: Learning the Craft of Qualitative Interviewing*, Sage, London and Thousand Oaks, CA.

Neuman, W.L. (2000) *Social Research Methods: Quantitative and Qualitative Approaches*, Ch. 13, 'Field Research', Boston, MA: Allyn & Bacon.

Oppenheim, A.N. (1992) *Questionnaire Design, Interviewing and Attitude Measurement*, Ch. 5, 'The Exploratory Interview' and Ch. 6, 'Standardized Interviewing', London: Pinter.

Robson, C. (2002) *Real World Research*, Ch. 9, 'Interviews', Oxford: Blackwell.

Tineke, A.A. (2001) 'Reflexive dialogues: A story about the development of injury prevention in two performing-arts schools', *Evaluation* 7(2): 238–252.

Wengraf, T. (2001) *Qualitative Research Interviewing: Biographic, Narrative and Semi-Structured Methods*, Sage, London and Thousand Oaks, CA.

Zikmund, W.G. (2003) *Business Research Methods*, Mason, OH: Cengage South-Western.

CHAPTER 12

USING QUESTIONNAIRES AND SCALES

LEARNING OBJECTIVES

At the end of this chapter the student should be able to:

- Design questionnaires and scales for different research projects.

- Discuss and explain the issues of validity and reliability in relation to questionnaire and scale design.

RESEARCH SKILLS

At the end of this chapter the student should, using the exercises on the accompanying online platform, be able to:

- Design a questionnaire for a given research project.

- Design a scale for a give research project.

- Name and explain three different scaling techniques.

The aim of this chapter is to explain the use of questionnaires and scales in data gathering. Questionnaires and scales are structured means of data gathering and they are used a great deal in quantitative research. Quantitative research produces quantitative data, which are numerical data or data that can readily be converted into numerical form. Qualitative data can be gathered with questionnaires, through the use of open questions. This chapter explains how to create questionnaires and scales, and when and how to use questionnaires and scales in a research project.

INTRODUCTION

As explained in previous chapters, data gathering techniques are part of the methodological framework, the third framework in the four frameworks approach to the design of the research project. The four frameworks approach to the research project facilitates the researcher in developing a logical and coherent, fully integrated research project. The first three frameworks of the four frameworks approach to research are laid out again in Figure 12.1.

The epistemological and ontological perspectives of the research project are, we know from our reading of Chapter 4, 'Understanding Research Philosophy', embedded in the philosophical perspective informing the research project, and consequently in the project's research methodology. As stated in Chapter 4 and in the previous two chapters, embedded in each statement of methodology are implicit statements or assumptions about the nature of reality (ontological assumptions) and implicit statements or assumptions about the kind of knowledge that will be generated by the research (epistemological assumptions). Questionnaires and **scales** are very precisely structured data gathering instruments; they are widely used in survey research. As stated above, they are used primarily in quantitative research to generate quantitative data, although qualitative data can be generated by questionnaires, through the use of open questions. Quantitative data is factual data. The gathering of quantitative data in a research project indicates a positivistic perspective in the research, and perhaps a positivistic philosophical framework for the research.

Scales
Specially designed, highly structured, very focused and usually short data collection instruments.

You will at some time in your life have filled in a questionnaire. You cannot open a bank account or join a library without filling in a questionnaire. Perhaps you have at some time completed a scale while participating in a research project. You will know that it is a simple thing to fill in a questionnaire and to complete a scale. In order to fill in a questionnaire, you simply read down through it, ticking boxes or putting numbers into boxes as you go. The simplicity of the design of the questionnaire or scale, from the respondent's point of view, is a tribute to the amount of work and reflection the researcher engaged in while compiling the questionnaire or scale.

The model of the research process demonstrates where in the research process questionnaires and scales are used. Questionnaires and scales, like observation, interviews and focus groups, explored in the previous two chapters, are data gathering methods. As Figure 12.2 shows, the selection and design of the data gathering methods for the research project generally takes place after the literature review has been completed

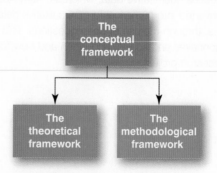

Figure 12.1   Three frameworks of the four frameworks approach to research

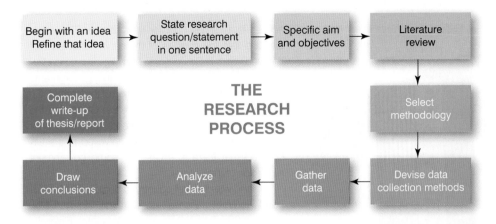

Figure 12.2   The research process

and decisions around methodology have been made. The researcher may have some ideas around data collection from the start of the project. However, these ideas are likely to change and/or develop over the course of the conceptualization of the research statement, the conduct of the literature review, and the design of the methodological framework for the research project. It is only at the point at which the methodology for the project, and the population and sample are finally decided upon, that the data gathering methods for the research project are finally selected and designed.

As you can see from the model, when the data collection methods are devised, the researcher then proceeds to use them to gather the data needed for the research project.

The text box below details different research projects related to internet usage globally. Among the sources quoted is a survey carried out for the BBC World Service. As you will see as you read through the extract presented below, the data

THE VALUE OF GOOD RESEARCH

Access to the internet

internet access is 'a fundamental right', BBC News (http://news.bbc.co.uk/2/hi/technology/8548190.stm)

I n an interesting news article, the BBC (http://news.bbc.co.uk/2/hi/technology/8548190.stm), detailed and explained a survey the BBC World Service had undertaken on the topic of internet access. The survey, which engaged with more than

27 000 adults across 26 countries, found strong support across all the participating countries for internet access. The survey was conducted by GlobeScan for the BBC. It revealed substantial disagreements regarding the issue of government control of some aspects of the internet.

Reporting on the study, Emma Barnett, writing in *The Telegraph* (08.03.2010), stated that 87 per cent of internet users (this rose to 90 per cent in Turkey), believed that access to the internet was a basic right, while more than 70 per cent of non-users believed that they should have access to the internet.

The findings of the survey were published as the United Nations (UN) pushes for universal web access. The Secretary General of the UN, Ban Ki-moon, cautions regularly against increasing attempts

Internet cafe © JVT/iStock

to suppress internet access (29.04.2010). In his Millennium Report (2000), the secretary general, among other priorities, listed the building of digital bridges as a priority. The call in the Millennium Report was specifically for the removal of regulatory and pricing impediments to internet access.

The International Telecommunication Union (ITU) (www.itu.int/en) is the leading UN agency for ICT. The current secretary general of ITU is Dr Hamadoun I. Touré. In his foreword on the web page of the ITU, Dr Touré outlines the dedication of ITU to the task of connecting everyone in the world to ICTs. He explains the ITU is particularly concerned with the need to connect people to ICTs who are not yet connected. A key endeavour of ITU as the UN specialized agency for ICT, we are told, is to 'fast-track the 2015 targets of the Millennium Goals' and to empower every person in terms of the capacity to seek and obtain information and knowledge.

According to the BBC news article, countries such as Finland and Estonia have already ruled that internet

access is a human right for their citizens. The article explains that the findings of the survey showed that the web users in South Korea and Nigeria who participated in the study strongly believed that governments should never be involved in regulation of the internet. On the other hand, a majority of those in China and the many European countries disagreed; we are told, for example, that over half of those surveyed in the UK believed that there is a case for some government regulation of the internet.

Finland was the first country to declare that broadband internet access is a legal right (CNN, 15.10.2009). The CNN news article quotes Finland's legislative counsellor for the Ministry of Transport and Communications who said that internet access is something that people cannot live without in a modern society; the Minister likened internet access to access to banking, electrical and water services. Whether or not internet access is a basic human right is an issue that is considered, discussed, debated, and indeed researched, globally.

References

Barnett, E. (2010) 'Four in five believe internet access is a fundamental right', 8 March, **www. telegraph.co.uk/technology/news/7397511/Four- in-five-believe-internet-access-is-a-fundamental- right.html**

Ahmed, S. (2009) 'Fast internet access becomes a legal right in Finland', 15 October, **http://edition. cnn.com/2009/TECH/10/15/finland.internet.rights/ index.html**

'Millennium Report of the Secretary General of the United Nations: Key Proposals', United Nations Department of Public Information, (DPI/2108) March 2000, **www.un.org/millennium/sg/report/**

Secretary-General's Foreword, International Telecommunications Union, **http://www.itu.int/net/ about/foreword.aspx** Accessed 03.06.2010.

'internet access is"a fundamental right"', *BBC News,* **http://news.bbc.co.uk/2/hi/8548190.stm**

'Governments must stand up for press freedom, public's right to know', United Nations Secretary General's address, World Press Freedom Day Observance, 29.04.2010 (OBV/875 PI/1934), **http://www.un.org/News/Press/docs/2010/obv875. doc.htm** Accessed 03.06.2010.

gathered through the survey was primarily quantitative data. The survey was very big. More than 27 000 people across 26 different countries participated in the research. It is interesting to consider this research, to consider how it was conducted, and what the research accomplished. As well as presenting the findings of the research in terms of the entire population of the study, some of the findings from individual countries were also presented. It is interesting also to consider the other sources quoted in the text box below, and the data they present and the concerns that they articulate. As well as learning something of the key concerns globally in relation to internet access by reading the material presented in the text box, you may develop some new ideas of your own for research projects.

A survey research methodology works well in large scale research projects. As explained in Chapter 7, surveys are often used in research conducted with large and/ or geographically spread populations. Questionnaires can be easily posted or emailed to such populations, or placed on the internet to allow for easy access globally. Online methods are commonly used, and they are very effective where the survey population has access to the technologies and the skills necessary to use those technologies.

There are very many software packages that facilitate the creation of questionnaires (see Figure 12.3) to be used in F2F research or in online research. Among these packages are Survey Monkey, Surveyspro, Snap Surveys Ltd and Question Pro. They are all useful and they all give help and direction in terms of question and question-naire design. The screen capture below details some of the questions asked in a questionnaire designed using Survey Monkey. As you can see, this software package allows for the use of a number of different kinds of questions, among them open and closed questions, multiple choice questions, **sentence completion exercises** and **rating scales**. The use of an online software package is also helpful in the aesthetics of a questionnaire or scale, providing different option in terms of organization and style. As well as providing for the design of data gathering instrument, an online package facilitates the administration of the instrument and the collation of results.

> **Sentence completion exercises**
> A projective techniques. The researcher starts a sentence and asks the respondent to complete it.

> **Rating scales**
> The researcher asks participants to rate different aspects or elements of the phenomenon under investigation.

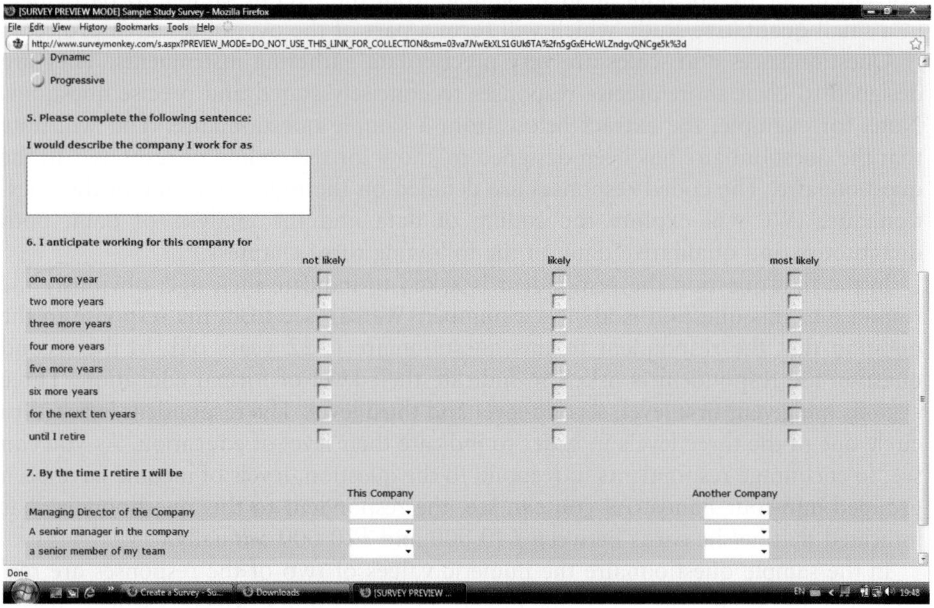

Figure 12.3 Screen capture of questionnaire developed in Survey Monkey. Reproduced with permission from SurveyMonkey.com © SurveyMonkey.com, LLC

Questionnaires and scales can be used in drop-and-collect situations where they are left with respondents and collected when the respondent has completed them. Questionnaires and scales can be administered to respondents in structured interviews conducted F2F, by telephone or online. There is a detailed explanation in Chapter 11 of how to carry out these interviews, and a discussion of their relative advantages and disadvantages.

QUESTIONNAIRES AND SCALES

When engaging a large population in a research project, it is not possible to engage every member of the population in in-depth research. The researcher must design a research instrument which facilitates a broad approach to researching the phenomenon, using a large number of respondents. A survey research methodology is an appropriate research methodology in such research. Survey research is situated within a framework of positivism, it is deductive and it is used primarily to generate quantitative data. Questionnaires and/or scales are appropriate data gathering instruments in such research. They are, as stated above, structured data gathering methods. They are structured to ensure that each respondent is asked the same simple, clear, concise and precise questions, and to ensure that the responses made to those questions/issues are also simple, clear, concise and precise.

The data gathered by researchers engaged in very large studies tends to be mostly or entirely quantitative data. Quantitative data are precise and concise, while qualitative data, on the other hand, tends to be complex, dense and often quite voluminous. Researchers tend not to gather much qualitative data from very large studies because if they did, there would just be too much data to analyze. So in studies with large numbers of participants, researchers tend to restrict the amount of qualitative data gathered by only including very few open questions in the data gathering instrument, or by engaging a small sample from the overall sample to participate in a small qualitative study which will form a part of the overall research project.

Questionnaires and scales are very precise data gathering instruments. They are designed to elicit short precise responses to concisely stated and precise questions. Note, for example, the extract below from a sample questionnaire. You will note that the questionnaire has been designed to allow for the coding of responses to the questionnaire. The coded responses are detailed on the right-hand side of the questionnaire. (We will explore the coding of data and the analysis of data, both quantitative and qualitative data, in the following three chapters.)

In the first question the respondent is asked to indicate their age; obviously the response to this question is always a number. We can see from the response to the question that the respondent to this questionnaire is 22 years old. In the second question the respondent is asked to indicate their level of formal education. Three options are given, first level, second level and third level. The respondent is asked to circle one of the three levels in order to indicate their level of education. As you can see, to encourage respondents to respond to the question, levels of income have been grouped into four bands. As you can see, the respondent to this questionnaire has indicated that he/she earns between £10 000 and £20 000 annually.

In the sample questionnaire the numeric values of two of the responses are real while one has been assigned by the researcher. Can you tell which is which? If you said that the numeric values (codes) 22 and 3 are real, while the numeric value (code)

Sample questionnaire   Code

Q1. What is your age? Please state   22 yrs   22

Q2. What is your level of formal education? Please circle   1st   2nd   (3rd)   3

Q3. What is your annual income? Please tick

Less than £10 000	☐
More than £10 000, less than £20 000	☐✓ 2
More than £20 000, less than £30 000	☐
More than £30 000, less than £40 000	☐

2 has been assigned by the researcher, you are correct. Coding assigned by the researcher is always assigned using a simple logic. In response to question three, the respondent selected the second option, so in coding this response the researcher assigned the number 2 as the **code** to signify this response. Codes and coding and the analysis of quantitative data are explored in detail in Chapter 14, 'Analysing Quantitative Data'.

The sample scale below (see Table 12.1) is an example of a **Likert scale**. Likert scales are named after the person who developed them, Rensis Likert, and are widely used in the measurement of attitudes. (Attitude research is the methodology in focus in this chapter.) The Likert scale is useful in that as well as measuring the direction of attitudes, it also measures the force of the attitudes. A Likert scale can be a three-point scale, or a five-point scale or a seven-point scale. The example below is of a five-point Likert scale; a three-point Likert scale would drop the two options, 'agree strongly', and 'disagree strongly'; in a seven-point Likert scale, two more options in terms of responses would be added on to the scale, for example 'agree very very strongly' and 'disagree very very strongly'. The more points in the scale, the more data can be gathered in terms of the strength of the attitudes held. In general, Likert

Code
Developed by the researcher for each of the responses to each of the questions asked in the course of the data gathering, in other words, for each piece of data gathered.

Likert scale
Developed by Rensis Likert. Used to measure the direction and force of attitudes on a three, five or seven point scale.

	Table 12.1 Sample Likert scale – measuring brand loyalty				
		Agree strongly	Agree	Non-committal	Disagree	Disagree strongly
1	I am loyal to one particular brand.		√			
2	I am not concerned so much about price; I would buy my brand regardless of the cost.			√		
3	If my local shop did not stock my brand, I would travel in order to be able to buy my brand.		√			

scales tend to have ten to 20 attitude statements. The sample scale shown here has just three attitude statements.

In order to respond to a Likert scale, the respondent simply reads down through each of the attitude statements, listed on the left, and then places a tick in the box that best corresponds to their attitude to that statement. As you can see, the respondent is quite loyal to one brand and while they would not buy the brand regardless of the cost of the brand, they would be prepared to travel beyond the local shop if necessary in order to be able to buy the brand.

The box feature below details a research project carried out using a Likert scale. You would find it helpful to source the original article to examine the survey methodology and the Likert scale used in the study. Worth noting also are the graphs at the end of the journal article and in particular the way the graphs are used to represent data.

REAL WORLD RESEARCH

A survey of 100 human resource professionals

'Total quality management meets human resource management: Perceptions of the shift towards high performance working'

This study by Keeble-Ramsay and Armitage (2010) was designed to test Watson's model of HPW (high performance working). Keeble-Ramsay and Armitage used a survey design to collect data over a 4 week long period in 2006 from 100 human resource professionals. The data gathering instrument was a seven-point Likert scale which, as the author's state, they adopted from Watson's model. A copy of the Likert scale used in the study is presented in an appendix of the journal article.

Keeble-Ramsay and Armitage, found that Watson's model for HPW was inconsistent with the choices of the respondents in their study. Their findings, they state, suggest that the professionals who participated in their study did not view current human resource practice within their own company to be within Watson's model of HPW practices. The authors concluded that their paper demonstrates a need for an understanding of the potential gap between employer's aspirations and employees perceptions of organizational practices.

Table 12.2 depicts a rating scale. A simple rating of any phenomenon can be a useful data gathering exercise. Using a rating scale, the researcher can ask participants in the research project to rate the phenomenon under investigation. The researcher can ask participants to rate as many or as few aspects of elements of the phenomenon under investigation as is useful for the purposes of the research. The rating scale is designed to gather ratings on an employee health and safety training programme. Respondents have been asked to rate different aspects of the training programme on a scale of 0 to 10.

Semantic differential scale
Uses opposite adjectives and asks respondents to indicate which of the adjectives best describes the phenomenon under investigation.

As you can see, this respondent has rated the delivery of the programme and the communication style of the presenter highly, and the content quite highly, while the relevance of the programme has been given only a medium rating (5 marks out of a possible 10).

Another useful scale is the **semantic differential scale**. A semantic differential scale uses opposite adjectives and asks respondents to indicate which of the adjectives best describes the phenomenon under investigation. A simple example of a semantic differential scale is shown in Figure 12.4.

As you can see, the brand 'Woolly Jumper' is very well perceived by the respondent who filled in this semantic differential scale.

Table 12.2 Rating scale employee Health and Safety training programme	
	Rating (0–10)
1 Please rate the content of the training programme.	8
2 Please rate the delivery of the training programme.	9
3 Please rate the relevance of the training programme.	5
4 Please rate the communication style of the presenter of the training programme.	9

Another scale is the **Bogardus social distance scale**, developed by psychologist E.S. Bogardus (see Table 12.3). The Bogardus social distance scale measures the social distance between different social and/or ethnic groups.

In using the Bogardus social distance scale, participants in the research simply indicate, by ticking or not ticking the boxes on the right of the scale, the degree to which they would be prejudiced against the population of the study, in the scale above, Irish people. As you can see, the respondent who filled in this scale is very well disposed to Irish people. The box feature below details an international business and tourism research project carried out using a revised version of the Bogardus social distance scale. The research project focused on the social distance between Austrian residents and Japanese and German tourists.

Bogardus social distance scale Developed by psychologist E.S. Bogardus. Measures the social distance between different social and/or ethnic groups.

Please indicate, by means of placing a tick on each line below, how you rate the brand 'Woolly Jumper'.

Hot √_:_:_:_:_:_:_: Cold
Good _√_:_:_:_:_:_:_: Bad
Fresh _√_:_:_:_:_:_: Tired

Figure 12.4   Semantic differential scale: Measuring perceptions of the brand 'Woolly Jumper'

Table 12.3 Bogardus social distance scale: Measuring prejudice against (in this case) Irish people	
I would admit an Irish person...	
Into my family by marriage	√
Into my club as a personal friend	√
To my street as a neighbour	√
To employment in my occupation	√
To employment in my workplace	√
As a colleague of mine in my workplace	√
As a visitor only to my workplace	
Would exclude from my workplace	

REAL WORLD RESEARCH

Using a revised version of the Bogardus social distance scale

'Social distance between residents and international tourists – Implications for international business', Sinkovics, R.R. and Penz, E. (2009)

The issue of social distance between residents and international tourists and the implications of this for international business was explored by Sinkovics and Penz (2009) using a revised version of the Bogardus social distance scale. The research focused on the attitudes of Austrian residents towards Japanese and German tourists. The removal of conflicts between residents and international tourists, according to the researchers, is vital for the improvement of economic outcomes in tourism. A survey methodology was used in the research. A quota sample of 449 respondents were engaged in the research. As indicated above, the data gathering instrument was a questionnaire which built on Bogardus' social distance scale. The questionnaire included 60 Likert-type statements on a seven-point scale, ranging from 1 'feeling very comfortable' to 7 'feeling very uncomfortable'. The participants in the research were asked in the questionnaire to imagine several situations in which they would meet tourists and to indicate on the scale how comfortable or uncomfortable they would feel in those situations. The research found that residents used social distance as a means of avoiding conflict. As the residents could not always manage spatial distance from tourists, they employed social distance as a means of managing their engagement with tourists. The researchers make recommendations on foot of the findings of their research for international business and tourism managers, designed to improve the social and economic performance of interactions between residents and tourists.

The journal article provides in an appendix a copy of the social distance scale used in the research. You should source the article and consider the methodology used in the research. As you read the article, critique the methodology used, the population, the sample, the sampling method and the questionnaire. Do you think the methodology the researchers developed and used was appropriate for this particular research project?

References

Sinkovics, R.R. and Penz, E. (2009) 'Social distance between residents and international tourists – Implications for international business', International Business Review 18(5): 457–469.

Vignettes
A projective technique. The researcher shows respondents images or narratives and respondents are asked to engage and respond to them.

Projective techniques
Are indirect techniques through which researchers probe the beliefs, attitudes and feelings of respondents.

PROJECTIVE TECHNIQUES

As well as questionnaires and scales, researchers also use projective techniques as data gathering methods. Projective techniques are indirect techniques through which researchers probe the beliefs, attitudes and feelings of respondents. **Vignettes** are an example of a **projective technique**. Using vignettes in research, the researcher presents the respondent with a story, a narrative, and asks the respondent to explain what is happening in the story or narrative to the researcher. The data are the responses the respondent makes to the story or narrative. The story or narrative does not need to be verbal, it can be visual. The researcher can present the participant with an image or a series of images, or a series of cartoons, or perhaps an advertisement or a series of advertisements (and so on) and ask the respondent to explain some aspect of the image(s). The response made by the respondent is their understanding of the meaning of the vignette. Their responses are the data gathered by the use of the data gathering method vignettes.

The box feature below details a research project in human resources management which was developed using vignettes and scaling techniques. Read the synopsis of the article presented below for an example of how vignettes and scales can be used in

REAL WORLD RESEARCH

How theory influences research

'Using vignettes and scales in human resource management research', Valentine *et al*. (2010)

In their research, Valentine *et al*. (2010), used two vignettes, both presenting questionable business situations, and they asked participants in the research to evaluate the ethics of both situations. Both of the vignettes presented were stories of an employee whose contract had been terminated because of blogging. The aim of this element of the research carried out by Valentine *et al*., was to establish and then compare and evaluate the moral reasoning of their respondents. The respondents were presented with the two vignettes, and asked to provide their opinions on the situations described in the vignettes on a seven-point scale, where 1 equalled 'strongly disagree' and 7 equalled 'strongly agree'.

In Appendix A in the journal article, 12 different scenarios are presented where employees were dismissed from their jobs for blogging. In Appendix B, the following synopsis of the methodology used in the research, projective techniques and scales, is presented.

Scenario 1

Heather maintains an internet blog (an online diary) in which she writes about a number of topics, mostly politics, but never work. A co-worker knows about Heather's blog and tells Heather's manager about the situation. Heather's manager reads the blog and is offended by some of the comments.

Action: The manager fires Heather because of the internet blog.

Scenario 2

Heather maintains an internet blog (an online diary) in which she writes about a number of topics, mostly politics. Heather occasionally 'gripes' about work in her blog (e.g., 'The guy in the cubicle next to me is a real jerk'). Heather uses a pseudonym on the blog and has never identified her employer, let alone what industry or city she works in. A co-worker knows about Heather's blog and tells Heather's manager about the situation. Heather's boss is upset that she has written about work on her blog.

Action: The manager fires Heather because of the internet blog.

The scale used is presented in the article as follows:

Ethical judgement

Next is a set of adjectives that allow you to evaluate the manager's action described in the situation.

1 Fair__:__:__:__:__:__:__: Unfair

2 Just__:__:__:__:__:__:__: Unjust

3 Morally right__:__:__:__:__:__:__:Not morally right

4 Acceptable to my family__:__:__:__:__:__:__: Unacceptable to my family

Unethical intention

How likely is it that you would engage in the manager's action described in the situation?

1 Likely__:__:__:__:__:__:__:Unlikely

2 Probable__:__:__:__:__:__:__:Improbable

3 Possible__:__:__:__:__:__:__:Impossible

4 Definitely would__:__:__:__:__:__:__:Definitely would not

Moral intensity

This scale was followed by a number of statements that described the situation.

1 The overall harm (if any) of the manager's action is very small.

2 Most people agree that the manager's action is wrong.

3 There is a very small likelihood that the manager's action will cause any harm.

4 The manager's action will not cause any harm in the immediate future.

5 If the manager and Heather are personal friends, the manager's action is wrong.

6 The manager's actions will harm very few people, (if any).

Corporate ethical values

1 Managers in my organization often engage in behaviours that I consider to be unethical.

2 In order to succeed in my organization, it is often necessary to compromise one's ethics.

3 Top management in my organization has let it be known in no uncertain terms that unethical behaviours will not be tolerated.

4 If a manager in my organization is discovered to have engaged in unethical behaviour that

results primarily in *personal gain* (rather than organizational gain), he/she will be promptly reprimanded.

5 If a manager in my organization is discovered to have engaged in unethical behaviour that results primarily in *organizational gain* (rather than personal gain), he/she will be promptly reprimanded.

As you read through the synopsis above, what thoughts have you had about these data gathering methods? If you were asked to critically engage with these data gathering methods as they were used in this research project, what issues would you high-light? What criticisms, if any, would you level at the attitude statements as they are presented in the section headed 'Moral intensity' and the section headed 'Corporate ethical values'? Now that you have read the synopsis above, do you think that you could use scales or projective techniques in your research project?

References

Valentine, S., Fleischman, G.M., Sprague, R. and Godkin, L. (2010) 'Exploring the ethicality of firing employees who blog', Human Resource Management 49(1): 87–108 © 2010 Wiley-Blackwell. Reproduced with permission via Rightslink.

business research. Then source and read the original article for a full understanding of how these scholars, Valentine *et al.* (2010), carried out their research using these data gathering methods.

Role play
A projective technique. Researcher and respondent take on character roles in a discussion.

Another projective technique used in research is **role play**. Here, the researcher facilitates respondents in some role-playing exercise, which is recorded, either on camera, or by some other means. The recording of the role play is the data. The researcher can also ask respondents or witnesses to write an account of the role play, of their experience of the role play, or of some other aspect of it. Such accounts also represent data for the research project. The researcher might decide to interview participants and witnesses about the role play, and/or the researcher to facilitate a focus group, or a series of focus groups, with participants and witnesses.

A very simple and useful projective technique is the sentence completion exercise. Sometimes sentence completion exercises stand alone, and sometimes they form part of a questionnaire. Often they are the final element of a questionnaire. In a sentence completion exercise, the researcher starts a sentence, and asks the respondent to complete it. There are three different examples on page 311.

Please complete the following sentence.
The training I received has:

_____

_____

_____

Please complete the following sentence.
My contribution to the company is:

_____

_____

_____

Please complete the following sentence.
I buy/I do not buy (delete as appropriate) *Woolly Jumper* products because:

_____

_____

_____

A sentence completion exercise can be used in relation to any aspect of the research. Note the sentence completion exercise in the questionnaire developed in Survey Monkey and illustrated in the screen capture (Figure 12.3). This exercise can also be a useful way to end a questionnaire because often by this time a respondent has a good flow of thoughts and ideas in mind with regard to the phenomenon under investigation. A sentence completion exercise gives respondents a simple and quick way to expressing their thoughts, feelings and attitudes regarding the phenomenon that is the subject of the research.

REAL WORLD RESEARCH

Focus on attitude research

The research methodology in focus in this chapter is attitude research. Attitude research, as the name suggests, is used in researching the attitudes of respondents to whatever is the focus of the research, for example the attitudes of respondents to an organization(s), to a product(s), to a service(s). The importance of attitudes and the value of studying attitudes lies primarily in the assumption that attitudes facilitate intention-forming and thus behaviour. Ajzen and Fishbein (1980), in their classic study in social psychology, modelled individual behaviour using four variables, beliefs, attitudes, intentions, and behaviour. The way in which a person behaves, according to this model, is an outcome of their beliefs, attitudes and intentions. As this is the case, the study of beliefs, attitudes and intentions is a means of predicting likely behaviours. According to Eagly and Chaiken (1993), because attitudes are believed to actually cause perceptions and behaviours, they have become a fundamental construct for social scientists. Clearly, the ability to predict likely behaviour is very useful in business and management. Attitude research has a wide application in market research and in research in human resources.

Daniel's research project

Daniel is studying for a degree in business management. In his research for his thesis, he has focused on the Scotland Rural Development Programme (SRDP) and the work within that programme of development officers helping farmers and others in rural Scotland to diversify into alternative enterprises. The alternative enterprises these officers are mostly concerned with are food production, tourism, forestry and fishing enterprises. Daniel's methodology is attitude research. His population is the entire population of development officers working on the SRDP. There are in total 100 officers. The aim of Daniel's research is to examine attitudes to alternative enterprises among these officers. His data gathering method is a one-to-one F2F interview using a structured questionnaire. He is developing a Likert scale that he intends to use as part of his study. The scale, as it is has been developed to date, is detailed below.

Scotland's agricultural development managers and alternative enterprises

My clients are interested in alternative enterprises
agree __;__;__;__;__; disagree

I regularly advise people on alternative enterprises
agree __;__;__;__;__; disagree

Many of my clients would like to be involved in alternative enterprises
agree __;__;__;__;__; disagree

Many of my clients are involved in alternative enterprises
agree __;__;__;__;__; disagree

I am fully confident that alternative enterprises are a viable means to security for rural dwellers
agree __;__;__;__;__; disagree

My organization is fully confident that alternative enterprises are a viable means to security for rural dwellers
agree __;__;__;__;__; disagree

The alternative enterprises my clients engage with are fully and thoroughly researched
agree __;__;__;__;__; disagree

My organization is committing the necessary resources for research
agree __;__;__;__;__; disagree

I have access to the most up-to-date data on alternative enterprises
agree __;__;__;__;__; disagree

Alternative enterprises strengthen the economic base of rural communities
agree __;__;__;__;__; disagree

Daniel is proposing to use this scale as part of a questionnaire. The questionnaire is made up of mostly yes/no type questions, i.e. questions to which the respondent will answer either 'Yes' or 'No'. The questionnaire also contains a semantic differential scale. In addition, Daniel is going to use projective techniques. He is going to use a sentence completion exercise and he is also proposing to use a vignette. The vignette he is proposing to use is a photograph which depicts a farm bed and breakfast enterprise. Daniel proposes asking his respondents to explain to him during the F2F interview what is happening in the photograph. While Daniel is proposing just one encounter with each respondent in his research, he is triangulating his research using 'between method triangulation'. The between method triangulation is accomplished with the use of a questionnaire, scales and projective techniques. In analysing his data, Daniel will be able to compare the findings from the questionnaire with the findings from the scales and the findings from the projective techniques. As defined in Chapter 2, 'Developing Research Skills', triangulation in social science research calls for more than one approach to answering the research question or responding to the research issue.

In relation to attitude research in particular, and survey research generally, you will find the following resources helpful.

Survey Resources Network (SRN). SRN is a service funded by the UK's Economic and Social Research Council (ESRC). The website provides extensive online resources for survey research (**http://surveynet.ac.uk/sm/introduction.asp**) Accessed 03.06.2010.

Surveyspro. This website provides examples of different kinds of questionnaires in their survey templates (**www.esurveyspro.com**) Accessed 03.06.2010.

What is an Employee Attitude Survey? This website provides information on human resources surveys and attitude research, **http://www.hr-survey.com/EmployeeAttitude.htm** Accessed 03.06.2010.

QuestionPro: Online Research Made Easy. This website provides online surveys and attitude research. On their 'Survey Questions' page, they give examples of different kinds of questions and scales (**www.questionpro.com/survey-questions.html**) Accessed 03.06.2010.

References

Ajzen, I. and Fishbein, M. (1980) *Understanding Attitudes and Predicting Social Behaviour*, Englewood Cliffs, NJ: Prentice Hall.

Eagly, A.H. and Chaiken, S. (1993) *The Psychology of Attitudes*, Forth Worth, TX: Harcourt Brace and Company.

THE ISSUES OF VALIDITY AND RELIABILITY

As stated in Chapter 11, the issues of validity and reliability are treated differently in quantitative research and qualitative research. In quantitative research, the researcher is primarily concerned with measurement and with the precision of the data gathering instruments they use or develop for use in their research projects. The issues of validity and reliability in quantitative research are explored in Table 12.4.

Table 12.4 Validity and reliability in quantitative research	
Validity	**Reliability**
The term validity in research, as defined in Chapter 2, is a question of how valid the research is, how logical, how truthful, how robust, how sound, how reasonable, how meaningful and how useful. The issue of validity in relation to data collection methods, **measurement validity**, refers to the degree to which the data collection methods, as they are designed, can accomplish what it is that they are designed to accomplish. There are different ways of establishing measurement validity: content validity, face validity, criterion related validity and construct validity.	The term reliability in research, as defined in Chapter 2, relates to the dependability of the research, to the degree to which the research can be repeated while obtaining consistent results. A data collection instrument in social science research is deemed reliable if it produces the same result again and again, over time and in different circumstances. A ruler, for example, is a reliable measure. If you use a ruler to measure the length and breadth of one of your shoes, you will get a particular result. If tomorrow you use the same ruler in the same measurement exercise, you will get the same result. If one of your friends uses a ruler to measure the length and breadth of the same shoe you measured, they will get the same result. The ruler is a dependable measure, it produces consistent results; it is a reliable instrument.
Using content validity the researcher establishes the validity of the data gathering method by ensuring that the phenomenon under investigation, as defined, or as outlined in the conceptual framework for the research project, is fully represented in the data gathering	There are three different kinds of reliability; stability reliability (sometimes referred to as the test re-test reliability), relates to whether or not the data collection instrument produces the same result over time; representative reliability relates to whether or not the data collection instrument produces the same result when

(Continued)

Table 12.4   Validity and reliability in quantitative research (continued)

instrument(s). Using face validity the researcher establishes that the data gathering instrument seems a reasonable measure of the phenomenon under investigation. The researcher can improve the face validity of a data gathering instrument by asking people with some expertise on the phenomenon, to judge whether or not the instrument is valid. The data gathering instrument can be changed and developed following their feedback. Using criterion related validity, also known as instrumental validity, the researcher uses some standard or criterion to measure the data gathering instrument against, for example, the researcher could use another data gathering instrument developed and validated by another (perhaps more established) researcher. Construct validity is applicable to data gathering instruments which have multiple indicators (questions/issues). In attempting to establish construct validity the researcher demonstrates how all of the indicators are consistent with each other and consistent with the phenomenon under investigation. The researcher ensures that the questions asked are relevant and pertinent to the phenomenon under investigation; that the data collection method designed is a complete and comprehensive examination of/reflection on the phenomenon under investigation.

applied to different subgroups in a population, testing the instrument on a sub-population of the population can establish whether or not the instrument has representative reliability; and equivalence reliability relates to whether or not when a lot of different items are used in a questionnaire, they all measure the phenomenon consistently. The **split-half method** is used to test for equivalence reliability. Using this method, the researcher divides the questionnaire into two halves, by randomly assigning all of the measures in the questionnaire to one half or the other, and then tests whether or not both halves yield consistent results. The **test re-test method** is also used as a means of estimating reliability. Using this method, the data gathering instrument (questionnaire or scale) is used in a pilot test, then, on another later occasion, the same pilot test is carried out with the same people. The two sets of responses are then compared for consistency. One problem with this method is that respondents may reflect on the first responses they gave and, as a consequence, they may give different, perhaps more mature responses, the second time. Researchers sometimes use a method called **inter coder reliability**. This is where there is more than one researcher, observer or coder. A measure is reliable if the observers or coders consistently agree with each other. This method of reliability is used often in content analysis. Inter coder reliability is tested by having two or more researchers, observers or coders measure the same phenomenon and then compare their results. If their results are consistent, inter coding can be deemed reliable.

The questionnaire and/or scale designed by the researcher must be a valid measure of the phenomenon under investigation. Every item in the questionnaire must be relevant. Every item in the questionnaire must be essential. The data gathering instrument must provide the data required for the research project. A pilot test can help improve the validity of a data gathering instrument. Replicating and/or building on the data gathering instruments developed by other researchers (these are to be found in the literature) helps improve validity.

Measuring at the most precise level possible will help improve reliability. Using clearly, precisely and simply defined items will help improve reliability. Using each item to measure only one concept will help. Using more than one item to measure each concept will help improve reliability. A pilot test can help improve the reliability of the data collection instrument. Replicating and/or building on the data gathering instruments developed by other researchers (these are to be found in the literature) helps improve reliability.

DESIGNING QUESTIONNAIRES AND SCALES

The researcher works hard at producing a questionnaire and/or a scale that will be valid and reliable, that will provide the data needed for the research project, and that will be simple for the respondent to the research to complete. In order to produce such a precise yet simple data gathering instrument, the researcher studies examples of questionnaires and scales in textbooks and in the literature and considers the data requirements of the research project. When you have collected a number of such questionnaires and scales, examine them.

- Study the way in which they are presented in terms of both organization and the aesthetics.
- Study the structure and the sequence of questions and items.
- Take note of which questions are asked first, and which questions came later.
- Study the words, concepts and language used.
- Examine the manner in which items and questions are presented.
- Take note of the manner in which the respondent was required to respond to the questions and items, ticking boxes, inputting words and/or numbers, writing phrases and/or sentences.
- Note the structure and presentation of the closed questions, and the way in which the respondent is required to respond to them.
- Note the structure and presentation of the open questions, and the way in which the respondent is required to respond to them.
- Note all of the different question formats in the questionnaires and scales you have gathered.
- Note **skips and filters** and the ways in which they are used.
- Note the length of the questionnaires and scales. Questionnaires and scales are designed to be concise and precise data gathering methods, they should be as long as is necessary, and as short as is possible.

The key issues when designing a questionnaire are:

1 The content of the questions.
2 The construction and presentation of each of the questions.
3 The order of the questions.
4 The length of the questionnaire.

The best guide to the design of an appropriate question or item, to begin with, is the conceptual framework of your research project. The conceptual framework of the research project is contained in the research question or statement of your project and it is the question or statement driving your research. If it is phrased as a question, you will need to find an answer to this question through your research; if it is phrased as a statement, you will need to respond fully to this statement through your research. When you begin to design a questionnaire for your research, you look at your research statement/question and from that you decide what it is precisely that you need to know. Look next at the aim and objectives of your research. Then consider the literature you have reviewed for the research project. Drawing on the literature, set about designing the series of questions and/or items that will elicit responses that will provide you with the data you need to complete your research.

As you think of possible research questions, imagine posing those questions to a member of your research population. Then try to imagine the kind of response that person might make to that research question. This is a useful exercise when attempt-

Measurement validity
Refers to the degree to which the data collection methods as they are designed can accomplish what it is that they are designed to accomplish.

Skips and filters
Devices used in questionnaires to allow respondents to skip over questions that do not relate to them.

Split-half method
Used to tests equivalence reliability. The researcher halves the questionnaire and then tests whether or not both halves yield consistent results.

Test re-test method
Used to estimate reliability. A questionnaire is used in a pilot test, then later, the same test is repeated and compared for consistency.

ing to generate research questions. When you have done this for a series of questions, examine the likely responses to see how well they fit with the data requirements of the research. This is an exercise in critical reflection. It is a good idea to record such critical reflections in your research diary. You will be able to use them in writing up your research, and in particular in writing the research methodology chapter of your thesis or section of your research report.

Inter coder reliability
Two or more researchers, observers or coders measure the same phenomenon and then compare their results. If their results are consistent, inter coding can be deemed reliable.

THE POLITICS AND PRACTICALITIES OF ASKING A QUESTION

As explained in the previous chapter, in quantitative research, the researcher decides what needs to be known, and designs a very precise data gathering instrument to gather data in order to create knowledge. In such a data gathering exercise, the researcher is the 'expert' and it is the researcher's understanding of and/or perspective on the phenomenon that is explored or examined in such research. In designing such a precise instrument, the researcher controls and even shapes the information that is gathered, and consequently the knowledge generated by the research project.

The critique of such approaches to research stems from what are perceived as power issues. The researcher has all the power and the researched are, in a sense, colonized by the researcher. Critics hold that the researcher outlines and explains the experiences and concerns of those researched, from within their own understanding of those experiences and concerns, instead of allowing those researched to themselves outline and explain their experiences and concerns. This is the essence of the politics of asking a question. Who is asking the question, from what or from whose perspective is the question framed, and why is the question being asked? These can all be substantial questions in social science research and can raise important issues.

Clearly a research project initiated and designed by a chief executive officer (CEO) in a company will be quite different from a research project initiated and designed by a trade union official in the same company. They hold different perspectives and are concerned with different issues with regard to the same company. Consequently, the issues they choose to study and the perspective within which they construct the study will be different. These are reasons why the researcher provides a justification for the choices and decisions made throughout the research process.

Quantitative research is said to be objective. In order to ensure that your research is objective, you must avoid bias. Bias in research, as defined in Chapter 11, is anything that contaminates or compromises the research. It is possible to bias research through the wording of the questions and items used in questionnaires and scales, and through the way in which respondents can be influenced in responding to those questions and items.

The researcher tackles these issues through the design of the data collection methods used in the research project, through the design of the questions asked of participants, and through the organization and management of data gathering for the research. There are very many issues in designing questions and only a few have been considered here (see Table 12.5). The important point is that you must critically engage with the words, concepts and language you use in the questions and items in your questionnaire and/or scale.

The presentation of the questionnaire should be simple, succinct, and professional. The spacing of the questions should be logical and aesthetically pleasing. In other words, the questionnaire should be attractive. This is important because the

Table 12.5 Issues in designing questions and items for questionnaires and scales	
Leading responses – the possibility of leading participants to a particular response through the way in which the question is framed	For example, 'Nike and Adidas are two of the most popular brands among third-level students in the UK. What brands would you name as being your top five favourite brands?' The use of the brand names Nike and Adidas in the research question works as a prompt for respondents. As these two brands have been introduced by the researcher into the research encounter, it is likely that the respondents will name these two brands as being among their five favourite brands. It is possible that the naming of the brands by the researcher might prompt respondents to deliberately avoid using these particular brand names as they name their top five. This is equally problematic. The problem is that the researcher has contaminated the research by prompting respondents through the use of particular brand names. For example, 'It has been established, in research and in the media, that the 'Fantastic Jersey' company uses child labour in the manufacture of their products. Do you support the brand 'Fantastic Jersey'?' It is unlikely that any respondent will admit to supporting a brand that uses child labour. So the researcher has contaminated responses to the research by designing a question that might lead responses.
Ambiguous questions	These are questions which have an unclear meaning, or questions that can have more than one possible meaning.
Complicated questions	Questions should be simple and clear, concise and precise.
Asking two questions, or more, in one question	For example, 'Please name your top five favourite brands, and explain why they are your favourites'. Here we have two questions in one. Always check that you have not done this when you are compiling a questionnaire, and if you have, re-phrase your question, turning that one question into two or more questions.
Potentially embarrassing questions and/or questions which you have no right to ask	Examples might be questions about how much money someone earns, questions about a person's sexual orientation, and so on. If you need to ask potentially sensitive questions, such as how much money the respondent earns, or how old the respondent is, it is helpful to aggregate the possible answers and then ask the respondent to indicate which range they belong to, rather than respond with a precise figure.
Asking unnecessary questions	Ensure that your questionnaire, or schedule of questions and/or issues to be explored, is succinct and relevant, and absolutely to the point. Do not gather unnecessary data.
Loaded words	Loaded words are words with a particularly strong emotional impact. For example, fascist is a loaded word, disease is a loaded word, mad is a loaded word, class is a loaded word. Other words are loaded too and perhaps they are not so apparent, e.g. poor is a loaded word.
Unclear or vague concepts	Concepts that are not clearly defined are problematic. 'Fat' is such a concept. By what standard can a person be described as being fat? Even medical definitions of obesity are contested. Another such concept is 'old'. Again, what is old? By what definition or standard is something or someone old?
Insulting words	Some words and phrases are simply insulting or even degrading. They should not be used. It is important to remember that a word or phrase that is perfectly acceptable in one culture may be quite unacceptable in another.

(Continued)

Table 12.5   Issues in designing questions and items for questionnaires and scales (continued)

Humour	As a rule, it is best to avoid humour completely. That is of course, unless humour is the topic of your research. Perceptions of what is funny vary from person to person as well as from culture to culture. As this is the case, it is best to avoid it completely.
Slang and colloquialisms	Many of the words and phrases we use every day are in fact either colloquial expressions, peculiar to who we are and where we've come from, or they are slang. While such language can be charming and colourful, the standard for language in a written account of a research project is formal. So a simple formal language should be used throughout. Avoid slang and colloquial words and expressions.
Ethnocentrism	Ensure that your questionnaire and/or scale is not ethnocentric. Ensure that the words, concepts, language you use in your questionnaire and/or scale are not ethnocentric. Ethnocentrism means viewing the world, and in this context consequently organizing and designing data collection for your research, from your own ethnic or cultural perspective.
Sexist, racist, ageist or disablist language	Do not use classist, sexist, racist, ageist, or diablist words, concepts or language in your questionnaire or scale. Ensure that you are not, through the language you use, discriminatory towards or displaying prejudice against any class, race or gender; younger people or older people; or people with different levels of physical and/or intellectual abilities.
Abbreviations and jargon	Do not use abbreviations or jargon. Make each question/item as simple and clear as possible. Use words concepts and phrases that will be familiar to your respondents.
Respondent bias	Three types of respondent bias are detailed and explained in Chapter 11, 'Using Interviews and Focus Groups'. They are acquiescent bias, social desirability bias and prestige bias.
Talking down to respondents	Do not 'talk down' to respondents, by treating them disrespectfully or by patronizing them.
Double negatives	Double negatives in a question or sentence can be confusing. Avoid using the word 'not' in a question, e.g. 'is it not true that ...'. Avoid negative questions.
Ask simple, easy-to-answer questions	Ask questions that the respondent will be easily able to answer. Don't ask too much of respondents; keep to a minimum the effort they will have to make in order to respond to the questionnaire.
Give clear instructions	Ensure that you give clear instructions to respondents. Make sure that respondents have all the instructions, direction and guidance they need in order to be able to properly and fully respond.

appearance of the questionnaire will influence people in terms of whether or not they respond to it. Questionnaires are often sent to respondents by post, or by internal mail or by email. When this happens, obviously the researcher is not at hand to encourage the respondent to respond to the questionnaire and it must appeal to the respondent, aesthetically as well as in terms of its content, and in the rationale for the questionnaire and the research. Creating aesthetically pleasing questionnaires takes a considerable amount of skill and time, but it is important to invest the time in this creative endeavour. As stated and illustrated at the start of this chapter, software designed to facilitate the creation of questionnaires and scales is very helpful.

A PILOT STUDY

A pilot study, as defined in Chapter 10, is a test of the design of the research project, or a test of the data gathering instrument(s) designed for the research. In general, all data gathering methods should be tested, and in your reading for the literature review and for the research methods element of your research, you will notice that almost every data collection method you come across will be subjected to a pilot study. This is because the assumptions researchers make about how research subjects will respond to the questions and items presented to them in the data gathering methods designed for the research project are not always correct. Therefore, researchers test the data collection methods they design to find out how, in reality, participants will respond to their questions.

A pilot study, as explained, is carried out using a small number of respondents. These respondents should be similar to the actual respondents in the study, but they should not be respondents in the study. Usually, pilot studies are carried out with five to 15 respondents, depending on the size of the study. In piloting a questionnaire and/or scale, the researcher wants to establish how respondents will respond to the questionnaire or scale. Will they clearly understand each item and question in the questionnaire or scale, and will the responses they give be the responses required?

Any issues that the pilot study throws up can be dealt with before the real study takes place. For example, the pilot study might establish that the respondents do not understand some element(s) of the data collection instrument. It might also reveal that respondents interpret some element(s) of the data collection instrument in a way other than the way the researcher had anticipated. The pilot study will show if there is any resistance among the respondents to any aspect of the data collection instrument.

REAL WORLD RESEARCH

Set backs and surprises in data gathering

One time, I was conducting research on the experiences of pupils of primary school education. I very carefully designed my research project and my research questions. One aspect of the classroom experience I was anxious to explore was that of participation in class. I decided that I would ask the pupils, as a measure of participation in class, how many times

they raised their hands in class. I stood in front of a classroom full of 8-year-olds, and I asked them how many times they put their hands up in class. They looked at me blankly. They did not know what I was talking about. They had never heard the phrase 'put your hand up'. They were not familiar with the concept of putting your hand up in class to indicate that you had something you wished to contribute to the class. When I was at primary school, if you had something to say in the classroom you indicated this by putting up your hand. That was then. Things have changed, perhaps classroom culture has changed or perhaps the culture of the class I was standing in front of was different from the culture of the classes I attended when I was at primary school. Whatever the case, the important point is that things often do not work in the field in the way that you imagine that they will work. It is important to be prepared for this. It can be very disconcerting for a researcher when data gathering does not go the way they anticipated it would. It is important to be flexible.

Whatever happens in the field should be recorded in your research diary. It is important to record what happens in as much detail as is possible and reasonable. It is important to examine what is happening in the field, and to attempt to understand what is happening in the field. Reporting such experiences in the thesis or in the report of the research will add to the value of your research. Record what is happening when it happens. You can interpret what has happened later.

RESPONSE RATES

Response rate
A count of the number of valid responses received to a data gathering exercise.

Researchers are very fundamentally concerned with response rates. A **response rate** in a research project is a count of the number of valid responses received to a data gathering exercise, for example the number of properly completed and returned questionnaires and/or scales. The higher the response rate the better. If every member of the study population or sample responds then the study will have a very complete data set. In F2F data gathering exercises, it is not unusual to achieve 100 per cent response rates, in telephone interviews it is not unusual to achieve 80 per cent response rates. In postal surveys and in online surveys, response rates are often considerably lower than this. If the response rate is, for example, 75 per cent, then there is no data on the attitudes or experiences of 25 per cent of the study population or sample. If the response rate is 25 per cent, then there is no data on the attitudes or experiences of 75 per cent of the study population or sample. The problem is that it is possible that the non-respondents vary in some way from the respondents in terms of their attitudes and experiences of the phenomenon being studied. Non-responses change the nature of the study and the claims that can be made about the study. If everyone responds, you can apply your findings confidently to the population of the study. The fewer the number of valid responses, the less confident you can be.

Generalizability
The application of the findings of a research project beyond the specific context of the study.

One claim that researchers sometimes make about their research is that it is generalizable. **Generalizability** in research is the application of the findings of a research project beyond the specific context of the study. In claiming that the findings of their research are generalizable, what the researcher means is that the findings and conclusions drawn from his/her study can be applied more generally. So if the researcher has studied, for example, the attitudes of financial controllers in companies in the UK to risk taking, they may claim that the findings of their study can be applied to financial controllers generally, i.e. to financial controllers across, and perhaps even beyond, the UK. The rule is, the bigger the sample population of the study, the more you can generalize. This is the reason why only quantitative research is said to be generalizable, if sound design and sampling procedures have been used. Qualitative research is said to be transferable rather than generalizable (see Table 11.4, Chapter 11). Researchers are often very focused on getting good response rates in their research and are active in encouraging as many responses as possible in order to be able to claim that their research is generalizable. Judgements about the number of responses necessary in order for a research project to be deemed valid vary from study to study. They vary in terms of the research being undertaken, the population of the study, the phenomenon being studied and the requirements of the study.

There are a number of ways through which response rates can be improved. Respondents can be contacted and encouraged to respond. Incentives can be given in order to improve response rates, although the value of the research, when clearly explained, is often incentive enough. Clear and persuasive information sheets and informed consent forms (see Chapter 3) can improve response rates, as can the presentation, format and layout of questionnaires and scales. More people can be encouraged to respond by clarity, simplicity and brevity in the design of the data gathering instrument. With postal questionnaires, the use of a covering letter, sending stamped addressed envelopes and addressing the envelopes containing postal questionnaires to a specific person can all help improve response rates. It is generally not a good idea to attempt to engage people in data gathering exercises during public or religious holidays. Courtesy will improve response rates.

CASE STUDY

'The role of celebrity in endorsing poverty reduction through international aid' Samman, E. *et al.* (2009)

The research project outlined in this journal article was designed to explore the strategy of celebrity endorsement which, the authors state, is gaining momentum in attempts to develop public awareness around the issue of poverty. An understanding of public perceptions, the authors contend, is important for international organizations intending to use celebrity endorsement in order to further their causes.

In the journal article, Samman *et al.* (2009) report the results of a preliminary survey conducted among

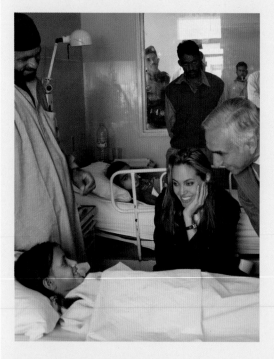

UNHCR Ambassador Angelina Jolie Tours Pakistan
© J Redden/UNHCR via Getty Images

100 members of the Irish public. The survey, as stated, was carried out 'to evaluate levels of awareness of celebrity involvement in international development work and the public's opinions about such involvement'.

The survey instrument, we are told, was semi-structured with some open-ended questions.

The focus of the survey, according to the article, was on respondents' ability to identify celebrities associated with international development work, and to elicit their opinions on those celebrities' perceived aims and knowledge of international development. The survey was designed to elicit data on whether or not such celebrity involvement influenced the respondents. The survey also sought the opinions of the respondents on the value of celebrity involvement generally.

The results, the author's state, suggest that respondents are generally able to distinguish between celebrities and their various causes. Most of the respondents, we are told, found celebrity involvement to be valuable in raising the profile of charities, though only a small number claimed to be personally influenced by such activity.

The respondents, according to the article, were fairly cynical as to the motives of most celebrities, whose involvement they felt served their own aims – namely publicity – first and foremost.

Most respondents, we are told, were more likely to be influenced by their perceptions of the character of the celebrity rather than their causes. 'They respected celebrities they felt were genuinely committed to the causes they espoused, but paradoxically, they felt such commitment was best demonstrated by the celebrity keeping a low profile and not actively seeking publicity.'

Long-term commitment to a given cause, the research found, was also highly regarded by the respondents to the survey.

Methodology

In the methodology section of the journal article, we are told that a brief survey was conducted among 100 respondents randomly selected from the Irish public.

❝ The survey was administered to 50 men and 50 women at commuter train stations (Dart) in central Dublin in January/February 2007. The respondents were asked to name up to three celebrities they believed to be associated with international development work, and to describe the celebrities' aims, their levels of knowledge, and whether they personally influenced the respondent. The survey also solicited the respondents' more general views regarding the value of celebrity involvement in international aid work and who were the beneficiaries of such involvement. Responses to the quantitative questions were entered into a database and analyzed using statistical software (SPSS).

The questionnaire – celebrity and international development work

1 Can you think of any celebrities associated with international aid work?
   (1)
   (2)
   (3)

2 What are they each trying to achieve?

Celebrity 1	Celebrity 2	Celebrity 3
(1)	(1)	(1)
(2)	(2)	(2)
(3)	(3)	(3)

3 How much do you think they know about international aid and development?

	Nothing (1)	A little (2)	A lot(3)
Celebrity 1			
Celebrity 2			
Celebrity 3			

4 Do they influence you? Yes/No. How?
   Celebrity 1
   Celebrity 2
   Celebrity 3

5 What is the value of them being involved in this sort of thing?

6 Who benefits from celebrities being involved in this work?

The research above was carried out using a survey methodology. As you can see from the questionnaire detailed above, the data collection instrument used in the research project is very simple, and it was used effectively. If you read the original article you will see the great use the researchers made of the data generated by this questionnaire. It is important to remember that the study was a preliminary study; this generally means that the researchers are planning a larger more robust study based on the experience and findings of this study.

The population of the research was a simple population. The population of the study was a population of Dublin commuters who were using the Dart service commuter train in Dublin city centre.

In the methodology section we are told that the sample of 100 participants was selected randomly. Can you critique that statement? Was the sample a random sample or a convenience sample? Can you provide a brief description of both sampling methods and briefly outline the differences between them?

The questionnaire contains examples of both open and closed questions. Can you identify the open and the closed questions?

Both quantitative and qualitative analyses of finding are presented in this journal article. Read these different approaches to data and document in your research diary the issues apparent to you and the ideas that come to you as you read.

Examine the article:

- for the manner in which the researchers constructed a theoretical framework for the project
- for the manner in which the project emerged from the theoretical framework
- for the way in which the quantitative data are presented in tables (in tabular form)
- for the way in which the findings of the research are knitted into the body of knowledge in this field.

References

Samman, E., McAuliffe, E. and MacLachlan, M. (2009) 'The role of celebrity in endorsing poverty reduction through international aid', *International* *Journal of Nonprofit and Voluntary Sector Marketing* 14(4): 137–148. © 2009 Wiley-Blackwell. Reproduced with permission via Rightslink.

CHAPTER REVIEW

This chapter focuses on the two data gathering methods, questionnaires and scales. The chapter highlights the importance of selecting appropriate data gathering methods for the research project. The appropriate data gathering methods for the research project are the data gathering methods that will provide the data required for the research. The different ways of designing and administering questionnaires and scales are explored and explained in the chapter. As well as questionnaires and scales, projective techniques of considered and explained and the use of projective techniques as data gathering methods is explored. The research methodology in focus in the chapter is attitude research. The issues of validity and reliability in quantitative research are explored and explained. The chapter examines the politics and the practicalities of asking a question. Research is essentially about asking questions and seeking answers to them. As we have seen in this chapter, asking can be a political act. Who gets the privilege of asking the question(s) in other words whose voice questions, and who gets to respond to questions, whose voice answers. The political problem is who gets to speak and who is silenced through the research process. As well as being a political issue, an issue of power, this is also an ethical issue. The best way to begin reflecting on questions to ask in the field work of the research project, as detailed in this chapter, is with a focus on the conceptual framework for the research project. The conceptual framework, as we know, is contained in the research question or the research statement. The conceptual framework for the research project contains all of the key concepts of the research project and it defines the focus of the research project. As this is the case, the questions asked in the field work for any research project will derive from the conceptual framework. They will also derive from the aim and objectives of the research. We have seen in this textbook how the theoretical framework for the research project is directed by the conceptual framework. As this is the case, the literature review carried out for the research project, which is directed by the conceptual framework, also provides issues for questions to be asked and explored in the field work for the research project.

Now update your interactive research diary with your notes and findings at www.cengage.co.uk/quinlan. Complete the activities provided to reinforce your understanding of this chapter.

END OF CHAPTER QUESTIONS

1 Why are questionnaires particularly useful with large, geographical spread populations?

2 List and explain the four key issues in designing a questionnaire.

3 Explain what a Likert scale is and design a ten-item Likert scale to measure attitudes to a new product.

4 Explain what a rating scale is and design a ten-item rating scale for a training programme.

5 What is a semantic differential scale? Give an example.

6 What is meant by the term 'sentence completion exercise'? Give an example.

7 Explain what vignettes are and briefly outline a small research project to be carried out using vignettes.

8 Explain the issues of validity and reliability in relation to quantitative research.

9 List and explain ten key issues in question design.

10 What is meant by the term response rate?

REFERENCES

Ajzen, I. and Fishbein, M. (1980) *Understanding Attitudes and Predicting Social Behaviour*, Englewood Cliffs, NJ: Prentice Hall.

BBC News, 'internet access is "a fundamental right"', **http://news.bbc.co.uk/2/hi/8548190.stm** Accessed 03.06.2010.

Eagly, A.H. and Chaiken, S. (1993) *The Psychology of Attitudes*, Forth Worth, TX: Harcourt Brace and Company.

Keeble-Ramsay, D. and Armitage, A. (2010) 'Total quality management meets human resource management: Perceptions of the shift towards high performance working', *Total Quality Management Journal* 22(1): 5–25.

QuestionPro: Online Research Made Easy, **www.questionpro.com/survey-questions.html** Accessed 03.06.2010.

Samman, E., McAuliffe, E. and MacLachlan, M. (2009) 'The role of celebrity in endorsing poverty reduction through international aid', *International Journal of Nonprofit and Voluntary Sector Marketing* 14(4): 137–148.

Sinkovics, R.R. and Penz, E. (2009) 'Social distance between residents and international tourists – Implications for international business', *International Business Review* 18(5): 457–469.

Snap Surveys Ltd, **www.snapsurveys.com**

Survey Monkey, **www.surveymonkey.com**

Survey Resources Network (SRN), **http://surveynet.ac.uk/srn/introduction.asp**

Surveyspro, **www.esurveyspro.com**

Valentine, S., Fleischman, G.M., Sprague, R. and Godkin, L. (2010) 'Exploring the ethicality of firing employees who blog', *Human Resource Management* 49(1): 87–108.

What is an Employee Attitude Survey?, **http://www.hr-survey.com/EmployeeAttitude.htm**

RECOMMENDED READING

Bell, J. (2000) Doing Your Research Project, Ch. 8, 'Designing and Administering Questionnaires', Maidenhead: Open University Press.

Collis, J. and Hussey, R. (2009) *Business Research: A Practical Guide for Undergraduate and Postgraduate Students*, Houndsmill: Palgrave Macmillan.

Creswell, J. (2003) *Research Design: Qualitative, Quantitative and Mixed Methods Approaches*, Ch. 9, 'Quantitative Methods', Thousand Oaks, CA: Sage.

Deacon, D., Pickering, M., Golding, P. and Murdock, G. (1999) *Researching Communications: A Practical Guide to Methods in Media and Cultural*

Analysis, Ch. 4, 'Asking Questions', Oxford: Oxford University Press.

Denscombe, M. (2003) *The Good Research Guide: For Small-scale Social Research Projects'* (2nd edn), Ch. 9, 'Questionnaires', Maidenhead: Open University Press.

de Vaus, D., (Ed), (2002) *'Surveys in Social Research',* 5th Ed., Routledge: London.

Easterby-Smith, M., Thorpe, R. and Jackson, P.R. (2008) *Management Research* (3rd edn), Ch. 9, 'Creating Quantitative Data', London: Sage.

Gill, J. and Johnson, P. (2006) *Research Methods for Managers*, Ch. 6, 'Survey Research Design', London: Sage.

Jankowicz, A.D. (2005) *Business Research Projects,* London: Cengage.

Kent, R. (2007) *Marketing Research, Approaches, Methods and Applications in Europe*, Ch. 6, 'Constructing Quantitative Data: Developing the Instruments of Data Capture' and Ch. 7, 'Constructing Quantitative Data: Selecting Methods', London: Cengage.

Meckel, M., Walters, D. and Baugh, P. (2005) 'Mixed-mode surveys using mail and web questionnaires', *Electronic Journal of Business Research Methods* 3(1): July 69–80.

Neuman, W.L. (2000) *Social Research Methods: Quantitative and Qualitative Approaches*, Ch. 10, 'Survey Research', Boston, CA: Allyn & Bacon.

Oppenheim, A.N. (1992) *Questionnaire Design, Interviewing and Attitude Measurement*, London: Pinter.

Robson, C. (2002) *Real World Research*, Ch. 8, 'Surveys and Questionnaires' and Ch. 10, 'Tests and Scales', Oxford: Blackwell.

Zikmund, W.G. (2003), *Business Research Methods,* Mason, OH: Cengage South-Western.

51,30%

13,40%   13,40%   51,3

MANAGING DATA AND INTRODUCING DATA ANALYSIS

The aim of this chapter is to introduce the student to data sets, and to the management and analysis of data. The chapter introduces the student to the different ways of analysing quantitative and qualitative data, and to the ways in which to begin to process of data analysis and the different ways of organising data analysis.

INTRODUCTION

In carrying out a research project, the researcher is attempting to explore or establish some phenomenon by gathering data (evidence) on that phenomenon. There are essentially two different kinds of data, quantitative and qualitative data. As we know, quantitative data are numerical data; data in the form of numbers or data that can readily be transformed into numerical form, while qualitative data are non-numerical data. A data set (or dataset) is the complete collection of data gathered for the research project.

As there are two different orders of data, quantitative data and qualitative data, there are two different approaches to data analysis. Quantitative data analysis is the analysis of numerical data using statistical methods. The computer software package **SPSS**, Statistical Package for the Social Sciences, is useful in the analysis of quantitative data. Qualitative data analysis does not draw on statistics or statistical methods; this is because qualitative data are non-numerical data. Qualitative data can be analyzed in a number of different ways:

SPSS
Statistical Package for the Social Sciences. A computer software package designed for the analysis of quantitative data.

- it can be analyzed in terms of content, textually, discursively, thematically, and/or semiotically

- it can be analyzed systematically and categorically as in a grounded theory approach to data analysis (Strauss and Corbin, 1990, 1998)

- it can be analyzed in terms of significant statements and meaning units, as in for example Moustakas' (1994) approach to analysing phenomenological data.

Computer Assisted Qualitative Data Analysis (CAQDAS)
Computer software designed to support qualitative data analysis.

Computer assisted qualitative data analysis software (**Computer Assisted Qualitative Data Analysis (CAQDAS)**) is a relatively recent development. Among the software packages available for qualitative data analysis are Atlas ti, NVivo and NUDIST.

In this chapter, as well as beginning to explore data analysis, we will learn a little about how to manage data when they have been gathered, or **data management**. Gathering the right data for the research project in a professional and scholarly manner takes considerable time and effort. It is also important that the data gathered be properly managed when it has been gathered. Some of the aspects of proper data management are fairly evident. For example, it is important not to lose data or to allow it to be stolen. One of the guarantees researchers are often obliged to make in applications for ethical approval for a research project is for the safe and secure management of data. In such applications, it is not enough for researchers to provide such guarantees; they must also clearly and in detail explain how they will accomplish this.

Data management
The correct, safe and secure management of data while data is being gathered, stored and analyzed.

Figure 13.1 details the research process. As can be seen, data analysis happens towards the end of the research process. Once the data have been analyzed, all that remains in the research process is to draw conclusions from the research and to finally write up and present the thesis or the written account of the research.

The text box below details the establishment of a new research institute, the Institute for New Economic Thought. The text box refers to an article in *The Times*, by Anatole Kaletsy (28.10.2009) which claimed that 'old' economics has died a death, and its demise is to be celebrated; as a consequence of its passing, a new economics has now to take its place. Hope for this new economics is supported by the establishment of the Institute for New Economic Thought. This new Institute,

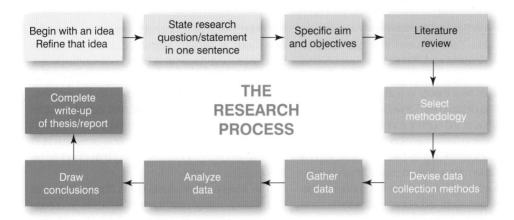

Figure 13.1   The research process

which is funded initially by George Soros and supported by a great number of distinguished academic economists, has been developed to provide new research and new theory in economics, and hopefully, given the recent global economic crisis, better and more accurate or more useful research and theory in economics.

THE VALUE OF GOOD RESEARCH

Three cheers for the death of old economics

'The Need for New Thinking, New Research and New Theory in Economics', Kaletsy A., *The Times*, 28.10.2009

It seems that we are moving towards a new way of thinking about economics. In an interesting article in *The Times*, Anatole Kaletsky states that one of the few benign consequences of the recent financial crisis was the exposure of modern economics as an emperor with no clothes. He wrote that many people, among them Nobel laureate economists, believed that economics had to be urgently re-invented. He believes that there is possibility for new thinking in economics with the help of the Institute for New Economic Thought (INET). INET (**http://ineteconomics.org/**) was founded in 2009 with a $50 million pledge from billionaire US

George Soros, Chairman of Soros Fund Management © Jeremy Sutton-Hibbert/Alamy

investor, George Soros. The non-profit organization is based in New York City and it is dedicated to developing new ideas and insights into economics and economic theory.

The need for new theory in economics is driven, according to the detail on INET's website, by a recognition of the failings of the current economic system and our ways of thinking about the recent global economic crisis. The mission of INET is 'to create an environment nourished by open discourse and critical thinking where the next generation of scholars has the support to go beyond our prevailing economic paradigms and advance the culture of change'.

A report by Alan Purkiss in *Bloomberg News* (2010), detailed that Soros is also helping to establish an economics institute at Oxford University. This initiative, according to Purkiss, is part of a campaign by Soros to push economic theory away from thinking that markets should be left to themselves. Such thinking Soros believes, led to the recent global financial crisis. Purkiss quotes Robert Johnson, a former managing director at Soros Fund Management LLC who is now in charge of INET, as saying that in the future a broader approach to economics is needed, an approach that will take into account the works of historians, sociologists, psychologists and political theorists, among other disciplines, when producing economic theory.

The hope for INET, according to Kaletsky, is that it might encourage original thinking in a profession where creativity has been stymied by intellectual and academic dogmas. In particular he is critical of economic models and he writes of the failure of economic models. He said that when policymakers turned to academic economists for guidance in the recent global financial crisis, they were essentially told that the economic models the academics were working with could not cope with the reality of the global crisis.

The three key problems with economic theory as highlighted by Kaletsky were the idea known as 'rational expectations', which held that capitalist economies with competitive labour markets do not need stabilizing by governments; the idea of 'efficient markets' which holds, as Kaletsky explains, that competitive finance always allocates resources in the most efficient way, reflecting all the best available information and forecasts about the future. The third idea was that economics which had for a long time been a largely descriptive study of human behaviour, had become a branch of mathematics. The application of mathematics and mathematical formulae to economics ensured, Kaletsky explains, that only the simplest and clearest conceptualizations of human behaviour could be used in mathematical models, as these are the only ones that fit in the mathematical models. Anything that didn't fit, he tells us, was ignored.

The worst political effects of the dogma of rational and efficient markets and the mathematical reductionism of economic modelling, as explained by Kaletsky, was that theoretical economics seemed to legitimize the most unjust effects and impacts of the markets. Huge levels of income inequality, for example, were readily explained and justified. They also became de-politicized. They were simply one result of the efficient workings of rational markets.

The inaugural conference of INET was held in King's College, Cambridge in April, 2010. Among the speakers at the conference were Dominique Strauss-Kahn, Managing Director of the International Monetary Fund (IMF), Adair Lord Turner, Chairman of the Financial Services Authority, and Joseph Stiglitz, Professor at Columbia University and Nobel laureate, as well as George Soros and Anatole Kaletsky. George Soros in his address concluded that it is not enough to study history, we must also learn the lessons of it. He said that we need to abandon rational expectations and the Efficient Market Hypothesis and build our theory of financial markets on the recognition that imperfect understanding, i.e. fallibility, is the human condition. All of the papers presented at the conference are available to view and read on the website, **http://ineteconomics.org/ initiatives/conferences/kings-college**.

In the news article in *The Times*, Kaletsky concluded that if the next generation of academic economists aspire to succeed Smith, Keynes and Hayek, rather than, as he says, ineffectually apeing Euclid, Newton and Einstein, then the venture that is INET will have been worthwhile.

References

Institute for New Economic Thinking (INET), **http:// ineteconomics.org** Accessed 03.06.2010.

Institute for New Economic Thinking, Conference Proceedings, April 2010, **http://ineteconomics. org/initiatives/conferences/kings-college/proceedings** Accessed 03.06.2010.

Kaletsky, A. (2009) 'Three cheers for the death of old economics: The orthodox mathematical model took no account of reality. The new George Soros Institute should bring back some sanity', *The Times*, 28 October.

Purkiss, A. (2010) 'Soros plans economics institute at Oxford University, *Times* says', 5 April, **http://**

www.bloomberg.com/apps/news? pid=20601102&sid=aKgAaKQObPhM Accessed 03.06.2010.

Soros, G. (2010) 'Anatomy of crisis – the living history of the last 30 years: Economic theory, politics and policy', presented at the INET Conference, King's College, April 8–11, 2010, **http:// ineteconomics.org/sites/inet.civicactions.net/files/ INET%20C%40K%20Paper%20Session%201% 20-%20Soros.pdf** Accessed 03.06.2010.

The article above considers the way in which orthodox economic theory failed the world, by not predicting the global economic downturn. The article is quite critical of experimental approaches to social research; note the references to Euclid, Newton and Einstein. Experimental design is the research methodology in focus in the next chapter, Chapter 14, 'Analysing Quantitative Data'. The article above welcomes the new institute, the INET, with the hope that it will provide new theories and more useful theories in economics.

One of the major roles of research is the generation of theory. The theory that is generated in research emerges from the data gathered for the research project, which comes from the questions asked in the data gathering process. These questions are generated by the researcher from their reading of the literature in the field, and from their very well conceptualized research statement or question that supports the entire research project. So the data gathered emerge from theory, and in turn the data gathered make a contribution to theory. And this, in a sense, is the full circle of the research project, and the research process (see Figure 13.1). As explained throughout this textbook, the four frameworks approach is a useful guide for the researcher to the research process.

Within the four frameworks approach to the research project, the researcher conceptualizes the research statement or question for the research project. Each of the important words and phrases in the research statement or question is a key concept in the research project. The key concepts in the conceptual framework guide the researcher in terms of the areas of literature they need to explore and examine for

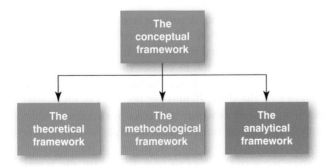

Figure 13.2   The four frameworks

the literature review. The key concepts can be used by the researcher to develop a framework of subheadings and sections in the literature review (see Chapter 6 'Reviewing the Literature'). If the researcher does use the key concepts in this way this will ensure that the literature review is properly focused on the research statement/question, and on the aim of the research.

The methodological framework for the research project is the detailed account that the researcher writes of the way in which the research was carried out. Each research project has its own unique methodology (see Chapter 7 'Understanding Research Methodology and Design'). In developing the research methodology for the research project, the researcher draws on their knowledge, including their reading of research methodology textbooks and methodologies used in other, published, research projects. Using all of these sources and supports, the researcher creates the unique methodological framework for their own research project.

The final framework in the four frameworks approach is the **analytical framework**. The researcher presents the analytical framework for the research project in the chapter on data analysis. This contains a full account of the analysis carried out on the data, and a complete presentation of the findings that emerge from that data analysis. The work of data analysis is a major project, which is undertaken at your desk. What goes into the data analysis chapter is a synopsis of all this analysis. There would simply be too much material to present it all in the data analysis chapter. In this synopsis, the researcher presents the key findings, the key data, and the key interpretations made in relation to the data. This is how the four frameworks approach to the research project provides the researcher with a guide throughout the research process.

The Four Frameworks
Conceptual Framework
Theoretical Framework
Methodological Framework
Analytical Framework

Analytical framework
Emerges from the conceptual framework, the theoretical framework and the methodological framework. Contained in the data analysis chapter in the thesis.

DATA AND DATA MANAGEMENT

Data management is an important issue. Data are the evidence that the researcher gathers for the research project and data management is about the proper management and the protection of data. There are many safety and security concerns in relation to data when they are being gathered, stored and analyzed.

If your data are electronically or digitally stored, you should make copies of the files. You need to back them up so that should anything happen to the originals, you have copies. It is of course important to ensure that the data and any copies of the data are secured.

Data can be lost or stolen. This can happen, for example, if you decide to move the data from your home to the university. Your car could be stolen, or the bag in which you are carrying the data could be lost or stolen. You might leave the bag behind on the bus, the train or taxi. A sudden strong gust of wind might blow away some of your questionnaires. As well as being careful not to lose data, it is important to ensure that data are not damaged in any way. If, for example, a questionnaire was torn or stained, the tear or stain might render the questionnaire illegible. As these examples demonstrate, moving data from one location to another creates risks to the security and integrity of the data. If moving the data is unavoidable, it is wise to make a plan which anticipates any potential risks or dangers posed to the data. Such a plan may simply involve some reflection on the risks involved in moving your data.

Every researcher should have a plan in place for the organization, safety and security, and management of the data to be gathered for the research project. This can be quite a simple plan, detailing how the data are to be recorded, where and how the data are to be stored, what precautions will be taken if the data are to be moved, and what plan is in place for the back-up of the data. This plan can usefully be detailed in a paragraph in the research methodology chapter of the thesis. Ideally, you should make a note of your reflections in your research diary. If you do this, you can use these notes to help you write the paragraph in your research methodology chapter to evidence the level of reflection that you engaged in regarding the safety and security of your data. A record should be kept of all of the data gathered for the project, and the research diary is a useful place to do this.

Each completed and returned questionnaire should be numbered and properly stored. Similarly, each interview or focus group should be numbered, stored electronically or digitally, and transcribed (typed up). The transcripts should be numbered and properly stored. For confidentiality purposes, the identities of the participants in the study should be concealed, if concealment is necessary. It will be necessary if the participants have been given a guarantee by the researcher that their participation in the research will remain anonymous. If this is the case, each of the questionnaires and interviews should have the real identity of the participant removed from the record and replaced with a coded identity for the participant. The researcher keeps a list of all of the real names of the participants and their code names and only the researcher and the supervisor of the research should have access to this list.

Every research project has its own unique ethical issues and concerns, in relation to data management as well as in relation to every other aspect of the research process. It is important to reflect on the uniqueness of your own research project and to consider the unique ethical issues in the management of your data.

The extract from the journal article detailed below considers the issue of research integrity within the context of a proposal for international standards for research integrity. As you read through the synopsis below, think about the conduct and management of your own research project, and in particular, think about your management of the data you have gathered for your research project. When you have read the synopsis of the article below, source the original article and read it through. It contains a lot of information on the issue of research integrity and some interesting examples of ethical issues in relation to the integrity of research.

REAL WORLD RESEARCH

How theory influences research

'International Standards for Research Integrity: An Idea Whose Time Has Come?' Resnik, D.B. (2009)

The author, Resnik, states that research integrity encompasses a wide range of topics relating to the ethical conduct of research. Among those topics he includes data management and data analysis.

International standards for the ethical conduct of research with human participants have, he writes, been in place since the adoption of the Nuremberg Code after the end of World War II; the Nuremberg Code was used in the Nuremberg trials of Nazi doctors and scientists accused of war crimes committed against prisoners in concentration camps who were used in human experiments.

In 2007, the Office of Research Integrity (ORI) and the European Science Foundation (ESF) held the first global forum on research integrity. The aim of the forum was to consider ways of harmonizing research misconduct policies and fostering ethical research. One of the reasons put forward in support of clear international integrity standards is that such standards can encourage the development of local standards. Resnik explains that countries that lack local standards for the conduct of research can use international standards as a model of the development of their own rules and policies, as some countries have used the Helsinki Declaration, adopted in 1964 by the World Medical Association and revised many times since, as a guide to developing their own policies.

Different countries, we are told, have different definitions of research misconduct. The US federal government, for example, defines research misconduct as fabrication, falsification or plagiarism (FFP). Norway defines research misconduct as FFP as well as other serious breaches of good scientific practice. Finland differentiates between fraud, which is defined as FFP, and research misconduct, which is defined as gross negligence and irresponsibility in the conduct of research.

There is a focus in the article on the issue of conflict of interest (COI). A conflict of interest can arise in research where a researcher has a vested interest in the findings of their research. This can arise when a researcher will materially benefit, for example through direct payment, through other funding such as grants and bursaries, or through career advancement. A conflict of interest issue can raise serious questions about a research project, and about the gathering, the management and the analysis of data in that research project and the findings and conclusions drawn from the research.

The final issue the author discusses is the issue of social responsibility, i.e. promoting good consequences for society and avoiding harmful ones. The author states that some of the most important ethical questions in scientific research have to do with social responsibility and he identifies several professional organizations with codes of ethics that encompass the social responsibilities of researchers.

Resnik believes that the development of international standards of research integrity is an idea whose time has come. In fact, he concludes that such standards are long overdue.

References

Resnik, D.B. (2009) 'International standards for research integrity: An idea whose time has come', *Accountability in Research* 16(4): 218–228.

The issue of plagiarism is dealt with in detail in Chapter 2 'Developing Research Skills' and ethics in research, including the codes of ethics of different professional bodies, is explored in detail in Chapter 3 'Understanding Research Ethics'. The proper management of data is clearly an ethical issue and the way in which data are managed is a reflection of the integrity of the researcher.

AN INTRODUCTION TO DATA ANALYSIS

In social research, data are either quantitative or qualitative. Some research projects generate quantitative data, some generate qualitative data, and some generate a mixture of both.

Quantitative data are numeric; they are data in the form of numbers or data that can readily be coded numerically. For example, you might ask research participants how old they are. In response they will tell you, for example, that they are 21 years old. The data you gather in response to this question are numeric and therefore they are quantitative data.

If you asked the same research participants to tell you how they celebrated their twenty-first birthdays, you would get in response very many different accounts of twenty-first birthday celebrations. These responses are qualitative and the data you gather in response to such a question are qualitative. It is possible, however, that there might be some quantitative element to these responses. For example, a respondent might say, 'I invited 30 friends to a party to celebrate my twenty-first birthday'. In this response we have a number, 30. Therefore, there is a quantitative element to the response. Whether or not that quantitative element is in anyway useful or meaningful in the research depends on what it is the researcher is trying to explore or establish in the research project. One number does not constitute data, it is just a detail. If very many or all of the respondents said that they had twenty-first birthday parties to which they invited a specific, stated, number of guests/friends, then the researcher has a range of data with which to work. This is more useful, and such a range of numbers does constitute data, rather than just detail. Whether or not these data are useful in the research project, again, depends on the focus of the research project. The qualitative responses of participants to such a question will be rich and complex and very individual. The stories they tell you, the researcher, in response to that question of how they celebrated their twenty-first birthdays, will be rich and personal and full of meaning for each of them. The responsibility of the researcher is to gather the responses properly, to manage them properly, keeping them safe and secure, and to adequately and expertly analyze them for the research project, and to report them thoroughly in the findings of the research.

Sometimes researchers gather both quantitative and qualitative data for their research project; this is known as a mixed-methods research project, or a mixed-methods approach to the research. As discussed earlier, there are many decisions to be made by the researcher in determining what data are required for the research project, where that data is or might be, and how best to gather it. As explained in previous chapters, the researcher designs the data collection methods for the research project. They are designed to suit the data requirements of the project, the data sources and/or the participants in the research project.

When you design the data gathering methods for the research project, you develop at the same time a sense of how the data will be analyzed. In your research diary you begin to develop a plan for data analysis, whether the data to be gathered are quantitative, qualitative or mixed. Your approach to data analysis will be determined by the kind of data you have to analyze. Sample size, as well as the kind of data gathered, has implications for the ways in which data can be analyzed. Large quantities of data are best analyzed using a computer, and, as explained above, there are different software packages specifically designed for the analysis of both quantitative and qualitative data. These software packages will be considered in detail in the following paragraphs and in the following two chapters, Chapter 14, 'Analysing Quantitative Data' and Chapter 15, 'Analysing Qualitative Data'.

Analysing quantitative data

Simple and small quantitative data sets can be analyzed by simply counting the numbers and calculating simple statistics in relation to them. Numbers can easily be counted, and the summaries of counted numbers can be meaningful. For example, let us consider again our small study of smokers, detailed in Chapter 4 'Understanding Research Philosophy'. Let us imagine that in response to this research we obtained the following data (see Table 13.1).

From this simple study we have gathered a lot of quantitative data and have calculated the **summarizing statistics** detailed in Table 13.1. The exercise was very simple, yet we have an impressive list of quantitative data. In calculating this data, we

Summarizing statistics Summarizing statistics are examples of descriptive statistics. Descriptive statistics are statistics that are used to describe data.

Table 13.1   Data gathered in response to cigarette smokers study
There are 30 students in the class in total
Of the 30 students, 10 are smokers
There are 16 female and 14 male students in the class
Of the 16 female students, 6 are smokers
Of the 14 male students, 4 are smokers
Of the 6 female smokers, 1 said that she had been smoking for 5 years, 2 said that they had been smoking for 4 years and 3 said that they had been smoking for 3 years
Of the 4 male smokers, 1 said that he had been smoking for 5 years, 1 said that he had been smoking for 3 years and 2 said that they had been smoking for 2 years

could simply use a pen and paper exercise. If we had more data, we might need to use a calculator. We might even use a spreadsheet. Even with the use of a calculator or a spreadsheet, it is still a very simple exercise, and yet it is a very useful one in terms of generating summarizing statistics.

If we had a lot of quantitative data, we might need to use a dedicated software package. The software package designed specifically for the analysis of quantitative data is called SPSS. SPSS is a very powerful tool in quantitative data analysis and is particularly useful in analysing larger data sets. It would, in fact, be very difficult to analyze a very large set of quantitative data without SPSS. SPSS works very well in the analysis of survey data. Using SPSS, the researcher first codes each response to each question in each questionnaire. Each response is coded as a number. The numeric code (the number) is then loaded (or inputted), into SPSS. When the participant in the research has completed and returned the questionnaire, the researcher codes the data in the questionnaire, and then loads the data, or inputs the data, from the question-naire into SPSS. When all of the completed questionnaires have been loaded or inputted, the researcher then uses the package to analyze the data.

The questionnaire below is the sample questionnaire detailed in Chapter 12 'Using Questionnaires and Scales', with one added question, the question on gender. You can see the coding of the responses, on the right-hand side of the sample questionnaire.

Sample questionnaire   Code

Q1. What is your age? Please state   22yrs   22

Q2. What is your level of formal education? Please circle   1st   2nd   ③rd   3

Q3. What is your annual income? Please tick

      Less than £10 000   ☐

      More than £10 000, less than £20 000   ☐√ 2

      More than £20 000, less than £30 000   ☐

      More than £30 000, less than £40 000   ☐

Q4. Please indicate your gender   Female ☐   Male ☐√ 2

Coding assigned by the researcher is always assigned using a simple logic. In response to question three, the respondent selected the second option, so in coding this response the researcher assigned the number 2 as the code to signify this response. Codes and coding and the analysis of quantitative data are explored in detail in Chapter 14, 'Analysing Quantitative Data'.

In coding each response as a number, the researcher assigns a numeric label, called a value label, to each value. For example, in the sample questionnaire, the fourth question relates to gender. The respondents to the questionnaire are asked to indicate in their response to the question whether they are male or female. The respondent ticks the appropriate box to respond to the question. The researcher in preparing these data for analysis, codes the response.

Sometimes, rather than coding responses in the questionnaire, researchers develop separate **coding keys** to go with the questionnaire. The coding key in Table 13.2 relates to the sample questionnaire above. The coding key becomes the researcher's key (or guide) to the data in SPSS.

Each question in the sample questionnaire relates to one variable. Age, gender, level of education and level of income are all variables. The third column in the coding key above is used to describe the variable. Variables have more than one value. Gender, for example has two values, female and male. Level of education, as coded in this questionnaire and coding key, has three values, 1st, 2nd and 3rd. Level of income, as coded in this questionnaire and coding key, has four values. The fourth column in the coding key is used to detail the labels (or codes) assigned to each value in each variable. When each value in each variable in the questionnaire has been labelled or coded, the questionnaire can be loaded, or inputted, into SPSS. The analysis of quantitative data using SPSS is considered in more detail in the following chapter, Chapter 14 'Analysing Quantitative Data'.

Coding keys
A guide to all of the codes used in coding data to input the data into a computer software program.

Table 13.2	Coding key: Sample questionnaire		
Question number	**Variable name**	**Variable description**	**Value labels**
Q1	Age	Age	Record number
Q2	Level of education	1st level	1
		2nd level	2
		3rd level	3
Q3	Level of income	‹ than £10 000	1
		› £10 000 ‹ £20 000	2
		› £20 000 ‹ £30 000	3
		› £30 000 ‹ £40 000	4
		(the four levels of income are aggregate measures)	
Q4	Gender	Female	1
		Male	2

When a researcher uses a pen and paper to analyze data and to calculate statistics, there can be issues with regard to data management. The researcher may simply make a mistake in their calculations, which may lead to a false reading, and a false reporting, of the data. Mistakes can also happen when the researcher uses a calculator. However, using a calculator may improve the accuracy of the calculations and make the calculations less laborious, which may mean that checking and re-checking the accuracy of the calculations may be relatively simple. This may help data management as well as data analysis.

When a researcher uses a computerized software package to aid data analysis, the computer, following the instructions of the researcher, conducts the analysis. This is known as computer assisted data analysis (CADA). CADA is a substantial aid in the analysis of large data sets. The computer has the capacity to store the analysis and the results of analysis, and with large data sets this is particularly invaluable. The computer stores data safely and securely, assuming that the computer itself is safe and secure. A computerized software package facilitates the cleaning of data. In checking accuracy in data and accuracy in the way in which data were loaded, researchers engage in cleaning data. Data are 'cleaned' in the software package to ensure that they are accurate.

REAL WORLD RESEARCH

Ensuring proper management and analysis of data

Miscalculating statistics, at the most basic level, simply means calculating the maths incorrectly. Such mistakes evidence very poor work, and they lead to misrepresentations of data. Through the publication of research, misrepresentations of data become more than misrepresentations of data, they become misrepresentations of populations.

If a researcher is not competent enough to analyze their data correctly, he/she may mismanage data and may, as a result, misrepresent their data and their research population.

Imagine, for example, that you are employed as a researcher in your university. Let us say, for instance, that the management of the university engages you to carry out research on overall levels of student satisfaction with the sports and leisure facilities in the university.

You decide to conduct a survey. You design a questionnaire to measure levels of satisfaction among the student body. You decide to study a sample of one-third of the students registered in the university; this is 3000 students. This is quite a big, seemingly robust, study. Your questionnaires are completed and returned. Because there is a great deal of interest among the students on campus in relation to the sports and leisure facilities in the university, you get a 60 per cent response rate. You code the responses and you load the data into SPSS.

However, in loading the data, you made a simple mistake and you didn't take the time to check the data and clean the data. As a result of this simple mistake, your correct reading of the incorrectly loaded data leads you to the conclusion that overall student satisfaction levels with the sports and leisure facilities are high. In fact, overall student satisfaction levels are low in relation to the sports and leisure facilities in the university.

The simple mistake which occurred in loading the data into SPSS has rendered the research useless. Actually, the research is worse than useless. It is damaging. It is likely that policy in the university around the provision of sports and leisure facilities for students will be based for some years to come on this research. But the research is flawed. It misrepresents the situation.

This is a simple example of the way in which mismanaged research can impact negatively on research populations.

Qualitative data

As stated above, qualitative data are non-numeric data. As such, qualitative data can come in almost any form. It can take the form of stated or articulated feelings, beliefs, opinions, perspectives. Qualitative data can be in the form of narratives or stories, images, drawings, maps, cartoons, paintings or photographs. As with quantitative data, there are a number of different ways in which qualitative data can be analyzed.

One simple approach to qualitative data analysis is to read through all of the data and while reading, make a list of all of the themes that occur in the data. The themes would be the key ideas or the key issues in the data that strike the researcher. The researcher continues reading the transcripts and recording themes until no new themes emerge. Then the researcher takes the complete list of themes and explores them with a view to collapsing themes together. In other words, the researcher tries to condense the list of themes by fitting themes together that seem to logically fit together. In this way, the list of themes becomes shorter and more manageable. When the researcher collapses themes together, it is sometimes necessary to conceptualize a new theme which will encompass all the themes collapsed together. This is a process of abstraction and, through it, the researcher takes a step away from the raw data, and a step towards an abstract or abstracted understanding of the data. Through a continuing and deepening process of abstraction, the researcher comes closer to the meaning of the data in relation to the overall aim of the research. As the researcher continues to collapse themes together, s/he move to deeper levels of abstraction in relation to the data, moving further and further away from the raw data. The researcher can colour-code the themes, perhaps assigning the colour red to the first theme, the colour yellow to the second theme, the colour green to the third theme, and so on. The researcher then reads through the transcripts assigning the colours to the parts of the data that represent each of the themes. In this way the researcher can see at a glance each of the themes as they are represented in the data. The researcher then decides how to tell the story of the data, based on this thematic analysis, in the written account of the analysis.

The decisions the researcher makes in relation to the story to be told are based on the overall aim of the research, the research statement or question, and the objectives of the research project. The researcher must maintain an appropriate focus while telling the story, the narrative, of the analyzed data, and so bring the research project full circle. At the start of the research project, the researcher asked a question, the research question. Now, when coming to the end of the research project, the researcher must answer that question. At the start of the research project, the researcher outlined a specific aim and a number of objectives. Now, in the narrative of the data analysis chapter, the researcher must begin to complete the accomplishment of that aim and those objectives. By maintaining a focus on the research question or statement and on the research aim and objectives, the researcher is not closed to any new important issue or aspect of the phenomenon under investigation to emerge from the data and the analysis of the data. Any such new, unanticipated finding or insight must be accommodated within the research project, although if the new finding is very substantial, it may require a shift in the focus of the project. If you find yourself in this position, you would need to seek direction from your research supervisor and/or your lecturer in research methodologies. Otherwise, it may be possible to accommodate this new insight by recommending further research.

The above is a very simple, yet valid and useful, approach to qualitative data analysis. This simple approach works well with small data sets. Such an approach will also work with large data sets. For the most efficient management of a large qualitative data set, a computerized qualitative data analysis software package, CAQDAS, is invaluable.

Computerized data analysis software packages are particularly helpful with managing data and data analysis. The software package stores the data and the analysis of the data so there is no need for large piles of printed data or colour-coded data. There is no need to move large quantities of paper about the desk or floor in order to carry out the analysis. The analysis can be done entirely on the computer, and stored and backed up there, too. As well as eliminating the hard (physical) work of dealing with data analysis on paper, using colour coding or some other kind of coding system, a computerized approach to data analysis is simpler and cleaner. As well as storing and analysing the data, the computer stores a memory of the analysis conducted on the data. When the data analysis process is computerized, there is less likelihood of data getting lost or simply missed in the analysis process. Qualitative data analysis is explored in detail in Chapter 15, 'Analysing Qualitative Data'.

THE VALUE OF GOOD RESEARCH

Focus on semiotics

Semiotics, as stated in Chapter 7, 'Understanding Research Methodology and Design' is the study of signs, their form, content and expression, in society. Signs in society are signs because they signify something. Anything that has signifying power, the power to signify, can be studied using semiotics. While traditionally semiotics focused on linguistics, on the study of the signifying capacity of language, more recently social scientists have engaged in the study of social semiotics.

Owyong (2009), in her research, used semiotics to explore the signifying potential of clothing. She contends in this journal article that clothes do more than meet our physical and physiological needs, they convey meanings in society that are beyond the superficial, meanings that enact and even create power relations between people. The aim of her research was to study the clothes people wear as a critical semiotic resource in the social construction of power relations. In her literature review, Owyong distinguishes between clothing and fashion; clothing is used generically to describe what people wear, while fashion is a style of dress temporarily worn by a discerning group in society. As she says, what is fashionable in one part of the world is not fashionable in another, and what is fashionable today may be considered dated or even *passé* tomorrow. To illustrate the point she discusses the wearing of knee-high socks by Japanese teenage girls in the 1990s, which they considered chic and fashionable, while at the same time, Singaporean teenage girls were trying hard to keep their socks hidden in their shoes, believing the appearance of shoes with no socks to be hip and trendy.

Owyong highlights the asymmetrical power relations that can be created by clothes. She points to the power relation between the hotel manager in a well-cut suit and the hotel cleaning staff in their nondescript uniforms. She highlights the power of the policeman's uniform. She demonstrates how different articles of clothing convey different messages; clothing reflects the power, or lack of power, of the wearer.

In her analysis, Owyong presents different case studies, among them a case study of the business suit. She presents a detailed analysis of the 'power suit' and the relative positions of men and women in relation to the wearing of power suits. She completes the presentation of her case studies with a consideration of the attire of superheroes such as Spiderman, Captain America and Luke Skywalker.

She concludes the article with the comment that, while Mark Twain said that 'clothes make the man', her study shows that the right clothes can make the man (and the woman) powerful.

The focus of Owyong's research is on clothing semiotics and the social construction of power relations. This research is relevant for human resource development, for business management as well as for marketing.

You will find the following resources useful in relation to semiotics and to the use of semiotics as a research methodology and/or a research method in your own research.

Koller, V. (2007) '"The world's local bank": Glocalisation as a strategy in corporate branding discourse', *Social Semiotics* 17(1): 111–131.

Semiotics for Beginners by David Chandler, **http://www.aber.ac.uk/media/Documents/S4B/**

The Semiotics, Advertising and Media website, created by Tom Streeter, University of Vermont, USA, **http://www.uvm.edu/~tstreete/semiotics_and_ads/**

Semiotics and Strategic Brand Management, by Laura Oswald, University of Illinois, **http://marketing-trends-congress.com/2009_cp/Materiali/Paper/Fr/Oswald.pdf**

Roland Barthes: Mythologies(1957), based on a series of three lectures by Tony McNeill, University of Sunderland, **http://seacoast.sunderland.ac.uk/~os0tmc/myth.htm**

The academic journals *American Journal of Semiotics, Applied Semiotics* and *Social Semiotics* are also useful.

THE FOUR STAGES OF DATA ANALYSIS

There are four stages in data analysis. The first stage is description, in which the researcher engages in a descriptive analysis of the data. The researcher describes the data, describing what it is that they see in the data. The second stage is interpretation. In this stage the researcher states what it is that they think that the data means.

The third stage is the conclusions stage. In this stage the researcher draws a major or minor conclusion from the data. In drawing conclusions, the researcher moves the interpretation along from stating what it is that that they see in the data, and what they think that means, to drawing some kind of conclusion about it. Conclusions are not just findings reiterated; in drawing conclusions, researchers move their thinking and reasoning along.

The conclusions that you draw as you go through the analysis are for the most part minor conclusions (see Table 13.3). They add up into, or they make a substantial contribution to, your major conclusion(s), which you state in the final chapter of the thesis, or in the final section of the report of the research.

Table 13.3 Drawing conclusions (an example)	
Describing data	Your data, for example, shows clearly that the students did not enjoy the module on research methodology.
Interpreting data	Your interpretation of these data is that there is some lack of fit between the research methodology module as it is currently presented and the needs of the students.
Drawing conclusions	The conclusion you draw is that the research methodology should be changed and improved.

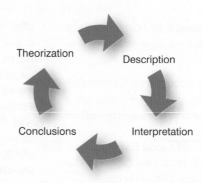

Figure 13.3   The four stages of analysis

Four stages of data analysis
Description, interpretation, conclusions and theorization.

The Four Frameworks
Conceptual Framework
Theoretical Framework
Methodological Framework
Analytical Framework

The fourth and final stage of the **four stages of data analysis** is the theorization stage. As we know, every research project conducted within academia, must make a contribution to knowledge. It is with this theorizing of the analysis that the researcher begins to make their contribution to theory, their contribution to the body of knowledge. In order to theorize their findings, the researcher looks back at their literature review and checks to see how their findings fit with the findings of the theorists detailed in that chapter. The researcher then demonstrates this in their data analysis chapter, or the section on findings in the report of the research, by stating how their finding fits with or contradicts the findings of other theorists, as detailed in their literature review. Whether the findings fit with or contradict the findings of others is unimportant. There may be temporal or cultural differences which can account for the researcher's findings contradicting the findings of others. The researcher tries as much as possible to link their work with the theory laid out in the literature review. The four stages of data analysis are demonstrated in the model above (see Figure 13.3).

In order to create the analytical framework for the research project, the fourth framework of the four frameworks approach, the researcher creates a structure for the chapter to contain the data analysis. This chapter is generally Chapter 4 in the thesis. Using the key concepts from the conceptual framework, the research statement/question, or the overall aim of the research project, and the key concepts and key issues to emerge from the theoretical framework, the review of the literature, with the key findings from the analysis of the data gathered for the research, the researcher constructs a framework for the presentation of the data analysis carried out for the research project. This is the analytical framework for the research project. It is detailed in the data analysis chapter.

YOUR RESEARCH
Data reduction

It is important when writing up the data analysis chapter, to remember that it is not necessary or appropriate, or even possible, to report every detail of the data or every element of data analysis. The process of data analysis is a process of data reduction. Through data reduction, data are transformed into more manageable formats. In writing up the data analysis chapter, the researcher reports only the most significant aspects of the analysis.

When the researcher gathers data, the data gathered are called raw data. Raw data, as defined in this chapter, are data which have yet to be ana-lyzed. In writing up the data analysis chapter, the researcher does not present raw data. The researcher carries out the analysis, and reports the key points, the key aspects, the key elements, the key themes, of the analyzed data.

The analytical framework is structured around a series of chapter subsections which are headed with subtitles. The subtitles and subsections provide the structure necessary for the narrative, or story, the researcher tells of analyzed data.

The researcher designs the data analysis chapter before beginning to write it, deciding how many subsections the chapter will have, what subtitle to use in each subsection, what material to use in each subsection, and in what order to present each subsection. The order in which the information is presented in the chapter is determined by the story or narrative that the researcher is developing. This narrative will be structured around the main argument, or the key point, the researcher is trying to make in the chapter. It is important therefore, to decide precisely what the key point or argument of the chapter is, and then structure the chapter around it.

Table 13.4 The structure of the data analysis chapter				
Total word count	**7000 words**	**5000 words**	**3000 words**	**1500 words**
Introduction	300 words	200 words	200 words	100 words
First subheading	2000 words, 4 paragraphs in each section, 500 words in each paragraph	1400 words, 3 paragraphs in each section, 350 words per paragraph	800 words, 3 paragraphs in each section, 250 words in each paragraph	400 words, 3 paragraphs in each section, 125 words in each paragraph
Second subheading	2000 words, 4 paragraphs in each section,500 words in each paragraph	1400 words 3 paragraphs in each section, 350 words per paragraph	800 words, 3 paragraphs in each section, 250 words in each paragraph	400 words, 3 paragraphs in each section, 125 words in each paragraph
Third subheading	2000 words, 4 paragraphs in each section,500 words in each paragraph	1400 words 3 paragraphs in each section, 350 words per paragraph	800 words, 3 paragraphs in each section, 250 words in each paragraph	400 words, 3 paragraphs in each section, 125 words in each paragraph
Summary/ Conclusion	500 words	500 words	300 words	200 words

Always try to write to a structure. The structure acts as a guide and will help you focus on the overall aim of the research project. The table below provides sample structures for the data analysis chapter.

The suggested word counts in Table 13.4 are designed to be a guide for you as you begin to plan and structure your data analysis chapter. If you do use one of the structures above for your data analysis chapter (the appropriate one for the word count you are allowed) then before you begin to write the chapter:

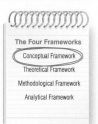

- you will have decided what it is that you are going to say in the chapter
- you will have decided on the main point or key argument you wish to make in the chapter
- you will have selected the particular aspects of your analyzed data that you wish to present in the chapter, and decided precisely where in the chapter each of these aspects fits best.

Using the four frameworks approach to the research, the key concepts in the conceptual framework are used to guide and direct the literature search for the literature review. The key concepts from the conceptual framework and the key issues to emerge from the literature review, together with the aim and objectives of the research, guide and direct the analysis of the data. In turn they guide and direct the structure of the data analysis chapter. Each of the subheadings in the data analysis chapter should reflect the key concepts of the research, as detailed in the research statement/question, in the overall aim of the research. The content of each of the subsections in the data analysis chapter is reflected in the subheading of the section.

THE VALUE OF GOOD RESEARCH

Carl's research project

Carl works as a manager for a High Street fashion company. The company has 250 retail outlets across the UK. In his research project for his degree in strategic business management, Karl has focused on the critical issues facing the company in the current economic climate. In order to examine this issue, Karl has conducted a survey. He has emailed a questionnaire to the managers of each of the 250 outlets. He has had a 90 per cent response rate to his questionnaire. He has loaded the responses to his questionnaire into SPSS and he has analyzed the data. Karl has spent 6 weeks analysing his data in SPSS and he is now ready to write up his data analysis chapter.

The aim of Karl's research is as follows: 'The aim of this survey is to identify and examine the critical issues facing this company in the current economic climate.' The aim of the research project contains all of the key concepts of the research project. These key concepts were used to search for literature for the literature review. The literature review with the conceptual framework for the research project was used to develop the questionnaire used in the survey. The analysis of the questionnaire was guided by the aim of the research project, the objectives of the research, the issues that emerged from the review of the literature, and the insights Karl developed from his work in analysing the data. From all of this, Karl developed a structure for his data analysis chapter. Karl has decided on key issues he is going to address in his presentation of his analysis of the data. He has decided what he is going to include in the chapter. He knows what data he is going to present in the data analysis chapter. He has decided on a narrative for the chapter. The word count for the chapter is 7000 words, this is given as guide, not an absolute word count. The structure Karl has designed for his data analysis chapter is as follows:

Introduction – (300 words)

First subheading – Critical issues facing the company (2000 words, in 4 paragraphs, 500 words in each paragraph)

Second subheading – The impact of the economic downturn (2000 words, in 4 paragraphs, 500 words in each paragraph)

Third subheading – Insights and ideas from retail outlet managers across the UK (2000 words, in 4 paragraphs, 500 words in each paragraph)

Fourth subheading – Dealing with the critical issues – a way forward (2000 words, in 4 paragraphs, 500 words in each paragraph)

Summary/Conclusion – (500 words)

Ask critical questions of data

When you have read through your data several times, you can begin the process of analysing it. A good way to begin the process of data analysis is to ask critical questions of the data. When you have organized your data into a data set ready for analysis, whether you have a large stack of interview transcripts or a smaller stack of completed questionnaires, or a data set in a computerized data analysis package, SPSS or NUDIST or Atlas ti or NVivo or some other software package, you can begin to think analytically about your data. Think about the issues that clearly and immediately emerge from your data. Think about the questions you could ask of the data in order to develop your thinking about it. The questions you ask of the data will primarily come from the conceptual framework for the project, which is contained in the research statement or question. They will come from the overall aim of the research, and the research objectives and from your review of the literature. Finally, some new questions will arise from the data itself, from your experiences in the gathering of it, what you observed, and the insights you developed in relation to the phenomenon under investigation through your experience in the field. From all of these sources, you will be able to generate good and useful questions with which to interrogate the data.

REAL WORLD RESEARCH

Shifts and changes in the research project

It is possible that the focus of your research will shift slightly as the research develops. If this happens, and it often does happen, then every aspect of the research project must shift slightly to accommodate this change, or these changes.

If you find that your research shifts or changes in a major way, then either your research project was not well-conceptualized to begin with, or in the course of your reading and/or reflection on the research, you encountered something substantial which you had not anticipated, and possibly could not have anticipated, or you had a major light bulb moment, a flash of insight that led you to substantially develop your research. If such a major shift occurs in your research, it is likely that you will have to go back to the start and re-design your research project to encompass this new insight. If, as this happens, you have been fortunate enough to make some substantial move forward in your thinking, then you will be on a very exciting research journey.

If you do need to make major changes, ask for advice, guidance and support, from your supervisor, your lecturer in research methods.

It is of the utmost importance that the analysis and the findings from the analysis are grounded in the data. This means that there must be evidence in the data for all of your descriptions, interpretations and conclusions. Everything that you state that you have found in your data must be clearly evident in the data itself. You must present data in the data analysis chapter, in tables, in figures, in direct quotes, in images, in whatever format the data you have gathered allows, to support your claims. You cannot make claims in your research, or for your research, that your data does not or cannot support. In other words, your findings must be grounded in the data. The purpose of the data analysis chapter is to clearly and completely detail your data, and the narrative you have created around your data and from your data. The key questions you should ask of the data analysis chapter are as follows:

1 What is the point of this chapter?
2 What point or argument am I making in this chapter?
3 How well and how clearly is this point or argument made in the chapter?
4 How well are the data used in the chapter to support this point or argument?
5 How well do the data support this main point or key argument?

You should be very clear about the argument or the point you are making in your data analysis chapter and you should make your argument or point very clearly. The argument or point you are making must also be a clear response to the overall aim of the research project.

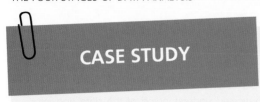

CASE STUDY

Managing and analysing data

An Exploratory Study of Multi Unit Restaurant Management Training: A Qualitative Perspective', Suboleski, S. *et al.* (2009)

I n this research, Suboleski *et al.* (2009) studied multi-unit restaurants (MURs) and multi-unit managers (MUMs). They state that a concern in many food service organizations is the lack of consistent training that is provided to MUMs. In this qualitative study they examined in-depth seven multi-unit organizations and the training they provided for their MUMs.

The data collection method used in the study was an open-ended interview process which, the authors stated, allowed for a detailed examination of the ways in which training was conducted and the specific training content delivered. Interviews were conducted with seven executives from seven of the top 100 MUR organizations in the USA. The interviews

Alfresco restaurant © Webphotgrapheer/iStock

were conducted over the phone during a 2 month period in 2005. The interviews were taped and the interview transcriptions underwent content analysis using the qualitative software package Atlas ti.

In an in-depth interview, the authors state the goal is to get as much information as possible from participants on a particular topic or subject area (Bogdan and Biklen, 2003). They explain that using the literature review as a foundation, an open-ended survey instrument was developed. They tell us that the survey instrument was reviewed by 'subject matter experts' and pilot tested by several training directors in MUR organizations in order to ensure that the content was complete and that the questions asked were clear and concise.

A purposive sampling approach was used in the study. Twelve executives were solicited to participate, in the end seven did participate, and seven interviews in total were carried out.

The data gathering instrument had both open-ended questions and demographic questions regarding the organization and the MUMs that work for the organization. The demographic questions, we are told, were developed to give each organization some kind of quantifiable description.

With respect to the open-ended questions, three specific dimensions of interest were addressed: the MUM's job, the MUM's employment, and the training the MUM received:

- In relation to the manager's job, questions were posed about the roles, duties, responsibilities and expectations of them.

- In relation to the manager's employment, questions were concerned with the criteria used in the organization for employing, promoting and developing managers.

- In relation to the manager's training, questions examined the training efforts or programs in place for managers and training plans in development for future programs for development of current managers and for new managers.

We are told that as more than one interviewer was used, and they both had their own unique style of creating a conversation with the respondents, there was a need to ensure consistency in the analysis of the data. This led to differences in the ways in which responses were generated. We are told that although the data gathering instrument was similar for each interview, different styles of interview prompted the researchers to use content analysis as the means by which the interview data were analyzed.

The interviews were conducted over the telephone. This was done to ensure consistency in the responses and to avoid possible bias by the interviewer being led by the physical responses, the body language, of the respondent. The interviews were organized to ensure that they were all conducted at the respondent's office or workspace. The interviews lasted between 60 and 90 minutes, and they were collected over a 2 month period in the spring of 2005. The seven interviews were carried out by two interviewers. Both interviewers were experienced in conducting in-depth interviews and in posing follow-up or probing questions in order to maximize the quality and depth of the responses.

We are told that, in keeping with the nature of a semi-structured interview, the goal of the interviewers was not to get all the questions in the instrument asked. Instead their focus was on gaining through the interviews an understanding of the participant's perspective of manager training and the role that it played in their organization.

A decision was made to tape all of the interviews. This was done in order to keep the data as pure and as complete as possible. Each of the seven interviews was transcribed promptly on completion by a professional transcriber. All conversations between the interviewers and respondents were transcribed so that the entire interaction, including all follow-up questions and probes, could be reviewed. The transcripts were reviewed to ensure that the different interviewer styles did not affect analysis.

In their analysis of the interview transcripts, the researchers focused on the words, phrases and themes in the data. They stated that, as recommended by Mehmetoglu and Altinay (2006), information from each participant was first analyzed separately to identify emerging themes within particular organizations. Then the themes that emerged from each respondent were compared across respondents in order to identify common beliefs or practices. The stated expectation was that such a multiple analysis approach would lead to a more sophisticated understanding of the data and information.

Analysis was completed using the program Atlas ti.

The authors explain that the three dimensions identified for the construction of the data gathering instrument – job, employment and training – were the major themes developed from the literature and they were the major themes used in the process of coding the data.

The following data were presented:

- Seven companies were interviewed (n = 7).
- The ages of these companies ranged from 5 years to 51 years, with the mean being 28.5 years.
- Only two of the companies were younger than 10 years old.
- Two of the companies were older than 25 years old.
- Two firms identified themselves as belonging to the quick-service hamburger market segment.
- The remaining five described themselves in terms of segment with the term 'casual'.
- Two of the companies identified themselves as part of the casual dining market segment.
- The remaining three identified themselves as fast casual, family-style casual, and full-service casual.
- The companies had anywhere from 32 to 1400 units.
- Two of the respondents held positions as directors of operations.
- One was a divisional vice president of operations.
- Three of the respondents were involved in training. Their titles were regional training director, vice president of management development and training, and field training specialist.

- One respondent was a vice president of human resources and was also directly involved with training.

- All of the participants were either MUMs themselves or directly involved with the training or supervision of MUMs within their organization.

- In four of the companies, MUMs were referred to as directors of operations.

- Two of the organizations called their MUMs multi-unit managers.

- One firm referred to the position by the title company business manager.

- The companies employed from 9 to 342 MUMs each.

- Two of the companies employed more than 100 MUMs, while four of the companies employed less than 25.

- The span of control, or number of properties for which each MUM was responsible, ranged from 3 to 11 per MUM.

- Three of the companies would not disclose the average age of their MUMs.

- The remaining four companies had MUMs ranging in age from 30 to 48 years old.

- Three companies would not disclose the gender breakdown of their MUMs.

- The remaining four companies had an overwhelming majority of male MUMs, ranging from 41 per cent to 100 per cent.

- Tenure of the MUMs in the organizations interviewed ranged from 2.5 years to 15 years.

Question The synopsis above of the research published by Suboleski *et al.* (2009) provides a good example of the detailed reflection on data, engagement with data, and management and analysis of data that researchers routinely undertake. Having read the synopsis above, what would you say are the main strengths and weaknesses of this study?

References

Suboleski, S., Kincaid, C.S. and Dipietro, R.B. (2009) 'An exploratory study of multi-unit restaurant management training: A qualitative perspective', *Journal of Human Resources in Hospitality & Tourism*, 8(2): 199–214.

CHAPTER REVIEW

This chapter considers data management and provides an introduction to data analysis. As detailed in the chapter, researchers gather quantitative data or qualitative data or a mixture of both. The appropriate management of data was shown in the chapter to be critical. In particular the safety and security of data are particular concerns. There are ethical concerns in the proper management of data, including particular ethical concerns around the security of data when research participants have been guaranteed anonymity. There are also particular ethical concerns in relation to the proper analysis of data and the possibility of research and research populations being misrepresented through mistakes in data analysis. Simple approaches to both quantitative and qualitative analyses are explored in the chapter. The use of computerized data analysis packages, SPSS for quantitative data, and NVivo, Atlas ti and NUDIST for qualitative data, are also considered. Four stages to the process of data analysis are presented in the chapter and explored. The four stages are description, interpretation, conclusion and theorization. The fourth framework in the four frameworks approach to research, the analytical framework, is presented here and discussed. An approach to planning and structuring the data analysis chapter is presented, and different options taking into account different allocated word counts for this chapter are outlined. The critical dimension of the presentation of analyzed data was shown to be the narrative or story of the data that the researcher decides to present in the data analysis chapter of the thesis, or in the data analysis section of the report of the research. This narrative must respond to the research question or statement. It must respond to the overall aim of the research and the objectives of the research.

Now update your interactive research diary with your notes and findings at www.cengage.co.uk/quinlan. Complete the activities provided to reinforce your understanding of this chapter.

END OF CHAPTER QUESTIONS

1 What is meant by the term data management?

2 Write a short paragraph on the key concerns in data management in a research project.

3 Describe a simple approach to quantitative data analysis.

4 Describe a simple approach to qualitative data analysis.

5 What are the four stages of the data analysis process, as explained in this chapter?

6 What is CADA, and what are the key advantages of CADA in data analysis?

7 What is SPSS, and what is it used for?

8 Explain in detail the acronym CAQDAS.

9 Explain the use of the analytical framework within the four frameworks approach to the research project.

10 Using the analytical framework and the sample structures for the data analysis chapter provided in this chapter, design a structure for the data analysis chapter of your research project.

REFERENCES

Chandler, D. 'Semiotics for beginners', http://www.aber.ac.uk/media/Documents/S4B/

Institute for New Economic Thinking (INET), http://ineteconomics.org Accessed 03.06.2010.

Institute for New Economic Thinking, Conference Proceedings, April 2010, http://ineteconomics.org/initiatives/conferences/kings-college/proceedings Accessed 03.06.2010.

Kaletsky, A. (2009) 'Three cheers for the death of old economics: The orthodox mathematical model took no account of reality. The new George Soros institute should bring back some sanity', *The Times*, 28 October.

Koller, V. (2007) '"The world's local bank": Glocalisation as a strategy in corporate branding discourse', *Social Semiotics* 17(1): 111–131.

McNeill, T. 'Roland Barthes: Mythologies (1957)', University of Sunderland, http://seacoast.sunderland.ac.uk/~os0tmc/myth.htm

Moustakas, C.E. (1994) *Phenomenological Research Methods*, Thousand Oaks, CA: Sage.

Oswald, L. 'Semiotics and Strategic Brand Management', University of Illinois, http://marketing-trends-congress.com/2009_cp/Materiali/Paper/Fr/Oswald.pdf

Owyong, Y.S.M. (2009) 'Clothing semiotics and the social construction of power relations', *Social Semiotics* 19(2): 191–211.

Purkiss, A. (2010) 'Soros plans economics institute at Oxford University, *Times* says', 5 April, http://www.bloomberg.com/apps/news?pid=20601102&-sid=aKgAaKQObPhM Accessed 03.06.2010.

Resnik, D.B. (2009) 'International standards for research integrity: An idea whose time has come', *Accountability in Research* 16(4): 218–228.Semiotics for Beginners by David Chandler, http://www.aber.ac.uk/media/Documents/S4B/

Semiotics for Beginners by David Chandler, http://www.aber.ac.uk/media/Documents/S4B/

Semiotics and Strategic Brand Management, by Laura Oswald, University of Illinois, http://marketing-trends-congress.com/2009_cp/Materiali/Paper/Fr/Oswald.pdf

Semiotics and Strategic Brand Management, by Laura Oswald, University of Illinois, http://marketing-trends-congress.com/2009_cp/Materiali/Paper/Fr/Oswald.pdf

Soros, G. (2010) 'Anatomy of crisis – the living history of the last 30 years: Economic theory, politics and policy', presented at the INET Conference, King's College, April 8–11, 2010, http://ineteconomics.org/sites/inet.civicactions.net/files/INET%20C%40K%20Paper%20Session%201%20-%20Soros.pdf Accessed 03.06.2010.

Strauss, A. and Corbin, J. (1990, 1998 edns), '*Basics of Qualitative Research: Techniques and Procedures for Developing Grounded Theory*', Thousand Oaks, CA: Sage.

Streeter, T. 'The Semiotics, advertising and media', University of Vermont, USA, http://www.uvm.edu/~tstreete/semiotics_and_ads/

Suboleski, S., Kincaid, C.S. and Dipietro, R.B. (2009) 'An exploratory study of multi-unit restaurant management training: A qualitative perspective', *Journal of Human Resources in Hospitality & Tourism*, 8(2): 199–214.

The Semiotics, Advertising and Media website, created by Tom Streeter, University of Vermont, USA, **http://www.uvm.edu/~tstreete/semiotics_ and_ads/**

RECOMMENDED READING

Bell, J. (2005) *Doing Your Research Project*, Part 111, *'Interpreting the Evidence and Reporting Findings'*, Maidenhead: Open University Press.

Collis, J. and Hussey, R. (2003) *Business Research*, Ch. 6, 'Collecting Original Data', Houndsmill: Palgrave Macmillan.

Creswell, J. (1998) *Qualitative Inquiry and Research Design: Choosing Among Five Traditions*, Ch. 8, 'Data Analysis and Representation', Thousand Oaks, CA: Sage.

Davis, D. (2005) *Business Research for Decision Making*, Ch. 12, 'Planning for Data Analysis', Mason, OH: Cengage South-Western.

Denscombe, M. (2003) *The Good Research Guide: For Small-scale Social Research Projects* (2nd edn), Part 111, 'Analysis', Maidenhead: Open University Press.

Easterby-Smith, M. Thorpe, R. and Jackson, P.R. (2008) *Management Research* (3rd edn), Ch. 8, 'Making Sense of Qualitative Data' and Ch. 10 'Making Sense of Quantitative Data', London: Sage.

Kessous, A. and Roux, E. (2008) 'A semiotic analysis of nostalgia as a connection to the past', *Qualitative Market Research* 11(2): 192–212.

Kane, E. and O'Reilly-De Brún, M. (2001) *Doing Your Own Research*, Ch. 15, 'Organising Your Qualitative Information', London: Marion Boyars Publishers.

Kent, R. (2007) *Marketing Research: Approaches, Methods and Applications in Europe*, Part III 'Data Analysis', London: Cengage.

Lewins, A. and Silver, C. (2007) *Using Software in Qualitative Research: A Step By Step Guide*, London: Sage.

Miles, M.B. and Huberman, A.M. (1994) *Qualitative Data Analysis* (2nd edn), London and Thousand Oaks, CA: Sage.

Neuman, W.L. (2005) *Social Research Methods: Quantitative and Qualitative Approaches*, Part Three 'Quantitative Data Collection and Analysis' and Part Four 'Qualitative Data Collection and Analysis', Boston, MA: Allyn & Bacon.

Oppenheim, A.N. (1992) *Questionnaire Design, Interviewing and Attitude Measurement*, London: Continuum.

Robson, C. (2002) *Real World Research* (2nd edn), Part IV, 'Dealing with the Data', Oxford: Blackwell.

White, B. (2000) *Dissertation Skills for Business and Management Students*, Ch. 8, 'Evaluating Research Results', London: Thomson.

Zikmund, W.G. (2003) *Business Research Methods*, Part 6 'Data Analysis and Presentation', Mason, OH: Cengage South-Western.

CHAPTER 14

ANALYZING QUANTITATIVE DATA

LEARNING OBJECTIVES

At the end of this chapter the student should be able to:

- Understand quantitative data analysis.

- Analyze quantitative data.

RESEARCH SKILLS

At the end of this chapter the student should, using the exercises on the accompanying online platform, be able to:

- Carry out an analysis of the data set presented.

- Critique the data provided in terms of the stated aim of the research project.

The aim of this chapter is to develop the focus on quantitative data and quantitative data analysis started in the previous chapter, and to teach you, the student, how to engage in quantitative data analysis. The chapter explains quantitative data analysis and the key concepts in quantitative data analysis. It demonstrates the processes involved in quantitative data analysis and basic statistical analysis. The use of visual displays of quantitative data analysis, charts and graphs, is explored and the importance of visual displays of quantitative data is explained.

INTRODUCTION

Quantitative data are numerical data and quantitative data analysis is the analysis of quantitative data using statistical methods. As you know from Chapter 13, basic quantitative data analysis can be carried out by simply adding up or summarizing the numbers in a data set. More complex quantitative data analysis can be carried out using a calculator or a spreadsheet, for example an Excel spreadsheet. Large quantitative data sets can be analyzed using the computer software package SPSS. The model of the research process (see Figure 14.1) illustrates where, in the research process, data analysis occurs. As you can see from the model, the researcher gathers data for the research project and then the researcher analyses that data. In the process of analysing data, the researcher interprets the data and finally the researcher comes to some conclusion(s) about the data.

The newspaper article below recommends to business owners and managers the use of an eco survey to establish how much energy their business uses and the cost of that energy. As explained in the article, using an eco-survey allows you to gather data on the ecological impact of your business. To help you analyze the data, you can plot the data on a graph or chart. Creating a graph or a chart from quantitative

THE VALUE OF GOOD RESEARCH

Environmentally friendly business © Peter Crowther/Ikon Images/ Getty Images

'If you only do one thing this week carry out an eco-survey', Finn, A. *The Guardian*, 16.11.2009

Extract

The secret to a more energy-efficient business is less complicated than you think – and starts with a simple eco-survey. Eco-surveys monitor the cost of energy use.

The eco message is everywhere, constantly extolling us to be greener, like some nagging spouse. Climate change will bring catastrophe if you just sit there doing nothing, you know. Turn out the lights. Recycle. Do this. Do that. But, while most big businesses employ environment managers to take care of these things, for those running small businesses, or for the self-employed, it can all be too much. There just isn't time to do everything. Where do you start? The trick is to pinpoint areas of unnecessary usage. You need to do an eco-survey.

An eco-survey can take many forms. The most affordable – but most cumbersome – method is to chart your energy usage by taking regular readings from your meter or getting your supplier to provide a detailed bill showing consumption at regular intervals. Once you have your figures, the Carbon Trust advises that you plot them on a chart, compare your energy usage with your business activities and investigate any suspicious areas. Does your energy graph show high usage during quiet periods for your business? Perhaps one particular piece of equipment that uses lots of energy is being left on. Get out your magnifying glass and track the culprit down.

Keeping a record is also useful for monitoring the effectiveness of any efficiency changes you make by allowing you to compare before and after graphs. Eco auditor Donnachadh McCarthy says that keeping tabs on your progress will motivate you to carry out the changes identified by a survey.

'Accountants say you pay attention to what you measure', he says. 'Seeing the stark figures brings home the effects of your efforts and encourages you to keep improving things. I try to get people to measure everything.'

Of course, being green is not just about saving energy. A full eco-survey should look at every aspect of your business. One option is to call in the professionals. An eco consultant such as McCarthy will spend a day or two assessing your firm's environmental impact and produce a report detailing where

you can improve and save money, and will make return visits to ensure the survey is being followed up.

If this is beyond your means, the Carbon Trust produces a wide range of 'walk around checklists' tailored to different industries. You can use these to assess everything from the efficiency of radiators to the use of fridges in restaurants. However, these can miss major factors, such as transport emissions, so to do the job properly you need to take a very broad view of your business and every part of its operation.

Until you know where the main problems lie, any attempt at going green is largely guesswork. Once you've done an effective eco survey and established your carbon footprint you may find a few targeted changes can make a big difference, both to your costs and your impact on the environment.

References

Finn, A. (2009) 'If you only do one thing this week carry out an eco-survey', *The Guardian*, 16 November. (c) Guardian News and Media Ltd 2009. Reproduced with permission.

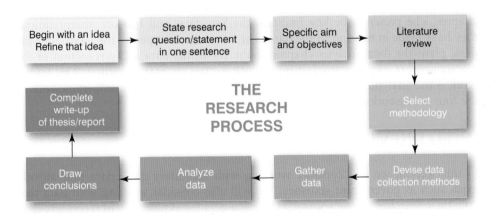

Figure 14.1   The research process

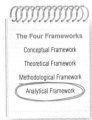

data is a useful and efficient way of presenting data. It often happens that a visual representation of data, in a graph and/or a chart, yields new insights into the data.

As the article explains, good research is the key to insight and understanding. Rather than relying on guesswork, carry out the research, gather good data and analyze it. The analysis of data and the presentation of that analysis, as explained in the previous chapter, provide the analytical framework for the research project. The analytical framework is the fourth and final framework in the four frameworks approach to

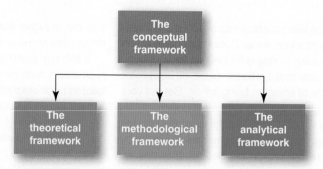

Figure 14.2   The Four Frameworks

the research project. The researcher presents the analytical framework for the research project in the chapter on data analysis in the thesis, or in the section on analysis in the report of the research. The chapter on data analysis contains a full account of the analysis carried out on the data, and a complete presentation of the findings that emerge from that data analysis. The four frameworks are detailed in Figure 14.2.

Data analysis is in itself, as explained in Chapter 13, a major project. The work of analysing data for the research project goes on for some time, for as much time as is necessary and for as much time as can be allowed. If you are using CADA, then the work of analysing your data takes place on your computer. If you are not using CADA, you will be analysing your data by hand. If this is the case, the work of analysing your data will take place at your desk, on the dining room table, on the kitchen table, on the living room floor. Wherever the work takes place, it is in-depth work, and is complex and time-consuming. What is presented in the data analysis chapter is a synopsis of this work.

The researcher presents a synopsis of their data analysis in the data analysis chapter, s/he presents the key findings, the key data, and the key interpretations they have made in relation to the data. The researcher, steeped in the analysis of the data, plans the data analysis chapter or the thesis, the data analysis section of the research report, and constructs a framework for this chapter or section. This framework is the analytical framework for the research project, the fourth framework in the four frameworks approach to the research project.

The Four Frameworks

Conceptual Framework

Theoretical Framework

Methodological Framework

Analytical Framework

WORKING WITH QUANTITATIVE DATA

In this section, we will consider working with secondary data, data that already exist, such as government statistics. We will also consider working with data that you, the researcher, create yourself. There is a detailed exploration of secondary data in Chapter 9, 'Using Secondary Data and Archival Sources'.

It is a good idea to browse through the data, relevant to your research, that is available on the websites of national and international organizations. This will give you a sense of what data is available, and may give you an idea for your research project. Working with an existing set of data is easier in one way than working with data you have created yourself, you don't have to go through the process of actually creating the data.

The screen captures (Figure 14.3 and Figure 14.4), depict data sourced from the UK Office of National Statistics. This office gathers quantitative data on different aspects of life and living in the UK. The following data is on employment. The table presented

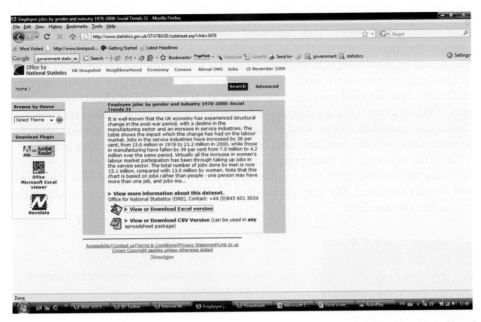

Figure 14.3 Reproduced with permission by the Office for National Statistics, from 'Employee jobs: by gender and industry 1978–2000', in Social Trends Vol. 31, Crown © Copyright 2009, Crown copyright material is reproduced under the terms of the Click-Use Licence. http://www.statistics.gov.uk/StatBase/ssdataset.asp?vlnk=3470&Pos=&ColRank=1 &Rank=272 Accessed 03.06.2010

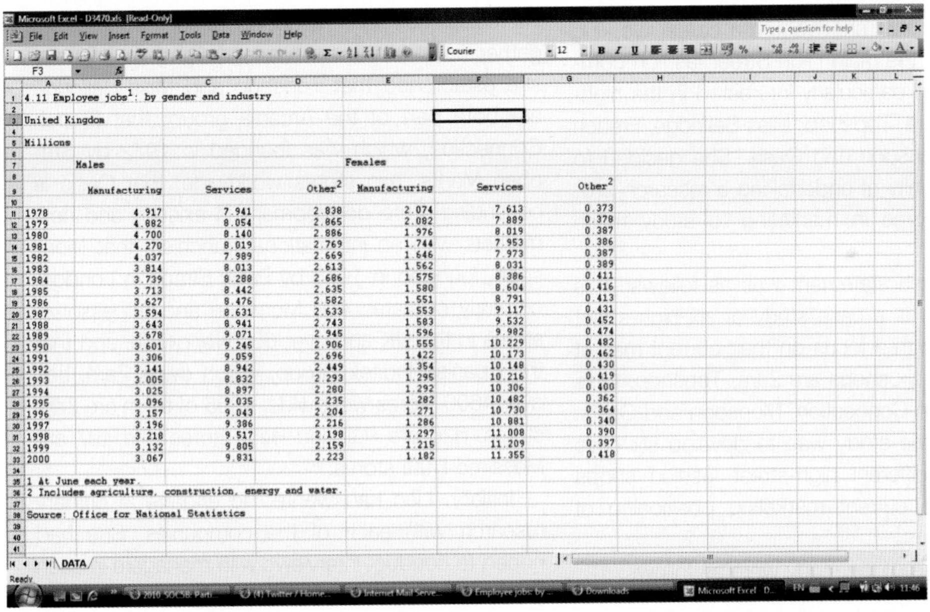

Figure 14.4 Reproduced with permission by the Office of National Statistics from Statistical Bulletin', Crown © Copyright 2009, Crown copyright material is reproduced under the terms of the Click-Use Licence; www.statistics.gov.uk/StatBase/ ssdataset.asp?vlnk=3470&Pos=&ColRank=1&Rank=272 Accessed 03.06.2010

in the screen capture (Figure 14.4) are data on jobs in terms of gender and industry, manufacturing services and other, between the years 1978 and 2000.

Data of this kind could be useful for an assignment in which you need a data set with which to demonstrate your ability to analyze data. It would be useful in a study of trends in employment, in relation to industry and/or in relation to gender, over the time period 1978–2000. This historical period might be of significance, if for example the focus of the study was on employment in the UK over that time period. The period might be useful in terms of providing background to a study, for example of changing patterns and trends in employment in the UK. For a contemporary study, the data detailed on page 381 are dated. It is limited in that it stops in the year 2000. In general, for a contemporary study, it is important to have the most up-to-date data possible. The process of gathering and collating data is time-consuming, so researchers use the best, the most recent data, the most suitable data available.

In order to create a quantitative data set, researchers develop questionnaires or scales themselves, or they use instruments that other researchers have developed and already validated. We have explored in previous chapters the ways in which the researcher creates data.

THE VALUE OF GOOD RESEARCH

Lian's research project

Lian decided that she wanted a career working with one of the main High Street fashion companies. She was particularly interested in the high-street chains Zara, Topshop, Miss Selfridge, French Connection, Monsoon and Oasis. She decided to use the opportunity of undertaking a research project for her degree in marketing to study these companies.

Lian's research statement was as follows: This research project is a case study of six high-street fashion shops with a focus on their current market positioning; the six shops are Zara, Topshop, Miss Selfridge, French Connection, Monsoon and Oasis.

The aim of the study was to develop six case studies of six different high-street fashion shops focused on the current marketing positioning of each of the shops.

The objectives of the study were as follows:

- To examine the branding of each of the shops.
- To explore, using secondary sources, the marketing positioning of each of the six shops.

- To examine customer perceptions of each of the six brands.
- To examine the current market positioning of the six brands through the attitudes and perceptions of customers.

Using a case study methodology, Lian developed six cases, one for each of the six shops that interested her. She used secondary sources to gather data on the six cases. Among other facts, she established that Topshop and Miss Selfridge are both part of the Arcadia group; that French Connection, which was founded in 1972 by Stephen Marks, has stores worldwide; that Oasis is continuing store development in existing and new markets with an international franchise; that Monsoon, founded in 1973 by Peter Simon in London, currently operates 400 Monsoon and Accessorize stores in the UK and over 600 worldwide; and that the Spanish Inditex Group, which owns Zara, has over 4600 stores worldwide, 1395 of them are Zara stores, 626 are Pull and Bear stores and 497 are Massimo Dutti stores.

Initially, Lian had wanted to engage in primary research with each of the companies. She had hoped to conduct interviews with managers in each of the shops. However, she didn't get any helpful or encouraging responses whenever she contacted the shops or the companies.

Lian decided, as an alternative, to interview customers of the shops. Using street intercept interviews, she engaged 120 customers in interviews,

20 customers for each of the six shops. She intercepted customers as they left the shops and invited them to participate in her study. She used a quota sampling method. Using this sampling method she continued to invite customers to engage in interview with her until she had her quota of 20 completed interviews with customers of each of the six shops. Lian used a structured questionnaire in the interviews which she had developed herself. The focus of the questionnaire, which was informed by her reading of the literature, was on customer brand perceptions, favourite stores, and shopping habits and patterns.

Lian's questionnaire is shown below. As you will see, Lian used a mixture of open and closed questions in the questionnaire. She gathered mostly quantitative data with the questionnaire, but she did gather some qualitative data. Can you identify the closed questions and the open questions? Can

you identify the questions designed to generate qualitative data?

Also detailed below is the coding key Lian developed to go with her questionnaire, it is included in Lian's questionnaire on the right side of the questionnaire.

Also presented below is an extract from Lian's data set. When Lian had gathered her data, she loaded it into SPSS. She used SPSS to analyze her data.

Lian found the process of loading the data into SPSS quite complex. To help her ensure that she loaded the data correctly, she decided to develop a separate coding key for her data. A copy of this coding key, developed as a separate document, is also shown below. When you examine this separate coding key, can you explain why Lian found it helpful?

QUESTIONNAIRE USED IN STREET INTERCEPT INTERVIEWS WITH HIGH STREET FASHION SHOPPERS

High Street Fashion – Shoppers' questionnaire
(Lian's research project.)

Code

Date:_____

Code
The side of the questionnaire contains the coding key for the questionnaire.

1 Location:_____　　　　　　　　　**1 2 3 4 5 6**

2 How often do you visit high street fashion shops like Zara and Topshop?

Every day ( )	1
Once or twice a week ( )	2
Once or twice a month ( )	3
Only when I must ( )	4
Other ( ) (please explain)	5

3 When you visit these shops do you tend to spend money in them?

All the time ( )	1
Sometimes ( )	2
Occasionally ( )	3
Never ( )	4

4 Do you ever shop online with any of these retailers?

Yes   1

No   2

5 With which of these shops have you shopped online?

Zara ( )   1

Topshop ( )   2

Miss Selfridge ( )   3

French Connection ( )   4

Monsoon ( )   5

Oasis ( )   6

Not applicable

6 Would you describe the experience generally as:

Very good ( )   1

Good ( )   2

OK ( )   3

Not good ( )   4

Bad ( )   5

Very bad ( )   6

Not applicable ( )   7

7 Please elaborate _____

8 On average, how much money do you spend per month in these shops?

Less than £20   1

More than £20–less than £50 2

More than £50–less than £100 3

More than £100–less than £200 4

More than £200   5

9 In the coming 12 months, do you anticipate spending more money or less money, or about the same amount of money in these shops?

More   1

Less   2

About the same amount   3

10 Please elaborate
_____

11 When you do shop, do you tend to buy mostly

Work clothes ( )   1

Party clothes ( )   2

Casual clothes ( )   3

Other, please elaborate ( ) 4

12 Which of the following adjectives would you apply to the 6 shops?

Exciting Fresh Adventurous Tired Old Safe

Zara	:__;__;__;__;__;	1 2 3 4 5 6
Topshop	:__;__;__;__;__;	1 2 3 4 5 6
Miss Selfridge	:__;__;__;__;__;	1 2 3 4 5 6
French Connection	:__;__;__;__;__;	1 2 3 4 5 6
Monsoon	:__;__;__;__;__;	1 2 3 4 5 6
Oasis	:__;__;__;__;__;	1 2 3 4 5 6

13 Please rank the shops in order, 1 = favourite, 6 = least favourite

Zara ( )	1 2 3 4 5 6
Topshop ( )	1 2 3 4 5 6
Miss Selfridge ( )	1 2 3 4 5 6
French Connection ( )	1 2 3 4 5 6
Monsoon ( )	1 2 3 4 5 6
Oasis ( )	1 2 3 4 5 6

14 Why is _____ your favourite of these shops?

15 Do you have any other favourite high street fashion shop, other than those named in this questionnaire?

Yes	1
No	2

16 Please elaborate: _____

17 Please complete the following sentences:

I would describe the brand Zara as:

_____

I would describe the brand Topshop as:

_____

I would describe the brand Miss Selfridge as:

_____

I would describe the brand French Connection as:

_____

I would describe the brand Monsoon as:

_____

I would describe the brand Oasis as:

_____

CODING KEY FOR HIGH STREET SHOPPERS' QUESTIONNAIRE (LIAN'S RESEARCH)

The coding key below (see Table 14.1) is the separate coding key that Lian developed to help her load her data into SPSS. Detailed in the coding key below, (see the top line in the coding key, reading from left to right) is the question number, which is taken from the questionnaire; the variable number, which is the number of the variable in SPSS; the variable name, which is simply the name of the variable; the variable description, which is a description of the variable; and the value labels, which are the codes assigned by the researcher to the different values in each of the variables. You will note from the coding key, the variable number does not track the question number, (see question number five).

Table 14.1   Coding key for high street shoppers' questionnaire (Lian's research)

Question number	Variable number	Variable name	Variable description		Value labels
1	V00001	Location	Zara		1
			Topshop		2
			Miss Selfridge		3
			French Connection		4
			Monsoon		5
			Oasis		6
2	V00002	How often do you visit high street fashion shops like Zara and Topshop?	Every day		1
			Once or twice a week		2
			Once or twice a month		3
			Only when I must		4
			Other/please explain		5
3	V00003	When you visit these shops do you tend to spend money in them?	Always		1
			Sometimes		2
			Occasionally		3
			Never		4
4	V00004	Do you ever shop online with any of these retailers?	Yes		1
			No		2
5	V00005	With which of these shops have you shopped online?	Zara		1
	V00006		Topshop		2
	V00007		Miss Selfridge		3
	V00008		French Connection		4
	V00009		Monsoon		5
	V00010		Oasis		6
			Not applicable		7
6	V00011	Would you describe the experience generally as:	Very good		1
			Good		2
			OK		3

Table 14.1	Coding key for high street shoppers' questionnaire (Lian's research) (continued)			
			Not good	4
			Bad	5
			Very bad	6
			Not applicable	7
7		Please elaborate		
8	V00012	On average, how much money do you spend per month in these shops?	Less than £20	1
			More than £20, less than £50	2
			More than £50, less than £100	3
			More than £100, less than £200	4
			More than £200	5
9	V00013	In the coming 12 months, do you anticipate spending more money or less money, or about the same amount of money, in these shops?	More money	1
			Less money	2
			About the same amount	3
10		Please elaborate		
11	V00014	When you do shop, do you tend to buy mostly:	Work clothes	1
			Party clothes	2
			Casual clothes	3
			Other, please elaborate	4
12	V00015	Which of the following adjectives would you apply to the 6 shops?	*Exciting/Fresh/ Adventurous/Tired/ Old/Safe*	
	V00016		Zara	1 2 3 4 5 6
	V00017		Topshop	1 2 3 4 5 6
	V00018		Miss Selfridge	1 2 3 4 5 6
	V00019		French Connection	1 2 3 4 5 6
	V00020		Monsoon	1 2 3 4 5 6
	V00021		Oasis	1 2 3 4 5 6
	V00022			
	V00023			
	V00024			
	V00025			
	V00026			
	V00027			
	V00028			
	V00029			

(Continued)

Table 14.1	Coding key for high street shoppers' questionnaire (Lian's research) (continued)			
	V00030			
	V00031			
	V00032			
13	V00033	Please rank the shops in order, 1 = favourite, 6 = least favourite	Zara	1 2 3 4 5 6
	V00034		Topshop	1 2 3 4 5 6
	V00035		Miss Selfridge	1 2 3 4 5 6
	V00036		French Connection	1 2 3 4 5 6
	V00037		Monsoon	1 2 3 4 5 6
	V00038		Oasis	1 2 3 4 5 6
14		Why is _____ your favourite of these shops?		
15	V00039	Do you have any other favourite high street fashion shop, other than those named in this questionnaire?	Yes	1
			No	2
16		Please elaborate:		
17		Sentence completion exercise		

It is important that you study this coding key. Try to understand the logic of the coding key. Read down through the coding key. Read it one question at a time. When you understand a question, move on to the next question. Ask for help with this exercise if you need help. Table 14.2 contains all of the data, as it appears in SPPS, for the first nine questionnaires of the 120 completed questionnaires Lian gathered for her research.

Take a moment to study the data set. The numbers, 1–9, down the left side of the data set relate to the questionnaire number. The number 1 signals that this line of data are from the first questionnaire, the number 2 signals that this line of data are from the second questionnaire, and so on. As you can see, the data set contains all of the data from the first nine questionnaires.

The line of data are read from left to right. Can you read the data? Use the questionnaire and the coding key to read the data. What does Var00001 relate to? If you said location, then you are correct. What does Var00005 relate to? If you said that it relates to the question 'With which of these shops have you shopped online?' you would be correct.

It is important to remember that the variable number does not track the question number. This is sometimes because there are open questions in the questionnaire, and the researcher, Lian in this case, has decided not to code these open questions for SPSS. This decision is made generally when there were too many different answers to the open questions. The answers to the open questions are analyzed using a qualitative data analysis process. A simple and useful approach to the analysis of qualitative data was presented in Chapter 13, 'Managing Data and Introducing Data

Table 14.2 Extract from the high street shoppers' data set (Lian's research project)

	var00001	var00002	var00003	var00004	var00005	var00006	var00007	var00008	var00009	var00010
1	2	3	1	1	7	7	7	7	7	7
2	3	2	1	1	1	2	3	4	5	6
3	4	1	1	1	1	2	3	7	7	7
4	1	4	2	1	5	3	1	2	6	7
5	2	5	1	1	4	2	3	1	9999	9999
6	6	3	3	2	7	7	7	7	7	7
7	5	2	1	1	4	3	5	1	2	9999
8	4	2	1	1	3	2	1	4	9999	9999
9	2	4	4	2	7	7	7	7	7	7

	var00011	var00012	var00013	var00014	var00015	var00016	var00017	var00018	var00019	var00020
1	7	1	1	2	1	2	3	1	2	3
2	3	3	2	2	1	2	3	1	2	3
3	2	2	2	1	1	2	3	1	2	3
4	1	4	3	2	1	2	3	1	2	3
5	1	3	3	3	4	5	6	4	5	6
6	7	4	1	1	9999	9999	9999	9999	9999	9999
7	2	5	2	4	1	2	3	9999	9999	9999
8	3	2	3	1	1	2	3	1	2	3
9	7	1	3	4	1	2	3	1	2	3

(Continued)

Table 14.2   Extract from the high street shoppers' data set (Lian's research project) (continued)

	var00021	var00022	var00023	var00024	var00025	var00026	var00027	var00028	var00029	var00030
1	1	2	3	1	2	3	1	2	3	1
2	1	2	3	1	2	3	1	2	3	1
3	1	2	3	1	2	3	1	2	3	1
4	1	2	3	9999	9999	9999	9999	9999	9999	9999
5	4	5	6	4	5	6	4	5	6	4
6	9999	9999	9999	1	2	3	1	2	3	1
7	9999	9999	9999	9999	9999	9999	9999	9999	9999	9999
8	9999	9999	9999	9999	9999	9999	1	2	3	9999
9	9999	9999	9999	1	2	3	9999	9999	9999	4

	var00031	var00032	var00033	var00034	var00035	var00036	var00037	var00038	var00039
1	2	3	1	2	6	5	4	3	2
2	2	3	1	2	6	5	4	3	1
3	2	3	1	3	5	4	6	2	2
4	9999	9999	1	2	3	6	5	4	1
5	5	6	6	2	3	4	5	6	2
6	2	3	2	5	4	1	2	3	1
7	9999	9999	2	3	4	5	1	6	2
8	9999	9999	2	3	5	5	1	6	2
9	5	6	1	2	3	6	5	4	1

Analysis'. The analysis of qualitative data is explored in detail in the following chapter, Chapter 15, 'Analysing Qualitative Data'.

It is sometimes possible to code qualitative data for SPSS. The question the researcher must ask her/himself is whether it is meaningful and useful to code the qualitative data for SPSS. If, for example, there were a relatively small number of respondents to the questionnaire, let us say less than 30, then it would be relatively easy to assign a numeric **value** to each of the responses. Or, if the researcher found on initially reading the responses to the question that there were a limited range of responses, then the responses could easily be categorized, and the categories could easily be coded for SPSS.

There is another reason why the variable number does not track the question number. This is because some questions require more than one response. For example, as demonstrated in the coding key above, question 12 in Lian's question-naire could, possibly, elicit 18 responses. This would happen if a respondent responded that each of the three positive adjectives or the three negative adjectives could be used to describe each of the six stores. It is important when loading data into SPSS that every response is included in the data set. When you are loading data into SPSS, ensure, as you load the data from the first questionnaire, that you leave a variable space along the line of data for every possible answer.

Loading the data is simple, but it does take time, and involves very precise, and some would say tedious, work. This is because the data must be loaded correctly, or the data will be rendered meaningless. Loading data correctly into any software package is a data management task. An example was given in the previous chapter, Chapter 13, 'Managing Data and Introducing Data Analysis', of one possible con-sequence of incorrectly coded data. Once the data are loaded into the software package, analysis of the data is relatively simple.

When analysing the data, the researcher uses the coding key with each of the questionnaires in order to de-code the data. Figure 14.5 is a screen capture taken from a data set in SPSS. The top line in the SPSS Data Editor contains commands very much

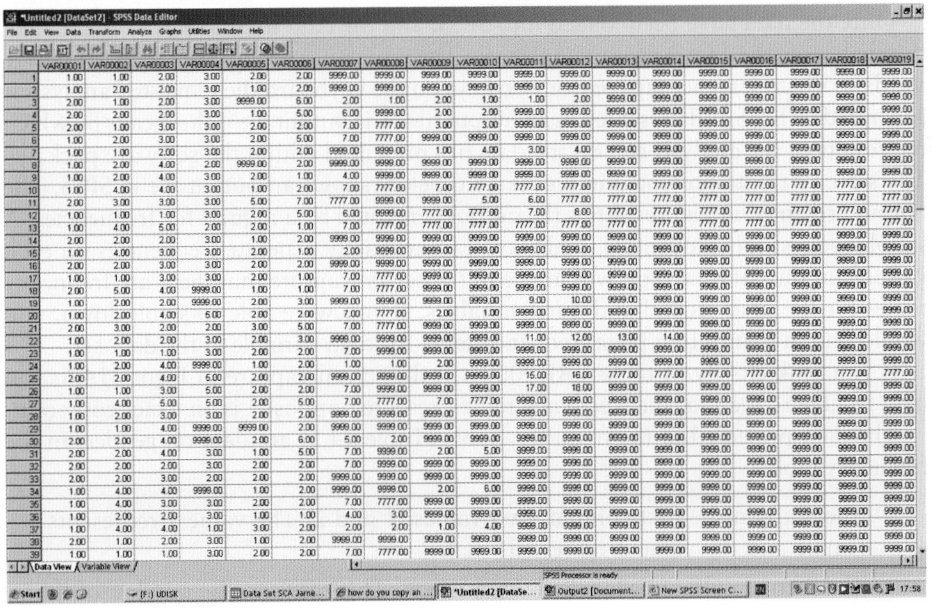

> **Value**
> Values make up different variables.

Figure 14.5   A data set in SPSS

like the commands in Microsoft Word or Excel. The commands are as follows: File, Edit, View, Data, Transform, Analyze, Graphs, Utiities, Window, Help. The command Analyze is used to run an analysis on the data in the data set. There is also a command called 'Graphs'. This command is used to generate graphs from the data in the data set. As explained earlier, the numbers down the left-hand side of the screen capture relate to individual questionnaires. As each completed questionnaire is returned to the researcher, the researcher numbers each questionnaire and loads it into SPSS. The number 1 refers to the first questionnaire, number 2 to the second, and so on.

Missing data Sometimes respondents do not answer all the questions when they fill in a questionnaire. It is possible that a question asked in the questionnaire might not be applicable to some respondents. When this is the case, there should be some means in the questionnaire for the respondent to indicate this; the respondent should be given a 'not applicable' option in the range of responses possible to that question or to those questions. It is important that respondents respond to each question. If respondents have not responded to questions in the questionnaire, for reasons other than the question asked not being applicable to them, then the researcher when coding the data must code the non-responses.

In coding for non-responses in SPSS, a good approach is to consistently use the same number to indicate non-responses. It is important to use a number that is not likely to be used otherwise in coding, so that the non-responses are immediately apparent. Using the number 7777, for example, is a good approach to coding for non-responses. When this is done, every time the researcher sees the number 7777 in the data set, they know straight away that that number indicates a non-response.

Similarly, in coding the response 'not applicable' the researcher might choose for example, the number 9999. Then every time the researcher sees the number 9999 in the data set, they know immediately that that question was not applicable to that respondent. If you look back at Lian's data set and at the screen capture of the SPSS data set, you will see that the numbers 7777 and 9999 appear in both data sets. Now you know what those numbers mean.

Once the data have been loaded into SPSS, and the data in SPSS has been cleaned, the analysis of the data is a very simple task. The researcher simply asks SPSS to analyze the data. The researcher taps one or two keys on the keyboard the requested analysis is generated by SPSS and presented in an output file. The output file is the means by which the results of the analysis run on the data are presented within the software package. The screen capture presented in Figure 14.6 below shows an output file in SPSS. The output presented in Figure 14.6 is the output generated by a request for frequencies. A simple request for frequencies in SPSS will immediately generate frequencies on each variable in the data set. You will notice in the screen capture that there are frequency tables for the first, second and third variables. If you were able to scroll down, you would find in that output file a frequency table for each variable in the data set.

If you look closely at table VAR00001 in the screen capture in Figure 14.6, you may be able to see that the frequency table presented opposite is an exact copy of it.

The data presented in the frequency table (Table 14.3) are data on gender. In the frequency table:

- There are in the first column, two values, 1 and 2. The value 1 represents female and the value 2 represents male.
- The second column is labelled 'Frequency'. This refers to the number of times, the frequency, with which both of the values are represented in the data set. As

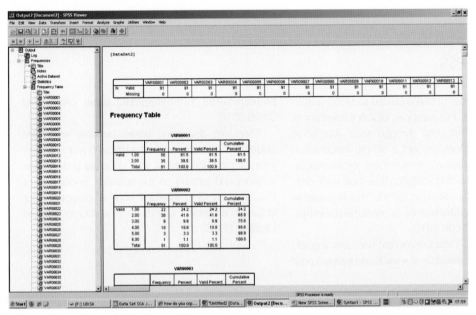

Figure 14.6   An SPSS output file generating frequencies

Table 14.3 VAR00001				
	Frequency	**Per cent**	**Valid per cent**	**Cumulative per cent**
Valid				
1.00	56	61.5	61.5	61.5
2.00	35	38.5	38.5	100.0
Total	91	100.0	100.0	

we can see, there are 56 females in this study and 35 males. In total, 91 people participated in this study.

- The third column is labelled 'Per cent'. The output in this column presents the values as percentages. As you can see, females account for 61.5% of respondents, and males account for 38.5% of respondents.

- The fourth column is labelled 'Valid per cent'. This column is the most widely used column in the frequency table. The output in this column presents the valid per cent, i.e. the percentage breakdown of respondents who actually answered the question.

- The fifth column is labelled 'Cumulative per cent'. The output in this column is a cumulative presentation of the valid per cents. In the frequency table above, the first per cent, 61.5% is added to the second per cent 38.5%, and this gives a total of 100%.

This is the format for every frequency table generated in SPSS. As explained in the previous chapter, it is neither necessary nor useful to detail all of the data when

YOUR RESEARCH
Guides to SPSS

There are a number of online guides to SPSS and to the use of SPSS. For example, UCLA (University of California, Los Angeles) through their Academic Technology Services present a simple introduction to descriptive statistics, frequencies, cross-tabulations and summarizing statistics (see below for definitions and explanations) in SPSS. This is available at **www.ats.ucla.edu/stat/Spss/modules/descript. htm** Accessed 03.06.2010.

Harvard – MIT Data Centre also presents a guide to SPSS. This is available at **www.hmdc.harvard.edu/**

projects/SPSS_Tutorial/spsstut.shtml   Accessed 03.06.2010.

There are also many books available which are guides to SPSS. These will be available in your university library. It may also be that your university provides the software and tutorials on the software. Enquire about this, and ask for a tutorial if none is provided. Your lecturer in research methods may be able to organise tutorial in SPSS.

writing up data analysis. The researcher must decide what to report, from all of the data available. The researcher reports the key aspects of the data and the most relevant data, in terms of the phenomenon under investigation.

Data management with SPSS SPSS, as well as helping the researcher analyze data, also serves as a tool for managing data. The data are secure within the software and may be password protected. The data within SPSS are all held within one file, which can and should be backed up. In order to load the data into SPSS, the researcher codes the data. While loading the data into SPSS, the researcher cleans the data. In cleaning the data, the researcher checks that the data are correct and that they are loaded correctly. Any errors in loading the data are corrected in cleaning the

REAL WORLD RESEARCH

the research, not the statistical analysis conducted on the data. Statistical analysis is simply a tool with which data may be investigated and analyzed. Statistical analyses are reported in the data analysis section of the thesis or report to support the narrative, the story the researcher is presenting about the analyzed data.

Whether you are using CADA or a pen and paper (with or without a calculator), it is important to keep a record of your thoughts, your reflections and your insights into your data as they form and develop. These notes, which you should for safety and security make and keep in your research diary, will provide you with many ideas in terms of the final story or narrative of the analysis to be presented in the data analysis chapter. There is, in Chapter 13, a detailed example of how to structure a data analysis chapter.

Presenting the analyzed data

It is important in data analysis to maintain a focus on the narrative to be told about the data. It is essential that the story or narrative told be logical and reasonable. Sometimes students fall into the trap of reporting the statistics, rather than the narrative. In reporting the narrative of the data, it is the data which are central to the narrative and the capacity of the data to respond to or illustrate the overall aim of

The ideas and insights that you get in relation to your data as you immerse yourself in your data in the data analysis phase of the research project will provide you with the narrative that you will present in the data analysis chapter in your thesis, or in the report of the research. You will be able to discern, from your notes and from the analysis conducted on the data, and from the research statement or question, the research hypothesis, the overall aim of the research project, precisely what narrative to present (what story to tell) about your data.

data. The data within SPSS have been rigorously coded and cleaned. Within the software the data can be easily, safely and securely stored, moved and used, as long as the computer and/or memory stick containing the data is secure. For ethical purposes, this level of data management is very valuable.

Variable
A characteristic with more than one value.

THE VARIABLE IN QUANTITATIVE DATA ANALYSIS

In quantitative analysis, as we have seen, the unit of measurement is the **variable**. In conducting quantitative research, we measure, control and/or manipulate variables. A variable is a characteristic with more than one value. As explained above, gender, for example, is a variable. There are two values (generally) in gender, male and female. Level of education is a variable. There are, let us say, three levels of education, primary, secondary, tertiary, and so in coding the values in the variable education, there would be three values to code.

There are different level variables: **nominal variables**, **ordinal variables** and **interval variables** (see Table 14.4). The different levels are important because they determine the kind of analysis that can be carried out on, or with, each variable.

Nominal variables
Each value is a distinct category and serves simply as a label. Categories cannot be ranked e.g. gender, nationality, race.

Ordinal variables
Values are ranked according to criteria e.g. social class (upper, middle, working).

Table 14.4 Nominal, ordinal and interval variables
Nominal is the lowest level of measurement. No assumptions can be made about relations between the values of a nominal level variable. The categories cannot be ranked. Each value is a distinct category and serves simply as a label. Examples of nominal level variables include gender, nationality, race, religion, type of business. A nominal scale simply involves putting the data into categories. A Yes/No scale is an example of a nominal scale.
Ordinal is the intermediate level of measurement. Values in ordinal level variables are ranked according to some criteria, in other words there is distance between the different values in the scale. While there is distance between the values, it is not possible to calculate or quantify the distance between the values. Level of education is an ordinal level variable. There are, we have said above, three levels of education. While we understand the distances between the different levels of education, it is not possible to mathematically measure those distances. The simplest ordinal level scale is a ranking. If you ask respondents to rank the tasks they undertake in their daily work in some order, for example, from the most important to the least important, you are asking them to create an ordinal scale of preference. In your questionnaire, if you ask respondents, for example, to rate their satisfaction with their job on a 5 point scale from very satisfied to very dissatisfied, you are using an ordinal scale.

Interval variables
Data with a meaningful and measurable distance between values e.g. an age.

(Continued)

Table 14.4   Nominal, ordinal and interval variables (continued)
Interval is the highest unit of measurement. Interval level variables are distributed in an even, continuous manner. In interval level variables, as well as scale there is meaningful and measurable distance between the values. Age is an example of an interval level variable. Income, when it is disaggregated, is an interval level variable. The difference between an interval level variable and an ordinal level variable is that there is meaningful distance between the values in an interval level variable. The distance between the values is equal. The distance between the values can be measured or quantified. A wide range of statistical analyses can be carried out on interval level data.

A **dichotomous variable** is one that has only two values. Gender is a dichotomous variable. Questions that elicit yes/no responses are dichotomous questions. The responses to such questions are dichotomous responses.

The effect is called the dependent variable. The assumed cause is called the **independent variable**. An **intervening variable** is the means by which the independent variable affects the dependent variable.

THE VALUE OF GOOD RESEARCH

Focus on experimental design

Experimental design, as explained in Chapter 7 'Understanding Research Methodology and Design' is the methodology used when conducting experiments. Field experiments are experiments which are conducted in real-life settings.

In true experiments, the independent variable is manipulated to test whether or not it has an effect on the dependent variable. The dependent variable is what is measured in an experiment; it is the variable that responds to the independent variable. The independent variable is the variable that is introduced or acted upon in some way in the experiment in order to produce some effect on the dependent variable. In a simple experiment, two groups are established, with individuals or units being randomly assigned to both groups. The two groups are pre-tested, and the dependent variable is measured. Then some programme or application, the independent variable, is applied to one group, the experimental group, and not

to the other group, the control group. Both groups are tested again; again the dependent variable is measured. If there is a difference in the experimental group but not in the control group, the programme or application applied to them, the independent variable is said to account for the difference.

In an experiment there can be more than one dependent variable (the variable(s) that are being acted upon) but there should only be one independent variable (the variable that is manipulated). In real life there are so many variables it can be difficult to establish precisely which variable(s) account for which changes. It can be difficult in social research to absolutely establish cause and effect, to establish precisely what/which cause brought about what/which effect. For example, you might want to study the impact of a training programme designed to bring about better communication in a company. You could establish two groups within the company, an experimental group and a control group. You pre-test both groups. You then administer the training to the experimental group but not to the control group. Then you test both groups again. You may suggest that any change evident in terms of communication in the experimental group is as a result of the training in communications given. However, this may not be the case. It could be simply the fact that the group spent time together (while undertaking the training), brought about improved communication in the group. In that case, the training itself is not responsible for the improved communication.

It can be difficult to establish precisely which variable(s) account for changes that occur in social science research and to establish precisely what/which cause brought about what/which effect.

The Hawthorne Experiments (1924–1933) are classic examples. Elton Mayo, a professor of industrial management at the Harvard Business School, studied worker behaviour at the Western Electrical Company's Hawthorne Works in Illinois, USA. The experiments Mayo carried out were designed to measure worker productivity. Mayo found that as he studied the workers, their productivity improved. What he realized was that the subjects of his experiments changed their performance in response to being observed. In other words, it was the experience of being observed that caused worker productivity to improve. This variable of being observed was an unforeseen variable in the experiments, yet it was the variable that brought about the change in worker behaviour. This discovery became known as 'the Hawthorne effect'. You can read about the Hawthorne experiments on the Harvard Business School website at **http://www.library.hbs.edu/hc/hawthorne/09.html** Accessed 03.06.2010.

You will find the following resources useful in relation to experimental design.

Trochim's (2006) website 'Research Methods: Knowledge Base', provides, as mentioned previously in the text, a clear introduction to experimental design. You will find this at **www.socialresearchmethods.net/kb/desexper.php** Accessed 03.06.2010.

The website of Science Olympiad also provides a good introduction to experimental design. You will find this at **http://soinc.org/exper_design_b** Accessed 03.06.2010.

BASIC STATISTICAL ANALYSIS

Statistics are used in quantitative data analysis for two purposes, description, using **descriptive statistics**, and prediction, using **inferential statistics**.

Descriptive statistics Descriptive statistics are used to describe the data gathered (www.socialresearchmethods.net/kb/statdesc.php). Summarizing statistics are examples of descriptive statistics. Each variable in the data gathered, gender, level of education, income, age, and so on, can be described using descriptive statistics. Using descriptive statistics, each variable can be described in a number of different ways. The most generally used descriptive statistics are frequencies, ranges, means, modes, medians and standard deviations. Table 14.5 names and explains the different descriptive statistics.

Inferential statistics With inferential statistics the researcher is trying to reach conclusions that extend beyond the data. Inferential statistics are used to infer, based on the study of a sample of a population, what the entire population might think, or do. **Statistical inference** uses the data gathered on a sample population to draw conclusions (or inferences) about the population from which the sample was drawn.

Inferential statistics are also used in quantitative data analysis for prediction (see Table 14.6). Prediction in quantitative data analysis is based on the science of probability. Inferential statistics are used, as explained by Trochim, to make judgements of the probability that an observed difference between groups is a dependable

Dichotomous variable
A variable with only two values.

Independent variable
In examining the relationship between two variables, the assumed cause is the independent variable.

Intervening variable
The means by which the independent variable affects the dependent variable.

Table 14.5 Descriptive statistics	
Measures of central tendency	
The mean	The mean is the arithmetic average. To calculate the mean, add up all the values, and divide the total by the number of values.
The mode	The mode is the most commonly occurring value in a range of values.
The median	The median is the middle value of a range of values
Measures of dispersion	
The range	The range is the minimum and maximum values in a range of data. For example, the age range was 21-years-old to 39-years-old. The youngest respondent was 21-years-old, and the oldest was 39-years-old. In another example, the turnover ranged from £300 000 to $40 000. The highest turnover was £300 000, the lowest was £40 000.
The interquartile range (IQR)	The interquartile range (IQR) is a robust measure of sample dispersion. It eliminates outliers by focusing on the difference between the first and third quartiles. Outliers are extreme measures that skew a distribution.
	The median, as explained above, is the middle value, and the IQR is the middle value of the lower and the upper halves of the data.
	For example, let us say that your population or sample ranges in age from 21 to 27 years, but you have one person who is aged 39. This one age is an extreme value, it is an outlier, and it will skew the distribution of the data. Using the IQR instead of the range eliminates such outliers, and in doing this, eliminates **skew** generated by outliers.
The standard deviation	The standard deviation measures the spread of data about the mean. It is used to compare sets of data that have the same mean but a different range of data.
	The standard deviation is calculated as the square root of the variance. Variance in a data set is the extent to which the values in the data set differ from the mean.
	A calculator that handles statistics will calculate standard deviation. To calculate the standard deviation by hand:
	1 Establish the mean in the range of data.
	2 Subtract the mean from each of the values to establish the deviation of the values from the mean.
	3 Square each deviation.
	4 Sum all the squares (add them up).
	5 Divide the sum by the number of data points, minus 1.
	6 Take the square root of that value. This is the standard deviation.
Other measures	
Percentages	Percentages are a particular kind of scale with measures of 1 to 100.
Ratios	A ratio can be calculated as follows, the ratio of number A to number B is defined as A divided by B.

Table 14.5 Descriptive statistics (continued)	
Proportions	Proportions are a type of ratio in which the denominator is the total number of cases.
Frequency distributions	A frequency distribution condenses information into a simple format which will allow the reader to picture the way in which the variable is distributed. We saw examples of frequency distribution tables in the screen capture, above, of the output file in SPSS (Figure 14.6).

Table 14.6 Inferential statistics	
T-tests	A t-test is used to decide if the means (the arithmetic averages) of two groups are statistically different from each other, for example the means of a control and experimental group. You will find a detailed explanation of the t-test on The Research Methods Knowledge Base website. You will find this at **www.socialresearchmethods.net.kb.stat_t.php.**
The ANOVA test the analysis of variance	There are similarities between the t-test and ANOVA. Both are used to test hypotheses about the differences (the variance) in the means in groups. While the t-test is used to test two means, ANOVA can be used to test the differences among the means of many groups at once. The purpose of one-way ANOVA is to test whether the means of different groups are common or different. Two-way ANOVA is used when the groups tested have two different defining characteristics, rather than one. MANOVA is a multivariate version of analysis of variance (MANOVA multiple analysis of variance). You will find a detailed explanation of ANOVA on the Columbia University Quantitative Methods in Social Sciences web page. You will find this at **http://ccnmtl.colombia.edu/projects/qmss/anova/ about_the_anova)test.html.**
Correlation tests	This is an often-used statistic. A correlation, according to Trochim's Research Methods Knowledge Base, is a single number that describes the degree of relationship between two variables. Correlation tests measure the extent to which an independent variable predicts a dependent variable. As well as explaining correlation tests, The Research Methods Knowledge Base works through a correlation example. You will find this at **www. socialresearchmethods.net/kb/statcorr.htm.**
Simple linear regression	Simple linear regression is like correlation, in that it too determines the extent to which an independent variable predicts a dependent variable, however, the simple linear regression also tells how well the line fits the data. The smaller the distance of the data from the regression line, the better the fit. According to the statistics guide of the Colorado State University, regression analysis attempts to determine the best 'fit' between two or more variables (**http://writing.colstate.edu/guides/research/stats/index.cfm**).
Multiple linear regression	Multiple linear regression measures how well multiple independent variables predict the value of a dependent variable. You will find a detailed explanation of multiple linear regression on the Columbia University web page of Quantitative Methods in Social Sciences, at **http://cnmtl.columbia.edu/projects/qmss/about_multiple_regression. html.**

difference or a difference that may have happened by chance in the study (**www. socialresearchmethods.net/kb/statinf.php**).

You may also find The Purdue Online Writing Lab's resource on 'Basic Inferential Statistics' helpful. You will find this at **http://owl.english.purdue.edu/owl/resource/ 672/05/** Accessed 03.06.2010.

When a researcher engages in quantitative analysis using inferential statistics, the sampling method used in selecting participants for the research project becomes critical. Probability sampling methods must be used. These sampling methods are designed to minimize biases and to ensure that the sample is as representative as possible of the population of the study. Probability sampling methods (and non-probability sampling methods) are outlined and explained in detail in Chapter 8, 'Understanding Research Methods, Populations and Sampling'.

The probability of any outcome is called the p-value. The p-value is written p followed by the actual value in brackets. For example $p = (0)$. The p-value is measured from 0 to 1, with 0 equalling complete certainty that the prediction will not occur, and 1 equalling complete certainty that the prediction will occur. For example, $p = 0.6$ would mean the likelihood of the prediction occurring is slightly greater than a likelihood of the prediction not occurring.

Hypothesis testing is commonly used in research in drawing inferences about a population based on **statistical analysis** of data drawn from a sample of that population. In hypothesis testing, a null hypothesis is a statement about the population of the study that the researcher wants to test. An alternative hypothesis is a challenging statement, or an alternative statement, against which the null hypothesis can be tested. In the first place the hypotheses are stated, and they must be mutually exclusive, i.e. if one is true the other must be false. Then the sample data are tested, using means, or t-tests, ANOVA or some other statistic. The results are interpreted, and the hypotheses are accepted or rejected (see Markova, 2009 for an example of a research project carried out using hypothesis testing). The online *Teach Yourself Statistics* website Stat Trek is helpful in relation to learning how to conduct statistical analyses and how to test hypotheses. You will find this website at **http://stattrek.com**. Also helpful is the Quantitative Methods in Social Sciences project on the Columbia University website. You will find this website at **http://ccnmtl.columbia.edu/projects/qmss/home.html** Accessed 03.06.2010.

Data analysis can be carried out using **univariate analysis**, the use of one variable in analysis; **bivariate analysis**, the use of two variables in analysis; and **multivariate analysis**, the use of three or more variables in analysis.

Univariate analysis is analysis of one variable. Using univariate analysis, each variable in the data set is analyzed individually, or one at a time. Methods for univariate analysis include: frequencies, **measures of central tendency** and **measures of dispersion**. Table 14.7 is an example of a frequency table generated in SPSS. It is an example of univariate analysis. We explored this table in detail earlier in this chapter.

Table 14.7 VAR00001				
	Frequency	**Per cent**	**Valid per cent**	**Cumulative per cent**
Valid				
1.00	56	61.5	61.5	61.5
2.00	35	38.5	38.5	100.0
Total	91	100.0	100.0	

Bivariate analysis is analysis conducted on two variables. Examples of the statistical analysis that can be carried out in bivariate analysis include **cross-tabulation**, one-way ANOVA, t-tests, correlation tests and simple linear regression.

Table 14.8 Cross-tabulating gender with level of education		
	Male	**Female**
1 level	4	5
2 level	25	30
3 level	55	60

Descriptive analysis
(below find three sentences outlining a typical analysis of the above table)

From the table above, it is clear that more than half of the respondents have third level education; to be precise, 55 male respondents and 60 female respondents have third level education. Twenty-five male respondents and 30 female respondents have been educated to second level. Only 5 female and 4 male respondents completed their formal education after first level.

Statistical analysis
Analysis of quantitative data through the use of statistics.

Univariate analysis
Analysis conducted on only one variable e.g. frequencies.

Bivariate analysis is
Analysis conducted on two variables e.g. chi-square tests, one-way ANOVA, t-tests, correlation, and simple regression.

Cross-tabulations (cross-tabs) are the means through which the joint distribution of two variables may be displayed. Cross-tabulations are easy to use and easy to understand. They can be used with any level of data, nominal, ordinal, interval. Cross-tabulations treat all data as categorical data (nominal level data).

Tables are useful in presenting data because they provide a means through which a great deal of data can be presented in a very succinct manner. They are useful too, in that tabulating data, like graphing data (see below), can produce fresh insights into the data. The **contingency table** above (see Table 14.8) details the cross-tabulation of the variable Gender, with the variable Level of Education.

Multivariate analysis is analysis conducted on three or more variables. Examples of statistics that can be used in multivariate analysis include multiple regression analysis and MANOVA multiple analysis of variance.

Multivariate analysis
Analysis conducted on more than two variables e.g. examples of multivariate statistics include multiple regression analysis.

GRAPHING DATA

Graphing data is an important facility in quantitative data analysis. Graphing data, like tabulating data, allows for the communication of large quantities of data in a very succinct manner. In addition, graphing data, or visually displaying data, can make trends and patterns in the data apparent. It does sometimes happen that researchers do not see particular trends or patterns in their data until they visually display the data by graphing it. Graphing data is as important to the process of data analysis as it is to the process of communicating data analysis. It is easy to graph data, for example, in Microsoft Excel and then the graph can be imported into the data analysis chapter in Microsoft Word. There is also, as detailed above, a facility in SPSS for graphing data. It would be a useful exercise to spend time exploring these facilities. Through a casual exploration of the facilities you will learn a lot about how they work, and you will get some good ideas about how you might use them in reporting your research. There are very many different kinds of graphs typically used with social science data. Some examples are presented on the next page.

Contingency table
A tabular representation of categorical data, (nominal level data).

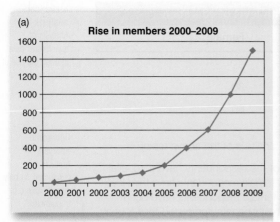

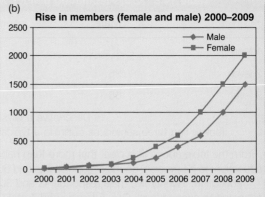

Figure 14.7 Line graphs depicting data on club membership over time
(a) Rise in members 2000–2009
(b) Rise in members (female and male 2000–2009)

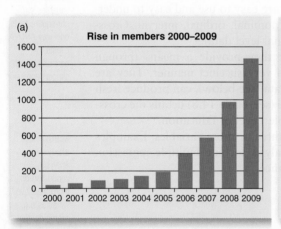

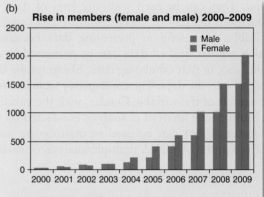

Figure 14.8 Bar charts depicting data on club membership over time
(a) Rise in members 2000-2009
(b) Rise in members (female and male 2000-2009)

Measures of central tendency
The mean: the arithmetic average; the mode: the most commonly occurring value; the median: the middle value of a range of values.

Line graph A line graph is used to visually display a line of data. Line graphs are useful in discerning trends in data and particularly trends over time. Figure 14.7 displays data on club membership over time, from 2000 to 2009. The graph on the right provides a gender breakdown on the data. In this graph we can see the relative rise in club membership of female and male members over the years 2000–2009. As you can see from the graph, while membership rates have risen consistently for both genders, the rise in female membership rates has been consistently higher than the rise in rates of male membership.

Bar chart A bar chart graphs data in tabular form. In Figure 14.8 the data on club membership is shown in bar charts. If you study both the line graphs, and the bar charts,

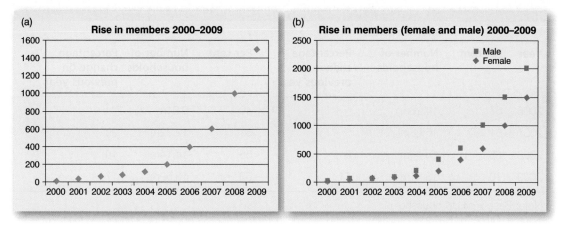

Figure 14.9 Scattergrams depicting data on club membership over time
(a) Rise in members 2000-2009
(b) Rise in members (female and male 2000-2009)

you will clearly see that both sets of visual data representations present the same data. The data on club membership is also presented in the scattergrams above.

Measures of dispersion
The interquartile range (IQR); the standard deviation.

Scattergrams In Figure 14.9 the graphs are scattergrams. A scattergram is a useful way of visually summarizing bivariate data. A scattergram gives a good representation of the relationship between two variables.

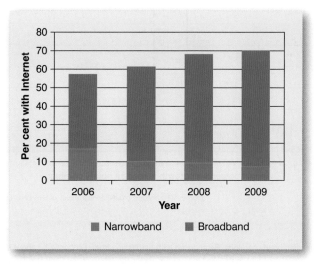

Figure 14.10 UK households with internet access 2006–2009
Source: Office for National Statistics, statistical bulletin *internet access households and individuals 2009*

Cross-tabulations (Cross-Tabs)
How joint distribution of two variables are displayed. Easy to use and understand.

Using graphs and tables taken from secondary sources Figure 14.10 details the number of UK households with narrowband and broadband internet access over

	Table 14.9	UK households with internet access 2006–2009					
	internet access			**Broadband**		
Year	Per cent	Number of households	Percentage change on previous year	Per cent	Number of households	Percentage change on previous year
2006	57	14.26m	–	40	9.91m	–
2007	61	15.23m	7	51	12.82m	29
2008	65	16.46m	8	56	14.14m	10
2009	70	18.31m	11	63	16.52m	17

Note: Base = all UK households
Source: Office for National Statistics, statistical bulletin *internet access households and individuals 2009*

the years 2006 to 2009. The table below the bar chart presents the same data in tabular form. The data are taken from the UK's Office for National Statistics Statistical Bulletin 'internet Access Households and Individuals 2009'. This bulletin contains a lot of data on internet access in the UK. You will find it at **www.statistics. gov.uk/statbase/Product.asp?vlnk=5672** Accessed 03.06.2010.

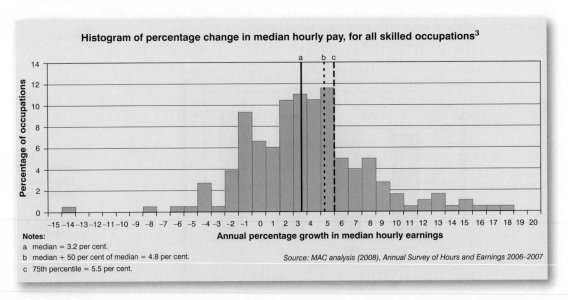

Figure 14.11   Annual percentage growth in median hourly earnings, Reproduced with permission from Economic & Labour Market Review, Vol. 3, No. 5, May 2009, Crown © Copyright 2009, Crown copyright material is reproduced under the terms of the Click-Use Licence

Table 14.9 presents these data on UK households with internet access in more detail. Figure 14.11 was taken from *The Economic & Labour Market Review* (Downs, 2009*)*. This is a publication of the UK's Office for National Statistics. You will find this publication at **http://www.statistics.gov.uk/cci/article.asp?id=2181** Accessed

03.06.2010. As you can see, the **histogram** shows the percentage change in median hourly pay, for all skilled occupations in the UK, 2006-2007. As we know, the median is the middle value of a range of values.

Clearly, there is a wealth of data in national and international databases that can be accessed and used as the sole source of data in a research project, or as supplementary sources of data in a research project. The key is to find data that are useful in terms of the research you are carrying out, and then to find a way to integrate that data in a meaningful way into your research.

A good way of learning how to present data is to examine how other researchers present data. You can do this by reading the theses in your library, and by finding journal articles which feature research similar to your own. Look at how these other researchers present their data. If you find one or more useful models, in terms of data presentation, try to model your own presentation of your data, or some aspects of your presentation of your data, on them. Reading the work of other researchers is one of the best ways of learning how to conduct and present research.

The research project presented below is a study of the research methodologies used in small business and entrepreneurial research and published in three journals over the time period 2001 to 2008. The journal article provides a critique of the research methodologies used in the research projects. The key issues in research methodology which are focused on in the article are sampling methods and issues of validity and reliability.

> **Histogram**
> Similar to a bar chart except that the bars in a histogram are side by side touching each other.

REAL WORLD RESEARCH

How theory influences research

'Research Methods in the Leading Small Business–Entrepreneurship Journals: A Critical Review with Recommendations for Future Research', Mullen, M.R. *et al.* (2009)

This article details a critique of the research methodologies used by small business and entrepreneurship researchers. The study gathered data from reports of research projects published in journal articles in three different journals, the *Journal of Small Business Management*, the *Journal of Business Venturing,* and *Entrepreneurship Theory and Practice.* The analysis carried out by Mullen *et al.* (2009), includes all of the articles published in the three journals between 2001 and 2008. There were in all 665 articles.

The stated objectives of the study were as follows:

- to discuss key methodological issues
- to assess recent methodological practice
- to identify current trends
- and to provide guidance for researchers in adopting existing and emerging research technologies.

Following a study by Chandler and Lyon (2001), Mullen *et al.* break their sample of articles into two broad categories, empirical and conceptual. Empirical studies are, they state, studies that include data and/or data analysis in the study while conceptual papers include theory/conceptual development, literature reviews and other treatments that do not gather or use data. Content analysis was the methodology used by Mullen *et al.* to examine the journal articles.

They found that there were in all 478 empirical studies and 187 conceptual papers. Of the 478 empirical papers, 50 were carried out using qualitative methods, case studies, interviews and observations. The qualitative studies accounted for seven per cent of all of the empirical research.

Almost three-quarters of all of the studies were quantitative ($n = 428$). In critiquing the quantitative studies, Mullen *et al.* focused on the sampling methods used, issues of validity and reliability, and the statistical methods used.

Across the three journals included in the study, there were in all 273 primary data studies. This represented 64 per cent of all quantitative studies, and 41 per cent of all small business/entrepreneurship research.

The primary data studies were divided into two groups, those carried out using a survey methodology, and those carried out using experimental design. Of the 273 primary data studies, only 13 studies, or 5 per cent of the primary data studies, had been carried out using experimental design. The remaining 260 studies were conducted using a survey methodology. Ninety-five per cent of all primary data studies, 61 percent of all empirical studies, and 39 percent of all small business/entrepreneurship studies relied on data gathered from surveys.

Secondary data, the researchers stated, were used in 155 papers, 36 per cent of all quantitative research and 24 per cent of all small business/entrepreneurship research.

Mullen *et al.* found that the researchers had used a wide range of statistical procedures to analyze their data. These statistical procedures included descriptive statistics, comparisons of means, the use of t-tests, correlation analysis, regression analysis and ANOVA and MANOVA.

The Mullen *et al.* study is interesting in terms of the focus of the study on the research methodologies used in small business and entrepreneurship research. As well as providing an analysis of the different methodological approaches used in the studies, the Mullen *et al.* study is interesting in terms of the critique it provides on those methodologies.

In conclusion Mullen *et al.* state that their review of all 655 studies published in the field of small business–entrepreneurship over the years 2001 to 2008 identifies improvements in the research methods used in the field of small business and entrepreneurship research, but also substantial methodological weaknesses.

Question Can you determine, from your reading of the journal article, the reasoning behind this conclusion? Based on your reading of the journal article, do you agree with this conclusion? Based on your reading of the journal article can you draw further conclusions? What further conclusions have you drawn?

References

Mullen, M.R., Budeva, D.G. and Doney, P.M. (2009) 'Research methods in the leading small business–entrepreneurship journals: A critical review with recommendations for future research', *Journal of Small Business Management* 47(3): 287–307.

THE FOUR STAGES IN THE DATA ANALYSIS PROCESS

It is important in quantitative data analysis, as it is in qualitative data analysis, to remember the four stages of the data analysis process, detailed and explained in-depth in the previous chapter, Chapter 13 'Managing Data and Introducing Data Analysis'. The four stages are as follows:

- The first stage calls for descriptive analysis. This is simply describing what it is that you see in the data.
- The second stage is interpretation; interpreting the data involves attempting to explain the meaning of what it is that you see in your data, as you have described it in the descriptive analysis.

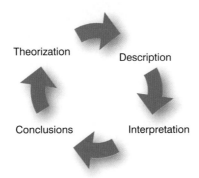

Figure 14.12   The four stages of analysis

- The third stage is the conclusions stage. In the conclusions stage, you move the interpretation along from stating what it is that you see in the data, and what you think that means, to drawing some kind of minor conclusion about that. The conclusions that you draw as you go along through the analysis are generally minor conclusions. They add up into, or they make a substantial contribution to, your overall conclusion(s). Your overall conclusion(s) are stated in the final chapter of the thesis, or in the final section of the report of the research project in the final chapter of the thesis.

- The fourth and final stage of the four stages of data analysis is theory or theorization. It is with this theorizing of the analysis that you begin to make your contribution to the body of knowledge. You look back at your literature review and you check to see how your findings fit with the findings of the theorists you have detailed in that chapter.

The means by which you draw findings from data, interpret those findings and draw conclusions from them are considered in detail in the final chapter of this textbook, Chapter 16, 'Drawing Conclusions and Writing Research'. Figure 14.12 illustrates the four stages in data analysis.

Table 14.10 Logic of the four frameworks approach to the research project	
The conceptual framework Contained in the research statement/ question and repeated again in the stated aim of the research.	The entire research project rests on the conceptual framework for the research project. The conceptual framework contains all of the key concepts in the research. The key concepts in the conceptual framework inform and guide the search for literature for the literature review, and they help structure the literature review.
The theoretical framework Contained in the literature review.	The literature review contains the theoretical framework for the research project. The structure and development of the literature review is guided and directed by the conceptual framework.

(Continued)

Table 14.10 Logic of the four frameworks approach to the research project (continued)	
The methodological framework Contained in the methodology section.	The methodological framework is contained in the methodology chapter of the thesis, or in the methodology section of the report of the research. The methodological framework contains all of the detail on how the research was carried out. The conceptual framework guides and directs the development of the theoretical framework. The conceptual framework with the theoretical framework guides and directs the development of the methodological framework. The conceptual framework, the aim and objectives of the research, and the theoretical framework inform, guide and direct the questions asked in the field work/data gathering for the research.
The analytical framework Contained in the data analysis chapter of the thesis/report.	The analytical framework is contained in the data analysis chapter of the thesis, or in the data analysis section of the report of the research. Data are gathered for the research project in order to respond to the research statement/question, the overall aim and the objectives of the research project. The focus of data analysis is on responding to the research statement/ question and the overall aim and objectives of the research. This ensures that the research project maintains focus, and it ensures that the researcher accomplishes what he/she set out to accomplish in undertaking the research as formally stated in the research aim and objectives.

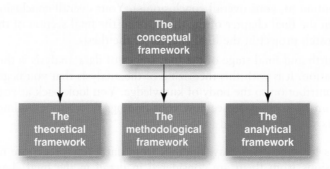

Figure 14.13   The four frameworks

As stated earlier in this chapter, you do not report every detail of your data. You select from your data (and your analysis of it) the key issues and aspects that you decide to present when writing up your analysis. The narrative (or story) that you tell about your data and your analysis of your data is dictated by your research statement or question, by the overall aim of your research, by the issues that emerged from your review of the literature, as well as by the data you gathered.

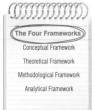

The four frameworks approach to research is designed to help the research maintain the focus of the research throughout the research process. The focus of the researcher throughout the research process should be on the research statement or question, the research hypothesis or the overall aim of the research project. The manner in which the four frameworks approach to the research process works is detailed once more in Figure 14.13.

The researcher must ensure that the data, the analysis of the data, and the data presented, all answer the research question, or all respond to the research statement, the research hypothesis, the overall aim of the research and the objectives of the research. Table 14.10 above explains once again the logic of the four frameworks approach.

CASE STUDY

A survey: Consumption of charity bracelets

'Consumers of charity bracelets: Cause-supporters or fashion-followers?', Yurchisin, J. et al. (2009)

Charity bracelet © IMAGEiN/Alamy

In this study, the researchers carried out a survey designed to compare the personal characteristics of buyers of rubber charity bracelets with those of non-buyers. The aim of the study was to develop a deeper understanding of the market success of rubber charity bracelets.

The survey was carried out on a convenience sample of 244 individuals in Texas and Iowa in the USA. The questionnaire used was divided into three sections. The first section was designed to assess participants' level of fashion involvement and celeb-rity involvement; the second section was designed to assess participants' attitudes toward the consumption of cause-related fashion products; and the third and final section was designed to facilitate the gathering of demographic data.

The authors state that the study provides useful information to manufacturers and sellers of cause-related products. They say that efforts to manufacture and sell cause-related products should focus on developing products that incorporate fashion trends with celebrity endorsers.

The article explains that one of the most popular fashion accessories in the USA in 2005 was a cause-related product: the silicone rubber charity bracelet (Dodes, 2005; Webster, 2005). These inexpensive, colourful, rubber bracelets, we are told, were sold by a variety of businesses (e.g. Nike, 7-Eleven, Hot Topic), and the proceeds or a portion of the proceeds of these sales were donated to specific charities (e.g. Lance Armstrong Foundation for cancer research, USO to support American troops stationed abroad, Hot Topic Foundation to support programmes and organizations that encourage youth involvement in art and music).

The article details that, according to the **LIVESTRONG** Lance Armstrong Foundation, more than 55 million people across the globe wear a yellow silicone band in support of people living with cancer (**LIVESTRONG**: 2007). With the overwhelming success of the rubber bracelet cause-related fashion product, the article explains, both for-profit and non-profit organizations located in the USA and around the globe are trying to develop new cause-related products that will be similarly popular in the upcoming seasons (Carnwath, 2006).

Thus, the authors suggest, a need exists among practitioners for information related to the consumers of rubber charity bracelets. They say that while general information has been collected about the consumers of ethical products and cause-related products (Cui *et al.*, 2003; Dickson and Littrell 1997), the unusually massive appeal of the rubber charity bracelet as a cause-related fashion product seems to warrant further investigation into the consumption of this particular cause-related product. The suggestion the authors make is that if practitioners can understand the reasons why consumers purchased the rubber charity bracelets, perhaps they can use this information to create similarly successful cause-related fashion products in the future.

They tell us that the purpose of their research was to survey rubber charity bracelet consumers by exploring their purchasing behaviour.

The demographic data presented in the article details that the majority of the participants in the research were female (86 per cent). Most participants indicated that they were either Caucasian American (76 per cent) or Hispanic American (17 per cent). The participants had a mean age of approximately 28 years, with a range of 18 to 65. We are told that although an attempt was made to obtain non-student participants, most participants were currently enrolled as undergraduate students (72 per cent). The number of rubber charity bracelets owned by participants ranged from 0 to 50, with a mean of 1.88. The average price paid by participants for each bracelet ranged from $0.00 to $20.00, with a mean of $2.55. The number of retail outlets where the bracelets were purchased ranged from 1 to 7, with an average of 2.71 outlets. The participants in the research indicated that they had purchased their bracelets most frequently from department stores (16.2 per cent); followed by speciality stores (15.3 per cent), discount retailers/mass merchandisers (14.7 per cent), internet websites (14.7 per cent), and boutiques (13.8 per cent).

In conclusion, the authors state that the results of their study indicate that the success of the rubber charity bracelet was based on different factors. They said that in the first place, the rubber charity bracelet is consistent with larger fashion trends, and in the second place it has an association with popularity celebrities. These two factors, the authors report, appeared to have contributed to the mass appeal of the rubber charity bracelet, particularly among individuals who were highly involved with fashion and celebrities.

The authors state that future efforts to manufacture cause-related products should focus on developing products that incorporate fashion trends. They also recommend that sellers of cause-related products could consider celebrity endorsers for effective marketing of their products.

We are told that the results of the study indicate that attitude toward purchasing a cause-related fashion product is not a good predictor of behaviour. The authors suggest that there may have been a social desirability bias where respondents showed support for particular causes and positive attitudes toward cause-related purchasing to please the researcher.

Question Can you explain what is meant by bias in research? Can you name and explain the main sources of bias in research?

References

Yurchisin, J., Yoo Jin, K. and Marcketti, S.B. (2009) 'Consumers of charity bracelets: Cause-supporters or fashion-followers?', *Journal of Fashion Marketing and Management* 13(3): 448–457.

CHAPTER REVIEW

The focus of this chapter was on quantitative data analysis. Simple approaches to data analysis were outlined and explained. As was demonstrated in the chapter, small simple data sets can be analyzed using a pen and paper, with perhaps the help of a calculator. More substantial quantitative data sets can be analyzed with the aid of a computer software package such as Microsoft Excel. The computer software package, SPSS as explained in the chapter, was designed for the analysis of quantitative social science data. This software package and the use of it was detailed and explained. The chapter demonstrates how to code data for SPSS and how to load data in SPSS. The critical importance of cleaning data loaded into SPSS for data analysis was emphasized. Both descriptive and inferential statistics are simply explained. The chapter explains the value of graphing data, both for presentation purposes and for the insights into data that can be gained from graphing data. The presentation of quantitative data in figures, graphs and tables is considered in the chapter. The four stages of the data analysis process are detailed and explained. The four stages are description, interpretation, conclusions and theorization. The fourth framework in the four frameworks approach to the research process, the analytical framework, is explained.

Now update your interactive research diary with your notes and findings at www.cengage.co.uk/quinlan. Complete the activities provided to reinforce your understanding of this chapter.

END OF CHAPTER QUESTIONS

1 What is a coding key?

2 What is a variable?

3 Explain the differences between nominal, ordinal and interval level variables.

4 Explain what is meant by the terms univariate, bivariate and multivariate analysis.

5 Explain the differences between descriptive and inferential statistics.

6 Name and explain ten descriptive statistics commonly used in quantitative data analysis and briefly outline how they are used in data analysis.

7 Name and explain five different inferential statistics and briefly outline how they are used in data analysis.

8 Explain why graphs and tables are used for the display and analysis of data

9 Outline and explain the key advantages to using SPSS in quantitative data analysis.

10 What is the analytical framework in the four frameworks approach to the research project, and explain how it helps the researcher maintain focus in the research project?

REFERENCES

Colorado State University, 'Writing guide: Introduction to statistics', http://writing.colstate.edu/guides/research/stats/index.cfm.

Columbia University, Columbia Center for New Media Teaching and Learning (CNMTL), 'Quantitative Methods in Social Sciences', Laymon, S. and Weiss, C., http://ccnmtl.columbia.edu/projects/qmss/home.html

Downs, A. (2009) 'Identifying shortage occupations in the UK', *Economic and Labour Market Review* 3(5): 23–29, www.statistics.gov.uk/cci/article.asp?id=2181 'Experimental design', The Science Olympiad, http://soinc.org/exper_design_b

Finn, A. (2009) 'If you only do one thing this week carry out an eco survey', *The Guardian*, 16 November.

Harvard – MIT Data Centre, 'Guide to SPSS', www.hmdc.harvard.edu/projects/SPSS_Tutorial/spsstut.shtml.

Hawthorne Experiments, Harvard Business School, http://www.library.hbs.edu/hc/hawthorne/09.html Accessed 03.06.2010.

Markova, G. (2009) 'Can human resource management make a big difference in a small company?', *International Journal of Strategic Management* 9 (2): 73–80.

Mullen, M.R., Budeva, D.G. and Doney, P.M. (2009) 'Research methods in the leading small business–entrepreneurship journals: A critical review with recommendations for future research', *Journal of Small Business Management* 47(3): 287–307.

Office for National Statistics, Statistical Bulletin 'internet access households and individuals 2009', www.statistics.gov.uk/statbase/Product.asp?vlnk=5672 Accessed 03.06.2010.

Purdue Online Writing Lab, 'Basic inferential statistics', http://owl.english.purdue.edu/owl/resource/672/05/

Stat Trek, 'Teach yourself statistics', http://stattrek.com

Trochim, W.M., The Research Methods Knowledge Base, 'Correlation', www.socialresearchmethods.net/kb/statcorr.php

— The Research Methods Knowledge Base, 'Experimental design', www.socialresearchmethods.net/kb/desexper.php

— The Research Methods Knowledge Base, 'Descriptive statistics', http://www.socialresearchmethods.net/kb/statdesc.php Accessed 03.06.2010.

— The Research Methods Knowledge Base, 'Inferential statistics', www.socialresearchmethods.net/kb/statinf.php

— The Research Methods Knowledge Base, 'The T-test', www.socialresearchmethods.net/kb/stat_t.php

UCLA 'Introduction to statistics', www.ats.ucla.edu/stat/Spss/modules/descript.htm

Yurchisin, J., Yoo Jin, K. and Marcketti, S.B. (2009) 'Consumers of charity bracelets: Cause-supporters or fashion-followers?', *Journal of Fashion Marketing and Management* 13(3): 448–457.

RECOMMENDED READING

Babbie, E. (1990) 'Survey Research Methods 2nd. Ed.', Wadsworth Publishing Co., Belmont, CA, USA.

Bell, J. (2005) *Doing your Research Project*, Ch. 12, 'Interpreting the Evidence and Reporting the Findings', Maidenhead: Open University Press.

Brengman, M. and Willems, K. (2009) 'Determinants of fashion store personality: A consumer perspective', *Journal of Product and Brand Management* 18(5): 346–355.

Collis, J. and Hussey, R. (2009) *Business Research: A Practical Guide for Undergraduate and Postgraduate Students*, Ch. 11, 'Analysing Data Using Descriptive Statistics' and Ch. 12, 'Analysing Data Using Inferential Statistics', Houndsmill: Palgrave Macmillan.

Creswell, J.W. (2003) *Research Design, Qualitative, Quantitative, and Mixed Methods Approaches*, (2nd edn), Ch. 9, 'Quantitative Methods', Thousand Oaks, CA: Sage.

Curwin, J. and Slater, R. (2004) *'Quantitative Methods: A Short Course'*, London: Cengage.

Daly, F., Hand, D.J., Jones, M.G., Lunn, A.D. and McConway, K.J. (1995) *Elements of Statistics*, Wokingham, UK: Addison Wesley.

Davis, D. (2005) *Business Research for Decision Making*, Part Five, 'Analytical Procedures', Mason, OH: Cengage South-Western.

Deacon, D., Pickering, M., Golding, P. and Murdock, G. (1999) *Researching Communications: A Practical Guide to Methods in Media and Cultural Analysis*, Ch. 5, 'Handling Numbers', and Ch. 6, 'Counting Contents', Oxford: Oxford University Press.

Easterby-Smith, M., Thorpe, R. and Jackson, P.R. (2008) *Management Research* (3rd edn), Ch. 10, 'Making Sense of Quantitative Data', and Ch. 11, 'Multivariate Analyses', London: Sage.

Kent, R. (2007) *Marketing Research: Approaches, Methods and Applications in Europe*, Ch. 11, 'Analysing Quantitative Data: Essential Descriptive Summaries of Single Variables', Ch. 12, 'Analysing Relationships Between Two Variables', Ch. 13, 'Making Statistical Inferences', and Ch. 14, 'Multivariate Analysis', London: Cengage.

Lee, N. and Lings, I. (2008) *Doing Business Research: A Guide to Theory and Practice*, Ch. 12, 'How and Why Statistics Work', Ch. 13, 'Quantitative Data Analysis I', and Ch. 14, 'Quantitative Data Analysis II', London: Sage.

Neuman, W., Lawrence (2000) *Social Research Methods: Quantitative and Qualitative Approaches*, Ch. 12, 'Analysis of Quantitative Data', Boston, MA: Allyn & Bacon.

Oppenheim, A.N. (1992) *Questionnaire Design, Interviewing and Attitude Measurement*, London: Pinter.

Robson, C. (2000) *Real World Research*, Ch. 13, 'The Analysis of Quantitative Data', Oxford: Blackwell.

Sutherland, E. (2009) 'Counting customers, subscribers and mobile phone numbers', *Info* 11(2): 6–23.

Zikmund, W.G. (2003) *Business Research Methods*, Part 6, 'Data Analysis and Presentation', Mason, OH: Cengage South-Western.

CHAPTER 15

ANALYZING QUALITATIVE DATA

LEARNING OBJECTIVES

At the end of this chapter the student should be able to:

- Understand qualitative data analysis.

- Be able to analyze qualitative data.

RESEARCH SKILLS

At the end of this chapter the student should, using the exercises on the accompanying online platform, be able to:

- Conduct an analysis of the data set presented.

- Critique the data provided in terms of the stated aim of the research project.

The aim of this chapter is to develop the focus on qualitative data and qualitative data analysis started in Chapter 13, 'Managing Data and Introducing Data Analysis', and to teach the student how to engage in qualitative data analysis. The chapter explains the key concepts and issues in qualitative data analysis, describes some of the different approaches to it, and demonstrates the processes and procedures involved. The student will learn in this chapter how to carry out qualitative data analysis.

INTRODUCTION

This chapter explains in detail what qualitative data are and how qualitative data are analyzed. The chapter outlines a simple approach to qualitative data analysis, and introduces the student to more complex approaches to qualitative data analysis. The use of CAQDAS software is explored in the chapter and three different software packages available for qualitative data analysis are considered, NVivo, Atlas ti and NUDIST. The centrality of language in qualitative data and qualitative data analysis is explored and explained. Different ways to present qualitative data and qualitative research findings in the thesis or research report are considered. Finally, the chapter explains how to blend together the findings from quantitative and qualitative research in the writing up of data analysis.

Figure 15.1 demonstrates once again where in the research process data analysis occurs. As you can see from the figure, the researcher gathers data, analyses that data, and then draws conclusions from the analyzed data in order to complete the research.

The newspaper article below details how a 50-year-old company used qualitative research to gain an understanding of what customers required and expected. In-depth qualitative research designed to examine the needs of customers was carried out. Through the research the purchase experience of customers was mapped out, step-by-step. Customer types were defined, different choices and behaviours on the part of customers were analyzed, and scenarios of the ideal customer experience were developed. The findings of the qualitative research provided the company with a complete rethink of the service provided for customers.

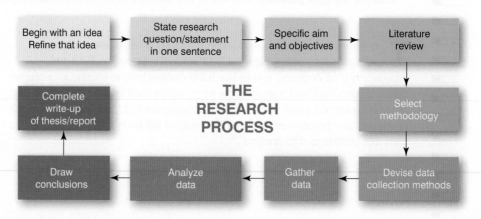

Figure 15.1   The research process

THE VALUE OF GOOD RESEARCH

'"People matter" is key message on the road to recovery', Trevett, N., *The Guardian*, 12.3.2010

Amplifon hearing aid specialists shop store in Norwich © T.M.O. Buildings/Alamy

Extract

By plotting the needs and desires of clients with great accuracy, service design is freeing up businesses to implement radical change in direct relation to what people want.

These are difficult times to do business. A toxic mix of recession, limited credit and consumers unwilling to spend, has created challenging conditions in every sector. Businesses are questioning themselves as never before in their search for competitive edge, if not survival. A sense of crisis is dissipating established mindsets and assumptions – and companies are discovering that people matter.

For all the talk of the importance of good customer service, in truth it is rare. Businesses don't really get it. And this is where service design can play its part: by helping a business to reach an in-depth understanding of its customers, and shape a service that meets their real, often unrecognized needs, service design can yield both financial rewards and satisfied consumers.

For Haluk Terzioglu, chief marketing executive of the Amplifon Group, the challenge was simple. Amplifon is an Italian worldwide retailer of customized hearing solutions, with 3000 points of sale in 14 countries. The group was, and is, the market leader in its sector, and Terzioglu wanted it to stay that way. That meant selling more hearing aids – but success depended on the customers' experience in the stores, and Terzioglu knew that the format that had worked for more than 50 years was no longer fit for purpose.

Amplifon's business has two aspects: medical and consumer. The products it sells are medical, and customers are both client and patient. The problem was that the medical aspect had become dominant; customers were walking into an environment that felt more like a clinic. A complete rethink was needed.

To gain an understanding of what customers required and expected, Terzioglu turned to design consultancy Continuum. Continuum conducted in-depth qualitative research into people's functional and emotional needs as they went through the process of buying a hearing aid. Continuum mapped the process out, step-by-step, defining customer types, analysing different choices and behaviours, and helping create scenarios that provided the ideal experience. Such an approach, Terzioglu believes, was a first, not only for Amplifon, but for the industry.

The resulting store design has united Amplifon's split personality. 'We have brought the two worlds together: retail and medical, emotional and rational,' says Terzioglu. 'The store is the visible expression of the new brand – welcoming, caring and proactive.'

The new format has won design awards, and, over the next 5 years, will roll out to all the group's stores.

References

Trevett, N. (2010) '"People matter" is key message on road to recovery', *The Guardian*, March 12, **www.guardian.co.uk/service-design/people-matter** Accessed 03.06.2010 © Guardian News & Media Ltd 2010. Reproduced with permission.

QUALITATIVE DATA ANALYSIS

Qualitative data analysis is the process through which qualitative data are analyzed. One of the main functions of qualitative data analysis is to develop as thick and rich and as complete an account of the phenomenon under investigation as possible. The concept of a **thick description** was introduced by Clifford Geertz in his book *The Interpretation of Cultures* (1973). This concept of a thick description is useful in relation to qualitative data analysis. The aim of the process of analysis in qualitative data analysis is to accomplish this thick description of the phenomenon under investigation.

Thick description Developed by Clifford Geertz, to explain the complex in-depth representation qualitative researchers attempt to accomplish when describing their research projects.

Qualitative researchers, rather than objectively studying the 'real' world, acknowledge multiple realities. Qualitative research is situated within a constructivist or interpretivist paradigm. Qualitative researchers hold that we co-construct our world, our understanding of reality, that we interpret the world individually and in our own way. In qualitative research, it is these subjective experiences and expressions of reality that the qualitative researcher tries to understand and describe.

The language of qualitative research and qualitative data analysis tends to be softer than the language of quantitative research and quantitative data analysis. In some respects, the language of quantitative research and quantitative data analysis is a technicist instrumentalist language. The vocabulary of quantitative research, for example, tends to include words like 'instrument', 'subject', 'experiment', and 'test'. In qualitative research, on the other hand, the word 'method' is often used instead of instrument. Rather than research subjects, qualitative researchers tend to talk about research participants; rather than experiment or test, qualitative researchers tend to 'explore', 'describe', 'detail' and 'construct'. There is an emphasis in qualitative research in signalling, throughout the research process and the writing up of the research, an acknowledgement of and a respect for the basic humanity of research participants and the circumstances of their lives.

Another striking difference in the reporting of quantitative and qualitative research is the presence of the researcher. In the reporting of quantitative research, there is no space for the researcher and the researcher is completely written out of the analysis. Qualitative research is very different. While the fundamental aim of qualitative research is to uncover the subjective meanings participants make of the phenomenon under investigation, there is an acknowledgement of the role that the researcher plays in creating meaning, through their essential selection, description and interpretation of the data they gather for the research project. This is because, within qualitative research, there is an explicit acknowledgement that data gathered is filtered through the consciousness of the researcher. In qualitative data analysis the researcher becomes subjectively immersed in the data and does not stand objectively apart from the data. As this is the case, there is a call within qualitative research for the researcher to provide a reflexive account of themselves within the research project.

Reflexivity In qualitative research, reflexivity calls for an acknowledgement on the part of the researcher of their role in the research project. The essential role of the researcher in interpreting the experiences of others in the qualitative research process calls for the perspective of the researcher in this process to be made explicit. This is done by the researcher through a reflexive process in which the researcher makes explicit the perspectives, understandings and decisions that guide them through the process of data analysis to the findings and conclusions of the research.

This is important in qualitative research because of the explicit acknowledgement in qualitative research that we are in relation to the phenomenon we are investigating impacts on how we study the phenomenon, how we interpret and make sense of it, and the conclusions we come to in relation to it. As this is the case, within qualitative research, there is a need for reflexivity on the part of the researcher. Reflexivity in qualitative research is the account that the researcher provides of themselves and their role in the construction of meaning in the research process.

Within qualitative data analysis, the researcher and the role of the researcher are evident and made evident, in a reflexive manner, in the way in which the report of the data analysis is written. It is a good exercise to use your research diary to develop notes of your ideas and thoughts on your reflexive engagement with your research project. These notes can be drawn on when you are writing a reflexive account of your engagement with your research project in the formal account of the research. We will explore this further in the next and final chapter, Chapter 16 'Drawing Conclusions and Writing Research'. When reading journal articles, it is useful to identify any differences in the language used in accounts of quantitative research projects and qualitative research projects, and to highlight the reflexive accounts that researchers in qualitative research projects give of themselves and their role(s) in the research.

Language Language is particularly important in qualitative data and qualitative data analysis as it is frequently through the study and analysis of the language of the participants in the study that the researchers conduct their research. The thick description that the researchers attempt to develop through data analysis is generated from and with the language of the participants in the study. In qualitative data analysis, rather than analysing and reporting numbers, researchers analyze language and they use language to give expression to their analyses. Many of the data collection methods used in qualitative research produce data that is language-based, for example interview and focus group transcripts of the oral testimony of participants.

In qualitative data analysis there are different approaches to the process of analysis, depending on the needs and design of the study. Qualitative data can be analyzed thematically, in terms of themes, or discursively, in terms of discourses. Qualitative data can be analyzed using a content analysis approach. Content analysis has application in both quantitative data analysis and qualitative data analysis. It means, simply, analysing the content of some phenomenon, photograph, cartoon, drawing, newspaper, magazine, film, or interview or focus group transcript. Qualitative data can be analyzed using a phenomenological approach, if the research project has been developed using a phenomenological methodology, and sometimes an argument can be made for using a phenomenological approach to data analysis in a research project which has not been developed using this methodology. Similarly, qualitative research can be analyzed using a grounded theory approach, if the research project has been developed using a grounded theory methodology, and sometimes this approach to data analysis can be appropriate in a research project which has not been developed using a ground theory methodology. **Narrative analysis** in qualitative data analysis calls for an analysis of the narratives in the data. Textual analysis calls for an analysis of the data as texts; data can be in the form of films, videos, television programmes, magazines, advertisements, photographs, clothes and graffiti, which can all be considered texts for the purposes of textual analysis. The key to selecting or developing an appropriate approach to qualitative data analysis, is to select or develop an approach which best suits, or fits, the research project.

Narrative analysis The analysis of data through the use of narratives.

THE FOUR STAGES OF DATA ANALYSIS

The four stages of data analysis (see Figure 15.2), as explained in the previous chapter, are description, interpretation, conclusions and theorization. In the first stage of data analysis, we describe what is there in the data, what is evident in the data. This first stage of data analysis is known as descriptive analysis. In the second stage, the interpretive stage, we try to interpret what is in the data. In interpreting the data, the researcher tries to uncover the meaning of the data, and tries to articulate that meaning. The question the researcher asks themselves is this – 'if this is what is in the data, what does that mean?' The third stage is the conclusions stage. In this stage the researcher draws minor conclusions from the data, as the process of data analysis unfolds. The question the researcher asks themselves in this stage is – 'if this is what the data says, and these are the possible meanings of that, what are the implications of that?' The researcher tries to tease out the implications of the data. The data may have different implications for different parties to the research, the participants in the research, the broader population of the study, the discipline, if there is a discipline, the area of business, if the research is situated within a particular area of business, and so on. The researcher tries to tease out the implications of the data for all of those parties.

The final stage in the four stages approach to data analysis is theorization. In this stage, the researcher looks back at the theoretical framework outlined in the literature review chapter or section of the study. The researcher examines the literature review to see if and how the findings of their study fit with or contradict the findings of the studies and the theorists as they have presented them in their literature review. The researcher, in writing the data analysis stage of the research, demonstrates how their findings fit with, or contradict, the findings of other (published) research projects. The researcher shows how, in the writing of the data analysis section or chapter of the research project, the research they are carrying out fits with the research published in the field or area. This is the process of theorization and it is the way in which the researcher knits their research into the body of knowledge. This is the way in which the researcher makes a contribution to the body of knowledge. Figure 15.2 details the four stages of analysis.

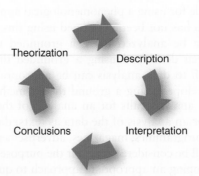

Figure 15.2   The four stages of analysis

The Analytical Framework

In the four frameworks approach to the research project the fourth and final framework is the analytical framework. As can be seen from Figure 15.3, the analytical framework takes its focus and direction from the conceptual framework for the research project. The conceptual framework for the research project is contained in the research statement or question. The conceptual framework contains all of the key concepts in the research project. The conceptual framework informs the development of the theoretical framework. Both the conceptual framework and the theoretical framework inform the methodological framework. They inform the selection and design of the methodology for the study, and this methodology, with the conceptual and theoretical frameworks, informs the data collection methods used in the study, the questions asked and the areas explored in the data gathering phase of the study. The methodological framework comprises the methodology, the data collection methods used in the project and all of the aspects of the process of carrying out the research. Finally, the analytical framework for the study is informed by the three preceding frameworks, the conceptual, theoretical and methodological frameworks.

The Four Frameworks
Conceptual Framework
Theoretical Framework
Methodological Framework
Analytical Framework

If the methodology used in the research is phenomenology, then the data analysis process will be phenomenological. Similarly, if the methodology is grounded theory, then the data analysis process will be a grounded theory process. If the methodology calls for the study of texts, then the process of analysis is likely to be textual analysis, and if the methodology calls for the gathering of narratives, then the process of analysis is likely to be narrative analysis. Sometimes the process of analysis to be used in the study is as clearly indicated as this, sometimes it is not. When the process of analysis is not so clearly indicated, the researcher develops an approach to analysis that best fits the research project. The approach to analysis, as well as being informed by the methodological framework, is informed by the conceptual framework. The conceptual framework guides the design and development of the process of data analysis for the research project. Along with the theoretical and methodological frameworks, it guides the design and development of the analytical framework for the project. The analytical framework is presented in the data analysis chapter of the thesis or in the data analysis section of the report of the research. The structure of the data analysis chapter, the subheadings in the chapter and the content of the subsections under each of the subheadings are informed by the conceptual framework, the theoretical framework, and the data gathered and analyzed for the research project. This four frameworks approach ensures that the focus is maintained throughout the

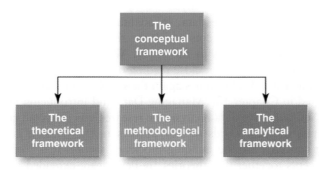

Figure 15.3   The four frameworks approach to the research project

Table 15.1 The four frameworks	
The conceptual framework Contained in the research statement/question and in the stated aim of the research.	The entire research project rests on the conceptual framework for the research project. The conceptual framework contains all of the key concepts in the research. The key concepts in the conceptual framework inform and guide the search for literature for the literature review, and they help structure the literature review.
The theoretical framework Contained in the literature review.	The literature review contains the theoretical framework for the research project. The structure and development of the literature review is guided and directed by the conceptual framework.
The methodological framework Contained in the methodology chapter of the thesis/report.	The methodological framework is contained in the methodology chapter of the thesis, or in the methodology section of the report of the research. The methodological framework contains all of the detail on how the research was carried out. The conceputal framework, the aim and objectives of the research, and the theoretical framework inform and direct data collection for the research. They inform, guide and direct the questions asked in the fieldwork/data gathering for the research.
The analytical framework Contained in the data analysis chapter of the thesis/report.	The analytical framework is contained in the data analysis chapter of the thesis, or in the data analysis section of the report of the research. Data are gathered for the research project in order to respond to the research statement/question, the overall aim and the objectives of the research project. The focus of data analysis is on responding to the research statement/question and the overall aim and objectives of the research. This ensures that the research project maintains focus, and it ensures that the researcher accomplishes what he/she set out to accomplish in undertaking the research and as formally stated in the research aim and objectives.

research process and it helps to ensure that the research project, as it develops, remains properly integrated (see Table 15.1).

A simple approach to qualitative data analysis

Basic qualitative data analysis begins with a close reading of the data. In order to achieve this, the researcher will read through the data over and over again. The researcher must become familiar with the data and eventually become immersed in the data. This close reading brings the researcher into the nuances of the data. The researcher must know and understand the data before they can begin to describe and analyze it. In qualitative data analysis (as in quantitative data analysis), the researcher engages in coding the data. In qualitative research, the codes used by the researcher are words or concepts which the researcher identifies in the data as relevant or even key or critical to the study. When the researcher has become immersed in the data through their close reading of the data, they begin this process of coding the data. Table 15.2 outlines again the simple approach to qualitative data analysis presented in Chapter 13, 'Managing Data and Introducing Data Analysis'.

In engaging in qualitative data analysis the researcher is above all concerned with the key concepts, the key words or key phrases in the data. It is important to remember that concepts are the building blocks of theory. It is from the work of connecting concepts together that theories are developed, extended or changed.

Table 15.2   A simple approach to qualitative data analysis

One simple approach to qualitative data analysis is to read through all of the data and whilst reading, make a list of all of the themes that occur in the data. The themes would be the key ideas or the key concepts that strike the researcher as important and relevant to the research, as he/she reads through the data transcripts. The researcher continues reading the transcripts and recording themes until no new themes emerge. Then the researcher takes the complete list of themes and explores them with a view to collapsing themes together. In other words, the researcher tries to condense the list of themes by fitting themes together that seem to logically fit together. In this way, the list of themes becomes shorter, and more manageable. When the researcher collapses themes together he/she needs to conceptualize a new theme, a theme which will encompass all the themes collapsed together. This process is a process of abstraction. Through this process, the researcher takes a step away from the raw data, and a step towards an abstract or abstracted understanding of the data. The researcher through this process of abstraction comes closer to the meaning of the data, the meaning of the data in relation to the overall aim of the research. The researcher moves to deeper levels of abstraction in relation to the data, moving further and further away from the raw data, as he/she continues to collapse themes together. The researcher can colour code the themes; in colour coding the themes, he/she assigns, arbitrarily, for example, the colour red to the first theme, the colour yellow to the second theme, the colour green to the third theme, and so on. The researcher then reads through the transcripts assigning the colours to the parts of the data that represent each of the themes. In this way the researcher can see at a glance each of the themes as they are represented in the data. The researcher then decides how to tell the story of the data, based on this thematic analysis, in the written account of the analysis presented in the data analysis chapter of the thesis or in the data analysis section of the report of the research.

This is the data analysis process that Lian used in analysing her qualitative data (see Lian's research project in Chapter 14 'Analyzing Quantitative Data').

1 The researcher engages in a process of attempting to group concepts together around key or core concepts.

2 Then the researcher groups the key or core concepts together in themes.

3 The researcher groups the themes together around key themes.

4 The researcher identifies the key themes in the data.

This process of analysis takes considerable reflection and engagement with the raw data. Eventually, the researcher presents an account of the project of data analysis, using the key themes that emerged in data analysis.

The research project should be fully integrated. The four frameworks approach to the research project is designed to facilitate the researcher in accomplishing this. Each aspect of the research process helps to build the next aspect. As this is the case, the themes that emerge from the process of data analysis should fit with the conceptual framework of the research project, and they should fit with the theoretical framework constructed by the researcher for the research project. This is not to say that the researcher should be closed to new and unanticipated concepts, themes and ideas that emerge from the data. The researcher should of course be open to new ideas, fresh insights and unanticipated concepts and themes in the data. These ideas, insights and concepts and themes, if and when they are discovered, can be incorporated into the research project. If they are substantial, they can be used to extend the focus of the research project, and if they are less substantial, they can be integrated into the structures that the researcher has provided for the analytical framework of the research project.

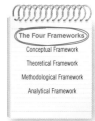

Other approaches to data analysis

Discourse analysis
The analysis of data through the use of discourses.

Thematic analysis
The analysis of data through the use of themes.

In **discourse analysis**, instead of themes, the researcher is focused on identifying and interpreting different discourses. The approach taken to analysis is the same or similar to the approach detailed above, but the focus is on discourses rather than themes. In narrative analysis, the researcher is focused on describing and interpreting the different narratives in the data. In semiotics, the researcher is focused on identifying signs in the data, and on describing and interpreting the way in which signs are used in the data, and the meanings of the signs in the data. Within semiotics the researcher uncovers the denotative (explicit) and the connotative (implicit) meanings of the data (see Bignell, 2002, Chapter 1). In image-based research, the images can be analyzed using **thematic analysis**, using discourse analysis, narrative analysis, textual analysis, content analysis or semiotic analysis. Image-based research could be used as the data gathering method, or as one of the data gathering methods, in many methodological approaches, for example, in a phenomenological, a grounded theory research project an action research project or in feminist research. As stated, the most appropriate approach to data analysis is based on what it is that the research project is attempting to accomplish, the methodology used in the research, the data collection methods used and the data gathered.

When the overall aim of a research project is to explore and describe how language is used in relation to a particular phenomenon, appropriate methodologies for such projects are methodologies which particularly focus on language. These include discourse analysis and narrative analysis. When the overall aim of a research project is to create a representation of some experience or culture, an appropriate methodology for such research is ethnography. Ethnography is the methodology in focus in Chapter 10 'Observation'. Data in ethnographic research can be analyzed thematically, discursively, semiotically, using discourse analysis, content analysis, and so on. The key, as always, is that the approach to data analysis used in the research project must fit with the research project. Sometimes the overall aim of a research project is specifically to develop theory. Grounded

Table 15.3 Data analysis in grounded theory research: Three stages in the data analysis process.
Open coding To begin with the researcher reads through the data a number of times to ensure that they are familiar with the data. In this first stage the researcher goes through the data coding for every concept that has meaning in relation to the research. The very many codes that emerge in this stage of the coding process are gathered together in categories. In a grounded theory research project, the fundamental aim of the research project is to generate theory from data. As this is the case, grounded theory researchers tend to draw their concepts and categories more from the language of the data gathered than from any literature reviewed for the research project. This is because the methodology is specifically designed to develop new theory.
Axial coding In this second stage the researcher looks for relationships in the data between the concepts that have emerged in the open coding process (the first stage). In this second stage the researcher is beginning to integrate the concepts under key concepts. So the number of concepts begins to narrow. At the same time, the researcher checks the data for concepts that did not emerge in the open coding stage. In this stage of data analysis the researcher begins to organize the different categories to emerge from the data in some order. The researcher asks critical questions of the data in order to thoroughly develop an account of the phenomenon under investigation. The researcher then looks for evidence in

(Continued)

	the data to support particular answers to the critical questions. All of this helps to deepen the analysis of the data.
Selective coding	In this third stage the researcher, having identified all of the categories and sub-categories in the data, now identifies the key category in the data. The core category in the data is described in all its dimensions and all of the properties of this core category are detailed. Then each of the other key categories in the data is related to this core category. The focus at this stage of the data analysis process is on developing and explicating a theory which details the phenomenon under investigation by connecting and explaining the relationships between each of the key categories to emerge from the analysis.

theory is an appropriate methodology for such projects. A particular approach to data analysis has been developed within grounded theory. Table 15.3 contains a very brief overview of a grounded theory approach to data analysis.

Grounded theory, as detailed above, is a good approach to data analysis. It facilitates in-depth data analysis. Adaptations of this grounded theory approach to data analysis are used in many research projects. Grounded theory is the methodology in focus in this chapter.

THE VALUE OF GOOD RESEARCH

Focus on ground theory methodology

Grounded theory (GT) methodology, as explained in Chapter 7 'Understanding Research Methodology and Design', is used when the specific focus of the research is on building theory from data. GT methodology is situated within a social constructivist paradigm, and it is rooted in symbolic interactionism. Very simply, symbolic interactionism is the formation of meaning between individuals through the ways in which they interact with each other.

GT was developed by Barney Glazer and Anselm Strauss (1967). Glaser and Strauss later split in their understanding of the methodology. Within Glaser's GT methodology, the methodology can draw on quantitative or qualitative methods, or both. Strauss and Corbin (2007), have more recently written on this methodology; they have presented the methodology as a qualitative methodology. (This is further

evidence of the great debates that exist and are ongoing in relation to research and research methodology in the social sciences.)

In an interesting journal article, Ng and Hase (2008), provide suggestions for doing a GT business research project. In the paper they provided guidelines and suggestions for beginner researchers and students on conducting a GT business research project. GT is, as they say, a systematic inductive approach to developing theory. The aim of GT research is to develop substantive theory from data that are gathered in real-world settings. The insights that a GT study produces, according to the authors, are contextual explanations for 'what's going on' rather than descriptions of 'what's going on'.

GT, the author's state, has a set of established principles for conducting research and interpreting data. These principles are laid out and discussed in the article. They are:

- Theory emerging from data: 'GT is not preconceived theory or a priori theory, it is theory grounded in data that are methodically acquired during the course of the research, (Glaser and Strauss, 1967: 32).

- Need to avoid preconceptions: as theory is 'discovered in the data', preconceived ideas are to be avoided. The researcher must approach the phenomenon with an open mind.

- The need to be theoretically sensitive: the researcher must have a capacity for conceptualization. They must be able to recognize and conceptualize patterns discovered in the data. This is essential if the research is to move beyond description to the conceptualization and development of theory.

- The constant comparison method of data analysis: this involves exploring similarities and differences in data gathered. Using constant comparison, categories are defined, relationships between categories are identified, and the identification of patterns is facilitated (Glaser, 2001). This process of constant comparison in data analysis continues until the core category has been identified. The core category, in Glaser's method, becomes the centre of the new emerging theory.

- An iterative research progression: Using an iterative approach to the research process, the researcher moves constantly between data collection and data analysis, from open coding to theoretical coding to data collection and back again to data analysis.

The main purpose and use of GT is to discover what is happening in relation to the research phenomenon, and to build a theory about that from the data gathered on/about that phenomenon.

It would be a useful exercise to source the article by Ng and Hase (2008) and read it through. It provides a thorough introduction to GT methodology and GT research in a business context.

References

Corbin, J. and Strauss, A. (2007) 'Basics of Qualitative Research: Techniques and Procedures for Developing Grounded Theory', Thousand Oaks, CA: Sage.

Glaser, B.G. (2001) The grounded theory perspective: Conceptualization contrasted with description', Mill Valley, CA: Sociology Press.

Grounded Theory: A Thumbnail Sketch', Bob Dick (2005), **www.scu.edu.au/schools/gcm/ar/arp/grounded. html** Accessed 03.06.2010.

Grounded Theory Review, an academic journal publishing research carried out using classic grounded theory methodology.

Partington, D. (2000) 'Building Grounded Theories of Management Action', *British Journal of Management,* 11 (2): 91–102.

Strauss, A. and Corbin, J. (1990, 1998 edns), 'Basics of Qualitative Research: Techniques and Procedures for Developing Grounded Theory' Thousand Oaks, CA: Sage.

The Grounded Theory Institute, **www.groundedtheory. com** Accessed 03.06.2010.

DATA ANALYSIS IN CASE STUDY RESEARCH: AN INTRODUCTION

The focus of phenomenological research is on the study of lived experience from the perspective of those living the experience. A phenomenological inquiry tries to uncover the meaning, the structure and the essence of a lived experience of the person or the group, or the community living the experience. Phenomenology is the research methodology in focus in Chapter 11 'Using Interviews and Focus Groups'. The main stages in data analysis in phenomenological research are shown in Table 15.4.

The process of analysis for phenomenological research detailed above has been developed specifically for that methodology. As can be seen, it is a quite distinct approach to data analysis. It is important that the researcher uses, and that they fully understand, the most appropriate approach to analysis for the data they have gathered. A great deal has been written about the different approaches to qualitative data analysis. You should source and read detailed and reliable material on the approach

Table 15.4	Data analysis in phenomenological research
First stage	In the first stage, the researcher examines their own beliefs, views, perspectives and assumptions regarding the phenomenon under investigation. Then the researcher sets those aside. This process is also known as **bracketing**. This is a way in phenomenological data analysis of performing the essential reflexivity of the qualitative research project.
Second stage	In the second stage of phenomenological data analysis, the researcher lists all of the significant statements in the data. This is called, in Moustakas (1994), terms, horizontalization of the data. The final list eliminates repetitive and overlapping statements. The statements will be significant in terms of the areas considered, examined and/or explored in the data gathering phase of the research. The researcher then clusters statements together in meaning units.
Third stage	In the third stage, using the meaning units the researcher develops a textual description of the phenomenon. Then the researcher develops a structural description of how the phenomenon was experienced. The researcher does this first to develop their own account of the experience. The researcher then does this for each participant in the research. After this, a description of the phenomenon is written which encompasses all of the experiences. Through this process, the researcher develops a thick description of the meaning, structure and essence of the experience.

Bracketing
The process through which the researcher acknowledges their preconceptions about the phenomenon under investigation.

to data analysis you propose using in your research project; this chapter is simply a general basic introduction to qualitative data analysis.

Data analysis in case study research

In case study research, data analysis involves making a thick description of the case being studied. Case study research generally calls for the analysis of multiple streams of data. The data may be quantitative or qualitative, or both. We dealt in detail with quantitative data analysis in the preceding chapter, Chapter 14, 'Analyzing Quantitative Data'. In this chapter 15, we have dealt in detail with the analysis of qualitative data. Within a case study methodology, a thematic approach to qualitative data analysis, as detailed earlier in this chapter, would be appropriate. (see Table 15.2). Content analysis, where appropriate, is used in case study research. The approach to data analysis used should be the approach best suited to the data. The important issues are the comprehensiveness and the validity of the data gathered on the case(s), and the quality of the analysis of that data. Tellis (1997), provides a simple and helpful account of data analysis in case study research. You will find this at **www. nova.edu/ssss/QR/QR3-2?tellis1.html**.

The box feature below is an interesting study of the role of branded products in nostalgia. The data gathering methods used consisted of two sets of interviews and a projective technique. The projective technique involved showing pictures of the products and brands named by the participants to them during the interviews in order to explore the thoughts and memories the products and brands evoke for the interviewees. Using a content analysis approach to data analysis the researchers analyzed the content of the interview transcripts in three different and distinct stages; in the first stage the transcripts were analyzed discursively (data analysis focused on the discourses in the data); in the second stage they were analyzed using a computer software package specifically designed to analyze words/vocabulary; and in the third stage a semiotic analysis of the texts (the interview transcripts) was carried out.

It would be a good idea to access this article online and to read it through. As you can see, a very thorough analysis was carried out. The three stages in data analysis enabled the researchers to immerse themselves in the data. The three stages provided different perspectives on the data and different insights into it. You can see in the

THE VALUE OF GOOD RESEARCH

'A semiotic analysis of nostalgia as a connection to the past', Kessous, A. and Roux, E. (2008)

In their research Kessous and Roux (2008) focused on a semiotic analysis of the meaning of nostalgia related to products and brands. Their research involved a two-stage interview process, each interviewee was interviewed twice. The interviews took place at 1 year intervals. Informants were interviewed about products and brands connected to nostalgic feelings. Pictures of products and brands evoked in the first interview were shown again in the second interview. Informants were asked to explain what came to mind for them when they looked at the pictures.

The interviews were taped and transcribed and based on the transcripts of the interviews, a three-step content analysis was performed.

The researchers state that content analysis was performed in three stages. First, all of the interviews were reviewed to identify discernable patterns as they emerged from the texts and to define a coding criterion. From this stage, the researchers distinguished first-time nostalgia from long-standing nostalgia. In the second stage the vocabulary the interviewees used when expressing nostalgic experiences was examined. In order to do this, a software package called Sphinx

Lexica was used. This software, according to the researchers, enabled a fast key word search of the transcripts. This, they said, made it possible to select the products/brands that were the most frequently mentioned, and these could then be related to their spatial-temporal-emotional-personal context (Helme-Guizon and Gavard-Perret, 2004). The researchers state that 'the simple description and quantification' of data quickly become sterile if not completed by a willingness to understand the meaning and the origin of frequency, textual structures, lexical associations or categories (Gavard-Perret and Moscarola, 1998). It was decided, we are told, that in a third stage in analysis a complementary semiotic approach was used to overcome this limitation (Benoit-Moreau, 2006).

The results of this study showed that some individuals are attached to special possessions, 'either replaceable (e.g. food) or irreplaceable (e.g. family jewels), which are rooted in a specific period of time, place or social situation (Grayson and Shulman, 2000)'. The researchers state that 'nostalgia connects objects, individuals and events across time and place (Holak and Havlena, 1992)'. They said that 'in each case, some symbolic reminder is sought so that the memories attached to the object will remain vivid and real'. They said that, 'furthermore, possessions derive their value by expressing or reinforcing the sense of self (Richins, 1994a,b; Mehta and Belk, 1991; Kleine *et al.*, 1995)'.

Through their analysis of the data gathered in the interviews, the researchers established that the interviewees experienced four nostalgic moments: everyday past, uniqueness, tradition and transition, and these were linked to specific brands and objects. In conclusion, the researchers suggested that these four distinct moments can provide a better understanding of the emotional attachment of consumers to brands and products.

References

Kessous, A. and Roux, E. (2008) 'A semiotic analysis of nostalgia as a connection to the past', *Qualitative Market Research* 11(2): 192–212.

extract above, how and where the researchers theorized their work, how and where they knitted the findings of their research into the findings of other researchers. The process of theorization is the fourth stage in data analysis in the four stages approach to data analysis, outlined above.

Presenting qualitative data

The key to the presentation of data is the story, or the narrative, the researcher is trying to tell in relation to the data. The narrative presented will be the narrative that best, and most completely, responds to the research question/statement, the aim and the objectives of the research. The researcher decides, based on the narrative to be presented, how to present the analysis of the data, and in what order the analyzed data should be presented. The data should be presented in the order in which the reader will best be able to make sense of it. As explained in Chapter 13 'Managing Data and Introducing Data Analysis', the researcher constructs a framework for the data analysis chapter

Table 15.5 Issues in presenting the analysis of qualitative data
The process of analysing data is a substantial and often a protracted process. The process of data analysis tends to generate very substantial amounts of material, i.e. the results of the analysis. It would not be possible to report all of the results of the analysis, or all of the findings from the analysis. What is reported is a synopsis of the analysis. This synopsis is presented in the data analysis chapter of the thesis, or in the data analysis section of the report of the research.
Clearly, the structure of the chapter will reflect the process of analysis undertaken. For example, a thematic analysis will be presented in themes.
The structure of a chapter on a phenomenological data analysis process will reflect the complexity of the lived experiences examined in the research. Analyzed data in a phenomenological study is presented in a natural fashion, in order to best describe the experience or phenomenon studied.
The structure of a GT data analysis process will evidence the GT process of data analysis and the emerging theory which the process is designed to generate. Analyzed data in a GT project will be presented in terms of the theory generated, with the core category presented first and the other categories then related to it.
The key to presenting data is to remain faithful in the presentation of the data to the methodology used in the research project. The manner in which analyzed data are presented in the thesis or report of the research should fit with research methodology used in the research project. The research methodology used in the research project will guide the process of analysis used in data analysis. The methodology and the data

Table 15.5   Issues in presenting qualitative data analysis (continued)
analysis procedure or process used should inform the manner in which the data are presented in the chapter.
Within the structure decided on for the data analysis chapter/section, analyzed data may be presented in terms of the most simple to the most complex, with the simplest elements of the data being presented first, followed by progressively more complex elements of the analysis. It may be presented in terms of the least important to the most important, with the least important data being presented first, followed by progressively more important data. It may be presented in terms of the most important data to the least important, with the most important aspects of data analysis being presented first, followed by progressively less important aspects of the data.
Data from a narrative analysis project will be presented in terms of narratives. The process of presenting data in narratives can be used in other research projects where narratives can be discerned in the data and where there is sense and logic in presenting data in this manner.
Data from a discourse analysis project will be presented in terms of discourses. The process of presenting data in discourses can be used in other research projects where discourses can be discerned in the data, and where there is sense and logic in presenting the data in this manner.
In quantitative research, the researcher uses numbers to support the analysis. In qualitative research, the researcher uses words and concepts and images to support the analysis. These words, concepts and images are drawn from the raw data, as numbers in quantitative analysis are drawn from the raw data. The words, concepts and images drawn from the raw data may be presented in the written account of the analysis in terms of direct quotes or in the form of photographs or still images or drawings, etc. Aspects of raw data are presented in the data analysis chapter to support the narrative unfolding in that chapter. This is done in the same way as numbers, statistics, graphs and charts are presented in the chapter on data analysis to support the narrative unfolding in that chapter about the quantitative data gathered for the research project.
In presenting qualitative data analysis, the researcher details the process of analysis and the outcome of the analysis and supports all of this with reference to the raw data, the quotes or images. In the writing of the analysis the researcher goes through the four stages of data analysis, description, interpretation, conclusion and theorization.
Data reduction and data display in quantitative data analysis are accomplished through the presentation of frequencies and other statistical presentations, through the presentation of tables, charts and figures. In qualitative analysis, data reduction and data display is accomplished through the presentation of direct quotes taken from the data. Data may be displayed in matrices. Data in the form of images may also be displayed.

based on the key areas/issues/themes in the narrative to be presented. The researcher creates a structure for the data analysis chapter. The researcher then presents the analysis within that structure. Table 15.5 below provides a succinct overview of the key issues in presenting the analysis of qualitative data.

Matrices
Data displays that the researcher creates for the purposes of reduction of qualitative data.

Matrices   A matrix (**matrices** is the plural) is a display that the researcher creates with their data. Like a table or a figure in quantitative data analysis, the construction of a matrix in qualitative data analysis can provide the researcher with new and fresh insights into their data. The researcher decides, based on their requirements and based, on the data available, how to construct the matrix, what form it should take, how many columns, rows and cells it should have, and so on. The researcher constructs a matrix for the data in

REAL WORLD RESEARCH

A thorough engagement with data analysis

It sometimes happens that students undertaking qualitative data analysis, instead of engaging in qualitative data analysis in an appropriately scholarly way and detailing in the written account of their research their scholarship in relation to qualitative data analysis, simply engage in a process of describing in the most basic way possible the data that they have gathered. Clearly, this is not acceptable.

In the paragraphs above there are introductions to some of the main approaches to analysing qualitative data. Enough detail is given to introduce the student to the different approaches to qualitative data analysis and to signal to the student some of the differences in those approaches. It would be necessary for every student, once a particular approach to qualitative data analysis has been decided upon, to read substantial detailed accounts of that process. In fact the student researcher is expected to become quite expert on the methodology and processes of data analysis they use in their research project, in the same way as they are expected to become quite expert on the phenomenon that is the focus of their research.

order to reduce and display the data. Through such displays the researcher may develop new insights into the data, into trends and patterns in the data, and into different relationships in the data. The case study at the end of this chapter details the research of Götze *et al.* (2009), who used diaries to study the impact that children have on their parents' purchase decisions. The article on which the case study is based provides an interesting example of a matrix of qualitative data. Miles and Huberman (1994) provide substantial guidance and support in terms of qualitative data analysis and the presentation of such data. They provide substantial guidence in terms of presenting data in matrices.

Mixed methods research

'Mixed methods' means that both quantitative and qualitative approaches are used in the research project. As we have seen, quantitative and qualitative research methodologies have different philosophical foundations and different epistemological and ontological assumptions. Arguments against mixed methods usually hold that these distinctions are not, or perhaps cannot be, observed in mixed methods research. You will notice as you read accounts of different research projects, that different methodologies and data gathering methods are used in different ways, to different effect, all of the time.

The researcher should have the necessary skills in both quantitative and qualitative research in order to undertake mixed methods research. The British Educational Research Association (bera) provides a very useful online resource on research and research methods (**www.bera.ac.uk/beraresources/methods/**). On their 'Methods' web page they provide a guide to mixed methods research (**www.bera.ac. uk/mixed-methods-research/**). On the 'Mixed Methods Research' page, there is a good discussion of mixed methods research and an overview of the theoretical and practical arguments for it. While it is possible, and indeed often advisable, to use mixed methods in research, it is important to understand the paradigmatic issues involved in such approaches. It is, as always, necessary to know what it is you are trying to accomplish with your research, and how the research methodologies and methods you employ in your research project will help you to do this.

If you have gathered and analyzed both quantitative and qualitative data, then both types of data will be presented in the data analysis chapter. Some researchers choose to present the findings of quantitative and qualitative data separately, presenting one first and then the other, and some choose to present them together. Either way, the key to presenting the analyzed data is always the narrative to be told of the data. To support the narrative, the researcher presents data, in the form of statistics, in tables and figures, in direct quotes, in images and in data matrices.

It is important when mixing or blending quantitative and qualitative data that the language used is sensitive to, and nuanced to, the different kinds of data being presented, and the different kinds and depths of experience being presented through the different kinds of data. As we know, the researcher is present in the presentation of the qualitative data, and absent in the presentation of the quantitative data. The researcher presents an objective account of quantitative data (whether or not any data or any research can be said to be really objective is debatable) and a subjective account of experiences that are documented and explored in qualitative data. The researcher must subtly blend both kinds of data and present them in ways that are sensitive to the underlying epistemological and ontological perspectives and concerns of both.

Cremer and Ramasamy (2009), understood very clearly what they could and could not accomplish with quantitative research, and what they would accomplish with qualitative research. It would be a good idea to source the article detailing their research and read it through. As you read, make a note of how and to what effect Cremer and Ramasamy used mixed methods in this study.

In the journal article detailed below, Alasuutari (2010), explores the rise and relevance of qualitative research. This is a very useful journal article. In it Alasuutari presents a very accessible account quantitative and qualitative research and the growth in recent decades in interest in mixed methods research.

REAL WORLD RESEARCH

How theory influences research

'The Rise and Relevance of Qualitative Research', Alasuutari, P. (2010)

In this journal article, the author, Alasuutari (2010), considers the rise of qualitative research. The paper provides a brief history of quantitative and qualitative social research which is followed by a detailed discussion of the evolution of qualitative research.

The article highlights a growth of interest, from the 1980s, in mixed methods research. The author highlights a new journal launched in this area in 2007, the *Journal of Mixed Methods Research*. The author highlights the fact that many qualitative researchers have incorporated different quantitative approaches, such as cross-tabulation of their data (Alasuutari, 1995; Silverman, 2002). He states that texts have appeared which go beyond the traditional qualitative–quantitative distinction. He says that there is increasingly in the social sciences a willingness to engage in different types of research practice.

The increased demand for quantitative research, he writes, is due in particular to the need for increased accountability in public expenditure and a requirement that research should serve policy ends. He says that the requirement that public policies and practices be grounded in evidence-based, scientifically validated research has grown in momentum since the early 1990s. This, he writes, has led to developments in the social sciences, among them the systematic review process.

He writes that while one faction of qualitative researchers rejects the idea of qualitative research as representations of truth and its policy relevance, and he references Denzin and Lincoln (2000) *Handbook of Qualitative Research* here, another faction has responded by trying to develop more rigorous and convincing arguments for their evidence and criteria against which such studies can be measured. He writes that the increased interest in mixed methods can be seen as part of the same developments, where researchers use both quantitative and qualitative methods in their research in order to improve overall the validity of their research.

Cremer and Ramasamy (2009) provide an interesting example of mixed methods research in their study of strategies for small internationalizing firms in China, (see above).

It is possible, Alasuutari believes, that the interest in, and increased employer need for, quantitative methods might make us miss the fact that qualitative methods have been consistently growing in strength. He says that a recent study (Payne *et al.*, 2004), shows that only about one in 20 published papers in mainstream British journals use quantitative analysis. He says the figures are the same for Finland, where he himself is based, and he says that a similar trend can be seen from the 1990s onward in Canada and the USA.

The paper asks why qualitative research has achieved such a strong position in social science research, in particular when the default assumption often is that scientifically sound research is research based on quantification and statistical analysis as in, for example, the randomized controlled trial (RCT), a methodology adopted from medicine. It is this question that Alasuutari addresses in his paper.

In an interesting insight he asserts that social science is more about running commentaries on changing societies than the accumulation of knowledge about a stable system. In other words, realities are not fixed but are fluid and ever changing.

It would be a useful exercise for you to source this article and read it through. The article clearly explains the development of both quantitative and qualitative social science research, the different contributions both make, and the issues in engaging in mixed methods research.

From your reading of the article, can you outline the relative strengths of quantitative and qualitative research? Can you explain the issues, as they are detailed in the article, in engaging in mixed methods research?

References

Reproduced with permission from ATLAS.ti Scientific Software Development GmbH 3 screenshots from **www. atlasti.com.** Accessed 03.06.2010

Computer assisted qualitative data analysis software (CAQDAS)

CAQDAS is particularly helpful with large data sets. Using CAQDAS, the computer software stores and manages the data. This is particularly important, as discussed in previous chapters, in terms of data management. When all of the qualitative data gathered for a research project is kept within a file in a computer software package, the data are relatively safe and easily secured. In addition, the management of the data throughout the process of data analysis is simple and safe. The process of analysis itself is highly organized within the structure of the data analysis package. Using a computer software package for qualitative data analysis, the data are coded using the software, making the process more organized and less liable to error. When analysing large quantities of qualitative data by hand, it is too easy to make mistakes, to overlook data, and to miss relevant issues or even critical issues within the data.

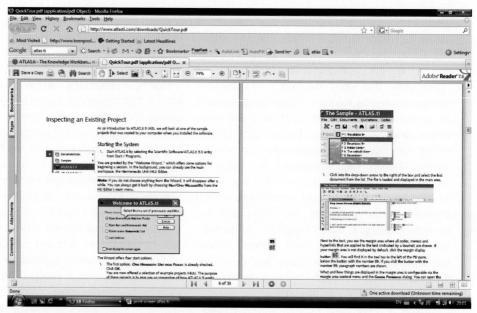

Figure 15.4   **www.atlasti.com**. Accessed 03.06.2010.

Figure 15.4 is from an online tutorial for Atlas ti, one of the main qualitative data analysis software packages. This software package has its own website **www.atlasti.com**. The website contains a lot of useful and interesting information about the software package, and most importantly, it provides tutorials and a free trial.

Using Atlas ti, each project is a distinct hermeneutic unit (HU). Within each HU, all of the files associated with the project are held. As well as the data files, there are files of quotes, codes and memos. These files of quotes, codes and memos are the means by which data are coded within Atlas ti. Documents, which are the transcripts of interviews, focus groups, etc. are assigned to the HU by the researcher. When they have been assigned, they can be coded and quotations can be created within them. The screen captures in Figure 15.5 are from a student project and show primary documents within Atlas ti which have been coded. They give a sense of what coded data looks like within the software.

Another software package designed for the analysis of qualitative data is NVivo. The website for NVivo is **www.qsrinternational.com** (accessed 03.06.2010). This website provides many different free online tutorials on the software. There are, for example, five tutorials for NVivo 8. The tutorials range from 20 minutes to 45 minutes in length and they cover different aspects of the software in the research process. The first tutorial provides an introduction to NVivo. The second shows you how to set up your project in NVivo and the third introduces you to the coding features in NVivo. The screen capture on page 436 (Figure 15.6) is taken from this tutorial; the name of the tutorial is 'Classifying your material into themes'.

If you have a substantial amount of qualitative data, you should use a software package to help you analyze your data. If you are interested in developing your research skills, whether or not you have substantial amounts of qualitative data, it is important to learn how to use one or more of the software packages designed for

Figure 15.5 The screen captures show primary documents within Atlas ti which have been coded. Reproduced with permission from ATLAS.ti Scientific Software Development GmbH 3 screenshots from www.atlasti.com

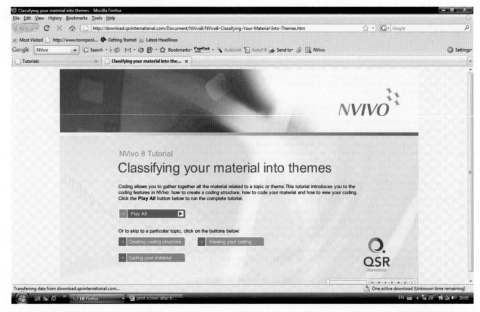

Figure 15.6   Classifying your material into themes. Screenshot from www.qsrinternational.com. Nvivo is designed and developed by QSR International Pty Ltd. Nvivo is a trademark or registered trademark of QSR International. Patent pending, www.qsrinternational.com, Reproduced with permission.

the analysis of qualitative data. It is likely that your university or college provides one or more of these software packages and probably has tutorials on how to use the software package. You should avail yourself of any such facilities whenever you can.

CASE STUDY

A Qualitative Study Using a Diary Method

The research project outlined below is a study of the influence that children have on their parents' purchasing behaviour. The data collection method used in the study is diary. In the study, 14 parents of young teenage children were asked to keep a diary for 2 weeks. They were asked to record in the diary purchase decisions they made in relation to innovative products, and the impact their young teenage children had on those decisions. The research project is interesting in terms of the data gathering method used and the data gathered using this method. The diary method, the researchers hold, is a good way of investigating phenomena that occur partly subconsciously. The diary is a method, they say, that eliminates a number of biases, interviewer bias, respondent bias and retrospection bias. The data in the dairies, the researchers contend, could not have been gathered using a questionnaire or in an interview. The synopsis presented below provides a good overview of the research. There is a great deal more useful and interesting detail on this study in the original article.

Mother and daughter shopping © Losevsky Pavel/Shutterstock

'Children's Impact on Innovation Decision-Making: A Diary Study', Götze, E, et al. (2009)

The researchers in this research project studied the impact that children have on their parents' purchasing behaviour. To gather data for the research project the researchers asked 14 parents to keep a diary in which they recorded their experiences in relation to their children influencing their purchasing behaviour. The value of the research, according to the researchers, is primarily in insights for marketers that this study provides.

We are told that over time, the influence of children has received increasing attention and studies have largely concentrated on the nature and extent of children's influence on parental consumer behaviour (Wells and Scieuto, 1966; Berey and Pollay, 1968; Isler et al., 1987). The literature reviewed for the study showed that children not only influence overall family decision-making, they are presumed

also to impact the purchase of innovative products (Cotte and Wood, 2004). As they are often more knowledgeable on certain novel products like consumer electronics or multimedia, they participate in the innovation-buying process quite actively (Ekstrom et al., 1987). The researchers show that children's influence on parental spending is a vast market. According to Kindel (1992), in the USA, children influence up to $360 million of parental spending. The researchers state that it is absolutely vital for companies to know whether and how children influence their parents with regard to the purchase and use of innovative products (Lee and Collins, 2000); and while it might be presumed that companies already know about children's impact, current research provides evidence to the contrary.

The researchers present the diary method as an excellent instrument for studying activities, events, behaviour and other phenomena that occur on a daily basis (DeLongis et al., 1992; Bolger et al., 2003) and in situ, i.e. within the context of a given situation (Bolger et al.). They hold that, in particular, activities that cannot be remembered or are not executed day-by-day are difficult to measure by conventional survey questions (Juster, 1986; Juster and Stafford, 1991; Kitterod, 2001). They say that the diary method allows people to express themselves in their own words and frequently report on the subject under investigation; and as respondents write their diary entry shortly after the activity to be recorded occurs, diaries can provide relevant and real records of experience. They say that although the diary method is not as common in research as other data collecting techniques, the number of scientific disciplines that use the diary method is wide and ranges from sociology to medicine and psychology (Grootaert, 1986; DeLongis I., 1992; Elliott, 1997; Johnson and Bytheway, 2002; Bolger et al., 2003). They do say however, that studies in marketing and market research that apply the diary method are still sparse (e.g. Sudman, 1964; Ehrenberg and Twyman, 1967; Sudman and Ferber, 1971).

This diary study was carried out in June 2005, in Austria. A total of 14 respondents were recruited by means of a snowball sampling method. A prerequisite for a participant to be recruited was that he/she was a parent of at least one 10 to 15-year-old child.

The researchers tell us that this age group was chosen as adolescents of this age have gained full cognitive development (Piaget, 1972), they understand the concept of money (Strauss, 1952), and they have already developed skills related to information processing (Ward *et al.*, 1977); compared to younger children, they have more experience with products and they have acquired some knowledge on consumer roles (Mangleburg, 1990).

All 14 parents in the sample agreed to keep the diary for 2 weeks. The diaries were booklets of A5 size. They were unstructured because the researchers wanted to give the parents as much freedom in reporting as possible. Before starting their diary, each family was visited personally and the method of diary writing was explained using a set of instructions.

The researchers decided that the first section of the diary was to focus on parent–child interaction related to consumerism. Purchase decisions were to be described in detail, i.e. discussions, planning, or execution of purchases. Participating parents were asked to report if the child expressed requests for any products, directly or indirectly, and they were asked to describe the circumstances of such requests. Parents were asked to note their reaction to such requests. In the second section of the diary, parents were asked to record the family's contact with products which were novel to the family, e.g. consumer electronics. In this section the researchers were interested in the children's influence on parental decision on the adoption of innovations. They were also to see if parents learned new skills from their children regarding new technology products.

The researchers stressed the importance of making entries daily and of also reporting events and activities seemingly minor or unimportant.

The data were analyzed using content analysis and an overview of the diary data is presented in the article in a tabular format.

According to the diary entries, children applied various strategies to influence their parents. However, children seem to stick with a specific strategy if it has worked before. So, the strategy used seems to depend on the child's characteristics as well as the (expected) parental response to it. Most often (for approximately a third of the products), the children used persuasion strategies, mainly reasonable requests or they provided their opinion on an innovation. Sometimes they would try to persuade their parents referring to 'everybody else', e.g. friends who own the innovative product, and sometimes they would simply beg for the product in question.

The researchers concluded that the diary reports showed that children influence parent's decisions on the adoption of innovation and that their influence is strongest in problem recognition (knowledge stage). They found that children who are more knowledgeable on certain products than their parents, or have mutual hobbies with their parents, exert considerable influence also in the information search (persuasion stage) and evaluations of alternatives stage (decision stage). Finally, they concurred with other researchers (Wilson and Wood, 2004), that it would be very useful to develop consumer decision-making typologies which specifically account for children's influence in these different phases.

You should source the original article and read it through. Note in particular as you read the original article, the matrix presented of the data collected and the direct quotes from respondents that are presented in the matrix. The researchers have done this, we are told, to maintain the 'individualism and subjectivity of each diary'.

Question What do you think of diaries as a means of gathering data? Why are the researchers concerned with maintaining the individualism and subjectivity of each diary?

References

Götze, E., Prange, C. and Uhrovska, I. (2009) 'Children's impact on innovation decision making: A diary study', *European Journal of Marketing* 43(1/2): 264–295.

CHAPTER REVIEW

W hile good quantitative research will provide numeric data and broad perspectives, good qualitative research can provide complex, rich and deep perspectives through the generation of non-numeric data.

This chapter explains in detail how qualitative data are analyzed. There are different ways of analysing qualitative data and the chapter provides a simple introduction to these different approaches. The use of software CAQDAS is explained and the centrality of language in qualitative data and qualitative data analysis is explored. The particular role and responsibilities of the researcher in qualitative data analysis is considered. The four stages approach to data analysis, description, interpretation, conclusions and theorization, are explained. The analytical framework, the fourth framework in the four frameworks approach to the research project, is further explored in this chapter. The use of direct quotes and visual displays in reporting data analysis is addressed and the use of data matrices in data reduction and data display in qualitative data analysis is explored. Finally, the chapter considers mixed methods research and explains how to blend together the findings from mixed methods research in the writing of research.

Now update your interactive research diary with your notes and findings at www.cengage.co.uk/quinlan. Complete the activities provided to reinforce your understanding of this chapter.

END OF CHAPTER QUESTIONS

1 Outline a simple approach to qualitative data analysis.

2 What are matrices and how are they used in qualitative data analysis?

3 Explain the fundamental importance of language in qualitative data analysis.

4 Explain the role of the researcher in qualitative data analysis.

5 Name and explain four different approaches to qualitative data analysis.

6 Sketch a model of the four stages in data analysis and explain how the model works.

7 What is the analytical framework in the four frameworks approach to the research project and how does it fit with the other frameworks in the four frameworks approach to the research project?

8 What is meant by the term mixed methods research?

9 Outline and explain the key issues and potential problems in mixed methods research.

10 Explain what is meant by the term CAQDAS and name two qualitative data analysis software packages. What are the key advantages to using CAQDAS?

REFERENCES

Alasuutari, P. (2010) 'The rise and relevance of qualitative research', *International Journal of Social Research Methodology* 13(2): 139–155.

Bignell, J. (2002) *Media Semiotics: An Introduction*, Oxford Road, Manchester: Manchester University Press.

Corbin, J. and Strauss, A.(2007) 'Basics of Qualitative Research: Techniques and Procedures for Developing Grounded Theory', Thousand Oaks, CA: Sage.

Cremer, R.D. and Ramasamy, B. (2009) 'Engaging China: Strategies for the small internationalizing firm', *Journal of Business Strategy* 30(6): 15–26.

Denzin, N.K. and Lincoln, Y.S. (2000) *Handbook of Qualitative Research*, Thousand Oaks, CA: Sage.

Dick, B. (2005) 'Grounded theory: A thumbnail sketch', **www.scu.edu.au/schools/gcm/ar/arp/grounded.html** Accessed 03.06.2010.

Glaser, B.G. (2001) 'The grounded theory perspective: Conceptualization contrasted with description', Mill Valley, CA: Sociology Press.

Glazer, B. and Strauss, A. (1967) 'The Discovery of Grounded Theory: Strategies for Qualitative Research', Chicago: Aldine Publishing Company.

Geertz, C. (1973) *The Interpretation of Cultures*, New York: Basic Books.

Götze, E., Prange, C. and Uhrovska, I. (2009) 'Children's impact on innovation decision making: A diary study', *European Journal of Marketing* 43(1/2): 264–295.

Journal of Mixed Methods Research, an academic journal publishing research carried out using mixed methods.

Kessous, A. and Roux, E. (2008) 'A semiotic analysis of nostalgia as a connection to the past', *Qualitative Market Research* 11(2): 192–212.

Miles, M.B. and Huberman, A.M. (1994) *Qualitative Data Analysis: An Expanded Sourcebook*, London and Thousand Oaks, CA: Sage.

Moustakas, C.E. (1994) *Phenomenological Research Methods*, Thousand Oaks, CA: Sage.

Ng, K. and Hase, S. (2008) 'Grounded suggestions for doing a grounded theory business research', *Electronic Journal of Business Research Methods* 6(2): 155–170.

Partington, D. (2000) 'Building Grounded Theories of Management Action', *British Journal of Management*, 11(2): 91–102.

Strauss, A. and Corbin, J. (1990, 1998 edns), 'Basics of Qualitative Research: Techniques and Procedures for Developing Grounded Theory', Thousand Oaks, CA: Sage.

The Grounded Theory Institute, **www.groundedtheory.com** Accessed 03.06.2010.

Tellis, W. (1997) 'Introduction to case study', *The Qualitative Report* 3(2), **www.nova.edu/ssss/QR/QR3-2?tellis1.html** Accessed 03.06.2010.

The British Educational Research Association (bera), 'Methods', **www.bera.ac.uk/beraresources/methods/** Accessed 03.06.2010.

The British Educational Research Association (bera), 'Mixed methods research', www.bera.ac.uk/mixed-methods-research/ Accessed 03.06.2010.

The Grounded Theory Institute, www.groundedtheory.com Accessed 03.06.2010.

Trevett, N. (2010) '"People matter" is key message on road to recovery', *The Guardian*, March 12, www.guardian.co.uk/service-design/people-matter Accessed 03.06.2010.

RECOMMENDED READING

Ball, M.S. and Smith, G.W.H. (1992) 'Analyzing visual data' (Paper), Qualitative Research Methods, Series 24, London: Sage.

Banks, M. (2007) *Using Visual Data in Qualitative Research*, London: Sage.

Bell, J. (2005) *Doing Your Research Project'*, Part III 'Interpreting the Evidence and Reporting the Findings', Maidenhead: Open University Press.

Corbin, J. and Strauss, A. (2008) *Basics of Qualitative Research*, Thousand Oaks, CA: Sage.

Creswell, J.W. (1998) *Qualitative Inquiry and Research Design: Choosing Among Five Traditions*, Ch. 8, 'Data Analysis and Representation', and Appendices B, C, D, E, and F, Thousand Oaks, CA: Sage.

Creswell, J.W. (2003) *Research Design, Qualitative, Quantitative, and Mixed Methods Approaches*, (2nd edn), Thousand Oaks, CA; London, UK; New Delhi, India: Sage.

Denscombe, M. (2005) *The Good Research Guide for Small-scale Research Projects*, Ch. 14, 'Qualitative Data', Maidenhead: Open University Press.

Fairclough, N. (1995) *Critical Discourse Analysis: The Critical Study of Language*, London: Longman.

Flick, U. (2009) 'An Introduction to Qualitative Research', 4th Ed., Sage: London.

Gray, D.E. (2009) 'Doing Research in the Real World', Chapter Eight, 'Research Design: Mixed Methods', Sage: London.

Hesse-Biber, S.N. (2010) 'Mixed Methods Research: Merging Theory with Practice', New York: The Guilford Press.

Lewins, A. and Silver, C. (2007) *Using Software in Qualitative Research*, London: Sage.

Miles, M.B. and Huberman, A.M. (1994) *Qualitative Data Analysis* (2nd edn), London and Thousand Oaks: Sage.

Neuman, W.L. (2000) *Social Research Methods: Quantitative and Qualitative Approaches*, Ch. 15, 'Analysis of Qualitative Data', Boston, MA: Allyn & Bacon.

Prosser, J. (2001) *Image-based Research: A Sourcebook for Qualitative Researchers*, Ch. 8, 'Photographs within the Sociological Research Process', London: Routledge.

Robson, C. (2000) *Real World Research*, Ch. 14, 'The Analysis of Qualitative Data', Oxford: Blackwell.

Rose, G. (0000) *Visual Methodologies*, London: Sage.

Seale, C. (2007) *The Quality of Qualitative Research*, Thousand Oaks, CA: Sage.

Silverman, D. (2001) 'Interpreting Qualitative Data: Methods for Analysing Talk, Text and Interaction', 2nd Ed., Sage: London.

Simpson, M. and Tuson, J. (2003) *Using Observation in Small-scale Research, a Beginner's Guide*, The SCRE Centre, Glasgow: University of Glasgow.

Van Leeuwen, T. (2005) *Introducing Social Semiotics*, London: Routledge.

CHAPTER 16

DRAWING CONCLUSIONS AND WRITING RESEARCH

LEARNING OBJECTIVES

At the end of this chapter the student should be able to:

- Conceptualize and present conclusions from research.

- Conceptualize and present recommendations for research projects.

- Be able to complete the final written report of a research project.

RESEARCH SKILLS

At the end of this chapter the student should, by using the exercises on the accompanying online platform, be able to:

- Explain what a conclusion is in a research project, and what conclusions represent in terms of the research endeavour.

- Explain how good and useful recommendations are conceptualized and presented.

- Critique the conclusions and recommendations from a given research project.

The aim of this chapter is to explain the concept of conclusions in research, to demonstrate how conclusions should be drawn and to help you, the student develop the skills needed to write a thesis. In this chapter, conclusions in research are explored and explained. The chapter demonstrates how conclusions are drawn in a research project and shows what conclusions are based on. The means by which the research project is brought full-circle is demonstrated by explaining how the conclusions of the research project respond to the research question or statement of the research project. The chapter explains how the final chapter of the thesis, or the final section of the research report, is designed to answer fully and completely the research question, or is designed to respond fully and completely to the research statement.

INTRODUCTION

This final chapter explains and demonstrates what conclusions are, how they are drawn and what they are based on, and what is meant by the implications of the conclusions of the research project. The process of theorizing conclusions is explained and demonstrated. The chapter explains and demonstrates how **recommendations** are made in a research project. The chapter also considers the process of writing a thesis and presents tips for writing and the writing process. The means by which the written research project fits together, how it is structured and designed is explained and demonstrated. The importance and the limitations of the **first draft** of the thesis and the importance of the work of editing in the production of the final draft of the thesis/report of the research is explained. The importance of sequence, of synthesis and of integration in the **final draft** of the thesis are considered. The model of the research project presented in Figure 16.1 shows how we have now come full circle in the research process. We are now at the stage of drawing conclusions from our research and are finally completing the writing up and presentation of the research.

The newspaper article in the feature box was written by the readers' editor of *The Guardian* newspaper. The article explains how two different accounts of one survey were published in the newspaper. The newspaper article demonstrates how it is possible, regardless of how practised you are, to get it wrong in the writing and presentation your research.

While *The Guardian* didn't 'get it wrong' exactly, they didn't precisely get it right either. They presented two different sets of results for the same survey, and Siobhain Butterworth, the readers' editor of *The Guardian*, explains in the following article how this happened. Butterworth's concluding point is useful for us in terms of this chapter. She states that the newspaper's weekender readers needed more information in order to be able to properly and fully understand the research as it was presented in the magazine section of the newspaper. It is important in writing and presenting research that the research is written and presented as fully and as completely as possible. The writing and the presentation of research should be done in such a way as to facilitate clear

Recommendations
The courses of action that the researcher recommends based on the findings and subsequent conclusions drawn from those findings.

First draft
The draft before the process of editing and getting feedback begins.

Final draft
The edited and polished fully integrated and correct copy of the thesis that is finally submitted for examination.

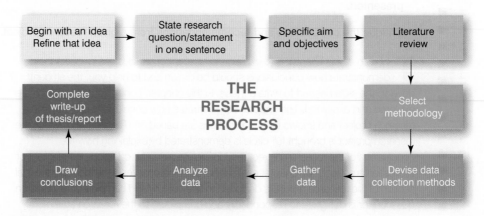

Figure 16.1   The research process

THE VALUE OF GOOD RESEARCH

An example of the potential complexities in reporting research

'The readers' editor on … 1000 teenagers, one survey, and two sets of results' Butterworth, S. *The Guardian*, 19.10.2009

This week we're discussing statistical confusion, so please sit up straight and pay attention. Why, asked a reader last week, did a news story in the main paper and a feature in *Weekend* magazine, published on the same day, give apparently conflicting findings from a survey about teenage boys?

The survey, by Echo Research, was commissioned by *The Guardian*'s magazine to go with

High school teenage soccer players © Jim Lane/Alamy

Simon Hattenstone's feature. He interviewed 19 young men for *Weekend*'s cover story, on Saturday 10 October, which challenged negative perceptions of this section of the population. 'I've read all the stereotypes about today's teenage boys, but my experience of them is virtually non-existent,' Hattenstone wrote. 'So I decided to immerse myself in Planet Teen Boy.'

The online poll used a panel of 1000 teenage boys living in England, Wales and Scotland as its base. Its key findings, some of which were highlighted in large type as pull quotes, made interesting reading: according to *Weekend* the poll found that 93% of teenage boys are happy in their social lives; 94% are happy in their home and family lives; 91% are happy in their school or work lives; 96% are ambitious about their future careers; and 95% believe their career prospects are good.

Hattenstone's news report, in the paper's main section the same day, presented a different set of results from the survey: 87% (not 93%) of teenage boys were happy in their social lives; 87% (not 94%) were happy in their family lives; 81% (not 91%) were happy at school or work; 88% (not 96%) were ambitious; and 88% (not 95%) believed they had good career prospects. Both sets of figures told the same story; the vast majority of teenage boys who took part in this survey said they were happy about their lives and prospects, but which findings were right?

The explanation for the disparity (part one) is as follows. Echo had provided only key findings to *Weekend*, but for the news story a full breakdown was requested so that the survey results could be shown in graphs and pie charts in the paper. The graphics editor noticed on the Friday (by which time *Weekend* had already been printed) that the visual representation of the survey didn't tally with the news story, which Hattenstone had based on the key findings. When he was alerted to the problem Hattenstone decided to refer to the detailed breakdown in his news report instead.

Still with me? Good. Then here is part two of the explanation. Echo says both sets of figures are correct and that they are different because the key findings produced for *Weekend* exclude people who gave the response 'neither agree nor disagree' to statements in the survey. Matt Painter, Echo's research director said: 'In the absence of an explicit "don't know" option in the survey, ["neither agree or disagree"] is really a proxy for "not sure/no opinion" … the figures in the magazine give a stronger picture by focusing solely on those respondents who have expressed an opinion.'

Painter said that after 'don't knows' were excluded the figures were 'rebased'. He illustrated how this was done by reference to the statement in the survey: 'I am ambitious about my future career'. To this statement 622/1000 (62%) responded 'strongly agree', 258 (26%) responded 'slightly agree', 81 (8%) responded 'neither agree nor disagree', 28 (3%) responded 'slightly disagree' and 11 (1%) opted for 'strongly disagree'. When the 81 who neither agreed nor disagreed were removed the base number of respondents changed from 1000 to 919 and when the percentages were recalculated 'strongly agree' rose to 68% and 'slightly agree' increased to 28% – producing an 'all agree' figure of 96%.

I have a concluding point. Even if we accept that rebasing to provide key findings was appropriate here (some of you may disagree), magazine readers needed more information. *Weekend*'s feature didn't say – because the journalists involved were not aware – that the figures had been rebased. Readers should have been told that the percentages it reported were for survey participants who expressed an opinion one way or the other.

References

Butterworth, S. (2009) 'The readers' editor on … 1000 teenagers, one survey, and two sets of results', *The Guardian*, 19 October.

and correct comprehension. The researcher writing up and presenting research is engaged in an exercise of communication with the reader. If the report is written for an academic audience, the communication should be structured to suit that audience. The final account of the research project should be communicated as fully, as comprehensively, and as clearly as possible.

THE FINAL CHAPTER – WRITING CONCLUSIONS AND DRAWING RECOMMENDATIONS

In the final chapter of the thesis, or the final section of the research report, the researcher presents the conclusions and recommendations of the research project. Usually, the final chapter of the thesis is relatively short. There is an exception, however, to this general rule. If, for example, a grounded theory methodology has been used in the research project, the final chapter will be a substantial chapter; it will contain a full and detailed outline and explanation of the theory developed through the research. Remember, GT methodology is specifically designed to facilitate the development of new theory which is grounded in the data gathered for the research project. In general the final chapter of the thesis/report of the research contains the overall conclusions drawn from the research, and the recommendations the researcher makes based on the conclusions drawn from the research.

All research undertaken within an academic setting must make a contribution to knowledge. Academic research, as explained in this textbook, emerges from a body of knowledge, and in turn, in makes a contribution to that body of knowledge. In the final chapter as well as presenting the findings of the research, the conclusions drawn from the research and the recommendations the researcher makes based on the research, the researcher theorizes the conclusions drawn from the research.

The process of theorizing conclusions is the same as the process of **theorization** in the four stages of data analysis. The four stages of data analysis, as explained in the previous three chapters, are description, interpretation, conclusion and theorization. In the process of theorising conclusions, the researcher draws on the work of other researchers and theorists and they knit their conclusions into the conclusions of these researchers and theorists. Through this process the researcher enriches the reporting of their conclusions.

> **Theorization**
> The researcher draws on the work of other researchers and theorists to enrich the reporting of their conclusions.

Conclusions in research

A conclusion is essentially a judgement, or a final decision. At the end of the research process, the researcher comes to a final conclusion, or several final conclusions, about the research. This final decision or final judgement will relate to, or respond to, the research question or statement, to the overall aim of the research project. We have seen throughout this textbook how the four frameworks approach to the research project facilitates the researcher in building the research project on the conceptual framework, the research statement or question, the overall aim of the research. Now in this final phase of the research project, the researcher conceptualizes the overall conclusion of the research project, which must emerge logically and validly from the analysis of the data gathered, and from the findings of the research in such a way as to ensure that the overall conclusion responds to the research question or statement and accomplishes the aim of the research.

The Four Frameworks
Conceptual Framework
Theoretical Framework
Methodological Framework
Analytical Framework

In presenting data analysis, you will remember, the researcher engages in the four stages of data analysis. First they describe the data, then they interpret the data, then they come to some minor conclusion about the data, and finally they theorize the data. In every step of presenting the analyzed data and the findings of the research, the researcher presents minor conclusions drawn from the research. All of these minor conclusions add up into the overall conclusion that the researcher draws from the research.

The overall conclusion that the researcher draws from the research is presented at the start of the final chapter, the chapter on conclusions and recommendations. This overall conclusion is a response to the research question or statement, a response to the overall aim of the research. It is the final accomplishment of the overall aim of the research project. It is the essential product of the research.

The overall conclusion from the research project is presented at the start of the final chapter, and it is thoroughly discussed and explained. This presentation, discussion and explanation of the overall conclusion is followed by the presentation and discussion of a number of main conclusions, all drawn from the overall conclusion.

The conclusions section in the final chapter of the thesis is the first part of the chapter. Following a brief introduction to the chapter, the conclusions are presented. The overall conclusion or overarching conclusion is presented and discussed first. Then the major conclusions are each detailed and discussed briefly. There then follows a general discussion of the conclusions, which are explored and examined. They are theorized. By this is meant that the researcher briefly explains how the conclusions that they have drawn from their research fit with or contradict the conclusions that other researchers and theorists (as detailed in the literature review) have drawn about their own research. In this way, the researcher connects their research to the research of others and makes a contribution to knowledge.

Table 16.1 demonstrates how conclusions are drawn from findings and how recommendations are made based on conclusions.

Table 16.1 Drawing conclusions and making recommendations		
Finding	**Conclusion**	**Recommendation**
One of the key findings of the research project was that all staff were dissatisfied with the professional development training provided by the company.	The professional development programme provided by the company is failing to meet the needs of staff.	Either the professional training programme provided should receive a substantial overhaul or a new professional development training programme should be provided.
One of the key findings of the research was that the junior managers felt isolated and unsupported.	The company is failing to maximize the resource that the junior managers represent.	A programme should be designed and put in place that will ensure that junior managers are properly supported.
All of the participants in the research agreed that the advertisement was attractive and engaging and they said that it would encourage them to purchase.	The advertisement is effective.	The new advertising campaign should be built around the advertisement.
The research found that the students had reduced disposable incomes.	This has implications for the amount of money students will spend on meals out.	Monitor sales and react promptly to any reduction in sales with deals and special offers.
The data showed that while income from product line A increased month on month over the year, income from product line B decreased substantially in the final 3 months of the study.	Product line A is a better seller than product line B.	Increase volume of product line A. Decrease volume of product line B. Continue monitoring sales levels. If sales of product line B continue to decline discontinue that product line.

The process demonstrated in the table is simplified. In reality, the conclusions drawn from findings can be very substantial and quite complex.

It is a good idea when writing the conclusions section of the final chapter to use your research diary to jot down the minor conclusions detailed in the data analysis chapter and the ideas and thoughts you have in relation to them. When you have done that, you should tease out the different aspects and elements of those conclusions. The more detail you can jot down in your research diary the better. Then, from the detail you can create (conceptualize), the overall conclusion you wish to present in your thesis. You can use the detail from your research diary to illustrate in your writing the complexity of the conclusion, which should reflect the complexity of the research undertaken. The style of the research project should be consistent throughout. For example, when writing the conclusions of a qualitative study, the richness of the data gathered should be reflected in the concluding chapter, as it was in the data analysis chapter.

Once again, it is a good idea to examine the manner in which conclusions are drawn and presented in research projects similar to the research project you are carrying out. The journal articles that you have been using to model your research on will be useful in terms of modelling your approach to the presentation of your conclusions. It is important to pay attention to the style of the presentation in these models as well as their content. It is useful, too, to examine other theses in the library. There is a need, as always, to be critical of any published research project

Table 16.2   Drawing conclusions and examples of the theorization process
The main conclusion drawn from the research is that the professional development training programme provided by the company for the staff of the company did not meet the requirements of the staff. This conclusion echoes the conclusion of Edwards (2009), Edwards and Burke (2008) and Clark *et al.* (2008). All of these researchers found that the professional development training programmes of the companies they studied did not meet the needs of the employees.
One of the conclusions drawn from the research is that the company is failing to maximize the resource that the junior managers represent. This conclusion is similar to the conclusion drawn by Bryant and Yong (2009) in their research who found that junior managers tended to be excluded from management meetings and isolated from each other through their geographic locations in the organizations.
The key conclusion of the research is that students have less disposable income. This conclusion coincides with the conclusions of Hughes (2009), Al Maheri (2009) and Merkeert (2009), all of whom have documented a retraction in levels of disposable income among third-level students.
The overall conclusion from the research is that the provision of incentives, in the form of special offers, did not impact on sales levels, and there was in fact no change in the level of sales over the period of the study. This conclusion challenges the conclusions of Marks and Henry (2009), Habite and Mehabby (2009), and Orlean and Tuti (2009), all of whom found that the use of incentives such as special offers does impact positively on sales levels.

that you might consider using as a model for your own work. When you have identified the models you think are suitable, it is a good idea to show them to your thesis supervisor or your lecturer in research methodologies and to ask their opinions on them in relation to your intention to use them as models for your own work.

As can be seen from the examples of theorization in Table 16.2, the researcher draws on the work of other researchers and theorists to enrich the reporting of their conclusions. At the same time they are connecting their work with the body of knowledge in their field and making their overall contribution to knowledge. The theorists that the researcher draws on should be detailed in the literature review of the research project. The researcher looks back at the literature review and sees how their research fits with the research detailed there. Then the researcher makes explicit connections between their research and the research of these other researchers. When the researcher has made the connections, the researcher then comes to a further conclusion(s).

The examples in Table 16.3 show how the process begins. The researcher continues to develop conclusions from the research until all of the possible conclusions that can be drawn from the research have been drawn. The researcher then edits the conclusions section to ensure that the most important conclusions are highlighted, and to make sure that the work fits within the word count allowed.

The entire research project is an exercise in logic. The conclusions that you come to in your research should be logical and reasonable. They should be based on the findings of the research project. The conclusions that you draw should be valid, sound and should stand up to scrutiny. They should be meaningful in terms of the overall aim and objectives of the research project.

Implications of conclusions When the conclusions have been presented, the implications of the conclusions should be explored. The implications of the conclusions are the meanings that the conclusions have for different parties or constituents to the research project. For example, in the professional development example above, the conclusions drawn will have implications for the company, for

Table 16.3   Coming to further conclusions

The main conclusion drawn from the research is that the professional development training programme provided by the company for the staff of the company did not meet the requirements of the staff. This conclusion echoes the conclusion of Edwards (2009), Edwards and Burke (2008) and Clark *et al.* (2008). These researchers found in their studies that the professional development training programmes of the companies they studied did not meet the needs of the employees.

There is clearly a real need for companies to pay particular attention to the utility and fitness for purpose of the professional development programmes they provide for staff.

One of the conclusions drawn from the research is that the company is failing to maximize the resource that the junior managers represent. This conclusion is similar to the conclusion drawn by Bryant and Yong (2009) who in their research found that junior managers tended to be excluded from management meetings, and isolated from each other through their geographic location in the organizations.

The evidence suggests that there is a serious problem in SMEs in the way in which they fail to properly and thoroughly engage junior managers, and through that failure, fail to properly and thoroughly maximize the resource that junior managers represent.

The key conclusion of the research is that students have less disposable income. This conclusion coincides with the conclusions of Hughes (2009), Al Maheri (2009) and Merkeert (2009), all of whom have documented a retraction in levels of disposable income among third level students.

It seems that there is a clear retraction in levels of disposable income among students and this will obviously have an impact across the board on small businesses providing services to students.

The overall conclusion from the research is that the provision of incentives, in the form of special offers, did not impact on sales levels. There was, in fact, no change in the level of sales over the period of the study. This conclusion challenges the conclusions of Marks and Henry (2009), Habite and Mehabby (2009), and Orlean and Tuti (2009), all of whom found that the use of incentives, such as special offers, does impact positively on sales levels.

It seems that although in general, incentives are an effective means of improving sales, this is by no means the rule. If there are special circumstances, as in the current study where there was a documented retraction in the level of disposable income available to the market, then incentives designed to improve sales may have only a limited effect, or perhaps no effect at all.

the people giving the training and for the staff undergoing the training. The company will have the cost of developing a new training programme, and then the benefits of the new training programme. The people delivering the training will either have to improve the training being provided, or lose the job of providing the training; there will be cost implications either way. The staff will no longer have to undergo training that they do not value, instead they will benefit from a new training programme. The staff are likely to feel encouraged and affirmed as a result of the company responding to their needs, which is likely to lead to staff renewing their commitment to the company. The company will benefit from renewed commitment from staff. These are all possible implications of that conclusion.

It is important to tease out the implications of all of the conclusions drawn from the research for every group of people, organization and entity affected by the research and the conclusions drawn from it. Once again, it is a good idea to do this in as much detail as possible. Your research diary is the place to record these thoughts, ideas and insights. Then when you have all of that detail, you can begin to plan and structure what you intend to report on the implications of the findings. Plan which implications to present, and where and how, and in what order, they would best be presented.

THE RECOMMENDATIONS OF THE STUDY

The recommendations of the study are the ways forward from the research. Recommendations are courses of action that the researcher recommends based on the findings of the research and the conclusions drawn from those findings. The recommendations, following a brief introduction, can be presented as a bullet list. The following points should be kept in mind when conceptualizing the recommendations for the study:

- Recommendations should be succinct.
- They should be meaningful in relation to the aim and objectives of the research.
- They should respond to the research question or statement.
- Recommendations should be do-able or achievable. There is no point in making recommendations that cannot possibly be put in action, perhaps because the necessary resources are not available, or because there would be too much opposition to them, or for other reasons.

Often a researcher will draw up a list of 20 or more recommendations in the process of listing all of the possible recommendations. It is a good idea to do this to begin with. Then, through a process of refining the recommendations, by collapsing some together, and by eliminating some, the researcher will produce a list of eight to ten meaningful recommendations for the research project.

The researcher may make separate recommendations for different constituents to the research. For example, using the example of the professional development training programme above, there might be recommendations for the company, for the training programme, for the trainers and for the staff of the company.

The research project detailed in the feature box below is useful here. In the journal article the aim of the research is clearly outlined. The aim of the research is to investigate the socialization experiences within the company of 30 newly hired engineers during the early stage of their employment with a large manufacturing company. The research was developed using a qualitative case study research design. The research questions are outlined, the sample is detailed as is the sampling method used. There is a good explanation and discussion in the article of the data collection and data analysis carried out. It is interesting to note how the different aspects of methodology are theorized, i.e. connected to other theories and theorists. The findings of the research are clearly presented and discussed and the implications of the findings for human resource development and socialization practices are presented and discussed. A number of recommendations are made (in the list of bullet points at the end of the article). You will notice that the recommendations are useful and do-able and reasonable and they are well-thought-out, well-written and well-presented. They are simple and clear, yet substantial and meaningful in relation to the research carried out.

THEORY IN RESEARCH

'How Newcomers Learn the Social Norms of an Organization: A Case Study of the Socialization of Newly Hired Engineers', Korte, R.F. (2009)

We are told that current scholarship views organizational socialization as a learning process that is primarily the responsibility of the newcomer. Yet Korte (2009) states that recent learning research recognizes the importance of the social interactions in the learning process. The study, we are told, investigated how newly hired engineers at a large manufacturing company learned job-related tasks and the social norms of the organization. The author states that, from the perspective of social exchange theory, two major findings emerged from the data:

1 Relationship building was the primary driver of socialization.

2 The work group was the primary context for socialization.

The author states that these findings challenge the current views of organizational socialization by accentuating the relational processes that mediate learning during socialization. He writes that when asked what he wished he had learned in school to better prepare for the workplace, one practising engineer lamented, 'I wish someone had taught me how to play the political game here'. He was referring to the unwritten rules governing behaviour—also known as the social norms of the organization.

Korte states that preliminary investigation of the experiences of engineers starting a new job indicated that the most troublesome experience was learning how to work within the informal social systems of the organization. He writes that in order to understand better the problems encountered by newcomers entering a workplace, his study investigated the experiences of 30 newly hired engineers during the early stage of their employment with a large manufacturing company.

The research methodology used was a qualitative case study research design. In justifying his use of this methodology, Korte writes that several authors describe a qualitative methodology as not only appropriate but also more likely to yield insights into complex social phenomena (Eisenhardt & Graebner, 2007; Patton, 2002; Silverman, 2005). He says that Stake (1995) described qualitative case study research as an appropriate design for acquiring in-depth understanding of the complex interactions and functions of people in the context of a specific situation. He writes that Yin (2003) described case study designs as relevant strategies for research questions of how and why, as well as relevant strategies for research focused on contemporary events within a real-life context and in which the researcher had little or no control over events. Thus, he says, the characteristics of the study (examining a complex social phenomenon in context) seemed most appropriate to a qualitative case study research design.

We are told that the organization participating in this study is one of the world's largest manufacturers, employing more than 250 000 people around the world. The company which is headquartered in the USA, has been, according to the article, a global engineering and sales leader for decades. Korte states that during the 2 years preceding the study the company hired nearly 200 new engineers, 30 of whom participated in the study. We are told that the participants in the study came from 26 work groups, and that while some of these work groups were well established, others were relatively new.

Three research questions guided the study. They were as follows:

1 How do new engineers learn the social norms of the organization?

2 What factors enable and constrain this learning process in the organization?

3 What factors determine how well new engineers learn and integrate into the workplace?

In terms of the sample used, Korte says that following the logic of theoretical or purposeful sampling (Patton, 2002; Strauss and Corbin, 1998), managers in the organization were asked to identify individuals to interview for the purpose of collecting rich, in-depth information addressing the research questions. He writes that the managers chose individuals according to length of employment, gender and experience. He explains that all of the participants had been with the company at least 6 months, and none had been employed with this company longer than 18 months. He explains that there were both men and women in the sample, and a mix of those who had previous job experience and those for whom this was the first job after graduating. We are told that the sample was composed of three groups:

- New graduates: 17 newly hired engineers starting their first job out of school.
- Experienced hires: 13 newly hired engineers with previous job experience.
- Managers: 6 managers of work groups with newly hired engineers.

Korte details that Seale (1999) in his discussion of quality in qualitative research, advocated the benefits of having research designs drawn from multiple paradigms. For example, Korte explains, Seale proposed a triangulation of methodologies to help minimize the biases of any one methodology in the biases of another methodology (e.g., using quantitative and qualitative methods to analyze the same data from different perspectives). Furthermore, he writes that Seale stated that use of multiple methodologies could help increase the understanding of a phenomenon.

Korte tells us that in his own study, 'avoiding the purist extremes of qualitative and quantitative methodologies', he used a blended approach to analyze the data collected under a qualitative case study research design. Data for the study was generated from semi-structured interviews conducted and recorded by the researcher following the critical incidents technique (Ellinger & Watkins, 1998; Flanagan, 1954; Gremler, 2004). He asked questions in the interviews which prompted participants to recall a specific event or incident in which they learned something about 'the way things work here'. He probed their responses using subsequent

questions designed to elicit detail on specifics: for example, What was the incident? What happened? Who was involved? What did the participant learn from this? He explains that in some cases, participants said there was not a specific incident. These participants recounted a series of small experiences that occurred over time which gave them an understanding of the norms of the organization. We are told that a professional transcriber converted the recorded interviews to text; the researcher checked the transcriptions for accuracy with the original recordings; and analysis of the interview transcripts followed qualitative analysis procedures recommended by Miles and Huberman (1994) and Strauss and Corbin (1998).

The process of data analysis used in the study was outlined as follows:

There were four steps in the qualitative data analysis process.

1 The researcher carefully read the transcripts and attached predetermined codes to specific statements that described learning and norms.

2 The researcher retrieved all statements coded as learning and norms, carefully re-read the retrieved statements, and proceeded to open code (Strauss & Corbin, 1998) the statements at a finer level of detail, staying close to the participants' language.

3 The researcher sorted the open codes into categories.

4 The researcher identified and described the categorical themes emerging from these data.

Korte explains that the emergent data indicated that relationship building was a critical process for newcomers. Furthermore, the data indicated that it was the quality of the relationships formed within the context of the work groups that enabled or constrained newcomer learning and integration into the workplace.

Korte tells us that the use of predetermined codes initially helped identify and categorize the experiences reported by newcomers into exchange and learning experiences related to the norms of the group. Then from these categories, common themes emerged that indicated how newcomers learned, what factors affected their learning, and how well they learned as they began their jobs. These themes are described by Korte in the findings section of the journal article.

He tells us that two major themes emerged from analysis of the data gathered from newcomers:

1 Relationship building was the primary driver of the socialization process – not individual capability for learning.

2 The work group was the primary context for socialization – not the organization.

He explains that the data indicated that the quality of relationship building between the newcomers and members of their work groups mediated the quality of learning by newcomers. He writes that overall, newcomers reported the necessity of building relationships with co-workers and their managers as a prerequisite for learning what to do and how to do it well.

Korte calculated frequency counts of learning incidents reported and attributed to different sources. He found that newcomers in the organization reported that co-workers were the primary source of learning the social norms of the work group (65% of learning incidents reported). We are told that newcomers also reported learning from managers (15%). Korte explains that the remaining learning interactions were reportedly self-directed, whereby newcomers relied on their personal knowledge and past experiences as a source of learning to understand and adapt to the social norms of the organization (18% of learning incidents reported).

The implications of the study for human resource development and socialization practices are teased out and several recommendations are made.

References

Korte, R.F. (2009) 'How newcomers learn the social norms of an organization: A case study of the socialization of newly hired engineers', *Human Resource Development Quarterly* 20(3): 285–306.

THE VALUE OF GOOD RESEARCH

Focus on life history

Life history, as explained in Chapter 7, 'Understanding Research Methodology and Design' is the research methodology used to compile biographies of different people or biographies of different companies, organisations, entities. This methodology could be used, for example, to understand the changes that have occurred in the lives of a group of people, or the changes that have occurred in the life of a company.

One particular kind of life history research is oral history. Oral history is a vocalized account of some historical experience given by a witness or participant in that experience. The most fundamental data collection method within a life history and an oral history research methodology is the life history interview.

The British Library has in its collection an oral history of Tesco, the supermarket chain. This oral history comprises 39 in-depth interviews with Tesco employees from the checkout staff to the chairman. According to the website of the British Library, this is 'an unparalleled collection of first-hand witness accounts from those working within a major British retailer'. You will find this project at **www.bl.uk/reshelp-prestype/sound/ohist/ohnls/nlstexco.html**. This oral history project, we are told, examines different functions across the business, distribution, information technology and personnel as well as retailing.

Other oral histories available in the British Library include an oral history of Barings Bank up to and including its collapse in 1995, oral histories of food and drink, documenting changes that have occurred in Britain's food industry over the course of the twentieth century, and an oral history project of the wine trade, comprising 42 life story interviews with workers in the wine trade.

Any business or business experience can usefully be studied using a life history or an oral history methodology. The contribution that such a project makes to knowledge rests on the quality of the research project, the insight the researcher brings to the project and the insights the researcher develops from the project.

You will find the following resources useful in relation to life history and oral history research methodologies.

National Life Stories: Tesco: An Oral History, British Library, **http://www.bl.uk/reshelp/findhelprestype/ sound/ohist/ohnls/nlstesco/tesco.html** Accessed 03.06.2010.

Oral History Research, University College Los Angeles (UCLA) Anderson School of Management, **http://www.anderson.ucla.edu/x1194.xml**

Oral History Collection, Columbia University, New York, **http://library.truman.edu/microforms/columbia_oral_ history.asp**

What is Oral History, **http://historymatters.gmu.edu/ mse/oral/what.html**, created by the American Social History Project, Centre for Media and Learning, City University New York. (CUNY).

WRITING THE RESEARCH PROJECT

The process of writing the research project is perhaps the most critical aspect of all aspects of the research process. It is through writing the research project that the researcher communicates the research, what it was about, how it was carried out, and what was accomplished through the research.

It is important to begin the process of writing the thesis as early as possible. Very rarely do researchers have enough time to conduct the research they wish to conduct (or at least this is usually how researchers feel). Because of this time constraint, it is important to get working on the research project as soon as possible. The research proposal is the first part of the research project. When the researcher has completed

Table 16.4 Chapter One: Introduction	
Research statement or question	This is the conceptual framework for the research project.
Aim and objectives	The aim is the research statement or question re-stated as an aim. The objectives (usually not less than two, no more than six) can be presented in bullet point form (a bullet point is a short phrase).
Population and sample	State the population of the research and the sample and sampling method, if a sample is used.
Methodology	State the methodology, explain it, the background to it, and provide a brief explanation as to why you are using it in this research project, i.e. justify your choice of methodology, explain why it is the most appropriate methodology for this research project?
Data collection methods	Introduce the data collection methods and briefly outline them. Explain why this method is the most appropriate/why these methods are the most appropriate methods for this study.
Rational for the research	Explain why you are undertaking this research and what it is that you hope to accomplish with the research.
Context for the research	Outline the context for the research. If you are undertaking the research as part of the requirements of a particular course of study, e.g. for a BSc. in Management, then state this. State where the study is being carried out. Any background detail you wish to provide for the study can be presented here in this section.

Table 16.5 Chapter Two: Literature review	
Introduction	A short introduction to the chapter.
	There may be two subsections or three, or four or five subsections. The sub-titles of the sub-sections are drawn from, or informed by, the conceptual framework.
First subheading	Each of the sub headings is an indication of the contents of that subsection. Remember that one or two words do not make good sub headings, develop a short (appropriate) phrase for each sub heading.
Second subheading	Each of the subsections deals with a different but related aspect or element of the conceptual framework.
Third subheading	The subsections are presented in a logical, meaningful order.
Summary	A brief summary of the chapter.

Table 16.6 Chapter Three: Methodology	
Introduction	Brief introduction to the chapter.
Research methodology	Theoretical background to the research methodology and a more detailed explanation of the methodology, following on from Chapter One. A justification of the methodology (an explanation of why the methodology is the appropriate methodology for this research project).
Population and sample	Detailed description of population and sample, sampling method used.
Data gathering methods	Detailed description and justification of data gathering methods.
Issues of validity and reliability	Detailed discussion of the issues of validity and reliability and how these are dealt with in regard to the data gathering methods used.
Triangulation	Has the research been triangulated, and if so how?
Pilot study	Detailed description of pilot study if pilot study has been carried out.
Gathering data	Detailed description of process of gathering data, any issues or problems encountered in data gathering and an explanation of how they were dealt with.
Data analysis	Detailed description of data analysis processes and procedures.
Ethical issues	Detailed discussion of ethical issues, routine ethical issues, informed consent and anonymity and confidentiality, as well as ethical issues specific to the research project. An honest, reflective account of how these issues were resolved.

a good research proposal, the research is off to a good start. The research proposal, with a little adaptation, can become the first chapter in the thesis, see Table 16.4.

The second chapter in the thesis is the literature review chapter and it contains the theoretical framework for the research project (see Table 16.5). The theoretical framework is built on the conceptual framework. The key concepts in the conceptual framework provide guidance and direction for the reading for the literature review and the structure of the literature review chapter.

The third chapter is the research methodology chapter and contains all of the information on how the research was carried out (see Table 16.6). This chapter contains the methodological framework for the research project, which is the third

Table 16.7 Chapter Four: Data analysis	
Introduction	A brief introduction to the contents of the chapter.
First subheading	There may be two subsections or three, or four or five subsections.
	Each of the subheadings is an indication of the contents of that subsection.
	Each of the subsections deals with a different but related aspect or element of the analysis or analytical framework.
Second subheading	The subsections are presented in a logical order, in the order which best suits the narrative, or story, the researcher wishes to tell from the analyzed data.
Third subheading	The narrative told will be the narrative which best describes or explains the phenomenon under investigation.
Summary	A brief summary of the contents of the chapter.

framework in the four frameworks approach. Every aspect of the methodological framework has to 'fit' with the research project, the methodology, the population and sample, the data gathering methods, the kind of data gathered, the way in which the data are analyzed, the ethical issues considered.

The fourth chapter is the data analysis chapter and contains the analytical framework for the research project (see Table 16.7). This is the fourth framework in the four frameworks approach to the research process. The chapter contains a synopsis of the analysis carried out on the data gathered for the research project. The structure of the chapter is based on the decisions the researcher makes about the story or narrative they wish to tell about the analyzed data, and the narrative told should be the one that best explains the phenomenon under investigation. Although the researcher does not report every detail of the analyzed data, the researcher does use all of the analyzed data to present the best possible account, providing the best possible insight into that phenomenon.

The final chapter is the chapter on conclusions and recommendations, see Table 16.8.

Table 16.8 Chapter Five: Conclusions and recommendations	
Introduction	A brief introduction to the contents of the chapter.
Conclusions	The overall conclusion of the research is stated. This conclusion responds to the research question or statement. The overall conclusion is theorized and the implications of it are drawn out. Then the overall conclusion is broken down into major conclusions. Each of these is discussed and theorized and the implications of each are drawn out. Finally, minor conclisions are reported, explained and theorised.
Limitations of the research	A short paragraph considering the limitations of the research is appropriate. The research should not be undermined by this paragraph. The paragraph is simply a brief acknowledgement of the limitations of the research.
Recommendations	The recommendations of the research are laid out in bullet points. A list of (about) ten well-conceptualized, carefully considered, useful and meaningful in terms of the research undertaken, recommendations are presented.
Final short paragraph	There is often a final short paragraph in this chapter which summarizes the research, and the accomplishments of the research. In this paragraph, the researcher can note or detail briefly what was accomplished by the research. They may also very briefly note what they themselves gained from the research.

Table 16.9 The thesis/report	
Title page	This page contains the title of the research, the name of the researcher, and any other detail necessary, such as the name of the university and school. The university or college will have a convention governing this page.
Acknowledgements	It is usual to acknowledge the help and support you received throughout the research. In general, your research supervisor would be thanked, participants in the research would be thanked, and any gatekeeper who facilitated the research would be thanked. In addition, it is customary to acknowledge the support of family and friends.
Abstract	This is a short one-paragraph summary of the thesis, for a 20 000 word thesis, the abstract would be less than 300 words long. It contains mention of all of the key concepts in the research project, the methodology and data gathering methods used, the main conclusion and key recommendations.
Table of contents	This is a detailed table of contents of the thesis complete with page numbers. Again the university or college will have a convention governing this page.
Introduction	The first chapter in the thesis/report, it is structured around the conceptual framework, the first framework in the four frameworks approach to the research project.
Literature review	The second chapter contains the theoretical framework.
Research methodology	The third chapter contains the methodological framework.
Data analysis	The fourth chapter contains the analytical framework.
Conclusions and recommendations	The fifth and final chapter contains the conclusions and recommendations.
Bibliography	Constitutes a complete list of all of the references in the text. Again, the university or college will have a convention governing the presentation of the references in the bibliography or list of references.
Appendices	Included in appendices are copies of letters written requesting access to research sites, letters written inviting participation in the research. You place copies of questionnaires, interview schedules, focus group schedules, observation schedules, and so on in appendices. Also placed in appendices are copies of informed consent forms. Long lists and big tables, graphs and charts, and other large images, are also placed in appendices.

List of references
A complete list of all of the works cited in your research project.

The bibliography or **List of references** follows the final chapter. The appendices (one appendix, appendices is the plural), follow the bibliography or list of references.

In terms of word count, the guidance usually given is that the word count for the completed thesis should come within a 10 per cent margin of the word count allowed. The title pages, the bibliography and the appendices tend not to be included in the word count, see Table 16.10.

Completing the first draft of the thesis is a major milestone. It is at this point that you can see the scale of the research project, and at first sight it is always impressive. Once the first draft of the thesis or report is complete, it is time to begin the process of rewriting and editing the thesis. It is at this stage, the polishing stage, that the final draft of the thesis comes into being. It is important to remember that the first draft is simply that, the first draft. A great deal of work goes into in producing the final draft

YOUR RESEARCH
Common research problems

One of the most common mistakes students make in writing research is that they do not take proper care with the language they use, or with spelling, grammar and syntax. Poorly written and poorly presented theses lose marks, and they lose a lot of marks, unnecessarily. The academic institution wherein English is the language used is merciless when it comes to written English and to preserving an appropriate standard of written English and this is the case whether or not English is the first language of the student. If you are studing within such an insititution and English is not your first language, you will have needed to assure the academic institution of your ability to study in English and write English to the appropriate standard in order to secure a place on the course of study. If you feel that your written English is not as good as it should be, then you should have someone proofread your work before you submit it for examination. In proofreading your work, this person will highlight for you any spelling mistakes, grammatical errors and errors of syntax in your work. You can then correct these mistakes before you submit the work.

A simple test: There is a deliberate error in each of the sentences below. Can you spot them? If you can't, you should get someone to proofread your work before you submit it for examination. (Answers at end of chapter).

There were too main reasons why the participants in the study did not enjoy the training programme.

Respondents anger over the refusal of the company to provide the information requested was evident.

Respondents indicated that they're anger was prompted by perceptions that the company was not listening to them.

'Your required to attend the training', was the actual wording on the document.

The government have decided to rescind all tax incentives.

It is easier to maintain correct grammar and syntax in short sentences. Meaning and sense can be lost when writing long sentences. When writing, use all of the aids to good clear writing available to you:

proper sentences and good spelling, good paragraphing, good headings and subheadings, and the use of bullet points when appropriate.

When you have finished writing a section, check back on it:

- Check for sentence structure, for syntax, grammatical errors and spelling errors.
- Check your paragraphing. Are the paragraphs too long, or are they too short? Remember, a paragraph is a substantial amount of information. Generally half a page is long enough for a paragraph.
- Critique your subheadings. Are they meaningful? Do they adequately indicate the content of that subsection?
- Are any of your sentences too long? If any sentence goes on for three lines or more it is too long. Try to break the long sentences down into two or more short sentences.

Perhaps the most important element of writing is the need to write to a point. When you are reading a section of your research, ask yourself, What point am I making here? Is it an important point? Is it as clear as it could be? Remember, in writing you are attempting to communicate. You have to structure your communication in such a way as to help the reader understand what it is that you are saying.

All of the points that you make in your writing should contribute to your overall argument. You should never lose sight of your overall argument. What is your overall argument? How well are you making that overall argument? Try to argue persuasively, in your writing.

Be careful to ensure that in your writing you are not evidencing biases, for example in terms of gender, race, ethnicity, culture or religion, in the way in which you use language.

It is important to get feedback on your writing. Check with your thesis supervisor that you are on the right track. There is nothing so dispiriting as to complete a large amount of work only to find that, for one reason or another, it is not to the standard required. It is better to check for feedback as you do

Table 16.10 Breakdown of typical word counts for theses and research projects				
Total word count	20 000 words	15 000 words	12 000 words	10 000 words
Introduction	2,000	1,200	1,000	1,000
Literature review	5,000	4,000	3,000	2,500
Research methodology	4,000	3,000	3,000	2,500
Data analysis	6,000	5,000	3,500	3,000
Conclusions and recommendations	3,000	1,800	1,500	1,000

of the thesis. It is a good idea to submit the first draft for formal feedback from your thesis supervisor. The feedback you receive should then be incorporated into the final draft of the thesis. If you have received feedback from your thesis supervisor throughout the different stages of the research process, there should not be any major surprises in the feedback you get on the first complete draft of the thesis.

It is important in the editing and polishing stage to take as much time as is needed to produce the final draft of the thesis. The work involves rewriting, editing and re-editing. Hopefully when you've finished this work you will have a complete, well-structured and well-integrated research project. You will have learned a great deal through the process of undertaking the research about the substantive area that is the focus of your research and about research methods. You will be able to draw on the knowledge and skills you have developed through the research process all through your career. I wish you great success.

CASE STUDY

'Why Do Management Practices Differ Across Firms and Countries?' Bloom, N. and Van Reenan, J.(2010)

In this paper, the authors present evidence to show that persistent differences in productivity at firm level and national level largely reflect variations in management practices. They say that, as British-born academics, they are used to reports that blame Britain's relatively low productivity on bad management. They say that this view is so common in the UK that it has generated a strong export industry of television shows on bad management. They cite *The Office*, an example of bad management in the wholesale sector, *Fawlty Towers*, an example of bad management in private services, and *Yes Minister*, an example of bad management in the public sector.

The authors, Bloom and Van Reenan (2010), have undertaken a large survey research program designed to measure management practices systematically across firms, industries and countries. In this paper, they explain how they measured management and they explore some of the basic patterns in their data. Their explanation, which they developed from their research, as to why management practices vary so much across firms and nations, rests on 'a combination of imperfectly competitive markets, family ownership of firms, regulations restricting management practices, and informational barriers'.

The ten conclusions they have come to based on their analysis of their data are as follows:

1 Firms with 'better' management practices tend to have better performance on a wide range of dimensions: they are larger, more productive, grow faster and have higher survival rates.

2 Management practices vary tremendously across firms and countries. Most of the difference in the average management score of a country is due to the size of the 'long tail' of very badly-managed firms. For example, relatively few US firms are very badly managed, while Brazil and India have many firms in that category.

3 Countries and firms specialize in different styles of management. For example, American firms score much higher than Swedish firms in incentives but are worse than Swedish firms in monitoring.

4 Strong product market competition appears to boost average management practices through a combination of eliminating the tail of badly-managed firms and pushing incumbents to improve their practices.

5 Multinationals are generally well-managed in every country. They also transplant their management styles abroad. For example, US multinationals located in the UK are better at incentives and worse at monitoring than Swedish multinationals in the UK.

6 Firms that export (but do not produce) overseas are better-managed than domestic

People in the Apple Store in Westfield, London © David Pearson/Alamy

non-exporters, but are worse-managed than multinationals.

7   Inherited family-owned firms who appoint a family member (especially the oldest son) as chief executive officer are very badly managed on average.

8   Government-owned firms are typically managed extremely badly. Firms with publicly quoted share prices or owned by private-equity firms are typically well managed.

9   Firms that more intensively use human capital, as measured by more educated workers, tend to have much better management practices.

10 At the country level, a relatively light touch in labour market regulation is associated with better use of incentives by management.

It is interesting that in this paper, we begin with a consideration of the conclusions, and then we move to reading about the research and the research methodology. The authors developed a new survey methodology. This is an interview-based evaluation tool that defines and scores from 1 (worst practice) to 5 (best practice) across 18

basic management practices. The survey instrument and the manner in which it was used in the study is explained in detail in the journal article.

The authors explain that their data is cross-sectional, across many firms and countries at roughly the same point in time. They present tables and graphs which highlight different trends and patterns in their data.

Questions What do you think of the conclusions drawn by Bloom and Van Reenan in this study? Can you see how these conclusions have emerged from the data gathered? What do you think of the recommendations they make for further research in the field of economics? In preparing your answer consider the work of Alasuutari (2010) as outlined in Chapter 15, 'Analysing Qualitative Data'. There are very many ideas in terms of possible research projects in the synopsis above and in the original journal article which you should source and read.

References

Bloom, N. and Van Reenan, J. (2010) 'Why do management practices differ across firms and countries?', Journal of Economic Perspectives 24(1): 203–224.

CHAPTER REVIEW

The aim of this chapter was to explain the processes involved in writing the research. A key point highlighted in the chapter is that it is important to begin writing the research as soon as possible. The process of writing the research should be ongoing throughout the research process. The completion of the first draft of the thesis is simply that, the completion of the first draft. There is a lot of work involved in writing and re-writing and editing and re-editing, in turning the first draft of the thesis into the final draft of the thesis. It is the final draft of the thesis that is submitted for examination. This chapter explains what conclusions are in research and it shows how conclusions are drawn in the research project. The chapter demonstrates that there is one overarching conclusion, and this responds to the research question or statement, the overall aim of the research project. This is a useful device in the work of bringing the research full circle. The overall conclusion of the research project must respond to the overall aim of the research. The overall conclusion is broken down into main conclusions, which are thoroughly examined and explored. They are theorized, by which is meant that they are connected to the body of knowledge. This is done by explicitly demonstrating how the conclusions fit with or contradict the conclusions of other researchers, whose work is detailed in the literature review chapter of the research project. The implications of conclusions, or the meaning(s) of conclusions for different constituents to the research are considered. In this chapter the means through which recommendations are conceptualized and then written in the final chapter of the thesis are explored. The process of writing a thesis is explained.

Now update your interactive research diary with your notes and findings at www.cengage.co.uk/quinlan. Complete the activities provided to reinforce your understanding of this chapter.

END OF CHAPTER QUESTIONS

1   What are conclusions and how are they drawn in a research project?

2   What is the role of the overall conclusion in the research project?

3   What is meant by the term 'theorizing conclusions'?

4   Explain the following statement: there are different conclusions for different constituents.

5   What are recommendations and how are they developed?

6   What is meant by the term 'the limitations of the research', in the context of the final chapter of the thesis or report of the research?

7   Illustrate, using examples, the differences between findings, conclusions and recommendations in research.

8   Outline and briefly explain the model of the research process.

9   Outline and briefly explain the four frameworks approach to the research process.

10   Explain the value of the research diary.

SPOT THE DELIBERATE ERROR

There were **too** (should be spelt two) main reasons why the participants in the study did not enjoy the training programme.

Respondents' anger (should be an apostrophe) anger over the refusal of the company to provide the information requested was evident.

Respondents indicated that **they're** anger (should be spelt their) was prompted by perceptions that the company was not listening to them.

'**Your** required (should be spelt You're) to attend the training', was the actual wording on the document.

The government **have** (should be has not have) decided to rescind all tax incentives.

REFERENCES

Alasuutari, P. (2010) 'The rise and relevance of qualitative research', *International Journal of Social Research Methodology* 13(2): 139–155.

Bloom, N. and Van Reenan, J. (2010) 'Why do management practices differ across firms and countries?', *Journal of Economic Perspectives* 24 (1): 203–224.

Butterworth, S. (2009) 'The readers' editor on … 1000 teenagers, one survey, and two sets of results', *The Guardian*, 19 October.

Korte, R.F. (2009) 'How newcomers learn the social norms of an organization: A case study of the socialization of newly hired engineers', *Human Resource Development Quarterly* 20(3): 285–306.

National Life Stories: Tesco: An Oral History, British Library, http://www.bl.uk/reshelp/findhelprestype/sound/ohist/ohnls/nlstesco/tesco.html Accessed 03.06.2010.

Oral History Collection, **Columbia University**, New York, http://library.truman.edu/microforms/columbia_oral_history.asp

Oral History Research, University College Los Angeles (UCLA) Anderson School of Management, http://www.anderson.ucla.edu/x1194.xml Accessed 03.06.2010.

What is Oral History, http://historymatters.gmu.edu/mse/oral/what.html, created by the American Social History Project, Centre for Media and Learning, City University New York (CUNY) Accessed 03.06.2010.

RECOMMENDED READING

Source and read five journal articles in business journals. Read the articles in particular for the theoretical frameworks (literature review), the methodologies and data collection methods used, the procedures for data analysis, the findings of the research and the conclusions drawn. Read the articles in particular for the style of writing, for the language used, and for the way in which in the articles the different research projects are presented, communicated to the audience.

Bell, J. (2005) *Doing Your Research Project*, Ch. 13, 'Writing the report', Maidenhead: Open University Press.

Creswell, J.W. (1998) *Qualitative Inquiry and Research Design: Choosing Among Five Traditions*, Ch. 11, 'Turning the Story' and 'Conclusion' and for the conclusions drawn from the five research projects detailed, read Appendices B, C, D, E, and F, Thousand Oaks, CA: Sage.

Collis, J. and Hussey, R. (2009) *Business Research: A Practical Guide for Undergraduate and Postgraduate Students*, Ch. 13, 'Writing up the Research', Houndsmill: Palgrave Macmillan.

Davies, D. (2005) *Business Research for Decision Making*, Ch. 17, 'Research Reporting and Evaluation', Mason, OH: Cengage South-Western.

Denscombe, M. (2003) *The Good Research Guide: For Small-scale Social Research Projects* (2nd edn), Ch. 15, 'Writing up the Research', Maidenhead: Open University Press.

Easterby-Smith, M., Thorpe, R. and Jackson, P.R. (2005) *Management Research* (3rd edn), Ch. 12, 'Writing and Disseminating Management Research', London: Sage.

Jankowicz, A.D., (2005) *Business Research Projects*, Ch. 13, 'Writing It Up', London: Cengage.

Kent, R. (2007) *Marketing Research, Approaches, Methods and Applications in Europe*, Ch. 18, 'Communicating the Results', London: Thomson.

methods@manchester: research methods in the social sciences, www.methods.manchester.ac.uk.

Miles, M.B. and Huberman, A.M. (1994) *Qualitative Data Analysis*, Ch. 10, 'Making Good Sense: Drawing and Verifying Conclusions', London and Thousand Oaks, CA: Sage.

Murray, R. (2003) *How to Write a Thesis*, Maidenhead: Open University Press.

Neuman, W.L. (2000) *Social Research Methods: Quantitative and Qualitative Approaches*, Ch. 16, 'Reviewing the Literature and Writing a Report', Boston, MA: Allyn & Bacon.

Robson, C. (2000) *Real World Research*, Ch. 15, 'Reporting on the Enquiry', Oxford: Blackwell.

White, B. (2000) *Dissertation Skills for Business and Management Students*, Ch. 9, 'Writing Up Your Dissertation', London: Thomson.

Zikmund, W. G. (2003) *Business Research Methods*, Ch. 25, 'Communicating Research Results: Report, Presentation and Follow-Up', Mason, OH: Cengage South-Western.

BIBLIOGRAPHY

Abercrombie, N., Hill, S. and Turner, B.S.(2000) *Penguin Dictionary of* Sociology(5thedn),Penguin Books.

Abrams, R. and Barrow, P. (2008) *The Successful Business Plan, Secrets and Strategies*, Capstone Publishing Ltd., Chichester: John Wiley & Sons.

Action Research Made Simple URL http://www.youtube.com/watch?v=Qg83f72_6Gw Accessed 31.08.2010.

Ajzen, I. and Fishbein, M. (1980) *Understanding Attitudes and Predicting Social Behaviour*, Englewood Cliffs, NJ: Prentice Hall.

Alasuutari, P. (2010) 'The rise and relevance of qualitative research', *International Journal of Social Research Methodology* 13(2): 139–155.

Allen, J. Dublin City University, 'DCU library citing and referencing: A guide for students' (2nd edn), http://www.library.dcu.ie/LibraryGuides/citing&refquide08.pdf Accessed 02.06.2010.

American Statistical Association's online guide 'What is a survey', www.whatisasurvey.info/ Accessed 02.06.2010.

Anderson, K. (2009) 'Ethnographic research: A key to strategy', http://hbr.org/2009/03/ethnographic-researcha-key-to-strategy/ar/1 Accessed 03.06.2010.

Andrews, M., Squire, C., and Tamboukou, M., (eds), (2008) *Doing Narrative Research*, Sage, London and Thousand Oaks, CA.

Atkinson, R. (1998) *The Life Story Interview* (Qualitative Research Methods Series 44), London: Sage.

Banks, M. (2007) *Using Visual Data in Qualitative Research*, London: Sage.

BBC News, 'internet access is "a fundamental right"', http://news.bbc.co.uk/2/hi/8548190.stm Accessed 03.06.2010.

BBC World Service Trust, 'Using content analysis to measure the influence of media development interventions: Elections training for journalists in Yemen', http://downloads.bbc.co.uk/worldservice/trust/pdf/bbcwst_research_series_yemen.pdf Accessed 02.06.2010.

Becker,H.S. (1974) 'Photography and sociology', *Studies in the Anthropology of Visual Communication* 1(1): 3–26.

Bell, J. (2005) *Doing Your Research Project*, Maidenhead: Open University Press.

Berger, P. and Luckman, T. (1966) *The Social Construction of Reality*, New York: Anchor Books.

Bignell, J. (2002) *Media Semiotics: An Introduction*, Oxford Road, Manchester: Manchester University Press.

Biloslavo, R. and Trnavčevič, A. (2009) 'Websites as tools of communication of a "green" company', *Management Decision* 47(7): 1158–1173.

Blackwell, E. (1996) *How to Prepare a Business Plan* (2nd edn), London: Kogan Page.

Bloom, N. and Van Reenan, J. (2010) 'Why do management practices differ across firms and countries?', *Journal of Economic Perspectives* 24 (1): 203–224.

Boje, D.M. (2001) *Narrative Methods for Organizational & Communication Research* (Series in Management Research), London: Sage.

Borenstein, M., Hedges, L.V., Higgins, J.P.T. and Rothstein, H.R. (2009) *Introduction to Meta Analysis*, Chichester: John Wiley & Sons Ltd.

Bourdieu, P. (1986) 'The Forms of Capital' in John-Richardson (ed.) *Handbook of Theory and Research for the Sociology of Education*, New York: Greenwood Press, pp. 241–258.

Bourdieu, P. (2001) *Masculine Domination*, California: Stanford University Press.

Bowen, G.A. (2009) 'Supporting a grounded theory with an audit trail: An illustration', *International Journal of Social Research Methodology* 12(4): 305–316.

Bowler, D. (1996) *Shanks: The Authorized Biography of Bill Shankly*, London: Orion.

Bradshaw, J. and Richardson, D. (2009) 'An index of child well-being in Europe', *Child Indicators Research* 2(3): 319–351.

Brotherton, B.(1999) (ed.), 'The Handbook of Contemporary Hospitality Management Research', New York: John Wiley & Sons.

Brydon-Miller, M., Greenwood, D. and Maguire, P. (2003) 'Why action research?', Action Research 1: 9-28.

Bryman, A. and Burgess, R.G. (1994) *Analysing Qualitative Data*, London: Routledge.

Bunch, K.J. (2007) 'Training failure as a consequence of organizational culture', *Human Resource Development Review* 6(2): 142–164.

Bunting, M. (2010) 'To tackle the last decades' myths, we must dust off the big moral questions: A robust debate on ethics is crucial to the pursuit of a good society in which individuals are more than mere economic units', *The Guardian*, 22 February.

Business Archives Council, **www.businessarchivescouncil.org.uk**

Butterworth, S. (2009) 'The readers' editor on ... 1000 teenagers, one survey, and two sets of results', *The Guardian*, 19 October.

CADAAD (Critical Approaches to Discourse Analysis Across Disciplines), **www.cadaad.org/** Accessed 02.06.2010.

Central Intelligence Agency (CIA), **www.cia.gov/**

Chan, G., Benner, P., Brykcynski, K.A. and Malone, R.E. (2010) *Interpretive Phenomenology in Health Care Research: Studying Social Practice, Lifeworlds, and Embodiment*, Sigma Theta Tau Intl., **http://www.nursinglibrary.org/Portal/CMSLite/GetFile.aspx?ContentID=103477&VersionID=115170** Accessed 03.06.2010.

Chandler, D. (2007) *Semiotics: The Basics*, London: Routledge.

Chandler, D. 'Semiotics for beginners', **http://www.aber.ac.uk/media/Documents/S4B/**

Channel 4 (2009) 'Crash: How long will it last?', *Dispatches* documentary, **http://www.channel4.com/programmes/dispatches/episode-guide/series-13/episode-2**

Child Poverty Action Group (CPAG) London(2009) 'The child well-being index', **http://www.cpag.org.uk/info/ChildWellbeingandChildPoverty.pdf** Accessed 03.06.2010.

Chou, A.Y. (2008) 'The role of knowledge sharing and trust in new product development outsourcing', *International Journal of Information Systems and Change Management*, 3(4) June: 301–313.

Clegg, S., Kornberger, M. and Rhodes, C. (2007) 'Business ethics as practice', *British Journal of Management* 18: 107–122.

Collier, J. Jr. and Collier, M. (1986) *Visual Anthropology: Photography as a Research Method*, New Mexico: University of New Mexico Press.

Colorado State University, 'Guide to narrative inquiry', **http://writing.colstate.edu/guides/research/observe/com3a2.cfm**

Colorado State University, 'Introduction to content analysis', **www.writing.colostate.edu/guides/research/content/index.cfm**

Colorado State University, 'Writing guide: Ethnography, observational research, and narrative inquiry', **http://writing.colstate.edu/guides/research/observe/**

Colorado State University, 'Writing guide: Introduction to statistics', **http://writing.colstate.edu/guides/research/stats/index.cfm.**

Columbia University, Columbia Center for New Media Teaching and Learning (CNMTL), 'Quantitative Methods in Social Sciences', Laymon, S. and Weiss, C., **http://ccnmtl.columbia.edu/projects/qmss/home.html**

Conklin, T.A. (2007) 'Method or madness: Phenomenology as knowledge creator', *Journal of Management Inquiry* 16(3): 275–287.

Connor, R.E. (2004) *Women, Accounting and Narrative: Keeping Books in Eighteenth-Century England*, London: Routledge.

Cope, J. (2005) 'Researching entrepreneurship through phenomenological inquiry: Philosophical and methodological issues, *International Journal of Small Business Management* 23(2): 163–189.

Corbin, J. and Strauss, A. (2008) *Basics of Qualitative Research*, Thousand Oaks, CA: Sage.

Corbin, J. and Strauss, A.(2007) 'Basics of Qualitative Research: Techniques and Procedures for Developing Grounded Theory', Thousand Oaks, CA: Sage.

Cote, J.A., McCullough, J. and Reilly, M. (1985) 'Effects of unexpected situations on behavior-intention differences: A garbology analysis', *The Journal of Consumer Research* 12(2): 188–194.

Cremer, R.D. and Ramasamy, B. (2009) 'Engaging China: Strategies for the small internationalizing firm', *Journal of Business Strategy* 30(6): 15–26.

Creswell, J. (2003) *Research Design: Qualitative, Quantitative and Mixed Methods Approaches*, Ch. 2, 'Review of the Literature', Thous and Oaks, CA: Sage.

Crick, M. (2002) *The Boss: The Many Sides of Alex Ferguson*, London: Simon and Schuster UK Ltd.

Crotty, M. (2005) *The Foundations of Social Research*, London: Sage.

Currell, S. (2010) 'The Canon: Middletown, by Robert and Helen Lynd', *Times Higher Educational Supplement*, 11 February.

Danto, E.A. (2008) *Historical Research*, Oxford, UK: Oxford University Press.

Davies, I.A., Doherty, B. and Knox, S. (2010) 'The rise and stall of a fair trade pioneer: The Cafédirect story', *Journal of Business Ethics* 92: 127–147.

Deacon, D.H., Golding, P., Pickering, M. and Murdock, G. (2007) *Researching Communications: A Practical Guide to Methods in Media and Cultural Analysis*, London: Hodder Arnold.

Denscombe, M. (2003) *The Good Research Guide: For Small-scale Social Research Projects* (2nd edn), Part 1, 'Strategies for Social Research', Milton Keynes, Buckingham: Open University Press.

Denzin, N. (1970) *The Research Act in Sociology*, Chicago: Aldine.

Denzin, N.K. (1970) 'The research act in sociology', Chicago, IL: Aldine.

Denzin, N.K. and Lincoln, Y.S. (2000) *Handbook of Qualitative Research*, Thousand Oaks, CA: Sage.

Dermody, J. and Scullion, R. (2004) 'Exploring the value of party political advertising for youth electoral engagement: An analysis of the 2001 British General Election advertising campaigns', *International Journal of Nonprofit and Voluntary Sector Marketing* 9(4): 361–379.

DeThomas, A. and Derammelaere, S. (2008) *Writing A Convincing Business Plan* (Barron's Business Library), New York: Barron's Educational Series.

Dick, B. (2005) 'Grounded theory: A thumbnail sketch', www.scu.edu.au/schools/gcm/ar/arp/grounded.html Accessed 03.06.2010.

Donaldson, T. (2003) 'Editor's comments: Taking ethics seriously? A mission now more possible', *Academy of Management Review*, 28: 363–366.

Downs, A. (2009) 'Identifying shortage occupations in the UK', *Economic and Labour Market Review* 3(5): 23–29, www.statistics.gov.uk/cci/article.asp?id=2181 'Experimental design', The Science Olympiad, http://soinc.org/exper_design_b

Duffy, B. (2005) 'The Analysis of Documentary Evidence', in J. Bell *Doing Your Research Project*, Ch.7, Maidenhead: Open University Press.

Eagly, A.H. and Chaiken, S. (1993) *The Psychology of Attitudes*, Forth Worth, TX: Harcourt Brace and Company.

Edwards, A. and Skinner, J. (2009) *Qualitative Research in Sports Management*, Oxford: Butterworth-Heinemann.

Ethnographic Research, Inc., www.ethnographic-research.com

Eurochild (2006) 'Ending child poverty within the EU: A review of the 2008–2010 national strategy reports on social protection and social inclusion', http://www.eurochild.org/fileadmin/user_upload/files/NAP_2008_-_2010/Ending_child_poverty.pdf Accessed 03.06.2010.

Eurochild (2007) 'Ending child poverty within the EU: A review of the 2008–2010 national strategy reports on social protection and social inclusion' (2nd edn), http://www.icyrnet.net/UserFiles/File/NAPs%20report%202006%20final.pdf Accessed 03.06.2010.

Exploring Online Research Methods, University of Leicester, www.geog.le.ac.uk/ORM/site/home.htm Accessed 02.06.2010.

Exploring Online Research Methods, University of Leicester, www.geog.le.ac.uk/ORM/site/home.htm Accessed 03.06.2010.

Fairclough, N. (1995) *Critical Discourse Analysis*, London, UK: Longman.

Fairclough, N. (1995) *Critical Discourse Analysis*, London: Longman.

Ferriss, S. and Young, M. (2008) *Chick Flicks: Contemporary Women at the Movies*, London and New York: Routledge.

Fetterman, D.M. (2010) *Ethnography: Step-by-Step* (3rd edn), Thousand Oaks, CA: Sage.

Finlay, L. (2009) 'Debating phenomenological research methods', *Phenomenology & Practice* 3 (1): 6–25, www.phandpr.org/index.php/pandp/article/viewFile/40/80 Accessed 03.06.2010.

Finn, A. (2009) 'If you only do one thing this week carry out an eco survey', *The Guardian*, 16 November.

Fletcher, D. (2007) '"Toy Story": The narrative world of entrepreneurship and the creation of interpretive communities', *Journal of Business Venturing* 22 (5): 649–672.

'Focus Groups', Channel 4 website, http://www.channel4.com/culture/microsites/W/wtc4/audience/focusgroups.html Accessed 03.06.2010.

Foucault, M. (1970) *The Order of Things*, New York: Pantheon.

Foucault, M. (1972) *Archaeology of Knowledge*, New York: Pantheon.

Fowler, F.J. (2002) *Survey Research Methods*, Thousand Oaks, CA: Sage.

Fowler, F.J. Jr (2009) *Survey Research Methods* (4th edn), Thousand Oaks, CA: Sage.

Geertz, C. (1973) *The Interpretation of Cultures*, New York: Basic Books.

Gibson, S.K. and Hanes, L.A. (2003) 'The contribution of phenomenology to HRD research', *Human Resource Development Review* 2(2): 181–205.

Giddens, A. (2001) *Sociology*, Cambridge: Polity.

Glaser, B. and Strauss, A.L. (1967) *The Discovery of Grounded Theory*, Chicago: Aldine.

Glaser, B.G. (2001) 'The grounded theory perspective: Conceptualization contrasted with description', Mill Valley, CA: Sociology Press.

Glazer, B. and Strauss, A. (1967) 'The Discovery of Grounded Theory: Strategies for Qualitative Research', Chicago: Aldine Publishing Company.

Goffman, E. (1979) *Gender Advertisements*, New York: Harper and Row.

Götze, E., Prange, C. and Uhrovska, I. (2009) 'Children's impact on innovation decision making: A diary study', *European Journal of Marketing* 43 (1/2): 264–295.

Grant, S. (2007) 'Learning through "being" and "doing"', *Action Research* 5(3): 265-274.

Groenewald, T. (2004) 'A phenomenological research design illustrated', *International Journal of Qualitative Methods* 3(1) 1–26. www.ualberta.ca/~backissues/3_1/pdf/groenewald.pdf Accessed 03.06.2010.

Guardian (2009) 'There's more to life than GDP', http://www.guardian.co.uk/news/datablog/2009/mar/24/g20-economics

Guba, E.G. and Lincoln, Y.S. (1994) 'Competing Paradigms in Qualitative Research', in N. Denzin and Y. Lincoln (eds), *Handbook of Qualitative Research*, Thousand Oaks, CA: Sage.

Guba, E.G. and Lincoln, Y.S. (1994) *Competing Paradigms in Qualitative Research*, http://create.alt.ed.nyu.edu/courses/3311/reading/10-guba_lincoln_94.pdf Accessed 03.06.2010.

Guba, G.G. and Lincoln, Y.S. (1994) 'Competing paradigms in qualitative research', http://ctl.iupui.edu/common/uploads/library/CTL/IDD443360.pdf Accessed 02.06.2010.

Gubrium, J.F. and Holstein, J.A. (2009) *Analyzing Narrative Reality*, Thousand Oaks, CA: Sage.

Hammersley, M. and Atkinson, P. (1995) *Ethnography*, London: Routledge.

Harper, D. (1996) 'Seeing sociology', *The American Sociologist* 37(3): 69–78.

Harper, D. (1998) 'An Argument for Visual Sociology', in J. Prosser (ed.), *Image-based Research*, pp. 24–41, London: Routledge and Falmer.

Harvard – MIT Data Centre, 'Guide to SPSS', www.hmdc.harvard.edu/projects/SPSS_Tutorial/spsstut.shtml.

Hawthorne Experiments, Harvard Business School, http://www.library.hbs.edu/hc/hawthorne/09.html Accessed 03.06.2010.

Helliar, C. and Bebbington, J. (2004) 'Taking ethics to heart: A discussion document by the Research Committee of The Institute of Chartered Accountants of Scotland', The Institute of Chartered Accountants of Scotland, http://www.icas.org.uk/site/cms/download/res_helliar_bebbington_Report.pdf Accessed 02.06.2010.

Hesse-Biber, S.N. (ed.) (2007) *Handbook of Feminist Research: Theory and Practice*, Thousand Oaks, CA: Sage.

Hesse-Biber, S.N. and Leavy, P.L. (2007) *Feminist Research Practice: A Primer*, Thousand Oaks, CA: Sage.

Hirsch, A. (2009) 'Should Sir Fred get away scotfree?', www.guardian.co.uk, 20 January.

Holt, R. and Macpherson, A. (2010) 'Sensemaking, rhetoric and the socially competent entrepreneur', *International Small Business Journal*, 28(1): 20–42.

Human Development Index, http://hdr.undp.org/en/site/ Accessed 03.06.2010.

Hutton, W. (2009) 'Hail the man who argues Britain should stop worrying about its debt', *The Observer*, 5 July.

Hutton, W. (2009) 'The banking system has shirked its ownership of risk, but governments must be generous if it is to survive', *The Banker*, www.the-banker.com Accessed 5 January 2009.

Institute for New Economic Thinking (INET), http://ineteconomics.org Accessed 03.06.2010.

Institute for New Economic Thinking, Conference Proceedings, April 2010, http://ineteconomics.org/initiatives/conferences/kings-college/proceedings Accessed 03.06.2010.

Jameson, D.A. (2009) 'Economic crises and financial disasters: The role of business communication', *Journal of Business Communication* 46: 499–509.

Johnson, P. and Smith, K. (1999) 'Contextualizing business ethics: Anomie and social life', *Human Relations*, 52: 1351–1375.

Johnson, R. (1993) *The Perfect Business Plan: All You Need To Get It Right First Time*, The Perfect Series, London: Century Business.

Journal of Mixed Methods Research, an academic journal publishing research carried out using mixed methods.

Kaletsky, A. (2009) 'Three cheers for the death of old economics: The orthodox mathematical model took no account of reality. The new George Soros institute should bring back some sanity', *The Times*, 28 October.

Katzenbach, J.R. and Smith, D.K. (2003) *The Wisdom of Teams: Creating the High-Performance Organization*, New York: McKinsey & Company.

Kaulio, M.A. and Uppvall, L. (2009) 'Critical incidents in R&D alliances: Uncovering leadership roles', *European Management Review* 6(3): 195–205.

Keeble-Ramsay, D. and Armitage, A. (2010) 'Total quality management meets human resource management: Perceptions of the shift towards high performance working', *Total Quality Management Journal* 22(1): 5–25.

Kent, T. (2010) 'The role of the museum shop in extending the visitor experience', *International Journal of Nonprofit and Voluntary Sector Marketing* 15(1): 67–77.

Kessous, A. and Roux, E. (2008) 'A semiotic analysis of nostalgia as a connection to the past', *Qualitative Market Research* 11(2): 192–212.

Kirca, A.H. and Yaprak, A. (2010) 'The use of meta analysis in international business research: Its current status and suggestions for better practice', *International Business Review* 19(2): 160–177.

Kohler Riessman, C. (2008) *Narrative Methods for the Human Sciences*, Thousand Oaks, CA: Sage.

Koller, V. (2007) '"The world's local bank": Glocalisation as a strategy in corporate branding discourse', *Social Semiotics* 17(1): 111–131.

Koo, R.C. (2008) *The Holy Grail of Macro Economics: Lessons from Japan's Great Recession*, Singapore: John Wiley & Sons.

Korte, R.F. (2009) 'How newcomers learn the social norms of an organization: A case study of the socialization of newly hired engineers', *Human Resource Development Quarterly* 20(3): 285–306.

Krippendorf, K. and Bock, M.A. (2009) *The Content Analysis Reader*, London: Sage.

Lee, J. (2009) 'Open mic: Professionalizing the rap career', *Ethnography* 10(4): 475–495.

Lee, R.M. (2000) *Unobtrusive Methods in Social Research*, Milton Keynes: Open University Press.

Lincoln, Y.S. and Guba, E.G. (1985) *Naturalistic Inquiry*, Newbury Park, CA: Sage.

Lipsey, M.W. and Wilson, D. (2000) *Practical Meta Analysis*, Thousand Oaks, CA: Sage.

Liu, S. and Meyer, L.M. (2008) 'Carnations and the floriculture industry: Documenting the cultivation and marketing of flowers in Colorado', *Journal of Archival Organization* 6(1): 6–23.

Maher, K. (2009) 'Is it time to kill the chick flick? Hollywood thinks that all women care about is weddings and shopping. Can anything stop the inane decline of the chick flick?', *The Times*, 3 February.

Marketing Online, www.marketing-online.co.uk Accessed 03.06.2010.

Markova, G. (2009) 'Can human resource management make a big difference in a small company?', *International Journal of Strategic Management* 9 (2): 73–80.

Martinez, E., Montaner, T. and Pina, J.M. (2009) 'Brand extension feedback: The role of advertising', *Journal of Business Research* 62(4): 405–414.

Mass Observation Archive, The Library, University of Sussex, www.massobs.org.uk

Mazza, C., Sahlin-Andersson, K. and Strandgaard Pedersen, J. (2005) 'European constructions of an American model: Developments of four MBA programmes', *Management Learning*, 36(4): 471–491.

McNeill, T. 'Roland Barthes: Mythologies (1957)', University of Sunderland, http://seacoast. sunderland.ac.uk/~os0tmc/myth.htm

McNiff, J. and Whitehead, J. (2009) *Doing and Writing Action Research*, London: Sage.

Media and Communications Studies, Aberystwyth University, 'Textual analysis', www.aber.ac.uk/ media/Sections/textan.html Accessed 02.06.2010.

Methodspace: Connecting the Research Community, Sage, www.methodspace.com Accessed 02.06.2010.

Methodspace: Connecting the Research Community, Sage, www.methodspace.com

Miles, M.B. and Huberman, A.M. (1994) *Qualitative Data Analysis: An Expanded Sourcebook*, London and Thousand Oaks, CA: Sage.

Millward, R. and Shoard, C. (2010) 'Does it matter that there are no women up for the Palme D'Or?', *The Observer*, 16 May.

Morgeson, F.P., Scott DeRue, D. and Karam, E.P. (2010) 'Leadership in teams: A functional approach to understanding leadership structures and processes', *Journal of Management* 36(1): 5–39.

Moustakas, C.E. (1994) *Phenomenological Research Methods*, Thousand Oaks, CA: Sage.

Mullen, M.R., Budeva, D.G. and Doney, P.M. (2009) 'Research methods in the leading small business– entrepreneurship journals: A critical review with recommendations for future research', *Journal of Small Business Management* 47(3): 287–307.

Murphy, P. (2009) *His Way: The Brian Clough Story*, London: Pan Books Ltd.

Nadin, S. and Cassell, C. (2006) 'The use of a research diary as a tool for reflexive practice: Some reflections from management research', *Qualitative Research in Accounting and Management* 4 (4): 208–217.

National Archives of Australia, www.naa.gov.au Accessed 03.06.2010.

National Archives of the UK, www.nationalarchives. gov.uk

National Archives of the USA, www.archives.gov/

National Life Stories: Tesco: An Oral History, British Library, http://www.bl.uk/reshelp/findhelprestype/ sound/ohist/ohnls/nlstesco/tesco.html Accessed 03.06.2010.

Neale, M.A., Mannix, E. and Sondak, H. (2002) *Toward Phenomenology of Groups and*

Group Membership, Vol. 4, Research on Managing Groups and Teams, Connecticut: Jai Press Inc.

Neuman, W.L. (2000) *Social Research Methods: Quantitative and Qualitative Approaches* (4th edn), Boston, MA: Allyn & Bacon.

Neuman, W.L. (2000) *Social Research Methods: Quantitative and Qualitative Approaches*, Boston: Allyn & Bacon.

Ng, K. and Hase, S. (2008) 'Grounded suggestions for doing a grounded theory business research', *Electronic Journal of Business ResearchMethods* 6 (2): 155–170.

O'Connell, C. (2009) 'Ocean census looks back to go forward', *Irish Times*, 28.05.2009.

OECD Family Database, Social Policy Division, Directorate of Employment, Labour and Social Affairs, (2005), 'PF1: Public spending on family benefits', http://www.oecd.org/dataoecd/45/46/37864391.pdf Accessed 03.06.2010.

Office for National Statistics, Statistical Bulletin 'internet access households and individuals 2009', www.statistics.gov.uk/statbase/Product.asp?vlnk=5672 Accessed 03.06.2010.

Oldfield, T. (2008) *Arsène Wenger: Pure Genius*, London: John Blake Publishing Ltd.

Oliver, J. and Eales, K. (2008) 'Re-evaluating the consequentialist perspective of using covert participant observation in management research', *Qualitative Market Research: An International Journal* 11(3): 344–357.

Oppenheim, A.N. (1998) *Questionnaire Design, Interviewing and Attitude Measurement*, London: Pinter.

Oral History Collection, Columbia University, New York, http://library.truman.edu/microforms/columbia_oral_history.asp

Oral History Research, University College Los Angeles (UCLA) Anderson School of Management, http://www.anderson.ucla.edu/x1194.xml Accessed 03.06.2010.

Organization for Economic Cooperation and Development (OECD), www.oecd.org

Oswald, L. 'Semiotics and Strategic Brand Management', University of Illinois, http://marketingtrends-congress.com/2009_cp/Materiali/Paper/Fr/Oswald.pdf

Owyong, Y.S.M. (2009) 'Clothing semiotics and the social construction of power relations', *Social Semiotics* 19(2): 191–211.

Parker, M. (ed.) (2003) 'Special issue on ethics politics and organization', *Organization*, Vol. 10(2).

Partington, D. (2000) 'Building Grounded Theories of Management Action', *British Journal of Management*, 11(2): 91–102.

Pink, S. (2006) Doing *Visual Ethnography* (2nd edn), London: Sage.

Plakoyiannaki, E. and Zotos, Y. (2009) 'Female role stereotypes in print advertising: Identifying associations with magazine and product categories', *European Journal of Marketing* 43(11/12): 1411–1434.

Porter, M. (1983) *Competitive Strategy*, London: Collier Macmillan, Free Press.

Porter, M. (1985) *Competitive Advantage*, London: Collier Macmillan, Free Press.

Porter, M. and Kramer, M. (2002) 'The competitive advantage of corporate philanthropy', *Harvard Business Review*, December, pp. 37–68.

Princeton University Survey Research Centre (PSRC), www.princeton.edu/~psrc/ Accessed 02.06.2010.

Prinson, L. (2008) *Anatomy of a Business Plan: The Step-by-Step Guide to Building a Business and Securing Your Company's Future*, California: Out of Your Mind ... and into the Marketplace Publishing Company.

Professor T.D.Wilson's online paper 'Alfred Schutz, phenomenology and research methodology for information behaviour', http://informationr.net/tdw/publ/papers/schutz02.html

Prosser, J. (1998) *Image-based Research*, London: Routledge.

Pullman, M.E. and Robson, S.K.A. (2007) 'Visual methods: Using photography to capture customers' experience with design', *Cornell Hotel and Restaurant Administration Quarterly*, 48(2): 121–144.

Purdue Online Writing Lab, 'Basic inferential statistics', http://owl.english.purdue.edu/owl/resource/672/05/

Purkiss, A. (2010) 'Soros plans economics institute at Oxford University, *Times* says', 5 April, http://www.bloomberg.com/apps/news?pid=20601102&-sid=aKgAaKQObPhM Accessed 03.06.2010.

QuestionPro: Online Research Made Easy, www.questionpro.com/survey-questions.html Accessed 03.06.2010.

Reid, D.J. and Reid, F.J.M. (2005) 'Online focus groups: An in-depth comparison of computer mediated and conventional focus group discussions', *International Journal of Market Research* 47(2): 131–262.

Reinvention: A Journal of Undergraduate Research, www.warwick.ac.uk

Research for Development, a free-to-access online database containing information about research projects supported by the Department for International Development UK, Department for

International Development (DFID), **www. research4development.info/index.asp** Accessed 02.06.2010.

Resnik, D.B. (2009) 'International standards for research integrity: An idea whose time has come', *Accountability in Research* 16(4): 218–228. Semiotics for Beginners by David Chandler, **http:// www.aber.ac.uk/media/Documents/S4B/** results', *The Guardian*, 19 October.

Rich, D. (2010) Moving from "what happened?" to "now what?" is vital for business', *Financial Times*, 4 February.

Richards, J. and Marks, A. (2007) 'Biting the hand that feeds: Social identity and resistance in restaurant teams', *International Journal of Business Science and Applied Management* 2(2): 41–57.

Richbell, S.M., Watts, H.D. and Wardle, P. (2006) 'Owner-managers and business planning in the small firm', *International Small Business Journal* 24(5): 496–514.

Riege, A.M. (2003) 'Validity and reliability tests in case study research: A literature review with "hands-on" applications for each research phase', *Qualitative Market Research*, 6(2): 75–86.

Roberts, D.D., Roberts, L.M., O'Neill, R.M. and Blake-Beard, S.D. (2008) 'The invisible work of managing visibility for social change: Insights from the leadership of Reverend Dr Martin Luther King Jr', *Business & Society* 47(4): December, 425–456.

Rose, G. (2001) *Visual Methodologies*, London: Sage.

Rose, G. (2007) *Visual Methodologies: An Introduction to the Interpretation of Visual Materials*, London and Thousand Oaks: Sage.

Russell, D.W. (2008) 'Nostalgic tourism', *Journal of Travel and Tourism Marketing* 25(2): October, 103–116.

Samman, E., McAuliffe, E. and MacLachlan, M. (2009) 'The role of celebrity in endorsing poverty reduction through international aid', *International Journal of Nonprofit and Voluntary Sector Marketing* 14(4): 137–148.

Schullery, N.M., Ickes, L. and Schullery, S.E. (2009) 'Employer preferences for résumés and cover letters', *Business Communication Quarterly* 72(2): 163–176.

Scott, J. (1990) *A Matter of Record: Documentary Sources in Social Research,* Oxford: Blackwell.

Scott, R. (2010) 'Cycling England scheme encourages bike users in towns', Transport Correspondent, *BBC News*, 23 February.

Seafish: The authority on seafood, **www.seafish.org** Accessed 02.06.2010.

Seager, A. and Stewart, H. (2010) 'Growth loses its place in the pursuit of happiness', *The Observer*, 10 January 2010.

Semiotics and Strategic Brand Management, by Laura Oswald, University of Illinois, **http:// marketing-trends-congress.com/2009_cp/Materiali/ Paper/Fr/Oswald.pdf**

Semiotics for Beginners by David Chandler, **http:// www.aber.ac.uk/media/Documents/S4B/**

Shankar, A., Elliot, R. and Fitchett, J.A. (2009) Identity, consumption, and narratives of identity', *Marketing Theory*, 9(1): 75.

Sinkovics, R.R. and Penz, E. (2009) 'Social distance between residents and international tourists – Implications for international business', *International Business Review* 18(5): 457–469.

Smith, J.A., Flowers, P. and Larkin, M. (2009) *Interpretative Phenomenological Analysis*, London: Sage.

Smithers, R. 'Scottish fish and chip shop named best in UK', *The Guardian*, 21.01.2010. Accessed 02.06.2010.

Snap Surveys Ltd, **www.snapsurveys.com**

Soros, G. (2010) 'Anatomy of crisis – the living history of the last 30 years: Economic theory, politics and policy', presented at the INET Conference, King's College, April 8–11, 2010, **http://ineteconomics.org/sites/inet.civicactions.net/ files/INET%20C%40K%20Paper%20Session%201% 20-%20Soros.pdf** Accessed 03.06.2010.

Soule, E. (2002) 'Managerial moral strategies? In search of a few good principals', *Academy of Management Review*, 27: 114–124.

Soy, S. (2006) 'The case study as a research method', www.ischool.utexas.edu/~ssoy/useusers/ l391.d1b.htm

Soy, S. (2006) *The Case Study as a Research Method*, **http://www.ischool.utexas.edu/~ssoy/usesusers/ l391d1b.htm** Accessed 02.06.2010.

Stat Trek, 'Teach yourself statistics', **http://stattrek.com**

Stat Trek, Teach yourself statistics, 'Tutorial on bias in survey sampling', (**http://stattrek.com/AP-Statistics-2/Survey-Sampling-Bias.aspx? Tutorial=AP**) Accessed 03.06.2010.

Strauss, A. and Corbin, J. (1990, 1998 edns), 'Basics of Qualitative Research: Techniques and Procedures for Developing Grounded Theory', Thousand Oaks, CA: Sage.

Strauss, A. and Corbin, J. (eds) (1997) *Grounded Theory in Practice*, London: Sage.

Streeter, T. 'The Semiotics, advertising and media', University of Vermont, USA, **http://www.uvm.edu/ ~tstreete/semiotics_and_ads/**

Suboleski, S., Kincaid, C.S. and Dipietro, R.B. (2009) 'An exploratory study of multi-unit restaurant management training: A qualitative perspective', *Journal of Human Resources in Hospitality & Tourism*, 8(2): 199–214.

Sudman, S. (1976) '*Applied sampling*', New York: Academic Press.

Survey Monkey, www.surveymonkey.com

Survey Resources Network (SRN), http://surveynet.ac.uk/srn/introduction.asp

Surveyspro, www.esurveyspro.com

Tellis, W. (1997) 'Introduction to case study', *The Qualitative Report* 3(2), www.nova.edu/ssss/QR/QR3-2?tellis1.html Accessed 03.06.2010.

The British Educational Research Association (bera), 'Methods', www.bera.ac.uk/beraresources/methods/ Accessed 03.06.2010.

The British Educational Research Association (bera), 'Mixed methods research', www.bera.ac.uk/mixedmethods-research/ Accessed 03.06.2010.

The Grounded Theory Institute, www.groundedtheory.com Accessed 03.06.2010.

The Institute of Chartered Accountants Scotland, www.icas.org.uk

The National Archive of the UK, www.nationalarchives.gov.uk

— The Research Methods Knowledge Base, 'Descriptive statistics', http://www.socialresearchmethods.net/kb/statdesc.php Accessed 03.06.2010.

— The Research Methods Knowledge Base, 'Experimental design', www.socialresearchmethods.net/kb/desexper.php

— The Research Methods Knowledge Base, 'Inferential statistics', www.socialresearchmethods.net/kb/statinf.php

— The Research Methods Knowledge Base, 'The T-test', www.socialresearchmethods.net/kb/stat_t.php

The Semiotics, Advertising and Media website, created by Tom Streeter, University of Vermont, USA, http://www.uvm.edu/~tstreete/semiotics_and_ads/

The University of Leeds 'Plagiarism awareness', www.ldu.leeds.ac.uk/plagiarism/ Accessed 02.06.2010.

The University of Oxford 'Plagiarism', www.admin.ox.ac.uk/epsc/plagiarism/ Accessed 02.06.2010.

The University Writing Centre, Wright State University, Ohio, USA, 'Textual analysis', http://www.wright.edu/academics/writingctr/resources/textualanalysis.html Accessed 02.06.2010.

The Walt Disney Company website 'Business standards and ethics', http://corporate.disney.go.com/corporate/cr_business_standards.html Accessed April 2009.

Thompson, P. (2000) *The Voice of the Past: Oral History* (3rd edn), Oxford: Oxford University Press.

Thorpe, V. (2009) 'The end of the age of FREE?', *The Observer*, 10 May.

Timonen, L. and Luoma-aho, V. (2010) 'Sector-based corporate citizenship', *Business Ethics: A European Review* 19(1) January: 1–13.

Tonge, A., Greer, L. and Lawton, A. (2003) 'The Enron story: You can fool some of the people some of the time', *Business Ethics, A European Review*, 12: 4–22.

Tope, D., Chamberlain, L.J., Crowley, M. and Hodson, R. (2005) 'The benefits of being there: Evidence from the literature on work', *Journal of Contemporary Ethnography* 34(4): 470–493.

Trevett, N. (2010) '"People matter" is key message on road to recovery', *The Guardian*, March 12, www.guardian.co.uk/service-design/people-matter Accessed 03.06.2010.

Trochim, W.M. (2006) *The Research Methods Knowledge Base* (2nd edn), www.socialresearchmethods.net/ Accessed 02.06.2010.

Trochim, W.M. (2006) *The Research Methods Knowledge Base* (2nd edn), www.socialresearchmethods.net/.

Trochim, W.M. *The Research Methods Knowledge Base*, 'Experimental design', www.socialresearchmethods.net/kb/desexper.php

Trochim, W.M., The Research Methods Knowledge Base, 'Correlation', www.socialresearchmethods.net/kb/statcorr.php

Trochim, William M. The Research Methods Knowledge Base, 2nd Edition. Internet WWW page, at URL: http://www.socialresearchmethods.net/kb/ (indirect measures, content analysis, and secondary analysis of data) (www.socialresearchmethods.net/kb.unobtrus.php)

Trott, P. (2008) *Innovation Management and New Product Development*, Harlow: Pearson.

UCLA 'Introduction to statistics', www.ats.ucla.edu/stat/Spss/modules/descript.htm

UCLA Anderson School of Management, Oral History Research, 'Entrepreneurs of the West', http://www.anderson.ucla.edu/x1194.xml Accessed 02.06.2010.

UK Office for National Statistics, http://www.ons.gov.uk/census/index.html Accessed 02.06.2010.

UK Office of National Statistics, (www.ons.gov.uk).

University of Pennsylvania, 'How to do ethnographic research: A simplified guide', www.sas.upenn.edu/anthro/anthro/cpiamethods

Unwin, E. (2007) 'Getting the picture: Programme awareness amongst film festival customers', *International Journal of Nonprofit and Voluntary Sector Marketing* 12(3): 231–245.

Valentine, S., Fleischman, G.M., Sprague, R. and Godkin, L. (2010) 'Exploring the ethicality of firing employees who blog', *Human Resource Management* 49(1): 87–108.

van Dijk, T.A. (1993) 'Principles of critical discourse analysis', *Discourse and Society* 4(2): 243–289.

van Leeuwen, T. (2005) *Introducing Social Semiotics*, London: Routledge.

Veiga, J. (2004) 'Bringing ethics into the mainstream: An introduction to the special topic', *Academy of Management Executive*, 18(2): 37–39.

Venkatraman, M. and Nelson, T. (2008) 'From servicescape to consumptionscape: A photoelicitation study of Starbucks in the New China', *Journal of International Business Studies* 39(6): 1010–1026.

Verma, S. (2009) 'Do all advertising appeals influence consumer purchase decision: An exploratory study', *Global Business Review* 10(1): 33-43.

Walton, J.K. (2010) 'New directions in business history: Themes, approaches and opportunities', *Business History* 52(1): 1–16.

Wang, J. (2006) 'Questions and the exercise of power', *Discourse and Society*, 7(4): 529–548.

Weaver, G. R., Treviño, L. K. and Cochran, P. L. (1999b) 'Corporate ethics practices in the mid-1990s: An empirical study of the fortune 1000', *Journal of Business Ethics*, 18: 283–294.

Werhane, P. H. (2000) 'Business ethics and the origins of contemporary capitalism: Economics and ethics in the work of Adam Smith and Herbert Spence', *Journal of Business Ethics*, 24: 185–198.

What is an Employee Attitude Survey?, http://www.hr-survey.com/EmployeeAttitude.htm

What is Oral History, http://historymatters.gmu.edu/mse/oral/what.html, created by the American Social History Project, Centre for Media and Learning, City University New York (CUNY) Accessed 03.06.2010.

Whitty, S.J. (2010) 'Project management artefacts and the emotions they evoke', *International Journal of Managing Projects in Business* 3(1): 22–45.

Wicks, A. C. and Freeman, R. E. (1998) 'Organization studies and the new pragmatism: Positivism, anti-positivism and the search for ethics', *Organization Science*, 9: 123–141.

Wodak, R., and Krzyzanowski, M., (eds), (2008) '*Qualitative Discourse Analysis in the Social Sciences*' Hampshire: Palgrave Macmillan.

'Women & Hollywood: from a feminist perspective', www.womenandhollywood.com

World Economic Forum, http://www.weforum.org/en/index.htm

'Writing case studies', provided by the Colorado State University, www.writing.colstate.edu/guides/research/casestudy

Wyke, N.'The UK's Top 10 fish and chip shops 2010', *Times Online*, 19.01.2010, http://www.timesonline.co.uk/tol/life_and_style/food_and_drink/article6998138.ece Accessed 02.06.2010.

Yin, R.K. (1989) *Case Study Research*, London: Sage.

Yin, R.K. (2008) *Case Study Research: Design and Methods*, London: Sage.

Yin, R.K. (2009) *Case Study Research: Design and Methods* (4th edn), Thousand Oaks, CA: Sage.

Yin, R.K. (2009) *Case Study Research: Design and Methods* 4, London: Sage.

Yuki, G. (2010) (7th edn), *Leadership in Organisations*, New Jersey, USA: Prentice Hall.

Yurchisin, J., Yoo Jin, K. and Marcketti, S.B. (2009) 'Consumers of charity bracelets: Cause-supporters or fashion-followers?', *Journal of Fashion Marketing and Management* 13(3): 448–457.

GLOSSARY

Access Access to data and access to the field of the research project.

Aim of your research To keep things simple, the aim of your research is your research statement/ question re-stated as an aim.

Aims and objectives A general statement of what you intend to accomplish. **Objectives** specify how you intend to accomplish this aim.

Analytical framework Emerges from the conceptual framework, the theoretical framework and the methodological framework. Contained in the data analysis chapter in the thesis.

Anonymity means free from identification.

Appendices Used to detail any document or artefact relevant to the research but not detailed in the body of the research project.

Bias Anything that contaminates or compromises the research or data.

Bibliography A list of all of the published work cited in the research project must all be listed in the bibliography.

Bivariate analysis is Analysis conducted on two variables e.g. chi-square tests, one-way ANOVA, t-tests, correlation, and simple regression

Bogardus social distance scale Developed by psychologist E.S. Bogardus. Measures the social distance between different social and/or ethnic groups.

Bracketing The process through which the researcher acknowledges their preconceptions about the phenomenon under investigation.

Case study methodology Useful in the in-depth study of bounded entities, such as an organization, or a single incident or event.

Closed questions Questions that elicit short responses, e.g. a yes/no. Often used to establish factual information.

Cluster sampling Used when the population of the study can be divided into discreet groups based on any particular characteristic, e.g. geographic location.

Code Developed by the researcher for each of the responses to each of the questions asked in the course of the data gathering, in other words, for each piece of data gathered.

Coding keys A guide to all of the codes used in coding data to input the data into a computer software program.

Computer Assisted Qualitative Data Analysis (CAQDAS) Computer software designed to support qualitative data analysis.

Concepts Every discipline and theory is made up of concepts, e.g. key ideas and key words.

Conclusion Essentially a judgement or a final decision.

Confidentiality The non-disclosure of certain information.

Contingency table A tabular representation of categorical data, (nominal level data).

Convenience sampling Using a this technique the researcher engages conveniently located participants.

Covert observation Carried out without the knowledge of those being observed.

Critical analysis Critical analysis is a questioning analytical approach to any phenomenon.

Critical engagement The process by which the researcher takes a critical perspective on the research being reviewed.

Critical perspective Is a reflective, thoughtful, evaluative perspective or view.

Crosstabulations (Cross-Tabs) How joint distribution of two variables are displayed. Easy to use and understand.

Cyclical process A cycle of research, as opposed to a linear (or straight line) process.

Data Information or evidence gathered for a research project.

Data analysis The process of exploring and examining data with a view to uncovering meaning. Data is analyzed in order to uncover patterns and trends.

Data collection methods The means by which data is gathered for a research project, e.g. observation, interviews, focus groups, questionnaires.

Data management The correct, safe and secure management of data while data is being gathered, stored and analyzed.

Data set A complete collection of interrelated data, e.g. all of the data in a research project.

Data stream Various data from different streams.

Dependent variable What is measured in an experiment. The variable that responds to the independent variable.

Descriptive statistics Used to describe variables in the data such as gender, education, income, age etc. Presented as percentages, ratios, ranges, averages, and standard deviations.

Dichotomous variable A variable with only two values.

Discourse analysis The analysis of data through the use of discourses.

Empirical Information or evidence gained from observation, experience or experiment.

Epistemology Relates to knowledge, to what constitutes knowledge, and to the processes through which knowledge is created.

Ethics Moral principles governing the conduct of an individual, a group, or an organization.

Field work The means by which data gathering is undertaken in order to provide primary data for a research project.

Final draft The edited and polished fully integrated and correct copy of the thesis that is finally submitted for examination.

First draft The draft before the process of editing and getting feedback begins.

Fit Every step in the research project, should 'fit' with the purpose and focus of the project, including the philosophical framework.

Five Forces Model for industry analysis A framework for industry analysis and business strategy developed by Professor Michael Porter.

Focus groups Data collection where a researcher uses a group of participants in a focused discussion on the issue under investigation, designed to produce new knowledge and new insights

Four frameworks approach An approach to carrying out research whereby the conceptual framework, shapes, supports and directs the other three frameworks.

Four stages of data analysis Description, interpretation, conclusions and theorization.

Gatekeeper Any person or structure that governs or controls access to people, places, structures and/or to organizations.

Generalizability The application of the findings of a research project beyond the specific context of the study.

Group dynamic Energy that develops naturally within a group. It can be positive or negative and is often affected by strong personalities.

Group interviews A researcher interviews the participants in a group.

Histogram Similar to a bar chart except that the bars in a histogram are side by side touching each other.

Hypothesis A predicted or expected answer to a research question.

Idea for a research project Your idea for your research project is properly expressed in your very wellconceptualized research statement or question.

Inclusion and exclusion criteria The criteria potential participants must meet in order to be included in the study. Exclusion criteria is the criteria on which potential participants will be excluded from participation in the study.

Independent variable In examining the relationship between two variables, the assumed cause is the independent variable.

Inferential statistics Inferential statistics infer, based on a study of a sample population, what the entire population might think, or do.

Informed consent Agreement given by a person to participate in some action, after being informed of the possible consequences.

Integrity The honesty and scholarship of the researcher in engaging with, conducting and concluding research.

Inter coder reliability Two or more researchers, observers or coders measure the same phenomenon and then compare their results. If their results are consistent, inter coding can be deemed reliable.

Interval variables Data with a meaningful and measurable distance between values e.g. an age.

Intervening variable The means by which the independent variable affects the dependent variable.

Interview schedule The list of questions the researcher develops to ask participants, or the list of points, or the key issues, the researcher develops to discuss/explore with participants.

Interviewer verification An interviewer gives each of the interviewees a transcript of their interview. Each interviewee then verifies that the transcript is an accurate record of their interview.

Interviews The social science researcher develops a series of questions or a series of points of interest to discuss with the interviewees.

Intrusion Unwarranted, unnecessary or unwelcome engagement on a person or place.

Judgemental sampling The researcher decides who to include in the research.

Justify The researcher is obliged to justify, or explain the choices they make in relation to the research they decide to undertake and their methodological choices.

Key concept A key idea, a word, or phrase.

Key word searches The researcher uses key words and/or concepts when searching for relevant literature.

Likert scale Developed by Rensis Likert. Used to measure the direction and force of attitudes on a three, five or seven point scale.

List of references A complete list of all of the works cited in your research project.

Literature review Always undertaken in order to embed the researcher and research project in the body of knowledge.

Literature Research that has already been carried out and published of research.

Longitudinal Research Research that takes place over a long period of time.

Matrices Data displays that the researcher creates for the purposes of reduction of qualitative data.

Measurement validity Refers to the degree to which the data collection methods as they are designed can accomplish what it is that they are designed to accomplish.

Measures of central tendency The mean: the arithmetic average; the mode: the most commonly occurring value; the median: the middle value of a range of values.

Measures of dispersion The interquartile range (IQR); the standard deviation.

Method Used to denote methodology and data collection such as data collection methods such as observation, interviews, focus groups, and questionnaires.

Methodological framework An outline and a justification of the methodology selected for the research project; e.g. justification of population, sample.

Methodological pyramid Shows how the fundamental philosophies and different data collection methods fit with the different methodologies.

Methodology The way in which the research is carried out, as means of supporting the philosophical assumptions that underpin the research project

Multivariate analysis Analysis conducted on more than two variables e.g. examples of multivariate statistics include multiple regression analysis.

Narrative analysis The analysis of data through the use of narratives.

Narrative research Narrative inquiry or narrative analysis is a research methodology that is used in the gathering and analysis of narratives (stories).

Nominal variables Each value is a distinct category and serves simply as a label. Categories cannot be ranked e.g. gender, nationality, race.

Non-participant observation Carried out when the researcher does not participate in the action or in the phenomenon being observed.

Non-probability sampling In situations where it is not possible to compile a complete sampling frame, researchers use nonprobability sampling techniques.

Objectives of the research The steps the researcher takes in order to accomplish the aim of the research.

Observation A data collection method where the researcher engages in observing and recording the phenomenon under investigation, or some part of the phenomenon under investigation.

Observation schedule An observation schedule, like an interview schedule, is a form or series of forms on which the results of an observation are recorded.

One-to-one interview The researcher interviews each participant, one at a time and in great depth and detail.

Online interviews Interviews conducted online. Can be synchronous or asynchronous.

Ontology relates to the study of being, the nature of being and our ways of being in the world.

Open questions Used to explore understandings, feelings and beliefs. Usually require thought and reflection generate longer responses.

Ordinal variables Values are ranked according to criteria e.g. social class (upper, middle, working).

Participant observation Carried out by the researcher when the researcher does participate in the action or in the phenomenon being observed.

Peer-reviewed sources Are published accounts of research which have been subjected to critical review by the peers of the authors of the research.

Philosophical framework The worldview within which the research is situated.

Photo-elicitation interview The researcher takes the interviewee through an exploration and analysis of a series of photographs.

Pilot study An aid to improving the rigour and the validity of the research. This is a test of the data gathering instrument(s) designed for the research.

Plagiarism The use and/or presentation of somebody else's work or ideas as your own. A serious offence and avoidable through proper referencing.

Population Every person who, or every entity which, could be included in the research.

Potential harms A potential harm is a harms that might occur.

Primary data Data directly observed or gathered by the researcher engaged in a research project.

Primary sources Sources that provide new insight into any phenomenon. Sometimes called original sources.

Privileged access Access to an individual or site which provides an advantage to those in securing access.

Probability sampling Each case, individual or element has an equal probability of being selected.

Projective techniques Are indirect techniques through which researchers probe the beliefs, attitudes and feelings of respondents.

Qualitative data Non-numerical data.

Qualitative data set A complete set of qualitative data used or to be used in a research project.

Qualitative research Qualitative research to focus on words rather than numbers in the collection of data. Qualitative research as a research strategy is inductive and subjective, constructivist and/or interpretivist.

Quantitative data Data in the form of numbers, numerical data.

Quantitative data set A complete set of quantitative data used or to be used in a research project.

Quantitative research Quantitative research usually focuses on the gathering of numeric data or data in numerical form, i.e. data in the form of numbers. Quantitative research is deductive. It is said to be objective and situated within a framework of positivism.

Questionnaires Questionnaires are structured means of gathering data.

Quota sampling The researcher fills a sample of participants in the research using different quota criteria.

Rating scales The researcher asks participants to rate different aspects or elements of the phenomenon under investigation.

Recommendations The courses of action that the researcher recommends based on the findings and subsequent conclusions drawn from those findings.

References Give details of the source of ideas or theories or models within literature.

Reflexivity Researcher's active thoughtful engagement with every aspect and development of their research, e.g. selfreflection, selfconsciousness, self-awareness.

Reliability The dependability of the research, to the degree to which the research can be repeated while obtaining consistent results.

Representation The degree to which a sample selected from a population can be said to be representative of that population.

Representative A sample selected from a population, under certain circumstances, is representative of that population.

Research ethics committee are convened by organizations to monitor and police the ethical standards of research projects in which the parent organization has some gatekeeping role.

Research idea This broad area within which you want to situate your research.

Research methodology Signals to the reader how the research was conducted, and what philosophical assumptions underpin the research.

Research methods Data collection methods.

Research process The means by which research is carried out.

Researchability A project is deemed researchable if the researcher has the time needed, the money required, if any money is required, and the access to data necessary to carry out and complete the research project

Researchable A project is **researchable** if you have the time, money, data and the level of access to the data needed.

Response rate A count of the number of valid responses received to a data gathering exercise.

Rigorous For a research project to be rigorous, it must adhere to the scientific principles of research. The research must be systematic and valid.

Rigour For a research project to be rigorous, it must adhere to the scientific principles of research, e.g. systematic and valid research.

Role play A projective technique. Researcher and respondent take on character roles in a discussion.

Sample A sample is a subset of a population. If probability sampling is used, the sample said to be representative of the population.

Sampling frame A complete list or chart of every individual, unit or case within the population.

Saturation point Saturation point is reached when the researcher gathering data for the project no longer hears any new thoughts, feelings, attitudes, emotions, intentions, etc. At this point continuing to engage participants would not be useful, necessary or ethically sound, as further participants will not add to the knowledge being generated.

Scales Specially designed, highly structured, very focused and usually short data collection instruments.

Scope In relation to scope, there are two dimensions in every research project. The two dimensions are breadth and depth. In deciding the scope of the project, the researcher does not want to attempt to do too much; however, the researcher does need to do enough.

Search strategy The plan the researcher makes for their search of the body of knowledge for relevant literature for their literature review.

Secondary data Data that already exists; it not created by the researcher.

Secondary sources Places and organizations, libraries, websites, books, reports and so on, that contain data and/or commentary and discussion on data.

Semantic differential scale Uses opposite adjectives and asks respondents to indicate which of the adjectives best describes the phenomenon under investigation.

Semi-structured observation Carried out when the researcher knows broadly speaking what aspects or elements of the research should or could be observed

Sentence completion exercises A projective techniques. The researcher starts a sentence and asks the respondent to complete it.

Simple random sampling Involves selecting a sample at random from a sampling frame.

Skew (Skew or skewness) A symmetry in the distribution of the data.

Skips and filters Devices used in questionnaires to allow respondents to skip over questions that do not relate to them.

Snowball sampling The researcher finds a suitable participant, asks them to recommend another participant and so on.

Social research paradigms Different perspectives taken by social scientists on the social world e.g. interpretivism and social constructionism.

Social research Research conducted by social scientists on some aspects of the social world. Can be inductive or deductive.

Split-half method Used to tests equivalence reliability. The researcher halves the questionnaire and then tests whether or not both halves yield consistent results.

SPSS Statistical Package for the Social Sciences. A computer software package designed for the analysis of quantitative data.

Statistical analysis Analysis of quantitative data through the use of statistics.

Statistical inference Uses the data gathered from a sample population to draw conclusions about the population.

Stratified sample A sample selected based on some known characteristic of the population, a characteristic which will have an impact on the research.

Structure The structure of a chapter, or any written work, is the way in which it is organized.

Structured observation Carried out when the researcher knows precisely what aspects or elements of the research project should or could be observed.

Summarizing statistics Summarizing statistics are examples of descriptive statistics. Descriptive statistics are statistics that are used to describe data.

Survey Used to denote survey research methodology in order to also used is particularly useful in facilitating the study of big populations and geographically scattered samples.

Systematic Systematic means there must be a system in place and the action is carried out in a systematic manner, using the system.

Systematic sampling Involves selecting items at systematic or regular intervals from the sampling frame.

Test re-test method Used to estimate reliability. A questionnaire is used in a pilot test, then later, the same test is repeated and compared for consistency.

The conceptual framework The entire research project rests on the conceptual framework, which is contained in the research statement or question.

The theoretical framework The framework the researcher builds from the literature (theory) s/he reviews for the research project.

thematic analysis The analysis of data through the use of themes.

Theorization The researcher draws on the work of other researchers and theorists to enrich the reporting of their conclusions.

Triangulation Studying the phenomenon under investigation from more than one perspective, e.g. researcher, theoretical, methodological triangulation.

Univariate analysis Analysis conducted on only one variable e.g. frequencies.

Unobtrusive observation Carried out unobtrusively, with or without the knowledge of the research participants.

Unstructured observations Carried out when the researcher does not know what aspects of elements of the action or the phenomenon should or could be observed.

Validity Relates to how logical, truthful, robust, sound, reasonable, meaningful and useful the research in question is.

Value Values make up different variables.

Variable A characteristic with more than one value.

Vignettes A projective technique. The researcher shows respondents images or narratives and respondents are asked to engage and respond to them.

Vulnerable populations Populations which have some vulnerability, in terms of their social position or their age or their state of well-being.

INDEX

access 263
action research (AR) 4, 14, 17, 181
   case study 28–30
aim of your research 138
aims and objectives 28, 42–3, 45, 57,
     138–9, 142, 143, 246, 273
analytical framework 6, 354, 379–80,
     408, 421
   see also four frameworks
     approach
anonymity 77
ANOVA 399
appendices 52
appendix 52
archival research 5, 185, 226,
     248–50
asynchronous online focus groups
     (OFG) 297
attitude research 4, 184–5, 331–3
axial coding 424–5

bar chart 402–3
between-method triangulation 40, 191
bias 289, 295–6, 336
bibliography 50–1
bivariate analysis 400
Bogardus social distance scale 327,
     328
bracketing 427

case studies
   action research 28–30
   celebrities and poverty reduction
     342–3
   child poverty 251–3
   consumption of charity bracelets
     409–10
   Imperial War Museum 312–13
   management practices 461–2
   managing/analyzing data 369–71
   methodological framework 192–6
   qualitative study using diary
     method 436–8
   random numbers 230–1
   research idea 276–8
   Walt Disney 86
case study 4, 14, 15, 38, 180, 223
   data analysis in 426–8
   documentary analysis 143–4

   focus on 74–5
   in practice 75–6
case study research 427–9
closed questions 291
cluster sampling 207, 209–10
code 383
coding 359
   qualitative data 391
coding keys 359, 386–95
Compte, Auguste 12
computer assisted data analysis
     (CADA) 360, 380
Computer Assisted Qualitative Data
     Analysis (CAQDAS) 350, 362,
     433–6
concepts 106–7
conceptual framework 6, 38, 135–6,
     154–5, 353–4, 407
   see also four frameworks
     approach
conclusions 5, 444, 458
   implications 449–50
   writing 446–50
conducting interviews 290–1
   breakdowns 294
   concluding 294
   contact interviewees 292
   group 293
   managing data 295
   method 291
   one-to-one/face-to-face (F2F)
     292–3
   online 293–4
   provide information 292
   sample selection 291–2
   schedule 291
   setting up 292
   telephone 293
confidentiality 77
constructivism 97
content analysis 14, 160–1, 183, 224
context for research 30, 58, 142, 144
contingency table 401
convenience sampling 211, 212
conventional inquiry 304
correlation tests 399
covert observation 219, 264
   in practice 266
critical analysis 131

critical engagement 163
critical incident technique 227–8
critical perspective 163
critical theory 94, 97
critique of interviews/focus groups
     309–11
cross-tabulation 400–1, 401
cycle of theory-research-knowledge
     115
cyclical process 16–17

data 5, 354–6
   access 20, 21
   critical questions 367–8
   evaluating utility of 247–8
   graphing 401–5
   loading 391
   missing 392–4
   presentation 150–1
   reduction 364–5
   safety/security 354–5
   unnecessary 81
   validity 47–8
data analysis 6, 164, 195, 356–7,
     391, 457, 458
   case study 369–71
   four stages 363–4, 406–8, 420
   in practice 360
   presenting 394–5
   qualitative 361–2, 422–3
   quantitative 357–60
   structure 364–6
   variable in quantitative data 395–6
data collection methods 4–5, 15–16,
     142, 189–90, 194, 203,
     218–29, 260–1, 284–5, 311,
     320–1, 323–4
   set back/surprise data gathering
     339–40
data management 295, 350, 354–6,
     360
   case study 369–71
   with SPSS 394–5
data set 244, 350
data stream 247
Datablog 150–3
decision-making 19, 179, 206,
     263, 265

dependent variable 226, 228
descriptive statistics 396, 398–9, 400
development 111
diaries 5, 10–11, 27, 39, 52–5, 56,
    224, 436–8
dichotomous variable 396, 397
discourse analysis 424
discourse analysis (DA) 184, 214–15,
    225
do no harm 72
documentary analysis 129–30, 184
    case study 143–4
documentary evidence 225
documentary research 5, 129–30, 184
Domino's Pizza 297
drop and collect questionnaires
    221–2, 324
Durkheim, Emile 12, 13

empirical 12
epistemology 13–14, 93–4, 97–8, 320
ethically reflective practitioner 76–7
ethics 25, 27, 67, 195–6, 311
    anonymity and confidentiality
        77–9
    codes 68
    debates on 68
    definition 68
    do no harm 72
    frameworks 68–9
    importance 70
    integrity 72
    issues and dilemmas 69–70, 74,
        80–1
    plagiarism 73
    power 73
    in practice 71–2, 329–30
    questions/prompts for ethical
        reflection 82–5
    in research 70, 72–3
    transparency 73
    validity 73
ethnographic research 4, 261
ethnography 14, 181, 269–70
evidence 47–8
exclusion criteria 207
experimental design 180–1, 353,
    396–7
experiments 226–7

face-to-face (F2F) focus group,
    conducting 299–300
face-to-face (F2F) interview 288–9,
    292–3
    audio-recorded 303
feminism 94, 97
feminist research 4, 186

field diaries 224
film research 5
final draft 444
first draft 444
fit 35, 37, 93
Five Forces Model for Industry
    Analysis 242–3
focus groups 4, 222, 284, 287,
    296–7
    advantages/disadvantages 298
    critiquing 309–11
    face-to-face 297, 299–300
    online 297
    in practice 286–7, 297
    schedules 301–3
formal observation 264
four frameworks approach 5–7, 177,
    228, 260, 353–4, 407–8
    creation 110–13, 139–40, 155–6
    outline 140–1
    research process and 9–10
    see also analytical framework;
        conceptual framework;
        methodological framework;
        theoretical framework
four stages of data analysis 364
    conclusions 363, 407, 420
    description 363, 406, 420
    interpretation 363, 406, 420
    theorization 364, 407, 420
frequency distributions 399
functionalism 94, 97

gatekeeper 20, 81
generalizability 340
graphing data 401–5
grounded theory (GT) 4, 14, 181–2
    data analysis 424–5
    methodology 425–6
group administered questionnaires
    222
group dynamic 287
group interviews 220, 289, 290, 293

Hawthorne Experiments 227
hermeneutics 97
histogram 405
historical analysis 182–3
historical data 13
historical research 182–3, 248–50
hypothesis 38
hypothesis testing 400

ideas for research project 124,
    126–33, 245–6
image-based research 4, 5, 109–10,
    185, 224–5

in practice 113–14
Imperial War Museum 312–13
inclusion criteria 207
independent variable 226, 228, 396,
    397
inferential statistics 396, 399, 400
informal observations 263–4
informed consent 77–9
integrity 27, 72, 355–6
inter coder reliability 334, 336
internet access 321–2
internet research 222–3
interpretivism 94, 97
interquartile range (IQR) 398
interval variable 395
intervening variable 396, 397
interview schedule 189, 291, 301–3
interviewee verification 303
interviewer verification 303
interviews 4, 13, 178
    conducting 290–5
    critiquing 309–11
    qualitative 192, 291
    quantitative research 290–1
    street intercept questionnaire
        383–5
    types 219–21, 287–90
intrusion 80

judgemental (purposive) sampling
    211–12
justify 93

key concept 6
key word searches 154–5
knowledge 98
    generation 104–5
    research-theory link 115

language 419
life history 5, 13, 183, 454–5
Likert scale 325
line graph 402
list of references 458
literature 150, 154
    source appropriate 45–7
literature appraisal
    conclusions 165
    data analysis 164
    findings 164
    introduction 164
    methodology 164
    overall 165
    recommendations 165
    review 164
literature review 4, 57–8, 456
    good and bad 46–7, 167–8

reading 163–5
sample 28–9, 143–4
writing 156–63
longitudinal 178

Marx, Karl 12
mass observation 261
matrices 430–1
mean 398
measurement validity 333, 335
measures of central tendency 398,
    400
measures of dispersion 398, 400
media research 95
    in practice 125–6, 202–3
median 398
meta-analysis 186
method 47
methodological framework 6, 140–1,
    228, 408
    case study 192–6
    creation 189–92
    data collection 189–90
    ethics 191
    explanation and justification 189
    population of study 189
    summary 192
    triangulation 190–1
    validity and reliability 190
    see also four frameworks
        approach
methodological pyramid 101–2, 177
methodological triangulation 40
methodology 4, 98–101, 456
    appropriate 187–8
missing data 392–4
mixed-methods research 357,
    431–2
mode 398
multiple linear regression 399
multiple reality 15
multivariate analysis 400, 401

narrative analysis 182, 188–9, 225,
    419
narrative inquiry 188–9
narrative research 5, 178, 182, 188–9
naturalistic inquiry 304
nominal variable 395
non-participative observation 264
non-probability sampling 207, 211
    techniques 211–13

objectives 42, 43
objectives of the research 138–9
observation 4, 191, 219, 260–1
    critique of 271–2

designing 272, 275
research methodology 273–4
rigour in 270–1
schedule 189
types 264–5
understanding 261, 263–4
using 265, 267–8
official analysis 131
one-to-one interview 219–20, 288–9,
    292–3
online focus groups (OFG) 297
online interviews 220–1, 289–90,
    293–4
    advantages/disadvantages
        298
online questionnaires 222
ontology 14, 93, 94, 320
open coding 424
open questions 291, 302
oral history 13, 14, 226
ordinal variable 395

participant observation 13, 219, 261,
    264
peer-reviewed sources 154
percentages 398
phenomenological research 426
    data analysis in 427
phenomenology 14, 100, 101, 182,
    308–9
    in practice 100
philosophical framework 93,
    96–101
photo-elicitation interview 288
pilot study 271, 339
plagiarism 48, 50, 73
population of the study 28, 57, 142,
    189, 194, 204
population/s 141, 195, 205, 213
Porter, Michael 242–3
positivism 12–13, 94, 97, 99
post-modernism 97
post-structuralism 97
postal questionnaires 221
potential harms 67
power 73
prediction 397, 399
primary data 238, 240–1, 263
    differentiating between
        primary and secondary
        data 241–3
printed material research 5
privileged access 80
probability sampling 207
    techniques 208–11
projective technique 5, 223–4,
    328–31
proportions 399

purposive (judgemental) sampling
    211–12

qualitative data 103, 104, 229
    analysis 350, 361–2
    coding 391
    presenting 429–31
qualitative data analysis 418–19
    simple 422–3
qualitative data set 244
qualitative research 229, 284
    conducting interviews 291
    difference with quantitative
        research 306
    validity/reliability 304–8
quantitative data 102, 103, 229, 378
    analysis 350, 357–60, 378
    variable in analysis 395–6
    working with 380–2
quantitative data set 247
quantitative research 229, 284, 320
    conducting interviews 290–1
    difference with qualitative
        research 306
    objectiveness of 336
    validity/reliability 304–8, 333–4
questionnaire design 334–6
    abbreviations/jargon 338
    ambiguous questions 337
    clear instructions 338
    complicated questions 337
    conceptual framework 225
    double negatives 338
    embarrassing questions 337
    ethnocentrism 338
    humour 338
    insulting words 337
    leading responses 337
    loaded words 337
    respondent bias 338
    sexist, racist, ageist, disablist
        language 338
    simple/easy-to-answer questions
        338
    slang/colloquialisms 338
    talking down to respondents 338
    two or more questions 337
    unclear/vague concepts 337
questionnaires 4, 191, 320, 324–5
    politics/practicalities of asking
        questions 336, 338
    presentation 336, 338
    street intercept interviews 383–5
    types 221–2
quota sampling 211, 212

random numbers 230–1
range 398
rating scales 323
rationale for research 30, 58–9, 142, 144
ratios 398
reality 13–15, 94
recommendations 444, 451, 458
references 166
reflexivity 77, 418–19
reliability 40, 190, 195
   quantitative research 304–8, 333–4
report 22–5, 458
representation 207, 211
research
   aims and objectives 138–9
   basic elements 97–101
   contribution to knowledge 238–9
   design 217–18
   different approaches 47
   four frameworks approach and 9–10
   good 7–9, 36, 66–7, 95, 125–6, 151–2, 160–1, 174–5, 188–9, 202–3, 214–15, 248–9, 262, 269–70, 297, 308–9, 351–2, 366–7, 378–9, 382–3, 396–7, 417, 425–6, 428–9, 445–6, 454
   influence of theory 21, 49, 105–6, 108–9, 133–4, 162–3, 178–9, 216–18, 243–4, 266, 307, 355–6, 405–6, 432–3, 452–4
   limiting scope of project 137–8
   methods 215–16
   philosophical underpinnings 96–7
   potential complexities in reporting 445–6
   problems 11–12, 176, 186–7, 188, 205, 303–4, 310, 459
   proposal 28, 57, 141–2
   theory-knowledge link 115
research diary 5, 10–11, 27, 39, 52–5, 56, 224
   case study 436–8
research ethics 25, 27
research ethics committee (REC) 78, 81–2
research idea 4, 35, 37, 126–33
   case study 276–8
   generating 245–6
   literature questions 127–8
   methodology and methods questions 128
   project questions 127

refining 136–7
   turning into research project 37
research methodology 14–16, 29, 142, 144, 164, 175, 176–8, 193–4, 246
   cyclical process of action 16–17
   formulation of researchable project 19–21
   in practice 58
   problems 17–19
   types 180–6
   writing up research 22–5
research process 4, 93–4, 96, 124, 150, 175, 239, 321, 379
   concepts 10
   literature review 10
   statement 9–10
research project 19–21, 37
   case study 57–9
   conclusions/recommendations 457
   data analysis 457
   introduction 455
   literature review 456
   methodology 456
   reflexivity 81
   shifts in 205–6, 367–8
   thesis/report 458
   writing 455–8
research statement 9–10, 111, 157, 246, 353
   development of 38–42
researchability 19, 37
researchable 37
researcher bias 295–6
researcher triangulation 40
respondent bias 296
response rate 211, 340
reviews, writing 156–63
rigour, rigorous 5, 270
role play 330

sample 141, 194, 206–7
   detailing 213
   random numbers 230–1
   size 210
sample literature review 139–40, 142, 143–4
sampling bias 296
sampling frame 207
sampling method 194
sampling with replacement 208
sampling techniques 207–13
sampling without replacement 208
saturation point 212

scales 5, 223, 320, 324, 325–7
   designing 334–6
   in practice 329–30
scattergrams 403
scope 38–9, 204, 205
search strategy 155
secondary data 238, 240–1
   appropriate use of 250
   differentiating between primary and secondary data 241–3
   ethics 250
   problems 250
   sourcing 244–7
secondary sources 223, 239, 242
   graphs and tables 403–5
selective coding 425
semantic differential scale 326
semi-structured interview/focus group schedule 301
semi-structured observation 268
semiotics 14, 225–6, 362–3
   in practice 428–9
sentence completion exercises 323, 330–1
simple linear regression 399
simple random sampling 207, 208
skew, skewness 400
skills 34
skips and filters 335, 336
SME (small and medium-sized enterprise) 111
snowball sampling 211, 212–13
social constructivism 13, 94
social research 12–14
social research paradigms 14
spidergrams 131, 132–3
split-half method 334, 335
SPSS (Statistical Package for the Social Sciences) 350, 358
   data management 394–5
   guides 394
standard deviation 398
statistical analysis 397–401, 470
   bivariate analysis 400
   cross-tabulation 401
   descriptive 397, 398–9
   hypothesis testing 400
   inferential 397, 399–400
   multivariate analysis 401
   univariate analysis 400
statistical inference 396, 400
stratified sample 208–9
   need for and use of 209
structuralism 97
structure 156, 364–6
structured interview/focus group schedule 301–3

structured observation 267, 268
subjective reality 15
summarizing statistics 357–8
survey 4, 14, 15, 41–2, 44, 180
    case study 57–9
    in practice 99, 378–9
symbolic interactionism 97
symbols 5
synchronous online focus groups
        (OFG) 297
systematic 260
systematic sampling 207, 208

T-tests 399
tables 401
telephone interviews 220, 285, 290,
        293
test re-test method 334, 335
textual analysis 185–6
thematic analysis 424
theoretical framework 6, 46, 407
    see also four frameworks
        approach
theoretical triangulation 40

theoretization 447
theorizing data 114–15
theory 104–5
    framework creation 110–13, 139–40
    generating 114–15, 353
    importance 106–9
    influence on research 49, 105–6,
        108–9, 133–4, 162–3, 178–9,
        216–18, 243–4, 266, 307,
        355–6, 405–6, 432–3, 452–4
    research-knowledge link 115
    uses in research 107–8
thesis 22–5, 458, 460
thick description 418
training 111
training and development 111
training and development for
        employees 111
transparency 73
triangulation 40–1, 190–1, 194–5

univariate analysis 400
unobtrusive methods 227

unobtrusive observation 267
unstructured observation 267, 268,
        273–4

validity 40, 73, 190, 195
    quantitative research 304–8,
        333–4
value 391
variable 228, 395
vignettes 328
    in practice 329–30
visual images 13
visual methods 224–5
vulnerable populations 80

Walt Disney Company 86
Weber, Max 12
within method triangulation 40
writing research project 455–8
writing reviews 156–63
writing standards 159